COPYRIGHT IN A GLOBAL INFORMATION ECONOMY

2009 Case and Statutory Supplement

ASPEN PUBLISHERS

COPYRIGHT IN A GLOBAL INFORMATION ECONOMY

2009 Case and Statutory Supplement

JULIE E. COHEN
Professor of Law
Georgetown University Law Center

LYDIA PALLAS LOREN
Jeffrey Bain Faculty Scholar
Professor of Law
Lewis and Clark Law School

RUTH L. OKEDIJI
William L. Prosser Professor of Law
University of Minnesota Law School

MAUREEN A. O'ROURKE
Dean and Professor of Law
Michaels Faculty Research Scholar
Boston University School of Law

Wolters Kluwer
Law & Business

AUSTIN   BOSTON   CHICAGO   NEW YORK   THE NETHERLANDS

Printed in the United States of America.

1 2 3 4 5 6 7 8 9 0

ISBN 978-0-7355-7932-3

About Wolters Kluwer Law & Business

Wolters Kluwer Law & Business is a leading provider of research information and workflow solutions in key specialty areas. The strengths of the individual brands of Aspen Publishers, CCH, Kluwer Law International, and Loislaw are aligned within Wolters Kluwer Law & Business to provide comprehensive, in-depth solutions and expert-authored content for the legal, professional, and education markets.

CCH was founded in 1913 and has served more than four generations of business professionals and their clients. The CCH products in the Wolters Kluwer Law & Business group are highly regarded electronic and print resources for legal, securities, antitrust, and trade regulation, government contracting, banking, pension, payroll, employment and labor, and healthcare reimbursement and compliance professionals.

Aspen Publishers is a leading information provider for attorneys, business professionals, and law students. Written by preeminent authorities, Aspen products offer analytical and practical information in a range of specialty practice areas from securities law and intellectual property to mergers and acquisitions and pension/benefits. Aspen's trusted legal education resources provide professors and students with high-quality, up-to-date, and effective resources for successful instruction and study in all areas of the law.

Kluwer Law International supplies the global business community with comprehensive English-language international legal information. Legal practitioners, corporate counsel, and business executives around the world rely on the Kluwer Law International journals, loose-leafs, books, and electronic products for authoritative information in many areas of international legal practice.

Loislaw is a premier provider of digitized legal content to small law firm practitioners of various specializations. Loislaw provides attorneys with the ability to quickly and efficiently find the necessary legal information they need, when and where they need it, by facilitating access to primary law as well as state-specific law, records, forms, and treatises.

Wolters Kluwer Law & Business, a unit of Wolters Kluwer, is headquartered in New York and Riverwoods, Illinois. Wolters Kluwer is a leading multinational publisher and information services company.

CONTENTS

Contents

Contents

Contents

Part I
United States Materials

A. United States Code, Title 17 — Copyrights

Chapter

Chapter 1. Subject Matter and Scope of Copyright

Sec.

§101. Definitions

Except as otherwise provided in this title, as used in this title, the following terms and their variant forms mean the following:

An "anonymous work" is a work on the copies or phonorecords of which no natural person is identified as author.

An "architectural work" is the design of a building as embodied in any tangible medium of expression, including a building, architectural plans, or drawings. The work includes the overall form as well as the arrangement and composition of spaces and elements in the design, but does not include individual standard features.

"Audiovisual works" are works that consist of a series of related images which are intrinsically intended to be shown by the use of machines or devices such as projectors, viewers, or electronic equipment, together with accompanying sounds, if any, regardless of the nature of the material objects, such as films or tapes, in which the works are embodied.

The "Berne Convention" is the Convention for the Protection of Literary and Artistic Works, signed at Berne, Switzerland, on September 9, 1886, and all acts, protocols, and revisions thereto.

The "best edition" of a work is the edition, published in the United States at any time before the date of deposit, that the Library of Congress determines to be most suitable for its purposes.

A person's "children" are that person's immediate offspring, whether legitimate or not, and any children legally adopted by that person.

A "collective work" is a work, such as a periodical issue, anthology, or encyclopedia, in which a number of contributions, constituting separate and independent works in themselves, are assembled into a collective whole.

A "compilation" is a work formed by the collection and assembling of preexisting materials or of data that are selected, coordinated, or arranged in such a way that the resulting work as a whole constitutes an original work of authorship. The term "compilation" includes collective works.

A "computer program" is a set of statements or instructions to be used directly or indirectly in a computer in order to bring about a certain result.

"Copies" are material objects, other than phonorecords, in which a work is fixed by any method now known or later developed, and from which the work can be perceived, reproduced, or otherwise communicated, either directly or with the aid of a machine or device. The term "copies" includes the material object, other than a phonorecord, in which the work is first fixed.

A "Copyright Royalty Judge" is a Copyright Royalty Judge appointed under section 802 of this title, and includes any individual serving as an interim Copyright Royalty Judge under such section.

"Copyright owner", with respect to any one of the exclusive rights comprised in a copyright, refers to the owner of that particular right.

A work is "created" when it is fixed in a copy or phonorecord for the first time; where a work is prepared over a period of time, the portion of it that has been fixed at any particular time constitutes the work as of that time, and where the work has been prepared in different versions, each version constitutes a separate work.

A "derivative work" is a work based upon one or more preexisting works, such as a translation, musical arrangement, dramatization, fictionalization, motion picture version, sound recording, art reproduction, abridgment, condensation, or any other form in which a work may be recast, transformed, or adapted. A work consisting of editorial revisions, annotations, elaborations, or other modifications, which, as a whole, represent an original work of authorship, is a "derivative work".

A "device", "machine", or "process" is one now known or later developed.

A "digital transmission" is a transmission in whole or in part in a digital or other non-analog format.

To "display" a work means to show a copy of it, either directly or by means of a film, slide, television image, or any other device or process or, in the case of a motion picture or other audiovisual work, to show individual images nonsequentially.

5

An "establishment" is a store, shop, or any similar place of business open to the general public for the primary purpose of selling goods or services in which the majority of the gross square feet of space that is nonresidential is used for that purpose, and in which nondramatic musical works are performed publicly.

A "food service or drinking establishment" is a restaurant, inn, bar, tavern, or any other similar place of business in which the public or patrons assemble for the primary purpose of being served food or drink, in which the majority of the gross square feet of space that is nonresidential is used for that purpose, and in which nondramatic musical works are performed publicly.

The term "financial gain" includes receipt, or expectation of receipt, of anything of value, including the receipt of other copyrighted works.

A work is "fixed" in a tangible medium of expression when its embodiment in a copy or phonorecord, by or under the authority of the author, is sufficiently permanent or stable to permit it to be perceived, reproduced, or otherwise communicated for a period of more than transitory duration. A work consisting of sounds, images, or both, that are being transmitted, is "fixed" for purposes of this title if a fixation of the work is being made simultaneously with its transmission.

The "Geneva Phonograms Convention" is the Convention for the Protection of Producers of Phonograms Against Unauthorized Duplication of Their Phonograms, concluded at Geneva, Switzerland, on October 29, 1971.

The "gross square feet of space" of an establishment means the entire interior space of that establishment, and any adjoining outdoor space used to serve patrons, whether on a seasonal basis or otherwise.

The terms "including" and "such as" are illustrative and not limitative.

An "international agreement" is —

(1) the Universal Copyright Convention;
(2) the Geneva Phonograms Convention;
(3) the Berne Convention;
(4) the WTO Agreement;
(5) the WIPO Copyright Treaty;
(6) the WIPO Performances and Phonograms Treaty; and
(7) any other copyright treaty to which the United States is a party.

A "joint work" is a work prepared by two or more authors with the intention that their contributions be merged into inseparable or interdependent parts of a unitary whole.

"Literary works" are works, other than audiovisual works, expressed in words, numbers, or other verbal or numerical symbols or indicia, regardless of the nature of the material objects, such as books, periodicals, manuscripts, phonorecords, film, tapes, disks, or cards, in which they are embodied.

"Motion pictures" are audiovisual works consisting of a series of related images which, when shown in succession, impart an impression of motion, together with accompanying sounds, if any.

The term "motion picture exhibition facility" means a movie theater, screening room, or other venue that is being used primarily for the exhibition of a copyrighted motion picture, if such exhibition is open to the public or is made to an assembled group of viewers outside of a normal circle of a family and its social acquaintances.

To "perform" a work means to recite, render, play, dance, or act it, either directly or by means of any device or process or, in the case of a motion picture or other audiovisual work, to show its images in any sequence or to make the sounds accompanying it audible.

A "performing rights society" is an association, corporation, or other entity that licenses the public performance of nondramatic musical works on behalf of copyright owners of such works, such as the American Society of Composers, Authors and Publishers (ASCAP), Broadcast Music, Inc. (BMI), and SESAC, Inc.

"Phonorecords" are material objects in which sounds, other than those accompanying a motion picture or other audiovisual work, are fixed by any method now known or later developed, and from which the sounds can be perceived, reproduced, or otherwise communicated, either directly or with the aid of a machine or device. The term "phonorecords" includes the material object in which the sounds are first fixed.

"Pictorial, graphic, and sculptural works" include two-dimensional and three-dimensional works of fine, graphic, and applied art, photographs, prints and art reproductions, maps, globes, charts, diagrams, models, and technical drawings, including architectural plans. Such works shall include works of artistic craftsmanship insofar as their form but not their mechanical or utilitarian aspects are concerned; the design of a useful article, as defined in this section, shall be considered a pictorial, graphic, or sculptural work only if, and only to the extent that, such design incorporates pictorial, graphic, or sculptural features that can be identified separately from, and are capable of existing independently of, the utilitarian aspects of the article.

For purposes of section 513, a "proprietor" is an individual, corporation, partnership, or other entity, as the case may be, that owns an establishment or a food service or drinking establishment, except that no owner or operator of a radio or television station licensed by the Federal Communications Commission, cable system or satellite carrier, cable or satellite carrier service or programmer, provider of online services or network access or the operator of facilities therefor, telecommunications company, or any other such audio or audiovisual service or programmer now known or as may be developed in the future, commercial subscription music service, or owner or operator of any other transmission service, shall under any circumstances be deemed to be a proprietor.

A "pseudonymous work" is a work on the copies or phonorecords of which the author is identified under a fictitious name.

"Publication" is the distribution of copies or phonorecords of a work to the public by sale or other transfer of ownership, or by rental, lease, or lending. The offering to distribute copies or phonorecords to a group of persons for purposes of further distribution, public performance, or public display, constitutes publication. A public performance or display of a work does not of itself constitute publication.

To perform or display a work "publicly" means —

(1) to perform or display it at a place open to the public or at any place where a substantial number of persons outside of a normal circle of a family and its social acquaintances is gathered; or

(2) to transmit or otherwise communicate a performance or display of the work to a place specified by clause (1) or to the public, by means of any device or process, whether the members of the public capable of receiving the performance or display receive it in the same place or in separate places and at the same time or at different times.

"Registration", for purposes of sections 205(c)(2), 405, 406, 410(d), 411, 412, and 506(e), means a registration of a claim in the original or the renewed and extended term of copyright.

"Sound recordings" are works that result from the fixation of a series of musical, spoken, or other sounds, but not including the sounds accompanying a motion picture or other audiovisual work, regardless of the nature of the material objects, such as disks, tapes, or other phonorecords, in which they are embodied.

"State" includes the District of Columbia and the Commonwealth of Puerto Rico, and any territories to which this title is made applicable by an Act of Congress.

A "transfer of copyright ownership" is an assignment, mortgage, exclusive license, or any other conveyance, alienation, or hypothecation of a copyright or of any of the exclusive rights comprised in a copyright, whether or not it is limited in time or place of effect, but not including a nonexclusive license.

A "transmission program" is a body of material that, as an aggregate, has been produced for the sole purpose of transmission to the public in sequence and as a unit.

To "transmit" a performance or display is to communicate it by any device or process whereby images or sounds are received beyond the place from which they are sent.

A "treaty party" is a country or intergovernmental organization other than the United States that is a party to an international agreement.

The "United States", when used in a geographical sense, comprises the several States, the District of Columbia and the Commonwealth of Puerto Rico, and the organized territories under the jurisdiction of the United States Government.

For purposes of section 411, a work is a "United States work" only if —

(1) in the case of a published work, the work is first published —

(A) in the United States;

(B) simultaneously in the United States and another treaty party or parties, whose law grants a term of copyright protection that is the same as or longer than the term provided in the United States;

(C) simultaneously in the United States and a foreign nation that is not a treaty party; or

(D) in a foreign nation that is not a treaty party, and all of the authors of the work are nationals, domiciliaries, or habitual residents of, or in the case of an audiovisual work legal entities with headquarters in, the United States;

(2) in the case of an unpublished work, all the authors of the work are nationals, domiciliaries, or habitual residents of the United States, or, in the

case of an unpublished audiovisual work, all the authors are legal entities with headquarters in the United States; or

(3) in the case of a pictorial, graphic, or sculptural work incorporated in a building or structure, the building or structure is located in the United States.

A "useful article" is an article having an intrinsic utilitarian function that is not merely to portray the appearance of the article or to convey information. An article that is normally a part of a useful article is considered a "useful article".

The author's "widow" or "widower" is the author's surviving spouse under the law of the author's domicile at the time of his or her death, whether or not the spouse has later remarried.

The "WIPO Copyright Treaty" is the WIPO Copyright Treaty concluded at Geneva, Switzerland, on December 20, 1996.

The "WIPO Performances and Phonograms Treaty" is the WIPO Performances and Phonograms Treaty concluded at Geneva, Switzerland, on December 20, 1996.

A "work of visual art" is —

(1) a painting, drawing, print or sculpture, existing in a single copy, in a limited edition of 200 copies or fewer that are signed and consecutively numbered by the author, or, in the case of a sculpture, in multiple cast, carved, or fabricated sculptures of 200 or fewer that are consecutively numbered by the author and bear the signature or other identifying mark of the author; or

(2) a still photographic image produced for exhibition purposes only, existing in a single copy that is signed by the author, or in a limited edition of 200 copies or fewer that are signed and consecutively numbered by the author.

A work of visual art does not include —

(A)(i) any poster, map, globe, chart, technical drawing, diagram, model, applied art, motion picture or other audiovisual work, book, magazine, newspaper, periodical, data base, electronic information service, electronic publication, or similar publication;

(ii) any merchandising item or advertising, promotional, descriptive, covering, or packaging material or container;

(iii) any portion or part of any item described in clause (i) or (ii);

(B) any work made for hire; or

(C) any work not subject to copyright protection under this title.

A "work of the United States Government" is a work prepared by an officer or employee of the United States Government as part of that person's official duties.

A "work made for hire" is —

(1)a work prepared by an employee within the scope of his or her employment; or

(2) a work specially ordered or commissioned for use as a contribution to a collective work, as a part of a motion picture or other audiovisual work, as a translation, as a supplementary work, as a compilation, as an instructional text, as a test, as answer material for a test, or as an atlas, if the parties expressly agree in a written instrument signed by them that the work shall be considered a work made for hire. For the purpose of the foregoing sentence, a "supplementary work" is a work prepared for publication as a secondary adjunct to a work by another author

for the purpose of introducing, concluding, illustrating, explaining, revising, commenting upon, or assisting in the use of the other work, such as forewords, afterwords, pictorial illustrations, maps, charts, tables, editorial notes, musical arrangements, answer material for tests, bibliographies, appendixes, and indexes, and an "instructional text" is a literary, pictorial, or graphic work prepared for publication and with the purpose of use in systematic instructional activities.

In determining whether any work is eligible to be considered a work made for hire under paragraph (2), neither the amendment contained in section 1011(d) of the Intellectual Property and Communications Omnibus Reform Act of 1999, as enacted by section 1000(a)(9) of Public Law 106-113, nor the deletion of the words added by that amendment—

      (A) shall be considered or otherwise given any legal significance, or

      (B) shall be interpreted to indicate congressional approval or disapproval of, or acquiescence in, any judicial determination,

by the courts or the Copyright Office. Paragraph (2) shall be interpreted as if both section 2(a)(1) of the Work Made For Hire and Copyright Corrections Act of 2000 and section 1011(d) of the Intellectual Property and Communications Omnibus Reform Act of 1999, as enacted by section 1000(a)(9) of Public Law 106-113, were never enacted, and without regard to any inaction or awareness by the Congress at any time of any judicial determinations.

The terms "WTO Agreement" and "WTO member country" have the meanings given those terms in paragraphs (9) and (10), respectively, of section 2 of the Uruguay Round Agreements Act.

§102. Subject matter of copyright: In general

(a) Copyright protection subsists, in accordance with this title, in original works of authorship fixed in any tangible medium of expression, now known or later developed, from which they can be perceived, reproduced, or otherwise communicated, either directly or with the aid of a machine or device. Works of authorship include the following categories:

(1) literary works;
(2) musical works, including any accompanying words;
(3) dramatic works, including any accompanying music;
(4) pantomimes and choreographic works;
(5) pictorial, graphic, and sculptural works;
(6) motion pictures and other audiovisual works;
(7) sound recordings; and
(8) architectural works.

(b) In no case does copyright protection for an original work of authorship extend to any idea, procedure, process, system, method of operation, concept, principle, or discovery, regardless of the form in which it is described, explained, illustrated, or embodied in such work.

10

§103. Subject matter of copyright: Compilations and derivative works

(a) The subject matter of copyright as specified by section 102 includes compilations and derivative works, but protection for a work employing pre-existing material in which copyright subsists does not extend to any part of the work in which such material has been used unlawfully.

(b) The copyright in a compilation or derivative work extends only to the material contributed by the author of such work, as distinguished from the pre-existing material employed in the work, and does not imply any exclusive right in the preexisting material. The copyright in such work is independent of, and does not affect or enlarge the scope, duration, ownership, or subsistence of, any copyright protection in the preexisting material.

§104. Subject matter of copyright: National origin

(a) Unpublished Works. — The works specified by sections 102 and 103, while unpublished, are subject to protection under this title without regard to the nationality or domicile of the author.

(b) Published Works. — The works specified by sections 102 and 103, when published, are subject to protection under this title if—

(1) on the date of first publication, one or more of the authors is a national or domiciliary of the United States, or is a national, domiciliary, or sovereign authority of a treaty party, or is a stateless person, wherever that person may be domiciled; or

(2) the work is first published in the United States or in a foreign nation that, on the date of first publication, is a treaty party; or

(3) the work is a sound recording that was first fixed in a treaty party; or

(4) the work is a pictorial, graphic, or sculptural work that is incorporated in a building or other structure, or an architectural work that is embodied in a building and the building or structure is located in the United States or a treaty party; or

(5) the work is first published by the United Nations or any of its specialized agencies, or by the Organization of American States; or

(6) the work comes within the scope of a Presidential proclamation. Whenever the President finds that a particular foreign nation extends, to works by authors who are nationals or domiciliaries of the United States or to works that are first published in the United States, copyright protection on substantially the same basis as that on which the foreign nation extends protection to works of its own nationals and domiciliaries and works first published in that nation, the President may by proclamation extend protection under this title to works of which one or more of the authors is, on the date of first publication, a national, domiciliary, or sovereign authority of that nation, or which was first published in that nation. The President may revise, suspend,

or revoke any such proclamation or impose any conditions or limitations on protection under a proclamation.

For purposes of paragraph (2), a work that is published in the United States or a treaty party within 30 days after publication in a foreign nation that is not a treaty party shall be considered to be first published in the United States or such treaty party, as the case may be.

(c) Effect of Berne Convention.—No right or interest in a work eligible for protection under this title may be claimed by virtue of, or in reliance upon, the provisions of the Berne Convention, or the adherence of the United States thereto. Any rights in a work eligible for protection under this title that derive from this title, other Federal or State statutes, or the common law, shall not be expanded or reduced by virtue of, or in reliance upon, the provisions of the Berne Convention, or the adherence of the United States thereto.

(d) Effect of Phonograms Treaties.—Notwithstanding the provisions of subsection (b), no works other than sound recordings shall be eligible for protection under this title solely by virtue of the adherence of the United States to the Geneva Phonograms Convention or the WIPO Performances and Phonograms Treaty.

§104A. Copyright in restored works

(a) Automatic Protection and Term.—

(1) Term.—

(A) Copyright subsists, in accordance with this section, in restored works, and vests automatically on the date of restoration.

(B) Any work in which copyright is restored under this section shall subsist for the remainder of the term of copyright that the work would have otherwise been granted in the United States if the work never entered the public domain in the United States.

(2) Exception.—Any work in which the copyright was ever owned or administered by the Alien Property Custodian and in which the restored copyright would be owned by a government or instrumentality thereof, is not a restored work.

(b) Ownership of Restored Copyright.—A restored work vests initially in the author or initial rightholder of the work as determined by the law of the source country of the work.

(c) Filing of Notice of Intent to Enforce Restored Copyright Against Reliance Parties.—On or after the date of restoration, any person who owns a copyright in a restored work or an exclusive right therein may file with the Copyright Office a notice of intent to enforce that person's copyright or exclusive right or may serve such a notice directly on a reliance party. Acceptance of a notice by the Copyright Office is effective as to any reliance parties but shall not create a presumption of the validity of any of the facts stated therein. Service on a reliance party is effective as to that reliance party and any other reliance parties with actual knowledge of such service and of the contents of that notice.

(d) Remedies for Infringement of Restored Copyrights. —

(1) Enforcement of Copyright in Restored Works in the Absence of a Reliance Party. — As against any party who is not a reliance party, the remedies provided in chapter 5 of this title shall be available on or after the date of restoration of a restored copyright with respect to an act of infringement of the restored copyright that is commenced on or after the date of restoration.

(2) Enforcement of Copyright in Restored Works as Against Reliance Parties. — As against a reliance party, except to the extent provided in paragraphs (3) and (4), the remedies provided in chapter 5 of this title shall be available, with respect to an act of infringement of a restored copyright, on or after the date of restoration of the restored copyright if the requirements of either of the following subparagraphs are met:

(A)(i) The owner of the restored copyright (or such owner's agent) or the owner of an exclusive right therein (or such owner's agent) files with the Copyright Office, during the 24-month period beginning on the date of restoration, a notice of intent to enforce the restored copyright; and

(ii)(I) the act of infringement commenced after the end of the 12-month period beginning on the date of publication of the notice in the Federal Register;

(II) the act of infringement commenced before the end of the 12-month period described in subclause (I) and continued after the end of that 12-month period, in which case remedies shall be available only for infringement occurring after the end of that 12-month period; or

(III) copies or phonorecords of a work in which copyright has been restored under this section are made after publication of the notice of intent in the Federal Register.

(B)(i) The owner of the restored copyright (or such owner's agent) or the owner of an exclusive right therein (or such owner's agent) serves upon a reliance party a notice of intent to enforce a restored copyright; and

(ii)(I) the act of infringement commenced after the end of the 12-month period beginning on the date the notice of intent is received;

(II) the act of infringement commenced before the end of the 12-month period described in subclause (I) and continued after the end of that 12-month period, in which case remedies shall be available only for the infringement occurring after the end of that 12-month period; or

(III) copies or phonorecords of a work in which copyright has been restored under this section are made after receipt of the notice of intent.

In the event that notice is provided under both subparagraphs (A) and (B), the 12-month period referred to in such subparagraphs shall run from the earlier of publication or service of notice.

(3) Existing Derivative Works. —

(A) In the case of a derivative work that is based upon a restored work and is created —

(i) before the date of the enactment of the Uruguay Round Agreements Act, if the source country of the restored work is an eligible country on such date, or

(ii) before the date on which the source country of the restored work becomes an eligible country, if that country is not an eligible country on such date of enactment,

a reliance party may continue to exploit that derivative work for the duration of the restored copyright if the reliance party pays to the owner of the restored copyright reasonable compensation for conduct which would be subject to a remedy for infringement but for the provisions of this paragraph.

(B) In the absence of an agreement between the parties, the amount of such compensation shall be determined by an action in United States district court, and shall reflect any harm to the actual or potential market for or value of the restored work from the reliance party's continued exploitation of the work, as well as compensation for the relative contributions of expression of the author of the restored work and the reliance party to the derivative work.

(4) Commencement of Infringement for Reliance Parties. — For purposes of section 412, in the case of reliance parties, infringement shall be deemed to have commenced before registration when acts which would have constituted infringement had the restored work been subject to copyright were commenced before the date of restoration.

(e) Notices of Intent to Enforce a Restored Copyright. —

(1) Notices of Intent Filed With the Copyright Office. —

(A)(i) A notice of intent filed with the Copyright Office to enforce a restored copyright shall be signed by the owner of the restored copyright or the owner of an exclusive right therein, who files the notice under subsection (d)(2)(A)(i) (hereafter in this paragraph referred to as the "owner"), or by the owner's agent, shall identify the title of the restored work, and shall include an English translation of the title and any other alternative titles known to the owner by which the restored work may be identified, and an address and telephone number at which the owner may be contacted. If the notice is signed by an agent, the agency relationship must have been constituted in a writing signed by the owner before the filing of the notice. The Copyright Office may specifically require in regulations other information to be included in the notice, but failure to provide such other information shall not invalidate the notice or be a basis for refusal to list the restored work in the Federal Register.

(ii) If a work in which copyright is restored has no formal title, it shall be described in the notice of intent in detail sufficient to identify it.

(iii) Minor errors or omissions may be corrected by further notice at any time after the notice of intent is filed. Notices of corrections for such minor errors or omissions shall be accepted after the period established in subsection (d)(2)(A)(i). Notices shall be published in the Federal Register pursuant to subparagraph (B).

(B)(i) The Register of Copyrights shall publish in the Federal Register, commencing not later than 4 months after the date of restoration for a particular nation and every 4 months thereafter for a period of 2 years, lists identifying restored works and the ownership thereof if a notice of intent to enforce a restored copyright has been filed.

(ii) Not less than 1 list containing all notices of intent to enforce shall be maintained in the Public Information Office of the Copyright Office and shall be available for public inspection and copying during regular business hours pursuant to sections 705 and 708.

(C) The Register of Copyrights is authorized to fix reasonable fees based on the costs of receipt, processing, recording, and publication of notices of intent to enforce a restored copyright and corrections thereto.

(D)(i) Not later than 90 days before the date the Agreement on Trade-Related Aspects of Intellectual Property referred to in section 101(d)(15) of the Uruguay Round Agreements Act enters into force with respect to the United States, the Copyright Office shall issue and publish in the Federal Register regulations governing the filing under this subsection of notices of intent to enforce a restored copyright.

(ii) Such regulations shall permit owners of restored copyrights to file simultaneously for registration of the restored copyright.

(2) Notices of Intent Served on a Reliance Party. —

(A) Notices of intent to enforce a restored copyright may be served on a reliance party at any time after the date of restoration of the restored copyright.

(B) Notices of intent to enforce a restored copyright served on a reliance party shall be signed by the owner or the owner's agent, shall identify the restored work and the work in which the restored work is used, if any, in detail sufficient to identify them, and shall include an English translation of the title, any other alternative titles known to the owner by which the work may be identified, the use or uses to which the owner objects, and an address and telephone number at which the reliance party may contact the owner. If the notice is signed by an agent, the agency relationship must have been constituted in writing and signed by the owner before service of the notice.

(3) Effect of Material False Statements. — Any material false statement knowingly made with respect to any restored copyright identified in any notice of intent shall make void all claims and assertions made with respect to such restored copyright.

(f) Immunity from Warranty and Related Liability. —

(1) In General. — Any person who warrants, promises, or guarantees that a work does not violate an exclusive right granted in section 106 shall not be liable for legal, equitable, arbitral, or administrative relief if the warranty, promise, or guarantee is breached by virtue of the restoration of copyright under this section, if such warranty, promise, or guarantee is made before January 1, 1995.

(2) Performances. — No person shall be required to perform any act if such performance is made infringing by virtue of the restoration of copyright under the provisions of this section, if the obligation to perform was undertaken before January 1, 1995.

(g) Proclamation of Copyright Restoration.—Whenever the President finds that a particular foreign nation extends, to works by authors who are nationals or domiciliaries of the United States, restored copyright protection on substantially the same basis as provided under this section, the President may by proclamation extend restored protection provided under this section to any work—

(1) of which one or more of the authors is, on the date of first publication, a national, domiciliary, or sovereign authority of that nation; or

(2) which was first published in that nation.

The President may revise, suspend, or revoke any such proclamation or impose any conditions or limitations on protection under such a proclamation.

(h) Definitions.—For purposes of this section and section 109(a):

(1) The term "date of adherence or proclamation" means the earlier of the date on which a foreign nation which, as of the date the WTO Agreement enters into force with respect to the United States, is not a nation adhering to the Berne Convention or a WTO member country, becomes—

(A) a nation adhering to the Berne Convention;

(B) a WTO member country;

(C) a nation adhering to the WIPO Copyright Treaty;

(D) a nation adhering to the WIPO Performances and Phonograms Treaty; or

(E) subject to a Presidential proclamation under subsection (g).

(2) The "date of restoration" of a restored copyright is—

(A) January 1, 1996, if the source country of the restored work is a nation adhering to the Berne Convention or a WTO member country on such date, or

(B) the date of adherence or proclamation, in the case of any other source country of the restored work.

(3) The term "eligible country" means a nation, other than the United States, that—

(A) becomes a WTO member country after the date of the enactment of the Uruguay Round Agreements Act;

(B) on such date of enactment is, or after such date of enactment becomes, a nation adhering to the Berne Convention;

(C) adheres to the WIPO Copyright Treaty;

(D) adheres to the WIPO Performances and Phonograms Treaty; or

(E) after such date of enactment becomes subject to a proclamation under subsection (g).

(4) The term "reliance party" means any person who—

(A) with respect to a particular work, engages in acts, before the source country of that work becomes an eligible country, which would have violated section 106 if the restored work had been subject to copyright protection, and who, after the source country becomes an eligible country, continues to engage in such acts;

(B) before the source country of a particular work becomes an eligible country, makes or acquires 1 or more copies or phonorecords of that work; or

(C) as the result of the sale or other disposition of a derivative work covered under subsection (d)(3), or significant assets of a person described in subparagraph (A) or (B), is a successor, assignee, or licensee of that person.

(5) The term "restored copyright" means copyright in a restored work under this section.

(6) The term "restored work" means an original work of authorship that —

(A) is protected under subsection (a);

(B) is not in the public domain in its source country through expiration of term of protection;

(C) is in the public domain in the United States due to —

(i) noncompliance with formalities imposed at any time by United States copyright law, including failure of renewal, lack of proper notice, or failure to comply with any manufacturing requirements;

(ii) lack of subject matter protection in the case of sound recordings fixed before February 15, 1972; or

(iii) lack of national eligibility;

(D) has at least one author or rightholder who was, at the time the work was created, a national or domiciliary of an eligible country, and if published, was first published in an eligible country and not published in the United States during the 30-day period following publication in such eligible country; and

(E) if the source country for the work is an eligible country solely by virtue of its adherence to the WIPO Performances and Phonograms Treaty, is a sound recording.

(7) The term "rightholder" means the person —

(A) who, with respect to a sound recording, first fixes a sound recording with authorization, or

(B) who has acquired rights from the person described in subparagraph (A) by means of any conveyance or by operation of law.

(8) The "source country" of a restored work is —

(A) a nation other than the United States;

(B) in the case of an unpublished work —

(i) the eligible country in which the author or rightholder is a national or domiciliary, or, if a restored work has more than 1 author or rightholder, of which the majority of foreign authors or rightholders are nationals or domiciliaries; or

(ii) if the majority of authors or rightholders are not foreign, the nation other than the United States which has the most significant contacts with the work; and

(C) in the case of a published work —

(i) the eligible country in which the work is first published, or

(ii) if the restored work is published on the same day in 2 or more eligible countries, the eligible country which has the most significant contacts with the work.

§105. Subject matter of copyright: United States Government works

Copyright protection under this title is not available for any work of the United States Government, but the United States Government is not precluded from receiving and holding copyrights transferred to it by assignment, bequest, or otherwise.

§106. Exclusive rights in copyrighted works

Subject to sections 107 through 122, the owner of copyright under this title has the exclusive rights to do and to authorize any of the following:

(1) to reproduce the copyrighted work in copies or phonorecords;

(2) to prepare derivative works based upon the copyrighted work;

(3) to distribute copies or phonorecords of the copyrighted work to the public by sale or other transfer of ownership, or by rental, lease, or lending;

(4) in the case of literary, musical, dramatic, and choreographic works, pantomimes, and motion pictures and other audiovisual works, to perform the copyrighted work publicly;

(5) in the case of literary, musical, dramatic, and choreographic works, pantomimes, and pictorial, graphic, or sculptural works, including the individual images of a motion picture or other audiovisual work, to display the copyrighted work publicly; and

(6) in the case of sound recordings, to perform the copyrighted work publicly by means of a digital audio transmission.

§106A. Rights of certain authors to attribution and integrity

(a) Rights of Attribution and Integrity. — Subject to section 107 and independent of the exclusive rights provided in section 106, the author of a work of visual art —

(1) shall have the right —

(A) to claim authorship of that work, and

(B) to prevent the use of his or her name as the author of any work of visual art which he or she did not create;

(2) shall have the right to prevent the use of his or her name as the author of the work of visual art in the event of a distortion, mutilation, or other modification of the work which would be prejudicial to his or her honor or reputation; and

(3) subject to the limitations set forth in section 113(d), shall have the right —

(A) to prevent any intentional distortion, mutilation, or other modification of that work which would be prejudicial to his or her honor or reputation, and any intentional distortion, mutilation, or modification of that work is a violation of that right, and

    (B) to prevent any destruction of a work of recognized stature, and any intentional or grossly negligent destruction of that work is a violation of that right.

    (b) Scope and Exercise of Rights. — Only the author of a work of visual art has the rights conferred by subsection (a) in that work, whether or not the author is the copyright owner. The authors of a joint work of visual art are coowners of the rights conferred by subsection (a) in that work.

    (c) Exceptions. —

    (1) The modification of a work of visual art which is the result of the passage of time or the inherent nature of the materials is not a distortion, mutilation, or other modification described in subsection (a)(3)(A).

    (2) The modification of a work of visual art which is the result of conservation, or of the public presentation, including lighting and placement, of the work is not a destruction, distortion, mutilation, or other modification described in subsection (a)(3) unless the modification is caused by gross negligence.

    (3) The rights described in paragraphs (1) and (2) of subsection (a) shall not apply to any reproduction, depiction, portrayal, or other use of a work in, upon, or in any connection with any item described in subparagraph (A) or (B) of the definition of "work of visual art" in section 101, and any such reproduction, depiction, portrayal, or other use of a work is not a destruction, distortion, mutilation, or other modification described in paragraph (3) of subsection (a).

    (d) Duration of Rights. —

    (1) With respect to works of visual art created on or after the effective date set forth in section 610(a) of the Visual Artists Rights Act of 1990, the rights conferred by subsection (a) shall endure for a term consisting of the life of the author.

    (2) With respect to works of visual art created before the effective date set forth in section 610(a) of the Visual Artists Rights Act of 1990, but title to which has not, as of such effective date, been transferred from the author, the rights conferred by subsection (a) shall be coextensive with, and shall expire at the same time as, the rights conferred by section 106.

    (3) In the case of a joint work prepared by two or more authors, the rights conferred by subsection (a) shall endure for a term consisting of the life of the last surviving author.

    (4) All terms of the rights conferred by subsection (a) run to the end of the calendar year in which they would otherwise expire.

    (e) Transfer and Waiver. —

    (1) The rights conferred by subsection (a) may not be transferred, but those rights may be waived if the author expressly agrees to such waiver in a written instrument signed by the author. Such instrument shall specifically identify the work, and uses of that work, to which the waiver applies, and the waiver shall apply only to the work and uses so identified. In the case of a joint work prepared by two or more authors, a waiver of rights under this paragraph made by one such author waives such rights for all such authors.

(2) Ownership of the rights conferred by subsection (a) with respect to a work of visual art is distinct from ownership of any copy of that work, or of a copyright or any exclusive right under a copyright in that work. Transfer of ownership of any copy of a work of visual art, or of a copyright or any exclusive right under a copyright, shall not constitute a waiver of the rights conferred by subsection (a). Except as may otherwise be agreed by the author in a written instrument signed by the author, a waiver of the rights conferred by subsection (a) with respect to a work of visual art shall not constitute a transfer of ownership of any copy of that work, or of ownership of a copyright or of any exclusive right under a copyright in that work.

§107. Limitations on exclusive rights: Fair use

Notwithstanding the provisions of sections 106 and 106A, the fair use of a copyrighted work, including such use by reproduction in copies or phonorecords or by any other means specified by that section, for purposes such as criticism, comment, news reporting, teaching (including multiple copies for classroom use), scholarship, or research, is not an infringement of copyright. In determining whether the use made of a work in any particular case is a fair use the factors to be considered shall include —

(1) the purpose and character of the use, including whether such use is of a commercial nature or is for nonprofit educational purposes;

(2) the nature of the copyrighted work;

(3) the amount and substantiality of the portion used in relation to the copyrighted work as a whole; and

(4) the effect of the use upon the potential market for or value of the copyrighted work.

The fact that a work is unpublished shall not itself bar a finding of fair use if such finding is made upon consideration of all the above factors.

§108. Limitations on exclusive rights: Reproduction by libraries and archives

(a) Except as otherwise provided in this title and notwithstanding the provisions of section 106, it is not an infringement of copyright for a library or archives, or any of its employees acting within the scope of their employment, to reproduce no more than one copy or phonorecord of a work, except as provided in subsections (b) and (c), or to distribute such copy or phonorecord, under the conditions specified by this section, if—

(1) the reproduction or distribution is made without any purpose of direct or indirect commercial advantage;

(2) the collections of the library or archives are (i) open to the public, or (ii) available not only to researchers affiliated with the library or archives or with

the institution of which it is a part, but also to other persons doing research in a specialized field; and

(3) the reproduction or distribution of the work includes a notice of copyright that appears on the copy or phonorecord that is reproduced under the provisions of this section, or includes a legend stating that the work may be protected by copyright if no such notice can be found on the copy or phonorecord that is reproduced under the provisions of this section.

(b) The rights of reproduction and distribution under this section apply to three copies or phonorecords of an unpublished work duplicated solely for purposes of preservation and security or for deposit for research use in another library or archives of the type described by clause (2) of subsection (a), if—

(1) the copy or phonorecord reproduced is currently in the collections of the library or archives; and

(2) any such copy or phonorecord that is reproduced in digital format is not otherwise distributed in that format and is not made available to the public in that format outside the premises of the library or archives.

(c) The right of reproduction under this section applies to three copies or phonorecords of a published work duplicated solely for the purpose of replacement of a copy or phonorecord that is damaged, deteriorating, lost, or stolen, or if the existing format in which the work is stored has become obsolete, if—

(1) the library or archives has, after a reasonable effort, determined that an unused replacement cannot be obtained at a fair price; and

(2) any such copy or phonorecord that is reproduced in digital format is not made available to the public in that format outside the premises of the library or archives in lawful possession of such copy.

For purposes of this subsection, a format shall be considered obsolete if the machine or device necessary to render perceptible a work stored in that format is no longer manufactured or is no longer reasonably available in the commercial marketplace.

(d) The rights of reproduction and distribution under this section apply to a copy, made from the collection of a library or archives where the user makes his or her request or from that of another library or archives, of no more than one article or other contribution to a copyrighted collection or periodical issue, or to a copy or phonorecord of a small part of any other copyrighted work, if—

(1) the copy or phonorecord becomes the property of the user, and the library or archives has had no notice that the copy or phonorecord would be used for any purpose other than private study, scholarship, or research; and

(2) the library or archives displays prominently, at the place where orders are accepted, and includes on its order form, a warning of copyright in accordance with requirements that the Register of Copyrights shall prescribe by regulation.

(e) The rights of reproduction and distribution under this section apply to the entire work, or to a substantial part of it, made from the collection of a library or archives where the user makes his or her request or from that of another library or archives, if the library or archives has first determined, on the basis of a reasonable investigation, that a copy or phonorecord of the copyrighted work cannot be obtained at a fair price, if —

(1) the copy or phonorecord becomes the property of the user, and the library or archives has had no notice that the copy or phonorecord would be used for any purpose other than private study, scholarship, or research; and

(2) the library or archives displays prominently, at the place where orders are accepted, and includes on its order form, a warning of copyright in accordance with requirements that the Register of Copyrights shall prescribe by regulation.

(f) Nothing in this section —

(1) shall be construed to impose liability for copyright infringement upon a library or archives or its employees for the unsupervised use of reproducing equipment located on its premises: *Provided,* That such equipment displays a notice that the making of a copy may be subject to the copyright law;

(2) excuses a person who uses such reproducing equipment or who requests a copy or phonorecord under subsection (d) from liability for copyright infringement for any such act, or for any later use of such copy or phonorecord, if it exceeds fair use as provided by section 107;

(3) shall be construed to limit the reproduction and distribution by lending of a limited number of copies and excerpts by a library or archives of an audiovisual news program, subject to clauses (1), (2), and (3) of subsection (a); or

(4) in any way affects the right of fair use as provided by section 107, or any contractual obligations assumed at any time by the library or archives when it obtained a copy or phonorecord of a work in its collections.

(g) The rights of reproduction and distribution under this section extend to the isolated and unrelated reproduction or distribution of a single copy or phonorecord of the same material on separate occasions, but do not extend to cases where the library or archives, or its employee —

(1) is aware or has substantial reason to believe that it is engaging in the related or concerted reproduction or distribution of multiple copies or phonorecords of the same material, whether made on one occasion or over a period of time, and whether intended for aggregate use by one or more individuals or for separate use by the individual members of a group; or

(2) engages in the systematic reproduction or distribution of single or multiple copies or phonorecords of material described in subsection (d): *Provided,* That nothing in this clause prevents a library or archives from participating in interlibrary arrangements that do not have, as their purpose or effect, that the library or archives receiving such copies or phonorecords for distribution does so in such aggregate quantities as to substitute for a subscription to or purchase of such work.

(h)(1) For purposes of this section, during the last 20 years of any term of copyright of a published work, a library or archives, including a nonprofit educational institution that functions as such, may reproduce, distribute, display, or perform in facsimile or digital form a copy or phonorecord of such work, or portions thereof, for purposes of preservation, scholarship, or research, if such library or archives has first determined, on the basis of a reasonable investigation, that none of the conditions set forth in subparagraphs (A), (B), and (C) of paragraph (2) apply.

(2) No reproduction, distribution, display, or performance is authorized under this subsection if —

(A) the work is subject to normal commercial exploitation;

(B) a copy or phonorecord of the work can be obtained at a reasonable price; or

(C) the copyright owner or its agent provides notice pursuant to regulations promulgated by the Register of Copyrights that either of the conditions set forth in subparagraphs (A) and (B) applies.

(3) The exemption provided in this subsection does not apply to any subsequent uses by users other than such library or archives.

(i) The rights of reproduction and distribution under this section do not apply to a musical work, a pictorial, graphic or sculptural work, or a motion picture or other audiovisual work other than an audiovisual work dealing with news, except that no such limitation shall apply with respect to rights granted by subsections (b), (c), and (h), or with respect to pictorial or graphic works published as illustrations, diagrams, or similar adjuncts to works of which copies are reproduced or distributed in accordance with subsections (d) and (e).

§109. Limitations on exclusive rights: Effect of transfer of particular copy or phonorecord

(a) Notwithstanding the provisions of section 106(3), the owner of a particular copy or phonorecord lawfully made under this title, or any person authorized by such owner, is entitled, without the authority of the copyright owner, to sell or otherwise dispose of the possession of that copy or phonorecord. Notwithstanding the preceding sentence, copies or phonorecords of works subject to restored copyright under section 104A that are manufactured before the date of restoration of copyright or, with respect to reliance parties, before publication or service of notice under section 104A(e), may be sold or otherwise disposed of without the authorization of the owner of the restored copyright for purposes of direct or indirect commercial advantage only during the 12-month period beginning on —

(1) the date of the publication in the Federal Register of the notice of intent filed with the Copyright Office under section 104A(d)(2)(A), or

(2) the date of the receipt of actual notice served under section 104A(d)(2)(B), whichever occurs first.

(b)(1)(A) Notwithstanding the provisions of subsection (a), unless authorized by the owners of copyright in the sound recording or the owner of copyright in a computer program (including any tape, disk, or other medium embodying such program), and in the case of a sound recording in the musical works embodied therein, neither the owner of a particular phonorecord nor any person in possession of a particular copy of a computer program (including any tape, disk, or other medium embodying such program), may, for the purposes of direct or indirect commercial advantage, dispose of, or authorize the disposal of, the possession of that phonorecord or computer program (including any tape, disk, or other medium embodying such program) by rental, lease, or lending, or by any other act or practice in the nature of rental, lease, or lending. Nothing in the preceding sentence shall apply to the rental, lease, or lending of a phonorecord for nonprofit purposes by a nonprofit library or nonprofit educational institution. The transfer of possession of a lawfully made copy of a computer program by a nonprofit educational institution to another nonprofit educational institution or to faculty, staff, and students does not constitute rental, lease, or lending for direct or indirect commercial purposes under this subsection.

(B) This subsection does not apply to —

(i) a computer program which is embodied in a machine or product and which cannot be copied during the ordinary operation or use of the machine or product; or

(ii) a computer program embodied in or used in conjunction with a limited purpose computer that is designed for playing video games and may be designed for other purposes.

(C) Nothing in this subsection affects any provision of chapter 9 of this title.

(2)(A) Nothing in this subsection shall apply to the lending of a computer program for nonprofit purposes by a nonprofit library, if each copy of a computer program which is lent by such library has affixed to the packaging containing the program a warning of copyright in accordance with requirements that the Register of Copyrights shall prescribe by regulation.

(B) Not later than three years after the date of the enactment of the Computer Software Rental Amendments Act of 1990, and at such times thereafter as the Register of Copyrights considers appropriate, the Register of Copyrights, after consultation with representatives of copyright owners and librarians, shall submit to the Congress a report stating whether this paragraph has achieved its intended purpose of maintaining the integrity of the copyright system while providing nonprofit libraries the capability to fulfill their function. Such report shall advise the Congress as to any information or recommendations that the Register of Copyrights considers necessary to carry out the purposes of this subsection.

(3) Nothing in this subsection shall affect any provision of the antitrust laws. For purposes of the preceding sentence, "antitrust laws" has the meaning given that term in the first section of the Clayton Act and includes section 5 of the Federal Trade Commission Act to the extent that section relates to unfair methods of competition.

(4) Any person who distributes a phonorecord or a copy of a computer program (including any tape, disk, or other medium embodying such program) in violation of paragraph (1) is an infringer of copyright under section 501 of this title and is subject to the remedies set forth in sections 502, 503, 504, and 505. Such violation shall not be a criminal offense under section 506 or cause such person to be subject to the criminal penalties set forth in section 2319 of title 18.

(c) Notwithstanding the provisions of section 106(5), the owner of a particular copy lawfully made under this title, or any person authorized by such owner, is entitled, without the authority of the copyright owner, to display that copy publicly, either directly or by the projection of no more than one image at a time, to viewers present at the place where the copy is located.

(d) The privileges prescribed by subsections (a) and (c) do not, unless authorized by the copyright owner, extend to any person who has acquired possession of the copy or phonorecord from the copyright owner, by rental, lease, loan, or otherwise, without acquiring ownership of it.

(e) Notwithstanding the provisions of sections 106(4) and 106(5), in the case of an electronic audiovisual game intended for use in coin-operated equipment, the owner of a particular copy of such a game lawfully made under this title, is entitled, without the authority of the copyright owner of the game, to publicly perform or display that game in coin-operated equipment, except that this subsection shall not apply to any work of authorship embodied in the audiovisual game if the copyright owner of the electronic audiovisual game is not also the copyright owner of the work of authorship.

§110. Limitations on exclusive rights: Exemption of certain performances and displays

Notwithstanding the provisions of section 106, the following are not infringements of copyright:

(1) performance or display of a work by instructors or pupils in the course of face-to-face teaching activities of a nonprofit educational institution, in a classroom or similar place devoted to instruction, unless, in the case of a motion picture or other audiovisual work, the performance, or the display of individual images, is given by means of a copy that was not lawfully made under this title, and that the person responsible for the performance knew or had reason to believe was not lawfully made;

(2) except with respect to a work produced or marketed primarily for performance or display as part of mediated instructional activities transmitted via digital networks, or a performance or display that is given by means of a copy or phonorecord that is not lawfully made and acquired under this title, and the transmitting government body or accredited nonprofit educational institution knew or had reason to believe was not lawfully made and acquired, the performance of a nondramatic literary or musical work or reasonable and limited portions of any other work, or display of a work in an amount comparable to that which is typically displayed in the course of a live classroom session, by or in the course of a transmission, if—

(A) the performance or display is made by, at the direction of, or under the actual supervision of an instructor as an integral part of a class session offered as a regular part of the systematic mediated instructional activities of a governmental body or an accredited nonprofit educational institution;

(B) the performance or display is directly related and of material assistance to the teaching content of the transmission;

(C) the transmission is made solely for, and, to the extent technologically feasible, the reception of such transmission is limited to —

(i) students officially enrolled in the course for which the transmission is made; or

(ii) officers or employees of governmental bodies as a part of their official duties or employment; and

(D) the transmitting body or institution —

(i) institutes policies regarding copyright, provides informational materials to faculty, students, and relevant staff members that accurately describe, and promote compliance with, the laws of the United States relating to copyright, and provides notice to students that materials used in connection with the course may be subject to copyright protection; and

(ii) in the case of digital transmissions —

(I) applies technological measures that reasonably prevent —

(aa) retention of the work in accessible form by recipients of the transmission from the transmitting body or institution for longer than the class session; and

(bb) unauthorized further dissemination of the work in accessible form by such recipients to others; and

(II) does not engage in conduct that could reasonably be expected to interfere with technological measures used by copyright owners to prevent such retention or unauthorized further dissemination;

(3) performance of a nondramatic literary or musical work or of a dramatico-musical work of a religious nature, or display of a work, in the course of services at a place of worship or other religious assembly;

(4) performance of a nondramatic literary or musical work otherwise than in a transmission to the public, without any purpose of direct or indirect commercial advantage and without payment of any fee or other compensation for the performance to any of its performers, promoters, or organizers, if—

(A) there is no direct or indirect admission charge; or

(B) the proceeds, after deducting the reasonable costs of producing the performance, are used exclusively for educational, religious, or charitable purposes and not for private financial gain, except where the copyright owner has served notice of objection to the performance under the following conditions:

(i) the notice shall be in writing and signed by the copyright owner or such owner's duly authorized agent; and

(ii) the notice shall be served on the person responsible for the performance at least seven days before the date of the performance, and shall state the reasons for the objection; and

(iii) the notice shall comply, in form, content, and manner of service, with requirements that the Register of Copyrights shall prescribe by regulation;

(5)(A) except as provided in subparagraph (B), communication of a transmission embodying a performance or display of a work by the public

26

reception of the transmission on a single receiving apparatus of a kind commonly used in private homes, unless —

(i) a direct charge is made to see or hear the transmission; or

(ii) the transmission thus received is further transmitted to the public;

(B) communication by an establishment of a transmission or retransmission embodying a performance or display of a nondramatic musical work intended to be received by the general public, originated by a radio or television broadcast station licensed as such by the Federal Communications Commission, or, if an audiovisual transmission, by a cable system or satellite carrier, if —

(i) in the case of an establishment other than a food service or drinking establishment, either the establishment in which the communication occurs has less than 2,000 gross square feet of space (excluding space used for customer parking and for no other purpose), or the establishment in which the communication occurs has 2,000 or more gross square feet of space (excluding space used for customer parking and for no other purpose) and —

(I) if the performance is by audio means only, the performance is communicated by means of a total of not more than 6 loudspeakers, of which not more than 4 loudspeakers are located in any 1 room or adjoining outdoor space; or

(II) if the performance or display is by audiovisual means, any visual portion of the performance or display is communicated by means of a total of not more than 4 audiovisual devices, of which not more than one audiovisual device is located in any 1 room, and no such audiovisual device has a diagonal screen size greater than 55 inches, and any audio portion of the performance or display is communicated by means of a total of not more than 6 loudspeakers, of which not more than 4 loudspeakers are located in any 1 room or adjoining outdoor space;

(ii) in the case of a food service or drinking establishment, either the establishment in which the communication occurs has less than 3,750 gross square feet of space (excluding space used for customer parking and for no other purpose), or the establishment in which the communication occurs has 3,750 gross square feet of space or more (excluding space used for customer parking and for no other purpose) and —

(I) if the performance is by audio means only, the performance is communicated by means of a total of not more than 6 loudspeakers, of which not more than 4 loudspeakers are located in any 1 room or adjoining outdoor space; or

(II) if the performance or display is by audiovisual means, any visual portion of the performance or display is communicated by means of a total of not more than 4 audiovisual devices, of which not more than 1 audiovisual device is located in any 1 room, and no such audiovisual device has a diagonal screen size greater than 55 inches, and any audio portion of the performance or display is communicated by means of a total of not more than 6 loudspeakers, of which not more than 4 loudspeakers are located in any 1 room or adjoining outdoor space;

(iii) no direct charge is made to see or hear the transmission or retransmission;

(iv) the transmission or retransmission is not further transmitted beyond the establishment where it is received; and

(v) the transmission or retransmission is licensed by the copyright owner of the work so publicly performed or displayed;

(6) performance of a nondramatic musical work by a governmental body or a nonprofit agricultural or horticultural organization, in the course of an annual agricultural or horticultural fair or exhibition conducted by such body or organization; the exemption provided by this clause shall extend to any liability for copyright infringement that would otherwise be imposed on such body or organization, under doctrines of vicarious liability or related infringement, for a performance by a concessionnaire, business establishment, or other person at such fair or exhibition, but shall not excuse any such person from liability for the performance;

(7) performance of a nondramatic musical work by a vending establishment open to the public at large without any direct or indirect admission charge, where the sole purpose of the performance is to promote the retail sale of copies or phonorecords of the work, or of the audiovisual or other devices utilized in such performance, and the performance is not transmitted beyond the place where the establishment is located and is within the immediate area where the sale is occurring;

(8) performance of a nondramatic literary work, by or in the course of a transmission specifically designed for and primarily directed to blind or other handicapped persons who are unable to read normal printed material as a result of their handicap, or deaf or other handicapped persons who are unable to hear the aural signals accompanying a transmission of visual signals, if the performance is made without any purpose of direct or indirect commercial advantage and its transmission is made through the facilities of: (i) a governmental body; or (ii) a noncommercial educational broadcast station (as defined in section 397 of title 47); or (iii) a radio subcarrier authorization (as defined in 47 CFR 73.293-73.295 and 73.593-73.595); or (iv) a cable system (as defined in section 111(f));

(9) performance on a single occasion of a dramatic literary work published at least ten years before the date of the performance, by or in the course of a transmission specifically designed for and primarily directed to blind or other handicapped persons who are unable to read normal printed material as a result of their handicap, if the performance is made without any purpose of direct or indirect commercial advantage and its transmission is made through the facilities of a radio subcarrier authorization referred to in clause (8) (iii), *Provided,* That the provisions of this clause shall not be applicable to more than one performance of the same work by the same performers or under the auspices of the same organization;

(10) notwithstanding paragraph (4), the following is not an infringement of copyright: performance of a nondramatic literary or musical work in the course of a social function which is organized and promoted by a nonprofit veterans' organization or a nonprofit fraternal organization to which the general public is not invited, but not including the invitees of the organizations, if the proceeds from the performance, after deducting the reasonable costs of producing the performance, are used exclusively for charitable purposes and not for financial gain. For purposes of this section the social functions of any college or university fraternity or sorority shall not be included unless the social function is held solely to raise funds for a specific charitable purpose; and

(11) the making imperceptible, by or at the direction of a member of a private household, of limited portions of audio or video content of a motion picture, during a performance in or transmitted to that household for private home viewing, from an authorized copy of the motion picture, or the creation or provision of a computer program or other technology that enables such making imperceptible and that is designed and marketed to be used, at the direction of a member of a private household, for such making imperceptible, if no fixed copy of the altered version of the motion picture is created by such computer program or other technology.

The exemptions provided under paragraph (5) shall not be taken into account in any administrative, judicial, or other governmental proceeding to set or adjust the royalties payable to copyright owners for the public performance or display of their works. Royalties payable to copyright owners for any public performance or display of their works other than such performances or displays as are exempted under paragraph (5) shall not be diminished in any respect as a result of such exemption.

In paragraph (2), the term "mediated instructional activities" with respect to the performance or display of a work by digital transmission under this section refers to activities that use such work as an integral part of the class experience, controlled by or under the actual supervision of the instructor and analogous to the type of performance or display that would take place in a live classroom setting. The term does not refer to activities that use, in 1 or more class sessions of a single course, such works as textbooks, course packs, or other material in any media, copies or phonorecords of which are typically purchased or acquired by the students in higher education for their independent use and retention or are typically purchased or acquired for elementary and secondary students for their possession and independent use.

For purposes of paragraph (2), accreditation —

(A) with respect to an institution providing post-secondary education, shall be as determined by a regional or national accrediting agency recognized by the Council on Higher Education Accreditation or the United States Department of Education; and

(B) with respect to an institution providing elementary or secondary education, shall be as recognized by the applicable state certification or licensing procedures.

For purposes of paragraph (2), no governmental body or accredited nonprofit educational institution shall be liable for infringement by reason of the transient or temporary storage of material carried out through the automatic technical process of a digital transmission of the performance or display of that material as authorized under paragraph (2). No such material stored on the system or network controlled or operated by the transmitting body or institution under this paragraph shall be maintained on such system or network in a manner ordinarily accessible to anyone other than anticipated recipients. No such copy shall be maintained on the system or network in a manner ordinarily accessible to such anticipated recipients for a longer period than is reasonably necessary to facilitate the transmissions for which it was made.

For purposes of paragraph (11), the term "making imperceptible" does not include the addition of audio or video content that is performed or displayed over or in place of existing content in a motion picture.

Nothing in paragraph (11) shall be construed to imply further rights under section 106 of this title, or to have any effect on defenses or limitations on rights granted under any other section of this title or under any other paragraph of this section.

§111. Limitations on exclusive rights: Secondary transmissions

(a) Certain Secondary Transmissions Exempted. — The secondary transmission of a performance or display of a work embodied in a primary transmission is not an infringement of copyright if—

(1) the secondary transmission is not made by a cable system, and consists entirely of the relaying, by the management of a hotel, apartment house, or similar establishment, of signals transmitted by a broadcast station licensed by the Federal Communications Commission, within the local service area of such station, to the private lodgings of guests or residents of such establishment, and no direct charge is made to see or hear the secondary transmission; or

(2) the secondary transmission is made solely for the purpose and under the conditions specified by clause (2) of section 110; or

(3) the secondary transmission is made by any carrier who has no direct or indirect control over the content or selection of the primary transmission or over the particular recipients of the secondary transmission, and whose activities with respect to the secondary transmission consist solely of providing wires, cables, or other communications channels for the use of others: *Provided,* That the provisions of this clause extend only to the activities of said carrier with respect to secondary transmissions and do not exempt from liability the activities of others with respect to their own primary or secondary transmissions;

(4) the secondary transmission is made by a satellite carrier pursuant to a statutory license under section 119; or

(5) the secondary transmission is not made by a cable system but is made by a governmental body, or other nonprofit organization, without any purpose of

direct or indirect commercial advantage, and without charge to the recipients of the secondary transmission other than assessments necessary to defray the actual and reasonable costs of maintaining and operating the secondary transmission service.

(b) Secondary Transmission of Primary Transmission to Controlled Group. — Notwithstanding the provisions of subsections (a) and (c), the secondary transmission to the public of a performance or display of a work embodied in a primary transmission is actionable as an act of infringement under section 501, and is fully subject to the remedies provided by sections 502 through 506, if the primary transmission is not made for reception by the public at large but is controlled and limited to reception by particular members of the public: *Provided,* however, That such secondary transmission is not actionable as an act of infringement if —

(1) the primary transmission is made by a broadcast station licensed by the Federal Communications Commission; and

(2) the carriage of the signals comprising the secondary transmission is required under the rules, regulations, or authorizations of the Federal Communications Commission; and

(3) the signal of the primary transmitter is not altered or changed in any way by the secondary transmitter.

(c) Secondary Transmissions by Cable Systems. —

(1) Subject to the provisions of clauses (2), (3), and (4) of this subsection and section 114(d), secondary transmissions to the public by a cable system of a performance or display of a work embodied in a primary transmission made by a broadcast station licensed by the Federal Communications Commission or by an appropriate governmental authority of Canada or Mexico shall be subject to statutory licensing upon compliance with the requirements of subsection (d) where the carriage of the signals comprising the secondary transmission is permissible under the rules, regulations, or authorizations of the Federal Communications Commission.

(2) Notwithstanding the provisions of clause (1) of this subsection, the willful or repeated secondary transmission to the public by a cable system of a primary transmission made by a broadcast station licensed by the Federal Communications Commission or by an appropriate governmental authority of Canada or Mexico and embodying a performance or display of a work is actionable as an act of infringement under section 501, and is fully subject to the remedies provided by sections 502 through 506, in the following cases:

(A) where the carriage of the signals comprising the secondary transmission is not permissible under the rules, regulations, or authorizations of the Federal Communications Commission; or

(B) where the cable system has not deposited the statement of account and royalty fee required by subsection (d).

(3) Notwithstanding the provisions of clause (1) of this subsection and subject to the provisions of subsection (e) of this section, the secondary transmission to the public by a cable system of a performance or display of a work embodied in a primary transmission made by a broadcast station licensed

by the Federal Communications Commission or by an appropriate governmental authority of Canada or Mexico is actionable as an act of infringement under section 501, and is fully subject to the remedies provided by sections 502 through 506 and section 510, if the content of the particular program in which the performance or display is embodied, or any commercial advertising or station announcements transmitted by the primary transmitter during, or immediately before or after, the transmission of such program, is in any way willfully altered by the cable system through changes, deletions, or additions, except for the alteration, deletion, or substitution of commercial advertisements performed by those engaged in television commercial advertising market research: *Provided,* That the research company has obtained the prior consent of the advertiser who has purchased the original commercial advertisement, the television station broadcasting that commercial advertisement, and the cable system performing the secondary transmission: *And provided further,* That such commercial alteration, deletion, or substitution is not performed for the purpose of deriving income from the sale of that commercial time.

(4) Notwithstanding the provisions of clause (1) of this subsection, the secondary transmission to the public by a cable system of a performance or display of a work embodied in a primary transmission made by a broadcast station licensed by an appropriate governmental authority of Canada or Mexico is actionable as an act of infringement under section 501, and is fully subject to the remedies provided by sections 502 through 506, if (A) with respect to Canadian signals, the community of the cable system is located more than 150 miles from the United States-Canadian border and is also located south of the forty-second parallel of latitude, or (B) with respect to Mexican signals, the secondary transmission is made by a cable system which received the primary transmission by means other than direct interception of a free space radio wave emitted by such broadcast television station, unless prior to April 15, 1976, such cable system was actually carrying, or was specifically authorized to carry, the signal of such foreign station on the system pursuant to the rules, regulations, or authorizations of the Federal Communications Commission.

(d) Statutory License for Secondary Transmissions by Cable Systems. —

(1) A cable system whose secondary transmissions have been subject to statutory licensing under subsection (c) shall, on a semiannual basis, deposit with the Register of Copyrights, in accordance with requirements that the Register shall prescribe by regulation —

(A) a statement of account, covering the six months next preceding, specifying the number of channels on which the cable system made secondary transmissions to its subscribers, the names and locations of all primary transmitters whose transmissions were further transmitted by the cable system, the total number of subscribers, the gross amounts paid to the cable system for the basic service of providing secondary transmissions of primary broadcast transmitters, and such other data as the Register of Copyrights may from time to time prescribe by regulation. In determining the total number of subscribers and the gross amounts paid to the cable system for the basic service of providing secondary transmissions of primary broadcast transmitters, the cable system shall not include subscribers and amounts collected from subscribers receiving secondary transmissions pursuant to section 119. Such statement shall also include a special statement of account covering any nonnetwork television programming that was carried by the cable system in whole or in part beyond the local service area of the primary transmitter, under rules, regulations, or authorizations of the Federal Communications Commission permitting the substitution or addition of signals under certain circumstances, together with logs showing the times, dates, stations, and programs involved in such substituted or added carriage; and

(B) except in the case of a cable system whose royalty is specified in subclause (C) or (D), a total royalty fee for the period covered by the statement, computed on the basis of specified percentages of the gross receipts from subscribers to the cable service during said period for the basic service of providing secondary transmissions of primary broadcast transmitters, as follows:

(i) 0.675 of 1 per centum of such gross receipts for the privilege of further transmitting any nonnetwork programming of a primary transmitter in whole or in part beyond the local service area of such primary transmitter, such amount to be applied against the fee, if any, payable pursuant to paragraphs (ii) through (iv);

(ii) 0.675 of 1 per centum of such gross receipts for the first distant signal equivalent;

(iii) 0.425 of 1 per centum of such gross receipts for each of the second, third, and fourth distant signal equivalents;

(iv) 0.2 of 1 per centum of such gross receipts for the fifth distant signal equivalent and each additional distant signal equivalent thereafter; and in computing the amounts payable under paragraph (ii) through (iv), above, any fraction of a distant signal equivalent shall be computed at its fractional value and, in the case of any cable system located partly within and partly without the local service area of a primary transmitter, gross receipts shall be limited to those gross receipts derived from subscribers located without the local service area of such primary transmitter; and

(C) if the actual gross receipts paid by subscribers to a cable system for the period covered by the statement for the basic service of providing secondary transmissions of primary broadcast transmitters total $80,000 or less, gross receipts of the cable system for the purpose of this subclause shall be computed by subtracting from such actual gross receipts the amount by which $80,000 exceeds such actual gross receipts, except that in no case shall a cable system's gross receipts be reduced to less than $3,000. The royalty fee payable under this subclause shall be 0.5 of 1 per centum, regardless of the number of distant signal equivalents, if any; and

(D) if the actual gross receipts paid by subscribers to a cable system for the period covered by the statement, for the basic service of providing secondary transmissions of primary broadcast transmitters, are more than $80,000 but less than $160,000, the royalty fee payable under this subclause shall be

(i) 0.5 of 1 per centum of any gross receipts up to $80,000; and

(ii) 1 per centum of any gross receipts in excess of $80,000 but less than $160,000, regardless of the number of distant signal equivalents, if any.

(2) The Register of Copyrights shall receive all fees deposited under this section and, after deducting the reasonable costs incurred by the Copyright Office under this section, shall deposit the balance in the Treasury of the United States, in such manner as the Secretary of the Treasury directs. All funds held by the Secretary of the Treasury shall be invested in interest-bearing United States securities for later distribution with interest by the Librarian of Congress upon authorization by the Copyright Royalty Judges.

(3) The royalty fees thus deposited shall, in accordance with the procedures provided by clause (4), be distributed to those among the following copyright owners who claim that their works were the subject of secondary transmissions by cable systems during the relevant semiannual period:

(A) any such owner whose work was included in a secondary transmission made by a cable system of a nonnetwork television program in whole or in part beyond the local service area of the primary transmitter; and

(B) any such owner whose work was included in a secondary transmission identified in a special statement of account deposited under clause (1)(A); and

(C) any such owner whose work was included in nonnetwork programming consisting exclusively of aural signals carried by a cable system in whole or in part beyond the local service area of the primary transmitter of such programs.

(4) The royalty fees thus deposited shall be distributed in accordance with the following procedures:

(A) During the month of July in each year, every person claiming to be entitled to statutory license fees for secondary transmissions shall file a claim with the Copyright Royalty Judges, in accordance with requirements that the Copyright Royalty Judges shall prescribe by regulation. Notwithstanding any provisions of the antitrust laws, for purposes of this clause any claimants may agree among themselves as to the proportionate division of statutory licensing fees among them, may lump their claims together and file them jointly or as a single claim, or may designate a common agent to receive payment on their behalf.

(B) After the first day of August of each year, the Copyright Royalty Judges shall, upon the recommendation of the Register of Copyrights, determine whether there exists a controversy concerning the distribution of royalty fees. If the Copyright Royalty Judges determine that no such controversy exists, the Copyright Royalty Judges shall authorize the Librarian of Congress to proceed to distribute such fees to the copyright owners entitled to receive them, or to their designated agents, subject to the deduction of reasonable administrative costs under this section. If the Copyright Royalty Judges find the existence of a controversy, the Copyright Royalty Judges shall, pursuant to chapter 8 of this title, conduct a proceeding to determine the distribution of royalty fees.

(C) During the pendency of any proceeding under this subsection, the Copyright Royalty Judges shall have the discretion to authorize the Librarian of Congress to proceed to distribute any amounts that are not in controversy.

(e) Nonsimultaneous Secondary Transmissions by Cable Systems. —

(1) Notwithstanding those provisions of the second paragraph of subsection (f) relating to nonsimultaneous secondary transmissions by a cable system, any such transmissions are actionable as an act of infringement under section 501, and are fully subject to the remedies provided by sections 502 through 506 and section 510, unless —

(A) the program on the videotape is transmitted no more than one time to the cable system's subscribers; and

(B) the copyrighted program, episode, or motion picture videotape, including the commercials contained within such program, episode, or picture, is transmitted without deletion or editing; and

(C) an owner or officer of the cable system

(i) prevents the duplication of the videotape while in the possession of the system,

(ii) prevents unauthorized duplication while in the possession of the facility making the videotape for the system if the system owns or controls the facility, or takes reasonable precautions to prevent such duplication if it does not own or control the facility,

(iii) takes adequate precautions to prevent duplication while the tape is being transported, and

(iv) subject to clause (2), erases or destroys, or causes the erasure or destruction of, the videotape; and

(D) within forty-five days after the end of each calendar quarter, an owner or officer of the cable system executes an affidavit attesting

(i) to the steps and precautions taken to prevent duplication of the videotape, and

(ii) subject to clause (2), to the erasure or destruction of all videotapes made or used during such quarter; and

(E) such owner or officer places or causes each such affidavit, and affidavits received pursuant to clause (2)(C), to be placed in a file, open to public inspection, at such system's main office in the community where the transmission is made or in the nearest community where such system maintains an office; and

(F) the nonsimultaneous transmission is one that the cable system would be authorized to transmit under the rules, regulations, and authorizations of the Federal Communications Commission in effect at the time of the nonsimultaneous transmission if the transmission had been made simultaneously, except that this subclause shall not apply to inadvertent or accidental transmissions.

(2) If a cable system transfers to any person a videotape of a program nonsimultaneously transmitted by it, such transfer is actionable as an act of infringement under section 501, and is fully subject to the remedies provided

by sections 502 through 506, except that, pursuant to a written, nonprofit contract providing for the equitable sharing of the costs of such videotape and its transfer, a videotape nonsimultaneously transmitted by it, in accordance with clause (1), may be transferred by one cable system in Alaska to another system in Alaska, by one cable system in Hawaii permitted to make such nonsimultaneous transmissions to another such cable system in Hawaii, or by one cable system in Guam, the Northern Mariana Islands, the Federated States of Micronesia, the Republic of Palau, or the Republic of the Marshall Islands, to another cable system in any of those three territories, if—

    (A) each such contract is available for public inspection in the offices of the cable systems involved, and a copy of such contract is filed, within thirty days after such contract is entered into, with the Copyright Office (which Office shall make each such contract available for public inspection); and

    (B) the cable system to which the videotape is transferred complies with clause (1)(A), (B), (C)(i), (iii), and (iv), and (D) through (F); and

    (C) such system provides a copy of the affidavit required to be made in accordance with clause (1)(D) to each cable system making a previous nonsimultaneous transmission of the same videotape.

    (3) This subsection shall not be construed to supersede the exclusivity protection provisions of any existing agreement, or any such agreement hereafter entered into, between a cable system and a television broadcast station in the area in which the cable system is located, or a network with which such station is affiliated.

    (4) As used in this subsection, the term "videotape", and each of its variant forms, means the reproduction of the images and sounds of a program or programs broadcast by a television broadcast station licensed by the Federal Communications Commission, regardless of the nature of the material objects, such as tapes or films, in which the reproduction is embodied.

    (f) Definitions. — As used in this section, the following terms and their variant forms mean the following:

A "primary transmission" is a transmission made to the public by the transmitting facility whose signals are being received and further transmitted by the secondary transmission service, regardless of where or when the performance or display was first transmitted.

A "secondary transmission" is the further transmitting of a primary transmission simultaneously with the primary transmission, or nonsimultaneously with the primary transmission if by a "cable system" not located in whole or in part within the boundary of the forty-eight contiguous States, Hawaii, or Puerto Rico: *Provided, however,* That a nonsimultaneous further transmission by a cable system located in Hawaii of a primary transmission shall be deemed to be a secondary transmission if the carriage of the television broadcast signal comprising such further transmission is permissible under the rules, regulations, or authorizations of the Federal Communications Commission.

A "cable system" is a facility, located in any State, Territory, Trust Territory, or Possession, that in whole or in part receives signals transmitted or programs broadcast by one or more television broadcast stations licensed by the Federal

Communications Commission, and makes secondary transmissions of such signals or programs by wires, cables, microwave, or other communications channels to subscribing members of the public who pay for such service. For purposes of determining the royalty fee under subsection (d)(1), two or more cable systems in contiguous communities under common ownership or control or operating from one headend shall be considered as one system.

The "local service area of a primary transmitter", in the case of a television broadcast station, comprises the area in which such station is entitled to insist upon its signal being retransmitted by a cable system pursuant to the rules, regulations, and authorizations of the Federal Communications Commission in effect on April 15, 1976, or such station's television market as defined in section 76.55(e) of title 47, Code of Federal Regulations (as in effect on September 18, 1993), or any modifications to such television market made, on or after September 18, 1993, pursuant to section 76.55(e) or 76.59 of title 47 of the Code of Federal Regulations, or in the case of a television broadcast station licensed by an appropriate governmental authority of Canada or Mexico, the area in which it would be entitled to insist upon its signal being retransmitted if it were a television broadcast station subject to such rules, regulations, and authorizations. In the case of a low power television station, as defined by the rules and regulations of the Federal Communications Commission, the "local service area of a primary transmitter" comprises the area within 35 miles of the transmitter site, except that in the case of such a station located in a standard metropolitan statistical area which has one of the 50 largest populations of all standard metropolitan statistical areas (based on the 1980 decennial census of population taken by the Secretary of Commerce), the number of miles shall be 20 miles. The "local service area of a primary transmitter", in the case of a radio broadcast station, comprises the primary service area of such station, pursuant to the rules and regulations of the Federal Communications Commission.

A "distant signal equivalent" is the value assigned to the secondary transmission of any nonnetwork television programming carried by a cable system in whole or in part beyond the local service area of the primary transmitter of such programming. It is computed by assigning a value of one to each independent station and a value of one-quarter to each network station and noncommercial educational station for the nonnetwork programming so carried pursuant to the rules, regulations, and authorizations of the Federal Communications Commission. The foregoing values for independent, network, and noncommercial educational stations are subject, however, to the following exceptions and limitations. Where the rules and regulations of the Federal Communications Commission require a cable system to omit the further transmission of a particular program and such rules and regulations also permit the substitution of another program embodying a performance or display of a work in place of the omitted transmission, or where such rules and regulations in effect on the date of enactment of this Act permit a cable system, at its election, to effect such deletion and substitution of a nonlive program or to carry additional programs not transmitted by primary transmitters within whose local service area the cable system is located, no value shall be assigned for the substituted or additional program; where the rules, regulations, or authorizations of the Federal Communications Commission in effect on the date of enactment of this Act permit a cable system, at its election, to omit the further transmission of a particular program and such rules, regulations, or authorizations also permit the substitution of another program embodying a performance or display of a work in place of the omitted transmission, the value assigned for the substituted or additional program shall be, in the case of a live program, the value of one full distant signal equivalent multiplied by a fraction that has as its numerator the number of days in the year in which such substitution occurs and as its denominator the number of days in the year. In the case of a station carried pursuant to the late-night or specialty programming rules of the Federal Communications Commission, or a station carried on a part-time basis where full-time carriage is not possible because the cable system lacks the activated channel capacity to retransmit on a full-time basis all signals which it is authorized to carry, the values for independent, network, and noncommercial educational stations set forth above, as the case may be, shall be multiplied by a fraction which is equal to the ratio of the broadcast hours of such station carried by the cable system to the total broadcast hours of the station.

A "network station" is a television broadcast station that is owned or operated by, or affiliated with, one or more of the television networks in the United States providing nationwide transmissions, and that transmits a substantial part of the programming supplied by such networks for a substantial part of that station's typical broadcast day.

An "independent station" is a commercial television broadcast station other than a network station.

A "noncommercial educational station" is a television station that is a noncommercial educational broadcast station as defined in section 397 of title 47.

§112. Limitations on exclusive rights: Ephemeral recordings

(a)(1) Notwithstanding the provisions of section 106, and except in the case of a motion picture or other audiovisual work, it is not an infringement of copyright for a transmitting organization entitled to transmit to the public a performance or display of a work, under a license, including a statutory license under section 114(f), or transfer of the copyright or under the limitations on exclusive rights in sound recordings specified by section 114(a) or for a transmitting organization that is a broadcast radio or television station licensed as such by the Federal Communications Commission and that makes a broadcast transmission of a performance of a sound recording in a digital format on a nonsubscription basis, to make no more than one copy or phonorecord of a particular transmission program embodying the performance or display, if —

(A) the copy or phonorecord is retained and used solely by the transmitting organization that made it, and no further copies or phonorecords are reproduced from it; and

(B) the copy or phonorecord is used solely for the transmitting organization's own transmissions within its local service area, or for purposes of archival preservation or security; and

(C) unless preserved exclusively for archival purposes, the copy or phonorecord is destroyed within six months from the date the transmission program was first transmitted to the public.

(2) In a case in which a transmitting organization entitled to make a copy or phonorecord under paragraph (1) in connection with the transmission to the public of a performance or display of a work is prevented from making such copy or phonorecord by reason of the application by the copyright owner of technical measures that prevent the reproduction of the work, the copyright owner shall make available to the transmitting organization the necessary means for permitting the making of such copy or phonorecord as permitted under that paragraph, if it is technologically feasible and economically reasonable for the copyright owner to do so. If the copyright owner fails to do so in a timely manner in light of the transmitting organization's reasonable business requirements, the transmitting organization shall not be liable for a violation of section 1201(a)(1) of this title for engaging in such activities as are necessary to make such copies or phonorecords as permitted under paragraph (1) of this subsection.

(b) Notwithstanding the provisions of section 106, it is not an infringement of copyright for a governmental body or other nonprofit organization entitled to transmit a performance or display of a work, under section 110(2) or under the limitations on exclusive rights in sound recordings specified by section 114(a), to make no more than thirty copies or phonorecords of a particular transmission program embodying the performance or display, if —

(1) no further copies or phonorecords are reproduced from the copies or phonorecords made under this clause; and

(2) except for one copy or phonorecord that may be preserved exclusively for archival purposes, the copies or phonorecords are destroyed within seven years from the date the transmission program was first transmitted to the public.

(c) Notwithstanding the provisions of section 106, it is not an infringement of copyright for a governmental body or other nonprofit organization to make for distribution no more than one copy or phonorecord, for each transmitting organization specified in clause (2) of this subsection, of a particular transmission program embodying a performance of a nondramatic musical work of a religious nature, or of a sound recording of such a musical work, if —

(1) there is no direct or indirect charge for making or distributing any such copies or phonorecords; and

(2) none of such copies or phonorecords is used for any performance other than a single transmission to the public by a transmitting organization entitled to transmit to the public a performance of the work under a license or transfer of the copyright; and

(3) except for one copy or phonorecord that may be preserved exclusively for archival purposes, the copies or phonorecords are all destroyed within one year from the date the transmission program was first transmitted to the public.

(d) Notwithstanding the provisions of section 106, it is not an infringement of copyright for a governmental body or other nonprofit organization entitled to transmit a performance of a work under section 110(8) to make no more than ten copies or phonorecords embodying the performance, or to permit the use of any such copy or phonorecord by any governmental body or nonprofit organization entitled to transmit a performance of a work under section 110(8), if—

(1) any such copy or phonorecord is retained and used solely by the organization that made it, or by a governmental body or nonprofit organization entitled to transmit a performance of a work under section 110(8), and no further copies or phonorecords are reproduced from it; and

(2) any such copy or phonorecord is used solely for transmissions authorized under section 110(8), or for purposes of archival preservation or security; and

(3) the governmental body or nonprofit organization permitting any use of any such copy or phonorecord by any governmental body or nonprofit organization under this subsection does not make any charge for such use.

(e) Statutory License. —

(1) A transmitting organization entitled to transmit to the public a performance of a sound recording under the limitation on exclusive rights specified by section 114(d)(1)(C)(iv) or under a statutory license in accordance with section 114(f) is entitled to a statutory license, under the conditions specified by this subsection, to make no more than 1 phonorecord of the sound recording (unless the terms and conditions of the statutory license allow for more), if the following conditions are satisfied:

(A) The phonorecord is retained and used solely by the transmitting organization that made it, and no further phonorecords are reproduced from it.

(B) The phonorecord is used solely for the transmitting organization's own transmissions originating in the United States under a statutory license in accordance with section 114(f) or the limitation on exclusive rights specified by section 114(d)(1)(C)(iv).

(C) Unless preserved exclusively for purposes of archival preservation, the phonorecord is destroyed within 6 months from the date the sound recording was first transmitted to the public using the phonorecord.

(D) Phonorecords of the sound recording have been distributed to the public under the authority of the copyright owner or the copyright owner authorizes the transmitting entity to transmit the sound recording, and the transmitting entity makes the phonorecord under this subsection from a phonorecord lawfully made and acquired under the authority of the copyright owner.

(2) Notwithstanding any provision of the antitrust laws, any copyright owners of sound recordings and any transmitting organizations entitled to a statutory license under this subsection may negotiate and agree upon royalty rates and license terms and conditions for making phonorecords of such sound recordings under this section and the proportionate division of fees paid among copyright owners, and may designate common agents to negotiate, agree to, pay, or receive such royalty payments.

(3) Proceedings under chapter 8 shall determine reasonable rates and terms of royalty payments for the activities specified by paragraph (1) during the 5-year period beginning on January 1 of the second year following the year

in which the proceedings are to be commenced, or such other period as the parties may agree. Such rates shall include a minimum fee for each type of service offered by transmitting organizations. Any copyright owners of sound recordings or any transmitting organizations entitled to a statutory license under this subsection may submit to the Copyright Royalty Judges licenses covering such activities with respect to such sound recordings. The parties to each proceeding shall bear their own costs.

(4) The schedule of reasonable rates and terms determined by the Copyright Royalty Judges shall, subject to paragraph (5), be binding on all copyright owners of sound recordings and transmitting organizations entitled to a statutory license under this subsection during the 5-year period specified in paragraph (3), or such other period as the parties may agree. Such rates shall include a minimum fee for each type of service offered by transmitting organizations. The Copyright Royalty Judges shall establish rates that most clearly represent the fees that would have been negotiated in the marketplace between a willing buyer and a willing seller. In determining such rates and terms, the Copyright Royalty Judges shall base their decision on economic, competitive, and programming information presented by the parties, including—

(A) whether use of the service may substitute for or may promote the sales of phonorecords or otherwise interferes with or enhances the copyright owner's traditional streams of revenue; and

(B) the relative roles of the copyright owner and the transmitting organization in the copyrighted work and the service made available to the public with respect to relative creative contribution, technological contribution, capital investment, cost, and risk.

In establishing such rates and terms, the Copyright Royalty Judges may consider the rates and terms under voluntary license agreements described in paragraphs (2) and (3). The Copyright Royalty Judges shall also establish requirements by which copyright owners may receive reasonable notice of the use of their sound recordings under this section, and under which records of such use shall be kept and made available by transmitting organizations entitled to obtain a statutory license under this subsection.

(5) License agreements voluntarily negotiated at any time between 1 or more copyright owners of sound recordings and 1 or more transmitting organizations entitled to obtain a statutory license under this subsection shall be given effect in lieu of any decision by the Librarian of Congress or determination by the Copyright Royalty Judges.

(6)(A) Any person who wishes to make a phonorecord of a sound recording under a statutory license in accordance with this subsection may do so without infringing the exclusive right of the copyright owner of the sound recording under section 106(1)—

(i) by complying with such notice requirements as the Copyright Royalty Judges shall prescribe by regulation and by paying royalty fees in accordance with this subsection; or

(ii) if such royalty fees have not been set, by agreeing to pay such royalty fees as shall be determined in accordance with this subsection.

(B) Any royalty payments in arrears shall be made on or before the 20th day of the month next succeeding the month in which the royalty fees are set.

(7) If a transmitting organization entitled to make a phonorecord under this subsection is prevented from making such phonorecord by reason of the application by the copyright owner of technical measures that prevent the reproduction of the sound recording, the copyright owner shall make available to the transmitting organization the necessary means for permitting the making of such phonorecord as permitted under this subsection, if it is technologically feasible and economically reasonable for the copyright owner to do so. If the copyright owner fails to do so in a timely manner in light of the transmitting organization's reasonable business requirements, the transmitting organization shall not be liable for a violation of section 1201(a)(1) of this title for engaging in such activities as are necessary to make such phonorecords as permitted under this subsection.

(8) Nothing in this subsection annuls, limits, impairs, or otherwise affects in any way the existence or value of any of the exclusive rights of the copyright owners in a sound recording, except as otherwise provided in this subsection, or in a musical work, including the exclusive rights to reproduce and distribute a sound recording or musical work, including by means of a digital phonorecord delivery, under section 106(1), 106(3), and 115, and the right to perform publicly a sound recording or musical work, including by means of a digital audio transmission, under sections 106(4) and 106(6).

(f)(1) Notwithstanding the provisions of section 106, and without limiting the application of subsection (b), it is not an infringement of copyright for a governmental body or other nonprofit educational institution entitled under section 110(2) to transmit a performance or display to make copies or phonorecords of a work that is in digital form and, solely to the extent permitted in paragraph (2), of a work that is in analog form, embodying the performance or display to be used for making transmissions authorized under section 110(2), if—

(A) such copies or phonorecords are retained and used solely by the body or institution that made them, and no further copies or phonorecords are reproduced from them, except as authorized under section 110(2); and

(B) such copies or phonorecords are used solely for transmissions authorized under section 110(2).

(2) This subsection does not authorize the conversion of print or other analog versions of works into digital formats, except that such conversion is permitted hereunder, only with respect to the amount of such works authorized to be performed or displayed under section 110(2), if—

(A) no digital version of the work is available to the institution; or

(B) the digital version of the work that is available to the institution is subject to technological protection measures that prevent its use for section 110(2).

(g) The transmission program embodied in a copy or phonorecord made under this section is not subject to protection as a derivative work under this title except with the express consent of the owners of copyright in the preexisting works employed in the program.

§113. Scope of exclusive rights in pictorial, graphic, and sculptural works

(a) Subject to the provisions of subsections (b) and (c) of this section, the exclusive right to reproduce a copyrighted pictorial, graphic, or sculptural work in copies under section 106 includes the right to reproduce the work in or on any kind of article, whether useful or otherwise.

(b) This title does not afford, to the owner of copyright in a work that portrays a useful article as such, any greater or lesser rights with respect to the making, distribution, or display of the useful article so portrayed than those afforded to such works under the law, whether title 17 or the common law or statutes of a State, in effect on December 31, 1977, as held applicable and construed by a court in an action brought under this title.

(c) In the case of a work lawfully reproduced in useful articles that have been offered for sale or other distribution to the public, copyright does not include any right to prevent the making, distribution, or display of pictures or photographs of such articles in connection with advertisements or commentaries related to the distribution or display of such articles, or in connection with news reports.

(d)(1) In a case in which—

(A) a work of visual art has been incorporated in or made part of a building in such a way that removing the work from the building will cause the destruction, distortion, mutilation, or other modification of the work as described in section 106A(a)(3), and

(B) the author consented to the installation of the work in the building either before the effective date set forth in section 610(a) of the Visual Artists Rights Act of 1990, or in a written instrument executed on or after such effective date that is signed by the owner of the building and the author and that specifies that installation of the work may subject the work to destruction, distortion, mutilation, or other modification, by reason of its removal, then the rights conferred by paragraphs (2) and (3) of section 106A(a) shall not apply.

(2) If the owner of a building wishes to remove a work of visual art which is a part of such building and which can be removed from the building without the destruction, distortion, mutilation, or other modification of the work as described in section 106A(a)(3), the author's rights under paragraphs (2) and (3) of section 106A(a) shall apply unless—

(A) the owner has made a diligent, good faith attempt without success to notify the author of the owner's intended action affecting the work of visual art, or

(B) the owner did provide such notice in writing and the person so notified failed, within 90 days after receiving such notice, either to remove the work or to pay for its removal.

For purposes of subparagraph (A), an owner shall be presumed to have made a diligent, good faith attempt to send notice if the owner sent such notice by registered mail to the author at the most recent address of the author that was recorded with the Register of Copyrights pursuant to paragraph (3). If the work is removed at the expense of the author, title to that copy of the work shall be deemed to be in the author.

(3) The Register of Copyrights shall establish a system of records whereby any author of a work of visual art that has been incorporated in or made part of a building, may record his or her identity and address with the Copyright Office. The Register shall also establish procedures under which any such author may update the information so recorded, and procedures under which owners of buildings may record with the Copyright Office evidence of their efforts to comply with this subsection.

§114. Scope of exclusive rights in sound recordings

(a) The exclusive rights of the owner of copyright in a sound recording are limited to the rights specified by clauses (1), (2), (3) and (6) of section 106, and do not include any right of performance under section 106(4).

(b) The exclusive right of the owner of copyright in a sound recording under clause (1) of section 106 is limited to the right to duplicate the sound recording in the form of phonorecords or copies that directly or indirectly recapture the actual sounds fixed in the recording. The exclusive right of the owner of copyright in a sound recording under clause (2) of section 106 is limited to the right to prepare a derivative work in which the actual sounds fixed in the sound recording are re-arranged, remixed, or otherwise altered in sequence or quality. The exclusive rights of the owner of copyright in a sound recording under clauses (1) and (2) of section 106 do not extend to the making or duplication of another sound recording that consists entirely of an independent fixation of other sounds, even though such sounds imitate or simulate those in the copyrighted sound recording. The exclusive rights of the owner of copyright in a sound recording under clauses (1), (2), and (3) of section 106 do not apply to sound recordings included in educational television and radio programs (as defined in section 397 of title 47) distributed or transmitted by or through public broadcasting entities (as defined by section 118 (g)): *Provided,* That copies or phonorecords of said programs are not commercially distributed by or through public broadcasting entities to the general public.

(c) This section does not limit or impair the exclusive right to perform publicly, by means of a phonorecord, any of the works specified by section 106(4).

(d) Limitations on Exclusive Right. — Notwithstanding the provisions of section 106(6) —

(1) Exempt transmissions and retransmissions. — The performance of a sound recording publicly by means of a digital audio transmission, other than as a part of an interactive service, is not an infringement of section 106(6) if the performance is part of —

(A) a nonsubscription broadcast transmission;

(B) a retransmission of a nonsubscription broadcast transmission: *Provided,* That, in the case of a retransmission of a radio station's broadcast transmission —

(i) the radio station's broadcast transmission is not willfully or repeatedly retransmitted more than a radius of 150 miles from the site of the radio broadcast transmitter, however —

(I) the 150 mile limitation under this clause shall not apply when a nonsubscription broadcast transmission by a radio station licensed by the Federal Communications Commission is retransmitted on a non-subscription basis by a terrestrial broadcast station, terrestrial translator, or terrestrial repeater licensed by the Federal Communications Commission; and

(II) in the case of a subscription retransmission of a non-subscription broadcast retransmission covered by subclause (I), the 150 mile radius shall be measured from the transmitter site of such broadcast retransmitter;

(ii) the retransmission is of radio station broadcast transmissions that are —

(I) obtained by the retransmitter over the air;

(II) not electronically processed by the retransmitter to deliver separate and discrete signals; and

(III) retransmitted only within the local communities served by the retransmitter;

(iii) the radio station's broadcast transmission was being retransmitted to cable systems (as defined in section 111(f)) by a satellite carrier on January 1, 1995, and that retransmission was being retransmitted by cable systems as a separate and discrete signal, and the satellite carrier obtains the radio station's broadcast transmission in an analog format: *Provided,* That the broadcast transmission being retransmitted may embody the programming of no more than one radio station; or

(iv) the radio station's broadcast transmission is made by a noncommercial educational broadcast station funded on or after January 1, 1995, under section 396(k) of the Communications Act of 1934 (47 U.S.C. 396(k)), consists solely of noncommercial educational and cultural radio programs, and the retransmission, whether or not simultaneous, is a nonsubscription terrestrial broadcast retransmission; or

(C) a transmission that comes within any of the following categories —

(i) a prior or simultaneous transmission incidental to an exempt transmission, such as a feed received by and then retransmitted by an exempt transmitter: *Provided,* That such incidental transmissions do not include any subscription transmission directly for reception by members of the public;

(ii) a transmission within a business establishment, confined to its premises or the immediately surrounding vicinity;

(iii) a retransmission by any retransmitter, including a multichannel video programming distributor as defined in section 602(12) of the Communications Act of 1934 (47 U.S.C. 522(12)), of a transmission by a transmitter licensed to publicly perform the sound recording as a part of that transmission, if the retransmission is simultaneous with the licensed transmission and authorized by the transmitter; or

(iv) a transmission to a business establishment for use in the ordinary course of its business: *Provided,* That the business recipient does not retransmit the transmission outside of its premises or the immediately surrounding vicinity, and that the transmission does not exceed the sound recording performance complement. Nothing in this clause shall limit the scope of the exemption in clause (ii).

(2) Statutory licensing of certain transmissions.—The performance of a sound recording publicly by means of a subscription digital audio transmission not exempt under paragraph (1), an eligible nonsubscription transmission, or a transmission not exempt under paragraph (1) that is made by a preexisting satellite digital audio radio service shall be subject to statutory licensing, in accordance with subsection (f) if—

(A)(i) the transmission is not part of an interactive service;

(ii) except in the case of a transmission to a business establishment, the transmitting entity does not automatically and intentionally cause any device receiving the transmission to switch from one program channel to another; and

(iii) except as provided in section 1002(e), the transmission of the sound recording is accompanied, if technically feasible, by the information encoded in that sound recording, if any, by or under the authority of the copyright owner of that sound recording, that identifies the title of the sound recording, the featured recording artist who performs on the sound recording, and related information, including information concerning the underlying musical work and its writer;

(B) in the case of a subscription transmission not exempt under paragraph (1) that is made by a preexisting subscription service in the same transmission medium used by such service on July 31, 1998, or in the case of a transmission not exempt under paragraph (1) that is made by a preexisting satellite digital audio radio service—

(i) the transmission does not exceed the sound recording performance complement; and

(ii) the transmitting entity does not cause to be published by means of an advance program schedule or prior announcement the titles of the specific sound recordings or phonorecords embodying such sound recordings to be transmitted; and

(C) in the case of an eligible nonsubscription transmission or a subscription transmission not exempt under paragraph (1) that is made by a new subscription service or by a preexisting subscription service other than in the same transmission medium used by such service on July 31, 1998—

(i) the transmission does not exceed the sound recording performance complement, except that this requirement shall not apply in the case of a retransmission of a broadcast transmission if the retransmission is made by a transmitting entity that does not have the right or ability to control the programming of the broadcast station making the broadcast transmission, unless—

(I) the broadcast station makes broadcast transmissions—

(aa) in digital format that regularly exceed the sound recording performance complement; or

(bb) in analog format, a substantial portion of which, on a weekly basis, exceed the sound recording performance complement; and

(II) the sound recording copyright owner or its representative has notified the transmitting entity in writing that broadcast transmissions of the copyright owner's sound recordings exceed the sound recording performance complement as provided in this clause;

(ii) the transmitting entity does not cause to be published, or induce or facilitate the publication, by means of an advance program schedule or prior announcement, the titles of the specific sound recordings to be transmitted, the phonorecords embodying such sound recordings, or, other than for illustrative purposes, the names of the featured recording artists, except that this clause does not disqualify a transmitting entity that makes a prior announcement that a particular artist will be featured within an unspecified future time period, and in the case of a retransmission of a broadcast transmission by a transmitting entity that does not have the right or ability to control the programming of the broadcast transmission, the requirement of this clause shall not apply to a prior oral announcement by the broadcast station, or to an advance program schedule published, induced, or facilitated by the broadcast station, if the transmitting entity does not have actual knowledge and has not received written notice from the copyright owner or its representative that the broadcast station publishes or induces or facilitates the publication of such advance program schedule, or if such advance program schedule is a schedule of classical music programming published by the broadcast station in the same manner as published by that broadcast station on or before September 30, 1998;

(iii) the transmission —

(I) is not part of an archived program of less than 5 hours duration;

(II) is not part of an archived program of 5 hours or greater in duration that is made available for a period exceeding 2 weeks;

(III) is not part of a continuous program which is of less than 3 hours duration; or

(IV) is not part of an identifiable program in which performances of sound recordings are rendered in a predetermined order, other than an archived or continuous program, that is transmitted at —

(aa) more than 3 times in any 2-week period that have been publicly announced in advance, in the case of a program of less than 1 hour in duration, or

(bb) more than 4 times in any 2-week period that have been publicly announced in advance, in the case of a program of 1 hour or more in duration, except that the requirement of this subclause shall not apply in the case of a retransmission of a broadcast transmission by a transmitting entity that does not have the right or ability to control the programming of the broadcast transmission, unless the transmitting entity is given notice in writing by the copyright owner of the sound recording that the broadcast station makes broadcast transmissions that regularly violate such requirement;

(iv) the transmitting entity does not knowingly perform the sound recording, as part of a service that offers transmissions of visual images contemporaneously with transmissions of sound recordings, in a manner that is likely to cause confusion, to cause mistake, or to deceive, as to the affiliation, connection, or association of the copyright owner or featured recording artist with the transmitting entity or a particular product or service advertised by the transmitting entity, or as to the origin, sponsorship, or approval by the copyright owner or featured recording artist of the activities of the transmitting entity other than the performance of the sound recording itself;

(v) the transmitting entity cooperates to prevent, to the extent feasible without imposing substantial costs or burdens, a transmission recipient or any other person or entity from automatically scanning the transmitting entity's transmissions alone or together with transmissions by other transmitting entities in order to select a particular sound recording to be transmitted to the transmission recipient, except that the requirement of this clause shall not apply to a satellite digital audio service that is in operation, or that is licensed by the Federal Communications Commission, on or before July 31, 1998;

(vi) the transmitting entity takes no affirmative steps to cause or induce the making of a phonorecord by the transmission recipient, and if the technology used by the transmitting entity enables the transmitting entity to limit the making by the transmission recipient of phonorecords of the transmission directly in a digital format, the transmitting entity sets such technology to limit such making of phonorecords to the extent permitted by such technology;

(vii) phonorecords of the sound recording have been distributed to the public under the authority of the copyright owner or the copyright owner authorizes the transmitting entity to transmit the sound recording, and the transmitting entity makes the transmission from a phonorecord lawfully made under the authority of the copyright owner, except that the requirement of this clause shall not apply to a retransmission of a broadcast transmission by a transmitting entity that does not have the right or ability to control the programming of the broadcast transmission, unless the transmitting entity is given notice in writing by the copyright owner of the sound recording that the broadcast station makes broadcast transmissions that regularly violate such requirement;

(viii) the transmitting entity accommodates and does not interfere with the transmission of technical measures that are widely used by sound recording copyright owners to identify or protect copyrighted works, and that are technically feasible of being transmitted by the transmitting entity without imposing substantial costs on the transmitting entity or resulting in perceptible aural or visual degradation of the digital signal, except that the requirement of this clause shall not apply to a satellite digital audio service that is in operation, or that is licensed under the authority of the Federal Communications Commission, on or before July 31, 1998, to the extent that such service has designed, developed, or made commitments to procure equipment or technology that is not compatible with such technical measures before such technical measures are widely adopted by sound recording copyright owners; and

(ix) the transmitting entity identifies in textual data the sound recording during, but not before, the time it is performed, including the title of the sound recording, the title of the phonorecord embodying such sound recording, if any, and the featured recording artist, in a manner to permit it to be displayed to the transmission recipient by the device or technology intended for receiving the service provided by the transmitting entity, except that the obligation in this clause shall not take effect until 1 year after the date of the enactment of the Digital Millennium Copyright Act and shall not apply in the case of a retransmission of a broadcast transmission by a transmitting entity that does not have the right or ability to control the programming of the broadcast transmission, or in the case in which devices or technology intended for receiving the service provided by the transmitting entity that have the capability to display such textual data are not common in the marketplace.

(3) Licenses for transmissions by interactive services. —

(A) No interactive service shall be granted an exclusive license under section 106(6) for the performance of a sound recording publicly by means of digital audio transmission for a period in excess of 12 months, except that with respect to an exclusive license granted to an interactive service by a licensor that holds the copyright to 1,000 or fewer sound recordings, the period of such license shall not exceed 24 months: *Provided,* however, That the grantee of such exclusive license shall be ineligible to receive another exclusive license for the performance of that sound recording for a period of 13 months from the expiration of the prior exclusive license.

(B) The limitation set forth in subparagraph (A) of this paragraph shall not apply if—

(i) the licensor has granted and there remain in effect licenses under section 106(6) for the public performance of sound recordings by means of digital audio transmission by at least 5 different interactive services; *Provided,* however, That each such license must be for a minimum of 10 percent of the copyrighted sound recordings owned by the licensor that have been licensed to interactive services, but in no event less than 50 sound recordings; or

(ii) the exclusive license is granted to perform publicly up to 45 seconds of a sound recording and the sole purpose of the performance is to promote the distribution or performance of that sound recording.

(C) Notwithstanding the grant of an exclusive or nonexclusive license of the right of public performance under section 106(6), an interactive service may not publicly perform a sound recording unless a license has been granted for the public performance of any copyrighted musical work contained in the sound recording: *Provided,* That such license to publicly perform the copyrighted musical work may be granted either by a performing rights society representing the copyright owner or by the copyright owner.

(D) The performance of a sound recording by means of a retransmission of a digital audio transmission is not an infringement of section 106(6) if—

(i) the retransmission is of a transmission by an interactive service licensed to publicly perform the sound recording to a particular member of the public as part of that transmission; and

(ii) the retransmission is simultaneous with the licensed transmission, authorized by the transmitter, and limited to that particular member of the public intended by the interactive service to be the recipient of the transmission.

(E) For the purposes of this paragraph—

(i) a "licensor" shall include the licensing entity and any other entity under any material degree of common ownership, management, or control that owns copyrights in sound recordings; and

(ii) a "performing rights society" is an association or corporation that licenses the public performance of nondramatic musical works on behalf of the copyright owner, such as the American Society of Composers, Authors and Publishers, Broadcast Music, Inc., and SESAC, Inc.

(4) Rights not otherwise limited.—

(A) Except as expressly provided in this section, this section does not limit or impair the exclusive right to perform a sound recording publicly by means of a digital audio transmission under section 106(6).

(B) Nothing in this section annuls or limits in any way—

(i) the exclusive right to publicly perform a musical work, including by means of a digital audio transmission, under section 106(4);

(ii) the exclusive rights in a sound recording or the musical work embodied therein under sections 106(1), 106(2) and 106(3); or

(iii) any other rights under any other clause of section 106, or remedies available under this title as such rights or remedies exist either before or after the date of enactment of the Digital Performance Right in Sound Recordings Act of 1995.

(C) Any limitations in this section on the exclusive right under section 106(6) apply only to the exclusive right under section 106(6) and not to any other exclusive rights under section 106. Nothing in this section shall be construed to annul, limit, impair or otherwise affect in any way the ability of the owner of a copyright in a sound recording to exercise the rights under sections 106(1), 106(2) and 106(3), or to obtain the remedies available under this title pursuant to such rights, as such rights and remedies exist either before or after the date of enactment of the Digital Performance Right in Sound Recordings Act of 1995.

(e) Authority for Negotiations.—

(1) Notwithstanding any provision of the antitrust laws, in negotiating statutory licenses in accordance with subsection (f), any copyright owners of sound recordings and any entities performing sound recordings affected by this section may negotiate and agree upon the royalty rates and license terms and conditions for the performance of such sound recordings and the proportionate division of fees paid among copyright owners, and may designate common agents on a nonexclusive basis to negotiate, agree to, pay, or receive payments.

(2) For licenses granted under section 106(6), other than statutory licenses, such as for performances by interactive services or performances that exceed the sound recording performance complement —

(A) copyright owners of sound recordings affected by this section may designate common agents to act on their behalf to grant licenses and receive and remit royalty payments: *Provided,* That each copyright owner shall establish the royalty rates and material license terms and conditions unilaterally, that is, not in agreement, combination, or concert with other copyright owners of sound recordings; and

(B) entities performing sound recordings affected by this section may designate common agents to act on their behalf to obtain licenses and collect and pay royalty fees: *Provided,* That each entity performing sound recordings shall determine the royalty rates and material license terms and conditions unilaterally, that is, not in agreement, combination, or concert with other entities performing sound recordings.

(f) Licenses for Certain Nonexempt Transmissions.

(1)(A) Proceedings under chapter 8 shall determine reasonable rates and terms of royalty payments for subscription transmissions by preexisting subscription services and transmissions by preexisting satellite digital audio radio services specified by subsection (d)(2) during the 5-year period beginning on January 1 of the second year following the year in which the proceedings are to be commenced, except in the case of a different transitional period provided under section 6(b)(3) of the Copyright Royalty and Distribution Reform Act of 2004, or such other period as the parties may agree. Such terms and rates shall distinguish among the different types of digital audio transmission services then in operation. Any copyright owners of sound recordings, preexisting subscription services, or preexisting satellite digital audio radio services may submit to the Copyright Royalty Judges licenses covering such subscription transmissions with respect to such sound recordings. The parties to each proceeding shall bear their own costs.

(B) In the absence of license agreements negotiated under subparagraph (A), during the 60-day period commencing 6 months after publication of the notice specified in subparagraph (A), and upon the filing of a petition in accordance with section 803(a)(1), the Librarian of Congress shall, pursuant to chapter 8, convene a copyright arbitration royalty panel to determine and publish in the Federal Register a schedule of rates and terms which, subject to paragraph (3), shall be binding on all copyright owners of sound recordings and entities performing sound recordings affected by this paragraph. In establishing rates and terms for preexisting subscription services and preexisting satellite digital audio radio services, in addition to the objectives set forth in section 801(b)(1), the copyright arbitration royalty panel may consider the rates and terms for comparable types of subscription digital audio transmission services and comparable circumstances under voluntary license agreements negotiated as provided in subparagraph (A).

(C)(i) Publication of a notice of the initiation of voluntary negotiation proceedings as specified in subparagraph (A) shall be repeated, in accordance with regulations that the Librarian of Congress shall prescribe —

(I) no later than 30 days after a petition is filed by any copyright owners of sound recordings, any preexisting subscription services, or any preexisting satellite digital audio radio services indicating that a new type of subscription digital audio transmission service on which sound recordings are performed is or is about to become operational; and

(II) in the first week of January 2001, and at 5-year intervals thereafter.

(ii) The procedures specified in subparagraph (B) shall be repeated, in accordance with regulations that the Librarian of Congress shall prescribe, upon filing of a petition in accordance with section 803(a)(1) during a 60-day period commencing —

(I) 6 months after publication of a notice of the initiation of voluntary negotiation proceedings under subparagraph (A) pursuant to a petition under clause (i)(I) of this subparagraph;

(II) on July 1, 2001, and at 5-year intervals thereafter.

(iii) The procedures specified in subparagraph (B) shall be concluded in accordance with section 802.

(2)(A) Proceedings under chapter 8 shall determine reasonable rates and terms of royalty payments for public performances of sound recordings by means of eligible nonsubscription transmission services and new subscription services specified by subsection (d)(2) during the 5-year period beginning on January 1 of the second year following the year in which the proceedings are to be commenced, except in the case of a different transitional period provided under section 6(b)(3) of the Copyright Royalty and Distribution Reform Act of 2004, or such other period as the parties may agree. Such rates and terms shall distinguish among the different types of eligible nonsubscription transmission services and new subscription services then in operation and shall include a minimum fee for each such type of service. Any copyright owners of sound recordings or any entities performing sound recordings affected by this paragraph may submit to the Copyright Royalty Judges licenses covering such eligible nonsubscription transmissions and new subscription services with respect to such sound recordings. The parties to each proceeding shall bear their own costs.

(B) In the absence of license agreements negotiated under subparagraph (A), during the 60-day period commencing 6 months after publication of the notice specified in subparagraph (A), and upon the filing of a petition in accordance with section 803(a)(1), the Librarian of Congress shall, pursuant to chapter 8, convene a copyright arbitration royalty panel to determine and publish in the Federal Register a schedule of rates and terms which, subject to paragraph (3), shall be binding on all copyright owners of sound recordings and entities performing sound recordings affected by this paragraph during the period beginning on the date of the enactment of the Digital Millennium Copyright Act and ending on December 31, 2000, or such other date as the parties may agree. Such rates and terms shall distinguish among the different types of eligible nonsubscription transmission services then in operation and shall include a minimum fee for each such type of service, such differences to be based on criteria including, but not limited to, the quantity and nature of the use of sound recordings and the degree to which use of the service may substitute for or may promote the purchase of phonorecords by consumers. In establishing rates and terms for transmissions by eligible nonsubscription services and new subscription services, the copyright arbitration royalty panel shall establish rates and terms that most clearly represent the rates and terms that would have been negotiated in the marketplace between a willing buyer and a willing seller. In determining such rates and terms, the copyright arbitration royalty panel shall base its decision on economic, competitive and programming information presented by the parties, including —

(i) whether use of the service may substitute for or may promote the sales of phonorecords or otherwise may interfere with or may enhance the sound recording copyright owner's other streams of revenue from its sound recordings; and

(ii) the relative roles of the copyright owner and the transmitting entity in the copyrighted work and the service made available to the public with respect to relative creative contribution, technological contribution, capital investment, cost, and risk.

In establishing such rates and terms, the copyright arbitration royalty panel may consider the rates and terms for comparable types of digital audio transmission services and comparable circumstances under voluntary license agreements described in subparagraph (A).

(C)(i) Publication of a notice of the initiation of voluntary negotiation proceedings as specified in subparagraph (A) shall be repeated in accordance with regulations that the Librarian of Congress shall prescribe —

(I) no later than 30 days after a petition is filed by any copyright owners of sound recordings or any eligible nonsubscription service or new subscription service indicating that a new type of eligible nonsubscription service or new subscription service on which sound recordings are performed is or is about to become operational; and

(II) in the first week of January 2000, and at 2-year intervals thereafter, except to the extent that different years for the repeating of such proceedings may be determined in accordance with subparagraph (A).

(ii) The procedures specified in subparagraph (B) shall be repeated, in accordance with regulations that the Librarian of Congress shall prescribe, upon filing of a petition in accordance with section 803(a)(1) during a 60-day period commencing —

(I) 6 months after publication of a notice of the initiation of voluntary negotiation proceedings under subparagraph (A) pursuant to a petition under clause (i)(I); or

(II) on July 1, 2000, and at 2-year intervals thereafter, except to the extent that different years for the repeating of such proceedings may be determined in accordance with subparagraph (A).

(iii) The procedures specified in subparagraph (B) shall be concluded in accordance with section 802.

(3) License agreements voluntarily negotiated at any time between 1 or more copyright owners of sound recordings and 1 or more entities performing sound recordings shall be given effect in lieu of any determination by a copyright arbitration royalty panel or decision by the Librarian of Congress.

(4)(A) The Librarian of Congress shall also establish requirements by which copyright owners may receive reasonable notice of the use of their sound recordings under this section, and under which records of such use shall be kept and made available by entities performing sound recordings.

(B) Any person who wishes to perform a sound recording publicly by means of a transmission eligible for statutory licensing under this subsection may do so without infringing the exclusive right of the copyright owner of the sound recording —

(i) by complying with such notice requirements as the Librarian of Congress shall prescribe by regulation and by paying royalty fees in accordance with this subsection; or

(ii) if such royalty fees have not been set, by agreeing to pay such royalty fees as shall be determined in accordance with this subsection.

(C) Any royalty payments in arrears shall be made on or before the twentieth day of the month next succeeding the month in which the royalty fees are set.

(5)(A) Not withstanding section 112(e) and the other provisions of this subsection, the receiving agent may enter into agreements for the reproduction and performance of sound recordings under section 112(e) and this section by any 1 or more commercial webcasters or noncommercial webcasters for a period of not more than 11 years beginning on January 1, 2005, that, once published in the Federal Register pursuant to subparagraph (B), shall be binding on all copyright owners of sound recordings and other persons entitled to payment under this section, in lieu of any determination by the Copyright Royalty Judges. Any such agreement for commercial webcasters may include provisions for payment of royalties on the basis of a percentage of revenue or expenses, or both, and include a minimum fee. Any such agreement may include other terms and conditions, including requirements by which copyright owners may receive notice of the use of their sound recordings and under which records of such use shall be kept and made available by commercial webcasters or noncommercial webcasters. The receiving agent shall be under no obligation to negotiate any such agreement. The receiving agent shall have no obligation to any copyright owner of sound recordings or any other person entitled to payment under this section in negotiating any such agreement, and no liability to any copyright owner of sound recordings or any other person entitled to payment under this section for having entered into such agreement.

(B) The Copyright Office shall cause to be published in the Federal Register any agreement entered into pursuant to subparagraph (A). Such publication shall include a statement containing the substance of subparagraph (C). Such agreements shall not be included in the Code of Federal Regulations. Thereafter, the terms of such agreement shall be available, as an option, to any commercial webcaster or noncommercial webcaster meeting the eligibility conditions of such agreement.

(C) Neither subparagraph (A) nor any provisions of any agreement entered into pursuant to subparagraph (A), including any rate structure, fees, terms, conditions, or notice and recordkeeping requirements set forth therein, shall be admissible as evidence or otherwise taken into account in any administrative, judicial, or other government proceeding involving the setting or adjustment of the royalties payable for the public performance or reproduction in ephemeral phonorecords or copies of sound recordings, the determination of terms or conditions related thereto, or the establishment of notice or recordkeeping requirements by the Copyright Royalty Judges under paragraph (4) or section 112(e)(4). It is the intent of Congress that any royalty rates, rate structure, definitions, terms, conditions, or notice and recordkeeping requirements, included in such agreements shall be considered as a compromise motivated by the unique business, economic and political circumstances of webcasters, copyright owners, and performers rather than as matters that would have been negotiated in the marketplace between a willing buyer and a willing seller, or otherwise meet the objectives set forth in section 801(b). This subparagraph shall not apply to the extent that the receiving agent and a webcaster that is a party to an agreement entered into pursuant to subparagraph (A) expressly authorize the submission of the agreement in a proceeding under this subsection.

(D) Nothing in the Webcaster Settlement Act of 2008 or any agreement entered into pursuant to subparagraph (A) shall be taken into account by the United States Court of Appeals for the District of Columbia Circuit in its review of the determination by the Copyright Royalty Judges of May 1, 2007, of rates and terms for the digital performance of sound recordings and ephemeral recordings, pursuant to sections 112 and 114.[1]

(E) As used in this paragraph —

(i) the term "noncommercial webcaster" means a webcaster that —

(I) is exempt from taxation under section 501 of the Internal Revenue Code of 1986 (26 U.S.C. 501);

(II) has applied in good faith to the Internal Revenue Service for exemption from taxation under section 501 of the Internal Revenue Code and has a commercially reasonable expectation that such exemption shall be granted; or

(III) is operated by a State or possession or any governmental entity or subordinate thereof, or by the United States or District of Columbia, for exclusively public purposes;

(ii) the term "receiving agent" shall have the meaning given that term in section 261.2 of title 37, Code of Federal Regulations, as published in the Federal Register on July 8, 2002; and

(iii) the term "webcaster" means a person or entity that has obtained a compulsory license under section 112 or 114[2] and the implementing regulations therefor to make eligible nonsubscription transmissions and ephemeral recordings.

(F) The authority to make settlements pursuant to subparagraph (A) shall expire February 15, 2009.

(g) Proceeds from Licensing of Transmissions. —

(1) Except in the case of a transmission licensed under a statutory license in accordance with subsection (f) of this section —

(A) a featured recording artist who performs on a sound recording that has been licensed for a transmission shall be entitled to receive payments from the copyright owner of the sound recording in accordance with the terms of the artist's contract; and

(B) a nonfeatured recording artist who performs on a sound recording that has been licensed for a transmission shall be entitled to receive payments from the copyright owner of the sound recording in accordance with the terms of the nonfeatured recording artist's applicable contract or other applicable agreement.

(2) An agent designated to distribute receipts from the licensing of transmissions in accordance with subsection (f) shall distribute such receipts as follows:

(A) 50 percent of the receipts shall be paid to the copyright owner of the exclusive right under section 106(6) of this title to publicly perform a sound recording by means of a digital audio transmission.

(B) 2 percent of the receipts shall be deposited in an escrow account managed by an independent administrator jointly appointed by copyright owners of sound recordings and the American Federation of Musicians (or any successor entity) to be distributed to nonfeatured musicians (whether or not members of the American Federation of Musicians) who have performed on sound recordings.

(C) 2 percent of the receipts shall be deposited in an escrow account managed by an independent administrator jointly appointed by copyright owners of sound recordings and the American Federation of Television and Radio Artists (or any successor entity) to be distributed to nonfeatured vocalists (whether or not members of the American Federation of Television and Radio Artists) who have performed on sound recordings.

(D) 45 percent of the receipts shall be paid, on a per sound recording basis, to the recording artist or artists featured on such sound recording (or the persons conveying rights in the artists' performance in the sound recordings).

(3) A nonprofit agent designated to distribute receipts from the licensing of transmissions in accordance with subsection (f) may deduct from any of its receipts, prior to the distribution of such receipts to any person or entity entitled thereto other than copyright owners and performers who have elected to receive royalties from another designated agent and have notified such nonprofit agent in writing of such election, the reasonable costs of such agent incurred after November 1, 1995, in —

(A) the administration of the collection, distribution, and calculation of the royalties;

(B) the settlement of disputes relating to the collection and calculation of the royalties; and

(C) the licensing and enforcement of rights with respect to the making of ephemeral recordings and performances subject to licensing under section 112 and this section, including those incurred in participating in negotiations or arbitration proceedings under section 112 and this section, except that all costs incurred relating to the section 112 ephemeral recordings right may only be deducted from the royalties received pursuant to section 112.

(4) Notwithstanding paragraph (3), any designated agent designated to distribute receipts from the licensing of transmissions in accordance with subsection (f) may deduct from any of its receipts, prior to the distribution of such receipts, the reasonable costs identified in paragraph (3) of such agent incurred after November 1, 1995, with respect to such copyright owners and performers who have entered with such agent a contractual relationship that specifies that such costs may be deducted from such royalty receipts.

(h) Licensing to Affiliates. —

(1) If the copyright owner of a sound recording licenses an affiliated entity the right to publicly perform a sound recording by means of a digital audio transmission under section 106(6), the copyright owner shall make the licensed sound recording available under section 106(6) on no less favorable terms and conditions to all bona fide entities that offer similar services, except that, if there are material differences in the scope of the requested license with respect to the type of service, the particular sound recordings licensed, the frequency of use, the number of subscribers served, or the duration, then the copyright owner may establish different terms and conditions for such other services.

(2) The limitation set forth in paragraph (1) of this subsection shall not apply in the case where the copyright owner of a sound recording licenses —

(A) an interactive service; or

(B) an entity to perform publicly up to 45 seconds of the sound recording and the sole purpose of the performance is to promote the distribution or performance of that sound recording.

(i) No effect on royalties for underlying works. — License fees payable for the public performance of sound recordings under section 106(6) shall not be taken into account in any administrative, judicial, or other governmental proceeding to set or adjust the royalties payable to copyright owners of musical works for the public performance of their works. It is the intent of Congress that royalties payable to copyright owners of musical works for the public performance of their works shall not be diminished in any respect as a result of the rights granted by section 106(6).

(j) Definitions. — As used in this section, the following terms have the following meanings:

(1) An "affiliated entity" is an entity engaging in digital audio transmissions covered by section 106(6), other than an interactive service, in which the licensor has any direct or indirect partnership or any ownership interest amounting to 5 percent or more of the outstanding voting or non-voting stock.

(2) An "archived program" is a predetermined program that is available repeatedly on the demand of the transmission recipient and that is performed in the same order from the beginning, except that an archived program shall not include a recorded event or broadcast transmission that makes no more than an incidental use of sound recordings, as long as such recorded event or broadcast transmission does not contain an entire sound recording or feature a particular sound recording.

(3) A "broadcast" transmission is a transmission made by a terrestrial broadcast station licensed as such by the Federal Communications Commission.

(4) A "continuous program" is a predetermined program that is continuously performed in the same order and that is accessed at a point in the program that is beyond the control of the transmission recipient.

(5) A "digital audio transmission" is a digital transmission as defined in section 101, that embodies the transmission of a sound recording. This term does not include the transmission of any audiovisual work.

(6) An "eligible nonsubscription transmission" is a noninteractive nonsubscription digital audio transmission not exempt under subsection (d)(1) that is made as part of a service that provides audio programming consisting, in whole or in part, of performances of sound recordings, including retransmissions of broadcast transmissions, if the primary purpose of the service is to provide to the public such audio or other entertainment programming, and the primary purpose of the service is not to sell, advertise, or promote particular products or services other than sound recordings, live concerts, or other music-related events.

(7) An "interactive service" is one that enables a member of the public to receive a transmission of a program specially created for the recipient, or on request, a transmission of a particular sound recording, whether or not as part of a program, which is selected by or on behalf of the recipient. The ability of individuals to request that particular sound recordings be performed for reception by the public at large, or in the case of a subscription service, by all subscribers of the service, does not make a service interactive, if the programming on each channel of the service does not substantially consist of sound recordings that are performed within 1 hour of the request or at a time designated by either the transmitting entity or the individual making such request. If an entity offers both interactive and noninteractive services (either concurrently or at different times), the noninteractive component shall not be treated as part of an interactive service.

(8) A "new subscription service" is a service that performs sound recordings by means of noninteractive subscription digital audio transmissions and that is not a preexisting subscription service or a preexisting satellite digital audio radio service.

(9) A "nonsubscription" transmission is any transmission that is not a subscription transmission.

(10) A "preexisting satellite digital audio radio service" is a subscription satellite digital audio radio service provided pursuant to a satellite digital audio radio service license issued by the Federal Communications Commission on or before July 31, 1998, and any renewal of such license to the extent of the scope of the original license, and may include a limited number of sample channels representative of the subscription service that are made available on a nonsubscription basis in order to promote the subscription service.

(11) A "preexisting subscription service" is a service that performs sound recordings by means of noninteractive audio-only subscription digital audio transmissions, which was in existence and was making such transmissions to the public for a fee on or before July 31, 1998, and may include a limited number of sample channels representative of the subscription service that are made available on a nonsubscription basis in order to promote the subscription service.

(12) A "retransmission" is a further transmission of an initial transmission, and includes any further retransmission of the same transmission. Except as provided in this section, a transmission qualifies as a "retransmission" only if it is simultaneous with the initial transmission. Nothing in this definition shall be construed to exempt a transmission that fails to satisfy a separate element required to qualify for an exemption under section 114(d)(1).

(13) The "sound recording performance complement" is the transmission during any 3-hour period, on a particular channel used by a transmitting entity, of no more than—

(A) 3 different selections of sound recordings from any one phonorecord lawfully distributed for public performance or sale in the United States, if no more than 2 such selections are transmitted consecutively; or

(B) 4 different selections of sound recordings—

(i) by the same featured recording artist; or

(ii) from any set or compilation of phonorecords lawfully distributed together as a unit for public performance or sale in the United States, if no more than three such selections are transmitted consecutively: *Provided,* That the transmission of selections in excess of the numerical limits provided for in clauses (A) and (B) from multiple phonorecords shall nonetheless qualify as a sound recording performance complement if the programming of the multiple phonorecords was not willfully intended to avoid the numerical limitations prescribed in such clauses.

(14) A "subscription" transmission is a transmission that is controlled and limited to particular recipients, and for which consideration is required to be paid or otherwise given by or on behalf of the recipient to receive the transmission or a package of transmissions including the transmission.

(15) A "transmission" is either an initial transmission or a retransmission.

§115. Scope of exclusive rights in nondramatic musical works: Compulsory license for making and distributing phonorecords

In the case of nondramatic musical works, the exclusive rights provided by clauses (1) and (3) of section 106, to make and to distribute phonorecords of such works, are subject to compulsory licensing under the conditions specified by this section.

(a) Availability and Scope of Compulsory License. —

(1) When phonorecords of a nondramatic musical work have been distributed to the public in the United States under the authority of the copyright owner, any other person, including those who make phonorecords or digital phonorecord deliveries, may, by complying with the provisions of this section, obtain a compulsory license to make and distribute phonorecords of the work. A person may obtain a compulsory license only if his or her primary purpose in making phonorecords is to distribute them to the public for private use, including by means of a digital phonorecord delivery. A person may not obtain a compulsory license for use of the work in the making of phonorecords duplicating a sound recording fixed by another, unless:

(i) such sound recording was fixed lawfully; and

(ii) the making of the phonorecords was authorized by the owner of copyright in the sound recording or, if the sound recording was fixed before February 15, 1972, by any person who fixed the sound recording pursuant to an express license from the owner of the copyright in the musical work or pursuant to a valid compulsory license for use of such work in a sound recording.

(2) A compulsory license includes the privilege of making a musical arrangement of the work to the extent necessary to conform it to the style or manner of interpretation of the performance involved, but the arrangement shall not change the basic melody or fundamental character of the work, and shall not be subject to protection as a derivative work under this title, except with the express consent of the copyright owner.

(b) Notice of Intention to Obtain Compulsory License. —

(1) Any person who wishes to obtain a compulsory license under this section shall, before or within thirty days after making, and before distributing any phonorecords of the work, serve notice of intention to do so on the copyright owner. If the registration or other public records of the Copyright Office do not identify the copyright owner and include an address at which notice can be served, it shall be sufficient to file the notice of intention in the Copyright Office. The notice shall comply, in form, content, and manner of service, with requirements that the Register of Copyrights shall prescribe by regulation.

(2) Failure to serve or file the notice required by clause (1) forecloses the possibility of a compulsory license and, in the absence of a negotiated license, renders the making and distribution of phonorecords actionable as acts of infringement under section 501 and fully subject to the remedies provided by sections 502 through 506 and 509.

(c) Royalty Payable Under Compulsory License.—

(1) To be entitled to receive royalties under a compulsory license, the copyright owner must be identified in the registration or other public records of the Copyright Office. The owner is entitled to royalties for phonorecords made and distributed after being so identified, but is not entitled to recover for any phonorecords previously made and distributed.

(2) Except as provided by clause (1), the royalty under a compulsory license shall be payable for every phonorecord made and distributed in accordance with the license. For this purpose, and other than as provided in paragraph (3), a phonorecord is considered "distributed" if the person exercising the compulsory license has voluntarily and permanently parted with its possession. With respect to each work embodied in the phonorecord, the royalty shall be either two and three-fourths cents, or one-half of one cent per minute of playing time or fraction thereof, whichever amount is larger.

(3)(A) A compulsory license under this section includes the right of the compulsory licensee to distribute or authorize the distribution of a phonorecord of a nondramatic musical work by means of a digital transmission which constitutes a digital phonorecord delivery, regardless of whether the digital transmission is also a public performance of the sound recording under section 106(6) of this title or of any nondramatic musical work embodied therein under section 106(4) of this title. For every digital phonorecord delivery by or under the authority of the compulsory licensee—

(i) on or before December 31, 1997, the royalty payable by the compulsory licensee shall be the royalty prescribed under paragraph (2) and chapter 8 of this title; and

(ii) on or after January 1, 1998, the royalty payable by the compulsory licensee shall be the royalty prescribed under subparagraphs (B) through (E) and chapter 8 of this title.

(B) Notwithstanding any provision of the antitrust laws, any copyright owners of nondramatic musical works and any persons entitled to obtain a compulsory license under subsection (a)(1) may negotiate and agree upon the terms and rates of royalty payments under this section and the proportionate division of fees paid among copyright owners, and may designate common agents on a nonexclusive basis to negotiate, agree to, pay or receive such royalty payments. Such authority to negotiate the terms and rates of royalty payments includes, but is not limited to, the authority to negotiate the year during which the royalty rates prescribed under this subparagraph and subparagraphs (C) through (E) and chapter 8 of this title shall next be determined.

(C) Proceedings under chapter 8 shall determine reasonable rates and terms of royalty payments for the activities specified by this section during the period beginning with the effective date of such rates and terms, but not earlier than January 1 of the second year following the year in which the petition requesting the proceeding is filed, and ending on the effective date of successor rates and terms, or such other period as the parties may agree. Such terms and rates shall distinguish between (i) digital phonorecord deliveries where the reproduction or distribution of a phonorecord is incidental to the transmission which constitutes the digital phonorecord delivery, and (ii) digital phonorecord deliveries in general. Any copyright owners of nondramatic musical works and any persons entitled to obtain a compulsory license under subsection (a)(1) may submit to the Copyright Royalty Judges licenses covering such activities. The parties to each proceeding shall bear their own costs.

(D) The schedule of reasonable rates and terms determined by the Copyright Royalty Judges shall, subject to subparagraph (E), be binding on all copyright owners of nondramatic musical works and persons entitled to obtain a compulsory license under subsection (a)(1) during the period specified in subparagraph (C), such other period as may be determined pursuant to subparagraphs (B) and (C), or such other period as the parties may agree. Such terms and rates shall distinguish between (i) digital phonorecord deliveries where the reproduction or distribution of a phonorecord is incidental to the transmission which constitutes the digital phonorecord delivery, and (ii) digital phonorecord deliveries in general. In addition to the objectives set forth in section 801(b)(1), in establishing such rates and terms, the Copyright Royalty Judges may consider rates and terms under voluntary license agreements described in subparagraphs (B) and (C). The royalty rates payable for a compulsory license for a digital phonorecord delivery under this section shall be established de novo and no precedential effect shall be given to the amount of the royalty payable by a compulsory licensee for digital phonorecord deliveries on or before December 31, 1997. The Copyright Royalty Judges shall also establish requirements by which copyright owners may receive reasonable notice of the use of their works under this section, and under which records of such use shall be kept and made available by persons making digital phonorecord deliveries.

(E)(i) License agreements voluntarily negotiated at any time between one or more copyright owners of nondramatic musical works and one or more persons entitled to obtain a compulsory license under subsection (a)(1) shall be given effect in lieu of any determination by the Librarian of Congress and Copyright Royalty Judges. Subject to clause (ii), the royalty rates determined pursuant to subparagraphs (C) and (D) shall be given effect as to digital phonorecord deliveries in lieu of any contrary royalty rates specified in a contract pursuant to which a recording artist who is the author of a nondramatic musical work grants a license under that person's exclusive rights in the musical work under paragraphs (1) and (3) of section 106 or commits another person to grant a license in that musical work under paragraphs (1) and (3) of section 106, to a person desiring to fix in a tangible medium of expression a sound recording embodying the musical work.

(ii) The second sentence of clause (i) shall not apply to —

(I) a contract entered into on or before June 22, 1995 and not modified thereafter for the purpose of reducing the royalty rates determined pursuant to subparagraphs (C) and (D) or of increasing the number of musical works within the scope of the contract covered by the reduced rates, except if a contract entered into on or before June 22, 1995, is modified thereafter for the purpose of increasing the number of musical works within the scope of the contract, any contrary royalty rates specified in the contract shall be given effect in lieu of royalty rates determined pursuant to subparagraphs (C) and (D) for the number of musical works within the scope of the contract as of June 22, 1995; and

(II) a contract entered into after the date that the sound recording is fixed in a tangible medium of expression substantially in a form intended for commercial release, if at the time the contract is entered into, the recording artist retains the right to grant licenses as to the musical work under paragraphs (1) and (3) of section 106.

(F) Except as provided in section 1002(e) of this title, a digital phonorecord delivery licensed under this paragraph shall be accompanied by the information encoded in the sound recording, if any, by or under the authority of the copyright owner of that sound recording, that identifies the title of the sound recording, the featured recording artist who performs on the sound recording, and related information, including information concerning the underlying musical work and its writer.

(G)(i) A digital phonorecord delivery of a sound recording is actionable as an act of infringement under section 501, and is fully subject to the remedies provided by sections 502 through 506, unless —

(I) the digital phonorecord delivery has been authorized by the copyright owner of the sound recording; and

(II) the owner of the copyright in the sound recording or the entity making the digital phonorecord delivery has obtained a compulsory license under this section or has otherwise been authorized by the copyright owner of the musical work to distribute or authorize the distribution, by means of a digital phonorecord delivery, of each musical work embodied in the sound recording.

(ii) Any cause of action under this subparagraph shall be in addition to those available to the owner of the copyright in the nondramatic musical work under subsection (c)(6) and section 106(4) and the owner of the copyright in the sound recording under section 106(6).

(H) The liability of the copyright owner of a sound recording for infringement of the copyright in a nondramatic musical work embodied in the sound recording shall be determined in accordance with applicable law, except that the owner of a copyright in a sound recording shall not be liable for a digital phonorecord delivery by a third party if the owner of the copyright in the sound recording does not license the distribution of a phonorecord of the nondramatic musical work.

(I) Nothing in section 1008 shall be construed to prevent the exercise of the rights and remedies allowed by this paragraph, paragraph (6), and chapter 5 in the event of a digital phonorecord delivery, except that no action alleging infringement of copyright may be brought under this title against a manufacturer, importer or distributor of a digital audio recording device, a digital audio recording medium, an analog recording device, or an analog recording medium, or against a consumer, based on the actions described in such section.

(J) Nothing in this section annuls or limits

(i) the exclusive right to publicly perform a sound recording or the musical work embodied therein, including by means of a digital transmission, under sections 106(4) and 106(6),

(ii) except for compulsory licensing under the conditions specified by this section, the exclusive rights to reproduce and distribute the sound recording and the musical work embodied therein under sections 106(1) and 106(3), including by means of a digital phonorecord delivery, or (iii) any other rights under any other provision of section 106, or remedies available under this title, as such rights or remedies exist either before or after the date of enactment of the Digital Performance Right in Sound Recordings Act of 1995.

(K) The provisions of this section concerning digital phonorecord deliveries shall not apply to any exempt transmissions or retransmissions under section 114(d)(1). The exemptions created in section 114(d)(1) do not expand or reduce the rights of copyright owners under section 106(1) through (5) with respect to such transmissions and retransmissions.

(4) A compulsory license under this section includes the right of the maker of a phonorecord of a nondramatic musical work under subsection (a)(1) to distribute or authorize distribution of such phonorecord by rental, lease, or lending (or by acts or practices in the nature of rental, lease, or lending). In addition to any royalty payable under clause (2) and chapter 8 of this title, a royalty shall be payable by the compulsory licensee for every act of distribution of a phonorecord by or in the nature of rental, lease, or lending, by or under the authority of the compulsory licensee. With respect to each nondramatic musical work embodied in the phonorecord, the royalty shall be a proportion of the revenue received by the compulsory licensee from every such act of distribution of the phonorecord under this clause equal to the proportion of the revenue received by the compulsory licensee from distribution of the phonorecord under clause (2) that is payable by a compulsory licensee under that clause and under chapter 8. The Register of Copyrights shall issue regulations to carry out the purpose of this clause.

(5) Royalty payments shall be made on or before the twentieth day of each month and shall include all royalties for the month next preceding. Each monthly payment shall be made under oath and shall comply with requirements that the Register of Copyrights shall prescribe by regulation. The Register shall also prescribe regulations under which detailed cumulative annual statements of account, certified by a certified public accountant, shall be filed for every compulsory license under this section. The regulations covering both the monthly and the annual statements of account shall prescribe the form, content, and manner of certification with respect to the number of records made and the number of records distributed.

(6) If the copyright owner does not receive the monthly payment and the monthly and annual statements of account when due, the owner may give written notice to the licensee that, unless the default is remedied within thirty days from the date of the notice, the compulsory license will be automatically terminated. Such termination renders either the making or the distribution, or both, of all phonorecords for which the royalty has not been paid, actionable as acts of infringement under section 501 and fully subject to the remedies provided by sections 502 through 506.

(d) Definition. — As used in this section, the following term has the following meaning: A "digital phonorecord delivery" is each individual delivery of a phonorecord by digital transmission of a sound recording which results in a specifically identifiable reproduction by or for any transmission recipient of a phonorecord of that sound recording, regardless of whether the digital transmission is also a public performance of the sound recording or any nondramatic musical work embodied therein. A digital phonorecord delivery does not result from a real-time, non-interactive subscription transmission of a sound recording where no reproduction of the sound recording or the musical work embodied therein is made from the inception of the transmission through to its receipt by the transmission recipient in order to make the sound recording audible.

§116. Negotiated licenses for public performances by means of coin-operated phonorecord players

(a) Applicability of Section. — This section applies to any nondramatic musical work embodied in a phonorecord.

(b) Negotiated Licenses. —

(1) Authority for negotiations. — Any owners of copyright in works to which this section applies and any operators of coin-operated phonorecord players may negotiate and agree upon the terms and rates of royalty payments for the performance of such works and the proportionate division of fees paid among copyright owners, and may designate common agents to negotiate, agree to, pay, or receive such royalty payments.

(2) Chapter 8 proceeding. — Parties not subject to such a negotiation may have the terms and rates and the division of fees described in paragraph (1) determined in a proceeding in accordance with the provisions of chapter 8.

(c) License agreements superior to determination by Copyright Royalty Judges. — License agreements between one or more copyright owners and one or more operators of coin-operated phonorecord players, which are negotiated in accordance with subsection (b), shall be given effect in lieu of any otherwise applicable determination by the Copyright Royalty Judges.

(d) Definitions. — As used in this section, the following terms mean the following:

(1) A "coin-operated phonorecord player" is a machine or device that—

(A) is employed solely for the performance of nondramatic musical works by means of phonorecords upon being activated by the insertion of coins, currency, tokens, or other monetary units or their equivalent;

(B) is located in an establishment making no direct or indirect charge for admission;

(C) is accompanied by a list which is comprised of the titles of all the musical works available for performance on it, and is affixed to the phonorecord player or posted in the establishment in a prominent position where it can be readily examined by the public; and

(D) affords a choice of works available for performance and permits the choice to be made by the patrons of the establishment in which it is located.

(2) An "operator" is any person who, alone or jointly with others —

(A) owns a coin-operated phonorecord player;

(B) has the power to make a coin-operated phonorecord player available for placement in an establishment for purposes of public performance; or

(C) has the power to exercise primary control over the selection of the musical works made available for public performance on a coin-operated phonorecord player.

§117. Limitations on exclusive rights: Computer programs

(a) Making of Additional Copy or Adaptation by Owner of Copy. — Notwithstanding the provisions of section 106, it is not an infringement for the owner of a copy of a computer program to make or authorize the making of another copy or adaptation of that computer program provided:

(1) that such a new copy or adaptation is created as an essential step in the utilization of the computer program in conjunction with a machine and that it is used in no other manner, or

(2) that such new copy or adaptation is for archival purposes only and that all archival copies are destroyed in the event that continued possession of the computer program should cease to be rightful.

(b) Lease, Sale, or Other Transfer of Additional Copy or Adaptation. — Any exact copies prepared in accordance with the provisions of this section may be leased, sold, or otherwise transferred, along with the copy from which such copies were prepared, only as part of the lease, sale, or other transfer of all rights in the program. Adaptations so prepared may be transferred only with the authorization of the copyright owner.

(c) Machine Maintenance or Repair. — Notwithstanding the provisions of section 106, it is not an infringement for the owner or lessee of a machine to make or authorize the making of a copy of a computer program if such copy is made solely by virtue of the activation of a machine that lawfully contains an authorized copy of the computer program, for purposes only of maintenance or repair of that machine, if —

(1) such new copy is used in no other manner and is destroyed immediately after the maintenance or repair is completed; and

(2) with respect to any computer program or part thereof that is not necessary for that machine to be activated, such program or part thereof is not

accessed or used other than to make such new copy by virtue of the activation of the machine.

(d) Definitions. — For purposes of this section —

(1) the "maintenance" of a machine is the servicing of the machine in order to make it work in accordance with its original specifications and any changes to those specifications authorized for that machine; and

(2) the "repair" of a machine is the restoring of the machine to the state of working in accordance with its original specifications and any changes to those specifications authorized for that machine.

§118. Scope of exclusive rights: Use of certain works in connection with noncommercial broadcasting

(a) The exclusive rights provided by section 106 shall, with respect to the works specified by subsection (b) and the activities specified by subsection (d), be subject to the conditions and limitations prescribed by this section.

(b) Notwithstanding any provision of the antitrust laws, any owners of copyright in published nondramatic musical works and published pictorial, graphic, and sculptural works and any public broadcasting entities, respectively, may negotiate and agree upon the terms and rates of royalty payments and the proportionate division of fees paid among various copyright owners, and may designate common agents to negotiate, agree to, pay, or receive payments.

(1) Any owner of copyright in a work specified in this subsection or any public broadcasting entity may submit to the Copyright Royalty Judges proposed licenses covering such activities with respect to such works.

(2) License agreements voluntarily negotiated at any time between one or more copyright owners and one or more public broadcasting entities shall be given effect in lieu of any determination by the Librarian of Congress or the Copyright Royalty Judges, if copies of such agreements are filed with the Copyright Royalty Judges within 30 days of execution in accordance with regulations that the Copyright Royalty Judges shall issue.

(3) Voluntary negotiation proceedings initiated pursuant to a petition filed under section 804(a) for the purpose of determining a schedule of terms and rates of royalty payments by public broadcasting entities to owners of copyright in works specified by this subsection and the proportionate division of fees paid among various copyright owners shall cover the 5-year period beginning on January 1 of the second year following the year in which the petition is filed. The parties to each negotiation proceeding shall bear their own costs.

(4) In the absence of license agreements negotiated under paragraph (2) or (3), the Copyright Royalty Judges shall, pursuant to chapter 8, conduct a proceeding to determine and publish in the Federal Register a schedule of rates and terms which, subject to paragraph (2), shall be binding on all owners of copyright in works specified by this subsection and public broadcasting entities, regardless of whether such copyright owners have submitted proposals

to the Copyright Royalty Judges. In establishing such rates and terms the Copyright Royalty Judges may consider the rates for comparable circumstances under voluntary license agreements negotiated as provided in paragraph (2) or (3). The Copyright Royalty Judges shall also establish requirements by which copyright owners may receive reasonable notice of the use of their works under this section, and under which records of such use shall be kept by public broadcasting entities.

(c) Subject to the terms of any voluntary license agreements that have been negotiated as provided by subsection (b)(2) or (3), a public broadcasting entity may, upon compliance with the provisions of this section, including the rates and terms established by the Copyright Royalty Judges under subsection (b)(4), engage in the following activities with respect to published nondramatic musical works and published pictorial, graphic, and sculptural works:

(1) performance or display of a work by or in the course of a transmission made by a noncommercial educational broadcast station referred to in subsection (f); and

(2) production of a transmission program, reproduction of copies or phonorecords of such a transmission program, and distribution of such copies or phonorecords, where such production, reproduction, or distribution is made by a nonprofit institution or organization solely for the purpose of transmissions specified in paragraph (1); and

(3) the making of reproductions by a governmental body or a nonprofit institution of a transmission program simultaneously with its transmission as specified in paragraph (1), and the performance or display of the contents of such program under the conditions specified by paragraph (1) of section 110, but only if the reproductions are used for performances or displays for a period of no more than seven days from the date of the transmission specified in paragraph (1), and are destroyed before or at the end of such period. No person supplying, in accordance with paragraph (2), a reproduction of a transmission program to governmental bodies or nonprofit institutions under this paragraph shall have any liability as a result of failure of such body or institution to destroy such reproduction: *Provided,* That it shall have notified such body or institution of the requirement for such destruction pursuant to this paragraph: *And provided further,* That if such body or institution itself fails to destroy such reproduction it shall be deemed to have infringed.

(d) Except as expressly provided in this subsection, this section shall have no applicability to works other than those specified in subsection (b). Owners of copyright in nondramatic literary works and public broadcasting entities may, during the course of voluntary negotiations, agree among themselves, respectively, as to the terms and rates of royalty payments without liability under the antitrust laws. Any such terms and rates of royalty payments shall be effective upon filing with the Copyright Royalty Judges, in accordance with regulations that the Copyright Royalty Judges shall prescribe as provided in section 803(b)(6).

(e) Nothing in this section shall be construed to permit, beyond the limits of fair use as provided by section 107, the unauthorized dramatization of a non-dramatic musical work, the production of a transmission program drawn to any substantial extent from a published compilation of pictorial, graphic, or sculptural works, or the unauthorized use of any portion of an audiovisual work.

(f) As used in this section, the term "public broadcasting entity" means a noncommercial educational broadcast station as defined in section 397 of title 47 and any nonprofit institution or organization engaged in the activities described in paragraph (2) of subsection (c).

§119. Limitations on exclusive rights: Secondary transmissions of superstations and network stations for private home viewing

(a) Secondary Transmissions by Satellite Carriers. —

(1) Superstations. — Subject to the provisions of paragraphs (5), (6), and (8) of this subsection and section 114(d), secondary transmissions of a performance or display of a work embodied in a primary transmission made by a superstation shall be subject to statutory licensing under this section if the secondary transmission is made by a satellite carrier to the public for private home viewing or for viewing in a commercial establishment, with regard to secondary transmissions the satellite carrier is in compliance with the rules, regulations, or authorizations of the Federal Communications Commission governing the carriage of television broadcast station signals, and the carrier makes a direct or indirect charge for each retransmission service to each household receiving the secondary transmission or to a distributor that has contracted with the carrier for direct or indirect delivery of the secondary transmission to the public for private home viewing or for viewing in a commercial establishment.

(2) Network stations. —

(A) In general. — Subject to the provisions of subparagraphs (B) and (C) of this paragraph and paragraphs (5), (6), (7), and (8) of this subsection and section 114(d), secondary transmissions of a performance or display of a work embodied in a primary transmission made by a network station shall be subject to statutory licensing under this section if the secondary transmission is made by a satellite carrier to the public for private home viewing, with regard to secondary transmissions the satellite carrier is in compliance with the rules, regulations, or authorizations of the Federal Communications Commission governing the carriage of television broadcast station signals, and the carrier makes a direct or indirect charge for such retransmission service to each subscriber receiving the secondary transmission.

(B) Secondary transmissions to unserved households. —

(i) In general. — The statutory license provided for in subparagraph (A) shall be limited to secondary transmissions of the signals of no more than two network stations in a single day for each television network to persons who reside in unserved households. The limitation in this clause shall not apply to secondary transmissions under paragraph (3).

(ii) Accurate determinations of eligibility. —

(I) Accurate predictive model. — In determining presumptively whether a person resides in an unserved household under subsection (d)(10)(A), a court shall rely on the Individual Location Longley-Rice model set forth by the Federal Communications Commission in Docket No. 98-201, as that model may be amended by the Commission over time under section 339(c)(3) of the Communications Act of 1934 to increase the accuracy of that model.

(II) Accurate measurements. — For purposes of site measurements to determine whether a person resides in an unserved household under subsection (d)(10)(A), a court shall rely on section 339(c)(4) of the Communications Act of 1934.

(iii) C-band exemption to unserved households. —

(I) In general. — The limitations of clause (i) shall not apply to any secondary transmissions by C-band services of network stations that a subscriber to C-band service received before any termination of such secondary transmissions before October 31, 1999.

(II) Definition. — In this clause the term "C-band service" means a service that is licensed by the Federal Communications Commission and operates in the Fixed Satellite Service under part 25 of title 47 of the Code of Federal Regulations.

(C) Exceptions. —

(i) States with single full-power network station. — In a State in which there is licensed by the Federal Communications Commission a single full-power station that was a network station on January 1, 1995, the statutory license provided for in subparagraph (A) shall apply to the secondary transmission by a satellite carrier of the primary transmission of that station to any subscriber in a community that is located within that State and that is not within the first 50 television markets as listed in the regulations of the Commission as in effect on such date (47 CFR 76.51).

(ii) States with all network stations and superstations in same local market. — In a State in which all network stations and superstations licensed by the Federal Communications Commission within that State as of January 1, 1995, are assigned to the same local market and that local market does not encompass all counties of that State, the statutory license provided under subparagraph (A) shall apply to the secondary transmission by a satellite carrier of the primary transmissions of such station to all subscribers in the State who reside in a local market that is within the first 50 major television markets as listed in the regulations of the Commission as in effect on such date (section 76.51 of title 47 of the Code of Federal Regulations).

(iii) Additional stations. — In the case of that State in which are located 4 counties that —

(I) on January 1, 2004, were in local markets principally comprised of counties in another State, and

(II) had a combined total of 41,340 television households, according to the U.S. Television Household Estimates by Nielsen Media Research for 2004, the statutory license provided under subparagraph (A) shall apply to secondary transmissions by a satellite carrier to subscribers in any such county of the primary transmissions of any network station located in that State, if the satellite carrier was making such secondary transmissions to any subscribers in that county on January 1, 2004.

(iv) Certain additional stations. — If 2 adjacent counties in a single State are in a local market comprised principally of counties located in another State, the statutory license provided for in subparagraph (A) shall apply to the secondary transmission by a satellite carrier to subscribers in those 2 counties of the primary transmissions of any network station located in the capital of the State in which such 2 counties are located, if—

(I) the 2 counties are located in a local market that is in the top 100 markets for the year 2003 according to Nielsen Media Research; and

(II) the total number of television households in the 2 counties combined did not exceed 10,000 for the year 2003 according to Nielsen Media Research.

(v) Applicability of royalty rates. — The royalty rates under subsection (b)(1)(B) apply to the secondary transmissions to which the statutory license under subparagraph (A) applies under clauses (i), (ii), (iii), and (iv).

(D) Submission of subscriber lists to networks. —

(i) Initial lists. — A satellite carrier that makes secondary transmissions of a primary transmission made by a network station pursuant to subparagraph (A) shall, 90 days after commencing such secondary transmissions, submit to the network that owns or is affiliated with the network station —

(I) a list identifying (by name and address, including street or rural route number, city, State, and zip code) all subscribers to which the satellite carrier makes secondary transmissions of that primary transmission to subscribers in unserved households; and

(II) a separate list, aggregated by designated market area (as defined in section 122(j)) (by name and address, including street or rural route number, city, State, and zip code), which shall indicate those subscribers being served pursuant to paragraph (3), relating to significantly viewed stations.

(ii) Monthly lists. — After the submission of the initial lists under clause (i), on the 15th of each month, the satellite carrier shall submit to the network —

(I) a list identifying (by name and address, including street or rural route number, city, State, and zip code) any persons who have been added or dropped as subscribers under clause (i)(I) since the last submission under clause (i); and

(II) a separate list, aggregated by designated market area (by name and street address, including street or rural route number, city, State, and zip code), identifying those subscribers whose service pursuant to paragraph (3), relating to significantly viewed stations, has been added or dropped.

(iii) Use of subscriber information. — Subscriber information submitted by a satellite carrier under this subparagraph may be used only for purposes of monitoring compliance by the satellite carrier with this subsection.

(iv) Applicability. — The submission requirements of this subparagraph shall apply to a satellite carrier only if the network to which the submissions are to be made places on file with the Register of Copyrights a document identifying the name and address of the person to whom such submissions are to be made. The Register shall maintain for public inspection a file of all such documents.

(3) Secondary transmissions of significantly viewed signals. —

(A) In general. — Notwithstanding the provisions of paragraph (2)(B), and subject to subparagraph (B) of this paragraph, the statutory license provided for in paragraphs (1) and (2) shall apply to the secondary transmission of the primary transmission of a network station or a superstation to a subscriber who resides outside the station's local market (as defined in section 122(j)) but within a community in which the signal has been determined by the Federal Communications Commission, to be significantly viewed in such community, pursuant to the rules, regulations, and authorizations of the Federal Communications Commission in effect on April 15, 1976, applicable to determining with respect to a cable system whether signals are significantly viewed in a community.

(B) Limitation. — Subparagraph (A) shall apply only to secondary transmissions of the primary transmissions of network stations and superstations to subscribers who receive secondary transmissions from a satellite carrier pursuant to the statutory license under section 122.

(C) Waiver. —

(i) In general. — A subscriber who is denied the secondary transmission of the primary transmission of a network station under subparagraph (B) may request a waiver from such denial by submitting a request, through the subscriber's satellite carrier, to the network station in the local market affiliated with the same network where the subscriber is located. The network station shall accept or reject the subscriber's request for a waiver within 30 days after receipt of the request. If the network station fails to accept or reject the subscriber's request for a waiver within that 30-day period, that network station shall be deemed to agree to the waiver request. Unless specifically stated by the network station, a waiver that was granted before the date of the enactment of the Satellite Home Viewer Extension and Reauthorization Act of 2004 under section 339(c)(2) of the Communications Act of 1934 shall not constitute a waiver for purposes of this subparagraph.

(ii) Sunset. — The authority under clause (i) to grant waivers shall terminate on December 31, 2008, and any such waiver in effect shall terminate on that date.

(4) Statutory license where retransmissions into local market available. —

(A) Rules for subscribers to analog signals under subsection (e) —

(i) For those receiving distant analog signals. — In the case of a subscriber of a satellite carrier who is eligible to receive the secondary transmission of the primary analog transmission of a network station solely by reason of subsection (e) (in this subparagraph referred to as a "distant analog signal"), and who, as of October 1, 2004, is receiving the distant analog signal of that network station, the following shall apply:

(I) In a case in which the satellite carrier makes available to the subscriber the secondary transmission of the primary analog transmission of a local network station affiliated with the same television network pursuant to the statutory license under section 122, the statutory license under paragraph (2) shall apply only to secondary transmissions by that satellite carrier to that subscriber of the distant analog signal of a station affiliated with the same television network —

(aa) if, within 60 days after receiving the notice of the satellite carrier under section 338(h)(1) of the Communications Act of 1934, the subscriber elects to retain the distant analog signal; but

(bb) only until such time as the subscriber elects to receive such local analog signal.

(II) Notwithstanding subclause (I), the statutory license under paragraph (2) shall not apply with respect to any subscriber who is eligible to receive the distant analog signal of a television network station solely by reason of subsection (e), unless the satellite carrier, within 60 days after the date of the enactment of the Satellite Home Viewer Extension and Reauthorization Act of 2004, submits to that television network a list, aggregated by designated market area (as defined in section 122(j)(2)(C)), that —

(aa) identifies that subscriber by name and address (street or rural route number, city, State, and zip code) and specifies the distant analog signals received by the subscriber; and

(bb) states, to the best of the satellite carrier's knowledge and belief, after having made diligent and good faith inquiries, that the subscriber is eligible under subsection (e) to receive the distant analog signals.

(ii) For those not receiving distant analog signals. — In the case of any subscriber of a satellite carrier who is eligible to receive the distant analog signal of a network station solely by reason of subsection (e) and who did not receive a distant analog signal of a station affiliated with the same network on October 1, 2004, the statutory license under paragraph (2) shall not apply to secondary transmissions by that satellite carrier to that subscriber of the distant analog signal of a station affiliated with the same network.

(B) Rules for other subscribers. — In the case of a subscriber of a satellite carrier who is eligible to receive the secondary transmission of the primary analog transmission of a network station under the statutory license under paragraph (2) (in this subparagraph referred to as a "distant analog signal"), other than subscribers to whom subparagraph (A) applies, the following shall apply:

(i) In a case in which the satellite carrier makes available to that subscriber, on January 1, 2005, the secondary transmission of the primary analog transmission of a local network station affiliated with the same television network pursuant to the statutory license under section 122, the statutory license under paragraph (2) shall apply only to secondary transmissions by that satellite carrier to that subscriber of the distant analog signal of a station affiliated with the same television network if the subscriber's satellite carrier, not later than March 1, 2005, submits to that television network a list, aggregated by designated market area (as defined in section 122(j)(2)(C)), that identifies that subscriber by name and address (street or rural route number, city, State, and zip code) and specifies the distant analog signals received by the subscriber.

(ii) In a case in which the satellite carrier does not make available to that subscriber, on January 1, 2005, the secondary transmission of the primary analog transmission of a local network station affiliated with the same television network pursuant to the statutory license under section 122, the statutory license under paragraph (2) shall apply only to secondary transmissions by that satellite carrier of the distant analog signal of a station affiliated with the same network to that subscriber if —

(I) that subscriber seeks to subscribe to such distant analog signal before the date on which such carrier commences to provide pursuant to the statutory license under section 122 the secondary transmissions of the primary analog transmission of stations from the local market of such local network station; and

(II) the satellite carrier, within 60 days after such date, submits to each television network a list that identifies each subscriber in that local market provided such an analog signal by name and address (street or rural route number, city, State, and zip code) and specifies the distant analog signals received by the subscriber.

(C) Future applicability. — The statutory license under paragraph (2) shall not apply to the secondary transmission by a satellite carrier of a primary analog transmission of a network station to a person who —

(i) is not a subscriber lawfully receiving such secondary transmission as of the date of the enactment of the Satellite Home Viewer Extension and Reauthorization Act of 2004; and

(ii) at the time such person seeks to subscribe to receive such secondary transmission, resides in a local market where the satellite carrier makes available to that person the secondary transmission of the primary analog transmission of a local network station affiliated with the same television network pursuant to the statutory license under section 122, and such secondary transmission of such primary transmission can reach such person.

(D) Special rules for distant digital signals. — The statutory license under paragraph (2) shall apply to secondary transmissions by a satellite carrier to a subscriber of primary digital transmissions of network stations if such secondary transmissions to such subscriber are permitted under section 339(a)(2)(D) of the Communications Act of 1934, as in effect on the day after the date of the enactment of the Satellite Home Viewer Extension and Reauthorization Act of 2004, except that the reference to section 73.683(a) of title 47, Code of Federal Regulations, referred to in section 339(a)(2)(D)(i)(I) shall refer to such section as in effect on the date of the enactment of the Satellite Home Viewer Extension and Reauthorization Act of 2004.

(E) Other provisions not affected. — This paragraph shall not affect the applicability of the statutory license to secondary transmissions under paragraph (3) or to unserved households included under paragraph (12).

(F) Waiver. — A subscriber who is denied the secondary transmission of a network station under subparagraph (C) or (D) may request a waiver from such denial by submitting a request, through the subscriber's satellite carrier, to the network station in the local market affiliated with the same network where the subscriber is located. The network station shall accept or reject the subscriber's request for a waiver within 30 days after receipt of the request. If the network station fails to accept or reject the subscriber's request for a waiver within that 30-day period, that network station shall be deemed to agree to the waiver request. Unless specifically stated by the network station, a waiver that was granted before the date of the enactment of the Satellite Home Viewer Extension and Reauthorization Act of 2004 under section 339(c)(2) of the Communications Act of 1934 shall not constitute a waiver for purposes of this subparagraph.

(G) Available defined. — For purposes of this paragraph, a satellite carrier makes available a secondary transmission of the primary transmission of a local station to a subscriber or person if the satellite carrier offers that secondary transmission to other subscribers who reside in the same zip code as that subscriber or person.

(5) Noncompliance with reporting and payment requirements. — Notwithstanding the provisions of paragraphs (1) and (2), the willful or repeated secondary transmission to the public by a satellite carrier of a primary transmission made by a superstation or a network station and embodying a performance or display of a work is actionable as an act of infringement under section 501, and is fully subject to the remedies provided by sections 502 through 506 and 509, where the satellite carrier has not deposited the statement of account and royalty fee required by subsection (b), or has failed to make the submissions to networks required by paragraph (2)(C).

(6) Willful alterations. — Notwithstanding the provisions of paragraphs (1) and (2), the secondary transmission to the public by a satellite carrier of a performance or display of a work embodied in a primary transmission made by a superstation or a network station is actionable as an act of infringement under section 501, and is fully subject to the remedies provided by sections 502 through 506 and section 510, if the content of the particular program in which the performance or display is embodied, or any commercial advertising or station announcement transmitted by the primary transmitter during, or immediately before or after, the transmission of such program, is in any way willfully altered by the satellite carrier through changes, deletions, or additions, or is combined with programming from any other broadcast signal.

(7) Violation of territorial restrictions on statutory license for network stations. —

(A) Individual violations. — The willful or repeated secondary transmission by a satellite carrier of a primary transmission made by a network station and embodying a performance or display of a work to a subscriber who is not eligible to receive the transmission under this section is actionable as an act of infringement under section 501 and is fully subject to the remedies provided by sections 502 through 506, except that —

(i) no damages shall be awarded for such act of infringement if the satellite carrier took corrective action by promptly withdrawing service from the ineligible subscriber, and

(ii) any statutory damages shall not exceed $5 for such subscriber for each month during which the violation occurred.

(B) Pattern of violations. — If a satellite carrier engages in a willful or repeated pattern or practice of delivering a primary transmission made by a network station and embodying a performance or display of a work to subscribers who are not eligible to receive the transmission under this section, then in addition to the remedies set forth in subparagraph (A) —

(i) if the pattern or practice has been carried out on a substantially nationwide basis, the court shall order a permanent injunction barring the secondary transmission by the satellite carrier, for private home viewing, of the primary transmissions of any primary network station affiliated with the same network, and the court may order statutory damages of not to exceed $250,000 for each 6-month period during which the pattern or practice was carried out; and

(ii) if the pattern or practice has been carried out on a local or regional basis, the court shall order a permanent injunction barring the secondary transmission, for private home viewing in that locality or region, by the satellite carrier of the primary transmissions of any primary network station affiliated with the same network, and the court may order statutory damages of not to exceed $250,000 for each 6-month period during which the pattern or practice was carried out.

(C) Previous subscribers excluded. — Subparagraphs (A) and (B) do not apply to secondary transmissions by a satellite carrier to persons who subscribed to receive such secondary transmissions from the satellite carrier or a distributor before November 16, 1988.

(D) Burden of proof. — In any action brought under this paragraph, the satellite carrier shall have the burden of proving that its secondary transmission of a primary transmission by a network station is to a subscriber who is eligible to receive the secondary transmission under this section.

(E) Exception. — The secondary transmission by a satellite carrier of a performance or display of a work embodied in a primary transmission made by a network station to subscribers who do not reside in unserved households shall not be an act of infringement if —

(i) the station on May 1, 1991, was retransmitted by a satellite carrier and was not on that date owned or operated by or affiliated with a television network that offered interconnected program service on a regular basis for 15 or more hours per week to at least 25 affiliated television licensees in 10 or more States;

(ii) as of July 1, 1998, such station was retransmitted by a satellite carrier under the statutory license of this section; and

(iii) the station is not owned or operated by or affiliated with a television network that, as of January 1, 1995, offered interconnected program service on a regular basis for 15 or more hours per week to at least 25 affiliated television licensees in 10 or more States.

(8) Discrimination by a satellite carrier. — Notwithstanding the provisions of paragraph (1), the willful or repeated secondary transmission to the public by a satellite carrier of a performance or display of a work embodied in a primary transmission made by a superstation or a network station is actionable as an act of infringement under section 501, and is fully subject to the remedies provided by sections 502 through 506, if the satellite carrier unlawfully discriminates against a distributor.

(9) Geographic limitation on secondary transmissions. — The statutory license created by this section shall apply only to secondary transmissions to households located in the United States.

(10) Loser pays for signal intensity measurement; recovery of measurement costs in a civil action. — In any civil action filed relating to the eligibility of subscribing households as unserved households —

(A) a network station challenging such eligibility shall, within 60 days after receipt of the measurement results and a statement of such costs, reimburse the satellite carrier for any signal intensity measurement that is conducted by that carrier in response to a challenge by the network station and that establishes the household is an unserved household; and

(B) a satellite carrier shall, within 60 days after receipt of the measurement results and a statement of such costs, reimburse the network station challenging such eligibility for any signal intensity measurement that is conducted by that station and that establishes the household is not an unserved household.

(11) Inability to conduct measurement. — If a network station makes a reasonable attempt to conduct a site measurement of its signal at a subscriber's household and is denied access for the purpose of conducting the measurement, and is otherwise unable to conduct a measurement, the satellite carrier shall within 60 days notice thereof, terminate service of the station's network to that household.

(12) Service to recreational vehicles and commercial trucks. —

(A) Exemption. —

(i) In general. — For purposes of this subsection, and subject to clauses (ii) and (iii), the term "unserved household" shall include —

(I) recreational vehicles as defined in regulations of the Secretary of Housing and Urban Development under section 3282.8 of title 24 of the Code of Federal Regulations; and

(II) commercial trucks that qualify as commercial motor vehicles under regulations of the Secretary of Transportation under section 383.5 of title 49 of the Code of Federal Regulations.

(ii) Limitation. — Clause (i) shall apply only to a recreational vehicle or commercial truck if any satellite carrier that proposes to make a secondary transmission of a network station to the operator of such a recreational vehicle or commercial truck complies with the documentation requirements under subparagraphs (B) and (C).

(iii) Exclusion. — For purposes of this subparagraph, the terms "recreational vehicle" and "commercial truck" shall not include any fixed dwelling, whether a mobile home or otherwise.

(B) Documentation requirements. — A recreational vehicle or commercial truck shall be deemed to be an unserved household beginning 10 days after the relevant satellite carrier provides to the network that owns or is affiliated with the network station that will be secondarily transmitted to the recreational vehicle or commercial truck the following documents:

(i) Declaration. — A signed declaration by the operator of the recreational vehicle or commercial truck that the satellite dish is permanently attached to the recreational vehicle or commercial truck, and will not be used to receive satellite programming at any fixed dwelling.

(ii) Registration. — In the case of a recreational vehicle, a copy of the current State vehicle registration for the recreational vehicle.

(iii) Registration and license. — In the case of a commercial truck, a copy of —

(I) the current State vehicle registration for the truck; and

(II) a copy of a valid, current commercial driver's license, as defined in regulations of the Secretary of Transportation under section 383 of title 49 of the Code of Federal Regulations, issued to the operator.

(C) Updated documentation requirements. — If a satellite carrier wishes to continue to make secondary transmissions to a recreational vehicle or commercial truck for more than a 2-year period, that carrier shall provide each network, upon request, with updated documentation in the form described under subparagraph (B) during the 90 days before expiration of that 2-year period.

(13) Statutory license contingent on compliance with FCC rules and remedial steps. — Notwithstanding any other provision of this section, the willful or repeated secondary transmission to the public by a satellite carrier of a primary transmission embodying a performance or display of a work made by a broadcast station licensed by the Federal Communications Commission is actionable as an act of infringement under section 501, and is fully subject to the remedies provided by sections 502 through 506, if, at the time of such transmission, the satellite carrier is not in compliance with the rules, regulations, and authorizations of the Federal Communications Commission concerning the carriage of television broadcast station signals.

(14) Waivers. — A subscriber who is denied the secondary transmission of a signal of a network station under subsection (a)(2)(B) may request a waiver from

such denial by submitting a request, through the subscriber's satellite carrier, to the network station asserting that the secondary transmission is prohibited. The network station shall accept or reject a subscriber's request for a waiver within 30 days after receipt of the request. If a television network station fails to accept or reject a subscriber's request for a waiver within the 30-day period after receipt of the request, that station shall be deemed to agree to the waiver request and have filed such written waiver. Unless specifically stated by the network station, a waiver that was granted before the date of the enactment of the Satellite Home Viewer Extension and Reauthorization Act of 2004 under section 339(c)(2) of the Communications Act of 1934, and that was in effect on such date of enactment, shall constitute a waiver for purposes of this paragraph.

(15) Carriage of low power television stations. —

(A) In general. — Notwithstanding paragraph (2)(B), and subject to subparagraphs (B) through (F) [sic] of this paragraph, the statutory license provided for in paragraphs (1) and (2) shall apply to the secondary transmission of the primary transmission of a network station or a superstation that is licensed as a low power television station, to a subscriber who resides within the same local market.

(B) Geographic limitation. —

(i) Network stations. — With respect to network stations, secondary transmissions provided for in subparagraph (A) shall be limited to secondary transmissions to subscribers who —

(I) reside in the same local market as the station originating the signal; and

(II) reside within 35 miles of the transmitter site of such station, except that in the case of such a station located in a standard metropolitan statistical area which has 1 of the 50 largest populations of all standard metropolitan statistical areas (based on the 1980 decennial census of population taken by the Secretary of Commerce), the number of miles shall be 20.

(ii) Superstations. — With respect to superstations, secondary transmissions provided for in subparagraph (A) shall be limited to secondary transmissions to subscribers who reside in the same local market as the station originating the signal.

(C) No applicability to repeaters and translators. — Secondary transmissions provided for in subparagraph (A) shall not apply to any low power television station that retransmits the programs and signals of another television station for more than 2 hours each day.

(D) Royalty fees. — Notwithstanding subsection (b)(1)(B), a satellite carrier whose secondary transmissions of the primary transmissions of a low power television station are subject to statutory licensing under this section shall have no royalty obligation for secondary transmissions to a subscriber who resides within 35 miles of the transmitter site of such station, except that in the case of such a station located in a standard metropolitan statistical area which has 1 of the 50 largest populations of all standard metropolitan statistical areas (based on the 1980 decennial census of population taken by the Secretary of Commerce), the number of miles shall be 20. Carriage of a superstation that is a low power television station within the station's local market, but outside of the 35-mile or 20-mile radius described in the preceding sentence, shall be subject to royalty payments under subsection (b)(1)(B).

(E) Limitation to subscribers taking local-into-local service. — Secondary transmissions provided for in subparagraph (A) may be made only to subscribers who receive secondary transmissions of primary transmissions from that satellite carrier pursuant to the statutory license under section 122, and only in conformity with the requirements under 340(b) of the Communications Act of 1934, as in effect on the date of the enactment of the Satellite Home Viewer Extension and Reauthorization Act of 2004.

(16) Restricted transmission of out-of-state distant network signals into certain markets. —

(A) Out-of-state network affiliates. — Notwithstanding any other provision of this title, the statutory license in this subsection and subsection (b) shall not apply to any secondary transmission of the primary transmission of a network station located outside of the State of Alaska to any subscriber in that State to whom the secondary transmission of the primary transmission of a television station located in that State is made available by the satellite carrier pursuant to section 122.

(B) Exception. — The limitation in subparagraph (A) shall not apply to the secondary transmission of the primary transmission of a digital signal of a network station located outside of the State of Alaska if at the time that the secondary transmission is made, no television station licensed to a community in the State and affiliated with the same network makes primary transmissions of a digital signal.

(b) Statutory License for Secondary Transmissions for Private Home Viewing. —

(1) Deposits with the Register of Copyrights. — A satellite carrier whose secondary transmissions are subject to statutory licensing under subsection (a) shall, on a semiannual basis, deposit with the Register of Copyrights, in accordance with requirements that the Register shall prescribe by regulation —

(A) a statement of account, covering the preceding 6-month period, specifying the names and locations of all superstations and network stations whose signals were retransmitted, at any time during that period, to subscribers as described in subsections (a)(1) and (a)(2), the total number of subscribers that received such retransmissions, and such other data as the Register of Copyrights may from time to time prescribe by regulation; and

(B) a royalty fee for that 6-month period, computed by multiplying the total number of subscribers receiving each secondary transmission of each superstation or network station during each calendar month by the appropriate rate in effect under this section.

Notwithstanding the provisions of subparagraph (B), a satellite carrier whose secondary transmissions are subject to statutory licensing under paragraph (1) or (2) of subsection (a) shall have no royalty obligation for secondary transmissions to a subscriber under paragraph (3) of such subsection.

(2) Investment of fees.—The Register of Copyrights shall receive all fees deposited under this section and, after deducting the reasonable costs incurred by the Copyright Office under this section (other than the costs deducted under paragraph (4)), shall deposit the balance in the Treasury of the United States, in such manner as the Secretary of the Treasury directs. All funds held by the Secretary of the Treasury shall be invested in interest-bearing securities of the United States for later distribution with interest by the Librarian of Congress as provided by this title.

(3) Persons to whom fees are distributed.—The royalty fees deposited under paragraph (2) shall, in accordance with the procedures provided by paragraph (4), be distributed to those copyright owners whose works were included in a secondary transmission made by a satellite carrier during the applicable 6-month accounting period and who file a claim with the Copyright Royalty Judges under paragraph (4).

(4) Procedures for distribution.—The royalty fees deposited under paragraph (2) shall be distributed in accordance with the following procedures:

(A) Filing of claims for fees.—During the month of July in each year, each person claiming to be entitled to statutory license fees for secondary transmissions shall file a claim with the Copyright Royalty Judges, in accordance with requirements that the Copyright Royalty Judges shall prescribe by regulation. For purposes of this paragraph, any claimants may agree among themselves as to the proportionate division of statutory license fees among them, may lump their claims together and file them jointly or as a single claim, or may designate a common agent to receive payment on their behalf.

(B) Determination of controversy; distributions.—After the first day of August of each year, the Copyright Royalty Judges shall determine whether there exists a controversy concerning the distribution of royalty fees. If the Copyright Royalty Judges determine that no such controversy exists, the Copyright Royalty Judges shall authorize the Librarian of Congress to proceed to distribute such fees to the copyright owners entitled to receive them, or to their designated agents, subject to the deduction of reasonable administrative costs under this section. If the Copyright Royalty Judges find the existence of a controversy, the Copyright Royalty Judges shall, pursuant to chapter 8 of this title, conduct a proceeding to determine the distribution of royalty fees.

(C) Withholding of fees during controversy.—During the pendency of any proceeding under this subsection, the Copyright Royalty Judges shall have the discretion to authorize the Librarian of Congress to proceed to distribute any amounts that are not in controversy.

(c) Adjustment of Royalty Fees.—

(1) Applicability and determination of royalty fees for analog signals.—

(A) Initial fee.—The appropriate fee for purposes of determining the royalty fee under subsection (b)(1)(B) for the secondary transmission of the primary analog transmissions of network stations and superstations shall be the appropriate fee set forth in part 258 of title 37, Code of

Federal Regulations, as in effect on July 1, 2004, as modified under this paragraph.

(B) Fee set by voluntary negotiation. — On or before January 2, 2005, the Librarian of Congress shall cause to be published in the Federal Register of the initiation of voluntary negotiation proceedings for the purpose of determining the royalty fee to be paid by satellite carriers for the secondary transmission of the primary analog transmission of network stations and superstations under subsection (b)(1)(B).

(C) Negotiations. — Satellite carriers, distributors, and copyright owners entitled to royalty fees under this section shall negotiate in good faith in an effort to reach a voluntary agreement or agreements for the payment of royalty fees. Any such satellite carriers, distributors and copyright owners may at any time negotiate and agree to the royalty fee, and may designate common agents to negotiate, agree to, or pay such fees. If the parties fail to identify common agents, the Librarian of Congress shall do so, after requesting recommendations from the parties to the negotiation proceeding. The parties to each negotiation proceeding shall bear the cost thereof.

(D) Agreements binding on parties; filing of agreements; public notice. —

(i) Voluntary agreements negotiated at any time in accordance with this paragraph shall be binding upon all satellite carriers, distributors, and copyright owners that a (sic) parties thereto. Copies of such agreements shall be filed with the Copyright Office within 30 days after execution in accordance with regulations that the Register of Copyrights shall prescribe.

(ii)(I) Within 10 days after publication in the Federal Register of a notice of the initiation of voluntary negotiation proceedings, parties who have reached a voluntary agreement may request that the royalty fees in that agreement be applied to all satellite carriers, distributors, and copyright owners without convening an arbitration proceeding pursuant to subparagraph (E).

(II) Upon receiving a request under subclause (I), the Librarian of Congress shall immediately provide public notice of the royalty fees from the voluntary agreement and afford parties an opportunity to state that they object to those fees.

(III) The Librarian shall adopt the royalty fees from the voluntary agreement for all satellite carriers, distributors, and copyright owners without convening an arbitration proceeding unless a party with an intent to participate in the arbitration proceeding and a significant interest in the outcome of that proceeding objects under subclause (II).

(E) Period agreement is in effect. — The obligation to pay the royalty fees established under a voluntary agreement which has been filed with the Copyright Office in accordance with this paragraph shall become effective on the date specified in the agreement, and shall remain in effect until December 31, 2009, or in accordance with the terms of the agreement, whichever is later.

(F) Fee set by compulsory arbitration. —

(i) Notice of initiation of proceedings. — On or before May 1, 2005, the Librarian of Congress shall cause notice to be published in the Federal Register of the initiation of arbitration proceedings for the purpose of determining the royalty fee to be paid for the secondary transmission of primary analog transmission of network stations and superstations under subsection (b)(1)(B) by satellite carriers and distributors

(I) in the absence of a voluntary agreement filed in accordance with subparagraph (D) that establishes royalty fees to be paid by all satellite carriers and distributors; or

(II) if an objection to the fees from a voluntary agreement submitted for adoption by the Librarian of Congress to apply to all satellite carriers, distributors, and copyright owners is received under subparagraph (D) from a party with an intent to participate in the arbitration proceeding and a significant interest in the outcome of that proceeding. Such arbitration proceeding shall be conducted under chapter 8 as in effect on the day before the date of the enactment of the Copyright Royalty and Distribution Act of 2004.

(ii) Establishment of royalty fees. — In determining royalty fees under this subparagraph, the copyright arbitration royalty panel appointed under chapter 8, as in effect on the day before the date of the enactment of the Copyright Royalty and Distribution Act of 2004 shall establish fees for the secondary transmissions of the primary analog transmission of network stations and superstations that most clearly represent the fair market value of secondary transmissions, except that the Librarian of Congress and any copyright arbitration royalty panel shall adjust those fees to account for the obligations of the parties under any applicable voluntary agreement filed with the Copyright Office pursuant to subparagraph (D). In determining the fair market value, the panel shall base its decision on economic, competitive, and programming information presented by the parties, including —

(I) the competitive environment in which such programming is distributed, the cost of similar signals in similar private and compulsory license marketplaces, and any special features and conditions of the retransmission marketplace;

(II) the economic impact of such fees on copyright owners and satellite carriers; and

(III) the impact on the continued availability of secondary transmissions to the public.

(iii) Period during which decision of arbitration panel or order of Librarian effective. — The obligation to pay the royalty fee established under a determination which —

(I) is made by a copyright arbitration royalty panel in an arbitration proceeding under this paragraph and is adopted by the Librarian of Congress under section 802(f), as in effect on the day before the date of the enactment of the Copyright Royalty and Distribution Act of 2004; or

(II) is established by the Librarian under section 802(f) as in effect on the day before such date of enactment shall be effective as of January 1, 2005.

(iv) Persons subject to royalty fee. — The royalty fee referred to in (iii) shall be binding on all satellite carriers, distributors and copyright owners, who are not party to a voluntary agreement filed with the Copyright Office under subparagraph (D).

(2) Applicability and determination of royalty fees for digital signals. — The process and requirements for establishing the royalty fee payable under subsection (b)(1)(B) for the secondary transmission of the primary digital transmissions of network stations and superstations shall be the same as that set forth in paragraph (1) for the secondary transmission of the primary analog transmission of network stations and superstations, except that —

(A) the initial fee under paragraph (1)(A) shall be the rates set forth in section 298.3(b)(1) and (2) of title 37, Code of Federal Regulations, as in effect on the date of the enactment of the Satellite Home Viewer Extension and Reauthorization Act of 2004, reduced by 22.5 percent;

(B) the notice of initiation of arbitration proceedings required in paragraph (1)(F)(i) shall be published on or before December 31, 2005; and

(C) the royalty fees that are established for the secondary transmission of the primary digital transmission of network stations and superstations in accordance with to (sic) the procedures set forth in paragraph (1)(F)(iii) and are payable under subsection (b)(1)(B) —

(i) shall be reduced by 22.5 percent; and

(ii) shall be adjusted by the Librarian of Congress on January 1, 2007, and on January 1 of each year thereafter, to reflect any changes occurring during the preceding 12 months in the cost of living as determined by the most recent Consumer Price Index (for all consumers and items) published by the Secretary of Labor.

(d) Definitions. — As used in this section —

(1) Distributor. — The term "distributor" means an entity which contracts to distribute secondary transmissions from a satellite carrier and, either as a single channel or in a package with other programming, provides the secondary transmission either directly to individual subscribers or indirectly through other program distribution entities in accordance with the provisions of this section.

(2) Network station. — The term "network station" means —

(A) a television station licensed by the Federal Communications Commission, including any translator station or terrestrial satellite station that rebroadcasts all or substantially all of the programming broadcast by a network station, that is owned or operated by, or affiliated with, one or more of the television networks in the United States which offer an interconnected program service on a regular basis for 15 or more hours per week to at least 25 of its affiliated television licensees in 10 or more States; or

(B) a noncommercial educational broadcast station (as defined in section 397 of the Communications Act of 1934 [47 U.S.C.A. §397]); except that the term does not include the signal of the Alaska Rural Communications Service, or any successor entity to that service.

(3) Primary network station. — The term "primary network station" means a network station that broadcasts or rebroadcasts the basic programming service of a particular national network.

(4) Primary transmission. — The term "primary transmission" has the meaning given that term in section 111(f) of this title.

(5) Private home viewing. — The term "private home viewing" means the viewing, for private use in a household by means of satellite reception equipment which is operated by an individual in that household and which serves only such household, of a secondary transmission delivered by a satellite carrier of a primary transmission of a television station licensed by the Federal Communications Commission.

(6) Satellite carrier. — The term "satellite carrier" means an entity that uses the facilities of a satellite or satellite service licensed by the Federal Communications Commission and operates in the Fixed-Satellite Service under part 25 of title 47 of the Code of Federal Regulations or the Direct Broadcast Satellite Service under part 100 of title 47 of the Code of Federal Regulations to establish and operate a channel of communications for point-to-multipoint distribution of television station signals, and that owns or leases a capacity or service on a satellite in order to provide such point-to-multipoint distribution, except to the extent that such entity provides such distribution pursuant to tariff under the Communications Act of 1934, other than for private home viewing.

(7) Secondary transmission. — The term "secondary transmission" has the meaning given that term in section 111(f) of this title.

(8) Subscriber. — The term "subscriber" means an individual who receives a secondary transmission service for private home viewing by means of a secondary transmission from a satellite carrier and pays a fee for the service, directly or indirectly, to the satellite carrier or to a distributor.

(9) Superstation. — The term "superstation" —

(A) means a television station, other than a network station, licensed by the Federal Communications Commission, that is secondarily transmitted by a satellite carrier; and

(B) except for purposes of computing the royalty fee, includes the Public Broadcasting Service satellite feed.

(10) Unserved household. — The term "unserved household", with respect to a particular television network, means a household that —

(A) cannot receive, through the use of a conventional, stationary, outdoor rooftop receiving antenna, an over-the-air signal of a primary network station affiliated with that network of Grade B intensity as defined by the Federal Communications Commission under section 73.683(a) of title 47 of the Code of Federal Regulations, as in effect on January 1, 1999;

(B) is subject to a waiver that meets the standards of subsection (a)(14) whether or not the waiver was granted before the date of the enactment of the Satellite Home Viewer Extension and Reauthorization Act of 2004;

(C) is a subscriber to whom subsection (e) applies;

(D) is a subscriber to whom subsection (a)(12) applies; or

(E) is a subscriber to whom the exemption under subsection (a)(2)(B)(iii) applies.

(11) Local market. — The term "local market" has the meaning given such term under section 122(j), except that with respect to a low power television station, the term "local market" means the designated market area in which the station is located.

(12) Low power television station. — The term "low power television station" means a low power television as defined under section 74.701(f) of title 47, Code of Federal Regulations, as in effect on June 1, 2004. For purposes of this paragraph, the term "low power television station" includes a low power television station that has been accorded primary status as a Class A television licensee under section 73.6001(a) of title 47, Code of Federal Regulations.

(13) Commercial establishment — The term "commercial establishment" —

(A) means an establishment used for commercial purposes, such as a bar, restaurant, private office, fitness club, oil rig, retail store, bank or other financial institution, supermarket, automobile or boat dealership, or any other establishment with a common business area; and

(B) does not include a multi-unit permanent or temporary dwelling where private home viewing occurs, such as a hotel, dormitory, hospital, apartment, condominium, or prison.

(e) Moratorium on Copyright Liability. — Until December 31, 2009, a subscriber who does not receive a signal of Grade A intensity (as defined in the regulations of the Federal Communications Commission under section 73.683(a) of title 47 of the Code of Federal Regulations, as in effect on January 1, 1999, or predicted by the Federal Communications Commission using the Individual Location Longley-Rice methodology described by the Federal Communications Commission in Docket No. 98-201) of a local network television broadcast station shall remain eligible to receive signals of network stations affiliated with the same network, if that subscriber had satellite service of such network signal terminated after July 11, 1998, and before October 31, 1999, as required by this section, or received such service on October 31, 1999.

(f) Expedited Consideration by Justice Department of Voluntary Agreements to Provide Satellite Secondary Transmissions to Local Markets. —

(1) In general. — In a case in which no satellite carrier makes available, to subscribers located in a local market, as defined in section 122(j)(2), the secondary transmission into that market of a primary transmission of one or more television broadcast stations licensed by the Federal Communications Commission, and two or more satellite carriers request a business review letter in accordance with section 50.6 of title 28, Code of Federal Regulations (as in effect on July 7, 2004), in order to assess the legality under the antitrust laws of proposed business conduct to make or carry out an agreement to provide such secondary transmission into such local market, the appropriate official of the Department of Justice shall respond to the request no later than 90 days after the date on which the request is received.

(2) Definition. — For purposes of this subsection, the term "antitrust laws" —

(A) has the meaning given that term in subsection (a) of the first section of the Clayton Act (15 U.S.C. 12(a)), except that such term includes section 5 of the Federal Trade Commission Act (15 U.S.C. 45) to the extent such section 5 applies to unfair methods of competition; and

(B) includes any State law similar to the laws referred to in paragraph (1).

§120. Scope of exclusive rights in architectural works

(a) Pictorial Representations Permitted. — The copyright in an architectural work that has been constructed does not include the right to prevent the making, distributing, or public display of pictures, paintings, photographs, or other pictorial representations of the work, if the building in which the work is embodied is located in or ordinarily visible from a public place.

(b) Alterations to and Destruction of Buildings. — Notwithstanding the provisions of section 106(2), the owners of a building embodying an architectural work may, without the consent of the author or copyright owner of the architectural work, make or authorize the making of alterations to such building, and destroy or authorize the destruction of such building.

§121. Limitations on exclusive rights: Reproduction for blind or other people with disabilities

(a) Notwithstanding the provisions of section 106, it is not an infringement of copyright for an authorized entity to reproduce or to distribute copies or phonorecords of a previously published, nondramatic literary work if such copies or phonorecords are reproduced or distributed in specialized formats exclusively for use by blind or other persons with disabilities.

(b)(1) Copies or phonorecords to which this section applies shall —

(A) not be reproduced or distributed in a format other than a specialized format exclusively for use by blind or other persons with disabilities;

(B) bear a notice that any further reproduction or distribution in a format other than a specialized format is an infringement; and

(C) include a copyright notice identifying the copyright owner and the date of the original publication.

(2) The provisions of this subsection shall not apply to standardized, secure, or norm-referenced tests and related testing material, or to computer programs, except the portions thereof that are in conventional human language (including descriptions of pictorial works) and displayed to users in the ordinary course of using the computer programs.

(c) Notwithstanding the provisions of section 106, it is not an infringement of copyright for a publisher of print instructional materials for use in elementary or secondary schools to create and distribute to the National Instructional Materials Access Center copies of the electronic files described in sections 612(a)(23)(C), 613(a)(6), and section 674(e) of the Individuals with Disabilities Education Act that contain the contents of print instructional materials using the National Instructional Material Accessibility Standard (as defined in section 674(e)(3) of that Act), if—

(1) the inclusion of the contents of such print instructional materials is required by any State educational agency or local educational agency;

(2) the publisher had the right to publish such print instructional materials in print formats; and

(3) such copies are used solely for reproduction or distribution of the contents of such print instructional materials in specialized formats.

(d) For purposes of this section, the term—

(1) "authorized entity" means a nonprofit organization or a governmental agency that has a primary mission to provide specialized services relating to training, education, or adaptive reading or information access needs of blind or other persons with disabilities;

(2) "blind or other persons with disabilities" means individuals who are eligible or who may qualify in accordance with the Act entitled "An Act to provide books for the adult blind", approved March 3, 1931 (2 U.S.C. 135a; 46 Stat. 1487) to receive books and other publications produced in specialized formats; and

(3) "print instructional materials" has the meaning given under section 674(e)(3)(C) of the Individuals with Disabilities Education Act; and

(4) "specialized formats" means—

(A) braille, audio, or digital text which is exclusively for use by blind or other persons with disabilities; and

(B) with respect to print instructional materials, includes large print formats when such materials are distributed exclusively for use by blind or other persons with disabilities.

§122. Limitations on exclusive rights: Secondary transmissions by satellite carriers within local markets

(a) Secondary Transmissions of Television Broadcast Stations by Satellite Carriers.—A secondary transmission of a performance or display of a work embodied in a primary transmission of a television broadcast station into the station's local market shall be subject to statutory licensing under this section if—

(1) the secondary transmission is made by a satellite carrier to the public;

(2) with regard to secondary transmissions, the satellite carrier is in compliance with the rules, regulations, or authorizations of the Federal Communications Commission governing the carriage of television broadcast station signals; and

(3) the satellite carrier makes a direct or indirect charge for the secondary transmission to—

(A) each subscriber receiving the secondary transmission; or

(B) a distributor that has contracted with the satellite carrier for direct or indirect delivery of the secondary transmission to the public.

(b) Reporting Requirements. —

(1) Initial lists. — A satellite carrier that makes secondary transmissions of a primary transmission made by a network station under subsection (a) shall, within 90 days after commencing such secondary transmissions, submit to the network that owns or is affiliated with the network station a list identifying (by name in alphabetical order and street address, including county and zip code) all subscribers to which the satellite carrier makes secondary transmissions of that primary transmission under subsection (a).

(2) Subsequent lists. — After the list is submitted under paragraph (1), the satellite carrier shall, on the 15th of each month, submit to the network a list identifying (by name in alphabetical order and street address, including county and zip code) any subscribers who have been added or dropped as subscribers since the last submission under this subsection.

(3) Use of subscriber information. — Subscriber information submitted by a satellite carrier under this subsection may be used only for the purposes of monitoring compliance by the satellite carrier with this section.

(4) Requirements of networks. — The submission requirements of this subsection shall apply to a satellite carrier only if the network to which the submissions are to be made places on file with the Register of Copyrights a document identifying the name and address of the person to whom such submissions are to be made. The Register of Copyrights shall maintain for public inspection a file of all such documents.

(c) No Royalty Fee Required. — A satellite carrier whose secondary transmissions are subject to statutory licensing under subsection (a) shall have no royalty obligation for such secondary transmissions.

(d) Noncompliance with Reporting and Regulatory Requirements. — Notwithstanding subsection (a), the willful or repeated secondary transmission to the public by a satellite carrier into the local market of a television broadcast station of a primary transmission embodying a performance or display of a work made by that television broadcast station is actionable as an act of infringement under section 501, and is fully subject to the remedies provided under sections 502 through 506, if the satellite carrier has not complied with the reporting requirements of subsection (b) or with the rules, regulations, and authorizations of the Federal Communications Commission concerning the carriage of television broadcast signals.

(e) Willful Alterations. — Notwithstanding subsection (a), the secondary transmission to the public by a satellite carrier into the local market of a television broadcast station of a performance or display of a work embodied in a primary transmission made by that television broadcast station is actionable as an act of infringement under section 501, and is fully subject to the remedies provided by sections 502 through 506 and section 510, if the content of the particular program in which the performance or display is embodied, or any commercial advertising or station announcement transmitted by the primary transmitter during, or immediately before or after, the transmission of such program, is in any way willfully altered by the satellite carrier through changes, deletions, or additions, or is combined with programming from any other broadcast signal.

(f) Violation of Territorial Restrictions on Statutory License for Television Broadcast Stations. —

(1) Individual violations. — The willful or repeated secondary transmission to the public by a satellite carrier of a primary transmission embodying a performance or display of a work made by a television broadcast station to a subscriber who does not reside in that station's local market, and is not subject to statutory licensing under section 119 or a private licensing agreement, is actionable as an act of infringement under section 501 and is fully subject to the remedies provided by sections 502 through 506, except that —

(A) no damages shall be awarded for such act of infringement if the satellite carrier took corrective action by promptly withdrawing service from the ineligible subscriber; and

(B) any statutory damages shall not exceed $5 for such subscriber for each month during which the violation occurred.

(2) Pattern of violations. — If a satellite carrier engages in a willful or repeated pattern or practice of secondarily transmitting to the public a primary transmission embodying a performance or display of a work made by a television broadcast station to subscribers who do not reside in that station's local market, and are not subject to statutory licensing under section 119 or a private licensing agreement, then in addition to the remedies under paragraph (1) —

(A) if the pattern or practice has been carried out on a substantially nationwide basis, the court —

(i) shall order a permanent injunction barring the secondary transmission by the satellite carrier of the primary transmissions of that television broadcast station (and if such television broadcast station is a network station, all other television broadcast stations affiliated with such network); and

(ii) may order statutory damages not exceeding $250,000 for each 6-month period during which the pattern or practice was carried out; and

(B) if the pattern or practice has been carried out on a local or regional basis with respect to more than one television broadcast station, the court —

(i) shall order a permanent injunction barring the secondary transmission in that locality or region by the satellite carrier of the primary transmissions of any television broadcast station; and

(ii) may order statutory damages not exceeding $250,000 for each 6-month period during which the pattern or practice was carried out.

(g) Burden of Proof. — In any action brought under subsection (f), the satellite carrier shall have the burden of proving that its secondary transmission of a primary transmission by a television broadcast station is made only to subscribers located within that station's local market or subscribers being served in compliance with section 119 or a private licensing agreement.

(h) Geographic Limitations on Secondary Transmissions. — The statutory license created by this section shall apply to secondary transmissions to locations in the United States.

(i) Exclusivity with Respect to Secondary Transmissions of Broadcast Stations by Satellite to Members of the Public. — No provision of section 111 or any other law (other than this section and section 119) shall be construed to contain any authorization, exemption, or license through which secondary transmissions by satellite carriers of programming contained in a primary transmission made by a television broadcast station may be made without obtaining the consent of the copyright owner.

(j) Definitions. — In this section —

(1) Distributor. — The term "distributor" means an entity which contracts to distribute secondary transmissions from a satellite carrier and, either as a single channel or in a package with other programming, provides the secondary transmission either directly to individual subscribers or indirectly through other program distribution entities.

(2) Local market. —

(A) In general. — The term "local market", in the case of both commercial and noncommercial television broadcast stations, means the designated market area in which a station is located, and —

(i) in the case of a commercial television broadcast station, all commercial television broadcast stations licensed to a community within the same designated market area are within the same local market; and

(ii) in the case of a noncommercial educational television broadcast station, the market includes any station that is licensed to a community within the same designated market area as the noncommercial educational television broadcast station.

(B) County of license. — In addition to the area described in subparagraph (A), a station's local market includes the county in which the station's community of license is located.

(C) Designated market area. — For purposes of subparagraph (A), the term "designated market area" means a designated market area, as determined by Nielsen Media Research and published in the 1999-2000 Nielsen Station Index Directory and Nielsen Station Index United States Television Household Estimates or any successor publication.

(D) Certain areas outside of any designated market area. — Any census area, borough, or other area in the State of Alaska that is outside of a designated market area, as determined by Nielsen Media Research, shall be deemed to be part of one of the local markets in the State of Alaska. A satellite carrier may determine which local market in the State of Alaska will be deemed to be the relevant local market in connection with each subscriber in such census area, borough, or other area.

(3) Network station; satellite carrier; secondary transmission. — The terms "network station", "satellite carrier", and "secondary transmission" have the meanings given such terms under section 119(d).

(4) Subscriber. — The term "subscriber" means a person who receives a secondary transmission service from a satellite carrier and pays a fee for the service, directly or indirectly, to the satellite carrier or to a distributor.

(5) Television broadcast station. — The term "television broadcast station" —

(A) means an over-the-air, commercial or noncommercial television broadcast station licensed by the Federal Communications Commission under subpart E of part 73 of title 47, Code of Federal Regulations, except that such term does not include a low-power or translator television station; and

(B) includes a television broadcast station licensed by an appropriate governmental authority of Canada or Mexico if the station broadcasts primarily in the English language and is a network station as defined in section 119(d)(2)(A).

Chapter 2. *Copyright Ownership and Transfer*

Sec.

§201. Ownership of copyright

(a) Initial Ownership. — Copyright in a work protected under this title vests initially in the author or authors of the work. The authors of a joint work are co-owners of copyright in the work.

(b) Works Made for Hire. — In the case of a work made for hire, the employer or other person for whom the work was prepared is considered the author for purposes of this title, and, unless the parties have expressly agreed otherwise in a written instrument signed by them, owns all of the rights comprised in the copyright.

(c) Contributions to Collective Works. — Copyright in each separate contribution to a collective work is distinct from copyright in the collective work as a whole, and vests initially in the author of the contribution. In the absence of an express transfer of the copyright or of any rights under it, the owner of copyright in the collective work is presumed to have acquired only the privilege of reproducing and distributing the contribution as part of that particular collective work, any revision of that collective work, and any later collective work in the same series.

(d) Transfer of Ownership. —

(1) The ownership of a copyright may be transferred in whole or in part by any means of conveyance or by operation of law, and may be bequeathed by will or pass as personal property by the applicable laws of intestate succession.

(2) Any of the exclusive rights comprised in a copyright, including any subdivision of any of the rights specified by section 106, may be transferred as provided by clause (1) and owned separately. The owner of any particular exclusive right is entitled, to the extent of that right, to all of the protection and remedies accorded to the copyright owner by this title.

(e) Involuntary Transfer. — When an individual author's ownership of a copyright, or of any of the exclusive rights under a copyright, has not previously been transferred voluntarily by that individual author, no action by any governmental body or other official or organization purporting to seize, expropriate, transfer, or exercise rights of ownership with respect to the copyright, or any of the exclusive rights under a copyright, shall be given effect under this title, except as provided under title 11.

§202. Ownership of copyright as distinct from ownership of material object

Ownership of a copyright, or of any of the exclusive rights under a copyright, is distinct from ownership of any material object in which the work is embodied. Transfer of ownership of any material object, including the copy or phonorecord in which the work is first fixed, does not of itself convey any rights in the copyrighted work embodied in the object; nor, in the absence of an agreement, does transfer of ownership of a copyright or of any exclusive rights under a copyright convey property rights in any material object.

§203. Termination of transfers and licenses granted by the author

(a) Conditions for Termination. — In the case of any work other than a work made for hire, the exclusive or nonexclusive grant of a transfer or license of copyright or of any right under a copyright, executed by the author on or after January 1, 1978, otherwise than by will, is subject to termination under the following conditions:

(1) In the case of a grant executed by one author, termination of the grant may be effected by that author or, if the author is dead, by the person or persons who, under clause (2) of this subsection, own and are entitled to exercise a total of more than one-half of that author's termination interest. In the case of a grant executed by two or more authors of a joint work, termination of the grant may be effected by a majority of the authors who executed it; if any of such authors is dead, the termination interest of any such author may be exercised as a unit by the person or persons who, under clause (2) of this subsection, own and are entitled to exercise a total of more than one-half of that author's interest.

(2) Where an author is dead, his or her termination interest is owned, and may be exercised, as follows:

(A) The widow or widower owns the author's entire termination interest unless there are any surviving children or grandchildren of the author, in which case the widow or widower owns one-half of the author's interest.

(B) The author's surviving children, and the surviving children of any dead child of the author, own the author's entire termination interest unless there is a widow or widower, in which case the ownership of one-half of the author's interest is divided among them.

(C) The rights of the author's children and grandchildren are in all cases divided among them and exercised on a per stirpes basis according to the number of such author's children represented; the share of the children of a dead child in a termination interest can be exercised only by the action of a majority of them.

(D) In the event that the author's widow or widower, children, and grandchildren are not living, the author's executor, administrator, personal representative, or trustee shall own the author's entire termination interest.

(3) Termination of the grant may be effected at any time during a period of five years beginning at the end of thirty-five years from the date of execution of the grant; or, if the grant covers the right of publication of the work, the period begins at the end of thirty-five years from the date of publication of the work under the grant or at the end of forty years from the date of execution of the grant, whichever term ends earlier.

(4) The termination shall be effected by serving an advance notice in writing, signed by the number and proportion of owners of termination interests required under clauses (1) and (2) of this subsection, or by their duly authorized agents, upon the grantee or the grantee's successor in title.

(A) The notice shall state the effective date of the termination, which shall fall within the five-year period specified by clause (3) of this subsection, and the notice shall be served not less than two or more than ten years before that date. A copy of the notice shall be recorded in the Copyright Office before the effective date of termination, as a condition to its taking effect.

(B) The notice shall comply, in form, content, and manner of service, with requirements that the Register of Copyrights shall prescribe by regulation.

(5) Termination of the grant may be effected notwithstanding any agreement to the contrary, including an agreement to make a will or to make any future grant.

(b) Effect of Termination. — Upon the effective date of termination, all rights under this title that were covered by the terminated grants revert to the author, authors, and other persons owning termination interests under clauses (1) and (2) of subsection (a), including those owners who did not join in signing the notice of termination under clause (4) of subsection (a), but with the following limitations:

(1) A derivative work prepared under authority of the grant before its termination may continue to be utilized under the terms of the grant after its termination, but this privilege does not extend to the preparation after the termination of other derivative works based upon the copyrighted work covered by the terminated grant.

(2) The future rights that will revert upon termination of the grant become vested on the date the notice of termination has been served as provided by clause (4) of subsection (a). The rights vest in the author, authors, and other persons named in, and in the proportionate shares provided by, clauses (1) and (2) of subsection (a).

(3) Subject to the provisions of clause (4) of this subsection, a further grant, or agreement to make a further grant, of any right covered by a terminated grant is valid only if it is signed by the same number and proportion of the owners, in whom the right has vested under clause (2) of this subsection, as are required to terminate the grant under clauses (1) and (2) of subsection (a). Such further grant or agreement is effective with respect to all of the persons in whom the right it covers has vested under clause (2) of this subsection, including those who did not join in signing it. If any person dies after rights under a terminated grant have vested in him or her, that person's legal representatives, legatees, or heirs at law represent him or her for purposes of this clause.

(4) A further grant, or agreement to make a further grant, of any right covered by a terminated grant is valid only if it is made after the effective date of the termination. As an exception, however, an agreement for such a further grant may be made between the persons provided by clause (3) of this subsection and the original grantee or such grantee's successor in title, after the notice of termination has been served as provided by clause (4) of subsection (a).

(5) Termination of a grant under this section affects only those rights covered by the grants that arise under this title, and in no way affects rights arising under any other Federal, State, or foreign laws.

(6) Unless and until termination is effected under this section, the grant, if it does not provide otherwise, continues in effect for the term of copyright provided by this title.

§204. Execution of transfers of copyright ownership

(a) A transfer of copyright ownership, other than by operation of law, is not valid unless an instrument of conveyance, or a note or memorandum of the transfer, is in writing and signed by the owner of the rights conveyed or such owner's duly authorized agent.

(b) A certificate of acknowledgment is not required for the validity of a transfer, but is prima facie evidence of the execution of the transfer if—

(1) in the case of a transfer executed in the United States, the certificate is issued by a person authorized to administer oaths within the United States; or

(2) in the case of a transfer executed in a foreign country, the certificate is issued by a diplomatic or consular officer of the United States, or by a person authorized to administer oaths whose authority is proved by a certificate of such an officer.

§205. Recordation of transfers and other documents

(a) Conditions for Recordation.—Any transfer of copyright ownership or other document pertaining to a copyright may be recorded in the Copyright Office if the document filed for recordation bears the actual signature of the person who executed it, or if it is accompanied by a sworn or official certification that it is a true copy of the original, signed document.

(b) Certificate of Recordation. — The Register of Copyrights shall, upon receipt of a document as provided by subsection (a) and of the fee provided by section 708, record the document and return it with a certificate of recordation.

(c) Recordation as Constructive Notice. — Recordation of a document in the Copyright Office gives all persons constructive notice of the facts stated in the recorded document, but only if—

(1) the document, or material attached to it, specifically identifies the work to which it pertains so that, after the document is indexed by the Register of Copyrights, it would be revealed by a reasonable search under the title or registration number of the work; and

(2) registration has been made for the work.

(d) Priority Between Conflicting Transfers. — As between two conflicting transfers, the one executed first prevails if it is recorded, in the manner required to give constructive notice under subsection (c), within one month after its execution in the United States or within two months after its execution outside the United States, or at any time before recordation in such manner of the later transfer. Otherwise the later transfer prevails if recorded first in such manner, and if taken in good faith, for valuable consideration or on the basis of a binding promise to pay royalties, and without notice of the earlier transfer.

(e) Priority Between Conflicting Transfer of Ownership and Nonexclusive License. — A nonexclusive license, whether recorded or not, prevails over a conflicting transfer of copyright ownership if the license is evidenced by a written instrument signed by the owner of the rights licensed or such owner's duly authorized agent, and if

(1) the license was taken before execution of the transfer; or

(2) the license was taken in good faith before recordation of the transfer and without notice of it.

Chapter 3. Duration of Copyright

Sec.

§301. Preemption with respect to other laws

(a) On and after January 1, 1978, all legal or equitable rights that are equivalent to any of the exclusive rights within the general scope of copyright as specified by section 106 in works of authorship that are fixed in a tangible medium of expression and come within the subject matter of copyright as specified by sections 102 and 103, whether created before or after that date and whether published or unpublished, are governed exclusively by this title. Thereafter, no person is entitled to any such right or equivalent right in any such work under the common law or statutes of any State.

(b) Nothing in this title annuls or limits any rights or remedies under the common law or statutes of any State with respect to —

(1) subject matter that does not come within the subject matter of copyright as specified by sections 102 and 103, including works of authorship not fixed in any tangible medium of expression; or

(2) any cause of action arising from undertakings commenced before January 1, 1978;

(3) activities violating legal or equitable rights that are not equivalent to any of the exclusive rights within the general scope of copyright as specified by section 106; or

(4) State and local landmarks, historic preservation, zoning, or building codes, relating to architectural works protected under section 102(a)(8).

(c) With respect to sound recordings fixed before February 15, 1972, any rights or remedies under the common law or statutes of any State shall not be annulled or limited by this title until February 15, 2067. The preemptive provisions of subsection (a) shall apply to any such rights and remedies pertaining to any cause of action arising from undertakings commenced on and after February 15, 2067. Notwithstanding the provisions of section 303, no sound recording fixed before February 15, 1972, shall be subject to copyright under this title before, on, or after February 15, 2067.

(d) Nothing in this title annuls or limits any rights or remedies under any other Federal statute.

(e) The scope of Federal preemption under this section is not affected by the adherence of the United States to the Berne Convention or the satisfaction of obligations of the United States thereunder.

(f)(1) On or after the effective date set forth in section 610(a) of the Visual Artists Rights Act of 1990, all legal or equitable rights that are equivalent to any of the rights conferred by section 106A with respect to works of visual art to which the rights conferred by section 106A apply are governed exclusively by section 106A and section 113(d) and the provisions of this title relating to such sections. Thereafter, no person is entitled to any such right or equivalent right in any work of visual art under the common law or statutes of any State.

(2) Nothing in paragraph (1) annuls or limits any rights or remedies under the common law or statutes of any State with respect to —

(A) any cause of action from undertakings commenced before the effective date set forth in section 610(a) of the Visual Artists Rights Act of 1990;

(B) activities violating legal or equitable rights that are not equivalent to any of the rights conferred by section 106A with respect to works of visual art; or

(C) activities violating legal or equitable rights which extend beyond the life of the author.

§302. Duration of copyright: Works created on or after January 1, 1978

(a) In General. — Copyright in a work created on or after January 1, 1978, subsists from its creation and, except as provided by the following subsections, endures for a term consisting of the life of the author and 70 years after the author's death.

(b) Joint Works. — In the case of a joint work prepared by two or more authors who did not work for hire, the copyright endures for a term consisting of the life of the last surviving author and 70 years after such last surviving author's death.

(c) Anonymous Works, Pseudonymous Works, and Works Made for Hire. — In the case of an anonymous work, a pseudonymous work, or a work made for hire, the copyright endures for a term of 95 years from the year of its first publication, or a term of 120 years from the year of its creation, whichever expires first. If, before the end of such term, the identity of one or more of the authors of an anonymous or pseudonymous work is revealed in the records of a registration made for that work under subsections (a) or (d) of section 408, or in the records provided by this subsection, the copyright in the work endures for the term specified by subsection (a) or (b), based on the life of the author or authors whose identity has been revealed. Any person having an interest in the copyright in an anonymous or pseudonymous work may at any time record, in records to be maintained by the Copyright Office for that purpose, a statement identifying one or more authors of the work; the statement shall also identify the person filing it, the nature of that person's interest, the source of the information recorded, and the particular work affected, and shall comply in form and content with requirements that the Register of Copyrights shall prescribe by regulation.

(d) Records Relating to Death of Authors. — Any person having an interest in a copyright may at any time record in the Copyright Office a statement of the date of death of the author of the copyrighted work, or a statement that the author is still living on a particular date. The statement shall identify the person filing it, the nature of that person's interest, and the source of the information recorded, and shall comply in form and content with requirements that the Register of Copyrights shall prescribe by regulation. The Register shall maintain current records of information relating to the death of authors of copyrighted works, based on such recorded statements and, to the extent the Register considers practicable, on data contained in any of the records of the Copyright Office or in other reference sources.

(e) Presumption as to Author's Death. — After a period of 95 years from the year of first publication of a work, or a period of 120 years from the year of its creation, whichever expires first, any person who obtains from the Copyright

Office a certified report that the records provided by subsection (d) disclose nothing to indicate that the author of the work is living, or died less than 70 years before, is entitled to the benefit of a presumption that the author has been dead for at least 70 years. Reliance in good faith upon this presumption shall be a complete defense to any action for infringement under this title.

§303. Duration of copyright: Works created but not published or copyrighted before January 1, 1978

(a) Copyright in a work created before January 1, 1978, but not theretofore in the public domain or copyrighted, subsists from January 1, 1978, and endures for the term provided by section 302. In no case, however, shall the term of copyright in such a work expire before December 31, 2002; and, if the work is published on or before December 31, 2002, the term of copyright shall not expire before December 31, 2047.

(b) The distribution before January 1, 1978, of a phonorecord shall not for any purpose constitute a publication of the musical work embodied therein.

§304. Duration of copyright: Subsisting copyrights

(a) Copyrights in Their First Term on January 1, 1978. —

(1)(A) Any copyright, in the first term of which is subsisting on January 1, 1978, shall endure for 28 years from the date it was originally secured.

(B) In the case of —

(i) any posthumous work or of any periodical, cyclopedic, or other composite work upon which the copyright was originally secured by the proprietor thereof, or

(ii) any work copyrighted by a corporate body (otherwise than as assignee or licensee of the individual author) or by an employer for whom such work is made for hire, the proprietor of such copyright shall be entitled to a renewal and extension of the copyright in such work for the further term of 67 years.

(C) In the case of any other copyrighted work, including a contribution by an individual author to a periodical or to a cyclopedic or other composite work —

(i) the author of such work, if the author is still living,

(ii) the widow, widower, or children of the author, if the author is not living,

(iii) the author's executors, if such author, widow, widower, or children are not living, or

(iv) the author's next of kin, in the absence of a will of the author, shall be entitled to a renewal and extension of the copyright in such work for a further term of 67 years.

(2)(A) At the expiration of the original term of copyright in a work specified in paragraph (1)(B) of this subsection, the copyright shall endure for a renewed and extended further term of 67 years, which —

> (i) if an application to register a claim to such further term has been made to the Copyright Office within 1 year before the expiration of the original term of copyright, and the claim is registered, shall vest, upon the beginning of such further term, in the proprietor of the copyright who is entitled to claim the renewal of copyright at the time the application is made; or

> (ii) if no such application is made or the claim pursuant to such application is not registered, shall vest, upon the beginning of such further term, in the person or entity that was the proprietor of the copyright as of the last day of the original term of copyright.

(B) At the expiration of the original term of copyright in a work specified in paragraph (1)(C) of this subsection, the copyright shall endure for a renewed and extended further term of 67 years, which —

> (i) if an application to register a claim to such further term has been made to the Copyright Office within 1 year before the expiration of the original term of copyright, and the claim is registered, shall vest, upon the beginning of such further term, in any person who is entitled under paragraph (1)(C) to the renewal and extension of the copyright at the time the application is made; or

> (ii) if no such application is made or the claim pursuant to such application is not registered, shall vest, upon the beginning of such further term, in any person entitled under paragraph (1)(C), as of the last day of the original term of copyright, to the renewal and extension of the copyright.

(3)(A) An application to register a claim to the renewed and extended term of copyright in a work may be made to the Copyright Office —

> (i) within 1 year before the expiration of the original term of copyright by any person entitled under paragraph (1)(B) or (C) to such further term of 67 years; and

> (ii) at any time during the renewed and extended term by any person in whom such further term vested, under paragraph (2)(A) or (B), or by any successor or assign of such person, if the application is made in the name of such person.

(B) Such an application is not a condition of the renewal and extension of the copyright in a work for a further term of 67 years.

(4)(A) If an application to register a claim to the renewed and extended term of copyright in a work is not made within 1 year before the expiration of the original term of copyright in a work, or if the claim pursuant to such application is not registered, then a derivative work prepared under authority of a grant of a transfer or license of the copyright that is made before the expiration of the original term of copyright may continue to be used under the terms of the grant during the renewed and extended term of copyright without infringing the copyright, except that such use does not extend to the preparation during such renewed and extended term of other derivative works based upon the copyrighted work covered by such grant.

(B) If an application to register a claim to the renewed and extended term of copyright in a work is made within 1 year before its expiration, and the claim is registered, the certificate of such registration shall constitute prima facie evidence as to the validity of the copyright during its renewed and extended term and of the facts stated in the certificate. The evidentiary weight to be accorded the certificates of a registration of a renewed and extended term of copyright made after the end of that 1-year period shall be within the discretion of the court.

(b) Copyrights in Their Renewal Term at the Time of the Effective Date of the Sonny Bono Copyright Term Extension Act. — Any copyright still in its renewal term at the time that the Sonny Bono Copyright Term Extension Act becomes effective shall have a copyright term of 95 years from the date copyright was originally secured.

(c) Termination of Transfers and Licenses Covering Extended Renewal Term. — In the case of any copyright subsisting in either its first or renewal term on January 1, 1978, other than a copyright in a work made for hire, the exclusive or nonexclusive grant of a transfer or license of the renewal copyright or any right under it, executed before January 1, 1978, by any of the persons designated by subsection (a)(1)(C) of this section, otherwise than by will, is subject to termination under the following conditions:

(1) In the case of a grant executed by a person or persons other than the author, termination of the grant may be effected by the surviving person or persons who executed it. In the case of a grant executed by one or more of the authors of the work, termination of the grant may be effected, to the extent of a particular author's share in the ownership of the renewal copyright, by the author who executed it or, if such author is dead, by the person or persons who, under clause (2) of this subsection, own and are entitled to exercise a total of more than one-half of that author's termination interest.

(2) Where an author is dead, his or her termination interest is owned, and may be exercised, as follows:

(A) The widow or widower owns the author's entire termination interest unless there are any surviving children or grandchildren of the author, in which case the widow or widower owns one-half of the author's interest.

(B) The author's surviving children, and the surviving children of any dead child of the author, own the author's entire termination interest unless there is a widow or widower, in which case the ownership of one-half of the author's interest is divided among them.

(C) The rights of the author's children and grandchildren are in all cases divided among them and exercised on a per stirpes basis according to the number of such author's children represented; the share of the children of a dead child in a termination interest can be exercised only by the action of a majority of them.

(D) In the event that the author's widow or widower, children, and grandchildren are not living, the author's executor, administrator, personal representative, or trustee shall own the author's entire termination interest.

(3) Termination of the grant may be effected at any time during a period of five years beginning at the end of fifty-six years from the date copyright was originally secured, or beginning on January 1, 1978, whichever is later.

(4) The termination shall be effected by serving an advance notice in writing upon the grantee or the grantee's successor in title. In the case of a grant executed by a person or persons other than the author, the notice shall be signed by all of those entitled to terminate the grant under clause (1) of this subsection, or by their duly authorized agents. In the case of a grant executed by one or more of the authors of the work, the notice as to any one author's share shall be signed by that author or his or her duly authorized agent or, if that author is dead, by the number and proportion of the owners of his or her termination interest required under clauses (1) and (2) of this subsection, or by their duly authorized agents.

(A) The notice shall state the effective date of the termination, which shall fall within the five-year period specified by clause (3) of this subsection, or, in the case of a termination under subsection (d), within the five-year period specified by subsection (d)(2), and the notice shall be served not less than two or more than ten years before that date. A copy of the notice shall be recorded in the Copyright Office before the effective date of termination, as a condition to its taking effect.

(B) The notice shall comply, in form, content, and manner of service, with requirements that the Register of Copyrights shall prescribe by regulation.

(5) Termination of the grant may be effected notwithstanding any agreement to the contrary, including an agreement to make a will or to make any future grant.

(6) In the case of a grant executed by a person or persons other than the author, all rights under this title that were covered by the terminated grant revert, upon the effective date of termination, to all of those entitled to terminate the grant under clause (1) of this subsection. In the case of a grant executed by one or more of the authors of the work, all of a particular author's rights under this title that were covered by the terminated grant revert, upon the effective date of termination, to that author or, if that author is dead, to the persons owning his or her termination interest under clause (2) of this subsection, including those owners who did not join in signing the notice of termination under clause (4) of this subsection. In all cases the reversion of rights is subject to the following limitations:

(A) A derivative work prepared under authority of the grant before its termination may continue to be utilized under the terms of the grant after its termination, but this privilege does not extend to the preparation after the termination of other derivative works based upon the copyrighted work covered by the terminated grant.

(B) The future rights that will revert upon termination of the grant become vested on the date the notice of termination has been served as provided by clause (4) of this subsection.

(C) Where the author's rights revert to two or more persons under clause (2) of this subsection, they shall vest in those persons in the proportionate shares provided by that clause. In such a case, and subject to the provisions of subclause (D) of this clause, a further grant, or agreement to make a further grant, of a particular author's share with respect to any right covered by a terminated grant is valid only if it is signed by the same number and proportion of the owners, in whom the right has vested under this clause, as are required to terminate the grant under clause (2) of this subsection. Such further grant or agreement is effective with respect to all of the persons in whom the right it covers has vested under this subclause, including those who did not join in signing it. If any person dies after rights under a terminated grant have vested in him or her, that person's legal representatives, legatees, or heirs at law represent him or her for purposes of this subclause.

(D) A further grant, or agreement to make a further grant, of any right covered by a terminated grant is valid only if it is made after the effective date of the termination. As an exception, however, an agreement for such a further grant may be made between the author or any of the persons provided by the first sentence of clause (6) of this subsection, or between the persons provided by subclause (C) of this clause, and the original grantee or such grantee's successor in title, after the notice of termination has been served as provided by clause (4) of this subsection.

(E) Termination of a grant under this subsection affects only those rights covered by the grant that arise under this title, and in no way affects rights arising under any other Federal, State, or foreign laws.

(F) Unless and until termination is effected under this subsection, the grant, if it does not provide otherwise, continues in effect for the remainder of the extended renewal term.

(d) Termination Rights Provided in Subsection (c) Which Have Expired on or Before the Effective Date of the Sonny Bono Copyright Term Extension Act. — In the case of any copyright other than a work made for hire, subsisting in its renewal term on the effective date of the Sonny Bono Copyright Term Extension Act for which the termination right provided in subsection (c) has expired by such date, where the author or owner of the termination right has not previously exercised such termination right, the exclusive or nonexclusive grant of a transfer or license of the renewal copyright or any right under it, executed before January 1, 1978, by any of the persons designated in subsection (a)(1)(C) of this section, other than by will, is subject to termination under the following conditions:

(1) The conditions specified in subsections (c)(1), (2), (4), (5), and (6) of this section apply to terminations of the last 20 years of copyright term as provided by the amendments made by the Sonny Bono Copyright Term Extension Act.

(2) Termination of the grant may be effected at any time during a period of 5 years beginning at the end of 75 years from the date copyright was originally secured.

§305. Duration of copyright: Terminal date

All terms of copyright provided by sections 302 through 304 run to the end of the calendar year in which they would otherwise expire.

Chapter 4. *Copyright Notice, Deposit, and Registration*

Sec.

§401. Notice of copyright: Visually perceptible copies

(a) General Provisions. — Whenever a work protected under this title is published in the United States or elsewhere by authority of the copyright owner, a notice of copyright as provided by this section may be placed on publicly distributed copies from which the work can be visually perceived, either directly or with the aid of a machine or device.

(b) Form of Notice. — If a notice appears on the copies, it shall consist of the following three elements:

(1) the symbol © (the letter C in a circle), or the word "Copyright", or the abbreviation "Copr."; and

(2) the year of first publication of the work; in the case of compilations or derivative works incorporating previously published material, the year date of first publication of the compilation or derivative work is sufficient. The year date may be omitted where a pictorial, graphic, or sculptural work, with accompanying text matter, if any, is reproduced in or on greeting cards, postcards, stationery, jewelry, dolls, toys, or any useful articles; and

(3) the name of the owner of copyright in the work, or an abbreviation by which the name can be recognized, or a generally known alternative designation of the owner.

(c) Position of Notice. — The notice shall be affixed to the copies in such manner and location as to give reasonable notice of the claim of copyright. The Register of Copyrights shall prescribe by regulation, as examples, specific methods of affixation and positions of the notice on various types of works that will satisfy this requirement, but these specifications shall not be considered exhaustive.

(d) Evidentiary Weight of Notice. — If a notice of copyright in the form and position specified by this section appears on the published copy or copies to which a defendant in a copyright infringement suit had access, then no weight shall be given to such a defendant's interposition of a defense based on innocent infringement in mitigation of actual or statutory damages, except as provided in the last sentence of section 504(c)(2).

§402. Notice of copyright: Phonorecords of sound recordings

(a) General Provisions. — Whenever a sound recording protected under this title is published in the United States or elsewhere by authority of the copyright owner, a notice of copyright as provided by this section may be placed on publicly distributed phonorecords of the sound recording.

(b) Form of Notice. — If a notice appears on the phonorecords, it shall consist of the following three elements:

(1) the symbol ℗ (the letter P in a circle); and

(2) the year of first publication of the sound recording; and

(3) the name of the owner of copyright in the sound recording, or an abbreviation by which the name can be recognized, or a generally known alternative designation of the owner; if the producer of the sound recording is named on the phonorecord labels or containers, and if no other name appears in conjunction with the notice, the producer's name shall be considered a part of the notice.

(c) Position of Notice. — The notice shall be placed on the surface of the phonorecord, or on the phonorecord label or container, in such manner and location as to give reasonable notice of the claim of copyright.

(d) Evidentiary Weight of Notice. — If a notice of copyright in the form and position specified by this section appears on the published phonorecord or phonorecords to which a defendant in a copyright infringement suit had access, then no weight shall be given to such a defendant's interposition of a defense based on innocent infringement in mitigation of actual or statutory damages, except as provided in the last sentence of section 504(c)(2).

§403. Notice of copyright: Publications incorporating United States Government works

Sections 401(d) and 402(d) shall not apply to a work published in copies or phonorecords consisting predominantly of one or more works of the United States Government unless the notice of copyright appearing on the published copies or phonorecords to which a defendant in the copyright infringement suit had access includes a statement identifying, either affirmatively or negatively, those portions of the copies or phonorecords embodying any work or works protected under this title.

§404. Notice of copyright: Contributions to collective works

(a) A separate contribution to a collective work may bear its own notice of copyright, as provided by sections 401 through 403. However, a single notice applicable to the collective work as a whole is sufficient to invoke the provisions of section 401(d) or 402(d), as applicable with respect to the separate contributions it contains (not including advertisements inserted on behalf of persons other than the owner of copyright in the collective work), regardless of the ownership of copyright in the contributions and whether or not they have been previously published.

(b) With respect to copies and phonorecords publicly distributed by authority of the copyright owner before the effective date of the Berne Convention Implementation Act of 1988, where the person named in a single notice applicable to a collective work as a whole is not the owner of copyright in a separate contribution that does not bear its own notice, the case is governed by the provisions of section 406(a).

§405. Notice of copyright: Omission of notice on certain copies and phonorecords

(a) Effect of Omission on Copyright. — With respect to copies and phonorecords publicly distributed by authority of the copyright owner before the effective date of the Berne Convention Implementation Act of 1988, the omission of the copyright notice described in sections 401 through 403 from copies or phonorecords publicly distributed by authority of the copyright owner does not invalidate the copyright in a work if —

    (1) the notice has been omitted from no more than a relatively small number of copies or phonorecords distributed to the public; or

    (2) registration for the work has been made before or is made within five years after the publication without notice, and a reasonable effort is made to add notice to all copies or phonorecords that are distributed to the public in the United States after the omission has been discovered; or

(3) the notice has been omitted in violation of an express requirement in writing that, as a condition of the copyright owner's authorization of the public distribution of copies or phonorecords, they bear the prescribed notice.

(b) Effect of Omission on Innocent Infringers. — Any person who innocently infringes a copyright, in reliance upon an authorized copy or phonorecord from which the copyright notice has been omitted and which was publicly distributed by authority of the copyright owner before the effective date of the Berne Convention Implementation Act of 1988, incurs no liability for actual or statutory damages under section 504 for any infringing acts committed before receiving actual notice that registration for the work has been made under section 408, if such person proves that he or she was misled by the omission of notice. In a suit for infringement in such a case the court may allow or disallow recovery of any of the infringer's profits attributable to the infringement, and may enjoin the continuation of the infringing undertaking or may require, as a condition for permitting the continuation of the infringing undertaking, that the infringer pay the copyright owner a reasonable license fee in an amount and on terms fixed by the court.

(c) Removal of Notice. — Protection under this title is not affected by the removal, destruction, or obliteration of the notice, without the authorization of the copyright owner, from any publicly distributed copies or phonorecords.

§406. Notice of copyright: Error in name or date on certain copies and phonorecords

(a) Error in Name. — With respect to copies and phonorecords publicly distributed by authority of the copyright owner before the effective date of the Berne Convention Implementation Act of 1988, where the person named in the copyright notice on copies or phonorecords publicly distributed by authority of the copyright owner is not the owner of copyright, the validity and ownership of the copyright are not affected. In such a case, however, any person who innocently begins an undertaking that infringes the copyright has a complete defense to any action for such infringement if such person proves that he or she was misled by the notice and began the undertaking in good faith under a purported transfer or license from the person named therein, unless before the undertaking was begun —

(1) registration for the work had been made in the name of the owner of copyright; or

(2) a document executed by the person named in the notice and showing the ownership of the copyright had been recorded.

The person named in the notice is liable to account to the copyright owner for all receipts from transfers or licenses purportedly made under the copyright by the person named in the notice.

(b) Error in Date. — When the year date in the notice on copies or phonorecords distributed before the effective date of the Berne Convention Implementation Act of 1988 by authority of the copyright owner is earlier than the year in which publication first occurred, any period computed from the year of first publication under section 302 is to be computed from the year in the notice.

Where the year date is more than one year later than the year in which publication first occurred, the work is considered to have been published without any notice and is governed by the provisions of section 405.

(c) Omission of Name or Date. — Where copies or phonorecords publicly distributed before the effective date of the Berne Convention Implementation Act of 1988 by authority of the copyright owner contain no name or no date that could reasonably be considered a part of the notice, the work is considered to have been published without any notice and is governed by the provisions of section 405 as in effect on the day before the effective date of the Berne Convention Implementation Act of 1988.

§407. Deposit of copies or phonorecords for Library of Congress

(a) Except as provided by subsection (c), and subject to the provisions of subsection (e), the owner of copyright or of the exclusive right of publication in a work published in the United States shall deposit, within three months after the date of such publication —

(1) two complete copies of the best edition; or

(2) if the work is a sound recording, two complete phonorecords of the best edition, together with any printed or other visually perceptible material published with such phonorecords.

Neither the deposit requirements of this subsection nor the acquisition provisions of subsection (e) are conditions of copyright protection.

(b) The required copies or phonorecords shall be deposited in the Copyright Office for the use or disposition of the Library of Congress. The Register of Copyrights shall, when requested by the depositor and upon payment of the fee prescribed by section 708, issue a receipt for the deposit.

(c) The Register of Copyrights may by regulation exempt any categories of material from the deposit requirements of this section, or require deposit of only one copy or phonorecord with respect to any categories. Such regulations shall provide either for complete exemption from the deposit requirements of this section, or for alternative forms of deposit aimed at providing a satisfactory archival record of a work without imposing practical or financial hardships on the depositor, where the individual author is the owner of copyright in a pictorial, graphic, or sculptural work and (i) less than five copies of the work have been published, or (ii) the work has been published in a limited edition consisting of numbered copies, the monetary value of which would make the mandatory deposit of two copies of the best edition of the work burdensome, unfair, or unreasonable.

(d) At any time after publication of a work as provided by subsection(a), the Register of Copyrights may make written demand for the required deposit on any of the persons obligated to make the deposit under subsection (a). Unless deposit is made within three months after the demand is received, the person or persons on whom the demand was made are liable —

(1) to a fine of not more than $250 for each work; and

(2) to pay into a specially designated fund in the Library of Congress the total retail price of the copies or phonorecords demanded, or, if no retail price has been fixed, the reasonable cost to the Library of Congress of acquiring them; and

(3) to pay a fine of $2,500, in addition to any fine or liability imposed under clauses (1) and (2), if such person willfully or repeatedly fails or refuses to comply with such a demand.

(e) With respect to transmission programs that have been fixed and transmitted to the public in the United States but have not been published, the Register of Copyrights shall, after consulting with the Librarian of Congress and other interested organizations and officials, establish regulations governing the acquisition, through deposit or otherwise, of copies or phonorecords of such programs for the collections of the Library of Congress.

(1) The Librarian of Congress shall be permitted, under the standards and conditions set forth in such regulations, to make a fixation of a transmission program directly from a transmission to the public, and to reproduce one copy or phonorecord from such fixation for archival purposes.

(2) Such regulations shall also provide standards and procedures by which the Register of Copyrights may make written demand, upon the owner of the right of transmission in the United States, for the deposit of a copy or phonorecord of a specific transmission program. Such deposit may, at the option of the owner of the right of transmission in the United States, be accomplished by gift, by loan for purposes of reproduction, or by sale at a price not to exceed the cost of reproducing and supplying the copy or phonorecord. The regulations established under this clause shall provide reasonable periods of not less than three months for compliance with a demand, and shall allow for extensions of such periods and adjustments in the scope of the demand or the methods for fulfilling it, as reasonably warranted by the circumstances. Willful failure or refusal to comply with the conditions prescribed by such regulations shall subject the owner of the right of transmission in the United States to liability for an amount, not to exceed the cost of reproducing and supplying the copy or phonorecord in question, to be paid into a specially designated fund in the Library of Congress.

(3) Nothing in this subsection shall be construed to require the making or retention, for purposes of deposit, of any copy or phonorecord of an unpublished transmission program, the transmission of which occurs before the receipt of a specific written demand as provided by clause (2).

(4) No activity undertaken in compliance with regulations prescribed under clauses (1) and (2) of this subsection shall result in liability if intended solely to assist in the acquisition of copies or phonorecords under this subsection.

§408. Copyright registration in general

(a) Registration Permissive. — At any time during the subsistence of the first term of copyright in any published or unpublished work in which the copyright was secured before January 1, 1978, and during the subsistence of any copyright secured on or after that date, the owner of copyright or of any exclusive right in the work may obtain registration of the copyright claim by delivering to the Copyright Office the deposit specified by this section, together with the application and fee specified by sections 409 and 708. Such registration is not a condition of copyright protection.

(b) Deposit for Copyright Registration. — Except as provided by subsection (c), the material deposited for registration shall include —

(1) in the case of an unpublished work, one complete copy or phonorecord;

(2) in the case of a published work, two complete copies or phonorecords of the best edition;

(3) in the case of a work first published outside the United States, one complete copy or phonorecord as so published;

(4) in the case of a contribution to a collective work, one complete copy or phonorecord of the best edition of the collective work.

Copies or phonorecords deposited for the Library of Congress under section 407 may be used to satisfy the deposit provisions of this section, if they are accompanied by the prescribed application and fee, and by any additional identifying material that the Register may, by regulation, require. The Register shall also prescribe regulations establishing requirements under which copies or phonorecords acquired for the Library of Congress under subsection (e) of section 407, otherwise than by deposit, may be used to satisfy the deposit provisions of this section.

(c) Administrative Classification and Optional Deposit. —

(1) The Register of Copyrights is authorized to specify by regulation the administrative classes into which works are to be placed for purposes of deposit and registration, and the nature of the copies or phonorecords to be deposited in the various classes specified. The regulations may require or permit, for particular classes, the deposit of identifying material instead of copies or phonorecords, the deposit of only one copy or phonorecord where two would normally be required, or a single registration for a group of related works. This administrative classification of works has no significance with respect to the subject matter of copyright or the exclusive rights provided by this title.

(2) Without prejudice to the general authority provided under clause (1), the Register of Copyrights shall establish regulations specifically permitting a single registration for a group of works by the same individual author, all first published as contributions to periodicals, including newspapers, within a twelve-month period, on the basis of a single deposit, application, and registration fee, under the following conditions:

(A) if the deposit consists of one copy of the entire issue of the periodical, or of the entire section in the case of a newspaper, in which each contribution was first published; and

(B) if the application identifies each work separately, including the periodical containing it and its date of first publication.

(3) As an alternative to separate renewal registrations under subsection (a) of section 304, a single renewal registration may be made for a group of works

by the same individual author, all first published as contributions to periodicals, including newspapers, upon the filing of a single application and fee, under all of the following conditions:

(A) the renewal claimant or claimants, and the basis of claim or claims under section 304(a), is the same for each of the works; and

(B) the works were all copyrighted upon their first publication, either through separate copyright notice and registration or by virtue of a general copyright notice in the periodical issue as a whole; and

(C) the renewal application and fee are received not more than twenty-eight or less than twenty-seven years after the thirty-first day of December of the calendar year in which all of the works were first published; and

(D) the renewal application identifies each work separately, including the periodical containing it and its date of first publication.

(d) Corrections and Amplifications.—The Register may also establish, by regulation, formal procedures for the filing of an application for supplementary registration, to correct an error in a copyright registration or to amplify the information given in a registration. Such application shall be accompanied by the fee provided by section 708, and shall clearly identify the registration to be corrected or amplified. The information contained in a supplementary registration augments but does not supersede that contained in the earlier registration.

(e) Published Edition of Previously Registered Work.—Registration for the first published edition of a work previously registered in unpublished form may be made even though the work as published is substantially the same as the unpublished version.

(f) Preregistration of works being prepared for commercial distribution.—

(1) Rulemaking.—Not later than 180 days after the date of enactment of this subsection, the Register of Copyrights shall issue regulations to establish procedures for preregistration of a work that is being prepared for commercial distribution and has not been published.

(2) Class of works.—The regulations established under paragraph (1) shall permit preregistration for any work that is in a class of works that the Register determines has had a history of infringement prior to authorized commercial distribution.

(3) Application for registration.—Not later than 3 months after the first publication of a work preregistered under this subsection, the applicant shall submit to the Copyright Office—

(A) an application for registration of the work;

(B) a deposit; and

(C) the applicable fee.

(4) Effect of untimely application.—An action under this chapter for infringement of a work preregistered under this subsection, in a case in which the infringement commenced no later than 2 months after the first publication of the work, shall be dismissed if the items described in paragraph (3) are not submitted to the Copyright Office in proper form within the earlier of—

(A) 3 months after the first publication of the work; or

(B) 1 month after the copyright owner has learned of the infringement.

§409. Application for copyright registration

The application for copyright registration shall be made on a form prescribed by the Register of Copyrights and shall include —

(1) the name and address of the copyright claimant;

(2) in the case of a work other than an anonymous or pseudonymous work, the name and nationality or domicile of the author or authors, and, if one or more of the authors is dead, the dates of their deaths;

(3) if the work is anonymous or pseudonymous, the nationality or domicile of the author or authors;

(4) in the case of a work made for hire, a statement to this effect;

(5) if the copyright claimant is not the author, a brief statement of how the claimant obtained ownership of the copyright;

(6) the title of the work, together with any previous or alternative titles under which the work can be identified;

(7) the year in which creation of the work was completed;

(8) if the work has been published, the date and nation of its first publication;

(9) in the case of a compilation or derivative work, an identification of any preexisting work or works that it is based on or incorporates, and a brief, general statement of the additional material covered by the copyright claim being registered;

(10) in the case of a published work containing material of which copies are required by section 601 to be manufactured in the United States, the names of the persons or organizations who performed the processes specified by subsection (c) of section 601 with respect to that material, and the places where those processes were performed; and

(11) any other information regarded by the Register of Copyrights as bearing upon the preparation or identification of the work or the existence, ownership, or duration of the copyright. If an application is submitted for the renewed and extended term provided for in section 304(a)(3)(A) and an original term registration has not been made, the Register may request information with respect to the existence, ownership, or duration of the copyright for the original term.

§410. Registration of claim and issuance of certificate

(a) When, after examination, the Register of Copyrights determines that, in accordance with the provisions of this title, the material deposited constitutes copyrightable subject matter and that the other legal and formal requirements of this title have been met, the Register shall register the claim and issue to the applicant a certificate of registration under the seal of the Copyright Office. The certificate shall contain the information given in the application, together with the number and effective date of the registration.

(b) In any case in which the Register of Copyrights determines that, in accordance with the provisions of this title, the material deposited does not constitute copyrightable subject matter or that the claim is invalid for any other reason, the Register shall refuse registration and shall notify the applicant in writing of the reasons for such refusal.

(c) In any judicial proceedings the certificate of a registration made before or within five years after first publication of the work shall constitute prima facie evidence of the validity of the copyright and of the facts stated in the certificate. The evidentiary weight to be accorded the certificate of a registration made thereafter shall be within the discretion of the court.

(d) The effective date of a copyright registration is the day on which an application, deposit, and fee, which are later determined by the Register of Copyrights or by a court of competent jurisdiction to be acceptable for registration, have all been received in the Copyright Office.

§411. Registration and civil infringement actions

(a) Except for an action brought for a violation of the rights of the author under section 106A(a), and subject to the provisions of subsection (b), no civil action for infringement of the copyright in any United States work shall be instituted until preregistration or registration of the copyright claim has been made in accordance with this title. In any case, however, where the deposit, application, and fee required for registration have been delivered to the Copyright Office in proper form and registration has been refused, the applicant is entitled to institute a civil action for infringement if notice thereof, with a copy of the complaint, is served on the Register of Copyrights. The Register may, at his or her option, become a party to the action with respect to the issue of registrability of the copyright claim by entering an appearance within sixty days after such service, but the Register's failure to become a party shall not deprive the court of jurisdiction to determine that issue.

(b)(1) A certificate of registration satisfies the requirements of this section and section 412, regardless of whether the certificate contains any inaccurate information, unless —

    (A) the inaccurate information was included on the application for copyright registration with knowledge that it was inaccurate; and

    (B) the inaccuracy of the information, if known, would have caused the Register of Copyrights to refuse registration.

    (2) In any case in which inaccurate information described under paragraph (1) is alleged, the court shall request the Register of Copyrights to advise the court whether the inaccurate information, if known, would have caused the Register of Copyrights to refuse registration.

    (3) Nothing in this subsection shall affect any rights, obligations, or requirements of a person related to information contained in a registration certificate, except for the institution of and remedies in infringement actions under this section and section 412.

(c) In the case of a work consisting of sounds, images, or both, the first fixation of which is made simultaneously with its transmission, the copyright owner may, either before or after such fixation takes place, institute an action for infringement under section 501, fully subject to the remedies provided by sections 502 through 505 and section 510, if, in accordance with requirements that the Register of Copyrights shall prescribe by regulation, the copyright owner—

(1) serves notice upon the infringer, not less than 48 hours before such fixation, identifying the work and the specific time and source of its first transmission, and declaring an intention to secure copyright in the work; and

(2) makes registration for the work, if required by subsection (a), within three months after its first transmission.

§412. Registration as prerequisite to certain remedies for infringement

In any action under this title, other than an action brought for a violation of the rights of the author under section 106A(a), an action for infringement of the copyright of a work that has been preregistered under section 408(f) before the commencement of the infringement and that has an effective date of registration not later than the earlier of 3 months after the first publication of the work or 1 month after the copyright owner has learned of the infringement, or an action instituted under section 411(c), no award of statutory damages or of attorney's fees, as provided by sections 504 and 505, shall be made for—

(1) any infringement of copyright in an unpublished work commenced before the effective date of its registration; or

(2) any infringement of copyright commenced after first publication of the work and before the effective date of its registration, unless such registration is made within three months after the first publication of the work.

Chapter 5. Copyright Infringement and Remedies

Sec.

§501. Infringement of copyright

(a) Anyone who violates any of the exclusive rights of the copyright owner as provided by sections 106 through 122 or of the author as provided in section 106A(a), or who imports copies or phonorecords into the United States in violation of section 602, is an infringer of the copyright or right of the author, as the case may be. For purposes of this chapter (other than section 506), any reference to copyright shall be deemed to include the rights conferred by section 106A(a). As used in this subsection, the term "anyone" includes any State, any instrumentality of a State, and any officer or employee of a State or instrumentality of a State acting in his or her official capacity. Any State, and any such instrumentality, officer, or employee, shall be subject to the provisions of this title in the same manner and to the same extent as any nongovernmental entity.

(b) The legal or beneficial owner of an exclusive right under a copyright is entitled, subject to the requirements of section 411, to institute an action for any infringement of that particular right committed while he or she is the owner of it. The court may require such owner to serve written notice of the action with a copy of the complaint upon any person shown, by the records of the Copyright Office or otherwise, to have or claim an interest in the copyright, and shall require that such notice be served upon any person whose interest is likely to be affected by a decision in the case. The court may require the joinder, and shall permit the intervention, of any person having or claiming an interest in the copyright.

(c) For any secondary transmission by a cable system that embodies a performance or a display of a work which is actionable as an act of infringement under subsection (c) of section 111, a television broadcast station holding a copyright or other license to transmit or perform the same version of that work shall, for purposes of subsection (b) of this section, be treated as a legal or beneficial owner if such secondary transmission occurs within the local service area of that television station.

(d) For any secondary transmission by a cable system that is actionable as an act of infringement pursuant to section 111(c)(3), the following shall also have standing to sue: (i) the primary transmitter whose transmission has been altered by the cable system; and (ii) any broadcast station within whose local service area the secondary transmission occurs.

(e) With respect to any secondary transmission that is made by a satellite carrier of a performance or display of a work embodied in a primary transmission and is actionable as an act of infringement under section 119(a)(5), a network station holding a copyright or other license to transmit or perform the same version of that work shall, for purposes of subsection (b) of this section, be treated as a legal or beneficial owner if such secondary transmission occurs within the local service area of that station.

(f)(1) With respect to any secondary transmission that is made by a satellite carrier of a performance or display of a work embodied in a primary transmission and is actionable as an act of infringement under section 122, a television broadcast station holding a copyright or other license to transmit or perform the same version of that work shall, for purposes of subsection (b) of this section, be treated as a legal or beneficial owner if such secondary transmission occurs within the local market of that station.

(2) A television broadcast station may file a civil action against any satellite carrier that has refused to carry television broadcast signals, as required under section 122(a)(2), to enforce that television broadcast station's rights under section 338(a) of the Communications Act of 1934.

§502.   Remedies for infringement: Injunctions

(a) Any court having jurisdiction of a civil action arising under this title may, subject to the provisions of section 1498 of title 28, grant temporary and final injunctions on such terms as it may deem reasonable to prevent or restrain infringement of a copyright.

(b) Any such injunction may be served anywhere in the United States on the person enjoined; it shall be operative throughout the United States and shall be enforceable, by proceedings in contempt or otherwise, by any United States court having jurisdiction of that person. The clerk of the court granting the injunction shall, when requested by any other court in which enforcement of the injunction is sought, transmit promptly to the other court a certified copy of all the papers in the case on file in such clerk's office.

§503.   Remedies for infringement: Impounding and disposition of infringing articles

(a)(1) At any time while an action under this title is pending, the court may order the impounding, on such terms as it may deem reasonable —

(A) of all copies or phonorecords claimed to have been made or used in violation of the exclusive right of the copyright owner;

(B) of all plates, molds, matrices, masters, tapes, film negatives, or other articles by means of which such copies of[*] phonorecords may be reproduced; and

(C) of records documenting the manufacture, sale, or receipt of things involved in any such violation, provided that any records seized under this subparagraph shall be taken into the custody of the court.

---

* [In original Pub. L. No. 110-403, probably should be "or". — Eds.]

(2) For impoundments of records ordered under paragraph (1)(C), the court shall enter an appropriate protective order with respect to discovery and use of any records or information that has been impounded. The protective order shall provide for appropriate procedures to ensure that confidential, private, proprietary, or privileged information contained in such records is not improperly disclosed or used.

(3) The relevant provisions of paragraphs (2) through (11) of section 34(d) of the Trademark Act (15 U.S.C. 1116(d)(2) through (11)) shall extend to any impoundment of records ordered under paragraph (1)(C) that is based upon an ex parte application, notwithstanding the provisions of rule 65 of the Federal Rules of Civil Procedure. Any references in paragraphs (2) through (11) of section 34(d) of the Trademark Act to section 32 of such Act shall be read as references to section 501 of this title, and references to use of a counterfeit mark in connection with the sale, offering for sale, or distribution of goods or services shall be read as references to infringement of a copyright.

(b) As part of a final judgment or decree, the court may order the destruction or other reasonable disposition of all copies or phonorecords found to have been made or used in violation of the copyright owner's exclusive rights, and of all plates, molds, matrices, masters, tapes, film negatives, or other articles by means of which such copies or phonorecords may be reproduced.

§504. Remedies for infringement: Damages and profits

(a) In General. — Except as otherwise provided by this title, an infringer of copyright is liable for either —

(1) the copyright owner's actual damages and any additional profits of the infringer, as provided by subsection (b); or

(2) statutory damages, as provided by subsection (c).

(b) Actual Damages and Profits. — The copyright owner is entitled to recover the actual damages suffered by him or her as a result of the infringement, and any profits of the infringer that are attributable to the infringement and are not taken into account in computing the actual damages. In establishing the infringer's profits, the copyright owner is required to present proof only of the infringer's gross revenue, and the infringer is required to prove his or her deductible expenses and the elements of profit attributable to factors other than the copyrighted work.

(c) Statutory Damages. —

(1) Except as provided by clause (2) of this subsection, the copyright owner may elect, at any time before final judgment is rendered, to recover, instead of actual damages and profits, an award of statutory damages for all infringements involved in the action, with respect to any one work, for which any one infringer is liable individually, or for which any two or more infringers are liable jointly and severally, in a sum of not less than $750 or more than $30,000 as the court considers just. For the purposes of this subsection, all the parts of a compilation or derivative work constitute one work.

(2) In a case where the copyright owner sustains the burden of proving, and the court finds, that infringement was committed willfully, the court in its

discretion may increase the award of statutory damages to a sum of not more than $150,000. In a case where the infringer sustains the burden of proving, and the court finds, that such infringer was not aware and had no reason to believe that his or her acts constituted an infringement of copyright, the court in its discretion may reduce the award of statutory damages to a sum of not less than $200. The court shall remit statutory damages in any case where an infringer believed and had reasonable grounds for believing that his or her use of the copyrighted work was a fair use under section 107, if the infringer was: (i) an employee or agent of a nonprofit educational institution, library, or archives acting within the scope of his or her employment who, or such institution, library, or archives itself, which infringed by reproducing the work in copies or phonorecords; or (ii) a public broadcasting entity which or a person who, as a regular part of the nonprofit activities of a public broadcasting entity (as defined in subsection (g) of section 118) infringed by performing a published nondramatic literary work or by reproducing a transmission program embodying a performance of such a work.

(3)(A) In a case of infringement, it shall be a rebuttable presumption that the infringement was committed willfully for purposes of determining relief if the violator, or a person acting in concert with the violator, knowingly provided or knowingly caused to be provided materially false contact information to a domain name registrar, domain name registry, or other domain name registration authority in registering, maintaining, or renewing a domain name used in connection with the infringement.

(B) Nothing in this paragraph limits what may be considered willful infringement under this subsection.

(C) For purposes of this paragraph, the term "domain name" has the meaning given that term in section 45 of the Act entitled "An Act to provide for the registration and protection of trademarks used in commerce, to carry out the provisions of certain international conventions, and for other purposes" approved July 5, 1946 (commonly referred to as the "Trademark Act of 1946"; 15 U.S.C. 1127).

(d) Additional Damages in Certain Cases. — In any case in which the court finds that a defendant proprietor of an establishment who claims as a defense that its activities were exempt under section 110(5) did not have reasonable grounds to believe that its use of a copyrighted work was exempt under such section, the plaintiff shall be entitled to, in addition to any award of damages under this section, an additional award of two times the amount of the license fee that the proprietor of the establishment concerned should have paid the plaintiff for such use during the preceding period of up to 3 years.

§505. Remedies for infringement: Costs and attorney's fees

In any civil action under this title, the court in its discretion may allow the recovery of full costs by or against any party other than the United States or an officer thereof. Except as otherwise provided by this title, the court may also award a reasonable attorney's fee to the prevailing party as part of the costs.

§506. Criminal offenses

(a) Criminal Infringement. —

(1) In general. — Any person who willfully infringes a copyright shall be punished as provided under section 2319 of title 18, if the infringement was committed —

(A) for purposes of commercial advantage or private financial gain;

(B) by the reproduction or distribution, including by electronic means, during any 180-day period, of 1 or more copies or phonorecords of 1 or more copyrighted works, which have a total retail value of more than $1,000; or

(C) by the distribution of a work being prepared for commercial distribution, by making it available on a computer network accessible to members of the public, if such person knew or should have known that the work was intended for commercial distribution.

(2) Evidence. — For purposes of this subsection, evidence of reproduction or distribution of a copyrighted work, by itself, shall not be sufficient to establish willful infringement of a copyright.

(3) Definition. — In this subsection, the term "work being prepared for commercial distribution" means —

(A) a computer program, a musical work, a motion picture or other audiovisual work, or a sound recording, if, at the time of unauthorized distribution —

(i) the copyright owner has a reasonable expectation of commercial distribution; and

(ii) the copies or phonorecords of the work have not been commercially distributed; or

(B) a motion picture, if, at the time of unauthorized distribution, the motion picture —

(i) has been made available for viewing in a motion picture exhibition facility; and

(ii) has not been made available in copies for sale to the general public in the United States in a format intended to permit viewing outside a motion picture exhibition facility.

(b) Forfeiture, Destruction, and Restitution. — Forfeiture, destruction, and restitution relating to this section shall be subject to section 2323 of title 18, to the extent provided in that section, in addition to any other similar remedies provided by law.

(c) Fraudulent Copyright Notice. — Any person who, with fraudulent intent, places on any article a notice of copyright or words of the same purport that such person knows to be false, or who, with fraudulent intent, publicly distributes or imports for public distribution any article bearing such notice or words that such person knows to be false, shall be fined not more than $2,500.

(d) Fraudulent Removal of Copyright Notice. — Any person who, with fraudulent intent, removes or alters any notice of copyright appearing on a copy of a copyrighted work shall be fined not more than $2,500.

(e) False Representation. — Any person who knowingly makes a false representation of a material fact in the application for copyright registration provided for by section 409, or in any written statement filed in connection with the application, shall be fined not more than $2,500.

(f) Rights of Attribution and Integrity. — Nothing in this section applies to infringement of the rights conferred by section 106A(a).

§507. Limitations on actions

(a) Criminal Proceedings. — Except as expressly provided otherwise in this title, no criminal proceeding shall be maintained under the provisions of this title unless it is commenced within 5 years after the cause of action arose.

(b) Civil Actions. — No civil action shall be maintained under the provisions of this title unless it is commenced within three years after the claim accrued.

§508. Notification of filing and determination of actions

(a) Within one month after the filing of any action under this title, the clerks of the courts of the United States shall send written notification to the Register of Copyrights setting forth, as far as is shown by the papers filed in the court, the names and addresses of the parties and the title, author, and registration number of each work involved in the action. If any other copyrighted work is later included in the action by amendment, answer, or other pleading, the clerk shall also send a notification concerning it to the Register within one month after the pleading is filed.

(b) Within one month after any final order or judgment is issued in the case, the clerk of the court shall notify the Register of it, sending with the notification a copy of the order or judgment together with the written opinion, if any, of the court.

(c) Upon receiving the notifications specified in this section, the Register shall make them a part of the public records of the Copyright Office.

§509. [Repealed.]

§510. Remedies for alteration of programming by cable systems

(a) In any action filed pursuant to section 111(c)(3), the following remedies shall be available:

(1) Where an action is brought by a party identified in subsections (b) or (c) of section 501, the remedies provided by sections 502 through 505, and the remedy provided by subsection (b) of this section; and

(2) When an action is brought by a party identified in subsection (d) of section 501, the remedies provided by sections 502 and 505, together with any actual damages suffered by such party as a result of the infringement, and the remedy provided by subsection (b) of this section.

(b) In any action filed pursuant to section 111(c)(3), the court may decree that, for a period not to exceed thirty days, the cable system shall be deprived of the benefit of a statutory license for one or more distant signals carried by such cable system.

§511. Liability of States, instrumentalities of States, and State officials for infringement of copyright

(a) In General. — Any State, any instrumentality of a State, and any officer or employee of a State or instrumentality of a State acting in his or her official capacity, shall not be immune, under the Eleventh Amendment of the Constitution of the United States or under any other doctrine of sovereign immunity, from suit in Federal Court by any person, including any governmental or nongovernmental entity, for a violation of any of the exclusive rights of a copyright owner provided by sections 106 through 122, for importing copies of phonorecords in violation of section 602, or for any other violation under this title.

(b) Remedies. — In a suit described in subsection (a) for a violation described in that subsection, remedies (including remedies both at law and in equity) are available for the violation to the same extent as such remedies are available for such a violation in a suit against any public or private entity other than a State, instrumentality of a State, or officer or employee of a State acting in his or her official capacity. Such remedies include impounding and disposition of infringing articles under section 503, actual damages and profits and statutory damages under section 504, costs and attorney's fees under section 505, and the remedies provided in section 510.

§512. Limitations on liability relating to material online

(a) Transitory Digital Network Communications. — A service provider shall not be liable for monetary relief, or, except as provided in subsection (j), for injunctive or other equitable relief, for infringement of copyright by reason of the provider's transmitting, routing, or providing connections for, material through a system or network controlled or operated by or for the service provider, or by reason of the intermediate and transient storage of that material in the course of such transmitting, routing, or providing connections, if—

(1) the transmission of the material was initiated by or at the direction of a person other than the service provider;

(2) the transmission, routing, provision of connections, or storage is carried out through an automatic technical process without selection of the material by the service provider;

(3) the service provider does not select the recipients of the material except as an automatic response to the request of another person;

(4) no copy of the material made by the service provider in the course of such intermediate or transient storage is maintained on the system or network in a manner ordinarily accessible to anyone other than anticipated recipients, and no such copy is maintained on the system or network in a manner ordinarily accessible to such anticipated recipients for a longer period than is reasonably necessary for the transmission, routing, or provision of connections; and

(5) the material is transmitted through the system or network without modification of its content.

(b) System Caching. —

(1) Limitation on liability. —A service provider shall not be liable for monetary relief, or, except as provided in subsection (j), for injunctive or other equitable relief, for infringement of copyright by reason of the intermediate and temporary storage of material on a system or network controlled or operated by or for the service provider in a case in which —

(A) the material is made available online by a person other than the service provider;

(B) the material is transmitted from the person described in subparagraph (A) through the system or network to a person other than the person described in subparagraph (A) at the direction of that other person; and

(C) the storage is carried out through an automatic technical process for the purpose of making the material available to users of the system or network who, after the material is transmitted as described in subparagraph (B), request access to the material from the person described in subparagraph (A),

if the conditions set forth in paragraph (2) are met.

(2) Conditions. —The conditions referred to in paragraph (1) are that —

(A) the material described in paragraph (1) is transmitted to the subsequent users described in paragraph (1)(C) without modification to its content from the manner in which the material was transmitted from the person described in paragraph (1)(A);

(B) the service provider described in paragraph (1) complies with rules concerning the refreshing, reloading, or other updating of the material when specified by the person making the material available online in accordance with a generally accepted industry standard data communications protocol for the system or network through which that person makes the material available, except that this subparagraph applies only if those rules are not used by the person described in paragraph (1)(A) to prevent or unreasonably impair the intermediate storage to which this subsection applies;

(C) the service provider does not interfere with the ability of technology associated with the material to return to the person described in paragraph (1)(A) the information that would have been available to that person if the material had been obtained by the subsequent users described in paragraph (1)(C) directly from that person, except that this subparagraph applies only if that technology —

(i) does not significantly interfere with the performance of the provider's system or network or with the intermediate storage of the material;

(ii) is consistent with generally accepted industry standard communications protocols; and

(iii) does not extract information from the provider's system or network other than the information that would have been available to the person described in paragraph (1)(A) if the subsequent users had gained access to the material directly from that person;

(D) if the person described in paragraph (1)(A) has in effect a condition that a person must meet prior to having access to the material, such as a condition based on payment of a fee or provision of a password or other information, the service provider permits access to the stored material in significant part only to users of its system or network that have met those conditions and only in accordance with those conditions; and

(E) if the person described in paragraph (1)(A) makes that material available online without the authorization of the copyright owner of the material, the service provider responds expeditiously to remove, or disable access to, the material that is claimed to be infringing upon notification of claimed infringement as described in subsection (c)(3), except that this subparagraph applies only if—

(i) the material has previously been removed from the originating site or access to it has been disabled, or a court has ordered that the material be removed from the originating site or that access to the material on the originating site be disabled; and

(ii) the party giving the notification includes in the notification a statement confirming that the material has been removed from the originating site or access to it has been disabled or that a court has ordered that the material be removed from the originating site or that access to the material on the originating site be disabled.

(c) Information Residing on Systems or Networks at Direction of Users. —

(1) In general. — A service provider shall not be liable for monetary relief, or, except as provided in subsection (j), for injunctive or other equitable relief, for infringement of copyright by reason of the storage at the direction of a user of material that resides on a system or network controlled or operated by or for the service provider, if the service provider—

(A)(i) does not have actual knowledge that the material or an activity using the material on the system or network is infringing;

(ii) in the absence of such actual knowledge, is not aware of facts or circumstances from which infringing activity is apparent; or

(iii) upon obtaining such knowledge or awareness, acts expeditiously to remove, or disable access to, the material;

(B) does not receive a financial benefit directly attributable to the infringing activity, in a case in which the service provider has the right and ability to control such activity; and

(C) upon notification of claimed infringement as described in paragraph (3), responds expeditiously to remove, or disable access to, the material that is claimed to be infringing or to be the subject of infringing activity.

(2) Designated agent. — The limitations on liability established in this subsection apply to a service provider only if the service provider has designated an agent to receive notifications of claimed infringement described in paragraph (3), by making available through its service, including on its website in a location accessible to the public, and by providing to the Copyright Office, substantially the following information:

(A) the name, address, phone number, and electronic mail address of the agent.

(B) other contact information which the Register of Copyrights may deem appropriate.

The Register of Copyrights shall maintain a current directory of agents available to the public for inspection, including through the Internet, in both electronic and hard copy formats, and may require payment of a fee by service providers to cover the costs of maintaining the directory.

(3) Elements of notification. —

(A) To be effective under this subsection, a notification of claimed infringement must be a written communication provided to the designated agent of a service provider that includes substantially the following:

(i) A physical or electronic signature of a person authorized to act on behalf of the owner of an exclusive right that is allegedly infringed.

(ii) Identification of the copyrighted work claimed to have been infringed, or, if multiple copyrighted works at a single online site are covered by a single notification, a representative list of such works at that site.

(iii) Identification of the material that is claimed to be infringing or to be the subject of infringing activity and that is to be removed or access to which is to be disabled, and information reasonably sufficient to permit the service provider to locate the material.

(iv) Information reasonably sufficient to permit the service provider to contact the complaining party, such as an address, telephone number, and, if available, an electronic mail address at which the complaining party may be contacted.

(v) A statement that the complaining party has a good faith belief that use of the material in the manner complained of is not authorized by the copyright owner, its agent, or the law.

(vi) A statement that the information in the notification is accurate, and under penalty of perjury, that the complaining party is authorized to act on behalf of the owner of an exclusive right that is allegedly infringed.

(B)(i) Subject to clause (ii), a notification from a copyright owner or from a person authorized to act on behalf of the copyright owner that fails to comply substantially with the provisions of subparagraph (A) shall not be considered under paragraph (1)(A) in determining whether a service provider has actual knowledge or is aware of facts or circumstances from which infringing activity is apparent.

(ii) In a case in which the notification that is provided to the service provider's designated agent fails to comply substantially with all the provisions of subparagraph (A) but substantially complies with clauses (ii), (iii), and (iv) of subparagraph (A), clause (i) of this subparagraph applies only if the service provider promptly attempts to contact the person making the notification or takes other reasonable steps to assist in the receipt of notification that substantially complies with all the provisions of subparagraph (A).

(d) Information Location Tools.—A service provider shall not be liable for monetary relief, or, except as provided in subsection (j), for injunctive or other equitable relief, for infringement of copyright by reason of the provider referring or linking users to an online location containing infringing material or infringing activity, by using information location tools, including a directory, index, reference, pointer, or hypertext link, if the service provider—

(1)(A) does not have actual knowledge that the material or activity is infringing;

(B) in the absence of such actual knowledge, is not aware of facts or circumstances from which infringing activity is apparent; or

(C) upon obtaining such knowledge or awareness, acts expeditiously to remove, or disable access to, the material;

(2) does not receive a financial benefit directly attributable to the infringing activity, in a case in which the service provider has the right and ability to control such activity; and

(3) upon notification of claimed infringement as described in subsection (c)(3), responds expeditiously to remove, or disable access to, the material that is claimed to be infringing or to be the subject of infringing activity, except that, for purposes of this paragraph, the information described in subsection (c)(3)(A)(iii) shall be identification of the reference or link, to material or activity claimed to be infringing, that is to be removed or access to which is to be disabled, and information reasonably sufficient to permit the service provider to locate that reference or link.

(e) Limitation on Liability of Nonprofit Educational Institutions.—

(1) When a public or other nonprofit institution of higher education is a service provider, and when a faculty member or graduate student who is an employee of such institution is performing a teaching or research function, for the purposes of subsections (a) and (b) such faculty member or graduate student shall be considered to be a person other than the institution, and for the purposes of subsections (c) and (d) such faculty member's or graduate student's knowledge or awareness of his or her infringing activities shall not be attributed to the institution, if—

(A) such faculty member's or graduate student's infringing activities do not involve the provision of online access to instructional materials that are or were required or recommended, within the preceding 3-year period, for a course taught at the institution by such faculty member or graduate student;

(B) the institution has not, within the preceding 3-year period, received more than 2 notifications described in subsection (c)(3) of claimed infringement by such faculty member or graduate student, and such notifications of claimed infringement were not actionable under subsection (f); and

(C) the institution provides to all users of its system or network informational materials that accurately describe, and promote compliance with, the laws of the United States relating to copyright.

(2) For the purposes of this subsection, the limitations on injunctive relief contained in subsections (j)(2) and (j)(3), but not those in (j)(1), shall apply.

(f) Misrepresentations. — Any person who knowingly materially misrepresents under this section —

(1) that material or activity is infringing, or

(2) that material or activity was removed or disabled by mistake or misidentification, shall be liable for any damages, including costs and attorneys' fees, incurred by the alleged infringer, by any copyright owner or copyright owner's authorized licensee, or by a service provider, who is injured by such misrepresentation, as the result of the service provider relying upon such misrepresentation in removing or disabling access to the material or activity claimed to be infringing, or in replacing the removed material or ceasing to disable access to it.

(g) Replacement of Removed or Disabled Material and Limitation on Other Liability. —

(1) No liability for taking down generally. — Subject to paragraph (2), a service provider shall not be liable to any person for any claim based on the service provider's good faith disabling of access to, or removal of, material or activity claimed to be infringing or based on facts or circumstances from which infringing activity is apparent, regardless of whether the material or activity is ultimately determined to be infringing.

(2) Exception. — Paragraph (1) shall not apply with respect to material residing at the direction of a subscriber of the service provider on a system or network controlled or operated by or for the service provider that is removed, or to which access is disabled by the service provider, pursuant to a notice provided under subsection (c)(1)(C), unless the service provider —

(A) takes reasonable steps promptly to notify the subscriber that it has removed or disabled access to the material;

(B) upon receipt of a counter notification described in paragraph (3), promptly provides the person who provided the notification under subsection (c)(1)(C) with a copy of the counter notification, and informs that person that it will replace the removed material or cease disabling access to it in 10 business days; and

(C) replaces the removed material and ceases disabling access to it not less than 10, nor more than 14, business days following receipt of the counter notice, unless its designated agent first receives notice from the person who submitted the notification under subsection (c)(1)(C) that such person has filed an action seeking a court order to restrain the subscriber from engaging in infringing activity relating to the material on the service provider's system or network.

(3) Contents of counter notification.—To be effective under this subsection, a counter notification must be a written communication provided to the service provider's designated agent that includes substantially the following:

(A) A physical or electronic signature of the subscriber.

(B) Identification of the material that has been removed or to which access has been disabled and the location at which the material appeared before it was removed or access to it was disabled.

(C) A statement under penalty of perjury that the subscriber has a good faith belief that the material was removed or disabled as a result of mistake or misidentification of the material to be removed or disabled.

(D) The subscriber's name, address, and telephone number, and a statement that the subscriber consents to the jurisdiction of Federal District Court for the judicial district in which the address is located, or if the subscriber's address is outside of the United States, for any judicial district in which the service provider may be found, and that the subscriber will accept service of process from the person who provided notification under subsection (c)(1)(C) or an agent of such person.

(4) Limitation on other liability.—A service provider's compliance with paragraph (2) shall not subject the service provider to liability for copyright infringement with respect to the material identified in the notice provided under subsection (c)(1)(C).

(h) Subpoena to Identify Infringer.—

(1) Request.—A copyright owner or a person authorized to act on the owner's behalf may request the clerk of any United States district court to issue a subpoena to a service provider for identification of an alleged infringer in accordance with this subsection.

(2) Contents of requests—The request may be made by filing with the clerk—

(A) a copy of a notification described in subsection (c)(3)(A);

(B) a proposed subpoena; and

(C) a sworn declaration to the effect that the purpose for which the subpoena is sought is to obtain the identity of an alleged infringer and that such information will only be used for the purpose of protecting rights under this title.

(3) Contents of subpoena.—The subpoena shall authorize and order the service provider receiving the notification and the subpoena to expeditiously disclose to the copyright owner or person authorized by the copyright owner information sufficient to identify the alleged infringer of the material described in the notification to the extent such information is available to the service provider.

(4) Basis for granting subpoena.—If the notification filed satisfies the provisions of subsection (c)(3)(A), the proposed subpoena is in proper form, and the accompanying declaration is properly executed, the clerk shall expeditiously issue and sign the proposed subpoena and return it to the requester for delivery to the service provider.

(5) Actions of service provider receiving subpoena. — Upon receipt of the issued subpoena, either accompanying or subsequent to the receipt of a notification described in subsection (c)(3)(A), the service provider shall expeditiously disclose to the copyright owner or person authorized by the copyright owner the information required by the subpoena, notwithstanding any other provision of law and regardless of whether the service provider responds to the notification.

(6) Rules applicable to subpoena. — Unless otherwise provided by this section or by applicable rules of the court, the procedure for issuance and delivery of the subpoena, and the remedies for noncompliance with the subpoena, shall be governed to the greatest extent practicable by those provisions of the Federal Rules of Civil Procedure governing the issuance, service, and enforcement of a subpoena duces tecum.

(i) Conditions for Eligibility. —

(1) Accommodation of technology. — The limitations on liability established by this section shall apply to a service provider only if the service provider —

(A) has adopted and reasonably implemented, and informs subscribers and account holders of the service provider's system or network of, a policy that provides for the termination in appropriate circumstances of subscribers and account holders of the service provider's system or network who are repeat infringers; and

(B) accommodates and does not interfere with standard technical measures.

(2) Definition. — As used in this subsection, the term "standard technical measures" means technical measures that are used by copyright owners to identify or protect copyrighted works and —

(A) have been developed pursuant to a broad consensus of copyright owners and service providers in an open, fair, voluntary, multi-industry standards process;

(B) are available to any person on reasonable and nondiscriminatory terms; and

(C) do not impose substantial costs on service providers or substantial burdens on their systems or networks.

(j) Injunctions. — The following rules shall apply in the case of any application for an injunction under section 502 against a service provider that is not subject to monetary remedies under this section:

(1) Scope of relief. —

(A) With respect to conduct other than that which qualifies for the limitation on remedies set forth in subsection (a), the court may grant injunctive relief with respect to a service provider only in one or more of the following forms:

(i) An order restraining the service provider from providing access to infringing material or activity residing at a particular online site on the provider's system or network.

(ii) An order restraining the service provider from providing access to a subscriber or account holder of the service provider's system or network who is engaging in infringing activity and is identified in the order, by terminating the accounts of the subscriber or account holder that are specified in the order.

(iii) Such other injunctive relief as the court may consider necessary to prevent or restrain infringement of copyrighted material specified in the order of the court at a particular online location, if such relief is the least burdensome to the service provider among the forms of relief comparably effective for that purpose.

(B) If the service provider qualifies for the limitation on remedies described in subsection (a), the court may only grant injunctive relief in one or both of the following forms:

(i) An order restraining the service provider from providing access to a subscriber or account holder of the service provider's system or network who is using the provider's service to engage in infringing activity and is identified in the order, by terminating the accounts of the subscriber or account holder that are specified in the order.

(ii) An order restraining the service provider from providing access, by taking reasonable steps specified in the order to block access, to a specific, identified, online location outside the United States.

(2) Considerations. — The court, in considering the relevant criteria for injunctive relief under applicable law, shall consider —

(A) whether such an injunction, either alone or in combination with other such injunctions issued against the same service provider under this subsection, would significantly burden either the provider or the operation of the provider's system or network;

(B) the magnitude of the harm likely to be suffered by the copyright owner in the digital network environment if steps are not taken to prevent or restrain the infringement;

(C) whether implementation of such an injunction would be technically feasible and effective, and would not interfere with access to noninfringing material at other online locations; and

(D) whether other less burdensome and comparably effective means of preventing or restraining access to the infringing material are available.

(3) Notice and ex parte orders. — Injunctive relief under this subsection shall be available only after notice to the service provider and an opportunity for the service provider to appear are provided, except for orders ensuring the preservation of evidence or other orders having no material adverse effect on the operation of the service provider's communications network.

(k) Definitions. —

(1) Service provider. —

(A) As used in subsection (a), the term "service provider" means an entity offering the transmission, routing, or providing of connections for digital online communications, between or among points specified by a user, of material of the user's choosing, without modification to the content of the material as sent or received.

(B) As used in this section, other than subsection (a), the term "service provider" means a provider of online services or network access, or the operator of facilities therefor, and includes an entity described in subparagraph (A).

(2) Monetary relief. — As used in this section, the term "monetary relief" means damages, costs, attorneys' fees, and any other form of monetary payment.

(l) Other Defenses Not Affected. — The failure of a service provider's conduct to qualify for limitation of liability under this section shall not bear adversely upon the consideration of a defense by the service provider that the service provider's conduct is not infringing under this title or any other defense.

(m) Protection of Privacy. — Nothing in this section shall be construed to condition the applicability of subsections (a) through (d) on —

(1) a service provider monitoring its service or affirmatively seeking facts indicating infringing activity, except to the extent consistent with a standard technical measure complying with the provisions of subsection (i); or

(2) a service provider gaining access to, removing, or disabling access to material in cases in which such conduct is prohibited by law.

(n) Construction. — Subsections (a), (b), (c), and (d) describe separate and distinct functions for purposes of applying this section. Whether a service provider qualifies for the limitation on liability in any one of those subsections shall be based solely on the criteria in that subsection, and shall not affect a determination of whether that service provider qualifies for the limitations on liability under any other such subsection.

§513. Determination of reasonable license fees for individual proprietors

In the case of any performing rights society subject to a consent decree which provides for the determination of reasonable license rates or fees to be charged by the performing rights society, notwithstanding the provisions of that consent decree, an individual proprietor who owns or operates fewer than 7 non-publicly traded establishments in which nondramatic musical works are performed publicly and who claims that any license agreement offered by that performing rights society is unreasonable in its license rate or fee as to that individual proprietor, shall be entitled to determination of a reasonable license rate or fee as follows:

(1) The individual proprietor may commence such proceeding for determination of a reasonable license rate or fee by filing an application in the applicable district court under paragraph (2) that a rate disagreement exists and by serving a copy of the application on the performing rights society. Such proceeding shall commence in the applicable district court within 90 days after the service of such copy, except that such 90-day requirement shall be subject to the administrative requirements of the court.

(2) The proceeding under paragraph (1) shall be held, at the individual proprietor's election, in the judicial district of the district court with jurisdiction over the applicable consent decree or in that place of holding court of a district court that is the seat of the Federal circuit (other than the Court of Appeals for the Federal Circuit) in which the proprietor's establishment is located.

(3) Such proceeding shall be held before the judge of the court with jurisdiction over the consent decree governing the performing rights society. At the discretion of the court, the proceeding shall be held before a special master or magistrate judge appointed by such judge. Should that consent decree provide for the appointment of an advisor or advisors to the court for any purpose, any such advisor shall be the special master so named by the court.

(4) In any such proceeding, the industry rate shall be presumed to have been reasonable at the time it was agreed to or determined by the court. Such presumption shall in no way affect a determination of whether the rate is being correctly applied to the individual proprietor.

(5) Pending the completion of such proceeding, the individual proprietor shall have the right to perform publicly the copyrighted musical compositions in the repertoire of the performing rights society by paying an interim license rate or fee into an interest bearing escrow account with the clerk of the court, subject to retroactive adjustment when a final rate or fee has been determined, in an amount equal to the industry rate, or, in the absence of an industry rate, the amount of the most recent license rate or fee agreed to by the parties.

(6) Any decision rendered in such proceeding by a special master or magistrate judge named under paragraph (3) shall be reviewed by the judge of the court with jurisdiction over the consent decree governing the performing rights society. Such proceeding, including such review, shall be concluded within 6 months after its commencement.

(7) Any such final determination shall be binding only as to the individual proprietor commencing the proceeding, and shall not be applicable to any other proprietor or any other performing rights society, and the performing rights society shall be relieved of any obligation of nondiscrimination among similarly situated music users that may be imposed by the consent decree governing its operations.

(8) An individual proprietor may not bring more than one proceeding provided for in this section for the determination of a reasonable license rate or fee under any license agreement with respect to any one performing rights society.

(9) For purposes of this section, the term "industry rate" means the license fee a performing rights society has agreed to with, or which has been determined by the court for, a significant segment of the music user industry to which the individual proprietor belongs.

Chapter 6. Manufacturing Requirements, Importation, and Exportation

Sec.

§601. Manufacture, importation, and public distribution of certain copies

(a) Prior to July 1, 1986, and except as provided by subsection (b), the importation into or public distribution in the United States of copies of a work consisting preponderantly of nondramatic literary material that is in the English language and is protected under this title is prohibited unless the portions consisting of such material have been manufactured in the United States or Canada.

(b) The provisions of subsection (a) do not apply—

(1) where, on the date when importation is sought or public distribution in the United States is made, the author of any substantial part of such material is neither a national nor a domiciliary of the United States or, if such author is a national of the United States, he or she has been domiciled outside the United States for a continuous period of at least one year immediately preceding that date; in the case of a work made for hire, the exemption provided by this clause does not apply unless a substantial part of the work was prepared for an employer or other person who is not a national or domiciliary of the United States or a domestic corporation or enterprise;

(2) where United States Customs and Border Protection is presented with an import statement issued under the seal of the Copyright Office, in which case a total of no more than two thousand copies of any one such work shall be allowed entry; the import statement shall be issued upon request to the copyright owner or to a person designated by such owner at the time of registration for the work under section 408 or at any time thereafter;

(3) where importation is sought under the authority or for the use, other than in schools, of the Government of the United States or of any State or political subdivision of a State;

(4) where importation, for use and not for sale, is sought—

(A) by any person with respect to no more than one copy of any work at any one time;

(B) by any person arriving from outside the United States, with respect to copies forming part of such person's personal baggage; or

(C) by an organization operated for scholarly, educational, or religious purposes and not for private gain, with respect to copies intended to form a part of its library;

(5) where the copies are reproduced in raised characters for the use of the blind; or

(6) where, in addition to copies imported under clauses (3) and (4) of this subsection, no more than two thousand copies of any one such work, which have not been manufactured in the United States or Canada, are publicly distributed in the United States; or

(7) where, on the date when importation is sought or public distribution in the United States is made—

(A) the author of any substantial part of such material is an individual and receives compensation for the transfer or license of the right to distribute the work in the United States; and

(B) the first publication of the work has previously taken place outside the United States under a transfer or license granted by such author to a transferee or licensee who was not a national or domiciliary of the United States or a domestic corporation or enterprise; and

(C) there has been no publication of an authorized edition of the work of which the copies were manufactured in the United States; and

(D) the copies were reproduced under a transfer or license granted by such author or by the transferee or licensee of the right of first publication as mentioned in subclause (B), and the transferee or the licensee of the right of reproduction was not a national or domiciliary of the United States or a domestic corporation or enterprise.

(c) The requirement of this section that copies be manufactured in the United States or Canada is satisfied if—

(1) in the case where the copies are printed directly from type that has been set, or directly from plates made from such type, the setting of the type and the making of the plates have been performed in the United States or Canada; or

(2) in the case where the making of plates by a lithographic or photoengraving process is a final or intermediate step preceding the printing of the copies, the making of the plates has been performed in the United States or Canada; and

(3) in any case, the printing or other final process of producing multiple copies and any binding of the copies have been performed in the United States or Canada.

(d) Importation or public distribution of copies in violation of this section does not invalidate protection for a work under this title. However, in any civil action or criminal proceeding for infringement of the exclusive rights to reproduce and distribute copies of the work, the infringer has a complete defense with respect to all of the nondramatic literary material comprised in the work and any other parts of the work in which the exclusive rights to reproduce and distribute copies are owned by the same person who owns such exclusive rights in the nondramatic literary material, if the infringer proves—

(1) that copies of the work have been imported into or publicly distributed in the United States in violation of this section by or with the authority of the owner of such exclusive rights; and

(2) that the infringing copies were manufactured in the United States or Canada in accordance with the provisions of subsection (c); and

(3) that the infringement was commenced before the effective date of registration for an authorized edition of the work, the copies of which have been manufactured in the United States or Canada in accordance with the provisions of subsection (c).

(e) In any action for infringement of the exclusive rights to reproduce and distribute copies of a work containing material required by this section to be manufactured in the United States or Canada, the copyright owner shall set forth in the complaint the names of the persons or organizations who performed the processes specified by subsection (c) with respect to that material, and the places where those processes were performed.

§602. Infringing importation or exportation of copies or phonorecords

(a) Infringing Importation or Exportation. —

(1) Importation. — Importation into the United States, without the authority of the owner of copyright under this title, of copies or phonorecords of a work that have been acquired outside the United States is an infringement of the exclusive right to distribute copies or phonorecords under section 106, actionable under section 501.

(2) Importation or exportation of infringing items. — Importation into the United States or exportation from the United States, without the authority of the owner of copyright under this title, of copies or phonorecords, the making of which either constituted an infringement of copyright, or which would have constituted an infringement of copyright if this title had been applicable, is an infringement of the exclusive right to distribute copies or phonorecords under section 106, actionable under sections 501 and 506.

(3) Exceptions. — This subsection does not apply to —

(A) importation or exportation of copies or phonorecords under the authority or for the use of the Government of the United States or of any State or political subdivision of a State, but not including copies or phonorecords for use in schools, or copies of any audiovisual work imported for purposes other than archival use;

(B) importation or exportation, for the private use of the importer or exporter and not for distribution, by any person with respect to no more than one copy or phonorecord of any one work at any one time, or by any person arriving from outside the United States or departing from the United States with respect to copies or phonorecords forming part of such person's personal baggage; or

(C) importation by or for an organization operated for scholarly, educational, or religious purposes and not for private gain, with respect to no more than one copy of an audiovisual work solely for its archival purposes, and no more than five copies or phonorecords of any other work for its library lending or archival purposes, unless the importation of such copies or phonorecords is part of an activity consisting of systematic reproduction or distribution, engaged in by such organization in violation of the provisions of section 108(g)(2).

(b) Import Prohibition. — In a case where the making of the copies or phonorecords would have constituted an infringement of copyright if this title had been applicable, their importation is prohibited. In a case where the copies or phonorecords were lawfully made, United States Customs and Border Protection has no authority to prevent their importation unless the provisions of section 601 are applicable. In either case, the Secretary of the Treasury is authorized to prescribe, by regulation, a procedure under which any person claiming an interest in the copyright in a particular work may, upon payment of a specified fee, be entitled to notification by the Customs Service of the importation of articles that appear to be copies or phonorecords of the work.

§603. Importation prohibitions: Enforcement and disposition of excluded articles

(a) The Secretary of the Treasury and the United States Postal Service shall separately or jointly make regulations for the enforcement of the provisions of this title prohibiting importation.

(b) These regulations may require, as a condition for the exclusion of articles under section 602 —

(1) that the person seeking exclusion obtain a court order enjoining importation of the articles; or

(2) that the person seeking exclusion furnish proof, of a specified nature and in accordance with prescribed procedures, that the copyright in which such person claims an interest is valid and that the importation would violate the prohibition in section 602; the person seeking exclusion may also be required to post a surety bond for any injury that may result if the detention or exclusion of the articles proves to be unjustified.

(c) Articles imported in violation of the importation prohibitions of this title are subject to seizure and forfeiture in the same manner as property imported in violation of the customs revenue laws. Forfeited articles shall be destroyed as directed by the Secretary of the Treasury or the court, as the case may be.

Chapter 7. Copyright Office

Sec.

§701. The Copyright Office: General responsibilities and organization

(a) All administrative functions and duties under this title, except as otherwise specified, are the responsibility of the Register of Copyrights as director of the Copyright Office of the Library of Congress. The Register of Copyrights, together with the subordinate officers and employees of the Copyright Office, shall be appointed by the Librarian of Congress, and shall act under the Librarian's general direction and supervision.

(b) In addition to the functions and duties set out elsewhere in this chapter, the Register of Copyrights shall perform the following functions:

(1) Advise Congress on national and international issues relating to copyright, other matters arising under this title, and related matters.

(2) Provide information and assistance to Federal departments and agencies and the Judiciary on national and international issues relating to copyright, other matters arising under this title, and related matters.

(3) Participate in meetings of international intergovernmental organizations and meetings with foreign government officials relating to copyright, other matters arising under this title, and related matters, including as a member of United States delegations as authorized by the appropriate Executive branch authority.

(4) Conduct studies and programs regarding copyright, other matters arising under this title, and related matters, the administration of the Copyright Office, or any function vested in the Copyright Office by law, including educational programs conducted cooperatively with foreign intellectual property offices and international intergovernmental organizations.

(5) Perform such other functions as Congress may direct, or as may be appropriate in furtherance of the functions and duties specifically set forth in this title.

(c) The Register of Copyrights shall adopt a seal to be used on and after January 1, 1978, to authenticate all certified documents issued by the Copyright Office.

(d) The Register of Copyrights shall make an annual report to the Librarian of Congress of the work and accomplishments of the Copyright Office during the previous fiscal year. The annual report of the Register of Copyrights shall be published separately and as a part of the annual report of the Librarian of Congress.

(e) Except as provided by section 706(b) and the regulations issued thereunder, all actions taken by the Register of Copyrights under this title are subject to the provisions of the Administrative Procedure Act of June 11, 1946, as amended (c. 324, 60 Stat. 237, title 5, United States Code, Chapter 5, Subchapter II and Chapter 7).

(f) The Register of Copyrights shall be compensated at the rate of pay in effect for level III of the Executive Schedule under section 5314 of title 5. The Librarian of Congress shall establish not more than four positions for Associate Registers of Copyrights, in accordance with the recommendations of the Register of Copyrights. The Librarian shall make appointments to such positions after consultation with the Register of Copyrights. Each Associate Register of Copyrights shall be paid at a rate not to exceed the maximum annual rate of basic pay payable for GS-18 of the General Schedule under section 5332 of title 5.

§702. Copyright Office regulations

The Register of Copyrights is authorized to establish regulations not inconsistent with law for the administration of the functions and duties made the responsibility of the Register under this title. All regulations established by the Register under this title are subject to the approval of the Librarian of Congress.

§703. Effective date of actions in Copyright Office

In any case in which time limits are prescribed under this title for the performance of an action in the Copyright Office, and in which the last day of the prescribed period falls on a Saturday, Sunday, holiday, or other nonbusiness day within the District of Columbia or the Federal Government, the action may be taken on the next succeeding business day, and is effective as of the date when the period expired.

§704. Retention and disposition of articles deposited in Copyright Office

(a) Upon their deposit in the Copyright Office under sections 407 and 408, all copies, phonorecords, and identifying material, including those deposited in connection with claims that have been refused registration, are the property of the United States Government.

(b) In the case of published works, all copies, phonorecords, and identifying material deposited are available to the Library of Congress for its collections, or for exchange or transfer to any other library. In the case of unpublished works, the Library is entitled, under regulations that the Register of Copyrights shall prescribe, to select any deposits for its collections or for transfer to the National Archives of the United States or to a Federal records center, as defined in section 2901 of title 44.

(c) The Register of Copyrights is authorized, for specific or general categories of works, to make a facsimile reproduction of all or any part of the material deposited under section 408, and to make such reproduction a part of the Copyright Office records of the registration, before transferring such material to the Library of Congress as provided by subsection (b), or before destroying or otherwise disposing of such material as provided by subsection (d).

(d) Deposits not selected by the Library under subsection (b), or identifying portions or reproductions of them, shall be retained under the control of the Copyright Office, including retention in Government storage facilities, for the longest period considered practicable and desirable by the Register of Copyrights and the Librarian of Congress. After that period it is within the joint discretion of the Register and the Librarian to order their destruction or other disposition; but, in the case of unpublished works, no deposit shall be knowingly or intentionally destroyed or otherwise disposed of during its term of copyright unless a facsimile reproduction of the entire deposit has been made a part of the Copyright Office records as provided by subsection (c).

(e) The depositor of copies, phonorecords, or identifying material under section 408, or the copyright owner of record, may request retention, under the control of the Copyright Office, of one or more of such articles for the full term of copyright in the work. The Register of Copyrights shall prescribe, by regulation, the conditions under which such requests are to be made and granted, and shall fix the fee to be charged under section 708(a)(10) if the request is granted.

§705. Copyright Office records: Preparation, maintenance, public inspection, and searching

(a) The Register of Copyrights shall ensure that records of deposits, registrations, recordations, and other actions taken under this title are maintained, and that indexes of such records are prepared.

(b) Such records and indexes, as well as the articles deposited in connection with completed copyright registrations and retained under the control of the Copyright Office, shall be open to public inspection.

(c) Upon request and payment of the fee specified by section 708, the Copyright Office shall make a search of its public records, indexes, and deposits, and shall furnish a report of the information they disclose with respect to any particular deposits, registrations, or recorded documents.

§706. Copies of Copyright Office records

(a) Copies may be made of any public records or indexes of the Copyright Office; additional certificates of copyright registration and copies of any public records or indexes may be furnished upon request and payment of the fees specified by section 708.

(b) Copies or reproductions of deposited articles retained under the control of the Copyright Office shall be authorized or furnished only under the conditions specified by the Copyright Office regulations.

§707. Copyright Office forms and publications

(a) Catalog of Copyright Entries. — The Register of Copyrights shall compile and publish at periodic intervals catalogs of all copyright registrations. These catalogs shall be divided into parts in accordance with the various classes of works, and the Register has discretion to determine, on the basis of practicability and usefulness, the form and frequency of publication of each particular part.

(b) Other Publications. — The Register shall furnish, free of charge upon request, application forms for copyright registration and general informational material in connection with the functions of the Copyright Office. The Register also has the authority to publish compilations of information, bibliographies, and other material he or she considers to be of value to the public.

(c) Distribution of Publications. — All publications of the Copyright Office shall be furnished to depository libraries as specified under section 1905 of title 44, and, aside from those furnished free of charge, shall be offered for sale to the public at prices based on the cost of reproduction and distribution.

§708. Copyright Office fees

(a) Fees. — Fees shall be paid to the Register of Copyrights —

(1) on filing each application under section 408 for registration of a copyright claim or for a supplementary registration, including the issuance of a certificate of registration if registration is made;

(2) on filing each application for registration of a claim for renewal of a subsisting copyright under section 304(a), including the issuance of a certificate of registration if registration is made;

(3) for the issuance of a receipt for a deposit under section 407;

(4) for the recordation, as provided by section 205, of a transfer of copyright ownership or other document;

(5) for the filing, under section 115(b), of a notice of intention to obtain a compulsory license;

(6) for the recordation, under section 302(c), of a statement revealing the identity of an author of an anonymous or pseudonymous work, or for the recordation, under section 302(d), of a statement relating to the death of an author;

(7) for the issuance, under section 706, of an additional certificate of registration;

(8) for the issuance of any other certification; and

(9) for the making and reporting of a search as provided by section 705, and for any related services.

The Register is authorized to fix fees for other services, including the cost of preparing copies of Copyright Office records, whether or not such copies are certified, based on the cost of providing the service.

(b) Adjustment of Fees. — The Register of Copyrights may, by regulation, adjust the fees for the services specified in paragraphs (1) through (9) of subsection (a) in the following manner:

(1) The Register shall conduct a study of the costs incurred by the Copyright Office for the registration of claims, the recordation of documents, and the provision of services. The study shall also consider the timing of any adjustment in fees and the authority to use such fees consistent with the budget.

(2) The Register may, on the basis of the study under paragraph (1), and subject to paragraph (5), adjust fees to not more than that necessary to cover the reasonable costs incurred by the Copyright Office for the services described in paragraph (1), plus a reasonable inflation adjustment to account for any estimated increase in costs.

(3) Any fee established under paragraph (2) shall be rounded off to the nearest dollar, or for a fee less than $12, rounded off to the nearest 50 cents.

(4) Fees established under this subsection shall be fair and equitable and give due consideration to the objectives of the copyright system.

(5) If the Register determines under paragraph (2) that fees should be adjusted, the Register shall prepare a proposed fee schedule and submit the schedule with the accompanying economic analysis to the Congress. The fees proposed by the Register may be instituted after the end of 120 days after the schedule is submitted to the Congress unless, within that 120-day period, a law is enacted stating in substance that the Congress does not approve the schedule.

(c) The fees prescribed by or under this section are applicable to the United States Government and any of its agencies, employees, or officers, but the Register of Copyrights has discretion to waive the requirement of this subsection in occasional or isolated cases involving relatively small amounts.

(d)(1) Except as provided in paragraph (2), all fees received under this section shall be deposited by the Register of Copyrights in the Treasury of the United States and shall be credited to the appropriations for necessary expenses of the Copyright Office. Such fees that are collected shall remain available until expended. The Register may, in accordance with regulations that he or she shall prescribe, refund any sum paid by mistake or in excess of the fee required by this section.

(2) In the case of fees deposited against future services, the Register of Copyrights shall request the Secretary of the Treasury to invest in interest-bearing securities in the United States Treasury any portion of the fees that, as determined by the Register, is not required to meet current deposit account demands. Funds from such portion of fees shall be invested in securities that

permit funds to be available to the Copyright Office at all times if they are determined to be necessary to meet current deposit account demands. Such investments shall be in public debt securities with maturities suitable to the needs of the Copyright Office, as determined by the Register of Copyrights, and bearing interest at rates determined by the Secretary of the Treasury, taking into consideration current market yields on outstanding marketable obligations of the United States of comparable maturities.

(3) The income on such investments shall be deposited in the Treasury of the United States and shall be credited to the appropriations for necessary expenses of the Copyright Office.

§709. Delay in delivery caused by disruption of postal or other services

In any case in which the Register of Copyrights determines, on the basis of such evidence as the Register may by regulation require, that a deposit, application, fee, or any other material to be delivered to the Copyright Office by a particular date, would have been received in the Copyright Office in due time except for a general disruption or suspension of postal or other transportation or communications services, the actual receipt of such material in the Copyright Office within one month after the date on which the Register determines that the disruption or suspension of such services has terminated, shall be considered timely.

Chapter 8. Proceedings by Copyright Royalty Judges

Sec.

§801. Copyright Royalty Judges; appointment and functions

(a) Appointment. — The Librarian of Congress shall appoint 3 full-time Copyright Royalty Judges, and shall appoint 1 of the 3 as the Chief Copyright Royalty Judge. The Librarian shall make appointments to such positions after consultation with the Register of Copyrights.

(b) Functions. — Subject to the provisions of this chapter, the functions of the Copyright Royalty Judges shall be as follows:

(1) To make determinations and adjustments of reasonable terms and rates of royalty payments as provided in sections 112(e), 114, 115, 116, 118, 119, and 1004. The rates applicable under sections 114(f)(1)(B), 115, and 116 shall be calculated to achieve the following objectives:

(A) To maximize the availability of creative works to the public.

(B) To afford the copyright owner a fair return for his or her creative work and the copyright user a fair income under existing economic conditions.

(C) To reflect the relative roles of the copyright owner and the copyright user in the product made available to the public with respect to relative creative contribution, technological contribution, capital investment, cost, risk, and contribution to the opening of new markets for creative expression and media for their communication.

(D) To minimize any disruptive impact on the structure of the industries involved and on generally prevailing industry practices.

(2) To make determinations concerning the adjustment of the copyright royalty rates under section 111 solely in accordance with the following provisions:

(A) The rates established by section 111(d)(1)(B) may be adjusted to reflect —

(i) national monetary inflation or deflation; or

(ii) changes in the average rates charged cable subscribers for the basic service of providing secondary transmissions to maintain the real constant dollar level of the royalty fee per subscriber which existed as of the date of October 19, 1976, except that —

(I) if the average rates charged cable system subscribers for the basic service of providing secondary transmissions are changed so that the average rates exceed national monetary inflation, no change in the rates established by section 111(d)(1)(B) shall be permitted; and

(II) no increase in the royalty fee shall be permitted based on any reduction in the average number of distant signal equivalents per subscriber.

The Copyright Royalty Judges may consider all factors relating to the maintenance of such level of payments, including, as an extenuating factor, whether the industry has been restrained by subscriber rate regulating authorities from increasing the rates for the basic service of providing secondary transmissions.

(B) In the event that the rules and regulations of the Federal Communications Commission are amended at any time after April 15, 1976, to permit the carriage by cable systems of additional television broadcast signals beyond the local service area of the primary transmitters of such signals, the royalty rates established by section 111(d)(1)(B) may be adjusted to ensure that the rates for the additional distant signal equivalents resulting from such carriage are reasonable in the light of the changes effected by the amendment to such rules and regulations. In determining the reasonableness of rates proposed following an amendment of Federal Communications Commission rules and regulations, the Copyright Royalty Judges shall consider, among other factors, the economic impact on copyright owners and users; except that no adjustment in royalty rates shall be made under this subparagraph with respect to any distant signal equivalent or fraction thereof represented by —

(i) carriage of any signal permitted under the rules and regulations of the Federal Communications Commission in effect on April 15, 1976, or the carriage of a signal of the same type (that is, independent, network, or noncommercial educational) substituted for such permitted signal; or

(ii) a television broadcast signal first carried after April 15, 1976, pursuant to an individual waiver of the rules and regulations of the Federal Communications Commission, as such rules and regulations were in effect on April 15, 1976.

(C) In the event of any change in the rules and regulations of the Federal Communications Commission with respect to syndicated and sports program exclusivity after April 15, 1976, the rates established by section 111(d)(1)(B) may be adjusted to assure that such rates are reasonable in light of the changes to such rules and regulations, but any such adjustment shall apply only to the affected television broadcast signals carried on those systems affected by the change.

(D) The gross receipts limitations established by section 111(d)(1)(C) and (D) shall be adjusted to reflect national monetary inflation or deflation or changes in the average rates charged cable system subscribers for the basic service of providing secondary transmissions to maintain the real constant dollar value of the exemption provided by such section, and the royalty rate specified therein shall not be subject to adjustment.

(3)(A) To authorize the distribution, under sections 111, 119, and 1007, of those royalty fees collected under sections 111, 119, and 1005, as the case may be, to the extent that the Copyright Royalty Judges have found that the distribution of such fees is not subject to controversy.

(B) In cases where the Copyright Royalty Judges determine that controversy exists, the Copyright Royalty Judges shall determine the distribution of such fees, including partial distributions, in accordance with section 111, 119, or 1007, as the case may be.

(C) Notwithstanding section 804(b)(8), the Copyright Royalty Judges, at any time after the filing of claims under section 111, 119, or 1007, may, upon motion of one or more of the claimants and after publication in the Federal Register of a request for responses to the motion from interested claimants, make a partial distribution of such fees, if, based upon all responses received during the 30-day period beginning on the date of such publication, the Copyright Royalty Judges conclude that no claimant entitled to receive such fees has stated a reasonable objection to the partial distribution, and all such claimants —

(i) agree to the partial distribution;

(ii) sign an agreement obligating them to return any excess amounts to the extent necessary to comply with the final determination on the distribution of the fees made under subparagraph (B);

(iii) file the agreement with the Copyright Royalty Judges; and

(iv) agree that such funds are available for distribution.

(D) The Copyright Royalty Judges and any other officer or employee acting in good faith in distributing funds under subparagraph (C) shall not be held liable for the payment of any excess fees under subparagraph (C). The Copyright Royalty Judges shall, at the time the final determination is made, calculate any such excess amounts.

(4) To accept or reject royalty claims filed under sections 111, 119, and 1007, on the basis of timeliness or the failure to establish the basis for a claim.

(5) To accept or reject rate adjustment petitions as provided in section 804 and petitions to participate as provided in section 803(b)(1) and (2).

(6) To determine the status of a digital audio recording device or a digital audio interface device under sections 1002 and 1003, as provided in section 1010.

(7)(A) To adopt as a basis for statutory terms and rates or as a basis for the distribution of statutory royalty payments, an agreement concerning such matters reached among some or all of the participants in a proceeding at any time during the proceeding, except that —

(i) the Copyright Royalty Judges shall provide to those that would be bound by the terms, rates, or other determination set by any agreement in a proceeding to determine royalty rates an opportunity to comment on the agreement and shall provide to participants in the proceeding under section 803(b)(2) that would be bound by the terms, rates, or other determination set by the agreement an opportunity to comment on the agreement and object to its adoption as a basis for statutory terms and rates; and

(ii) the Copyright Royalty Judges may decline to adopt the agreement as a basis for statutory terms and rates for participants that are not parties to the agreement, if any participant described in clause (i) objects to the agreement and the Copyright Royalty Judges conclude, based on the record before them if one exists, that the agreement does not provide a reasonable basis for setting statutory terms or rates.

(B) License agreements voluntarily negotiated pursuant to section 112(e)(5), 114(f)(3), 115(c)(3)(E)(i), 116(c), or 118(b)(2) that do not result in statutory terms and rates shall not be subject to clauses (i) and (ii) of subparagraph (A).

(C) Interested parties may negotiate and agree to, and the Copyright Royalty Judges may adopt, an agreement that specifies as terms notice and recordkeeping requirements that apply in lieu of those that would otherwise apply under regulations.

(8) To perform other duties, as assigned by the Register of Copyrights within the Library of Congress, except as provided in section 802(g), at times

when Copyright Royalty Judges are not engaged in performing the other duties set forth in this section.

(c) Rulings.—The Copyright Royalty Judges may make any necessary procedural or evidentiary rulings in any proceeding under this chapter and may, before commencing a proceeding under this chapter, make any such rulings that would apply to the proceedings conducted by the Copyright Royalty Judges.

(d) Administrative Support.—The Librarian of Congress shall provide the Copyright Royalty Judges with the necessary administrative services related to proceedings under this chapter.

(e) Location in Library of Congress.—The offices of the Copyright Royalty Judges and staff shall be in the Library of Congress.

(f) Effective Date of Actions.— On and after the date of the enactment of the Copyright Royalty and Distribution Reform Act of 2004, in any case in which time limits are prescribed under this title for performance of an action with or by the Copyright Royalty Judges, and in which the last day of the prescribed period falls on a Saturday, Sunday, holiday, or other nonbusiness day within the District of Columbia or the Federal Government, the action may be taken on the next succeeding business day, and is effective as of the date when the period expired.

§802. Copyright Royalty Judgeships; staff

(a) Qualifications of Copyright Royalty Judges.—

(1) In general.—Each Copyright Royalty Judge shall be an attorney who has at least 7 years of legal experience. The Chief Copyright Royalty Judge shall have at least 5 years of experience in adjudications, arbitrations, or court trials. Of the other 2 Copyright Royalty Judges, 1 shall have significant knowledge of copyright law, and the other shall have significant knowledge of economics. An individual may serve as a Copyright Royalty Judge only if the individual is free of any financial conflict of interest under subsection (h).

(2) Definition.—In this subsection, the term "adjudication" has the meaning given that term in section 551 of title 5, but does not include mediation.

(b) Staff.—The Chief Copyright Royalty Judge shall hire 3 full-time staff members to assist the Copyright Royalty Judges in performing their functions.

(c) Terms.—The individual first appointed as the Chief Copyright Royalty Judge shall be appointed to a term of 6 years, and of the remaining individuals first appointed as Copyright Royalty Judges, 1 shall be appointed to a term of 4 years, and the other shall be appointed to a term of 2 years. Thereafter, the terms of succeeding Copyright Royalty Judges shall each be 6 years. An individual serving as a Copyright Royalty Judge may be reappointed to subsequent terms. The term of a Copyright Royalty Judge shall begin when the term of the predecessor of that Copyright Royalty Judge ends. When the term of office of a Copyright Royalty Judge ends, the individual serving that term may continue to serve until a successor is selected.

(d) Vacancies or Incapacity. —

(1) Vacancies. — If a vacancy should occur in the position of Copyright Royalty Judge, the Librarian of Congress shall act expeditiously to fill the vacancy, and may appoint an interim Copyright Royalty Judge to serve until another Copyright Royalty Judge is appointed under this section. An individual appointed to fill the vacancy occurring before the expiration of the term for which the predecessor of that individual was appointed shall be appointed for the remainder of that term.

(2) Incapacity. — In the case in which a Copyright Royalty Judge is temporarily unable to perform his or her duties, the Librarian of Congress may appoint an interim Copyright Royalty Judge to perform such duties during the period of such incapacity.

(e) Compensation. —

(1) Judges. — The Chief Copyright Royalty Judge shall receive compensation at the rate of basic pay payable for level AL-1 for administrative law judges pursuant to section 5372(b) of title 5, and each of the other two Copyright Royalty Judges shall receive compensation at the rate of basic pay payable for level AL-2 for administrative law judges pursuant to such section. The compensation of the Copyright Royalty Judges shall not be subject to any regulations adopted by the Office of Personnel Management pursuant to its authority under section 5376(b)(1) of title 5.

(2) Staff members. — Of the staff members appointed under subsection (b) —

(A) the rate of pay of 1 staff member shall be not more than the basic rate of pay payable for level 10 of GS-15 of the General Schedule;

(B) the rate of pay of 1 staff member shall be not less than the basic rate of pay payable for GS-13 of the General Schedule and not more than the basic rate of pay payable for level 10 of GS-14 of such Schedule; and

(C) the rate of pay for the third staff member shall be not less than the basic rate of pay payable for GS-8 of the General Schedule and not more than the basic rate of pay payable for level 10 of GS-11 of such Schedule.

(3) Locality pay. — All rates of pay referred to under this subsection shall include locality pay.

(f) Independence of Copyright Royalty Judge.

(1) In making determinations. —

(A) In general. —

(i) Subject to subparagraph (B) and clause (ii) of this subparagraph, the Copyright Royalty Judges shall have full independence in making determinations concerning adjustments and determinations of copyright royalty rates and terms, the distribution of copyright royalties, the acceptance or rejection of royalty claims, rate adjustment petitions, and petitions to participate, and in issuing other rulings under this title, except that the Copyright Royalty Judges may consult with the Register of Copyrights on any matter other than a question of fact.

(ii) One or more Copyright Royalty Judges may, or by motion to the Copyright Royalty Judges, any participant in a proceeding may, request from the Register of Copyrights an interpretation of any material questions of substantive law that relate to the construction of provisions of this title and arise in the course of the proceeding. Any request for a written interpretation shall be in writing and on the record, and reasonable provision shall be made to permit participants in the proceeding to comment on the material questions of substantive law in a manner that minimizes duplication and delay. Except as provided in subparagraph (B), the Register of Copyrights shall deliver to the Copyright Royalty Judges a written response within 14 days after the receipt of all briefs and comments from the participants. The Copyright Royalty Judges shall apply the legal interpretation embodied in the response of the Register of Copyrights if it is timely delivered, and the response shall be included in the record that accompanies the final determination. The authority under this clause shall not be construed to authorize the Register of Copyrights to provide an interpretation of questions of procedure before the Copyright Royalty Judges, the ultimate adjustments and determinations of copyright royalty rates and terms, the ultimate distribution of copyright royalties, or the acceptance or rejection of royalty claims, rate adjustment petitions, or petitions to participate in a proceeding.

(B) Novel questions. —

(i) In any case in which a novel material question of substantive law concerning an interpretation of those provisions of this title that are the subject of the proceeding is presented, the Copyright Royalty Judges shall request a decision of the Register of Copyrights, in writing, to resolve such novel question. Reasonable provision shall be made for comment on such request by the participants in the proceeding, in such a way as to minimize duplication and delay. The Register of Copyrights shall transmit his or her decision to the Copyright Royalty Judges within 30 days after the Register of Copyrights receives all of the briefs or comments of the participants. Such decision shall be in writing and included by the Copyright Royalty Judges in the record that accompanies their final determination. If such a decision is timely delivered to the Copyright Royalty Judges, the Copyright Royalty Judges shall apply the legal determinations embodied in the decision of the Register of Copyrights in resolving material questions of substantive law.

(ii) In clause (i), a "novel question of law" is a question of law that has not been determined in prior decisions, determinations, and rulings described in section 803(a).

(C) Consultation. — Notwithstanding the provisions of subparagraph (A), the Copyright Royalty Judges shall consult with the Register of Copyrights with respect to any determination or ruling that would require that any act be performed by the Copyright Office, and any such determination or ruling shall not be binding upon the Register of Copyrights.

(D) Review of legal conclusions by the Register of Copyrights. — The Register of Copyrights may review for legal error the resolution by the Copyright Royalty Judges of a material question of substantive law under this title that underlies or is contained in a final determination of the Copyright Royalty Judges. If the Register of Copyrights concludes, after taking into consideration the views of the participants in the proceeding, that any resolution reached by the Copyright Royalty Judges was in material error, the Register of Copyrights shall issue a written decision correcting such legal error, which shall be made part of the record of the proceeding. The Register of Copyrights shall issue such written decision not later than 60 days after the date on which the final determination by the Copyright Royalty Judges is issued. Additionally, the Register of Copyrights shall cause to be published in the Federal Register such written decision, together with a specific identification of the legal conclusion of the Copyright Royalty Judges that is determined to be erroneous. As to conclusions of substantive law involving an interpretation of the statutory provisions of this title, the decision of the Register of Copyrights shall be binding as precedent upon the Copyright Royalty Judges in subsequent proceedings under this chapter. When a decision has been rendered pursuant to this subparagraph, the Register of Copyrights may, on the basis of and in accordance with such decision, intervene as of right in any appeal of a final determination of the Copyright Royalty Judges pursuant to section 803(d) in the United States Court of Appeals for the District of Columbia Circuit. If, prior to intervening in such an appeal, the Register of Copyrights gives notification to, and undertakes to consult with, the Attorney General with respect to such intervention, and the Attorney General fails, within a reasonable period after receiving such notification, to intervene in such appeal, the Register of Copyrights may intervene in such appeal in his or her own name by any attorney designated by the Register of Copyrights for such purpose. Intervention by the Register of Copyrights in his or her own name shall not preclude the Attorney General from intervening on behalf of the United States in such an appeal as may be otherwise provided or required by law.

(E) Effect on judicial review. — Nothing in this section shall be interpreted to alter the standard applied by a court in reviewing legal determinations involving an interpretation or construction of the provisions of this title or to affect the extent to which any construction or interpretation of the provisions of this title shall be accorded deference by a reviewing court.

(2) Performance appraisals.

(A) In general. — Notwithstanding any other provision of law or any regulation of the Library of Congress, and subject to subparagraph (B), the Copyright Royalty Judges shall not receive performance appraisals.

(B) Relating to sanction or removal. — To the extent that the Librarian of Congress adopts regulations under subsection (h) relating to the sanction or removal of a Copyright Royalty Judge and such regulations require documentation to establish the cause of such sanction or removal, the Copyright Royalty Judge may receive an appraisal related specifically to the cause of the sanction or removal.

(g) Inconsistent Duties Barred. — No Copyright Royalty Judge may undertake duties that conflict with his or her duties and responsibilities as a Copyright Royalty Judge.

(h) Standards of Conduct. — The Librarian of Congress shall adopt regulations regarding the standards of conduct, including financial conflict of interest and restrictions against ex parte communications, which shall govern the Copyright Royalty Judges and the proceedings under this chapter.

(i) Removal or Sanction. — The Librarian of Congress may sanction or remove a Copyright Royalty Judge for violation of the standards of conduct adopted under subsection (h), misconduct, neglect of duty, or any disqualifying physical or mental disability. Any such sanction or removal may be made only after notice and opportunity for a hearing, but the Librarian of Congress may suspend the Copyright Royalty Judge during the pendency of such hearing. The Librarian shall appoint an interim Copyright Royalty Judge during the period of any such suspension.

§803. Proceedings of Copyright Royalty Judges

(a) Proceedings. —

(1) In General. — The Copyright Royalty Judges shall act in accordance with this title, and to the extent not inconsistent with this title, in accordance with subchapter II of chapter 5 of title 5, in carrying out the purposes set forth in section 801. The Copyright Royalty Judges shall act in accordance with regulations issued by the Copyright Royalty Judges and the Librarian of Congress, and on the basis of a written record, prior determinations and interpretations of the Copyright Royalty Tribunal, Librarian of Congress, the Register of Copyrights, copyright arbitration royalty panels (to the extent those determinations are not inconsistent with a decision of the Librarian of Congress or the Register of Copyrights), and the Copyright Royalty Judges (to the extent those determinations are not inconsistent with a decision of the Register of Copyrights that was timely delivered to the Copyright Royalty Judges pursuant to section 802(f)(1)(A) or (B), or with a decision of the Register of Copyrights pursuant to section 802(f)(1)(D)), under this chapter, and decisions of the court of appeals under this chapter before, on, or after the effective date of the Copyright Royalty and Distribution Reform Act of 2004.

(2) Judges Acting as Panel and Individually. — The Copyright Royalty Judges shall preside over hearings in proceedings under this chapter en banc. The Chief Copyright Royalty Judge may designate a Copyright Royalty Judge to preside individually over such collateral and administrative proceedings, and over such proceedings under paragraphs (1) through (5) of subsection (b), as the Chief Judge considers appropriate.

(3) Determinations. — Final determinations of the Copyright Royalty Judges in proceedings under this chapter shall be made by majority vote. A Copyright Royalty Judge dissenting from the majority on any determination under this chapter may issue his or her dissenting opinion, which shall be included with the determination.

(b) Procedures. —

(1) Initiation. —

(A) Call for Petitions to Participate. —

(i) The Copyright Royalty Judges shall cause to be published in the Federal Register notice of commencement of proceedings under this chapter, calling for the filing of petitions to participate in a proceeding under this chapter for the purpose of making the relevant determination under section 111, 112, 114, 115, 116, 118, 119, 1004, or 1007, as the case may be —

(I) promptly upon a determination made under section 804(a);

(II) by no later than January 5 of a year specified in paragraph (2) of section 804(b) for the commencement of proceedings;

(III) by no later than January 5 of a year specified in subparagraph (A) or (B) of paragraph (3) of section 804(b) for the commencement of proceedings, or as otherwise provided in subparagraph (A) or (C) of such paragraph for the commencement of proceedings;

(IV) as provided under section 804(b)(8); or

(V) by no later than January 5 of a year specified in any other provision of section 804(b) for the filing of petitions for the commencement of proceedings, if a petition has not been filed by that date, except that the publication notice requirement shall not apply in the case of proceedings under section 111 that are scheduled to commence in 2005.

(ii) Petitions to participate shall be filed by no later than 30 days after publication of notice of commencement of a proceeding under clause (i), except that the Copyright Royalty Judges may, for substantial good cause shown and if there is no prejudice to the participants that have already filed petitions, accept late petitions to participate at any time up to the date that is 90 days before the date on which participants in the proceeding are to file their written direct statements. Notwithstanding the preceding sentence, petitioners whose petitions are filed more than 30 days after publication of notice of commencement of a proceeding are not eligible to object to a settlement reached during the voluntary negotiation period under paragraph (3), and any objection filed by such a petitioner shall not be taken into account by the Copyright Royalty Judges.

(B) Petitions to Participate. — Each petition to participate in a proceeding shall describe the petitioner's interest in the subject matter of the proceeding. Parties with similar interests may file a single petition to participate.

(2) Participation in General. — Subject to paragraph (4), a person may participate in a proceeding under this chapter, including through the submission of briefs or other information, only if —

(A) that person has filed a petition to participate in accordance with paragraph (1) (either individually or as a group under paragraph (1)(B));

(B) the Copyright Royalty Judges have not determined that the petition to participate is facially invalid;

(C) the Copyright Royalty Judges have not determined, sua sponte or on the motion of another participant in the proceeding, that the person lacks a significant interest in the proceeding; and

(D) the petition to participate is accompanied by either —

(i) in a proceeding to determine royalty rates, a filing fee of $150; or

(ii) in a proceeding to determine distribution of royalty fees —

(I) a filing fee of $150; or

(II) a statement that the petitioner (individually or as a group) will not seek a distribution of more than $1000, in which case the amount distributed to the petitioner shall not exceed $1000.

(3) Voluntary Negotiation Period. —

(A) Commencement of proceedings. —

(i) Rate adjustment proceeding. — Promptly after the date for filing of petitions to participate in a proceeding, the Copyright Royalty Judges shall make available to all participants in the proceeding a list of such participants and shall initiate a voluntary negotiation period among the participants.

(ii) Distribution proceeding. — Promptly after the date for filing of petitions to participate in a proceeding to determine the distribution of royalties, the Copyright Royalty Judges shall make available to all participants in the proceeding a list of such participants. The initiation of a voluntary negotiation period among the participants shall be set at a time determined by the Copyright Royalty Judges.

(B) Length of Proceedings. — The voluntary negotiation period initiated under subparagraph (A) shall be 3 months.

(C) Determination of Subsequent Proceedings. — At the close of the voluntary negotiation proceedings, the Copyright Royalty Judges shall, if further proceedings under this chapter are necessary, determine whether and to what extent paragraphs (4) and (5) will apply to the parties.

(4) Small Claims Procedure in Distribution Proceedings. —

(A) In General. — If, in a proceeding under this chapter to determine the distribution of royalties, the contested amount of a claim is $10,000 or less, the Copyright Royalty Judges shall decide the controversy on the basis of the filing of the written direct statement by the participant, the response by any opposing participant, and 1 additional response by each such party.

(B) Bad Faith Inflation of Claim. — If the Copyright Royalty Judges determine that a participant asserts in bad faith an amount in controversy in excess of $10,000 for the purpose of avoiding a determination under the procedure set forth in subparagraph (A), the Copyright Royalty Judges shall impose a fine on that participant in an amount not to exceed the difference between the actual amount distributed and the amount asserted by the participant.

(5) Paper Proceedings. — The Copyright Royalty Judges in proceedings under this chapter may decide, sua sponte or upon motion of a participant, to determine issues on the basis of the filing of the written direct statement by the participant, the response by any opposing participant, and one additional response by each such participant. Prior to making such decision to proceed on such a paper record only, the Copyright Royalty Judges shall offer to all parties

to the proceeding the opportunity to comment on the decision. The procedure under this paragraph —

(A) shall be applied in cases in which there is no genuine issue of material fact, there is no need for evidentiary hearings, and all participants in the proceeding agree in writing to the procedure; and

(B) may be applied under such other circumstances as the Copyright Royalty Judges consider appropriate.

(6) Regulations. —

(A) In General. — The Copyright Royalty Judges may issue regulations to carry out their functions under this title. All regulations issued by the Copyright Royalty Judges are subject to the approval of the Librarian of Congress. Not later than 120 days after Copyright Royalty Judges or interim Copyright Royalty Judges, as the case may be, are first appointed after the enactment of the Copyright Royalty and Distribution Reform Act of 2004, such judges shall issue regulations to govern proceedings under this chapter.

(B) Interim Regulations. — Until regulations are adopted under subparagraph (A), the Copyright Royalty Judges shall apply the regulations in effect under this chapter on the day before the effective date of the Copyright Royalty and Distribution Reform Act of 2004, to the extent such regulations are not inconsistent with this chapter, except that functions carried out under such regulations by the Librarian of Congress, the Register of Copyrights, or copyright arbitration royalty panels that, as of such date of enactment, are to be carried out by the Copyright Royalty Judges under this chapter, shall be carried out by the Copyright Royalty Judges under such regulations.

(C) Requirements. — Regulations issued under subparagraph (A) shall include the following:

(i) The written direct statements and written rebuttal statements of all participants in a proceeding under paragraph (2) shall be filed by a date specified by the Copyright Royalty Judges, which, in the case of written direct statements, may be not earlier than 4 months, and not later than 5 months, after the end of the voluntary negotiation period under paragraph (3). Notwithstanding the preceding sentence, the Copyright Royalty Judges may allow a participant in a proceeding to file an amended written direct statement based on new information received during the discovery process, within 15 days after the end of the discovery period specified in clause (iv).

(ii)(I) Following the submission to the Copyright Royalty Judges of written direct statements and written rebuttal statements by the participants in a proceeding under paragraph (2), the Copyright Royalty Judges, after taking into consideration the views of the participants in the proceeding, shall determine a schedule for conducting and completing discovery.

(II) In this chapter, the term "written direct statements" means witness statements, testimony, and exhibits to be presented in the proceedings, and such other information that is necessary to establish terms and rates, or the distribution of royalty payments, as the case may be, as set forth in regulations issued by the Copyright Royalty Judges.

(iii) Hearsay may be admitted in proceedings under this chapter to the extent deemed appropriate by the Copyright Royalty Judges.

(iv) Discovery in connection with written direct statements shall be permitted for a period of 60 days, except for discovery ordered by the Copyright Royalty Judges in connection with the resolution of motions, orders, and disputes pending at the end of such period. The Copyright Royalty Judges may order a discovery schedule in connection with written rebuttal statements.

(v) Any participant under paragraph (2) in a proceeding under this chapter to determine royalty rates may request of an opposing participant nonprivileged documents directly related to the written direct statement or written rebuttal statement of that participant. Any objection to such a request shall be resolved by a motion or request to compel production made to the Copyright Royalty Judges in accordance with regulations adopted by the Copyright Royalty Judges. Each motion or request to compel discovery shall be determined by the Copyright Royalty Judges, or by a Copyright Royalty Judge when permitted under subsection (a)(2). Upon such motion, the Copyright Royalty Judges may order discovery pursuant to regulations established under this paragraph.

(vi)(I) Any participant under paragraph (2) in a proceeding under this chapter to determine royalty rates may, by means of written motion or on the record, request of an opposing participant or witness other relevant information and materials if, absent the discovery sought, the Copyright Royalty Judges' resolution of the proceeding would be substantially impaired. In determining whether discovery will be granted under this clause, the Copyright Royalty Judges may consider —

(aa) whether the burden or expense of producing the requested information or materials outweighs the likely benefit, taking into account the needs and resources of the participants, the importance of the issues at stake, and the probative value of the requested information or materials in resolving such issues;

(bb) whether the requested information or materials would be unreasonably cumulative or duplicative, or are obtainable from another source that is more convenient, less burdensome, or less expensive; and

(cc) whether the participant seeking discovery has had ample opportunity by discovery in the proceeding or by other means to obtain the information sought.

(II) This clause shall not apply to any proceeding scheduled to commence after December 31, 2010.

(vii) In a proceeding under this chapter to determine royalty rates, the participants entitled to receive royalties shall collectively be permitted to take no more than 10 depositions and secure responses to no more than 25 interrogatories, and the participants obligated to pay royalties shall collectively be permitted to take no more than 10 depositions and secure responses to no more than 25 interrogatories. The Copyright Royalty Judges shall resolve any disputes among similarly aligned participants to allocate the number of depositions or interrogatories permitted under this clause.

(viii) The rules and practices in effect on the day before the effective date of the Copyright Royalty and Distribution Reform Act of 2004, relating to discovery in proceedings under this chapter to determine the distribution of royalty fees, shall continue to apply to such proceedings on and after such effective date.

(ix) In proceedings to determine royalty rates, the Copyright Royalty Judges may issue a subpoena commanding a participant or witness to appear and give testimony, or to produce and permit inspection of documents or tangible things, if the Copyright Royalty Judges' resolution of the proceeding would be substantially impaired by the absence of such testimony or production of documents or tangible things. Such subpoena shall specify with reasonable particularity the materials to be produced or the scope and nature of the required testimony. Nothing in this clause shall preclude the Copyright Royalty Judges from requesting the production by a nonparticipant of information or materials relevant to the resolution by the Copyright Royalty Judges of a material issue of fact.

(x) The Copyright Royalty Judges shall order a settlement conference among the participants in the proceeding to facilitate the presentation of offers of settlement among the participants. The settlement conference shall be held during a 21-day period following the 60-day discovery period specified in clause (iv) and shall take place outside the presence of the Copyright Royalty Judges.

(xi) No evidence, including exhibits, may be submitted in the written direct statement or written rebuttal statement of a participant without a sponsoring witness, except where the Copyright Royalty Judges have taken official notice, or in the case of incorporation by reference of past records, or for good cause shown.

(c) Determination of Copyright Royalty Judges. —

(1) Timing. —The Copyright Royalty Judges shall issue their determination in a proceeding not later than 11 months after the conclusion of the 21-day settlement conference period under subsection (b)(6)(C)(x), but, in the case of a proceeding to determine successors to rates or terms that expire on a specified date, in no event later than 15 days before the expiration of the then current statutory rates and terms.

(2) Rehearings. —

(A) In General. —The Copyright Royalty Judges may, in exceptional cases, upon motion of a participant in a proceeding under subsection (b)(2), order a rehearing, after the determination in the proceeding is issued under paragraph (1), on such matters as the Copyright Royalty Judges determine to be appropriate.

(B) Timing for Filing Motion. —Any motion for a rehearing under subparagraph (A) may only be filed within 15 days after the date on which the Copyright Royalty Judges deliver to the participants in the proceeding their initial determination.

(C) Participation by Opposing Party Not Required. — In any case in which a rehearing is ordered, any opposing party shall not be required to participate in the rehearing, except that nonparticipation may give rise to the limitations with respect to judicial review provided for in subsection (d)(1).

(D) No Negative Inference. — No negative inference shall be drawn from lack of participation in a rehearing.

(E) Continuity of Rates and Terms. —

(i) If the decision of the Copyright Royalty Judges on any motion for a rehearing is not rendered before the expiration of the statutory rates and terms that were previously in effect, in the case of a proceeding to determine successors to rates and terms that expire on a specified date, then —

(I) the initial determination of the Copyright Royalty Judges that is the subject of the rehearing motion shall be effective as of the day following the date on which the rates and terms that were previously in effect expire; and

(II) in the case of a proceeding under section 114(f)(1)(C) or 114(f)(2)(C), royalty rates and terms shall, for purposes of section 114(f)(4)(B), be deemed to have been set at those rates and terms contained in the initial determination of the Copyright Royalty Judges that is the subject of the rehearing motion, as of the date of that determination.

(ii) The pendency of a motion for a rehearing under this paragraph shall not relieve persons obligated to make royalty payments who would be affected by the determination on that motion from providing the statements of account and any reports of use, to the extent required, and paying the royalties required under the relevant determination or regulations.

(iii) Notwithstanding clause (ii), whenever royalties described in clause (ii) are paid to a person other than the Copyright Office, the entity designated by the Copyright Royalty Judges to which such royalties are paid by the copyright user (and any successor thereto) shall, within 60 days after the motion for rehearing is resolved or, if the motion is granted, within 60 days after the rehearing is concluded, return any excess amounts previously paid to the extent necessary to comply with the final determination of royalty rates by the Copyright Royalty Judges. Any underpayment of royalties resulting from a rehearing shall be paid within the same period.

(3) Contents of Determination. — A determination of the Copyright Royalty Judges shall be supported by the written record and shall set forth the findings of fact relied on by the Copyright Royalty Judges. Among other terms adopted in a determination, the Copyright Royalty Judges may specify notice and recordkeeping requirements of users of the copyrights at issue that apply in lieu of those that would otherwise apply under regulations.

(4) Continuing Jurisdiction. — The Copyright Royalty Judges may issue an amendment to a written determination to correct any technical or clerical errors in the determination or to modify the terms, but not the rates, of royalty payments in response to unforeseen circumstances that would frustrate the proper implementation of such determination. Such amendment shall be set forth in a written addendum to the determination that shall be distributed to the participants of the proceeding and shall be published in the Federal Register.

(5) Protective Order. — The Copyright Royalty Judges may issue such orders as may be appropriate to protect confidential information, including orders excluding confidential information from the record of the determination that is published or made available to the public, except that any terms or rates of royalty payments or distributions may not be excluded.

(6) Publication of Determination. — By no later than the end of the 60-day period provided in section 802(f)(1)(D), the Librarian of Congress shall cause the determination, and any corrections thereto, to be published in the Federal Register. The Librarian of Congress shall also publicize the determination and corrections in such other manner as the Librarian considers appropriate, including, but not limited to, publication on the Internet. The Librarian of Congress shall also make the determination, corrections, and the accompanying record available for public inspection and copying.

(7) Late Payment. — A determination of the Copyright Royalty Judges may include terms with respect to late payment, but in no way shall such terms prevent the copyright holder from asserting other rights or remedies provided under this title.

(d) Judicial Review. —

(1) Appeal. — Any determination of the Copyright Royalty Judges under subsection (c) may, within 30 days after the publication of the determination in the Federal Register, be appealed, to the United States Court of Appeals for the District of Columbia Circuit, by any aggrieved participant in the proceeding under subsection (b)(2) who fully participated in the proceeding and who would be bound by the determination. Any participant that did not participate in a rehearing may not raise any issue that was the subject of that rehearing at any stage of judicial review of the hearing determination. If no appeal is brought within that 30-day period, the determination of the Copyright Royalty Judges shall be final, and the royalty fee or determination with respect to the distribution of fees, as the case may be, shall take effect as set forth in paragraph (2).

(2) Effect of Rates. —

(A) Expiration on Specified Date. — When this title provides that the royalty rates and terms that were previously in effect are to expire on a specified date, any adjustment or determination by the Copyright Royalty Judges of successor rates and terms for an ensuing statutory license period shall be effective as of the day following the date of expiration of the rates and terms that were previously in effect, even if the determination of the Copyright Royalty Judges is rendered on a later date. A licensee shall be obligated to continue making payments under the rates and terms previously in effect until such time as rates and terms for the successor period are established. Whenever royalties pursuant to this section are paid to a person other than the Copyright Office, the entity designated by the Copyright Royalty Judges to which such royalties are paid by the copyright user (and any successor thereto) shall, within 60 days after the final determination of the Copyright Royalty Judges establishing rates and terms for a successor period or the exhaustion of all rehearings or appeals of such determination, if any, return any excess amounts previously paid to the extent necessary to comply with the final determination of royalty rates. Any underpayment of royalties by a copyright user shall be paid to the entity designated by the Copyright Royalty Judges within the same period.

(B) Other Cases. — In cases where rates and terms have not, prior to the inception of an activity, been established for that particular activity under the relevant license, such rates and terms shall be retroactive to the inception of activity under the relevant license covered by such rates and terms. In other cases where rates and terms do not expire on a specified date, successor rates and terms shall take effect on the first day of the second month that begins after the publication of the determination of the Copyright Royalty Judges in the Federal Register, except as otherwise provided in this title, or by the Copyright Royalty Judges, or as agreed by the participants in a proceeding that would be bound by the rates and terms. Except as otherwise provided in this title, the rates and terms, to the extent applicable, shall remain in effect until such successor rates and terms become effective.

(C) Obligation to Make Payments. —

(i) The pendency of an appeal under this subsection shall not relieve persons obligated to make royalty payments under section 111, 112, 114, 115, 116, 118, 119, or 1003, who would be affected by the determination on appeal, from —

(I) providing the applicable statements of account and reports of use; and

(II) paying the royalties required under the relevant determination or regulations.

(ii) Notwithstanding clause (i), whenever royalties described in clause (i) are paid to a person other than the Copyright Office, the entity designated by the Copyright Royalty Judges to which such royalties are paid by the copyright user (and any successor thereto) shall, within 60 days after the final resolution of the appeal, return any excess amounts previously paid (and interest thereon, if ordered pursuant to paragraph (3)) to the extent necessary to comply with the final determination of royalty rates on appeal. Any underpayment of royalties resulting from an appeal (and interest thereon, if ordered pursuant to paragraph (3)) shall be paid within the same period.

(3) Jurisdiction of Court. — section 706 of title 5 shall apply with respect to review by the court of of appeals under this section. If the court modifies or vacates a determination of the Copyright Royalty Judges, the court may enter its own determination with respect to the amount or distribution of royalty fees and costs, and order the repayment of any excess fees, the payment of any underpaid fees, and the payment of interest pertaining respectively thereto, in accordance with its final judgment. The court may also vacate the determination of the Copyright Royalty Judges and remand the case to the Copyright Royalty Judges for further proceedings in accordance with subsection (a).

(e) Administrative Matters. —

(1) Deduction of Costs of Library of Congress and Copyright Office from Filing Fees. —

(A) Deduction from Filing Fees. — The Librarian of Congress may, to the extent not otherwise provided under this title, deduct from the filing fees collected under subsection (b) for a particular proceeding under this chapter the reasonable costs incurred by the Librarian of Congress, the Copyright Office, and the Copyright Royalty Judges in conducting that proceeding, other than the salaries of the Copyright Royalty Judges and the 3 staff members appointed under section 802(b).

(B) Authorization of Appropriations. — There are authorized to be appropriated such sums as may be necessary to pay the costs incurred under this chapter not covered by the filing fees collected under subsection (b). All funds made available pursuant to this subparagraph shall remain available until expended.

(2) Positions Required For Administration of Compulsory Licensing. — Section 307 of the Legislative Branch Appropriations Act, 1994, shall not apply to employee positions in the Library of Congress that are required to be filled in order to carry out section 111, 112, 114, 115, 116, 118, or 119 or chapter 10.

§804. Institution of proceedings

(a) Filing of Petition. — With respect to proceedings referred to in paragraphs (1) and (2) of section 801(b) concerning the determination or adjustment of royalty rates as provided in sections 111, 112, 114, 115, 116, 118, 119, and 1004, during the calendar years specified in the schedule set forth in subsection (b), any owner or user of a copyrighted work whose royalty rates are specified by this title, or are established under this chapter before or after the enactment of the Copyright Royalty and Distribution Reform Act of 2004, may file a petition with the Copyright Royalty Judges declaring that the petitioner requests a determination or adjustment of the rate. The Copyright Royalty Judges shall make a determination as to whether the petitioner has such a significant interest in the royalty rate in which a determination or adjustment is requested. If the Copyright Royalty Judges determine that the petitioner has such a significant interest, the Copyright Royalty Judges shall cause notice of this determination, with the reasons for such determination, to be published in the Federal Register, together with the notice of commencement of proceedings under this chapter. With respect to proceedings under paragraph (1) of section 801(b) concerning the determination or adjustment of royalty rates as provided in sections 112 and 114, during the calendar years specified in the schedule set forth in subsection (b), the Copyright Royalty Judges shall cause notice of commencement of proceedings under this chapter to be published in the Federal Register as provided in section 803(b)(1)(A).

(b) Timing of Proceedings. —

(1) Section 111 Proceedings. —

(A) A petition described in subsection (a) to initiate proceedings under section 801(b)(2) concerning the adjustment of royalty rates under section 111 to which subparagraph (A) or (D) of section 801(b)(2) applies may be filed during the year 2005 and in each subsequent fifth calendar year.

(B) In order to initiate proceedings under section 801(b)(2) concerning the adjustment of royalty rates under section 111 to which subparagraph (B) or (C) of section 801(b)(2) applies, within 12 months after an event described in either of those subsections, any owner or user of a copyrighted work whose royalty rates are specified by section 111, or by a rate established under this chapter before or after the enactment of the Copyright Royalty and Distribution Reform Act of 2004, may file a petition with the Copyright Royalty Judges declaring that the petitioner requests an adjustment of the rate. The Copyright Royalty Judges shall then proceed as set forth in subsection (a) of this section. Any change in royalty rates made under this chapter pursuant to this subparagraph may be reconsidered in the year 2005, and each fifth calendar year thereafter, in accordance with the provisions in section 801(b)(2)(B) or (C), as the case may be. A petition for adjustment of rates established by section 111(d)(1)(B) as a result of a change in the rules and regulations of the Federal Communications Commission shall set forth the change on which the petition is based.

(C) Any adjustment of royalty rates under section 111 shall take effect as of the first accounting period commencing after the publication of the determination of the Copyright Royalty Judges in the Federal Register, or on such other date as is specified in that determination.

(2) Certain Section 112 Proceedings. — Proceedings under this chapter shall be commenced in the year 2007 to determine reasonable terms and rates of royalty payments for the activities described in section 112(e)(1) relating to the limitation on exclusive rights specified by section 114(d)(1)(C)(iv), to become effective on January 1, 2009. Such proceedings shall be repeated in each subsequent fifth calendar year.

(3) Section 114 and Corresponding 112 Proceedings. —

(A) For Eligible Nonsubscription Services and New Subscription Services. — Proceedings under this chapter shall be commenced as soon as practicable after the date of enactment of the Copyright Royalty and Distribution Reform Act of 2004 to determine reasonable terms and rates of royalty payments under sections 114 and 112 for the activities of eligible nonsubscription transmission services and new subscription services, to be effective for the period beginning on January 1, 2006, and ending on December 31, 2010. Such proceedings shall next be commenced in January 2009 to determine reasonable terms and rates of royalty payments, to become effective on January 1, 2011. Thereafter, such proceedings shall be repeated in each subsequent fifth calendar year.

(B) For Preexisting Subscription and Satellite Digital Audio Radio Services. — Proceedings under this chapter shall be commenced in January 2006 to determine reasonable terms and rates of royalty payments under sections 114 and 112 for the activities of preexisting subscription services, to be effective during the period beginning on January 1, 2008, and ending on December 31, 2012, and preexisting satellite digital audio radio services, to be effective during the period beginning on January 1, 2007, and ending on December 31, 2012. Such proceedings shall next be commenced in 2011 to determine reasonable terms and rates of royalty payments, to become effective on January 1, 2013. Thereafter, such proceedings shall be repeated in each subsequent fifth calendar year.

(C)(i) Notwithstanding any other provision of this chapter, this subparagraph shall govern proceedings commenced pursuant to section 114(f)(1)(C) and 114(f)(2)(C) concerning new types of services.

(ii) Not later than 30 days after a petition to determine rates and terms for a new type of service is filed by any copyright owner of sound recordings, or such new type of service, indicating that such new type of service is or is about to become operational, the Copyright Royalty Judges shall issue a notice for a proceeding to determine rates and terms for such service.

(iii) The proceeding shall follow the schedule set forth in subsections (b), (c), and (d) of section 803, except that—

(I) the determination shall be issued by not later than 24 months after the publication of the notice under clause (ii); and

(II) the decision shall take effect as provided in subsections (c)(2) and (d)(2) of section 803 and section 114(f)(4)(B)(ii) and (C).

(iv) The rates and terms shall remain in effect for the period set forth in section 114(f)(1)(C) or 114(f)(2)(C), as the case may be.

(4) Section 115 Proceedings.—A petition described in subsection (a) to initiate proceedings under section 801(b)(1) concerning the adjustment or determination of royalty rates as provided in section 115 may be filed in the year 2006 and in each subsequent fifth calendar year, or at such other times as the parties have agreed under section 115(c)(3)(B) and (C).

(5) Section 116 Proceedings.—

(A) A petition described in subsection (a) to initiate proceedings under section 801(b) concerning the determination of royalty rates and terms as provided in section 116 may be filed at any time within 1 year after negotiated licenses authorized by section 116 are terminated or expire and are not replaced by subsequent agreements.

(B) If a negotiated license authorized by section 116 is terminated or expires and is not replaced by another such license agreement which provides permission to use a quantity of musical works not substantially smaller than the quantity of such works performed on coin-operated phonorecord players during the 1-year period ending March 1, 1989, the Copyright Royalty Judges shall, upon petition filed under paragraph (1) within 1 year after such termination or expiration, commence a proceeding to promptly establish an interim royalty rate or rates for the public performance by means of a coin-operated phonorecord player of nondramatic musical works embodied in phonorecords which had been subject to the terminated or expired negotiated license agreement. Such rate or rates shall be the same as the last such rate or rates and shall remain in force until the conclusion of proceedings by the Copyright Royalty Judges, in accordance with section 803, to adjust the royalty rates applicable to such works, or until superseded by a new negotiated license agreement, as provided in section 116(b).

(6) Section 118 Proceedings.—A petition described in subsection (a) to initiate proceedings under section 801(b)(1) concerning the determination of reasonable terms and rates of royalty payments as provided in section 118 may be filed in the year 2006 and in each subsequent fifth calendar year.

(7) Section 1004 Proceedings.—A petition described in subsection (a) to initiate proceedings under section 801(b)(1) concerning the adjustment of reasonable royalty rates under section 1004 may be filed as provided in section 1004(a)(3).

(8) Proceedings Concerning Distribution of Royalty Fees.—With respect to proceedings under section 801(b)(3) concerning the distribution of royalty fees in certain circumstances under section 111, 119, or 1007, the Copyright Royalty Judges shall, upon a determination that a controversy exists concerning such distribution, cause to be published in the Federal Register notice of commencement of proceedings under this chapter.

§805. General rule for voluntarily negotiated agreements

Any rates or terms under this title that—

(1) are agreed to by participants to a proceeding under section 803(b)(3),

(2) are adopted by the Copyright Royalty Judges as part of a determination under this chapter, and

(3) are in effect for a period shorter than would otherwise apply under a determination pursuant to this chapter, shall remain in effect for such period of time as would otherwise apply under such determination, except that the Copyright Royalty Judges shall adjust the rates pursuant to the voluntary negotiations to reflect national monetary inflation during the additional period the rates remain in effect.

Chapter 9. Protection of Semiconductor Chip Products

Sec.

§901. Definitions

(a) As used in this chapter—

(1) a "semiconductor chip product" is the final or intermediate form of any product—

(A) having two or more layers of metallic, insulating, or semiconductor material, deposited or otherwise placed on, or etched away or otherwise removed from, a piece of semiconductor material in accordance with a predetermined pattern; and

(B) intended to perform electronic circuitry functions;

(2) a "mask work" is a series of related images, however fixed or encoded—

(A) having or representing the predetermined, three-dimensional pattern of metallic, insulating, or semiconductor material present or removed from the layers of a semiconductor chip product; and

(B) in which series the relation of the images to one another is that each image has the pattern of the surface of one form of the semiconductor chip product;

(3) a mask work is "fixed" in a semiconductor chip product when its embodiment in the product is sufficiently permanent or stable to permit the mask work to be perceived or reproduced from the product for a period of more than transitory duration;

(4) to "distribute" means to sell, or to lease, bail, or otherwise transfer, or to offer to sell, lease, bail, or otherwise transfer;

(5) to "commercially exploit" a mask work is to distribute to the public for commercial purposes a semiconductor chip product embodying the mask work; except that such term includes an offer to sell or transfer a semiconductor chip product only when the offer is in writing and occurs after the mask work is fixed in the semiconductor chip product;

(6) the "owner" of a mask work is the person who created the mask work, the legal representative of that person if that person is deceased or under a legal incapacity, or a party to whom all the rights under this chapter of such person or representative are transferred in accordance with section 903(b); except that, in the case of a work made within the scope of a person's employment, the owner is the employer for whom the person created the mask work or a party to whom all the rights under this chapter of the employer are transferred in accordance with section 903(b);

(7) an "innocent purchaser" is a person who purchases a semiconductor chip product in good faith and without having notice of protection with respect to the semiconductor chip product;

(8) having "notice of protection" means having actual knowledge that, or reasonable grounds to believe that, a mask work is protected under this chapter; and

(9) an "infringing semiconductor chip product" is a semiconductor chip product which is made, imported, or distributed in violation of the exclusive rights of the owner of a mask work under this chapter.

(b) For purposes of this chapter, the distribution or importation of a product incorporating a semiconductor chip product as a part thereof is a distribution or importation of that semiconductor chip product.

§902. Subject matter of protection

(a)(1) Subject to the provisions of subsection (b), a mask work fixed in a semiconductor chip product, by or under the authority of the owner of the mask work, is eligible for protection under this chapter if—

(A) on the date on which the mask work is registered under section 908, or is first commercially exploited anywhere in the world, whichever occurs first, the owner of the mask work is (i) a national or domiciliary of the United States, (ii) a national, domiciliary, or sovereign authority of a foreign nation that is a party to a treaty affording protection to mask works to which the United States is also a party, or (iii) a stateless person, wherever that person may be domiciled;

(B) the mask work is first commercially exploited in the United States; or

(C) the mask work comes within the scope of a Presidential proclamation issued under paragraph (2).

(2) Whenever the President finds that a foreign nation extends, to mask works of owners who are nationals or domiciliaries of the United States protection (A) on substantially the same basis as that on which the foreign nation extends protection to mask works of its own nationals and domiciliaries and mask works first commercially exploited in that nation, or (B) on substantially the same basis as provided in this chapter, the President may by proclamation extend protection under this chapter to mask works (i) of owners who are, on the date on which the mask works are registered under section 908, or the date on which the mask works are first commercially exploited anywhere in the world, whichever occurs first, nationals, domiciliaries, or sovereign authorities of that nation, or (ii) which are first commercially exploited in that nation. The President may revise, suspend, or revoke any such proclamation or impose any conditions or limitations on protection extended under any such proclamation.

(b) Protection under this chapter shall not be available for a mask work that—

(1) is not original; or

(2) consists of designs that are staple, commonplace, or familiar in the semiconductor industry, or variations of such designs, combined in a way that, considered as a whole, is not original.

(c) In no case does protection under this chapter for a mask work extend to any idea, procedure, process, system, method of operation, concept, principle, or discovery, regardless of the form in which it is described, explained, illustrated, or embodied in such work.

§903. Ownership, transfer, licensing, and recordation

(a) The exclusive rights in a mask work subject to protection under this chapter belong to the owner of the mask work.

(b) The owner of the exclusive rights in a mask work may transfer all of those rights, or license all or less than all of those rights, by any written instrument signed by such owner or a duly authorized agent of the owner. Such rights may be transferred or licensed by operation of law, may be bequeathed by will, and may pass as personal property by the applicable laws of intestate succession.

(c)(1) Any document pertaining to a mask work may be recorded in the Copyright Office if the document filed for recordation bears the actual signature of the person who executed it, or if it is accompanied by a sworn or official certification that it is a true copy of the original, signed document. The Register of Copyrights shall, upon receipt of the document and the fee specified pursuant to section 908(d), record the document and return it with a certificate of recordation. The recordation of any transfer or license under this paragraph gives all persons constructive notice of the facts stated in the recorded document concerning the transfer or license.

(2) In any case in which conflicting transfers of the exclusive rights in a mask work are made, the transfer first executed shall be void as against a subsequent transfer which is made for a valuable consideration and without notice of the first transfer, unless the first transfer is recorded in accordance with paragraph (1) within three months after the date on which it is executed, but in no case later than the day before the date of such subsequent transfer.

(d) Mask works prepared by an officer or employee of the United States Government as part of that person's official duties are not protected under this chapter, but the United States Government is not precluded from receiving and holding exclusive rights in mask works transferred to the Government under subsection (b).

§904. Duration of protection

(a) The protection provided for a mask work under this chapter shall commence on the date on which the mask work is registered under section 908, or the date on which the mask work is first commercially exploited anywhere in the world, whichever occurs first.

(b) Subject to subsection (c) and the provisions of this chapter, the protection provided under this chapter to a mask work shall end ten years after the date on which such protection commences under subsection (a).

(c) All terms of protection provided in this section shall run to the end of the calendar year in which they would otherwise expire.

§905. Exclusive rights in mask works

The owner of a mask work provided protection under this chapter has the exclusive rights to do and to authorize any of the following:
(1) to reproduce the mask work by optical, electronic, or any other means;
(2) to import or distribute a semiconductor chip product in which the mask work is embodied; and
(3) to induce or knowingly to cause another person to do any of the acts described in paragraphs (1) and (2).

§906. Limitation on exclusive rights: Reverse engineering; first sale

(a) Notwithstanding the provisions of section 905, it is not an infringement of the exclusive rights of the owner of a mask work for —
(1) a person to reproduce the mask work solely for the purpose of teaching, analyzing, or evaluating the concepts or techniques embodied in the mask work or the circuitry, logic flow, or organization of components used in the mask work; or
(2) a person who performs the analysis or evaluation described in paragraph (1) to incorporate the results of such conduct in an original mask work which is made to be distributed.

(b) Notwithstanding the provisions of section 905(2), the owner of a particular semiconductor chip product made by the owner of the mask work, or by any person authorized by the owner of the mask work, may import, distribute, or otherwise dispose of or use, but not reproduce, that particular semiconductor chip product without the authority of the owner of the mask work.

§907. Limitation on exclusive rights: Innocent infringement

(a) Notwithstanding any other provision of this chapter, an innocent purchaser of an infringing semiconductor chip product —
(1) shall incur no liability under this chapter with respect to the importation or distribution of units of the infringing semiconductor chip product that occurs before the innocent purchaser has notice of protection with respect to the mask work embodied in the semiconductor chip product; and

(2) shall be liable only for a reasonable royalty on each unit of the infringing semiconductor chip product that the innocent purchaser imports or distributes after having notice of protection with respect to the mask work embodied in the semiconductor chip product.

(b) The amount of the royalty referred to in subsection (a)(2) shall be determined by the court in a civil action for infringement unless the parties resolve the issue by voluntary negotiation, mediation, or binding arbitration.

(c) The immunity of an innocent purchaser from liability referred to in subsection (a)(1) and the limitation of remedies with respect to an innocent purchaser referred to in subsection (a)(2) shall extend to any person who directly or indirectly purchases an infringing semiconductor chip product from an innocent purchaser.

(d) The provisions of subsections (a), (b), and (c) apply only with respect to those units of an infringing semiconductor chip product that an innocent purchaser purchased before having notice of protection with respect to the mask work embodied in the semiconductor chip product.

§908. Registration of claims of protection

(a) The owner of a mask work may apply to the Register of Copyrights for registration of a claim of protection in a mask work. Protection of a mask work under this chapter shall terminate if application for registration of a claim of protection in the mask work is not made as provided in this chapter within two years after the date on which the mask work is first commercially exploited anywhere in the world.

(b) The Register of Copyrights shall be responsible for all administrative functions and duties under this chapter. Except for section 708, the provisions of chapter 7 of this title relating to the general responsibilities, organization, regulatory authority, actions, records, and publications of the Copyright Office shall apply to this chapter, except that the Register of Copyrights may make such changes as may be necessary in applying those provisions to this chapter.

(c) The application for registration of a mask work shall be made on a form prescribed by the Register of Copyrights. Such form may require any information regarded by the Register as bearing upon the preparation or identification of the mask work, the existence or duration of protection of the mask work under this chapter, or ownership of the mask work. The application shall be accompanied by the fee set pursuant to subsection (d) and the identifying material specified pursuant to such subsection.

(d) The Register of Copyrights shall by regulation set reasonable fees for the filing of applications to register claims of protection in mask works under this chapter, and for other services relating to the administration of this chapter or the rights under this chapter, taking into consideration the cost of providing those services, the benefits of a public record, and statutory fee schedules under this title. The Register shall also specify the identifying material to be deposited in connection with the claim for registration.

(e) If the Register of Copyrights, after examining an application for registration, determines, in accordance with the provisions of this chapter, that the application relates to a mask work which is entitled to protection under this chapter, then the Register shall register the claim of protection and issue to the applicant a certificate of registration of the claim of protection under the seal of the Copyright Office. The effective date of registration of a claim of protection shall be the date on which an application, deposit of identifying material, and fee, which are determined by the Register of Copyrights or by a court of competent jurisdiction to be acceptable for registration of the claim, have all been received in the Copyright Office.

(f) In any action for infringement under this chapter, the certificate of registration of a mask work shall constitute prima facie evidence (1) of the facts stated in the certificate, and (2) that the applicant issued the certificate has met the requirements of this chapter, and the regulations issued under this chapter, with respect to the registration of claims.

(g) Any applicant for registration under this section who is dissatisfied with the refusal of the Register of Copyrights to issue a certificate of registration under this section may seek judicial review of that refusal by bringing an action for such review in an appropriate United States district court not later than sixty days after the refusal. The provisions of chapter 7 of title 5 shall apply to such judicial review. The failure of the Register of Copyrights to issue a certificate of registration within four months after an application for registration is filed shall be deemed to be a refusal to issue a certificate of registration for purposes of this subsection and section 910(b)(2), except that, upon a showing of good cause, the district court may shorten such four-month period.

§909. Mask work notice

(a) The owner of a mask work provided protection under this chapter may affix notice to the mask work, and to masks and semiconductor chip products embodying the mask work, in such manner and location as to give reasonable notice of such protection. The Register of Copyrights shall prescribe by regulation, as examples, specific methods of affixation and positions of notice for purposes of this section, but these specifications shall not be considered exhaustive. The affixation of such notice is not a condition of protection under this chapter, but shall constitute prima facie evidence of notice of protection.

(b) The notice referred to in subsection (a) shall consist of—

(1) the words "mask work", the symbol *M*, or the symbol M (the letter M in a circle); and

(2) the name of the owner or owners of the mask work or an abbreviation by which the name is recognized or is generally known.

§910. Enforcement of exclusive rights

(a) Except as otherwise provided in this chapter, any person who violates any of the exclusive rights of the owner of a mask work under this chapter, by conduct in or affecting commerce, shall be liable as an infringer of such rights. As used in this subsection, the term "any person" includes any State, any instrumentality of a State, and any officer or employee of a State or instrumentality of a State acting in his or her official capacity. Any State, and any such instrumentality, officer, or employee, shall be subject to the provisions of this chapter in the same manner and to the same extent as any nongovernmental entity.

(b)(1) The owner of a mask work protected under this chapter, or the exclusive licensee of all rights under this chapter with respect to the mask work, shall, after a certificate of registration of a claim of protection in that mask work has been issued under section 908, be entitled to institute a civil action for any infringement with respect to the mask work which is committed after the commencement of protection of the mask work under section 904(a).

(2) In any case in which an application for registration of a claim of protection in a mask work and the required deposit of identifying material and fee have been received in the Copyright Office in proper form and registration of the mask work has been refused, the applicant is entitled to institute a civil action for infringement under this chapter with respect to the mask work if notice of the action, together with a copy of the complaint, is served on the Register of Copyrights, in accordance with the Federal Rules of Civil Procedure. The Register may, at his or her option, become a party to the action with respect to the issue of whether the claim of protection is eligible for registration by entering an appearance within sixty days after such service, but the failure of the Register to become a party to the action shall not deprive the court of jurisdiction to determine that issue.

(c)(1) The Secretary of the Treasury and the United States Postal Service shall separately or jointly issue regulations for the enforcement of the rights set forth in section 905 with respect to importation. These regulations may require, as a condition for the exclusion of articles from the United States, that the person seeking exclusion take any one or more of the following actions:

(A) Obtain a court order enjoining, or an order of the International Trade Commission under section 337 of the Tariff Act of 1930 excluding, importation of the articles.

(B) Furnish proof that the mask work involved is protected under this chapter and that the importation of the articles would infringe the rights in the mask work under this chapter.

(C) Post a surety bond for any injury that may result if the detention or exclusion of the articles proves to be unjustified.

(2) Articles imported in violation of the rights set forth in section 905 are subject to seizure and forfeiture in the same manner as property imported in violation of the customs laws. Any such forfeited articles shall be destroyed as directed by the Secretary of the Treasury or the court, as the case may be, except that the articles may be returned to the country of export whenever it is shown to the

satisfaction of the Secretary of the Treasury that the importer had no reasonable grounds for believing that his or her acts constituted a violation of the law.

§911. Civil actions

(a) Any court having jurisdiction of a civil action arising under this chapter may grant temporary restraining orders, preliminary injunctions, and permanent injunctions on such terms as the court may deem reasonable to prevent or restrain infringement of the exclusive rights in a mask work under this chapter.

(b) Upon finding an infringer liable, to a person entitled under section 910(b)(1) to institute a civil action, for an infringement of any exclusive right under this chapter, the court shall award such person actual damages suffered by the person as a result of the infringement. The court shall also award such person the infringer's profits that are attributable to the infringement and are not taken into account in computing the award of actual damages. In establishing the infringer's profits, such person is required to present proof only of the infringer's gross revenue, and the infringer is required to prove his or her deductible expenses and the elements of profit attributable to factors other than the mask work.

(c) At any time before final judgment is rendered, a person entitled to institute a civil action for infringement may elect, instead of actual damages and profits as provided by subsection (b), an award of statutory damages for all infringements involved in the action, with respect to any one mask work for which any one infringer is liable individually, or for which any two or more infringers are liable jointly and severally, in an amount not more than $250,000 as the court considers just.

(d) An action for infringement under this chapter shall be barred unless the action is commenced within three years after the claim accrues.

(e)(1) At any time while an action for infringement of the exclusive rights in a mask work under this chapter is pending, the court may order the impounding, on such terms as it may deem reasonable, of all semiconductor chip products, and any drawings, tapes, masks, or other products by means of which such products may be reproduced, that are claimed to have been made, imported, or used in violation of those exclusive rights. Insofar as practicable, applications for orders under this paragraph shall be heard and determined in the same manner as an application for a temporary restraining order or preliminary injunction.

(2) As part of a final judgment or decree, the court may order the destruction or other disposition of any infringing semiconductor chip products, and any masks, tapes, or other articles by means of which such products may be reproduced.

(f) In any civil action arising under this chapter, the court in its discretion may allow the recovery of full costs, including reasonable attorneys' fees, to the prevailing party.

(g)(1) Any State, any instrumentality of a State, and any officer or employee of a State or instrumentality of a State acting in his or her official capacity, shall not be immune, under the Eleventh Amendment of the Constitution of the United States or under any other doctrine of sovereign immunity, from suit in Federal court by any person, including any governmental or nongovernmental entity, for a violation of any of the exclusive rights of the owner of a mask work under this chapter, or for any other violation under this chapter.

(2) In a suit described in paragraph (1) for a violation described in that paragraph, remedies (including remedies both at law and in equity) are available for the violation to the same extent as such remedies are available for such a violation in a suit against any public or private entity other than a State, instrumentality of a State, or officer or employee of a State acting in his or her official capacity. Such remedies include actual damages and profits under subsection (b), statutory damages under subsection (c), impounding and disposition of infringing articles under subsection (e), and costs and attorney's fees under subsection (f).

§912. Relation to other laws

(a) Nothing in this chapter shall affect any right or remedy held by any person under chapters 1 through 8 or 10 of this title, or under title 35.

(b) Except as provided in section 908(b) of this title, references to "this title" or "title 17" in chapters 1 through 8 or 10 of this title shall be deemed not to apply to this chapter.

(c) The provisions of this chapter shall preempt the laws of any State to the extent those laws provide any rights or remedies with respect to a mask work which are equivalent to those rights or remedies provided by this chapter, except that such preemption shall be effective only with respect to actions filed on or after January 1, 1986.

(d) Notwithstanding subsection (c), nothing in this chapter shall detract from any rights of a mask work owner, whether under Federal law (exclusive of this chapter) or under the common law or the statutes of a State, heretofore or hereafter declared or enacted, with respect to any mask work first commercially exploited before July 1, 1983.

§913. Transitional provisions

(a) No application for registration under section 908 may be filed, and no civil action under section 910 or other enforcement proceeding under this chapter may be instituted, until sixty days after the date of the enactment of this chapter.

(b) No monetary relief under section 911 may be granted with respect to any conduct that occurred before the date of the enactment of this chapter, except as provided in subsection (d).

(c) Subject to subsection (a), the provisions of this chapter apply to all mask works that are first commercially exploited or are registered under this chapter, or both, on or after the date of the enactment of this chapter.

(d)(1) Subject to subsection (a), protection is available under this chapter to any mask work that was first commercially exploited on or after July 1, 1983, and before the date of the enactment of this chapter, if a claim of protection in the mask work is registered in the Copyright Office before July 1, 1985, under section 908.

(2) In the case of any mask work described in paragraph (1) that is provided protection under this chapter, infringing semiconductor chip product units manufactured before the date of the enactment of this chapter may, without liability under sections 910 and 911, be imported into or distributed in the United States, or both, until two years after the date of registration of the mask work under section 908, but only if the importer or distributor, as the case may be, first pays or offers to pay the reasonable royalty referred to in section 907(a)(2) to the mask work owner, on all such units imported or distributed, or both, after the date of the enactment of this chapter.

(3) In the event that a person imports or distributes infringing semiconductor chip product units described in paragraph (2) of this subsection without first paying or offering to pay the reasonable royalty specified in such paragraph, or if the person refuses or fails to make such payment, the mask work owner shall be entitled to the relief provided in sections 910 and 911.

§914. International transitional provisions

(a) Notwithstanding the conditions set forth in subparagraphs (A) and (C) of section 902(a)(1) with respect to the availability of protection under this chapter to nationals, domiciliaries, and sovereign authorities of a foreign nation, the Secretary of Commerce may, upon the petition of any person, or upon the Secretary's own motion, issue an order extending protection under this chapter to such foreign nationals, domiciliaries, and sovereign authorities if the Secretary finds —

(1) that the foreign nation is making good faith efforts and reasonable progress toward —

(A) entering into a treaty described in section 902(a)(1)(A); or

(B) enacting or implementing legislation that would be in compliance with subparagraph (A) or (B) of section 902(a)(2); and

(2) that the nationals, domiciliaries, and sovereign authorities of the foreign nation, and persons controlled by them, are not engaged in the misappropriation, or unauthorized distribution or commercial exploitation, of mask works; and

(3) that issuing the order would promote the purposes of this chapter and international comity with respect to the protection of mask works.

(b) While an order under subsection (a) is in effect with respect to a foreign nation, no application for registration of a claim for protection in a mask work under this chapter may be denied solely because the owner of the mask work is a national, domiciliary, or sovereign authority of that foreign nation, or solely because the mask work was first commercially exploited in that foreign nation.

(c) Any order issued by the Secretary of Commerce under subsection (a) shall be effective for such a period as the Secretary designates in the order, except that no such order may be effective after that date on which the authority of the Secretary of Commerce terminates under subsection (e). The effective date of any such order shall also be designated in the order. In the case of an order issued upon the petition of a person, such effective date may be no earlier than the date on which the Secretary receives such petition.

(d)(1) Any order issued under this section shall terminate if—

(A) the Secretary of Commerce finds that any of the conditions set forth in paragraphs (1), (2), and (3) of subsection (a) no longer exist; or

(B) mask works of nationals, domiciliaries, and sovereign authorities of that foreign nation or mask works first commercially exploited in that foreign nation become eligible for protection under subparagraph (A) or (C) of section 902(a)(1).

(2) Upon the termination or expiration of an order issued under this section, registrations of claims of protection in mask works made pursuant to that order shall remain valid for the period specified in section 904.

(e) The authority of the Secretary of Commerce under this section shall commence on the date of the enactment of this chapter, and shall terminate on July 1, 1995.

(f)(1) The Secretary of Commerce shall promptly notify the Register of Copyrights and the Committees on the Judiciary of the Senate and the House of Representatives of the issuance or termination of any order under this section, together with a statement of the reasons for such action. The Secretary shall also publish such notification and statement of reasons in the Federal Register.

(2) Two years after the date of the enactment of this chapter, the Secretary of Commerce, in consultation with the Register of Copyrights, shall transmit to the Committees on the Judiciary of the Senate and the House of Representatives a report on the actions taken under this section and on the current status of international recognition of mask work protection. The report shall include such recommendations for modifications of the protection accorded under this chapter to mask works owned by nationals, domiciliaries, or sovereign authorities of foreign nations as the Secretary, in consultation with the Register of Copyrights, considers would promote the purposes of this chapter and international comity with respect to mask work protection. Not later than July 1, 1994, the Secretary of Commerce, in consultation with the Register of Copyrights, shall transmit to the Committees on the Judiciary of the Senate and the House of Representatives a report updating the matters contained in the report transmitted under the preceding sentence.

Chapter 10. Digital Audio Recording Devices and Media

Subchapter A — Definitions

Sec.

Subchapter B — Copying Controls

Sec.

Subchapter C — Royalty Payments

Sec.

Subchapter D — Prohibition on Certain Infringement Actions, Remedies, and Arbitration

Sec.

SUBCHAPTER A — DEFINITIONS

§1001. Definitions

As used in this chapter, the following terms have the following meanings:

(1) A "digital audio copied recording" is a reproduction in a digital recording format of a digital musical recording, whether that reproduction is made directly from another digital musical recording or indirectly from a transmission.

(2) A "digital audio interface device" is any machine or device that is designed specifically to communicate digital audio information and related interface data to a digital audio recording device through a nonprofessional interface.

(3) A "digital audio recording device" is any machine or device of a type commonly distributed to individuals for use by individuals, whether or not included with or as part of some other machine or device, the digital recording function of which is designed or marketed for the primary purpose of, and that is capable of, making a digital audio copied recording for private use, except for —

(A) professional model products, and

(B) dictation machines, answering machines, and other audio recording equipment that is designed and marketed primarily for the creation of sound recordings resulting from the fixation of nonmusical sounds.

(4)(A) A "digital audio recording medium" is any material object in a form commonly distributed for use by individuals, that is primarily marketed or most commonly used by consumers for the purpose of making digital audio copied recordings by use of a digital audio recording device.

(B) Such term does not include any material object —

(i) that embodies a sound recording at the time it is first distributed by the importer or manufacturer; or

(ii) that is primarily marketed and most commonly used by consumers either for the purpose of making copies of motion pictures or other audiovisual works or for the purpose of making copies of nonmusical literary works, including computer programs or data bases.

(5)(A) A "digital musical recording" is a material object —

(i) in which are fixed, in a digital recording format, only sounds, and material, statements, or instructions incidental to those fixed sounds, if any, and

(ii) from which the sounds and material can be perceived, reproduced, or otherwise communicated, either directly or with the aid of a machine or device.

(B) A "digital musical recording" does not include a material object —

(i) in which the fixed sounds consist entirely of spoken word recordings, or

(ii) in which one or more computer programs are fixed, except that a digital musical recording may contain statements or instructions constituting the fixed sounds and incidental material, and statements or instructions to be used directly or indirectly in order to bring about the perception, reproduction, or communication of the fixed sounds and incidental material.

(C) For purposes of this paragraph —

(i) a "spoken word recording" is a sound recording in which are fixed only a series of spoken words, except that the spoken words may be accompanied by incidental musical or other sounds, and

(ii) the term "incidental" means related to and relatively minor by comparison.

(6) "Distribute" means to sell, lease, or assign a product to consumers in the United States, or to sell, lease, or assign a product in the United States for ultimate transfer to consumers in the United States.

(7) An "interested copyright party" is —

(A) the owner of the exclusive right under section 106(1) of this title to reproduce a sound recording of a musical work that has been embodied in a digital musical recording or analog musical recording lawfully made under this title that has been distributed;

(B) the legal or beneficial owner of, or the person that controls, the right to reproduce in a digital musical recording or analog musical recording a musical work that has been embodied in a digital musical recording or analog musical recording lawfully made under this title that has been distributed;

(C) a featured recording artist who performs on a sound recording that has been distributed; or

(D) any association or other organization —

(i) representing persons specified in subparagraph (A), (B), or (C), or

(ii) engaged in licensing rights in musical works to music users on behalf of writers and publishers.

(8) To "manufacture" means to produce or assemble a product in the United States. A "manufacturer" is a person who manufactures.

(9) A "music publisher" is a person that is authorized to license the reproduction of a particular musical work in a sound recording.

(10) A "professional model product" is an audio recording device that is designed, manufactured, marketed, and intended for use by recording professionals in the ordinary course of a lawful business, in accordance with such requirements as the Secretary of Commerce shall establish by regulation.

(11) The term "serial copying" means the duplication in a digital format of a copyrighted musical work or sound recording from a digital reproduction of a digital musical recording. The term "digital reproduction of a digital musical recording" does not include a digital musical recording as distributed, by authority of the copyright owner, for ultimate sale to consumers.

(12) The "transfer price" of a digital audio recording device or a digital audio recording medium —

(A) is, subject to subparagraph (B) —

(i) in the case of an imported product, the actual entered value at United States Customs (exclusive of any freight, insurance, and applicable duty), and

(ii) in the case of a domestic product, the manufacturer's transfer price (FOB the manufacturer, and exclusive of any direct sales taxes or excise taxes incurred in connection with the sale); and

(B) shall, in a case in which the transferor and transferee are related entities or within a single entity, not be less than a reasonable arms-length price under the principles of the regulations adopted pursuant to section 482 of the Internal Revenue Code of 1986, or any successor provision to such section.

(13) A "writer" is the composer or lyricist of a particular musical work.

SUBCHAPTER B — COPYING CONTROLS

§1002. Incorporation of copying controls

(a) Prohibition on Importation, Manufacture, and Distribution. — No person shall import, manufacture, or distribute any digital audio recording device or digital audio interface device that does not conform to —

(1) the Serial Copy Management System;

(2) a system that has the same functional characteristics as the Serial Copy Management System and requires that copyright and generation status information be accurately sent, received, and acted upon between devices using the system's method of serial copying regulation and devices using the Serial Copy Management System; or

(3) any other system certified by the Secretary of Commerce as prohibiting unauthorized serial copying.

(b) Development of Verification Procedure. — The Secretary of Commerce shall establish a procedure to verify, upon the petition of an interested party, that a system meets the standards set forth in subsection (a)(2).

(c) Prohibition on Circumvention of the System. — No person shall import, manufacture, or distribute any device, or offer or perform any service, the primary purpose or effect of which is to avoid, bypass, remove, deactivate, or otherwise circumvent any program or circuit which implements, in whole or in part, a system described in subsection (a).

(d) Encoding of Information on Digital Musical Recordings. —

(1) Prohibition on encoding inaccurate information. — No person shall encode a digital musical recording of a sound recording with inaccurate information relating to the category code, copyright status, or generation status of the source material for the recording.

(2) Encoding of copyright status not required. — Nothing in this chapter requires any person engaged in the importation or manufacture of digital musical recordings to encode any such digital musical recording with respect to its copyright status.

(e) Information Accompanying Transmissions in Digital Format. — Any person who transmits or otherwise communicates to the public any sound recording in digital format is not required under this chapter to transmit or otherwise communicate the information relating to the copyright status of the sound recording. Any such person who does transmit or otherwise communicate such copyright status information shall transmit or communicate such information accurately.

Subchapter C — Royalty Payments

§1003. Obligation to make royalty payments

(a) Prohibition on Importation and Manufacture. — No person shall import into and distribute, or manufacture and distribute, any digital audio recording device or digital audio recording medium unless such person records the notice specified by this section and subsequently deposits the statements of account and applicable royalty payments for such device or medium specified in section 1004.

(b) Filing of Notice. — The importer or manufacturer of any digital audio recording device or digital audio recording medium, within a product category or utilizing a technology with respect to which such manufacturer or importer has not previously filed a notice under this subsection, shall file with the Register of Copyrights a notice with respect to such device or medium, in such form and content as the Register shall prescribe by regulation.

(c) Filing of Quarterly and Annual Statements of Account. —

(1) Generally. — Any importer or manufacturer that distributes any digital audio recording device or digital audio recording medium that it manufactured or imported shall file with the Register of Copyrights, in such form and content as the Register shall prescribe by regulation, such quarterly and annual statements of account with respect to such distribution as the Register shall prescribe by regulation.

(2) Certification, verification, and confidentiality. — Each such statement shall be certified as accurate by an authorized officer or principal of the importer or manufacturer. The Register shall issue regulations to provide for the verification and audit of such statements and to protect the confidentiality of the information contained in such statements. Such regulations shall provide for the disclosure, in confidence, of such statements to interested copyright parties.

(3) Royalty payments. — Each such statement shall be accompanied by the royalty payments specified in section 1004.

§1004. Royalty payments

(a) Digital Audio Recording Devices. —

(1) Amount of payment. — The royalty payment due under section 1003 for each digital audio recording device imported into and distributed in the United States, or manufactured and distributed in the United States, shall be 2 percent of the transfer price. Only the first person to manufacture and distribute or import and distribute such device shall be required to pay the royalty with respect to such device.

(2) Calculation for devices distributed with other devices. — With respect to a digital audio recording device first distributed in combination with one or more devices, either as a physically integrated unit or as separate components, the royalty payment shall be calculated as follows:

(A) If the digital audio recording device and such other devices are part of a physically integrated unit, the royalty payment shall be based on the transfer price of the unit, but shall be reduced by any royalty payment made on any digital audio recording device included within the unit that was not first distributed in combination with the unit.

(B) If the digital audio recording device is not part of a physically integrated unit and substantially similar devices have been distributed separately at any time during the preceding 4 calendar quarters, the royalty payment shall be based on the average transfer price of such devices during those 4 quarters.

(C) If the digital audio recording device is not part of a physically integrated unit and substantially similar devices have not been distributed separately at any time during the preceding 4 calendar quarters, the royalty payment shall be based on a constructed price reflecting the proportional value of such device to the combination as a whole.

(3) Limits on royalties. — Notwithstanding paragraph (1) or (2), the amount of the royalty payment for each digital audio recording device shall not be less than $1 nor more than the royalty maximum. The royalty maximum shall be $8 per device, except that in the case of a physically integrated unit containing more than 1 digital audio recording device, the royalty maximum for such unit shall be $12. During the 6th year after the effective date of this chapter, and not more than once each year thereafter, any interested copyright party may petition the Copyright Royalty Judges to increase the royalty maximum and, if more than 20 percent of the royalty payments are at the relevant royalty maximum, the Copyright Royalty Judges shall prospectively increase such royalty maximum with the goal of having no more than 10 percent of such payments at the new royalty maximum; however the amount of any such increase as a percentage of the royalty maximum shall in no event exceed the percentage increase in the Consumer Price Index during the period under review.

(b) Digital Audio Recording Media. — The royalty payment due under section 1003 for each digital audio recording medium imported into and distributed in the United States, or manufactured and distributed in the United States, shall be 3 percent of the transfer price. Only the first person to manufacture and distribute or import and distribute such medium shall be required to pay the royalty with respect to such medium.

§1005.　Deposit of royalty payments and deduction of expenses

The Register of Copyrights shall receive all royalty payments deposited under this chapter and, after deducting the reasonable costs incurred by the Copyright Office under this chapter, shall deposit the balance in the Treasury of the United States as offsetting receipts, in such manner as the Secretary of the Treasury directs. All funds held by the Secretary of the Treasury shall be invested in interest-bearing United States securities for later distribution with interest under section 1007. The Register may, in the Register's discretion, 4 years after the close of any calendar year, close out the royalty payments account for that calendar year, and may treat any funds remaining in such account and any subsequent deposits that would otherwise be attributable to that calendar year as attributable to the succeeding calendar year.

§1006. Entitlement to royalty payments

(a) Interested Copyright Parties. — The royalty payments deposited pursuant to section 1005 shall, in accordance with the procedures specified in section 1007, be distributed to any interested copyright party —

(1) whose musical work or sound recording has been —

(A) embodied in a digital musical recording or an analog musical recording lawfully made under this title that has been distributed, and

(B) distributed in the form of digital musical recordings or analog musical recordings or disseminated to the public in transmissions, during the period to which such payments pertain; and

(2) who has filed a claim under section 1007.

(b) Allocation of Royalty Payments to Groups. — The royalty payments shall be divided into 2 funds as follows:

(1) The sound recordings fund. — 66⅔ percent of the royalty payments shall be allocated to the Sound Recordings Fund. 2⅝ percent of the royalty payments allocated to the Sound Recordings Fund shall be placed in an escrow account managed by an independent administrator jointly appointed by the interested copyright parties described in section 1001(7)(A) and the American Federation of Musicians (or any successor entity) to be distributed to nonfeatured musicians (whether or not members of the American Federation of Musicians or any successor entity) who have performed on sound recordings distributed in the United States. 1⅜ percent of the royalty payments allocated to the Sound Recordings Fund shall be placed in an escrow account managed by an independent administrator jointly appointed by the interested copyright parties described in section 1001(7)(A) and the American Federation of Television and Radio Artists (or any successor entity) to be distributed to nonfeatured vocalists (whether or not members of the American Federation of Television and Radio Artists or any successor entity) who have performed on sound recordings distributed in the United States. 40 percent of the remaining royalty payments in the Sound Recordings Fund shall be distributed to the interested copyright parties described in section 1001(7)(C), and 60 percent of such remaining royalty payments shall be distributed to the interested copyright parties described in section 1001(7)(A).

(2) The musical works fund. —

(A) 33⅓ percent of the royalty payments shall be allocated to the Musical Works Fund for distribution to interested copyright parties described in section 1001(7)(B).

(B)(i) Music publishers shall be entitled to 50 percent of the royalty payments allocated to the Musical Works Fund.

(ii) Writers shall be entitled to the other 50 percent of the royalty payments allocated to the Musical Works Fund.

(c) Allocation of Royalty Payments Within Groups. — If all interested copyright parties within a group specified in subsection (b) do not agree on a voluntary proposal for the distribution of the royalty payments within each group, the Copyright Royalty Judges shall, pursuant to the procedures specified under section 1007(c), allocate royalty payments under this section based on the extent to which, during the relevant period —

(1) for the Sound Recordings Fund, each sound recording was distributed in the form of digital musical recordings or analog musical recordings; and

(2) for the Musical Works Fund, each musical work was distributed in the form of digital musical recordings or analog musical recordings or disseminated to the public in transmissions.

§1007   Procedures for distributing royalty payments

(a) Filing of Claims and Negotiations. —

(1) Filing of claims. — During the first 2 months of each calendar year, every interested copyright party seeking to receive royalty payments to which such party is entitled under section 1006 shall file with the Copyright Royalty Judges a claim for payments collected during the preceding year in such form and manner as the Copyright Royalty Judges shall prescribe by regulation.

(2) Negotiations. — Notwithstanding any provision of the antitrust laws, for purposes of this section interested copyright parties within each group specified in section 1006(b) may agree among themselves to the proportionate division of royalty payments, may lump their claims together and file them jointly or as a single claim, or may designate a common agent, including any organization described in section 1001(7)(D), to negotiate or receive payment on their behalf; except that no agreement under this subsection may modify the allocation of royalties specified in section 1006(b).

(b) Distribution of Payments in the Absence of a Dispute. — After the period established for the filing of claims under subsection (a), in each year, the Copyright Royalty Judges shall determine whether there exists a controversy concerning the distribution of royalty payments under section 1006(c). If the Copyright Royalty Judges determine that no such controversy exists, the Copyright Royalty Judges shall, within 30 days after such determination, authorize the distribution of the royalty payments as set forth in the agreements regarding the distribution of royalty payments entered into pursuant to subsection (a). The Librarian of Congress shall, before such royalty payments are distributed, deduct the reasonable administrative costs incurred under this section.

(c) Resolution of Disputes. — If the Copyright Royalty Judges find the existence of a controversy, the Copyright Royalty Judges shall, pursuant to chapter 8 of this title, conduct a proceeding to determine the distribution of royalty payments. During the pendency of such a proceeding, the Copyright Royalty Judges shall withhold from distribution an amount sufficient to satisfy all claims with respect to which a controversy exists, but shall, to the extent feasible, authorize the distribution of any amounts that are not in controversy. The Librarian of Congress shall, before such royalty payments are distributed, deduct the reasonable administrative costs incurred under this section.

SUBCHAPTER D — PROHIBITION ON CERTAIN INFRINGEMENT ACTIONS, REMEDIES, AND ARBITRATION

§1008. Prohibition on certain infringement actions

No action may be brought under this title alleging infringement of copyright based on the manufacture, importation, or distribution of a digital audio recording device, a digital audio recording medium, an analog recording device, or an analog recording medium, or based on the noncommercial use by a consumer of such a device or medium for making digital musical recordings or analog musical recordings.

§1009. Civil remedies

(a) Civil Actions. — Any interested copyright party injured by a violation of section 1002 or 1003 may bring a civil action in an appropriate United States district court against any person for such violation.

(b) Other Civil Actions. — Any person injured by a violation of this chapter may bring a civil action in an appropriate United States district court for actual damages incurred as a result of such violation.

(c) Powers of the Court. — In an action brought under subsection (a), the court —

(1) may grant temporary and permanent injunctions on such terms as it deems reasonable to prevent or restrain such violation;

(2) in the case of a violation of section 1002, or in the case of an injury resulting from a failure to make royalty payments required by section 1003, shall award damages under subsection (d);

(3) in its discretion may allow the recovery of costs by or against any party other than the United States or an officer thereof; and

(4) in its discretion may award a reasonable attorney's fee to the prevailing party.

(d) Award of Damages. —

(1) Damages for section 1002 or 1003 violations. —

(A) Actual damages. —

(i) In an action brought under subsection (a), if the court finds that a violation of section 1002 or 1003 has occurred, the court shall award to the complaining party its actual damages if the complaining party elects such damages at any time before final judgment is entered.

(ii) In the case of section 1003, actual damages shall constitute the royalty payments that should have been paid under section 1004 and deposited under section 1005. In such a case, the court, in its discretion, may award an additional amount of not to exceed 50 percent of the actual damages.

(B) Statutory damages for section 1002 violations. —

(i) Device. — A complaining party may recover an award of statutory damages for each violation of section 1002(a) or (c) in the sum of not more than $2,500 per device involved in such violation or per device on which a service prohibited by section 1002(c) has been performed, as the court considers just.

(ii) Digital musical recording. — A complaining party may recover an award of statutory damages for each violation of section 1002(d) in the sum of not more than $25 per digital musical recording involved in such violation, as the court considers just.

(iii) Transmission. — A complaining party may recover an award of damages for each transmission or communication that violates section 1002(e) in the sum of not more than $10,000, as the court considers just.

(2) Repeated violations. — In any case in which the court finds that a person has violated section 1002 or 1003 within 3 years after a final judgment against that person for another such violation was entered, the court may increase the award of damages to not more than double the amounts that would otherwise be awarded under paragraph (1), as the court considers just.

(3) Innocent violations of section 1002. — The court in its discretion may reduce the total award of damages against a person violating section 1002 to a sum of not less than $250 in any case in which the court finds that the violator was not aware and had no reason to believe that its acts constituted a violation of section 1002.

(e) Payment of Damages. — Any award of damages under subsection (d) shall be deposited with the Register pursuant to section 1005 for distribution to interested copyright parties as though such funds were royalty payments made pursuant to section 1003.

(f) Impounding of Articles. — At any time while an action under subsection (a) is pending, the court may order the impounding, on such terms as it deems reasonable, of any digital audio recording device, digital musical recording, or device specified in section 1002(c) that is in the custody or control of the alleged violator and that the court has reasonable cause to believe does not comply with, or was involved in a violation of, section 1002.

(g) Remedial Modification and Destruction of Articles. — In an action brought under subsection (a), the court may, as part of a final judgment or decree finding a violation of section 1002, order the remedial modification or the destruction of any digital audio recording device, digital musical recording, or device specified in section 1002(c) that —

(1) does not comply with, or was involved in a violation of, section 1002, and

(2) is in the custody or control of the violator or has been impounded under subsection (f).

§1010. Determination of certain disputes

(a) Scope of Determination. — Before the date of first distribution in the United States of a digital audio recording device or a digital audio interface device, any party manufacturing, importing, or distributing such device, and any interested copyright party may mutually agree to petition the Copyright Royalty Judges to determine whether such device is subject to section 1002, or the basis on which royalty payments for such device are to be made under section 1003.

(b) Initiation of Proceedings. — The parties under subsection (a) shall file the petition with the Copyright Royalty Judges requesting the commencement of a proceeding. Within 2 weeks after receiving such a petition, the Chief Copyright Royalty Judge shall cause notice to be published in the Federal Register of the initiation of the proceeding.

(c) Stay of Judicial Proceedings. — Any civil action brought under section 1009 against a party to a proceeding under this section shall, on application of one of the parties to the proceeding, be stayed until completion of the proceeding.

(d) Proceeding. — The Copyright Royalty Judges shall conduct a proceeding with respect to the matter concerned, in accordance with such procedures as the Copyright Royalty Judges may adopt. The Copyright Royalty Judges shall act on the basis of a fully documented written record. Any party to the proceeding may submit relevant information and proposals to the Copyright Royalty Judges. The parties to the proceeding shall each bear their respective costs of participation.

(e) Judicial Review. — Any determination of the Copyright Royalty Judges under subsection (d) may be appealed, by a party to the proceeding, in accordance with section 803(d) of this title. The pendency of an appeal under this subsection shall not stay the determination of the Copyright Royalty Judges. If the court modifies the determination of the Copyright Royalty Judges, the court shall have jurisdiction to enter its own decision in accordance with its final judgment. The court may further vacate the determination of the Copyright Royalty Judges and remand the case for proceedings as provided in this section.

Chapter 11. Sound Recordings and Music Videos

Sec.

§1101.   Unauthorized fixation and trafficking in sound recordings and music videos

(a) Unauthorized Acts. — Anyone who, without the consent of the performer or performers involved —

(1) fixes the sounds or sounds and images of a live musical performance in a copy or phonorecord, or reproduces copies or phonorecords of such a performance from an unauthorized fixation,

(2) transmits or otherwise communicates to the public the sounds or sounds and images of a live musical performance, or

(3) distributes or offers to distribute, sells or offers to sell, rents or offers to rent, or traffics in any copy or phonorecord fixed as described in paragraph (1), regardless of whether the fixations occurred in the United States, shall be subject to the remedies provided in sections 502 through 505, to the same extent as an infringer of copyright.

(b) Definition. — As used in this section, the term "traffic in" means transport, transfer, or otherwise dispose of, to another, as consideration for anything of value, or make or obtain control of with intent to transport, transfer, or dispose of.

(c) Applicability. — This section shall apply to any act or acts that occur on or after the date of the enactment of the Uruguay Round Agreements Act.

(d) State Law Not Preempted. — Nothing in this section may be construed to annul or limit any rights or remedies under the common law or statutes of any State.

Chapter 12.   Copyright Protection and Management Systems

Sec.

§1201.   Circumvention of copyright protection systems

(a) Violations Regarding Circumvention of Technological Measures. —

(1)(A) No person shall circumvent a technological measure that effectively controls access to a work protected under this title. The prohibition contained in the preceding sentence shall take effect at the end of the 2-year period beginning on the date of the enactment of this chapter.

(B) The prohibition contained in subparagraph (A) shall not apply to persons who are users of a copyrighted work which is in a particular class of works, if such persons are, or are likely to be in the succeeding 3-year period, adversely affected by virtue of such prohibition in their ability to make noninfringing uses of that particular class of works under this title, as determined under subparagraph (C).

(C) During the 2-year period described in subparagraph (A), and during each succeeding 3-year period, the Librarian of Congress, upon the recommendation of the Register of Copyrights, who shall consult with the Assistant Secretary for Communications and Information of the Department of Commerce and report and comment on his or her views in making such recommendation, shall make the determination in a rulemaking proceeding for purposes of subparagraph (B) of whether persons who are users of a copyrighted work are, or are likely to be in the succeeding 3-year period, adversely affected by the prohibition under subparagraph (A) in their ability to make noninfringing uses under this title of a particular class of copyrighted works. In conducting such rule making, the Librarian shall examine —

(i) the availability for use of copyrighted works;

(ii) the availability for use of works for nonprofit archival, preservation, and educational purposes;

(iii) the impact that the prohibition on the circumvention of technological measures applied to copyrighted works has on criticism, comment, news reporting, teaching, scholarship, or research;

(iv) the effect of circumvention of technological measures on the market for or value of copyrighted works; and

(v) such other factors as the Librarian considers appropriate.

(D) The Librarian shall publish any class of copyrighted works for which the Librarian has determined, pursuant to the rulemaking conducted under subparagraph (C), that noninfringing uses by persons who are users of a copyrighted work are, or are likely to be, adversely affected, and the prohibition contained in subparagraph (A) shall not apply to such users with respect to such class of works for the ensuing 3-year period.

(E) Neither the exception under subparagraph (B) from the applicability of the prohibition contained in subparagraph (A), nor any determination made in a rulemaking conducted under subparagraph (C), may be used as a defense in any action to enforce any provision of this title other than this paragraph.

(2) No person shall manufacture, import, offer to the public, provide, or otherwise traffic in any technology, product, service, device, component, or part thereof, that —

(A) is primarily designed or produced for the purpose of circumventing a technological measure that effectively controls access to a work protected under this title;

(B) has only limited commercially significant purpose or use other than to circumvent a technological measure that effectively controls access to a work protected under this title; or

(C) is marketed by that person or another acting in concert with that person with that person's knowledge for use in circumventing a technological measure that effectively controls access to a work protected under this title.

(3) As used in this subsection —

(A) to "circumvent a technological measure" means to descramble a scrambled work, to decrypt an encrypted work, or otherwise to avoid, bypass, remove, deactivate, or impair a technological measure, without the authority of the copyright owner; and

(B) a technological measure "effectively controls access to a work" if the measure, in the ordinary course of its operation, requires the application of information, or a process or a treatment, with the authority of the copyright owner, to gain access to the work.

(b) Additional Violations. —

(1) No person shall manufacture, import, offer to the public, provide, or otherwise traffic in any technology, product, service, device, component, or part thereof, that —

(A) is primarily designed or produced for the purpose of circumventing protection afforded by a technological measure that effectively protects a right of a copyright owner under this title in a work or a portion thereof;

(B) has only limited commercially significant purpose or use other than to circumvent protection afforded by a technological measure that effectively protects a right of a copyright owner under this title in a work or a portion thereof; or

(C) is marketed by that person or another acting in concert with that person with that person's knowledge for use in circumventing protection afforded by a technological measure that effectively protects a right of a copyright owner under this title in a work or a portion thereof.

(2) As used in this subsection —

(A) to "circumvent protection afforded by a technological measure" means avoiding, bypassing, removing, deactivating, or otherwise impairing a technological measure; and

(B) a technological measure "effectively protects a right of a copyright owner under this title" if the measure, in the ordinary course of its operation, prevents, restricts, or otherwise limits the exercise of a right of a copyright owner under this title.

(c) Other Rights, Etc., Not Affected. —

(1) Nothing in this section shall affect rights, remedies, limitations, or defenses to copyright infringement, including fair use, under this title.

(2) Nothing in this section shall enlarge or diminish vicarious or contributory liability for copyright infringement in connection with any technology, product, service, device, component, or part thereof.

(3) Nothing in this section shall require that the design of, or design and selection of parts and components for, a consumer electronics, telecommunications, or computing product provide for a response to any particular technological measure, so long as such part or component, or the product in which such part or component is integrated, does not otherwise fall within the prohibitions of subsection (a)(2) or (b)(1).

(4) Nothing in this section shall enlarge or diminish any rights of free speech or the press for activities using consumer electronics, telecommunications, or computing products.

(d) Exemption for Nonprofit Libraries, Archives, and Educational Institutions. —

(1) A nonprofit library, archives, or educational institution which gains access to a commercially exploited copyrighted work solely in order to make a good faith determination of whether to acquire a copy of that work for the sole purpose of engaging in conduct permitted under this title shall not be in violation of subsection (a)(1)(A). A copy of a work to which access has been gained under this paragraph —

(A) may not be retained longer than necessary to make such good faith determination; and

(B) may not be used for any other purpose.

(2) The exemption made available under paragraph (1) shall only apply with respect to a work when an identical copy of that work is not reasonably available in another form.

(3) A nonprofit library, archives, or educational institution that willfully for the purpose of commercial advantage or financial gain violates paragraph (1) —

(A) shall, for the first offense, be subject to the civil remedies under section 1203; and

(B) shall, for repeated or subsequent offenses, in addition to the civil remedies under section 1203, forfeit the exemption provided under paragraph (1).

(4) This subsection may not be used as a defense to a claim under subsection (a)(2) or (b), nor may this subsection permit a nonprofit library, archives, or educational institution to manufacture, import, offer to the public, provide, or otherwise traffic in any technology, product, service, component, or part thereof, which circumvents a technological measure.

(5) In order for a library or archives to qualify for the exemption under this subsection, the collections of that library or archives shall be —

(A) open to the public; or

(B) available not only to researchers affiliated with the library or archives or with the institution of which it is a part, but also to other persons doing research in a specialized field.

(e) Law Enforcement, Intelligence, and Other Government Activities. — This section does not prohibit any lawfully authorized investigative, protective, information security, or intelligence activity of an officer, agent, or employee of the

United States, a State, or a political subdivision of a State, or a person acting pursuant to a contract with the United States, a State, or a political subdivision of a State. For purposes of this subsection, the term "information security" means activities carried out in order to identify and address the vulnerabilities of a government computer, computer system, or computer network.

(f) Reverse Engineering. —

(1) Notwithstanding the provisions of subsection (a)(1)(A), a person who has lawfully obtained the right to use a copy of a computer program may circumvent a technological measure that effectively controls access to a particular portion of that program for the sole purpose of identifying and analyzing those elements of the program that are necessary to achieve interoperability of an independently created computer program with other programs, and that have not previously been readily available to the person engaging in the circumvention, to the extent any such acts of identification and analysis do not constitute infringement under this title.

(2) Notwithstanding the provisions of subsections (a)(2) and (b), a person may develop and employ technological means to circumvent a technological measure, or to circumvent protection afforded by a technological measure, in order to enable the identification and analysis under paragraph (1), or for the purpose of enabling interoperability of an independently created computer program with other programs, if such means are necessary to achieve such interoperability, to the extent that doing so does not constitute infringement under this title.

(3) The information acquired through the acts permitted under paragraph (1), and the means permitted under paragraph (2), may be made available to others if the person referred to in paragraph (1) or (2), as the case may be, provides such information or means solely for the purpose of enabling interoperability of an independently created computer program with other programs, and to the extent that doing so does not constitute infringement under this title or violate applicable law other than this section.

(4) For purposes of this subsection, the term "interoperability" means the ability of computer programs to exchange information, and of such programs mutually to use the information which has been exchanged.

(g) Encryption Research. —

(1) Definitions. — For purposes of this subsection —

(A) the term "encryption research" means activities necessary to identify and analyze flaws and vulnerabilities of encryption technologies applied to copyrighted works, if these activities are conducted to advance the state of knowledge in the field of encryption technology or to assist in the development of encryption products; and

(B) the term "encryption technology" means the scrambling and descrambling of information using mathematical formulas or algorithms.

(2) Permissible acts of encryption research. — Notwithstanding the provisions of subsection (a)(1)(A), it is not a violation of that subsection for a person to circumvent a technological measure as applied to a copy, phonorecord, performance, or display of a published work in the course of an act of good faith encryption research if—

(A) the person lawfully obtained the encrypted copy, phonorecord, performance, or display of the published work;

(B) such act is necessary to conduct such encryption research;

(C) the person made a good faith effort to obtain authorization before the circumvention; and

(D) such act does not constitute infringement under this title or a violation of applicable law other than this section, including section 1030 of title 18 and those provisions of title 18 amended by the Computer Fraud and Abuse Act of 1986.

(3) Factors in determining exemption. — In determining whether a person qualifies for the exemption under paragraph (2), the factors to be considered shall include —

(A) whether the information derived from the encryption research was disseminated, and if so, whether it was disseminated in a manner reasonably calculated to advance the state of knowledge or development of encryption technology, versus whether it was disseminated in a manner that facilitates infringement under this title or a violation of applicable law other than this section, including a violation of privacy or breach of security;

(B) whether the person is engaged in a legitimate course of study, is employed, or is appropriately trained or experienced, in the field of encryption technology; and

(C) whether the person provides the copyright owner of the work to which the technological measure is applied with notice of the findings and documentation of the research, and the time when such notice is provided.

(4) Use of technological means for research activities. — Notwithstanding the provisions of subsection (a)(2), it is not a violation of that subsection for a person to —

(A) develop and employ technological means to circumvent a technological measure for the sole purpose of that person performing the acts of good faith encryption research described in paragraph (2); and

(B) provide the technological means to another person with whom he or she is working collaboratively for the purpose of conducting the acts of good faith encryption research described in paragraph (2) or for the purpose of having that other person verify his or her acts of good faith encryption research described in paragraph (2).

(5) Report to Congress. — Not later than 1 year after the date of the enactment of this chapter, the Register of Copyrights and the Assistant Secretary for Communications and Information of the Department of Commerce shall jointly report to the Congress on the effect this subsection has had on —

(A) encryption research and the development of encryption technology;

(B) the adequacy and effectiveness of technological measures designed to protect copyrighted works; and

(C) protection of copyright owners against the unauthorized access to their encrypted copyrighted works.

The report shall include legislative recommendations, if any.

(h) Exceptions Regarding Minors. — In applying subsection (a) to a component or part, the court may consider the necessity for its intended and actual incorporation in a technology, product, service, or device, which —

(1) does not itself violate the provisions of this title; and

(2) has the sole purpose to prevent the access of minors to material on the Internet.

(i) Protection of Personally Identifying Information. —

(1) Circumvention permitted. — Notwithstanding the provisions of subsection (a)(1)(A), it is not a violation of that subsection for a person to circumvent a technological measure that effectively controls access to a work protected under this title, if —

(A) the technological measure, or the work it protects, contains the capability of collecting or disseminating personally identifying information reflecting the online activities of a natural person who seeks to gain access to the work protected;

(B) in the normal course of its operation, the technological measure, or the work it protects, collects or disseminates personally identifying information about the person who seeks to gain access to the work protected, without providing conspicuous notice of such collection or dissemination to such person, and without providing such person with the capability to prevent or restrict such collection or dissemination;

(C) the act of circumvention has the sole effect of identifying and disabling the capability described in subparagraph (A), and has no other effect on the ability of any person to gain access to any work; and

(D) the act of circumvention is carried out solely for the purpose of preventing the collection or dissemination of personally identifying information about a natural person who seeks to gain access to the work protected, and is not in violation of any other law.

(2) Inapplicability to certain technological measures. — This subsection does not apply to a technological measure, or a work it protects, that does not collect or disseminate personally identifying information and that is disclosed to a user as not having or using such capability.

(j) Security Testing. —

(1) Definition. — For purposes of this subsection, the term "security testing" means accessing a computer, computer system, or computer network, solely for the purpose of good faith testing, investigating, or correcting, a security flaw or vulnerability, with the authorization of the owner or operator of such computer, computer system, or computer network.

(2) Permissible acts of security testing. — Notwithstanding the provisions of subsection (a)(1)(A), it is not a violation of that subsection for a person to engage in an act of security testing, if such act does not constitute infringement under this title or a violation of applicable law other than this section, including

section 1030 of title 18 and those provisions of title 18 amended by the Computer Fraud and Abuse Act of 1986.

(3) Factors in determining exemption. — In determining whether a person qualifies for the exemption under paragraph (2), the factors to be considered shall include —

(A) whether the information derived from the security testing was used solely to promote the security of the owner or operator of such computer, computer system or computer network, or shared directly with the developer of such computer, computer system, or computer network; and

(B) whether the information derived from the security testing was used or maintained in a manner that does not facilitate infringement under this title or a violation of applicable law other than this section, including a violation of privacy or breach of security.

(4) Use of technological means for security testing. — Notwithstanding the provisions of subsection (a)(2), it is not a violation of that subsection for a person to develop, produce, distribute or employ technological means for the sole purpose of performing the acts of security testing described in subsection (a)(2), provided such technological means does not otherwise violate subsection (a)(2).

(k) Certain Analog Devices and Certain Technological Measures. —

(1) Certain analog devices. —

(A) Effective 18 months after the date of the enactment of this chapter, no person shall manufacture, import, offer to the public, provide or otherwise traffic in any —

(i) VHS format analog video cassette recorder unless such recorder conforms to the automatic gain control copy control technology;

(ii) 8mm format analog video cassette camcorder unless such camcorder conforms to the automatic gain control technology;

(iii) Beta format analog video cassette recorder, unless such recorder conforms to the automatic gain control copy control technology, except that this requirement shall not apply until there are 1,000 Beta format analog video cassette recorders sold in the United States in any one calendar year after the date of the enactment of this chapter;

(iv) 8mm format analog video cassette recorder that is not an analog video cassette camcorder, unless such recorder conforms to the automatic gain control copy control technology, except that this requirement shall not apply until there are 20,000 such recorders sold in the United States in any one calendar year after the date of the enactment of this chapter; or

(v) analog video cassette recorder that records using an NTSC format video input and that is not otherwise covered under clauses (i) through (iv), unless such device conforms to the automatic gain control copy control technology.

(B) Effective on the date of the enactment of this chapter, no person shall manufacture, import, offer to the public, provide or otherwise traffic in —

(i) any VHS format analog video cassette recorder or any 8mm format analog video cassette recorder if the design of the model of such recorder has been modified after such date of enactment so that a model of recorder that previously conformed to the automatic gain control copy control technology no longer conforms to such technology; or

(ii) any VHS format analog video cassette recorder, or any 8mm format analog video cassette recorder that is not an 8mm analog video cassette camcorder, if the design of the model of such recorder has been modified after such date of enactment so that a model of recorder that previously conformed to the four-line colorstripe copy control technology no longer conforms to such technology.

Manufacturers that have not previously manufactured or sold a VHS format analog video cassette recorder, or an 8mm format analog cassette recorder, shall be required to conform to the four-line colorstripe copy control technology in the initial model of any such recorder manufactured after the date of the enactment of this chapter, and thereafter to continue conforming to the four-line colorstripe copy control technology. For purposes of this subparagraph, an analog video cassette recorder "conforms to" the four-line colorstripe copy control technology if it records a signal that, when played back by the playback function of that recorder in the normal viewing mode, exhibits, on a reference display device, a display containing distracting visible lines through portions of the viewable picture.

(2) Certain encoding restrictions. — No person shall apply the automatic gain control copy control technology or colorstripe copy control technology to prevent or limit consumer copying except such copying —

(A) of a single transmission, or specified group of transmissions, of live events or of audiovisual works for which a member of the public has exercised choice in selecting the transmissions, including the content of the transmissions or the time of receipt of such transmissions, or both, and as to which such member is charged a separate fee for each such transmission or specified group of transmissions;

(B) from a copy of a transmission of a live event or an audiovisual work if such transmission is provided by a channel or service where payment is made by a member of the public for such channel or service in the form of a subscription fee that entitles the member of the public to receive all of the programming contained in such channel or service;

(C) from a physical medium containing one or more prerecorded audiovisual works; or

(D) from a copy of a transmission described in subparagraph (A) or from a copy made from a physical medium described in subparagraph (C).

In the event that a transmission meets both the conditions set forth in subparagraph (A) and those set forth in subparagraph (B), the transmission shall be treated as a transmission described in subparagraph (A).

(3) Inapplicability.—This subsection shall not—

(A) require any analog video cassette camcorder to conform to the automatic gain control copy control technology with respect to any video signal received through a camera lens;

(B) apply to the manufacture, importation, offer for sale, provision of, or other trafficking in, any professional analog video cassette recorder; or

(C) apply to the offer for sale or provision of, or other trafficking in, any previously owned analog video cassette recorder, if such recorder was legally manufactured and sold when new and not subsequently modified in violation of paragraph (1)(B).

(4) Definitions.—For purposes of this subsection:

(A) An "analog video cassette recorder" means a device that records, or a device that includes a function that records, on electromagnetic tape in an analog format the electronic impulses produced by the video and audio portions of a television program, motion picture, or other form of audiovisual work.

(B) An "analog video cassette camcorder" means an analog video cassette recorder that contains a recording function that operates through a camera lens and through a video input that may be connected with a television or other video playback device.

(C) An analog video cassette recorder "conforms" to the automatic gain control copy control technology if it—

(i) detects one or more of the elements of such technology and does not record the motion picture or transmission protected by such technology; or

(ii) records a signal that, when played back, exhibits a meaningfully distorted or degraded display.

(D) The term "professional analog video cassette recorder" means an analog video cassette recorder that is designed, manufactured, marketed, and intended for use by a person who regularly employs such a device for a lawful business or industrial use, including making, performing, displaying, distributing, or transmitting copies of motion pictures on a commercial scale.

(E) The terms "VHS format," "8mm format," "Beta format," "automatic gain control copy control technology," "colorstripe copy control technology," "four-line version of the colorstripe copy control technology," and "NTSC" have the meanings that are commonly understood in the consumer electronics and motion picture industries as of the date of the enactment of this chapter.

(5) Violations.—Any violation of paragraph (1) of this subsection shall be treated as a violation of subsection (b)(1) of this section. Any violation of paragraph (2) of this subsection shall be deemed an "act of circumvention" for the purposes of section 1203(c)(3)(A) of this chapter.

§1202. Integrity of copyright management information

(a) False Copyright Management Information.—No person shall knowingly and with the intent to induce, enable, facilitate, or conceal infringement—

(1) provide copyright management information that is false, or

(2) distribute or import for distribution copyright management information that is false.

(b) Removal or Alteration of Copyright Management Information.—No person shall, without the authority of the copyright owner or the law—

(1) intentionally remove or alter any copyright management information,

(2) distribute or import for distribution copyright management information knowing that the copyright management information has been removed or altered without authority of the copyright owner or the law, or

(3) distribute, import for distribution, or publicly perform works, copies of works, or phonorecords, knowing that copyright management information has been removed or altered without authority of the copyright owner or the law,

knowing, or, with respect to civil remedies under section 1203, having reasonable grounds to know, that it will induce, enable, facilitate, or conceal an infringement of any right under this title.

(c) Definition.—As used in this section, the term "copyright management information" means any of the following information conveyed in connection with copies or phonorecords of a work or performances or displays of a work, including in digital form, except that such term does not include any personally identifying information about a user of a work or of a copy, phonorecord, performance, or display of a work:

(1) The title and other information identifying the work, including the information set forth on a notice of copyright.

(2) The name of, and other identifying information about, the author of a work.

(3) The name of, and other identifying information about, the copyright owner of the work, including the information set forth in a notice of copyright.

(4) With the exception of public performances of works by radio and television broadcast stations, the name of, and other identifying information about, a performer whose performance is fixed in a work other than an audiovisual work.

(5) With the exception of public performances of works by radio and television broadcast stations, in the case of an audiovisual work, the name of, and other identifying information about, a writer, performer, or director who is credited in the audiovisual work.

(6) Terms and conditions for use of the work.

(7) Identifying numbers or symbols referring to such information or links to such information.

(8) Such other information as the Register of Copyrights may prescribe by regulation, except that the Register of Copyrights may not require the provision of any information concerning the user of a copyrighted work.

(d) Law Enforcement, Intelligence, and Other Government Activities. — This section does not prohibit any lawfully authorized investigative, protective, information security, or intelligence activity of an officer, agent, or employee of the United States, a State, or a political subdivision of a State, or a person acting pursuant to a contract with the United States, a State, or a political subdivision of a State. For purposes of this subsection, the term "information security" means activities carried out in order to identify and address the vulnerabilities of a government computer, computer system, or computer network.

(e) Limitations on Liability. —

(1) Analog transmissions. — In the case of an analog transmission, a person who is making transmissions in its capacity as a broadcast station, or as a cable system, or someone who provides programming to such station or system, shall not be liable for a violation of subsection (b) if —

(A) avoiding the activity that constitutes such violation is not technically feasible or would create an undue financial hardship on such person; and

(B) such person did not intend, by engaging in such activity, to induce, enable, facilitate, or conceal infringement of a right under this title.

(2) Digital transmissions. —

(A) If a digital transmission standard for the placement of copyright management information for a category of works is set in a voluntary, consensus standard-setting process involving a representative cross-section of broadcast stations or cable systems and copyright owners of a category of works that are intended for public performance by such stations or systems, a person identified in paragraph (1) shall not be liable for a violation of subsection (b) with respect to the particular copyright management information addressed by such standard if —

(i) the placement of such information by someone other than such person is not in accordance with such standard; and

(ii) the activity that constitutes such violation is not intended to induce, enable, facilitate, or conceal infringement of a right under this title.

(B) Until a digital transmission standard has been set pursuant to subparagraph (A) with respect to the placement of copyright management information for a category of works, a person identified in paragraph (1) shall not be liable for a violation of subsection (b) with respect to such copyright management information, if the activity that constitutes such violation is not intended to induce, enable, facilitate, or conceal infringement of a right under this title, and if —

(i) the transmission of such information by such person would result in a perceptible visual or aural degradation of the digital signal; or

(ii) the transmission of such information by such person would conflict with —

(I) an applicable government regulation relating to transmission of information in a digital signal;

(II) an applicable industry-wide standard relating to the transmission of information in a digital signal that was adopted by a voluntary consensus standards body prior to the effective date of this chapter; or

(III) an applicable industry-wide standard relating to the transmission of information in a digital signal that was adopted in a voluntary, consensus standards-setting process open to participation by a representative cross-section of broadcast stations or cable systems and copyright owners of a category of works that are intended for public performance by such stations or systems.

(3) Definitions. — As used in this subsection —

(A) the term "broadcast station" has the meaning given that term in section 3 of the Communications Act of 1934 (47 U.S.C. 153); and

(B) the term "cable system" has the meaning given that term in section 602 of the Communications Act of 1934 (47 U.S.C. 522).

§1203.   Civil remedies

(a) Civil Actions. — Any person injured by a violation of section 1201 or 1202 may bring a civil action in an appropriate United States district court for such violation.

(b) Powers of the Court. — In an action brought under subsection (a), the court —

(1) may grant temporary and permanent injunctions on such terms as it deems reasonable to prevent or restrain a violation, but in no event shall impose a prior restraint on free speech or the press protected under the 1st amendment to the Constitution;

(2) at any time while an action is pending, may order the impounding, on such terms as it deems reasonable, of any device or product that is in the custody or control of the alleged violator and that the court has reasonable cause to believe was involved in a violation;

(3) may award damages under subsection (c);

(4) in its discretion may allow the recovery of costs by or against any party other than the United States or an officer thereof;

(5) in its discretion may award reasonable attorney's fees to the prevailing party; and

(6) may, as part of a final judgment or decree finding a violation, order the remedial modification or the destruction of any device or product involved in the violation that is in the custody or control of the violator or has been impounded under paragraph (2).

(c) Award of Damages. —

(1) In general. — Except as otherwise provided in this title, a person committing a violation of section 1201 or 1202 is liable for either —

(A) the actual damages and any additional profits of the violator, as provided in paragraph (2), or

(B) statutory damages, as provided in paragraph (3).

(2) Actual damages.—The court shall award to the complaining party the actual damages suffered by the party as a result of the violation, and any profits of the violator that are attributable to the violation and are not taken into account in computing the actual damages, if the complaining party elects such damages at any time before final judgment is entered.

(3) Statutory damages.—(A) At any time before final judgment is entered, a complaining party may elect to recover an award of statutory damages for each violation of section 1201 in the sum of not less than $200 or more than $2,500 per act of circumvention, device, product, component, offer, or performance of service, as the court considers just.

(B) At any time before final judgment is entered, a complaining party may elect to recover an award of statutory damages for each violation of section 1202 in the sum of not less than $2,500 or more than $25,000.

(4) Repeated violations.—In any case in which the injured party sustains the burden of proving, and the court finds, that a person has violated section 1201 or 1202 within three years after a final judgment was entered against the person for another such violation, the court may increase the award of damages up to triple the amount that would otherwise be awarded, as the court considers just.

(5) Innocent violations.—

(A) In general.—The court in its discretion may reduce or remit the total award of damages in any case in which the violator sustains the burden of proving, and the court finds, that the violator was not aware and had no reason to believe that its acts constituted a violation.

(B) Nonprofit library, archives, educational institutions, or public broadcasting entities.—

(i) Definition.—In this subparagraph, the term "public broadcasting entity" has the meaning given such term under section 118(g).

(ii) In general.—In the case of a nonprofit library, archives, educational institution, or public broadcasting entity, the court shall remit damages in any case in which the library, archives, educational institution, or public broadcasting entity sustains the burden of proving, and the court finds, that the library, archives, educational institution, or public broadcasting entity was not aware and had no reason to believe that its acts constituted a violation.

§1204. Criminal offenses and penalties

(a) In General.—Any person who violates section 1201 or 1202 willfully and for purposes of commercial advantage or private financial gain—

(1) shall be fined not more than $500,000 or imprisoned for not more than 5 years, or both, for the first offense; and

(2) shall be fined not more than $1,000,000 or imprisoned for not more than 10 years, or both, for any subsequent offense.

(b) Limitation for Nonprofit Library, Archives, Educational Institution, or Public Broadcasting Entity. — Subsection (a) shall not apply to a nonprofit library, archives, educational institution, or public broadcasting entity (as defined under section 118(g)).

(c) Statute of Limitations. — No criminal proceeding shall be brought under this section unless such proceeding is commenced within 5 years after the cause of action arose.

§1205. Savings clause

Nothing in this chapter abrogates, diminishes, or weakens the provisions of, nor provides any defense or element of mitigation in a criminal prosecution or civil action under, any Federal or State law that prevents the violation of the privacy of an individual in connection with the individual's use of the Internet.

Chapter 13. Protection of Original Designs

Sec.

§1301. Designs protected

(a) Designs Protected. —

(1) In general. — The designer or other owner of an original design of a useful article which makes the article attractive or distinctive in appearance to the purchasing or using public may secure the protection provided by this chapter upon complying with and subject to this chapter.

(2) Vessel features. — The design of a vessel hull, deck, or combination of a hull and deck, including a plug or mold, is subject to protection under this chapter, notwithstanding section 1302(4).

(3) Exceptions. — Department of Defense rights in a registered design under this chapter, including the right to build to such registered design, shall be determined solely by operation of section 2320 of title 10 or by the instrument under which the design was developed for the United States Government.

(b) Definitions. — For the purpose of this chapter, the following terms have the following meanings:

(1) A design is "original" if it is the result of the designer's creative endeavor that provides a distinguishable variation over prior work pertaining to similar articles which is more than merely trivial and has not been copied from another source.

(2) A "useful article" is a vessel hull or deck, including a plug or mold, which in normal use has an intrinsic utilitarian function that is not merely to portray the appearance of the article or to convey information. An article which normally is part of a useful article shall be deemed to be a useful article.

(3) A "vessel" is a craft —

(A) that is designed and capable of independently steering a course on or through water through its own means of propulsion; and

(B) that is designed and capable of carrying and transporting one or more passengers.

(4) A "hull" is the exterior frame or body of a vessel, exclusive of the deck, superstructure, masts, sails, yards, rigging, hardware, fixtures, and other attachments.

(5) A "plug" means a device or model used to make a mold for the purpose of exact duplication, regardless of whether the device or model has an intrinsic utilitarian function that is not only to portray the appearance of the product or to convey information.

(6) A "mold" means a matrix or form in which a substance for material is used, regardless of whether the matrix or form has an intrinsic utilitarian function that is not only to portray the appearance of the product or to convey information.

(7) A "deck" is the horizontal surface of a vessel that covers the hull, including exterior cabin and cockpit surfaces, and exclusive of masts, sails, yards, rigging, hardware, fixtures, and other attachments.

§1302.   Designs not subject to protection

Protection under this chapter shall not be available for a design that is —
(1) not original;
(2) staple or commonplace, such as a standard geometric figure, a familiar symbol, an emblem, or a motif, or another shape, pattern, or configuration which has become standard, common, prevalent, or ordinary;
(3) different from a design excluded by paragraph (2) only in insignificant details or in elements which are variants commonly used in the relevant trades;
(4) dictated solely by a utilitarian function of the article that embodies it; or
(5) embodied in a useful article that was made public by the designer or owner in the United States or a foreign country more than 2 years before the date of the application for registration under this chapter.

§1303.   Revisions, adaptations, and rearrangements

Protection for a design under this chapter shall be available notwithstanding the employment in the design of subject matter excluded from protection under section 1302 if the design is a substantial revision, adaptation, or rearrangement of such subject matter. Such protection shall be independent of any subsisting protection in subject matter employed in the design, and shall not be construed as securing any right to subject matter excluded from protection under this chapter or as extending any subsisting protection under this chapter.

§1304.   Commencement of protection

The protection provided for a design under this chapter shall commence upon the earlier of the date of publication of the registration under section 1313(a) or the date the design is first made public as defined by section 1310(b).

§1305. Term of protection

(a) In General — Subject to subsection (b), the protection provided under this chapter for a design shall continue for a term of 10 years beginning on the date of the commencement of protection under section 1304.

(b) Expiration. — All terms of protection provided in this section shall run to the end of the calendar year in which they would otherwise expire.

(c) Termination of Rights. — Upon expiration or termination of protection in a particular design under this chapter, all rights under this chapter in the design shall terminate, regardless of the number of different articles in which the design may have been used during the term of its protection.

§1306. Design notice

(a) Contents of Design Notice. —

(1) Whenever any design for which protection is sought under this chapter is made public under section 1310(b), the owner of the design shall, subject to the provisions of section 1307, mark it or have it marked legibly with a design notice consisting of —

(A) the words "Protected Design", the abbreviation "Prot'd Des.", or the letter "D" with a circle, or the symbol "*D*";

(B) the year of the date on which protection for the design commenced; and

(C) the name of the owner, an abbreviation by which the name can be recognized, or a generally accepted alternative designation of the owner.

Any distinctive identification of the owner may be used for purposes of subparagraph (C) if it has been recorded by the Administrator before the design marked with such identification is registered.

(2) After registration, the registration number may be used instead of the elements specified in subparagraphs (B) and (C) of paragraph (1).

(b) Location of Notice. — The design notice shall be so located and applied as to give reasonable notice of design protection while the useful article embodying the design is passing through its normal channels of commerce.

(c) Subsequent Removal of Notice. — When the owner of a design has complied with the provisions of this section, protection under this chapter shall not be affected by the removal, destruction, or obliteration by others of the design notice on an article.

§1307. Effect of omission of notice

(a) Actions with Notice. — Except as provided in subsection (b), the omission of the notice prescribed in section 1306 shall not cause loss of the protection under this chapter or prevent recovery for infringement under this chapter against any person who, after receiving written notice of the design protection, begins an undertaking leading to infringement under this chapter.

(b) Actions without Notice.—The omission of the notice prescribed in section 1306 shall prevent any recovery under section 1323 against a person who began an undertaking leading to infringement under this chapter before receiving written notice of the design protection. No injunction shall be issued under this chapter with respect to such undertaking unless the owner of the design reimburses that person for any reasonable expenditure or contractual obligation in connection with such undertaking that was incurred before receiving written notice of the design protection, as the court in its discretion directs. The burden of providing written notice of design protection shall be on the owner of the design.

§1308. Exclusive rights

The owner of a design protected under this chapter has the exclusive right to—

(1) make, have made, or import, for sale or for use in trade, any useful article embodying that design; and

(2) sell or distribute for sale or for use in trade any useful article embodying that design.

§1309. Infringement

(a) Acts of Infringement.—Except as provided in subsection (b), it shall be infringement of the exclusive rights in a design protected under this chapter for any person, without the consent of the owner of the design, within the United States and during the term of such protection, to—

(1) make, have made, or import, for sale or for use in trade, any infringing article as defined in subsection (e); or

(2) sell or distribute for sale or for use in trade any such infringing article.

(b) Acts of Sellers and Distributors.—A seller or distributor of an infringing article who did not make or import the article shall be deemed to have infringed on a design protected under this chapter only if that person—

(1) induced or acted in collusion with a manufacturer to make, or an importer to import such article, except that merely purchasing or giving an order to purchase such article in the ordinary course of business shall not of itself constitute such inducement or collusion; or

(2) refused or failed, upon the request of the owner of the design, to make a prompt and full disclosure of that person's source of such article, and that person orders or reorders such article after receiving notice by registered or certified mail of the protection subsisting in the design.

(c) Acts without Knowledge.—It shall not be infringement under this section to make, have made, import, sell, or distribute, any article embodying a design which was created without knowledge that a design was protected under this chapter and was copied from such protected design.

(d) Acts in Ordinary Course of Business.—A person who incorporates into that person's product of manufacture an infringing article acquired from others in the ordinary course of business, or who, without knowledge of the protected design embodied in an infringing article, makes or processes the infringing article for the account of another person in the ordinary course of business, shall not be deemed to have infringed the rights in that design under this chapter except under a condition contained in paragraph (1) or (2) of subsection (b). Accepting an order or reorder from the source of the infringing article shall be deemed ordering or reordering within the meaning of subsection (b)(2).

(e) Infringing Article Defined.—As used in this section, an "infringing article" is any article the design of which has been copied from a design protected under this chapter, without the consent of the owner of the protected design. An infringing article is not an illustration or picture of a protected design in an advertisement, book, periodical, newspaper, photograph, broadcast, motion picture, or similar medium. A design shall not be deemed to have been copied from a protected design if it is original and not substantially similar in appearance to a protected design.

(f) Establishing Originality.—The party to any action or proceeding under this chapter who alleges rights under this chapter in a design shall have the burden of establishing the design's originality whenever the opposing party introduces an earlier work which is identical to such design, or so similar as to make prima facie showing that such design was copied from such work.

(g) Reproduction for Teaching or Analysis.—It is not an infringement of the exclusive rights of a design owner for a person to reproduce the design in a useful article or in any other form solely for the purpose of teaching, analyzing, or evaluating the appearance, concepts, or techniques embodied in the design, or the function of the useful article embodying the design.

§1310. Application for registration

(a) Time Limit for Application for Registration.—Protection under this chapter shall be lost if application for registration of the design is not made within 2 years after the date on which the design is first made public.

(b) When Design Is Made Public.—A design is made public when an existing useful article embodying the design is anywhere publicly exhibited, publicly distributed, or offered for sale or sold to the public by the owner of the design or with the owner's consent.

(c) Application by Owner of Design.—Application for registration may be made by the owner of the design.

(d) Contents of Application.—The application for registration shall be made to the Administrator and shall state—

(1) the name and address of the designer or designers of the design;

(2) the name and address of the owner if different from the designer;

(3) the specific name of the useful article embodying the design;

(4) the date, if any, that the design was first made public, if such date was earlier than the date of the application;

(5) affirmation that the design has been fixed in a useful article; and

(6) such other information as may be required by the Administrator.

The application for registration may include a description setting forth the salient features of the design, but the absence of such a description shall not prevent registration under this chapter.

(e) Sworn Statement. — The application for registration shall be accompanied by a statement under oath by the applicant or the applicant's duly authorized agent or representative, setting forth, to the best of the applicant's knowledge and belief —

(1) that the design is original and was created by the designer or designers named in the application;

(2) that the design has not previously been registered on behalf of the applicant or the applicant's predecessor in title; and

(3) that the applicant is the person entitled to protection and to registration under this chapter.

If the design has been made public with the design notice prescribed in section 1306, the statement shall also describe the exact form and position of the design notice.

(f) Effect of Errors. —

(1) Error in any statement or assertion as to the utility of the useful article named in the application under this section, the design of which is sought to be registered, shall not affect the protection secured under this chapter.

(2) Errors in omitting a joint designer or in naming an alleged joint designer shall not affect the validity of the registration, or the actual ownership or the protection of the design, unless it is shown that the error occurred with deceptive intent.

(g) Design Made in Scope of Employment. — In a case in which the design was made within the regular scope of the designer's employment and individual authorship of the design is difficult or impossible to ascribe and the application so states, the name and address of the employer for whom the design was made may be stated instead of that of the individual designer.

(h) Pictorial Representation of Design. — The application for registration shall be accompanied by two copies of a drawing or other pictorial representation of the useful article embodying the design, having one or more views, adequate to show the design, in a form and style suitable for reproduction, which shall be deemed a part of the application.

(i) Design in More Than One Useful Article. — If the distinguishing elements of a design are in substantially the same form in different useful articles, the design shall be protected as to all such useful articles when protected as to one of them, but not more than one registration shall be required for the design.

(j) Application for More Than One Design. — More than one design may be included in the same application under such conditions as may be prescribed by the Administrator. For each design included in an application the fee prescribed for a single design shall be paid.

§1311. Benefit of earlier filing date in foreign country

An application for registration of a design filed in the United States by any person who has, or whose legal representative or predecessor or successor in title has, previously filed an application for registration of the same design in a foreign country which extends to designs of owners who are citizens of the United States, or to applications filed under this chapter, similar protection to that provided under this chapter shall have that same effect as if filed in the United States on the date on which the application was first filed in such foreign country, if the application in the United States is filed within 6 months after the earliest date on which any such foreign application was filed.

§1312. Oaths and acknowledgements

(a) In General. — Oaths and acknowledgments required by this chapter —
  (1) may be made —
    (A) before any person in the United States authorized by law to administer oaths; or
    (B) when made in a foreign country, before any diplomatic or consular officer of the United States authorized to administer oaths, or before any official authorized to administer oaths in the foreign country concerned, whose authority shall be proved by a certificate of a diplomatic or consular officer of the United States; and
  (2) shall be valid if they comply with the laws of the State or country where made.

(b) Written Declaration in Lieu of Oath. —
  (1) The Administrator may by rule prescribe that any document which is to be filed under this chapter in the Office of the Administrator and which is required by any law, rule, or other regulation to be under oath, may be subscribed to by a written declaration in such form as the Administrator may prescribe, and such declaration shall be in lieu of the oath otherwise required.
  (2) Whenever a written declaration under paragraph (1) is used, the document containing the declaration shall state that willful false statements are punishable by fine or imprisonment, or both, pursuant to section 1001 of title 18, and may jeopardize the validity of the application or document or a registration resulting therefrom.

§1313. Examination of application and issue or refusal of registration

(a) Determination of Registrability of Design; Registration. — Upon the filing of an application for registration in proper form under section 1310, and upon payment of the fee prescribed under section 1316, the Administrator shall determine whether or not the application relates to a design which on its face appears to be subject to protection under this chapter, and, if so, the Register shall register the design. Registration under this subsection shall be announced by publication. The date of registration shall be the date of publication.

(b) Refusal to Register; Reconsideration. — If, in the judgment of the Administrator, the application for registration relates to a design which on its face is not subject to protection under this chapter, the Administrator shall send to the applicant a notice of refusal to register and the grounds for the refusal. Within 3 months after the date on which the notice of refusal is sent, the applicant may, by written request, seek reconsideration of the application. After consideration of such a request, the Administrator shall either register the design or send to the applicant a notice of final refusal to register.

(c) Application to Cancel Registration. — Any person who believes he or she is or will be damaged by a registration under this chapter may, upon payment of the prescribed fee, apply to the Administrator at any time to cancel the registration on the ground that the design is not subject to protection under this chapter, stating the reasons for the request. Upon receipt of an application for cancellation, the Administrator shall send to the owner of the design, as shown in the records of the Office of the Administrator, a notice of the application, and the owner shall have a period of 3 months after the date on which such notice is mailed in which to present arguments to the Administrator for support of the validity of the registration. The Administrator shall also have the authority to establish, by regulation, conditions under which the opposing parties may appear and be heard in support of their arguments. If, after the periods provided for the presentation of arguments have expired, the Administrator determines that the applicant for cancellation has established that the design is not subject to protection under this chapter, the Administrator shall order the registration stricken from the record. Cancellation under this subsection shall be announced by publication, and notice of the Administrator's final determination with respect to any application for cancellation shall be sent to the applicant and to the owner of record. Costs of the cancellation procedure under this subsection shall be borne by the nonprevailing party or parties, and the Administrator shall have the authority to assess and collect such costs.

§1314. Certification of registration

Certificates of registration shall be issued in the name of the United States under the seal of the Office of the Administrator and shall be recorded in the official records of the Office. The certificate shall state the name of the useful article, the date of filing of the application, the date of registration, and the date the design was made public, if earlier than the date of filing of the application, and shall contain a reproduction of the drawing or other pictorial representation of the design. If a description of the salient features of the design appears in the application, the description shall also appear in the certificate. A certificate of registration shall be admitted in any court as prima facie evidence of the facts stated in the certificate.

§1315. Publication of announcements and indexes

(a) Publications of the Administrator. — The Administrator shall publish lists and indexes of registered designs and cancellations of designs and may also publish the drawings or other pictorial representations of registered designs for sale or other distribution.

(b) File of Representatives of Registered Designs. — The Administrator shall establish and maintain a file of the drawings or other pictorial representations of registered designs. The file shall be available for use by the public under such conditions as the Administrator may prescribe.

§1316. Fees

The Administrator shall by regulation set reasonable fees for the filing of applications to register designs under this chapter and for other services relating to the administration of this chapter, taking into consideration the cost of providing these services and the benefit of a public record.

§1317. Regulations

The Administrator may establish regulations for the administration of this chapter.

§1318. Copies of records

Upon payment of the prescribed fee, any person may obtain a certified copy of any official record of the Office of the Administrator that relates to this chapter. That copy shall be admissible in evidence with the same effect as the original.

§1319. Correction of errors in certificates

The Administrator may, by a certificate of correction under seal, correct any error in a registration incurred through the fault of the Office, or, upon payment of the required fee, any error of a clerical or typographical nature occurring in good faith but not through the fault of the Office. Such registration, together with the certificate, shall thereafter have the same effect as if it had been originally issued in such corrected form.

§1320.   Ownership and transfer

(a) Property Right in Design. — The property right in a design subject to protection under this chapter shall vest in the designer, the legal representatives of a deceased designer or of one under legal incapacity, the employer for whom the designer created the design in the case of a design made within the regular scope of the designer's employment, or a person to whom the rights of the designer or of such employer have been transferred. The person in whom the property right is vested shall be considered the owner of the design.

(b) Transfer of Property Right. — The property right in a registered design, or a design for which an application for registration has been or may be filed, may be assigned, granted, conveyed, or mortgaged by an instrument in writing, signed by the owner, or may be bequeathed by will.

(c) Oath or Acknowledgment of Transfer. — An oath or acknowledgment under section 1312 shall be prima facie evidence of the execution of an assignment, grant, conveyance, or mortgage under subsection (b).

(d) Recordation of Transfer. — An assignment, grant, conveyance, or mortgage under subsection (b) shall be void as against any subsequent purchaser or mortgagee for a valuable consideration, unless it is recorded in the Office of the Administrator within 3 months after its date of execution or before the date of such subsequent purchase or mortgage.

§1321.   Remedy for infringement

(a) In General. — The owner of a design is entitled, after issuance of a certificate of registration of the design under this chapter, to institute an action for any infringement of the design.

(b) Review of Refusal to Register. —

(1) Subject to paragraph (2), the owner of a design may seek judicial review of a final refusal of the Administrator to register the design under this chapter by bringing a civil action, and may in the same action, if the court adjudges the design subject to protection under this chapter, enforce the rights in that design under this chapter.

(2) The owner of a design may seek judicial review under this section if —

(A) the owner has previously duly filed and prosecuted to final refusal an application in proper form for registration of the design;

(B) the owner causes a copy of the complaint in the action to be delivered to the Administrator within 10 days after the commencement of the action; and

(C) the defendant has committed acts in respect to the design which would constitute infringement with respect to a design protected under this chapter.

(c) Administrator as Party to Action. — The Administrator may, at the Administrator's option, become a party to the action with respect to the issue of registrability of the design claim by entering an appearance within 60 days after being served with the complaint, but the failure of the Administrator to become a party shall not deprive the court of jurisdiction to determine that issue.

(d) Use of Arbitration to Resolve Dispute. — The parties to an infringement dispute under this chapter, within such time as may be specified by the Administrator by regulation, may determine the dispute, or any aspect of the dispute, by arbitration. Arbitration shall be governed by title 9. The parties shall give notice of any arbitration award to the Administrator, and such award shall, as between the parties to the arbitration, be dispositive of the issues to which it relates. The arbitration award shall be unenforceable until such notice is given. Nothing in this subsection shall preclude the Administrator from determining whether a design is subject to registration in a cancellation proceeding under section 1313(c).

§1322. Injunctions

(a) In General. — A court having jurisdiction over actions under this chapter may grant injunctions in accordance with the principles of equity to prevent infringement of a design under this chapter, including, in its discretion, prompt relief by temporary restraining orders and preliminary injunctions.

(b) Damages for Injunctive Relief Wrongfully Obtained. — A seller or distributor who suffers damage by reason of injunctive relief wrongfully obtained under this section has a cause of action against the applicant for such injunctive relief and may recover such relief as may be appropriate, including damages for lost profits, cost of materials, loss of good will, and punitive damages in instances where the injunctive relief was sought in bad faith, and, unless the court finds extenuating circumstances, reasonable attorney's fees.

§1323. Recovery for infringement

(a) Damages. — Upon a finding for the claimant in an action for infringement under this chapter, the court shall award the claimant damages adequate to compensate for the infringement. In addition, the court may increase the damages to such amount, not exceeding $50,000 or $1 per copy, whichever is greater, as the court determines to be just. The damages awarded shall constitute compensation and not a penalty. The court may receive expert testimony as an aid to the determination of damages.

(b) Infringer's Profits. — As an alternative to the remedies provided in subsection (a), the court may award the claimant the infringer's profits resulting from the sale of the copies if the court finds that the infringer's sales are reasonably related to the use of the claimant's design. In such a case, the claimant shall be required to prove only the amount of the infringer's sales and the infringer shall be required to prove its expenses against such sales.

(c) Statute of Limitations. — No recovery under subsection (a) or (b) shall be had for any infringement committed more than 3 years before the date on which the complaint is filed.

(d) Attorney's Fees. — In an action for infringement under this chapter, the court may award reasonable attorney's fees to the prevailing party.

(e) Disposition of Infringing and Other Articles. — The court may order that all infringing articles, and any plates, molds, patterns, models, or other means specifically adapted for making the articles, be delivered up for destruction or other disposition as the court may direct.

§1324. Power of court over registration

In any action involving the protection of a design under this chapter, the court, when appropriate, may order registration of a design under this chapter or the cancellation of such a registration. Any such order shall be certified by the court to the Administrator, who shall make an appropriate entry upon the record.

§1325. Liability for action on registration fraudulently obtained

Any person who brings an action for infringement knowing that registration of the design was obtained by a false or fraudulent representation materially affecting the rights under this chapter, shall be liable in the sum of $10,000, or such part of that amount as the court may determine. That amount shall be to compensate the defendant and shall be charged against the plaintiff and paid to the defendant, in addition to such costs and attorney's fees of the defendant as may be assessed by the court.

§1326. Penalty for false marking

(a) In General. — Whoever, for the purpose of deceiving the public, marks upon, applies to, or uses in advertising in connection with an article made, used, distributed, or sold, a design which is not protected under this chapter, a design notice specified in section 1306, or any other words or symbols importing that the design is protected under this chapter, knowing that the design is not so protected, shall pay a civil fine of not more than $500 for each such offense.

(b) Suit by Private Persons. — Any person may sue for the penalty established by subsection (a), in which event one-half of the penalty shall be awarded to the person suing and the remainder shall be awarded to the United States.

§1327. Penalty for false representation

Whoever knowingly makes a false representation materially affecting the rights obtainable under this chapter for the purpose of obtaining registration of a design under this chapter shall pay a penalty of not less than $500 and not more than $1,000, and any rights or privileges that individual may have in the design under this chapter shall be forfeited.

§1328. Enforcement by Treasury and Postal Service

(a) Regulations. — The Secretary of the Treasury and the United States Postal Service shall separately or jointly issue regulations for the enforcement of the rights set forth in section 1308 with respect to importation. Such regulations may require, as a condition for the exclusion of articles from the United States, that the person seeking exclusion take any one or more of the following actions:

(1) Obtain a court order enjoining, or an order of the International Trade Commission under section 337 of the Tariff Act of 1930 excluding, importation of the articles.

(2) Furnish proof that the design involved is protected under this chapter and that the importation of the articles would infringe the rights in the design under this chapter.

(3) Post a surety bond for any injury that may result if the detention or exclusion of the articles proves to be unjustified.

(b) Seizure and Forfeiture. — Articles imported in violation of the rights set forth in section 1308 are subject to seizure and forfeiture in the same manner as property imported in violation of the customs laws. Any such forfeited articles shall be destroyed as directed by the Secretary of the Treasury or the court, as the case may be, except that the articles may be returned to the country of export whenever it is shown to the satisfaction of the Secretary of the Treasury that the importer had no reasonable grounds for believing that his or her acts constituted a violation of the law.

§1329. Relation to design patent law

The issuance of a design patent under title 35, United States Code, for an original design for an article of manufacture shall terminate any protection of the original design under this chapter.

§1330. Common law and other rights unaffected

Nothing in this chapter shall annul or limit —

(1) common law or other rights or remedies, if any, available to or held by any person with respect to a design which has not been registered under this chapter; or

(2) any right under the trademark laws or any right protected against unfair competition.

§1331. Administrator; Office of the Administrator

In this chapter, the "Administrator" is the Register of Copyrights, and the "Office of the Administrator" and the "Office" refer to the Copyright Office of the Library of Congress.

§1332. No retroactive effect

Protection under this chapter shall not be available for any design that has been made public under section 1310(b) before the effective date of this chapter.

B. United States Code, Title 18 — Crimes and Criminal Procedure

§2318. Trafficking in counterfeit labels, illicit labels, or counterfeit documentation or packaging[1]

(a)(1) Whoever, in any of the circumstances described in subsection (c), knowingly traffics in —

(A) a counterfeit label or illicit label affixed to, enclosing, or accompanying, or designed to be affixed to, enclose, or accompany —

(i) a phonorecord;

(ii) a copy of a computer program;

(iii) a copy of a motion picture or other audiovisual work;

(iv) a copy of a literary work;

(v) a copy of a pictorial, graphic, or sculptural work;

(vi) a work of visual art; or

(vii) documentation or packaging; or

(B) counterfeit documentation or packaging, shall be fined under this title or imprisoned for not more than 5 years, or both.

(b) As used in this section —

(1) the term "counterfeit label" means an identifying label or container that appears to be genuine, but is not;

(2) the term "traffic" has the same meaning as in section 2320(e) of this title;

(3) the terms "copy", "phonorecord", "motion picture", "computer program", "audiovisual work", "literary work", "pictorial, graphic, or sculptural work", "sound recording", "work of visual art", and "copyright owner" have, respectively, the meanings given those terms in section 101 (relating to definitions) of title 17;

(4) the term "illicit label" means a genuine certificate, licensing document, registration card, or similar labeling component —

---

1. Eds. Note: As provided in 18 U.S.C. §3571, the maximum fine for an individual is $250,000, and the maximum fine for an organization is $500,000.

(A) that is used by the copyright owner to verify that a phonorecord, a copy of a computer program, a copy of a motion picture or other audiovisual work, a copy of a literary work, a copy of a pictorial, graphic, or sculptural work, a work of visual art, or documentation or packaging is not counterfeit or infringing of any copyright; and

(B) that is, without the authorization of the copyright owner—

(i) distributed or intended for distribution not in connection with the copy, phonorecord, or work of visual art to which such labeling component was intended to be affixed by the respective copyright owner; or

(ii) in connection with a genuine certificate or licensing document, knowingly falsified in order to designate a higher number of licensed users or copies than authorized by the copyright owner, unless that certificate or document is used by the copyright owner solely for the purpose of monitoring or tracking the copyright owner's distribution channel and not for the purpose of verifying that a copy or phonorecord is noninfringing;

(5) the term "documentation or packaging" means documentation or packaging, in physical form, for a phonorecord, copy of a computer program, copy of a motion picture or other audiovisual work, copy of a literary work, copy of a pictorial, graphic, or sculptural work, or work of visual art; and

(6) the term "counterfeit documentation or packaging" means documentation or packaging that appears to be genuine, but is not.

(c) The circumstances referred to in subsection (a) of this section are—

(1) the offense is committed within the special maritime and territorial jurisdiction of the United States; or within the special aircraft jurisdiction of the United States (as defined in section 46501 of title 49);

(2) the mail or a facility of interstate or foreign commerce is used or intended to be used in the commission of the offense;

(3) the counterfeit label or illicit label is affixed to, encloses, or accompanies, or is designed to be affixed to, enclose, or accompany—

(A) a phonorecord of a copyrighted sound recording or copyrighted musical work;

(B) a copy of a copyrighted computer program;

(C) a copy of a copyrighted motion picture or other audiovisual work;

(D) a copy of a literary work;

(E) a copy of a pictorial, graphic, or sculptural work;

(F) a work of visual art; or

(G) copyrighted documentation or packaging; or

(4) the counterfeited documentation or packaging is copyrighted.

(d) Forfeiture and Destruction of Property; Restitution.—Forfeiture, destruction, and restitution relating to this section shall be subject to section 2323, to the extent provided in that section, in addition to any other similar remedies provided by law.

(e) Civil Remedies.—

(1) In General.—Any copyright owner who is injured, or is threatened with injury, by a violation of subsection (a) may bring a civil action in an appropriate United States district court.

(2) Discretion of Court.—In any action brought under paragraph (1), the court—

(A) may grant 1 or more temporary or permanent injunctions on such terms as the court determines to be reasonable to prevent or restrain a violation of subsection (a);

(B) at any time while the action is pending, may order the impounding, on such terms as the court determines to be reasonable, of any article that is in the custody or control of the alleged violator and that the court has reasonable cause to believe was involved in a violation of subsection (a); and

(C) may award to the injured party—

(i) reasonable attorney fees and costs; and

(ii)(I) actual damages and any additional profits of the violator, as provided in paragraph (3); or

(II) statutory damages, as provided in paragraph (4).

(3) Actual Damages and Profits.—

(A) In General.—The injured party is entitled to recover—

(i) the actual damages suffered by the injured party as a result of a violation of subsection (a), as provided in subparagraph (B) of this paragraph; and

(ii) any profits of the violator that are attributable to a violation of subsection (a) and are not taken into account in computing the actual damages.

(B) Calculation of Damages.—The court shall calculate actual damages by multiplying—

(i) the value of the phonorecords, copies, or works of visual art which are, or are intended to be, affixed with, enclosed in, or accompanied by any counterfeit labels, illicit labels, or counterfeit documentation or packaging, by

(ii) the number of phonorecords, copies, or works of visual art which are, or are intended to be, affixed with, enclosed in, or accompanied by any counterfeit labels, illicit labels, or counterfeit documentation or packaging.

(C) Definition.—For purposes of this paragraph, the "value" of a phonorecord, copy, or work of visual art is—

(i) in the case of a copyrighted sound recording or copyrighted musical work, the retail value of an authorized phonorecord of that sound recording or musical work;

(ii) in the case of a copyrighted computer program, the retail value of an authorized copy of that computer program;

(iii) in the case of a copyrighted motion picture or other audiovisual work, the retail value of an authorized copy of that motion picture or audiovisual work;

(iv) in the case of a copyrighted literary work, the retail value of an authorized copy of that literary work;

(v) in the case of a pictorial, graphic, or sculptural work, the retail value of an authorized copy of that work; and

(vi) in the case of a work of visual art, the retail value of that work.

(4) Statutory Damages. — The injured party may elect, at any time before final judgment is rendered, to recover, instead of actual damages and profits, an award of statutory damages for each violation of subsection (a) in a sum of not less than $2,500 or more than $25,000, as the court considers appropriate.

(5) Subsequent Violation. — The court may increase an award of damages under this subsection by 3 times the amount that would otherwise be awarded, as the court considers appropriate, if the court finds that a person has subsequently violated subsection (a) within 3 years after a final judgment was entered against that person for a violation of that subsection.

(6) Limitation on Actions. — A civil action may not be commenced under section unless it is commenced within 3 years after the date on which the claimant discovers the violation of subsection (a).

§2319. Criminal infringement of a copyright[2]

(a) Any person who violates section 506(a) (relating to criminal offenses) of title 17 shall be punished as provided in subsections (b), (c), and (d) and such penalties shall be in addition to any other provisions of title 17 or any other law.

(b) Any person who commits an offense under section 506(a)(1)(A) of title 17 —

(1) shall be imprisoned not more than 5 years, or fined in the amount set forth in this title, or both, if the offense consists of the reproduction or distribution, including by electronic means, during any 180-day period, of at least 10 copies or phonorecords, of 1 or more copyrighted works, which have a total retail value of more than $2,500;

(2) shall be imprisoned not more than 10 years, or fined in the amount set forth in this title, or both, if the offense is a felony and is a second or subsequent offense under subsection (a); and

(3) shall be imprisoned not more than 1 year, or fined in the amount set forth in this title, or both, in any other case.

(c) Any person who commits an offense under section 506(a)(1)(B) of title 17 —

(1) shall be imprisoned not more than 3 years, or fined in the amount set forth in this title, or both, if the offense consists of the reproduction or distribution of 10 or more copies or phonorecords of 1 or more copyrighted works, which have a total retail value of $2,500 or more;

(2) shall be imprisoned not more than 6 years, or fined in the amount set forth in this title, or both, if the offense is a felony and is a second or subsequent offense under subsection (a); and

2. Eds. Note: In 1997, the No Electronic Theft Act directed the United States Sentencing Commission to "ensure that the applicable guideline range for a defendant convicted of a crime against intellectual property . . . is sufficiently stringent to deter such a crime" and to "ensure that the guidelines provide for consideration of the retail value and quantity of the items with respect to which the crime against intellectual property was committed." Pub. L. No. 105-147, 111 Stat. 2678 (1997).

(3) shall be imprisoned not more than 1 year, or fined in the amount set forth in this title, or both, if the offense consists of the reproduction or distribution of 1 or more copies or phonorecords of 1 or more copyrighted works, which have a total retail value of more than $1,000.

(d) Any person who commits an offense under section 506(a)(1)(C) of title 17—

(1) shall be imprisoned not more than 3 years, fined under this title, or both;

(2) shall be imprisoned not more than 5 years, fined under this title, or both, if the offense was committed for purposes of commercial advantage or private financial gain;

(3) shall be imprisoned not more than 6 years, fined under this title, or both, if the offense is a felony and is a second or subsequent offense under subsection (a); and

(4) shall be imprisoned not more than 10 years, fined under this title, or both, if the offense is a felony and is a second or subsequent offense under paragraph (2).

(e)(1) During preparation of the presentence report pursuant to Rule 32(c) of the Federal Rules of Criminal Procedure, victims of the offense shall be permitted to submit, and the probation officer shall receive, a victim impact statement that identifies the victim of the offense and the extent and scope of the injury and loss suffered by the victim, including the estimated economic impact of the offense on that victim.

(2) Persons permitted to submit victim impact statements shall include—

(A) producers and sellers of legitimate works affected by conduct involved in the offense;

(B) holders of intellectual property rights in such works; and

(C) the legal representatives of such producers, sellers, and holders.

(f) As used in this section—

(1) the terms "phonorecord" and "copies" have, respectively, the meanings set forth in section 101 (relating to definitions) of title 17;

(2) the terms "reproduction" and "distribution" refer to the exclusive rights of a copyright owner under clauses (1) and (3) respectively of section 106 (relating to exclusive rights in copyrighted works), as limited by sections 107 through 122, of title 17;

(3) the term "financial gain" has the meaning given the term in section 101 of title 17; and

(4) the term "work being prepared for commercial distribution" has the meaning given the term in section 506(a) of title 17.

§2319A. Unauthorized fixation of and trafficking in sound recordings and music videos of live musical performances

(a) Offense.—Whoever, without the consent of the performer or performers involved, knowingly and for purposes of commercial advantage or private financial gain—

(1) fixes the sounds or sounds and images of a live musical performance in a copy or phonorecord, or reproduces copies or phonorecords of such a performance from an unauthorized fixation;

(2) transmits or otherwise communicates to the public the sounds or sounds and images of a live musical performance; or

(3) distributes or offers to distribute, sells or offers to sell, rents or offers to rent, or traffics in any copy or phonorecord fixed as described in paragraph (1), regardless of whether the fixations occurred in the United States; shall be imprisoned for not more than 5 years or fined in the amount set forth in this title, or both, or if the offense is a second or subsequent offense, shall be imprisoned for not more than 10 years or fined in the amount set forth in this title, or both.

(b) Forfeiture and Destruction of Property; Restitution. — Forfeiture, destruction, and restitution relating to this section shall be subject to section 2323, to the extent provided in that section, in addition to any other similar remedies provided by law.

(c) Seizure and Forfeiture. — If copies or phonorecords of sounds or sounds and images of a live musical performance are fixed outside of the United States without the consent of the performer or performers involved, such copies or phonorecords are subject to seizure and forfeiture in the United States in the same manner as property imported in violation of the customs laws. The Secretary of Homeland Security shall issue regulations by which any performer may, upon payment of a specified fee, be entitled to notification by United States Customs and Border Protection of the importation of copies or phonorecords that appear to consist of unauthorized fixations of the sounds or sounds and images of a live musical performance.

(d) Victim Impact Statement. —

(1) During preparation of the presentence report pursuant to Rule 32(c) of the Federal Rules of Criminal Procedure, victims of the offense shall be permitted to submit, and the probation officer shall receive, a victim impact statement that identifies the victim of the offense and the extent and scope of the injury and loss suffered by the victim, including the estimated economic impact of the offense on that victim.

(2) Persons permitted to submit victim impact statements shall include —

(A) producers and sellers of legitimate works affected by conduct involved in the offense;

(B) holders of intellectual property rights in such works; and

(C) the legal representatives of such producers, sellers, and holders.

(e) Definitions. — As used in this section —

(1) the terms "copy", "fixed", "musical work", "phonorecord", "reproduce", "sound recordings", and "transmit" mean those terms within the meaning of title 17; and

(2) the term "traffic" has the same meaning as in section 2320(e) of this title.

(f) Applicability. — This section shall apply to any Act or Acts that occur on or after the date of the enactment of the Uruguay Round Agreements Act.

§2319B. Unauthorized recording of motion pictures in a motion picture exhibition facility

(a) Offense. — Any person who, without the authorization of the copyright owner, knowingly uses or attempts to use an audiovisual recording device to transmit or make a copy of a motion picture or other audiovisual work protected under title 17, or any part thereof, from a performance of such work in a motion picture exhibition facility, shall—

(1) be imprisoned for not more than 3 years, fined under this title, or both; or

(2) if the offense is a second or subsequent offense, be imprisoned for no more than 6 years, fined under this title, or both.

The possession by a person of an audiovisual recording device in a motion picture exhibition facility may be considered as evidence in any proceeding to determine whether that person committed an offense under this subsection, but shall not, by itself, be sufficient to support a conviction of that person for such offense.

(b) Forfeiture and Destruction of Property; Restitution. — Forfeiture, destruction, and restitution relating to this section shall be subject to section 2323, to the extent provided in that section, in addition to any other similar remedies provided by law.

(c) Authorized Activities. — This section does not prevent any lawfully authorized investigative, protective, or intelligence activity by an officer, agent, or employee of the United States, a State, or a political subdivision of a State, or by a person acting under a contract with the United States, a State, or a political subdivision of a State.

(d) Immunity for Theaters. — With reasonable cause, the owner or lessee of a motion picture exhibition facility where a motion picture or other audiovisual work is being exhibited, the authorized agent or employee of such owner or lessee, the licensor of the motion picture or other audiovisual work being exhibited, or the agent or employee of such licensor—

(1) may detain, in a reasonable manner and for a reasonable time, any person suspected of a violation of this section with respect to that motion picture or audiovisual work for the purpose of questioning or summoning a law enforcement officer; and

(2) shall not be held liable in any civil or criminal action arising out of a detention under paragraph (1).

(e) Victim Impact Statement. —

(1) In general. — During the preparation of the presentence report under rule 32(c) of the Federal Rules of Criminal Procedure, victims of an offense under this section shall be permitted to submit to the probation officer a victim impact statement that identifies the victim of the offense and the extent and scope of the injury and loss suffered by the victim, including the estimated economic impact of the offense on that victim.

(2) Contents. — A victim impact statement submitted under this subsection shall include—

    (A) producers and sellers of legitimate works affected by conduct involved in the offense;

    (B) holders of intellectual property rights in the works described in subparagraph (A); and

    (C) the legal representatives of such producers, sellers, and holders.

    (f) State Law Not Preempted. — Nothing in this section may be construed to annul or limit any rights or remedies under the laws of any State.

    (g) Definitions. — In this section, the following definitions shall apply:

    (1) Title 17 definitions. — The terms "audiovisual work", "copy", "copyright owner", "motion picture", "motion picture exhibition facility", and "transmit" have, respectively, the meanings given those terms in section 101 of title 17.

    (2) Audiovisual recording device. — The term "audiovisual recording device" means a digital or analog photographic or video camera, or any other technology or device capable of enabling the recording or transmission of a copyrighted motion picture or other audiovisual work, or any part thereof, regardless of whether audiovisual recording is the sole or primary purpose of the device.

§2323. Forfeiture, destruction, and restitution

    (a) Civil Forfeiture. —

    (1) Property Subject to Forfeiture. — The following property is subject to forfeiture to the United States Government:

    (A) Any article, the making or trafficking of which is, prohibited under section 506 of title 17, or section 2318, 2319, 2319A, 2319B, or 2320, or chapter 90, of this title.

    (B) Any property used, or intended to be used, in any manner or part to commit or facilitate the commission of an offense referred to in subparagraph (A).

    (C) Any property constituting or derived from any proceeds obtained directly or indirectly as a result of the commission of an offense referred to in subparagraph (A).

    (2) Procedures. — The provisions of chapter 46 relating to civil forfeitures shall extend to any seizure or civil forfeiture under this section. For seizures made under this section, the court shall enter an appropriate protective order with respect to discovery and use of any records or information that has been seized. The protective order shall provide for appropriate procedures to ensure that confidential, private, proprietary, or privileged information contained in such records is not improperly disclosed or used. At the conclusion of the forfeiture proceedings, unless otherwise requested by an agency of the United States, the court shall order that any property forfeited under paragraph (1) be destroyed, or otherwise disposed of according to law.

    (b) Criminal Forfeiture. —

    (1) Property Subject to Forfeiture. — The court, in imposing sentence on a person convicted of an offense under section 506 of title 17, or section 2318,

2319, 2319A, 2319B, or 2320, or chapter 90, of this title, shall order, in addition to any other sentence imposed, that the person forfeit to the United States Government any property subject to forfeiture under subsection (a) for that offense.

(2) Procedures.—

(A) In General.—The forfeiture of property under paragraph (1), including any seizure and disposition of the property and any related judicial or administrative proceeding, shall be governed by the procedures set forth in section 413 of the Comprehensive Drug Abuse Prevention and Control Act of 1970 (21 U.S.C. 853), other than subsection (d) of that section.

(B) Destruction.—At the conclusion of the forfeiture proceedings, the court, unless otherwise requested by an agency of the United States shall order that any—

(i) forfeited article or component of an article bearing or consisting of a counterfeit mark be destroyed or otherwise disposed of according to law; and

(ii) infringing items or other property described in subsection (a)(1)(A) and forfeited under paragraph (1) of this subsection be destroyed or otherwise disposed of according to law.

(c) Restitution.—When a person is convicted of an offense under section 506 of title 17 or section 2318, 2319, 2319A, 2319B, or 2320, or chapter 90, of this title, the court, pursuant to sections 3556, 3663A, and 3664 of this title, shall order the person to pay restitution to any victim of the offense as an offense against property referred to in section 3663A(c)(1)(A)(ii) of this title.

C. United States Code, Title 28 — Judiciary and Judicial Procedure

§1338. Patents, plant variety protection, copyrights, mask works, designs, trademarks, and unfair competition

(a) The district courts shall have original jurisdiction of any civil action arising under any Act of Congress relating to patents, plant variety protection, copyrights and trademarks. Such jurisdiction shall be exclusive of the courts of the states in patent, plant variety protection and copyright cases.

(b) The district courts shall have original jurisdiction of any civil action asserting a claim of unfair competition when joined with a substantial and related claim under the copyright, patent, plant variety protection or trademark laws.

(c) Subsections (a) and (b) apply to exclusive rights in mask works under chapter 9 of title 17, and to exclusive rights in designs under chapter 13 of title 17, to the same extent as such subsections apply to copyrights.

§1400. Patents and copyrights, mask works, and designs

(a) Civil actions, suits, or proceedings arising under any Act of Congress relating to copyrights or exclusive rights in mask works or designs may be instituted in the district in which the defendant or his agent resides or may be found.

(b) Any civil action for patent infringement may be brought in the judicial district where the defendant resides, or where the defendant has committed acts of infringement and has a regular and established place of business.

§1498. Patent and copyright cases

. . .

(b) Hereafter, whenever the copyright in any work protected under the copyright laws of the United States shall be infringed by the United States, by a corporation owned or controlled by the United States, or by a contractor, sub-contractor, or any person, firm, or corporation acting for the Government and with the authorization or consent of the Government, the exclusive action which may be brought for such infringement shall be an action by the copyright owner against the United States in the Court of Federal Claims for the recovery of his reasonable and entire compensation as damages for such infringement, including the minimum statutory damages as set forth in section 504(c) of title 17, United States Code: *Provided*, That a Government employee shall have a right of action against the Government under this subsection except where he was in a position to order, influence, or induce use of the copyrighted work by the Government: *Provided, however*, That this subsection shall not confer a right of action on any copyright owner or any assignee of such owner with respect to any copyrighted work prepared by a person while in the employment or service of the United States, where the copyrighted work was prepared as a part of the official functions of the employee, or in the preparation of which Government time, material, or facilities were used: *And provided further*, That before such action against the United States has been instituted the appropriate corporation owned or controlled by the United States or the head of the appropriate department or agency of the Government, as the case may be, is authorized to enter into an agreement with the copyright owner in full settlement and compromise for the damages accruing to him by reason of such infringement and to settle the claim administratively out of available appropriations.

Except as otherwise provided by law, no recovery shall be had for any infringement of a copyright covered by this subsection committed more than three years prior to the filing of the complaint or counterclaim for infringement in the action, except that the period between the date of receipt of a written claim for compensation by the Department or agency of the Government or corporation owned or controlled by the United States, as the case may be, having authority to settle such claim and the date of mailing by the Government of a notice to the claimant that his claim has been denied shall not be counted as a part of the three years, unless suit is brought before the last-mentioned date.

(c) The provisions of this section shall not apply to any claim arising in a foreign country. . . .

(e) Subsections (b) and (c) of this section apply to exclusive rights in mask works under chapter 9 of title 17, and to exclusive rights in designs under chapter 13 of title 17, to the same extent as such subsections apply to copyrights.

224

E. Table of Contents of Code of Federal Regulations, Title 37—Patents, Trademarks, and Copyrights

Complete regulations can be found on the web at *http://www.copyright.gov/title 37/*.

CHAPTER II—COPYRIGHT OFFICE, LIBRARY OF CONGRESS

SUBCHAPTER A—COPYRIGHT OFFICE AND PROCEDURES

Part 201—General Provisions

Sec.

Part 202 — Preregistration and Registration of Claims to Copyright

Sec.

Part 203 — Freedom of Information Act: Policies and Procedures

Sec.

Part 204 — Privacy Act: Policies and Procedures

Sec.

Part 205 — Legal Processes

SUBPART A — GENERAL PROVISIONS

Sec.

SUBPART B — SERVICE OF PROCESS

Sec.

SUBPART C — TESTIMONY BY EMPLOYEES AND PRODUCTION OF DOCUMENTS IN LEGAL PROCEEDINGS IN WHICH THE OFFICE IS NOT A PARTY

Sec.

Part 211 — Mask Work Protection

Sec.

Part 212

Sec.

SUBCHAPTER B — COPYRIGHT ARBITRATION ROYALTY PANEL RULES AND PROCEDURES

Part 251 — Copyright Arbitration Royalty Panel Rules of Procedure

CHAPTER III — COPYRIGHT ROYALTY BOARD, LIBRARY OF CONGRESS

SUBCHAPTER A — GENERAL PROVISIONS

SUBCHAPTER B — COPYRIGHT ROYALTY JUDGES RULES AND PROCEDURES

SUBCHAPTER C — SUBMISSION of ROYALTY CLAIMS

Part II

International Materials

A. Berne Convention for the Protection of Literary and Artistic Works

Paris Act of July 24, 1971, as amended on September 28, 1979
Berne Convention for the Protection of Literary and Artistic Works of September 9, 1886, completed at PARIS on May 4, 1896, revised at BERLIN on November 13, 1908, completed at BERNE on March 20, 1914, revised at ROME on June 2, 1928, at BRUSSELS on June 26, 1948, at STOCKHOLM on July 14, 1967, and at PARIS on July 24, 1971.

The countries of the Union, being equally animated by the desire to protect, in as effective and uniform a manner as possible, the rights of authors in their literary and artistic works,

Recognizing the importance of the work of the Revision Conference held at Stockholm in 1967,

Have resolved to revise the Act adopted by the Stockholm Conference, while maintaining without change Articles 1 to 20 and 22 to 26 of that Act.

Consequently, the undersigned Plenipotentiaries, having presented their full powers, recognized as in good and due form, have agreed as follows:

Article 1

The countries to which this Convention applies constitute a Union for the protection of the rights of authors in their literary and artistic works.

Article 2

(1) The expression "literary and artistic works" shall include every production in the literary, scientific and artistic domain, whatever may be the mode or form of its expression, such as books, pamphlets and other writings; lectures, addresses, sermons and other works of the same nature; dramatic or dramatico-musical works; choreographic works and entertainments in dumb show; musical compositions with or without words; cinematographic works to which are assimilated works expressed by a process analogous to cinematography; works of drawing, painting, architecture, sculpture, engraving and lithography; photographic works to which

are assimilated works expressed by a process analogous to photography; works of applied art; illustrations, maps, plans, sketches and three-dimensional works relative to geography, topography, architecture or science.

(2) It shall, however, be a matter for legislation in the countries of the Union to prescribe that works in general or any specified categories of works shall not be protected unless they have been fixed in some material form.

(3) Translations, adaptations, arrangements of music and other alterations of a literary or artistic work shall be protected as original works without prejudice to the copyright in the original work.

(4) It shall be a matter for legislation in the countries of the Union to determine the protection to be granted to official texts of a legislative, administrative and legal nature, and to official translations of such texts.

(5) Collections of literary or artistic works such as encyclopaedias and anthologies which, by reason of the selection and arrangement of their contents, constitute intellectual creations shall be protected as such, without prejudice to the copyright in each of the works forming part of such collections.

(6) The works mentioned in this article shall enjoy protection in all countries of the Union. This protection shall operate for the benefit of the author and his successors in title.

(7) Subject to the provisions of Article 7(4) of this Convention, it shall be a matter for legislation in the countries of the Union to determine the extent of the application of their laws to works of applied art and industrial designs and models, as well as the conditions under which such works, designs and models shall be protected. Works protected in the country of origin solely as designs and models shall be entitled in another country of the Union only to such special protection as is granted in that country to designs and models; however, if no such special protection is granted in that country, such works shall be protected as artistic works.

(8) The protection of this Convention shall not apply to news of the day or to miscellaneous facts having the character of mere items of press information.

Article 2bis

(1) It shall be a matter for legislation in the countries of the Union to exclude, wholly or in part, from the protection provided by the preceding Article political speeches and speeches delivered in the course of legal proceedings.

(2) It shall also be a matter for legislation in the countries of the Union to determine the conditions under which lectures, addresses and other works of the same nature which are delivered in public may be reproduced by the press, broadcast, communicated to the public by wire and made the subject of public communication as envisaged in Article 11bis (1) of this Convention, when such use is justified by the informatory purpose.

(3) Nevertheless, the author shall enjoy the exclusive right of making a collection of his works mentioned in the preceding paragraphs.

Article 3

(1) The protection of this Convention shall apply to:

(a) authors who are nationals of one of the countries of the Union, for their works, whether published or not;

(b) authors who are not nationals of one of the countries of the Union, for their works first published in one of those countries, or simultaneously in a country outside the Union and in a country of the Union.

(2) Authors who are not nationals of one of the countries of the Union but who have their habitual residence in one of them shall, for the purposes of this Convention, be assimilated to nationals of that country.

(3) The expression "published works" means works published with the consent of their authors, whatever may be the means of manufacture of the copies, provided that the availability of such copies has been such as to satisfy the reasonable requirements of the public, having regard to the nature of the work. The performance of a dramatic, dramatico-musical, cinematographic or musical work, the public recitation of a literary work, the communication by wire or the broadcasting of literary or artistic works, the exhibition of a work of art and the construction of a work of architecture shall not constitute publication.

(4) A work shall be considered as having been published simultaneously in several countries if it has been published in two or more countries within thirty days of its first publication.

Article 4

The protection of this Convention shall apply, even if the conditions of Article 3 are not fulfilled, to:

(a) authors of cinematographic works the maker of which has his headquarters or habitual residence in one of the countries of the Union;

(b) authors of works of architecture erected in a country of the Union or of other artistic works incorporated in a building or other structure located in a country of the Union.

Article 5

(1) Authors shall enjoy, in respect of works for which they are protected under this Convention, in countries of the Union other than the country of origin, the rights which their respective laws do now or may hereafter grant to their nationals, as well as the rights specially granted by this Convention.

(2) The enjoyment and the exercise of these rights shall not be subject to any formality; such enjoyment and such exercise shall be independent of the existence of protection in the country of origin of the work. Consequently, apart from the provisions of this Convention, the extent of protection, as well as the means of

redress afforded to the author to protect his rights, shall be governed exclusively by the laws of the country where protection is claimed.

(3) Protection in the country of origin is governed by domestic law. However, when the author is not a national of the country of origin of the work for which he is protected under this Convention, he shall enjoy in that country the same rights as national authors.

(4) The country of origin shall be considered to be:

(a) in the case of works first published in a country of the Union, that country; in the case of works published simultaneously in several countries of the Union which grant different terms of protection, the country whose legislation grants the shortest term of protection;

(b) in the case of works published simultaneously in a country outside the Union and in a country of the Union, the latter country;

(c) in the case of unpublished works or of works first published in a country outside the Union, without simultaneous publication in a country of the Union, the country of the Union of which the author is a national, provided that:

(i) when these are cinematographic works the maker of which has his headquarters or his habitual residence in a country of the Union, the country of origin shall be that country, and

(ii) when these are works of architecture erected in a country of the Union or other artistic works incorporated in a building or other structure located in a country of the Union, the country of origin shall be that country.

Article 6

(1) Where any country outside the Union fails to protect in an adequate manner the works of authors who are nationals of one of the countries of the Union, the latter country may restrict the protection given to the works of authors who are, at the date of the first publication thereof, nationals of the other country and are not habitually resident in one of the countries of the Union. If the country of first publication avails itself of this right, the other countries of the Union shall not be required to grant to works thus subjected to special treatment a wider protection than that granted to them in the country of first publication.

(2) No restrictions introduced by virtue of the preceding paragraph shall affect the rights which an author may have acquired in respect of a work published in a country of the Union before such restrictions were put into force.

(3) The countries of the Union which restrict the grant of copyright in accordance with this Article shall give notice thereof to the Director General of the World Intellectual Property Organization (hereinafter designated as "the Director General") by a written declaration specifying the countries in regard to which protection is restricted, and the restrictions to which rights of authors who are nationals of those countries are subjected. The Director General shall immediately communicate this declaration to all the countries of the Union.

Article 6bis

(1) Independently of the author's economic rights, and even after the transfer of the said rights, the author shall have the right to claim authorship of the work and to object to any distortion, mutilation or other modification of, or other derogatory action in relation to, the said work, which would be prejudicial to his honor or reputation.

(2) The rights granted to the author in accordance with the preceding paragraph shall, after his death, be maintained, at least until the expiry of the economic rights, and shall be exercisable by the persons or institutions authorized by the legislation of the country where protection is claimed. However, those countries whose legislation, at the moment of their ratification of or accession to this Act, does not provide for the protection after the death of the author of all the rights set out in the preceding paragraph may provide that some of these rights may, after his death, cease to be maintained.

(3) The means of redress for safeguarding the rights granted by this Article shall be governed by the legislation of the country where protection is claimed.

Article 7

(1) The term of protection granted by this Convention shall be the life of the author and fifty years after his death.

(2) However, in the case of cinematographic works, the countries of the Union may provide that the term of protection shall expire fifty years after the work has been made available to the public with the consent of the author, or, failing such an event within fifty years from the making of such a work, fifty years after the making.

(3) In the case of anonymous or pseudonymous works, the term of protection granted by this Convention shall expire fifty years after the work has been lawfully made available to the public. However, when the pseudonym adopted by the author leaves no doubt as to his identity, the term of protection shall be that provided in paragraph (1). If the author of an anonymous or pseudonymous work discloses his identity during the above-mentioned period, the term of protection applicable shall be that provided in paragraph (1). The countries of the Union shall not be required to protect anonymous or pseudonymous works in respect of which it is reasonable to presume that their author has been dead for fifty years.

(4) It shall be a matter for legislation in the countries of the Union to determine the term of protection of photographic works and that of works of applied art in so far as they are protected as artistic works; however, this term shall last at least until the end of a period of twenty-five years from the making of such a work.

(5) The term of protection subsequent to the death of the author and the terms provided by paragraphs (2), (3) and (4) shall run from the date of death or of the event referred to in those paragraphs, but such terms shall always be deemed to begin on the first of January of the year following the death or such event.

(6) The countries of the Union may grant a term of protection in excess of those provided by the preceding paragraphs.

(7) Those countries of the Union bound by the Rome Act of this Convention which grant, in their national legislation in force at the time of signature of the present Act, shorter terms of protection than those provided for in the preceding paragraphs shall have the right to maintain such terms when ratifying or acceding to the present Act.

(8) In any case, the term shall be governed by the legislation of the country where protection is claimed; however, unless the legislation of that country otherwise provides, the term shall not exceed the term fixed in the country of origin of the work.

Article 7bis

The provisions of the preceding Article shall also apply in the case of a work of joint authorship, provided that the terms measured from the death of the author shall be calculated from the death of the last surviving author.

Article 8

Authors of literary and artistic works protected by this Convention shall enjoy the exclusive right of making and of authorizing the translation of their works throughout the term of protection of their rights in the original works.

Article 9

(1) Authors of literary and artistic works protected by this Convention shall have the exclusive right of authorizing the reproduction of these works, in any manner or form.

(2) It shall be a matter for legislation in the countries of the Union to permit the reproduction of such works in certain special cases, provided that such reproduction does not conflict with a normal exploitation of the work and does not unreasonably prejudice the legitimate interests of the author.

(3) Any sound or visual recording shall be considered as a reproduction for the purposes of this Convention.

Article 10

(1) It shall be permissible to make quotations from a work which has already been lawfully made available to the public, provided that their making is compatible with fair practice, and their extent does not exceed that justified by the purpose, including quotations from newspaper articles and periodicals in the form of press summaries.

(2) It shall be a matter for legislation in the countries of the Union, and for special agreements existing or to be concluded between them, to permit the utilization, to the extent justified by the purpose, of literary or artistic works by way of illustration in publications, broadcasts or sound or visual recordings for teaching, provided such utilization is compatible with fair practice.

(3) Where use is made of works in accordance with the preceding paragraphs of this Article, mention shall be made of the source, and of the name of the author if it appears thereon.

Article 10bis

(1) It shall be a matter for legislation in the countries of the Union to permit the reproduction by the press, the broadcasting or the communication to the public by wire of articles published in newspapers or periodicals on current economic, political or religious topics, and of broadcast works of the same character, in cases in which the reproduction, broadcasting or such communication thereof is not expressly reserved. Nevertheless, the source must always be clearly indicated; the legal consequences of a breach of this obligation shall be determined by the legislation of the country where protection is claimed.

(2) It shall also be a matter for legislation in the countries of the Union to determine the conditions under which, for the purpose of reporting current events by means of photography, cinematography, broadcasting or communication to the public by wire, literary or artistic works seen or heard in the course of the event may, to the extent justified by the informatory purpose, be reproduced and made available to the public.

Article 11

(1) Authors of dramatic, dramatico-musical and musical works shall enjoy the exclusive right of authorizing:

    (i) the public performance of their works, including such public performance by any means or process;

    (ii) any communication to the public of the performance of their works.

(2) Authors of dramatic or dramatico-musical works shall enjoy, during the full term of their rights in the original works, the same rights with respect to translations thereof.

Article 11bis

(1) Authors of literary and artistic works shall enjoy the exclusive right of authorizing:

    (i) the broadcasting of their works or the communication thereof to the public by any other means of wireless diffusion of signs, sounds or images;

(ii) any communication to the public by wire or by rebroadcasting of the broadcast of the work, when this communication is made by an organization other than the original one;

(iii) the public communication by loudspeaker or any other analogous instrument transmitting, by signs, sounds or images, the broadcast of the work.

(2) It shall be a matter for legislation in the countries of the Union to determine the conditions under which the rights mentioned in the preceding paragraph may be exercised, but these conditions shall apply only in the countries where they have been prescribed. They shall not in any circumstances be prejudicial to the moral rights of the author, nor to his right to obtain equitable remuneration which, in the absence of agreement, shall be fixed by competent authority.

(3) In the absence of any contrary stipulation, permission granted in accordance with paragraph (1) of this Article shall not imply permission to record, by means of instruments recording sounds or images, the work broadcast. It shall, however, be a matter for legislation in the countries of the Union to determine the regulations for ephemeral recordings made by a broadcasting organization by means of its own facilities and used for its own broadcasts. The preservation of these recordings in official archives may, on the ground of their exceptional documentary character, be authorized by such legislation.

Article 11ter

(1) Authors of literary works shall enjoy the exclusive right of authorizing:

(i) the public recitation of their works, including such public recitation by any means or process;

(ii) any communication to the public of the recitation of their works.

(2) Authors of literary works shall enjoy, during the full term of their rights in the original works, the same rights with respect to translations thereof.

Article 12

Authors of literary or artistic works shall enjoy the exclusive right of authorizing adaptations, arrangements and other alterations of their works.

Article 13

(1) Each country of the Union may impose for itself reservations and conditions on the exclusive right granted to the author of a musical work and to the author of any words, the recording of which together with the musical work has already been authorized by the latter, to authorize the sound recording of that musical work, together with such words, if any; but all such reservations and conditions shall apply only in the countries which have imposed them and shall not, in any circumstances, be prejudicial to the rights of these authors to obtain equitable remuneration which, in the absence of agreement, shall be fixed by competent authority.

(2) Recordings of musical works made in a country of the Union in accordance with Article 13(3) of the Convention signed at Rome on June 2, 1928, and at Brussels on June 26, 1948, may be reproduced in that country without the permission of the author of the musical work until a date two years after that country becomes bound by this Act.

(3) Recordings made in accordance with paragraphs (1) and (2) of this Article and imported without permission from the parties concerned into a country where they are treated as infringing recordings shall be liable to seizure.

Article 14

(1) Authors of literary or artistic works shall have the exclusive right of authorizing:

(i) the cinematographic adaptation and reproduction of these works, and the distribution of the works thus adapted or reproduced;

(ii) the public performance and communication to the public by wire of the works thus adapted or reproduced.

(2) The adaptation into any other artistic form of a cinematographic production derived from literary or artistic works shall, without prejudice to the authorization of the author of the cinematographic production, remain subject to the authorization of the authors of the original works.

(3) The provisions of Article 13(1) shall not apply.

Article 14bis

(1) Without prejudice to the copyright in any work which may have been adapted or reproduced, a cinematographic work shall be protected as an original work. The owner of copyright in a cinematographic work shall enjoy the same rights as the author of an original work, including the rights referred to in the preceding Article.

(2)(a) Ownership of copyright in a cinematographic work shall be a matter for legislation in the country where protection is claimed.

****(b) However, in the countries of the Union which, by legislation, include among the owners of copyright in a cinematographic work authors who have brought contributions to the making of the work, such authors, if they have undertaken to bring such contributions, may not, in the absence of any contrary or special stipulation, object to the reproduction, distribution, public performance, communication to the public by wire, broadcasting or any other communication to the public, or to the subtitling or dubbing of texts, of the work.

(c) The question whether or not the form of the undertaking referred to above should, for the application of the preceding subparagraph (b), be in a written agreement or a written act of the same effect shall be a matter for the legislation of the country where the maker of the cinematographic work has his headquarters or habitual residence. However, it shall be a matter for the legislation of the country of the Union where protection is claimed to provide that the said undertaking shall be in a written agreement or a written act of the same effect. The countries whose legislation so provides shall notify the Director General by means of a written declaration, which will be immediately communicated by him to all the other countries of the Union.

(d) By "contrary or special stipulation" is meant any restrictive condition which is relevant to the aforesaid undertaking.

(3) Unless the national legislation provides to the contrary, the provisions of paragraph (2)(b) above shall not be applicable to authors of scenarios, dialogues and musical works created for the making of the cinematographic work, nor to the principal director thereof. However, those countries of the Union whose legislation does not contain rules providing for the application of the said paragraph (2)(b) to such director shall notify the Director General by means of a written declaration, which will be immediately communicated by him to all the other countries of the Union.

Article 14ter

(1) The author, or after his death the persons or institutions authorized by national legislation, shall, with respect to original works of art and original manuscripts of writers and composers, enjoy the inalienable right to an interest in any sale of the work subsequent to the first transfer by the author of the work.

(2) The protection provided by the preceding paragraph may be claimed in a country of the Union only if legislation in the country to which the author belongs so permits, and to the extent permitted by the country where this protection is claimed.

(3) The procedure for collection and the amounts shall be matters for determination by national legislation.

Article 15

(1) In order that the author of a literary or artistic work protected by this Convention shall, in the absence of proof to the contrary, be regarded as such, and consequently be entitled to institute infringement proceedings in the countries of the Union, it shall be sufficient for his name to appear on the work in the usual manner. This paragraph shall be applicable even if this name is a pseudonym, where the pseudonym adopted by the author leaves no doubt as to his identity.

(2) The person or body corporate whose name appears on a cinematographic work in the usual manner shall, in the absence of proof to the contrary, be presumed to be the maker of the said work.

(3) In the case of anonymous and pseudonymous works, other than those referred to in paragraph (1) above, the publisher whose name appears on the work shall, in the absence of proof to the contrary, be deemed to represent the author, and in this capacity shall be entitled to protect and enforce the author's rights. The

provisions of this paragraph shall cease to apply when the author reveals his identity and establishes his claim to authorship of the work.

(4)(a) In the case of unpublished works where the identity of the author is unknown, but where there is every ground to presume that he is a national of a country of the Union, it shall be a matter for legislation in that country to designate the competent authority which shall represent the author and shall be entitled to protect and enforce his rights in the countries of the Union.

(b) Countries of the Union which make such designation under the terms of this provision shall notify the Director General by means of a written declaration giving full information concerning the authority thus designated. The Director General shall at once communicate this declaration to all other countries of the Union.

Article 16

(1) Infringing copies of a work shall be liable to seizure in any country of the Union where the work enjoys legal protection.

(2) The provisions of the preceding paragraph shall also apply to reproductions coming from a country where the work is not protected, or has ceased to be protected.

(3) The seizure shall take place in accordance with the legislation of each country.

Article 17

The provisions of this Convention cannot in any way affect the right of the Government of each country of the Union to permit, to control, or to prohibit by legislation or regulation, the circulation, presentation, or exhibition of any work or production in regard to which the competent authority may find it necessary to exercise that right.

Article 18

(1) This Convention shall apply to all works which, at the moment of its coming into force, have not yet fallen into the public domain in the country of origin through the expiry of the term of protection.

(2) If, however, through the expiry of the term of protection which was previously granted, a work has fallen into the public domain of the country where protection is claimed, that work shall not be protected anew.

(3) The application of this principle shall be subject to any provisions contained in special conventions to that effect existing or to be concluded between countries of the Union. In the absence of such provisions, the respective countries shall determine, each in so far as it is concerned, the conditions of application of this principle.

(4) The preceding provisions shall also apply in the case of new accessions to the Union and to cases in which protection is extended by the application of Article 7 or by the abandonment of reservations.

Article 19

The provisions of this Convention shall not preclude the making of a claim to the benefit of any greater protection which may be granted by legislation in a country of the Union.

Article 20

The Governments of the countries of the Union reserve the right to enter into special agreements among themselves, in so far as such agreements grant to authors more extensive rights than those granted by the Convention, or contain other provisions not contrary to this Convention. The provisions of existing agreements which satisfy these conditions shall remain applicable.

Article 21

(1) Special provisions regarding developing countries are included in the Appendix.

(2) Subject to the provisions of Article 28(1)(b), the Appendix forms an integral part of this Act.

Article 22

(1)(a) The Union shall have an Assembly consisting of those countries of the Union which are bound by Articles 22 to 26.

(b) The Government of each country shall be represented by one delegate, who may be assisted by alternate delegates, advisors, and experts.

(c) The expenses of each delegation shall be borne by the Government which has appointed it.

(2)(a) The Assembly shall:

(i) deal with all matters concerning the maintenance and development of the Union and the implementation of this Convention;

(ii) give directions concerning the preparation for conferences of revision to the International Bureau of Intellectual Property (hereinafter designated as "the International Bureau") referred to in the Convention Establishing the World Intellectual Property Organization (hereinafter designated as "the Organization"), due account being taken of any comments made by those countries of the Union which are not bound by Articles 22 to 26;

(iii) review and approve the reports and activities of the Director General of the Organization concerning the Union, and give him all necessary instructions concerning matters within the competence of the Union;

(iv) elect the members of the Executive Committee of the Assembly;

(v) review and approve the reports and activities of its Executive Committee, and give instructions to such Committee;

(vi) determine the program and adopt the biennial budget of the Union, and approve its final accounts;

(vii) adopt the financial regulations of the Union;

(viii) establish such committees of experts and working groups as may be necessary for the work of the Union;

(ix) determine which countries not members of the Union and which intergovernmental and international non-governmental organizations shall be admitted to its meetings as observers;

(x) adopt amendments to Articles 22 to 26;

(xi) take any other appropriate action designed to further the objectives of the Union;

(xii) exercise such other functions as are appropriate under this Convention;

(xiii) subject to its acceptance, exercise such rights as are given to it in the Convention establishing the Organization.

(b) With respect to matters which are of interest also to other Unions administered by the Organization, the Assembly shall make its decisions after having heard the advice of the Coordination Committee of the Organization.

(3)(a) Each country member of the Assembly shall have one vote.

(b) One-half of the countries members of the Assembly shall constitute a quorum.

(c) Notwithstanding the provisions of subparagraph (b), if, in any session, the number of countries represented is less than one-half but equal to or more than one-third of the countries members of the Assembly, the Assembly may make decisions but, with the exception of decisions concerning its own procedure, all such decisions shall take effect only if the following conditions are fulfilled. The International Bureau shall communicate the said decisions to the countries members of the Assembly which were not represented and shall invite them to express in writing their vote or abstention within a period of three months from the date of the communication. If, at the expiration of this period, the number of countries having thus expressed their vote or abstention attains the number of countries which was lacking for attaining the quorum in the session itself, such decisions shall take effect provided that at the same time the required majority still obtains.

(d) Subject to the provisions of Article 26(2), the decisions of the Assembly shall require two-thirds of the votes cast.

(e) Abstentions shall not be considered as votes.

(f) A delegate may represent, and vote in the name of, one country only.

(g) Countries of the Union not members of the Assembly shall be admitted to its meetings as observers.

(4)(a) The Assembly shall meet once in every second calendar year in ordinary session upon convocation by the Director General and, in the absence of exceptional circumstances, during the same period and at the same place as the General Assembly of the Organization.

(b) The Assembly shall meet in extraordinary session upon convocation by the Director General, at the request of the Executive Committee or at the request of one-fourth of the countries members of the Assembly.

(5) The Assembly shall adopt its own rules of procedure.

Article 23

(1) The Assembly shall have an Executive Committee.

(2)(a) The Executive Committee shall consist of countries elected by the Assembly from among countries members of the Assembly. Furthermore, the country on whose territory the Organization has its headquarters shall, subject to the provisions of Article 25(7)(b), have an ex officio seat on the Committee.

(b) The Government of each country member of the Executive Committee shall be represented by one delegate, who may be assisted by alternate delegates, advisors, and experts.

(c) The expenses of each delegation shall be borne by the Government which has appointed it.

(3) The number of countries members of the Executive Committee shall correspond to one-fourth of the number of countries members of the Assembly. In establishing the number of seats to be filled, remainders after division by four shall be disregarded.

(4) In electing the members of the Executive Committee, the Assembly shall have due regard to an equitable geographical distribution and to the need for countries party to the Special Agreements which might be established in relation with the Union to be among the countries constituting the Executive Committee.

(5)(a) Each member of the Executive Committee shall serve from the close of the session of the Assembly which elected it to the close of the next ordinary session of the Assembly.

(b) Members of the Executive Committee may be re-elected, but not more than two-thirds of them.

(c) The Assembly shall establish the details of the rules governing the election and possible re-election of the members of the Executive Committee.

(6)(a) The Executive Committee shall:

(i) prepare the draft agenda of the Assembly;

(ii) submit proposals to the Assembly respecting the draft program and biennial budget of the Union prepared by the Director General;

(iii) [*deleted*]

(iv) submit, with appropriate comments, to the Assembly the periodical reports of the Director General and the yearly audit reports on the accounts;

(v) in accordance with the decisions of the Assembly and having regard to circumstances arising between two ordinary sessions of the Assembly, take all necessary measures to ensure the execution of the program of the Union by the Director General;

(vi) perform such other functions as are allocated to it under this Convention.

(b) With respect to matters which are of interest also to other Unions administered by the Organization, the Executive Committee shall make its decisions after having heard the advice of the Coordination Committee of the Organization.

(7)(a) The Executive Committee shall meet once a year in ordinary session upon convocation by the Director General, preferably during the same period and at the same place as the Coordination Committee of the Organization.

(b) The Executive Committee shall meet in extraordinary session upon convocation by the Director General, either on his own initiative, or at the request of its Chairman or one-fourth of its members.

(8)(a) Each country member of the Executive Committee shall have one vote.

(b) One-half of the members of the Executive Committee shall constitute a quorum.

(c) Decisions shall be made by a simple majority of the votes cast.

(d) Abstentions shall not be considered as votes.

(e) A delegate may represent, and vote in the name of, one country only.

(9) Countries of the Union not members of the Executive Committee shall be admitted to its meetings as observers.

(10) The Executive Committee shall adopt its own rules of procedure.

Article 24

(1)(a) The administrative tasks with respect to the Union shall be performed by the International Bureau, which is a continuation of the Bureau of the Union united with the Bureau of the Union established by the International Convention for the Protection of Industrial Property.

(b) In particular, the International Bureau shall provide the secretariat of the various organs of the Union.

(c) The Director General of the Organization shall be the chief executive of the Union and shall represent the Union.

(2) The International Bureau shall assemble and publish information concerning the protection of copyright. Each country of the Union shall promptly communicate to the International Bureau all new laws and official texts concerning the protection of copyright.

(3) The International Bureau shall publish a monthly periodical.

(4) The International Bureau shall, on request, furnish information to any country of the Union on matters concerning the protection of copyright.

(5) The International Bureau shall conduct studies, and shall provide services, designed to facilitate the protection of copyright.

(6) The Director General and any staff member designated by him shall participate, without the right to vote, in all meetings of the Assembly, the Executive

Committee and any other committee of experts or working group. The Director General, or a staff member designated by him, shall be ex officio secretary of these bodies.

(7)(a) The International Bureau shall, in accordance with the directions of the Assembly and in cooperation with the Executive Committee, make the preparations for the conferences of revision of the provisions of the Convention other than Articles 22 to 26.

(b) The International Bureau may consult with intergovernmental and international non-governmental organizations concerning preparations for conferences of revision.

(c) The Director General and persons designated by him shall take part, without the right to vote, in the discussions at these conferences.

(8) The International Bureau shall carry out any other tasks assigned to it.

Article 25

(1)(a) The Union shall have a budget.

(b) The budget of the Union shall include the income and expenses proper to the Union, its contribution to the budget of expenses common to the Unions, and, where applicable, the sum made available to the budget of the Conference of the Organization.

(c) Expenses not attributable exclusively to the Union but also to one or more other Unions administered by the Organization shall be considered as expenses common to the Unions. The share of the Union in such common expenses shall be in proportion to the interest the Union has in them.

(2) The budget of the Union shall be established with due regard to the requirements of coordination with the budgets of the other Unions administered by the Organization.

(3) The budget of the Union shall be financed from the following sources: (i) contributions of the countries of the Union; (ii) fees and charges due for services performed by the International Bureau in relation to the Union; (iii) sale of, or royalties on, the publications of the International Bureau concerning the Union; (iv) gifts, bequests, and subventions; (v) rents, interests, and other miscellaneous income.

(4)(a) For the purpose of establishing its contribution towards the budget, each country of the Union shall belong to a class, and shall pay its annual contributions on the basis of a number of units fixed as follows:

Class I 25
Class II 20
Class III 15
Class IV 10
Class V 5
Class VI 3
Class VII 1

(b) Unless it has already done so, each country shall indicate, concurrently with depositing its instrument of ratification or accession, the class to which it wishes to belong. Any country may change class. If it chooses a lower class, the country must announce it to the Assembly at one of its ordinary sessions. Any such change shall take effect at the beginning of the calendar year following the session.

(c) The annual contribution of each country shall be an amount in the same proportion to the total sum to be contributed to the annual budget of the Union by all countries as the number of its units is to the total of the units of all contributing countries.

(d) Contributions shall become due on the first of January of each year.

(e) A country which is in arrears in the payment of its contributions shall have no vote in any of the organs of the Union of which it is a member if the amount of its arrears equals or exceeds the amount of the contributions due from it for the preceding two full years. However, any organ of the Union may allow such a country to continue to exercise its vote in that organ if, and as long as, it is satisfied that the delay in payment is due to exceptional and unavoidable circumstances.

(f) If the budget is not adopted before the beginning of a new financial period, it shall be at the same level as the budget of the previous year, in accordance with the financial regulations.

(5) The amount of the fees and charges due for services rendered by the International Bureau in relation to the Union shall be established, and shall be reported to the Assembly and the Executive Committee, by the Director General.

(6)(a) The Union shall have a working capital fund which shall be constituted by a single payment made by each country of the Union. If the fund becomes insufficient, an increase shall be decided by the Assembly.

(b) The amount of the initial payment of each country to the said fund or of its participation in the increase thereof shall be a proportion of the contribution of that country for the year in which the fund is established or the increase decided.

(c) The proportion and the terms of payment shall be fixed by the Assembly on the proposal of the Director General and after it has heard the advice of the Coordination Committee of the Organization.

(7)(a) In the headquarters agreement concluded with the country on the territory of which the Organization has its headquarters, it shall be provided that, whenever the working capital fund is insufficient, such country shall grant advances. The amount of these advances and the conditions on which they are granted shall be the subject of separate agreements, in each case, between such country and the Organization. As long as it remains under the obligation to grant advances, such country shall have an ex officio seat on the Executive Committee.

(b) The country referred to in subparagraph (a) and the Organization shall each have the right to denounce the obligation to grant advances, by written notification. Denunciation shall take effect three years after the end of the year in which it has been notified.

(8) The auditing of the accounts shall be effected by one or more of the countries of the Union or by external auditors, as provided in the financial regulations. They shall be designated, with their agreement, by the Assembly.

Article 26

(1) Proposals for the amendment of Articles 22, 23, 24, 25, and the present Article, may be initiated by any country member of the Assembly, by the Executive Committee, or by the Director General. Such proposals shall be communicated by the Director General to the member countries of the Assembly at least six months in advance of their consideration by the Assembly.

(2) Amendments to the Articles referred to in paragraph (1) shall be adopted by the Assembly. Adoption shall require three-fourths of the votes cast, provided that any amendment of Article 22, and of the present paragraph, shall require four-fifths of the votes cast.

(3) Any amendment to the Articles referred to in paragraph (1) shall enter into force one month after written notifications of acceptance, effected in accordance with their respective constitutional processes, have been received by the Director General from three-fourths of the countries members of the Assembly at the time it adopted the amendment. Any amendment to the said Articles thus accepted shall bind all the countries which are members of the Assembly at the time the amendment enters into force, or which become members thereof at a subsequent date, provided that any amendment increasing the financial obligations of countries of the Union shall bind only those countries which have notified their acceptance of such amendment.

Article 27

(1) This Convention shall be submitted to revision with a view to the introduction of amendments designed to improve the system of the Union.

(2) For this purpose, conferences shall be held successively in one of the countries of the Union among the delegates of the said countries.

(3) Subject to the provisions of Article 26 which apply to the amendment of Articles 22 to 26, any revision of this Act, including the Appendix, shall require the unanimity of the votes cast.

Article 28

(1)(a) Any country of the Union which has signed this Act may ratify it, and, if it has not signed it, may accede to it. Instruments of ratification or accession shall be deposited with the Director General.

(b) Any country of the Union may declare in its instrument of ratification or accession that its ratification or accession shall not apply to Articles 1 to 21 and the Appendix, provided that, if such country has previously made a declaration under Article VI(1) of the Appendix, then it may declare in the said instrument only that its ratification or accession shall not apply to Articles 1 to 20.

(c) Any country of the Union which, in accordance with subparagraph (b), has excluded provisions therein referred to from the effects of its ratification or accession may at any later time declare that it extends the effects of its ratification or accession to those provisions. Such declaration shall be deposited with the Director General.

(2)(a) Articles 1 to 21 and the Appendix shall enter into force three months after both of the following two conditions are fulfilled:

(i) at least five countries of the Union have ratified or acceded to this Act without making a declaration under paragraph (1)(b),

(ii) France, Spain, the United Kingdom of Great Britain and Northern Ireland, and the United States of America, have become bound by the Universal Copyright Convention as revised at Paris on July 24, 1971.

(b) The entry into force referred to in subparagraph (a) shall apply to those countries of the Union which, at least three months before the said entry into force, have deposited instruments of ratification or accession not containing a declaration under paragraph (1)(b).

(c) With respect to any country of the Union not covered by subparagraph (b) and which ratifies or accedes to this Act without making a declaration under paragraph (1)(b), Articles 1 to 21 and the Appendix shall enter into force three months after the date on which the Director General has notified the deposit of the relevant instrument of ratification or accession, unless a subsequent date has been indicated in the instrument deposited. In the latter case, Articles 1 to 21 and the Appendix shall enter into force with respect to that country on the date thus indicated.

(d) The provisions of subparagraphs (a) to (c) do not affect the application of Article VI of the Appendix.

(3) With respect to any country of the Union which ratifies or accedes to this Act with or without a declaration made under paragraph (1)(b), Articles 22 to 38 shall enter into force three months after the date on which the Director General has notified the deposit of the relevant instrument of ratification or accession, unless a subsequent date has been indicated in the instrument deposited. In the latter case, Articles 22 to 38 shall enter into force with respect to that country on the date thus indicated.

Article 29

(1) Any country outside the Union may accede to this Act and thereby become party to this Convention and a member of the Union. Instruments of accession shall be deposited with the Director General.

(2)(a) Subject to subparagraph (b), this Convention shall enter into force with respect to any country outside the Union three months after the date on which the Director General has notified the deposit of its instrument of accession, unless a subsequent date has been indicated in the instrument deposited. In the latter case, this Convention shall enter into force with respect to that country on the date thus indicated.

(b) If the entry into force according to subparagraph (a) precedes the entry into force of Articles 1 to 21 and the Appendix according to Article 28(2)(a), the said country shall, in the meantime, be bound, instead of by Articles 1 to 21 and the Appendix, by Articles 1 to 20 of the Brussels Act of this Convention.

Article 29bis

Ratification of or accession to this Act by any country not bound by Articles 22 to 38 of the Stockholm Act of this Convention shall, for the sole purposes of Article 14(2) of the Convention establishing the Organization, amount to ratification of or accession to the said Stockholm Act with the limitation set forth in Article 28(1)(b)(i) thereof.

Article 30

(1) Subject to the exceptions permitted by paragraph (2) of this article, by Article 28(1)(b), by Article 33(2), and by the Appendix, ratification or accession shall automatically entail acceptance of all the provisions and admission to all the advantages of this Convention.

(2)(a) Any country of the Union ratifying or acceding to this Act may, subject to Article V(2) of the Appendix, retain the benefit of the reservations it has previously formulated on condition that it makes a declaration to that effect at the time of the deposit of its instrument of ratification or accession.

(b) Any country outside the Union may declare, in acceding to this Convention and subject to Article V(2) of the Appendix, that it intends to substitute, temporarily at least, for Article 8 of this Act concerning the right of translation, the provisions of Article 5 of the Union Convention of 1886, as completed at Paris in 1896, on the clear understanding that the said provisions are applicable only to translations into a language in general use in the said country. Subject to Article I(6)(b) of the Appendix, any country has the right to apply, in relation to the right of translation of works whose country of origin is a country availing itself of such a reservation, a protection which is equivalent to the protection granted by the latter country.

(c) Any country may withdraw such reservations at any time by notification addressed to the Director General.

Article 31

(1) Any country may declare in its instrument of ratification or accession, or may inform the Director General by written notification at any time thereafter, that this Convention shall be applicable to all or part of those territories, designated in the declaration or notification, for the external relations of which it is responsible.

(2) Any country which has made such a declaration or given such a notification may, at any time, notify the Director General that this Convention shall cease to be applicable to all or part of such territories.

(3)(a) Any declaration made under paragraph (1) shall take effect on the same date as the ratification or accession in which it was included, and any notification given under that paragraph shall take effect three months after its notification by the Director General.

(b) Any notification given under paragraph (2) shall take effect twelve months after its receipt by the Director General.

(4) This article shall in no way be understood as implying the recognition or tacit acceptance by a country of the Union of the factual situation concerning a territory to which this Convention is made applicable by another country of the Union by virtue of a declaration under paragraph (1).

Article 32

(1) This Act shall, as regards relations between the countries of the Union, and to the extent that it applies, replace the Berne Convention of September 9, 1886, and the subsequent Acts of revision. The Acts previously in force shall continue to be applicable, in their entirety or to the extent that this Act does not replace them by virtue of the preceding sentence, in relations with countries of the Union which do not ratify or accede to this Act.

(2) Countries outside the Union which become party to this Act shall, subject to paragraph (3), apply it with respect to any country of the Union not bound by this Act or which, although bound by this Act, has made a declaration pursuant to Article 28(1)(b). Such countries recognize that the said country of the Union, in its relations with them:

(i) may apply the provisions of the most recent Act by which it is bound, and

(ii) subject to Article I(6) of the Appendix, has the right to adapt the protection to the level provided for by this Act.

(3) Any country which has availed itself of any of the faculties provided for in the Appendix may apply the provisions of the Appendix relating to the faculty or faculties of which it has availed itself in its relations with any other country of the Union which is not bound by this Act, provided that the latter country has accepted the application of the said provisions.

Article 33

(1) Any dispute between two or more countries of the Union concerning the interpretation or application of this Convention, not settled by negotiation, may, by any one of the countries concerned, be brought before the International Court of Justice by application in conformity with the Statute of the Court, unless the countries concerned agree on some other method of settlement. The country bringing the dispute before the Court shall inform the International Bureau; the International Bureau shall bring the matter to the attention of the other countries of the Union.

(2) Each country may, at the time it signs this Act or deposits its instrument of ratification or accession, declare that it does not consider itself bound by the

provisions of paragraph (1). With regard to any dispute between such country and any other country of the Union, the provisions of paragraph (1) shall not apply.

(3) Any country having made a declaration in accordance with the provisions of paragraph (2) may, at any time, withdraw its declaration by notification addressed to the Director General.

Article 34

(1) Subject to Article 29bis, no country may ratify or accede to earlier Acts of this Convention once Articles 1 to 21 and the Appendix have entered into force.

(2) Once Articles 1 to 21 and the Appendix have entered into force, no country may make a declaration under Article 5 of the Protocol Regarding Developing Countries attached to the Stockholm Act.

Article 35

(1) This Convention shall remain in force without limitation as to time.

(2) Any country may denounce this Act by notification addressed to the Director General. Such denunciation shall constitute also denunciation of all earlier Acts and shall affect only the country making it, the Convention remaining in full force and effect as regards the other countries of the Union.

(3) Denunciation shall take effect one year after the day on which the Director General has received the notification.

(4) The right of denunciation provided by this article shall not be exercised by any country before the expiration of five years from the date upon which it becomes a member of the Union.

Article 36

(1) Any country party to this Convention undertakes to adopt, in accordance with its constitution, the measures necessary to ensure the application of this Convention.

(2) It is understood that, at the time a country becomes bound by this Convention, it will be in a position under its domestic law to give effect to the provisions of this Convention.

Article 37

(1)(a) This Act shall be signed in a single copy in the French and English languages and, subject to paragraph (2), shall be deposited with the Director General.

(b) Official texts shall be established by the Director General, after consultation with the interested Governments, in the Arabic, German, Italian,

Portuguese and Spanish languages, and such other languages as the Assembly may designate.

(c) In case of differences of opinion on the interpretation of the various texts, the French text shall prevail.

(2) This Act shall remain open for signature until January 31, 1972. Until that date, the copy referred to in paragraph (1)(a) shall be deposited with the Government of the French Republic.

(3) The Director General shall certify and transmit two copies of the signed text of this Act to the Governments of all countries of the Union and, on request, to the Government of any other country.

(4) The Director General shall register this Act with the Secretariat of the United Nations.

(5) The Director General shall notify the Governments of all countries of the Union of signatures, deposits of instruments of ratification or accession and any declarations included in such instruments or made pursuant to Articles 28(1)(c), 30(2)(a) and (b), and 33(2), entry into force of any provisions of this Act, notifications of denunciation, and notifications pursuant to Articles 30(2)(c), 31(1) and (2), 33(3), and 38(1), as well as the Appendix.

Article 38

(1) Countries of the Union which have not ratified or acceded to this Act and which are not bound by Articles 22 to 26 of the Stockholm Act of this Convention may, until April 26, 1975, exercise, if they so desire, the rights provided under the said Articles as if they were bound by them. Any country desiring to exercise such rights shall give written notification to this effect to the Director General; this notification shall be effective on the date of its receipt. Such countries shall be deemed to be members of the Assembly until the said date.

(2) As long as all the countries of the Union have not become Members of the Organization, the International Bureau of the Organization shall also function as the Bureau of the Union, and the Director General as the Director of the said Bureau.

(3) Once all the countries of the Union have become Members of the Organization, the rights, obligations, and property, of the Bureau of the Union shall devolve on the International Bureau of the Organization.

APPENDIX

SPECIAL PROVISIONS REGARDING DEVELOPING COUNTRIES

Article I

(1) Any country regarded as a developing country in conformity with the established practice of the General Assembly of the United Nations which ratifies

or accedes to this Act, of which this Appendix forms an integral part, and which, having regard to its economic situation and its social or cultural needs, does not consider itself immediately in a position to make provision for the protection of all the rights as provided for in this Act, may, by a notification deposited with the Director General at the time of depositing its instrument of ratification or accession or, subject to Article V(1)(c), at any time thereafter, declare that it will avail itself of the faculty provided for in Article II, or of the faculty provided for in Article III, or of both of those faculties. It may, instead of availing itself of the faculty provided for in Article II, make a declaration according to Article V(1)(a).

(2)(a) Any declaration under paragraph (1) notified before the expiration of the period of ten years from the entry into force of Articles 1 to 21 and this Appendix according to Article 28(2) shall be effective until the expiration of the said period. Any such declaration may be renewed in whole or in part for periods of ten years each by a notification deposited with the Director General not more than fifteen months and not less than three months before the expiration of the ten-year period then running.

(b) Any declaration under paragraph (1) notified after the expiration of the period of ten years from the entry into force of Articles 1 to 21 and this Appendix according to Article 28(2) shall be effective until the expiration of the ten-year period then running. Any such declaration may be renewed as provided for in the second sentence of subparagraph (a).

(3) Any country of the Union which has ceased to be regarded as a developing country as referred to in paragraph (1) shall no longer be entitled to renew its declaration as provided in paragraph (2), and, whether or not it formally withdraws its declaration, such country shall be precluded from availing itself of the faculties referred to in paragraph (1) from the expiration of the ten-year period then running or from the expiration of a period of three years after it has ceased to be regarded as a developing country, whichever period expires later.

(4) Where, at the time when the declaration made under paragraph (1) or (2) ceases to be effective, there are copies in stock which were made under a license granted by virtue of this Appendix, such copies may continue to be distributed until their stock is exhausted.

(5) Any country which is bound by the provisions of this Act and which has deposited a declaration or a notification in accordance with Article 31(1) with respect to the application of this Act to a particular territory, the situation of which can be regarded as analogous to that of the countries referred to in paragraph (1), may, in respect of such territory, make the declaration referred to in paragraph (1) and the notification of renewal referred to in paragraph (2). As long as such declaration or notification remains in effect, the provisions of this Appendix shall be applicable to the territory in respect of which it was made.

(6)(a) The fact that a country avails itself of any of the faculties referred to in paragraph (1) does not permit another country to give less protection to works of which the country of origin is the former country than it is obliged to grant under Articles 1 to 20.

(b) The right to apply reciprocal treatment provided for in Article 30(2)(b), second sentence, shall not, until the date on which the period applicable under

Article I(3) expires, be exercised in respect of works the country of origin of which is a country which has made a declaration according to Article V(1)(a).

Article II

(1) Any country which has declared that it will avail itself of the faculty provided for in this Article shall be entitled, so far as works published in printed or analogous forms of reproduction are concerned, to substitute for the exclusive right of translation provided for in Article 8 a system of non-exclusive and non-transferable licenses, granted by the competent authority under the following conditions and subject to Article IV.

(2)(a) Subject to paragraph (3), if, after the expiration of a period of three years, or of any longer period determined by the national legislation of the said country, commencing on the date of the first publication of the work, a translation of such work has not been published in a language in general use in that country by the owner of the right of translation, or with his authorization, any national of such country may obtain a license to make a translation of the work in the said language and publish the translation in printed or analogous forms of reproduction.

(b) A license under the conditions provided for in this Article may also be granted if all the editions of the translation published in the language concerned are out of print.

(3)(a) In the case of translations into a language which is not in general use in one or more developed countries which are members of the Union, a period of one year shall be substituted for the period of three years referred to in paragraph (2)(a).

(b) Any country referred to in paragraph (1) may, with the unanimous agreement of the developed countries which are members of the Union and in which the same language is in general use, substitute, in the case of translations into that language, for the period of three years referred to in paragraph (2)(a) a shorter period as determined by such agreement but not less than one year. However, the provisions of the foregoing sentence shall not apply where the language in question is English, French or Spanish. The Director General shall be notified of any such agreement by the Governments which have concluded it.

(4)(a) No license obtainable after three years shall be granted under this Article until a further period of six months has elapsed, and no license obtainable after one year shall be granted under this Article until a further period of nine months has elapsed

(i) from the date on which the applicant complies with the requirements mentioned in Article IV(1), or

(ii) where the identity or the address of the owner of the right of translation is unknown, from the date on which the applicant sends, as provided for in Article IV(2), copies of his application submitted to the authority competent to grant the license.

(b) If, during the said period of six or nine months, a translation in the language in respect of which the application was made is published by the owner of the right of translation or with his authorization, no license under this Article shall be granted.

(5) Any license under this Article shall be granted only for the purpose of teaching, scholarship or research.

(6) If a translation of a work is published by the owner of the right of translation or with his authorization at a price reasonably related to that normally charged in the country for comparable works, any license granted under this Article shall terminate if such translation is in the same language and with substantially the same content as the translation published under the licence. Any copies already made before the license terminated may continue to be distributed until their stock is exhausted.

(7) For works which are composed mainly of illustrations, a license to make and publish a translation of the text and to reproduce and publish the illustrations may be granted only if the conditions of Article III are also fulfilled.

(8) No licence shall be granted under this Article when the author has withdrawn from circulation all copies of his work.

(9)(a) A license to make a translation of a work which has been published in printed or analogous forms of reproduction may also be granted to any broadcasting organization having its headquarters in a country referred to in paragraph (1), upon an application made to the competent authority of that country by the said organization, provided that all of the following conditions are met:

(i) the translation is made from a copy made and acquired in accordance with the laws of the said country;

(ii) the translation is only for use in broadcasts intended exclusively for teaching or for the dissemination of the results of specialized technical or scientific research to experts in a particular profession;

(iii) the translation is used exclusively for the purposes referred to in condition (ii) through broadcasts made lawfully and intended for recipients on the territory of the said country, including broadcasts made through the medium of sound or visual recordings lawfully and exclusively made for the purpose of such broadcasts;

(iv) all uses made of the translation are without any commercial purpose.

(b) Sound or visual recordings of a translation which was made by a broadcasting organization under a license granted by virtue of this paragraph may, for the purposes and subject to the conditions referred to in subparagraph (a) and with the agreement of that organization, also be used by any other broadcasting organization having its headquarters in the country whose competent authority granted the license in question.

(c) Provided that all of the criteria and conditions set out in subparagraph (a) are met, a license may also be granted to a broadcasting organization to translate any text incorporated in an audio-visual fixation where such fixation was itself prepared and published for the sole purpose of being used in connection with systematic instructional activities.

(d) Subject to subparagraphs (a) to (c), the provisions of the preceding paragraphs shall apply to the grant and exercise of any license granted under this paragraph.

Article III

(1) Any country which has declared that it will avail itself of the faculty provided for in this Article shall be entitled to substitute for the exclusive right of reproduction provided for in Article 9 a system of non-exclusive and non-transferable licenses, granted by the competent authority under the following conditions and subject to Article IV.

(2)(a) If, in relation to a work to which this article applies by virtue of paragraph (7), after the expiration of

(i) the relevant period specified in paragraph (3), commencing on the date of first publication of a particular edition of the work, or

(ii) any longer period determined by national legislation of the country referred to in paragraph (1), commencing on the same date, copies of such edition have not been distributed in that country to the general public or in connection with systematic instructional activities, by the owner of the right of reproduction or with his authorization, at a price reasonably related to that normally charged in the country for comparable works, any national of such country may obtain a license to reproduce and publish such edition at that or a lower price for use in connection with systematic instructional activities.

(b) A license to reproduce and publish an edition which has been distributed as described in subparagraph (a) may also be granted under the conditions provided for in this Article if, after the expiration of the applicable period, no authorized copies of that edition have been on sale for a period of six months in the country concerned to the general public or in connection with systematic instructional activities at a price reasonably related to that normally charged in the country for comparable works.

(3) The period referred to in paragraph (2)(a)(i) shall be five years, except that

(i) for works of the natural and physical sciences, including mathematics, and of technology, the period shall be three years;

(ii) for works of fiction, poetry, drama and music, and for art books, the period shall be seven years.

(4)(a) No license obtainable after three years shall be granted under this article until a period of six months has elapsed

(i) from the date on which the applicant complies with the requirements mentioned in Article IV(1), or

(ii) where the identity or the address of the owner of the right of reproduction is unknown, from the date on which the applicant sends, as provided for in Article IV(2), copies of his application submitted to the authority competent to grant the license.

(b) Where licenses are obtainable after other periods and Article IV(2) is applicable, no license shall be granted until a period of three months has elapsed from the date of the dispatch of the copies of the application.

(c) If, during the period of six or three months referred to in subparagraphs (a) and (b), a distribution as described in paragraph (2)(a) has taken place, no license shall be granted under this article.

(d) No license shall be granted if the author has withdrawn from circulation all copies of the edition for the reproduction and publication of which the license has been applied for.

(5) A license to reproduce and publish a translation of a work shall not be granted under this Article in the following cases:

(i) where the translation was not published by the owner of the right of translation or with his authorization, or

(ii) where the translation is not in a language in general use in the country in which the license is applied for.

(6) If copies of an edition of a work are distributed in the country referred to in paragraph (1) to the general public or in connection with systematic instructional activities, by the owner of the right of reproduction or with his authorization, at a price reasonably related to that normally charged in the country for comparable works, any license granted under this article shall terminate if such edition is in the same language and with substantially the same content as the edition which was published under the said license. Any copies already made before the license terminates may continue to be distributed until their stock is exhausted.

(7)(a) Subject to subparagraph (b), the works to which this Article applies shall be limited to works published in printed or analogous forms of reproduction.

(b) This Article shall also apply to the reproduction in audio-visual form of lawfully made audio-visual fixations including any protected works incorporated therein and to the translation of any incorporated text into a language in general use in the country in which the license is applied for, always provided that the audio-visual fixations in question were prepared and published for the sole purpose of being used in connection with systematic instructional activities.

Article IV

(1) A license under Article II or Article III may be granted only if the applicant, in accordance with the procedure of the country concerned, establishes either that he has requested, and has been denied, authorization by the owner of the right to make and publish the translation or to reproduce and publish the edition, as the case may be, or that, after due diligence on his part, he was unable to find the owner of the right. At the same time as making the request, the applicant shall inform any national or international information center referred to in paragraph (2).

(2) If the owner of the right cannot be found, the applicant for a license shall send, by registered airmail, copies of his application, submitted to the authority competent to grant the license, to the publisher whose name appears on the work and to any national or international information center which may have been designated, in a notification to that effect deposited with the Director General, by the Government of the country in which the publisher is believed to have his principal place of business.

(3) The name of the author shall be indicated on all copies of the translation or reproduction published under a license granted under Article II or Article III. The title of the work shall appear on all such copies. In the case of a translation, the original title of the work shall appear in any case on all the said copies.

(4)(a) No license granted under Article II or Article III shall extend to the export of copies, and any such license shall be valid only for publication of the translation or of the reproduction, as the case may be, in the territory of the country in which it has been applied for.

(b) For the purposes of subparagraph (a), the notion of export shall include the sending of copies from any territory to the country which, in respect of that territory, has made a declaration under Article I(5).

(c) Where a governmental or other public entity of a country which has granted a license to make a translation under Article II into a language other than English, French or Spanish sends copies of a translation published under such license to another country, such sending of copies shall not, for the purposes of subparagraph (a), be considered to constitute export if all of the following conditions are met:

(i) the recipients are individuals who are nationals of the country whose competent authority has granted the license, or organizations grouping such individuals;

(ii) the copies are to be used only for the purpose of teaching, scholarship or research;

(iii) the sending of the copies and their subsequent distribution to recipients is without any commercial purpose; and

(iv) the country to which the copies have been sent has agreed with the country whose competent authority has granted the license to allow the receipt, or distribution, or both, and the Director General has been notified of the agreement by the Government of the country in which the license has been granted.

(5) All copies published under a license granted by virtue of Article II or Article III shall bear a notice in the appropriate language stating that the copies are available for distribution only in the country or territory to which the said license applies.

(6)(a) Due provision shall be made at the national level to ensure

(i) that the license provides, in favour of the owner of the right of translation or of reproduction, as the case may be, for just compensation that is consistent with standards of royalties normally operating on licenses freely negotiated between persons in the two countries concerned, and

(ii) payment and transmittal of the compensation: should national currency regulations intervene, the competent authority shall make all efforts, by the use of international machinery, to ensure transmittal in internationally convertible currency or its equivalent.

(b) Due provision shall be made by national legislation to ensure a correct translation of the work, or an accurate reproduction of the particular edition, as the case may be.

Article V

(1)(a) Any country entitled to make a declaration that it will avail itself of the faculty provided for in Article II may, instead, at the time of ratifying or acceding to this Act:

(i) if it is a country to which Article 30(2)(a) applies, make a declaration under that provision as far as the right of translation is concerned;

(ii) if it is a country to which Article 30(2)(a) does not apply, and even if it is not a country outside the Union, make a declaration as provided for in Article 30(2)(b), first sentence.

(b) In the case of a country which ceases to be regarded as a developing country as referred to in Article I(1), a declaration made according to this paragraph shall be effective until the date on which the period applicable under Article I(3) expires.

(c) Any country which has made a declaration according to this paragraph may not subsequently avail itself of the faculty provided for in Article II even if it withdraws the said declaration.

(2) Subject to paragraph (3), any country which has availed itself of the faculty provided for in Article II may not subsequently make a declaration according to paragraph (1).

(3) Any country which has ceased to be regarded as a developing country as referred to in Article I(1) may, not later than two years prior to the expiration of the period applicable under Article I(3), make a declaration to the effect provided for in Article 30(2)(b), first sentence, notwithstanding the fact that it is not a country outside the Union. Such declaration shall take effect at the date on which the period applicable under Article I(3) expires.

Article VI

(1) Any country of the Union may declare, as from the date of this Act, and at any time before becoming bound by Articles 1 to 21 and this Appendix:

(i) if it is a country which, were it bound by Articles 1 to 21 and this Appendix, would be entitled to avail itself of the faculties referred to in Article I(1), that it will apply the provisions of Article II or of Article III or of both to works whose country of origin is a country which, pursuant to (ii) below, admits the application of those Articles to such works, or which is bound by Articles 1 to 21 and this Appendix; such declaration may, instead of referring to Article II, refer to Article V;

(ii) that it admits the application of this Appendix to works of which it is the country of origin by countries which have made a declaration under (i) above or a notification under Article I.

(2) Any declaration made under paragraph (1) shall be in writing and shall be deposited with the Director General. The declaration shall become effective from the date of its deposit.

B. General Agreement on Tariffs and Trade: Final Act Embodying the Results of the Uruguay Round of Negotiations

(Done at Marrakesh, April 15, 1994)

ANNEX 1C: AGREEMENT ON TRADE-RELATED ASPECTS OF INTELLECTUAL PROPERTY RIGHTS

Members,

Desiring to reduce distortions and impediments to international trade, and taking into account the need to promote effective and adequate protection of intellectual property rights, and to ensure that measures and procedures to enforce intellectual property rights do not themselves become barriers to legitimate trade;

Recognizing, to this end, the need for new rules and disciplines concerning:

(a) the applicability of the basic principles of GATT 1994 and of relevant international intellectual property agreements or conventions;

(b) the provision of adequate standards and principles concerning the availability, scope and use of trade-related intellectual property rights;

(c) the provision of effective and appropriate means for the enforcement of trade-related intellectual property rights, taking into account differences in national legal systems;

(d) the provision of effective and expeditious procedures for the multilateral prevention and settlement of disputes between governments; and

(e) transitional arrangements aiming at the fullest participation in the results of the negotiations;

Recognizing the need for a multilateral framework of principles, rules and disciplines dealing with international trade in counterfeit goods;

Recognizing that intellectual property rights are private rights;

Recognizing the underlying public policy objectives of national systems for the protection of intellectual property, including developmental and technological objectives;

Recognizing also the special needs of the least-developed country Members in respect of maximum flexibility in the domestic implementation of laws and regulations in order to enable them to create a sound and viable technological base;

Emphasizing the importance of reducing tensions by reaching strengthened commitments to resolve disputes on trade-related intellectual property issues through multilateral procedures;

Desiring to establish a mutually supportive relationship between the WTO and the World Intellectual Property Organization (referred to in this Agreement as "WIPO") as well as other relevant international organizations;

Hereby agree as follows:

PART I. GENERAL PROVISIONS AND BASIC PRINCIPLES

Article 1. Nature and Scope of Obligations

1. Members shall give effect to the provisions of this Agreement. Members may, but shall not be obliged to, implement in their domestic law more extensive protection than is required by this Agreement, provided that such protection does not contravene the provisions of this Agreement. Members shall be free to determine the appropriate method of implementing the provisions of this Agreement within their own legal system and practice.

2. For the purposes of this Agreement, the term "intellectual property" refers to all categories of intellectual property that are the subject of Sections 1 through 7 of Part II.

3. Members shall accord the treatment provided for in this Agreement to the nationals of other Members.[1] In respect of the relevant intellectual property right, the nationals of other Members shall be understood as those natural or legal persons that would meet the criteria for eligibility for protection provided for in the Paris Convention (1967), the Berne Convention (1971), the Rome Convention and the Treaty on Intellectual Property in Respect of Integrated Circuits, were all Members of the WTO members of those conventions.[2] Any Member availing itself of the

---

1. When "nationals" are referred to in this Agreement, they shall be deemed, in the case of a separate customs territory Member of the WTO, to mean persons, natural or legal, who are domiciled or have a real and effective industrial or commercial establishment in that customs territory.

2. In this Agreement, "Paris Convention" refers to the Paris Convention for the Protection of Industrial Property; "Paris Convention (1967)" refers to the Stockholm Act of this Convention of 14 July 1967. "Berne Convention" refers to the Berne Convention for the Protection of Literary and Artistic Works; "Berne Convention (1971)" refers to the Paris Act of this Convention of 24 July 1971. "Rome Convention" refers to the International Convention for the Protection of Performers, Producers of Phonograms and Broadcasting Organizations, adopted at Rome on 26 October 1961. "Treaty on Intellectual Property in Respect of Integrated Circuits" (IPIC Treaty) refers to the Treaty on Intellectual Property in Respect of Integrated Circuits, adopted at Washington on 26 May 1989. "WTO Agreement" refers to the Agreement Establishing the WTO.

possibilities provided in paragraph 3 of Article 5 or paragraph 2 of Article 6 of the Rome Convention shall make a notification as foreseen in those provisions to the Council for Trade-Related Aspects of Intellectual Property Rights (the "Council for TRIPS").

Article 2. *Intellectual Property Conventions*

1. In respect of Parts II, III and IV of this Agreement, Members shall comply with Articles 1 through 12, and Article 19, of the Paris Convention (1967).

2. Nothing in Parts I to IV of this Agreement shall derogate from existing obligations that Members may have to each other under the Paris Convention, the Berne Convention, the Rome Convention and the Treaty on Intellectual Property in Respect of Integrated Circuits.

Article 3. *National Treatment*

1. Each Member shall accord to the nationals of other Members treatment no less favourable than that it accords to its own nationals with regard to the protection[3] of intellectual property, subject to the exceptions already provided in, respectively, the Paris Convention (1967), the Berne Convention (1971), the Rome Convention or the Treaty on Intellectual Property in Respect of Integrated Circuits. In respect of performers, producers of phonograms and broadcasting organizations, this obligation only applies in respect of the rights provided under this Agreement. Any Member availing itself of the possibilities provided in Article 6 of the Berne Convention (1971) or paragraph 1(b) of Article 16 of the Rome Convention shall make a notification as foreseen in those provisions to the Council for TRIPS.

2. Members may avail themselves of the exceptions permitted under paragraph 1 in relation to judicial and administrative procedures, including the designation of an address for service or the appointment of an agent within the jurisdiction of a Member, only where such exceptions are necessary to secure compliance with laws and regulations which are not inconsistent with the provisions of this Agreement and where such practices are not applied in a manner which would constitute a disguised restriction on trade.

Article 4. *Most-Favoured-Nation Treatment*

With regard to the protection of intellectual property, any advantage, favour, privilege or immunity granted by a Member to the nationals of any other country shall be accorded immediately and unconditionally to the nationals of all other

---

3. For the purposes of Articles 3 and 4, "protection" shall include matters affecting the availability, acquisition, scope, maintenance and enforcement of intellectual property rights as well as those matters affecting the use of intellectual property rights specifically addressed in this Agreement.

Members. Exempted from this obligation are any advantage, favour, privilege or immunity accorded by a Member:

(a) deriving from international agreements on judicial assistance or law enforcement of a general nature and not particularly confined to the protection of intellectual property;

(b) granted in accordance with the provisions of the Berne Convention (1971) or the Rome Convention authorizing that the treatment accorded be a function not of national treatment but of the treatment accorded in another country;

(c) in respect of the rights of performers, producers of phonograms and broadcasting organizations not provided under this Agreement;

(d) deriving from international agreements related to the protection of intellectual property which entered into force prior to the entry into force of the WTO Agreement, provided that such agreements are notified to the Council for TRIPS and do not constitute an arbitrary or unjustifiable discrimination against nationals of other Members.

Article 5. Multilateral Agreements on Acquisition or Maintenance of Protection

The obligations under Articles 3 and 4 do not apply to procedures provided in multilateral agreements concluded under the auspices of WIPO relating to the acquisition or maintenance of intellectual property rights.

Article 6. Exhaustion

For the purposes of dispute settlement under this Agreement, subject to the provisions of Articles 3 and 4 nothing in this Agreement shall be used to address the issue of the exhaustion of intellectual property rights.

Article 7. Objectives

The protection and enforcement of intellectual property rights should contribute to the promotion of technological innovation and to the transfer and dissemination of technology, to the mutual advantage of producers and users of technological knowledge and in a manner conducive to social and economic welfare, and to a balance of rights and obligations.

Article 8. Principles

1. Members may, in formulating or amending their laws and regulations, adopt measures necessary to protect public health and nutrition, and to promote the public interest in sectors of vital importance to their socio-economic and technological development, provided that such measures are consistent with the provisions of this Agreement.

2. Appropriate measures, provided that they are consistent with the provisions of this Agreement, may be needed to prevent the abuse of intellectual property rights by right holders or the resort to practices which unreasonably restrain trade or adversely affect the international transfer of technology.

PART II.   STANDARDS CONCERNING THE AVAILABILITY, SCOPE AND USE OF INTELLECTUAL PROPERTY RIGHTS

Section 1:   Copyright and Related Rights

Article 9.   Relation to the Berne Convention

1. Members shall comply with Articles 1 through 21 of the Berne Convention (1971) and the Appendix thereto. However, Members shall not have rights or obligations under this Agreement in respect of the rights conferred under Article 6bis of that Convention or of the rights derived therefrom.

2. Copyright protection shall extend to expressions and not to ideas, procedures, methods of operation or mathematical concepts as such.

Article 10.   Computer Programs and Compilations of Data

1. Computer programs, whether in source or object code, shall be protected as literary works under the Berne Convention (1971).

2. Compilations of data or other material, whether in machine readable or other form, which by reason of the selection or arrangement of their contents constitute intellectual creations shall be protected as such. Such protection, which shall not extend to the data or material itself, shall be without prejudice to any copyright subsisting in the data or material itself.

Article 11.   Rental Rights

In respect of at least computer programs and cinematographic works, a Member shall provide authors and their successors in title the right to authorize or to prohibit the commercial rental to the public of originals or copies of their copyright works. A Member shall be excepted from this obligation in respect of cinematographic works unless such rental has led to widespread copying of such works which is materially impairing the exclusive right of reproduction conferred in that Member on authors and their successors in title. In respect of computer programs, this obligation does not apply to rentals where the program itself is not the essential object of the rental.

Article 12. Term of Protection

Whenever the term of protection of a work, other than a photographic work or a work of applied art, is calculated on a basis other than the life of a natural person, such term shall be no less than 50 years from the end of the calendar year of authorized p ublication, or, failing such authorized publication within 50 years from the making of the work, 50 years from the end of the calendar year of making.

Article 13. Limitations and Exceptions

Members shall confine limitations or exceptions to exclusive rights to certain special cases which do not conflict with a normal exploitation of the work and do not unreasonably prejudice the legitimate interests of the right holder.

Article 14. Protection of Performers, Producers of Phonograms (Sound Recordings) and Broadcasting Organizations

1. In respect of a fixation of their performance on a phonogram, performers shall have the possibility of preventing the following acts when undertaken without their authorization: the fixation of their unfixed performance and the reproduction of such fixation. Performers shall also have the possibility of preventing the following acts when undertaken without their authorization: the broadcasting by wireless means and the communication to the public of their live performance.

2. Producers of phonograms shall enjoy the right to authorize or prohibit the direct or indirect reproduction of their phonograms.

3. Broadcasting organizations shall have the right to prohibit the following acts when undertaken without their authorization: the fixation, the reproduction of fixations, and the rebroadcasting by wireless means of broadcasts, as well as the communication to the public of television broadcasts of the same. Where Members do not grant such rights to broadcasting organizations, they shall provide owners of copyright in the subject matter of broadcasts with the possibility of preventing the above acts, subject to the provisions of the Berne Convention (1971).

4. The provisions of Article 11 in respect of computer programs shall apply *mutatis mutandis* to producers of phonograms and any other right holders in phonograms as determined in a Member's law. If on 15 April 1994 a Member has in force a system of equitable remuneration of right holders in respect of the rental of phonograms, it may maintain such system provided that the commercial rental of phonograms is not giving rise to the material impairment of the exclusive rights of reproduction of right holders.

5. The term of the protection available under this Agreement to performers and producers of phonograms shall last at least until the end of a period of 50 years computed from the end of the calendar year in which the fixation was made or the performance took place. The term of protection granted pursuant to

paragraph 3 shall last for at least 20 years from the end of the calendar year in which the broadcast took place.

6. Any Member may, in relation to the rights conferred under paragraphs 1, 2 and 3, provide for conditions, limitations, exceptions and reservations to the extent permitted by the Rome Convention. However, the provisions of Article 18 of the Berne Convention (1971) shall also apply, *mutatis mutandis*, to the rights of performers and producers of phonograms in phonograms.

. . .

Section 4:   Industrial Designs

Article 25.   Requirements for Protection

1. Members shall provide for the protection of independently created industrial designs that are new or original. Members may provide that designs are not new or original if they do not significantly differ from known designs or combinations of known design features. Members may provide that such protection shall not extend to designs dictated essentially by technical or functional considerations.

2. Each Member shall ensure that requirements for securing protection for textile designs, in particular in regard to any cost, examination or publication, do not unreasonably impair the opportunity to seek and obtain such protection. Members shall be free to meet this obligation through industrial design law or through copyright law.

Article 26.   Protection

1. The owner of a protected industrial design shall have the right to prevent third parties not having the owner's consent from making, selling or importing articles bearing or embodying a design which is a copy, or substantially a copy, of the protected design, when such acts are undertaken for commercial purposes.

2. Members may provide limited exceptions to the protection of industrial designs, provided that such exceptions do not unreasonably conflict with the normal exploitation of protected industrial designs and do not unreasonably prejudice the legitimate interests of the owner of the protected design, taking account of the legitimate interests of third parties.

3. The duration of protection available shall amount to at least 10 years.

. . .

PART III. ENFORCEMENT OF INTELLECTUAL PROPERTY RIGHTS

Section 1: General Obligations

Article 41.

1. Members shall ensure that enforcement procedures as specified in this Part are available under their law so as to permit effective action against any act of infringement of intellectual property rights covered by this Agreement, including expeditious remedies to prevent infringements and remedies which constitute a deterrent to further infringements. These procedures shall be applied in such a manner as to avoid the creation of barriers to legitimate trade and to provide for safeguards against their abuse.

2. Procedures concerning the enforcement of intellectual property rights shall be fair and equitable. They shall not be unnecessarily complicated or costly, or entail unreasonable time-limits or unwarranted delays.

3. Decisions on the merits of a case shall preferably be in writing and reasoned. They shall be made available at least to the parties to the proceeding without undue delay. Decisions on the merits of a case shall be based only on evidence in respect of which parties were offered the opportunity to be heard.

4. Parties to a proceeding shall have an opportunity for review by a judicial authority of final administrative decisions and, subject to jurisdictional provisions in a Member's law concerning the importance of a case, of at least the legal aspects of initial judicial decisions on the merits of a case. However, there shall be no obligation to provide an opportunity for review of acquittals in criminal cases.

5. It is understood that this Part does not create any obligation to put in place a judicial system for the enforcement of intellectual property rights distinct from that for the enforcement of law in general, nor does it affect the capacity of Members to enforce their law in general. Nothing in this Part creates any obligation with respect to the distribution of resources as between enforcement of intellectual property rights and the enforcement of law in general.

Section 2: Civil and Administrative Procedures and Remedies

Article 42. Fair and Equitable Procedures

Members shall make available to right holders[11] civil judicial procedures concerning the enforcement of any intellectual property right covered by this Agreement. Defendants shall have the right to written notice which is timely and contains

---

11. For the purpose of this Part, the term "right holder" includes federations and associations having legal standing to assert such rights.

sufficient detail, including the basis of the claims. Parties shall be allowed to be represented by independent legal counsel, and procedures shall not impose overly burdensome requirements concerning mandatory personal appearances. All parties to such procedures shall be duly entitled to substantiate their claims and to present all relevant evidence. The procedure shall provide a means to identify and protect confidential information, unless this would be contrary to existing constitutional requirements.

Article 43. Evidence

1. The judicial authorities shall have the authority, where a party has presented reasonably available evidence sufficient to support its claims and has specified evidence relevant to substantiation of its claims which lies in the control of the opposing party, to order that this evidence be produced by the opposing party, subject in appropriate cases to conditions which ensure the protection of confidential information.

2. In cases in which a party to a proceeding voluntarily and without good reason refuses access to, or otherwise does not provide necessary information within a reasonable period, or significantly impedes a procedure relating to an enforcement action, a Member may accord judicial authorities the authority to make preliminary and final determinations, affirmative or negative, on the basis of the information presented to them, including the complaint or the allegation presented by the party adversely affected by the denial of access to information, subject to providing the parties an opportunity to be heard on the allegations or evidence.

Article 44. Injunctions

1. The judicial authorities shall have the authority to order a party to desist from an infringement, *inter alia* to prevent the entry into the channels of commerce in their jurisdiction of imported goods that involve the infringement of an intellectual property right, immediately after customs clearance of such goods. Members are not obliged to accord such authority in respect of protected subject matter acquired or ordered by a person prior to knowing or having reasonable grounds to know that dealing in such subject matter would entail the infringement of an intellectual property right.

2. Notwithstanding the other provisions of this Part and provided that the provisions of Part II specifically addressing use by governments, or by third parties authorized by a government, without the authorization of the right holder are complied with, Members may limit the remedies available against such use to payment of remuneration in accordance with subparagraph (h) of Article 31. In other cases, the remedies under this Part shall apply or, where these remedies are inconsistent with a Member's law, declaratory judgments and adequate compensation shall be available.

Article 45.   Damages

1. The judicial authorities shall have the authority to order the infringer to pay the right holder damages adequate to compensate for the injury the right holder has suffered because of an infringement of that person's intellectual property right by an infringer who knowingly, or with reasonable grounds to know, engaged in infringing activity.

2. The judicial authorities shall also have the authority to order the infringer to pay the right holder expenses, which may include appropriate attorney's fees. In appropriate cases, Members may authorize the judicial authorities to order recovery of profits and/or payment of pre-established damages even where the infringer did not knowingly, or with reasonable grounds to know, engage in infringing activity.

Article 46.   Other Remedies

In order to create an effective deterrent to infringement, the judicial authorities shall have the authority to order that goods that they have found to be infringing be, without compensation of any sort, disposed of outside the channels of commerce in such a manner as to avoid any harm caused to the right holder, or, unless this would be contrary to existing constitutional requirements, destroyed. The judicial authorities shall also have the authority to order that materials and implements the predominant use of which has been in the creation of the infringing goods be, without compensation of any sort, disposed of outside the channels of commerce in such a manner as to minimize the risks of further infringements. In considering such requests, the need for proportionality between the seriousness of the infringement and the remedies ordered as well as the interests of third parties shall be taken into account. In regard to counterfeit trademark goods, the simple removal of the trademark unlawfully affixed shall not be sufficient, other than in exceptional cases, to permit release of the goods into the channels of commerce.

Article 47.   Right of Information

Members may provide that the judicial authorities shall have the authority, unless this would be out of proportion to the seriousness of the infringement, to order the infringer to inform the right holder of the identity of third persons involved in the production and distribution of the infringing goods or services and of their channels of distribution.

Article 48.   Indemnification of the Defendant

1. The judicial authorities shall have the authority to order a party at whose request measures were taken and who has abused enforcement procedures to provide to a party wrongfully enjoined or restrained adequate compensation for the injury suffered because of such abuse. The judicial authorities shall also have the

authority to order the applicant to pay the defendant expenses, which may include appropriate attorney's fees.

2. In respect of the administration of any law pertaining to the protection or enforcement of intellectual property rights, Members shall only exempt both public authorities and officials from liability to appropriate remedial measures where actions are taken or intended in good faith in the course of the administration of that law.

Article 49. Administrative Procedures

To the extent that any civil remedy can be ordered as a result of administrative procedures on the merits of a case, such procedures shall conform to principles equivalent in substance to those set forth in this Section.

Section 3: Provisional Measures

Article 50.

1. The judicial authorities shall have the authority to order prompt and effective provisional measures:

(a) to prevent an infringement of any intellectual property right from occurring, and in particular to prevent the entry into the channels of commerce in their jurisdiction of goods, including imported goods immediately after customs clearance;

(b) to preserve relevant evidence in regard to the alleged infringement.

2. The judicial authorities shall have the authority to adopt provisional measures *inaudita altera parte* where appropriate, in particular where any delay is likely to cause irreparable harm to the right holder, or where there is a demonstrable risk of evidence being destroyed.

3. The judicial authorities shall have the authority to require the applicant to provide any reasonably available evidence in order to satisfy themselves with a sufficient degree of certainty that the applicant is the right holder and that the applicant's right is being infringed or that such infringement is imminent, and to order the applicant to provide a security or equivalent assurance sufficient to protect the defendant and to prevent abuse.

4. Where provisional measures have been adopted *inaudita altera parte*, the parties affected shall be given notice, without delay after the execution of the measures at the latest. A review, including a right to be heard, shall take place upon request of the defendant with a view to deciding, within a reasonable period after the notification of the measures, whether these measures shall be modified, revoked or confirmed.

5. The applicant may be required to supply other information necessary for the identification of the goods concerned by the authority that will execute the provisional measures.

6. Without prejudice to paragraph 4, provisional measures taken on the basis of paragraphs 1 and 2 shall, upon request by the defendant, be revoked or otherwise cease to have effect, if proceedings leading to a decision on the merits of the case are not initiated within a reasonable period, to be determined by the judicial authority ordering the measures where a Member's law so permits or, in the absence of such a determination, not to exceed 20 working days or 31 calendar days, whichever is the longer.

7. Where the provisional measures are revoked or where they lapse due to any act or omission by the applicant, or where it is subsequently found that there has been no infringement or threat of infringement of an intellectual property right, the judicial authorities shall have the authority to order the applicant, upon request of the defendant, to provide the defendant appropriate compensation for any injury caused by these measures.

8. To the extent that any provisional measure can be ordered as a result of administrative procedures, such procedures shall conform to principles equivalent in substance to those set forth in this Section.

Section 4:   Special Requirements Related to Border Measures[12]

Article 51.   Suspension of Release by Customs Authorities

Members shall, in conformity with the provisions set out below, adopt procedures[13] to enable a right holder, who has valid grounds for suspecting that the importation of counterfeit trademark or pirated copyright goods[14] may take place, to lodge an application in writing with competent authorities, administrative or judicial, for the suspension by the customs authorities of the release into free circulation of such goods. Members may enable such an application to be made in respect of goods which involve other infringements of intellectual property rights, provided that the requirements of this Section are met. Members

---

12. Where a Member has dismantled substantially all controls over movement of goods across its border with another Member with which it forms part of a customs union, it shall not be required to apply the provisions of this Section at that border.

13. It is understood that there shall be no obligation to apply such procedures to imports of goods put on the market in another country by or with the consent of the right holder, or to goods in transit.

14. For the purposes of this Agreement:

(a) "counterfeit trademark goods" shall mean any goods, including packaging, bearing without authorization a trademark which is identical to the trademark validly registerd in respect of such goods, or which cannot be distinguished in its essential aspects from such a trademark, and which thereby infringes the rights of the owner of the trademark in question under the law of the country of importation;

(b) "pirated copyright goods" shall mean any goods which are copies made without the consent of the right holder or person duly authorized by the right holder in the country of production and which are made directly or indirectly from an article where the making of that copy would have constituted an infringement of a copyright or a related right under the law of the country of importation.

may also provide for corresponding procedures concerning the suspension by the customs authorities of the release of infringing goods destined for exportation from their territories.

Article 52. Application

Any right holder initiating the procedures under Article 51 shall be required to provide adequate evidence to satisfy the competent authorities that, under the laws of the country of importation, there is *prima facie* an infringement of the right holder's intellectual property right and to supply a sufficiently detailed description of the goods to make them readily recognizable by the customs authorities. The competent authorities shall inform the applicant within a reasonable period whether they have accepted the application and, where determined by the competent authorities, the period for which the customs authorities will take action.

Article 53. Security or Equivalent Assurance

1. The competent authorities shall have the authority to require an applicant to provide a security or equivalent assurance sufficient to protect the defendant and the competent authorities and to prevent abuse. Such security or equivalent assurance shall not unreasonably deter recourse to these procedures.

2. Where pursuant to an application under this Section the release of goods involving industrial designs, patents, layout-designs or undisclosed information into free circulation has been suspended by customs authorities on the basis of a decision other than by a judicial or other independent authority, and the period provided for in Article 55 has expired without the granting of provisional relief by the duly empowered authority, and provided that all other conditions for importation have been complied with, the owner, importer, or consignee of such goods shall be entitled to their release on the posting of a security in an amount sufficient to protect the right holder for any infringement. Payment of such security shall not prejudice any other remedy available to the right holder, it being understood that the security shall be released if the right holder fails to pursue the right of action within a reasonable period of time.

Article 54. Notice of Suspension

The importer and the applicant shall be promptly notified of the suspension of the release of goods according to Article 51.

Article 55. Duration of Suspension

If, within a period not exceeding 10 working days after the applicant has been served notice of the suspension, the customs authorities have not been informed that proceedings leading to a decision on the merits of the case have been initiated by a party other than the defendant, or that the duly empowered authority has taken provisional measures prolonging the suspension of the release of the goods, the goods shall be released, provided that all other conditions for importation or exportation have been complied with; in appropriate cases, this time-limit may be extended by another 10 working days. If proceedings leading to a decision on the merits of the case have been initiated, a review, including a right to be heard, shall take place upon request of the defendant with a view to deciding, within a reasonable period, whether these measures shall be modified, revoked or confirmed. Notwithstanding the above, where the suspension of the release of goods is carried out or continued in accordance with a provisional judicial measure, the provisions of paragraph 6 of Article 50 shall apply.

Article 56. Indemnification of the Importer and of the Owner of the Goods

Relevant authorities shall have the authority to order the applicant to pay the importer, the consignee and the owner of the goods appropriate compensation for any injury caused to them through the wrongful detention of goods or through the detention of goods released pursuant to Article 55.

Article 57. Right of Inspection and Information

Without prejudice to the protection of confidential information, Members shall provide the competent authorities the authority to give the right holder sufficient opportunity to have any goods detained by the customs authorities inspected in order to substantiate the right holder's claims. The competent authorities shall also have authority to give the importer an equivalent opportunity to have any such goods inspected. Where a positive determination has been made on the merits of a case, Members may provide the competent authorities the authority to inform the right holder of the names and addresses of the consignor, the importer and the consignee and of the quantity of the goods in question.

Article 58. Ex Officio Action

Where Members require competent authorities to act upon their own initiative and to suspend the release of goods in respect of which they have acquired *prima facie* evidence that an intellectual property right is being infringed:

(a) the competent authorities may at any time seek from the right holder any information that may assist them to exercise these powers;

(b) the importer and the right holder shall be promptly notified of the suspension. Where the importer has lodged an appeal against the suspension with the competent authorities, the suspension shall be subject to the conditions, *mutatis mutandis*, set out at Article 55;

(c) Members shall only exempt both public authorities and officials from liability to appropriate remedial measures where actions are taken or intended in good faith.

Article 59. Remedies

Without prejudice to other rights of action open to the right holder and subject to the right of the defendant to seek review by a judicial authority, competent authorities shall have the authority to order the destruction or disposal of infringing goods in accordance with the principles set out in Article 46. In regard to counterfeit trademark goods, the authorities shall not allow the re-exportation of the infringing goods in an unaltered state or subject them to a different customs procedure, other than in exceptional circumstances.

Article 60. De Minimis Imports

Members may exclude from the application of the above provisions small quantities of goods of a non-commercial nature contained in travellers' personal luggage or sent in small consignments.

Section 5:   Criminal Procedures

Article 61.

Members shall provide for criminal procedures and penalties to be applied at least in cases of wilful trademark counterfeiting or copyright piracy on a commercial scale. Remedies available shall include imprisonment and/or monetary fines sufficient to provide a deterrent, consistently with the level of penalties applied for crimes of a corresponding gravity. In appropriate cases, remedies available shall also include the seizure, forfeiture and destruction of the infringing goods and of any materials and implements the predominant use of which has been in the commission of the offence. Members may provide for criminal procedures and penalties to be applied in other cases of infringement of intellectual property rights, in particular where they are committed wilfully and on a commercial scale.

PART IV.   ACQUISITION AND MAINTENANCE OF INTELLECTUAL PROPERTY RIGHTS AND RELATED INTER-PARTES PROCEDURES

Article 62.

1. Members may require, as a condition of the acquisition or maintenance of the intellectual property rights provided for under Sections 2 through 6 of Part II,

compliance with reasonable procedures and formalities. Such procedures and formalities shall be consistent with the provisions of this Agreement.

2. Where the acquisition of an intellectual property right is subject to the right being granted or regist ered, Members shall ensure that the procedures for grant or registration, subject to compliance with the substantive conditions for acquisition of the right, permit the granting or registration of the right within a reasonable period of time so as to avoid unwarranted curtailment of the period of protection.

3. Article 4 of the Paris Convention (1967) shall apply *mutatis mutandis* to service marks.

4. Procedures concerning the acquisition or maintenance of intellectual property rights and, where a Member's law provides for such procedures, administrative revocation and *inter partes* procedures such as opposition, revocation and cancellation, shall be governed by the general principles set out in paragraphs 2 and 3 of Article 41.

5. Final administrative decisions in any of the procedures referred to under paragraph 4 shall be subject to review by a judicial or quasi-judicial authority. However, there shall be no obligation to provide an opportunity for such review of decisions in cases of unsuccessful opposition or administrative revocation, provided that the grounds for such procedures can be the subject of invalidation procedures.

PART V. DISPUTE PREVENTION AND SETTLEMENT

Article 63. Transparency

1. Laws and regulations, and final judicial decisions and administrative rulings of general application, made effective by a Member pertaining to the subject matter of this Agreement (the availability, scope, acquisition, enforcement and prevention of the abuse of intellectual property rights) shall be published, or where such publication is not practicable made publicly available, in a national language, in such a manner as to enable governments and right holders to become acquainted with them. Agreements concerning the subject matter of this Agreement which are in force between the government or a governmental agency of a Member and the government or a governmental agency of another Member shall also be published.

2. Members shall notify the laws and regulations referred to in paragraph 1 to the Council for TRIPS in order to assist that Council in its review of the operation of this Agreement. The Council shall attempt to minimize the burden on Members in carrying out this obligation and may decide to waive the obligation to notify such laws and regulations directly to the Council if consultations with WIPO on the establishment of a common register containing these laws and regulations are successful. The Council shall also consider in this connection any action

required regarding notifications pursuant to the obligations under this Agreement stemming from the provisions of Article 6*ter* of the Paris Convention (1967).

3. Each Member shall be prepared to supply, in response to a written request from another Member, information of the sort referred to in paragraph 1. A Member, having reason to believe that a specific judicial decision or administrative ruling or bilateral agreement in the area of intellectual property rights affects its rights under this Agreement, may also request in writing to be given access to or be informed in sufficient detail of such specific judicial decisions or administrative rulings or bilateral agreements.

4. Nothing in paragraphs 1, 2 and 3 shall require Members to disclose confidential information which would impede law enforcement or otherwise be contrary to the public interest or would prejudice the legitimate commercial interests of particular enterprises, public or private.

Article 64. Dispute Settlement

1. The provisions of Articles XXII and XXIII of GATT 1994 as elaborated and applied by the Dispute Settlement Understanding shall apply to consultations and the settlement of disputes under this Agreement except as otherwise specifically provided herein.

2. Subparagraphs 1(b) and 1(c) of Article XXIII of GATT 1994 shall not apply to the settlement of disputes under this Agreement for a period of five years from the date of entry into force of the WTO Agreement.

3. During the time period referred to in paragraph 2, the Council for TRIPS shall examine the scope and modalities for complaints of the type provided for under subparagraphs 1(b) and 1(c) of Article XXIII of GATT 1994 made pursuant to this Agreement, and submit its recommendations to the Ministerial Conference for approval. Any decision of the Ministerial Conference to approve such recommendations or to extend the period in paragraph 2 shall be made only by consensus, and approved recommendations shall be effective for all Members without further formal acceptance process.

PART VI. TRANSITIONAL ARRANGEMENTS

Article 65. Transitional Arrangements

1. Subject to the provisions of paragraphs 2, 3 and 4, no Member shall be obliged to apply the provisions of this Agreement before the expiry of a general period of one year following the date of entry into force of the WTO Agreement.

2. A developing country Member is entitled to delay for a further period of four years the date of application, as defined in paragraph 1, of the provisions of this Agreement other than Articles 3, 4 and 5.

3. Any other Member which is in the process of transformation from a centrally-planned into a market, free-enterprise economy and which is undertaking

structural reform of its intellectual property system and facing special problems in the preparation and implementation of intellectual property laws and regulations, may also benefit from a period of delay as foreseen in paragraph 2.

4. To the extent that a developing country Member is obliged by this Agreement to extend product patent protection to areas of technology not so protectable in its territory on the general date of application of this Agreement for that Member, as defined in paragraph 2, it may delay the application of the provisions on product patents of Section 5 of Part II to such areas of technology for an additional period of five years.

5. A Member availing itself of a transitional period under paragraphs 1, 2, 3 or 4 shall ensure that any changes in its laws, regulations and practice made during that period do not result in a lesser degree of consistency with the provisions of this Agreement.

Article 66.   Least-Developed Country Members

1. In view of the special needs and requirements of least-developed country Members, their economic, financial and administrative constraints, and their need for flexibility to create a viable technological base, such Members shall not be required to apply the provisions of this Agreement, other than Articles 3, 4 and 5, for a period of 10 years from the date of application as defined under paragraph 1 of Article 65. The Council for TRIPS shall, upon duly motivated request by a least-developed country Member, accord extensions of this period.

2. Developed country Members shall provide incentives to enterprises and institutions in their territories for the purpose of promoting and encouraging technology transfer to least-developed country Members in order to enable them to create a sound and viable technological base.

Article 67.   Technical Cooperation

In order to facilitate the implementation of this Agreement, developed country Members shall provide, on request and on mutually agreed terms and conditions, technical and financial cooperation in favour of developing and least-developed country Members. Such cooperation shall include assistance in the preparation of laws and regulations on the protection and enforcement of intellectual property rights as well as on the prevention of their abuse, and shall include support regarding the establishment or reinforcement of domestic offices and agencies relevant to these matters, including the training of personnel. . . .

C. WIPO Copyright Treaty

Adopted by the Diplomatic Conference on December 20, 1996*

Preamble

The Contracting Parties,

Desiring to develop and maintain the protection of the rights of authors in their literary and artistic works in a manner as effective and uniform as possible,

Recognizing the need to introduce new international rules and clarify the interpretation of certain existing rules in order to provide adequate solutions to the questions raised by new economic, social, cultural and technological developments,

Recognizing the profound impact of the development and convergence of information and communication technologies on the creation and use of literary and artistic works,

Emphasizing the outstanding significance of copyright protection as an incentive for literary and artistic creation,

Recognizing the need to maintain a balance between the rights of authors and the larger public interest, particularly education, research and access to information, as reflected in the Berne Convention,

Have agreed as follows:

Article 1.   Relation to the Berne Convention

(1) This Treaty is a special agreement within the meaning of Article 20 of the Berne Convention for the Protection of Literary and Artistic Works, as regards Contracting Parties that are countries of the Union established by that Convention. This Treaty shall not have any connection with treaties other than the Berne Convention, nor shall it prejudice any rights and obligations under any other treaties.

---

* Reproduced with the permission of the World Intellectual Property Organization (WIPO), the owner of the copyright. The Secretariat of WIPO assumes no liability or responsibility with regard to the transformation or translation of this data.

(2) Nothing in this Treaty shall derogate from existing obligations that Contracting Parties have to each other under the Berne Convention for the Protection of Literary and Artistic Works.

(3) Hereinafter, "Berne Convention" shall refer to the Paris Act of July 24, 1971 of the Berne Convention for the Protection of Literary and Artistic Works.

(4) Contracting Parties shall comply with Articles 1 to 21 and the Appendix of the Berne Convention.

Article 2.   Scope of Copyright Protection

Copyright protection extends to expressions and not to ideas, procedures, methods of operation or mathematical concepts as such.

Article 3.   Application of Articles 2 to 6 of the Berne Convention

Contracting Parties shall apply *mutatis mutandis* the provisions of Articles 2 to 6 of the Berne Convention in respect of the protection provided for in this Treaty.

Article 4.   Computer Programs

Computer programs are protected as literary works within the meaning of Article 2 of the Berne Convention. Such protection applies to computer programs, whatever may be the mode or form of their expression.

Article 5.   Compilations of Data (Databases)

Compilations of data or other material, in any form, which by reason of the selection or arrangement of their contents constitute intellectual creations, are protected as such. This protection does not extend to the data or the material itself and is without prejudice to any copyright subsisting in the data or material contained in the compilation.

Article 6.   Right of Distribution

(1) Authors of literary and artistic works shall enjoy the exclusive right of authorizing the making available to the public of the original and copies of their works through sale or other transfer of ownership.

(2) Nothing in this Treaty shall affect the freedom of Contracting Parties to determine the conditions, if any, under which the exhaustion of the right in paragraph (1) applies after the first sale or other transfer of ownership of the original or a copy of the work with the authorization of the author.

Article 7. Right of Rental

(1) Authors of

    (i) computer programs;

    (ii) cinematographic works; and

    (iii) works embodied in phonograms, as determined in the national law of Contracting Parties,

    shall enjoy the exclusive right of authorizing commercial rental to the public of the originals or copies of their works.

(2) Paragraph (1) shall not apply

    (i) in the case of computer programs, where the program itself is not the essential object of the rental; and

    (ii) in the case of cinematographic works, unless such commercial rental has led to widespread copying of such works materially impairing the exclusive right of reproduction.

(3) Notwithstanding the provisions of paragraph (1), a Contracting Party that, on April 15, 1994, had and continues to have in force a system of equitable remuneration of authors for the rental of copies of their works embodied in phonograms may maintain that system provided that the commercial rental of works embodied in phonograms is not giving rise to the material impairment of the exclusive right of reproduction of authors.

Article 8. Right of Communication to the Public

Without prejudice to the provisions of Articles 11(1)(ii), 11*bis* (1)(i) and (ii), 11*ter*(1)(ii), 14(1)(ii) and 14*bis*(1) of the Berne Convention, authors of literary and artistic works shall enjoy the exclusive right of authorizing any communication to the public of their works, by wire or wireless means, including the making available to the public of their works in such a way that members of the public may access these works from a place and at a time individually chosen by them.

Article 9. Duration of the Protection of Photographic Works

In respect of photographic works, the Contracting Parties shall not apply the provisions of Article 7(4) of the Berne Convention.

Article 10. Limitations and Exceptions

(1) Contracting Parties may, in their national legislation, provide for limitations of or exceptions to the rights granted to authors of literary and artistic works under this Treaty in certain special cases that do not conflict with a normal exploitation of the work and do not unreasonably prejudice the legitimate interests of the author.

(2) Contracting Parties shall, when applying the Berne Convention, confine any limitations of or exceptions to rights provided for therein to certain special cases that do not conflict with a normal exploitation of the work and do not unreasonably prejudice the legitimate interests of the author.

Article 11.   Obligations concerning Technological Measures

Contracting Parties shall provide adequate legal protection and effective legal remedies against the circumvention of effective technological measures that are used by authors in connection with the exercise of their rights under this Treaty or the Berne Convention and that restrict acts, in respect of their works, which are not authorized by the authors concerned or permitted by law.

Article 12.   Obligations concerning Rights Management Information

(1) Contracting Parties shall provide adequate and effective legal remedies against any person knowingly performing any of the following acts knowing, or with respect to civil remedies having reasonable grounds to know, that it will induce, enable, facilitate or conceal an infringement of any right covered by this Treaty or the Berne Convention:

(i) to remove or alter any electronic rights management information without authority;

(ii) to distribute, import for distribution, broadcast or communicate to the public, without authority, works or copies of works knowing that electronic rights management information has been removed or altered without authority.

(2) As used in this Article, "rights management information" means information which identifies the work, the author of the work, the owner of any right in the work, or information about the terms and conditions of use of the work, and any numbers or codes that represent such information, when any of these items of information is attached to a copy of a work or appears in connection with the communication of a work to the public.

Article 13.   Application in Time

Contracting Parties shall apply the provisions of Article 18 of the Berne Convention to all protection provided for in this Treaty.

Article 14.   Provisions on Enforcement of Rights

(1) Contracting Parties undertake to adopt, in accordance with their legal systems, the measures necessary to ensure the application of this Treaty.

(2) Contracting Parties shall ensure that enforcement procedures are available under their law so as to permit effective action against any act of infringement of rights covered by this Treaty, including expeditious remedies to prevent infringements and remedies which constitute a deterrent to further infringements.

Article 15. Assembly

(1)(a) The Contracting Parties shall have an Assembly.

(b) Each Contracting Party shall be represented by one delegate who may be assisted by alternate delegates, advisors and experts.

(c) The expenses of each delegation shall be borne by the Contracting Party that has appointed the delegation. The Assembly may ask the World Intellectual Property Organization (hereinafter referred to as "WIPO") to grant financial assistance to facilitate the participation of delegations of Contracting Parties that are regarded as developing countries in conformity with the established practice of the General Assembly of the United Nations or that are countries in transition to a market economy.

(2)(a) The Assembly shall deal with matters concerning the maintenance and development of this Treaty and the application and operation of this Treaty.

(b) The Assembly shall perform the function allocated to it under Article 17(2) in respect of the admission of certain intergovernmental organizations to become party to this Treaty.

(c) The Assembly shall decide the convocation of any diplomatic conference for the revision of this Treaty and give the necessary instructions to the Director General of WIPO for the preparation of such diplomatic conference.

(3)(a) Each Contracting Party that is a State shall have one vote and shall vote only in its own name.

(b) Any Contracting Party that is an intergovernmental organization may participate in the vote, in place of its Member States, with a number of votes equal to the number of its Member States which are party to this Treaty. No such intergovernmental organization shall participate in the vote if any one of its Member States exercises its right to vote and *vice versa*.

(4) The Assembly shall meet in ordinary session once every two years upon convocation by the Director General of WIPO.

(5) The Assembly shall establish its own rules of procedure, including the convocation of extraordinary sessions, the requirements of a quorum and, subject to the provisions of this Treaty, the required majority for various kinds of decisions.

Article 16. International Bureau

The International Bureau of WIPO shall perform the administrative tasks concerning the Treaty.

Article 17. Eligibility for Becoming Party to the Treaty

(1) Any Member State of WIPO may become party to this Treaty.

(2) The Assembly may decide to admit any intergovernmental organization to become party to this Treaty which declares that it is competent in respect of, and has its own legislation binding on all its Member States on, matters covered

by this Treaty and that it has been duly authorized, in accordance with its internal procedures, to become party to this Treaty.

(3) The European Community, having made the declaration referred to in the preceding paragraph in the Diplomatic Conference that has adopted this Treaty, may become party to this Treaty.

Article 18.   Rights and Obligations under the Treaty

Subject to any specific provisions to the contrary in this Treaty, each Contracting Party shall enjoy all of the rights and assume all of the obligations under this Treaty.

Article 19.   Signature of the Treaty

This Treaty shall be open for signature until December 31, 1997, by any Member State of WIPO and by the European Community.

Article 20.   Entry into Force of the Treaty

This Treaty shall enter into force three months after 30 instruments of ratification or accession by States have been deposited with the Director General of WIPO.

Article 21.   Effective Date of Becoming Party to the Treaty

This Treaty shall bind

(i) the 30 States referred to in Article 20, from the date on which this Treaty has entered into force;

(ii) each other State from the expiration of three months from the date on which the State has deposited its instrument with the Director General of WIPO;

(iii) the European Community, from the expiration of three months after the deposit of its instrument of ratification or accession if such instrument has been deposited after the entry into force of this Treaty according to Article 20, or, three months after the entry into force of this Treaty if such instrument has been deposited before the entry into force of this Treaty;

(iv) any other intergovernmental organization that is admitted to become party to this Treaty, from the expiration of three months after the deposit of its instrument of accession.

Article 22.   No Reservations to the Treaty

No reservation to this Treaty shall be admitted.

Article 23.   Denunciation of the Treaty

This Treaty may be denounced by any Contracting Party by notification addressed to the Director General of WIPO. Any denunciation shall take effect one year from the date on which the Director General of WIPO received the notification.

Article 24.   Languages of the Treaty

(1) This Treaty is signed in a single original in English, Arabic, Chinese, French, Russian and Spanish languages, the versions in all these languages being equally authentic.

(2) An official text in any language other than those referred to in paragraph (1) shall be established by the Director General of WIPO on the request of an interested party, after consultation with all the interested parties. For the purposes of this paragraph, "interested party" means any Member State of WIPO whose official language, or one of whose official languages, is involved and the European Community, and any other intergovernmental organization that may become party to this Treaty, if one of its official languages is involved.

Article 25.   Depositary

The Director General of WIPO is the depositary of this Treaty.

Agreed Statements Concerning the WIPO Copyright Treaty

Adopted by the Diplomatic Conference on December 20,1996

Concerning Article 1(4)

The reproduction right, as set out in Article 9 of the Berne Convention, and the exceptions permitted thereunder, fully apply in the digital environment, in particular to the use of works in digital form. It is understood that the storage of a protected work in digital form in an electronic medium constitutes a reproduction within the meaning of Article 9 of the Berne Convention.

Concerning Article 3

It is understood that in applying Article 3 of this Treaty, the expression "country of the Union" in Articles 2 to 6 of the Berne Convention will be read as if it were a reference to a Contracting Party to this Treaty, in the application of those Berne Articles in respect of protection provided for in this Treaty. It is also understood that the expression "country outside the Union" in those Articles in the Berne Convention will, in the same circumstances, be read as if it were a reference to a country that is not a Contracting Party to this Treaty, and that "this Convention" in Articles 2 (8), 2*bis*(2), 3, 4 and 5 of the Berne Convention will be read as if it were a reference to the Berne Convention and this Treaty. Finally, it is understood that a reference in Articles 3 to 6 of the Berne Convention to a "national of one of the countries of the Union" will, when these Articles are applied to this Treaty, mean, in regard to an intergovernmental organization that is a Contracting Party to this Treaty, a national of one of the countries that is member of that organization.

Concerning Article 4

The scope of protection for computer programs under Article 4 of this Treaty, read with Article 2, is consistent with Article 2 of the Berne Convention and on a par with the relevant provisions of the TRIPS Agreement.

Concerning Article 5

The scope of protection for compilations of data (databases) under Article 5 of this Treaty, read with Article 2, is consistent with Article 2 of the Berne Convention and on a par with the relevant provisions of the TRIPS Agreement.

Concerning Articles 6 and 7

As used in these Articles, the expressions "copies" and "original and copies," being subject to the right of distribution and the right of rental under the said Articles, refer exclusively to fixed copies that can be put into circulation as tangible objects.

Concerning Article 7

It is understood that the obligation under Article 7(1) does not require a Contracting Party to provide an exclusive right of commercial rental to authors who, under that Contracting Party's law, are not granted rights in respect of phonograms. It is understood that this obligation is consistent with Article 14(4) of the TRIPS Agreement.

Concerning Article 8

It is understood that the mere provision of physical facilities for enabling or making a communication does not in itself amount to communication within the meaning of this Treaty or the Berne Convention. It is further understood that nothing in Article 8 precludes a Contracting Party from applying Article 11*bis*(2).

Concerning Article 10

It is understood that the provisions of Article 10 permit Contracting Parties to carry forward and appropriately extend into the digital environment limitations and exceptions in their national laws which have been considered acceptable under the Berne Convention. Similarly, these provisions should be understood to permit Contracting Parties to devise new exceptions and limitations that are appropriate in the digital network environment.

It is also understood that Article 10(2) neither reduces nor extends the scope of applicability of the limitations and exceptions permitted by the Berne Convention.

Concerning Article 12

It is understood that the reference to "infringement of any right covered by this Treaty or the Berne Convention" includes both exclusive rights and rights of remuneration.

It is further understood that Contracting Parties will not rely on this Article to devise or implement rights management systems that would have the effect of imposing formalities which are not permitted under the Berne Convention or this Treaty, prohibiting the free movement of goods or impeding the enjoyment of rights under this Treaty.

D. WIPO Performances and Phonograms Treaty

Adopted by the Diplomatic Conference on December 20, 1996[*]

Preamble

The Contracting Parties,

Desiring to develop and maintain the protection of the rights of performers and producers of phonograms in a manner as effective and uniform as possible,

Recognizing the need to introduce new international rules in order to provide adequate solutions to the questions raised by economic, social, cultural and technological developments,

Recognizing the profound impact of the development and convergence of information and communication technologies on the production and use of performances and phonograms,

Recognizing the need to maintain a balance between the rights of performers and producers of phonograms and the larger public interest, particularly education, research and access to information,

Have agreed as follows:

Chapter I. General Provisions

Article 1. Relation to Other Conventions

(1) Nothing in this Treaty shall derogate from existing obligations that Contracting Parties have to each other under the International Convention for the Protection of Performers, Producers of Phonograms and Broadcasting Organizations done in Rome, October 26, 1961 (hereinafter the "Rome Convention").

---

[*] Reproduced with the permission of the World Intellectual Property Organization (WIPO), the owner of the copyright. The Secretariat of WIPO assumes no liability or responsibility with regard to the transformation or translation of this data.

(2) Protection granted under this Treaty shall leave intact and shall in no way affect the protection of copyright in literary and artistic works. Consequently, no provision of this Treaty may be interpreted as prejudicing such protection.

(3) This Treaty shall not have any connection with, nor shall it prejudice any rights and obligations under, any other treaties.

Article 2. Definitions

For the purposes of this Treaty:

(a) "performers" are actors, singers, musicians, dancers, and other persons who act, sing, deliver, declaim, play in, interpret, or otherwise perform literary or artistic works or expressions of folklore;

(b) "phonogram" means the fixation of the sounds of a performance or of other sounds, or of a representation of sounds, other than in the form of a fixation incorporated in a cinematographic or other audiovisual work;

(c) "fixation" means the embodiment of sounds, or of the representations thereof, from which they can be perceived, reproduced or communicated through a device;

(d) "producer of a phonogram" means the person, or the legal entity, who or which takes the initiative and has the responsibility for the first fixation of the sounds of a performance or other sounds, or the representations of sounds;

(e) "publication" of a fixed performance or a phonogram means the offering of copies of the fixed performance or the phonogram to the public, with the consent of the rightholder, and provided that copies are offered to the public in reasonable quantity;

(f) "broadcasting" means the transmission by wireless means for public reception of sounds or of images and sounds or of the representations thereof; such transmission by satellite is also "broadcasting"; transmission of encrypted signals is "broadcasting" where the means for decrypting are provided to the public by the broadcasting organization or with its consent;

(g) "communication to the public" of a performance or a phonogram means the transmission to the public by any medium, otherwise than by broadcasting, of sounds of a performance or the sounds or the representations of sounds fixed in a phonogram. For the purposes of Article 15, "communication to the public" includes making the sounds or representations of sounds fixed in a phonogram audible to the public.

Article 3. Beneficiaries of Protection under this Treaty

(1) Contracting Parties shall accord the protection provided under this Treaty to the performers and producers of phonograms who are nationals of other Contracting Parties.

(2) The nationals of other Contracting Parties shall be understood to be those performers or producers of phonograms who would meet the criteria for

eligibility for protection provided under the Rome Convention, were all the Contracting Parties to this Treaty Contracting States of that Convention. In respect of these criteria of eligibility, Contracting Parties shall apply the relevant definitions in Article 2 of this Treaty.

(3) Any Contracting Party availing itself of the possibilities provided in Article 5(3) of the Rome Convention or, for the purposes of Article 5 of the same Convention, Article 17 thereof shall make a notification as foreseen in those provisions to the Director General of the World Intellectual Property Organization (WIPO).

Article 4. National Treatment

(1) Each Contracting Party shall accord to nationals of other Contracting Parties, as defined in Article 3(2), the treatment it accords to its own nationals with regard to the exclusive rights specifically granted in this Treaty, and to the right to equitable remuneration provided for in Article 15 of this Treaty.

(2) The obligation provided for in paragraph (1) does not apply to the extent that another Contracting Party makes use of the reservations permitted by Article 15(3) of this Treaty.

Chapter II. Rights of Performers

Article 5. Moral Rights of Performers

(1) Independently of a performer's economic rights, and even after the transfer of those rights, the performer shall, as regards his live aural performances or performances fixed in phonograms, have the right to claim to be identified as the performer of his performances, except where omission is dictated by the manner of the use of the performance, and to object to any distortion, mutilation or other modification of his performances that would be prejudicial to his reputation.

(2) The rights granted to a performer in accordance with paragraph (1) shall, after his death, be maintained, at least until the expiry of the economic rights, and shall be exercisable by the persons or institutions authorized by the legislation of the Contracting Party where protection is claimed. However, those Contracting Parties whose legislation, at the moment of their ratification of or accession to this Treaty, does not provide for protection after the death of the performer of all rights set out in the preceding paragraph may provide that some of these rights will, after his death, cease to be maintained.

(3) The means of redress for safeguarding the rights granted under this Article shall be governed by the legislation of the Contracting Party where protection is claimed.

Article 6. Economic Rights of Performers in their Unfixed Performances

Performers shall enjoy the exclusive right of authorizing, as regards their performances:

(i) the broadcasting and communication to the public of their unfixed performances except where the performance is already a broadcast performance; and

(ii) the fixation of their unfixed performances.

Article 7. Right of Reproduction

Performers shall enjoy the exclusive right of authorizing the direct or indirect reproduction of their performances fixed in phonograms, in any manner or form.

Article 8. Right of Distribution

(1) Performers shall enjoy the exclusive right of authorizing the making available to the public of the original and copies of their performances fixed in phonograms through sale or other transfer of ownership.

(2) Nothing in this Treaty shall affect the freedom of Contracting Parties to determine the conditions, if any, under which the exhaustion of the right in paragraph (1) applies after the first sale or other transfer of ownership of the original or a copy of the fixed performance with the authorization of the performer.

Article 9. Right of Rental

(1) Performers shall enjoy the exclusive right of authorizing the commercial rental to the public of the original and copies of their performances fixed in phonograms as determined in the national law of Contracting Parties, even after distribution of them by, or pursuant to, authorization by the performer.

(2) Notwithstanding the provisions of paragraph (1), a Contracting Party that, on April 15, 1994, had and continues to have in force a system of equitable remuneration of performers for the rental of copies of their performances fixed in phonograms, may maintain that system provided that the commercial rental of phonograms is not giving rise to the material impairment of the exclusive right of reproduction of performers.

Article 10. Right of Making Available of Fixed Performances

Performers shall enjoy the exclusive right of authorizing the making available to the public of their performances fixed in phonograms, by wire or wireless means, in such a way that members of the public may access them from a place and at a time individually chosen by them.

Chapter III.   Rights of Producers of Phonograms

Article 11.   Right of Reproduction

Producers of phonograms shall enjoy the exclusive right of authorizing the direct or indirect reproduction of their phonograms, in any manner or form.

Article 12.   Right of Distribution

(1) Producers of phonograms shall enjoy the exclusive right of authorizing the making available to the public of the original and copies of their phonograms through sale or other transfer of ownership.

(2) Nothing in this Treaty shall affect the freedom of Contracting Parties to determine the conditions, if any, under which the exhaustion of the right in paragraph (1) applies after the first sale or other transfer of ownership of the original or a copy of the phonogram with the authorization of the producer of the phonogram.

Article 13.   Right of Rental

(1) Producers of phonograms shall enjoy the exclusive right of authorizing the commercial rental to the public of the original and copies of their phonograms, even after distribution of them by or pursuant to authorization by the producer.

(2) Notwithstanding the provisions of paragraph (1), a Contracting Party that, on April 15, 1994, had and continues to have in force a system of equitable remuneration of producers of phonograms for the rental of copies of their phonograms, may maintain that system provided that the commercial rental of phonograms is not giving rise to the material impairment of the exclusive rights of reproduction of producers of phonograms.

Article 14.   Right of Making Available of Phonograms

Producers of phonograms shall enjoy the exclusive right of authorizing the making available to the public of their phonograms, by wire or wireless means, in such a way that members of the public may access them from a place and at a time individually chosen by them.

Chapter IV.   Common Provisions

Article 15.   Right to Remuneration for Broadcasting and Communication to the Public

(1) Performers and producers of phonograms shall enjoy the right to a single equitable remuneration for the direct or indirect use of phonograms published for commercial purposes for broadcasting or for any communication to the public.

(2) Contracting Parties may establish in their national legislation that the single equitable remuneration shall be claimed from the user by the performer or by the producer of a phonogram or by both. Contracting Parties may enact national legislation that, in the absence of an agreement between the performer and the producer of a phonogram, sets the terms according to which performers and producers of phonograms shall share the single equitable remuneration.

(3) Any Contracting Party may in a notification deposited with the Director General of WIPO, declare that it will apply the provisions of paragraph (1) only in respect of certain uses, or that it will limit their application in some other way, or that it will not apply these provisions at all.

(4) For the purposes of this Article, phonograms made available to the public by wire or wireless means in such a way that members of the public may access them from a place and at a time individually chosen by them shall be considered as if they had been published for commercial purposes.

Article 16. Limitations and Exceptions

(1) Contracting Parties may, in their national legislation, provide for the same kinds of limitations or exceptions with regard to the protection of performers and producers of phonograms as they provide for, in their national legislation, in connection with the protection of copyright in literary and artistic works.

(2) Contracting Parties shall confine any limitations of or exceptions to rights provided for in this Treaty to certain special cases which do not conflict with a normal exploitation of the performance or phonogram and do not unreasonably prejudice the legitimate interests of the performer or of the producer of the phonogram.

Article 17. Term of Protection

(1) The term of protection to be granted to performers under this Treaty shall last, at least, until the end of a period of 50 years computed from the end of the year in which the performance was fixed in a phonogram.

(2) The term of protection to be granted to producers of phonograms under this Treaty shall last, at least, until the end of a period of 50 years computed from the end of the year in which the phonogram was published, or failing such publication within 50 years from fixation of the phonogram, 50 years from the end of the year in which the fixation was made.

Article 18. Obligations concerning Technological Measures

Contracting Parties shall provide adequate legal protection and effective legal remedies against the circumvention of effective technological measures that are used by performers or producers of phonograms in connection with the exercise of their rights under this Treaty and that restrict acts, in respect of their performances or phonograms, which are not authorized by the performers or the producers of phonograms concerned or permitted by law.

Article 19. Obligations concerning Rights Management Information

(1) Contracting Parties shall provide adequate and effective legal remedies against any person knowingly performing any of the following acts knowing, or with respect to civil remedies having reasonable grounds to know, that it will induce, enable, facilitate or conceal an infringement of any right covered by this Treaty:

(i) to remove or alter any electronic rights management information without authority;

(ii) to distribute, import for distribution, broadcast, communicate or make available to the public, without authority, performances, copies of fixed performances or phonograms knowing that electronic rights management information has been removed or altered without authority.

(2) As used in this Article, "rights management information" means information which identifies the performer, the performance of the performer, the producer of the phonogram, the phonogram, the owner of any right in the performance or phonogram, or information about the terms and conditions of use of the performance or phonogram, and any numbers or codes that represent such information, when any of these items of information is attached to a copy of a fixed performance or a phonogram or appears in connection with the communication or making available of a fixed performance or a phonogram to the public.

Article 20. Formalities

The enjoyment and exercise of the rights provided for in this Treaty shall not be subject to any formality.

Article 21. Reservations

Subject to the provisions of Article 15(3), no reservations to this Treaty shall be permitted.

Article 22. Application in Time

(1) Contracting Parties shall apply the provisions of Article 18 of the Berne Convention, *mutatis mutandis*, to the rights of performers and producers of phonograms provided for in this Treaty.

(2) Notwithstanding paragraph (1), a Contracting Party may limit the application of Article 5 of this Treaty to performances which occurred after the entry into force of this Treaty for that Party.

Article 23. Provisions on Enforcement of Rights

(1) Contracting Parties undertake to adopt, in accordance with their legal systems, the measures necessary to ensure the application of this Treaty.

(2) Contracting Parties shall ensure that enforcement procedures are available under their law so as to permit effective action against any act of infringement of rights covered by this Treaty, including expeditious remedies to prevent infringements and remedies which constitute a deterrent to further infringements.

Chapter V. Administrative and Final Clauses

Article 24. Assembly

(1)(a) The Contracting Parties shall have an Assembly.

(b) Each Contracting Party shall be represented by one delegate who may be assisted by alternate delegates, advisors and experts.

(c) The expenses of each delegation shall be borne by the Contracting Party that has appointed the delegation. The Assembly may ask WIPO to grant financial assistance to facilitate the participation of delegations of Contracting Parties that are regarded as developing countries in conformity with the established practice of the General Assembly of the United Nations or that are countries in transition to a market economy.

(2)(a) The Assembly shall deal with matters concerning the maintenance and development of this Treaty and the application and operation of this Treaty.

(b) The Assembly shall perform the function allocated to it under Article 26(2) in respect of the admission of certain intergovernmental organizations to become party to this Treaty.

(c) The Assembly shall decide the convocation of any diplomatic conference for the revision of this Treaty and give the necessary instructions to the Director General of WIPO for the preparation of such diplomatic conference.

(3)(a) Each Contracting Party that is a State shall have one vote and shall vote only in its own name.

(b) Any Contracting Party that is an intergovernmental organization may participate in the vote, in place of its Member States, with a number of votes equal to the number of its Member States which are party to this Treaty. No such intergovernmental organization shall participate in the vote if any one of its Member States exercises its right to vote and vice versa.

(4) The Assembly shall meet in ordinary session once every two years upon convocation by the Director General of WIPO.

(5) The Assembly shall establish its own rules of procedure, including the convocation of extraordinary sessions, the requirements of a quorum and, subject to the provisions of this Treaty, the required majority for various kinds of decisions.

Article 25. International Bureau

The International Bureau of WIPO shall perform the administrative tasks concerning the Treaty.

Article 26. Eligibility for Becoming Party to the Treaty

(1) Any Member State of WIPO may become party to this Treaty.

(2) The Assembly may decide to admit any intergovernmental organization to become party to this Treaty which declares that it is competent in respect of, and has its own legislation binding on all its Member States on, matters covered by this Treaty and that it has been duly authorized, in accordance with its internal procedures, to become party to this Treaty.

(3) The European Community, having made the declaration referred to in the preceding paragraph in the Diplomatic Conference that has adopted this Treaty, may become party to this Treaty.

Article 27. Rights and Obligations under the Treaty

Subject to any specific provisions to the contrary in this Treaty, each Contracting Party shall enjoy all of the rights and assume all of the obligations under this Treaty.

Article 28. Signature of the Treaty

This Treaty shall be open for signature until December 31, 1997, by any Member State of WIPO and by the European Community.

Article 28. Entry into Force of the Treaty

This Treaty shall enter into force three months after 30 instruments of ratification or accession by States have been deposited with the Director General of WIPO.

Article 30. Effective Date of Becoming Party to the Treaty

This Treaty shall bind

(i) the 30 States referred to in Article 29, from the date on which this Treaty has entered into force;

(ii) each other State from the expiration of three months from the date on which the State has deposited its instrument with the Director General of WIPO;

(iii) the European Community, from the expiration of three months after the deposit of its instrument of ratification or accession if such instrument has been deposited after the entry into force of this Treaty according to Article 29, or, three months after the entry into force of this Treaty if such instrument has been deposited before the entry into force of this Treaty;

(iv) any other intergovernmental organization that is admitted to become party to this Treaty, from the expiration of three months after the deposit of its instrument of accession.

Article 31. Denunciation of the Treaty

This Treaty may be denounced by any Contracting Party by notification addressed to the Director General of WIPO. Any denunciation shall take effect one year from the date on which the Director General of WIPO received the notification.

Article 32. Languages of the Treaty

(1) This Treaty is signed in a single original in English, Arabic, Chinese, French, Russian and Spanish languages, the versions in all these languages being equally authentic.

(2) An official text in any language other than those referred to in paragraph (1) shall be established by the Director General of WIPO on the request of an interested party, after consultation with all the interested parties. For the purposes of this paragraph, "interested party" means any Member State of WIPO whose official language, or one of whose official languages, is involved and the European Community, and any other intergovernmental organization that may become party to this Treaty, if one of its official languages is involved.

Article 33. Depositary

The Director General of WIPO is the depositary of this Treaty.

Agreed Statements Concerning the WIPO Performances and Phonograms Treaty

Adopted by the Diplomatic Conference on December 20, 1996

Concerning Article 1

It is understood that Article 1(2) clarifies the relationship between rights in phonograms under this Treaty and copyright in works embodied in the phonograms. In cases where authorization is needed from both the author of a work embodied in the phonogram and a performer or producer owning rights in the phonogram, the need for the authorization of the author does not cease to exist because the authorization of the performer or producer is also required, and vice versa.

It is further understood that nothing in Article 1(2) precludes a Contracting Party from providing exclusive rights to a performer or producer of phonograms beyond those required to be provided under this Treaty.

Concerning Article 2(b)

It is understood that the definition of phonogram provided in Article 2(b) does not suggest that rights in the phonogram are in any way affected through their incorporation into a cinematographic or other audiovisual work.

Concerning Articles 2(e), 8, 9, 12, and 13

As used in these Articles, the expressions "copies" and "original and copies," being subject to the right of distribution and the right of rental under the said Articles, refer exclusively to fixed copies that can be put into circulation as tangible objects.

Concerning Article 3

It is understood that the reference in Articles 5(a) and 16(a)(iv) of the Rome Convention to "national of another Contracting State" will, when applied to this Treaty, mean, in regard to an intergovernmental organization that is a Contracting Party to this Treaty, a national of one of the countries that is a member of that organization.

Concerning Article 3(2)

For the application of Article 3(2), it is understood that fixation means the finalization of the master tape ("bande-mère").

Concerning Articles 7, 11, and 16

The reproduction right, as set out in Articles 7 and 11, and the exceptions permitted thereunder through Article 16, fully apply in the digital environment, in particular to the use of performances and phonograms in digital form. It is understood that the storage of a protected performance or phonogram in digital form in an electronic medium constitutes a reproduction within the meaning of these Articles.

Concerning Article 15

It is understood that Article 15 does not represent a complete resolution of the level of rights of broadcasting and communication to the public that should be enjoyed by performers and phonogram producers in the digital age. Delegations were unable to achieve consensus on differing proposals for aspects of exclusivity to be provided in certain circumstances or for rights to be provided without the possibility of reservations, and have therefore left the issue to future resolution.

Concerning Article 15

It is understood that Article 15 does not prevent the granting of the right conferred by this Article to performers of folklore and producers of phonograms recording folklore where such phonograms have not been published for commercial gain.

Concerning Article 16

The agreed statement concerning Article 10 (on Limitations and Exceptions) of the WIPO Copyright Treaty is applicable *mutatis mutandis* also to Article 16 (on Limitations and Exceptions) of the WIPO Performances and Phonograms Treaty.

Concerning Article 19

The agreed statement concerning Article 12 (on Obligations concerning Rights Management Information) of the WIPO Copyright Treaty is applicable *mutatis mutandis* also to Article 19 (on Obligations concerning Rights Management Information) of the WIPO Performances and Phonograms Treaty.

Part III
European Union Materials

A. Council Directive 91/250/EEC of 14 May 1991 on the legal protection of computer programs

THE COUNCIL OF THE EUROPEAN COMMUNITIES,

Having regard to the Treaty establishing the European Economic Community and in particular Article 100a thereof,

Having regard to the proposal from the Commission,

In cooperation with the European Parliament,

Having regard to the opinion of the Economic and Social Committee,

Whereas computer programs are at present not clearly protected in all Member States by existing legislation and such protection, where it exists, has different attributes;

Whereas the development of computer programs requires the investment of considerable human, technical and financial resources while computer programs can be copied at a fraction of the cost needed to develop them independently;

Whereas computer programs are playing an increasingly important role in a broad range of industries and computer program technology can accordingly be considered as being of fundamental importance for the Community's industrial development;

Whereas certain differences in the legal protection of computer programs offered by the laws of the Member States have direct and negative effects on the functioning of the common market as regards computer programs and such differences could well become greater as Member States introduce new legislation on this subject;

Whereas existing differences having such effects need to be removed and new ones prevented from arising, while differences not adversely affecting the functioning of the common market to a substantial degree need not be removed or prevented from arising;

Whereas the Community's legal framework on the protection of computer programs can accordingly in the first instance be limited to establishing that Member States should accord protection to computer programs under copyright law as literary works and, further, to establishing who and what should be protected, the exclusive rights on which protected persons should be able to rely in order to authorize or prohibit certain acts and for how long the protection should apply;

Whereas, for the purpose of this Directive, the term 'computer program' shall include programs in any form, including those which are incorporated into hardware; whereas this term also includes preparatory design work leading to the development of a computer program provided that the nature of the preparatory work is such that a computer program can result from it at a later stage;

Whereas, in respect of the criteria to be applied in determining whether or not a computer program is an original work, no tests as to the qualitative or aesthetic merits of the program should be applied;

Whereas the Community is fully committed to the promotion of international standardization;

Whereas the function of a computer program is to communicate and work together with other components of a computer system and with users and, for this purpose, a logical and, where appropriate, physical interconnection and interaction is required to permit all elements of software and hardware to work with other software and hardware and with users in all the ways in which they are intended to function;

Whereas the parts of the program which provide for such interconnection and interaction between elements of software and hardware are generally known as 'interfaces';

Whereas this functional interconnection and interaction is generally known as 'interoperability'; whereas such interoperability can be defined as the ability to exchange information and mutually to use the information which has been exchanged;

Whereas, for the avoidance of doubt, it has to be made clear that only the expression of a computer program is protected and that ideas and principles which underlie any element of a program, including those which underlie its interfaces, are not protected by copyright under this Directive;

Whereas, in accordance with this principle of copyright, to the extent that logic, algorithms and programming languages comprise ideas and principles, those ideas and principles are not protected under this Directive;

Whereas, in accordance with the legislation and jurisprudence of the Member States and the international copyright conventions, the expression of those ideas and principles is to be protected by copyright;

Whereas, for the purposes of this Directive, the term 'rental' means the making available for use, for a limited period of time and for profit-making purposes, of a computer program or a copy thereof;

Whereas this term does not include public lending, which, accordingly, remains outside the scope of this Directive; Whereas the exclusive rights of the author to prevent the unauthorized reproduction of his work have to be subject to a limited exception in the case of a computer program to allow the reproduction technically necessary for the use of that program by the lawful acquirer;

Whereas this means that the acts of loading and running necessary for the use of a copy of a program which has been lawfully acquired, and the act of correction of its errors, may not be prohibited by contract;

Whereas, in the absence of specific contractual provisions, including when a copy of the program has been sold, any other act necessary for the use of the copy of a program may be performed in accordance with its intended purpose by a lawful acquirer of that copy;

Whereas a person having a right to use a computer program should not be prevented from performing acts necessary to observe, study or test the functioning of the program, provided that these acts do not infringe the copyright in the program;

Whereas the unauthorized reproduction, translation, adaptation or transformation of the form of the code in which a copy of a computer program has been made available constitutes an infringement of the exclusive rights of the author;

Whereas, nevertheless, circumstances may exist when such a reproduction of the code and translation of its form within the meaning of Article 4 (a) and (b) are indispensable to obtain the necessary information to achieve the interoperability of an independently created program with other programs;

Whereas it has therefore to be considered that in these limited circumstances only, performance of the acts of reproduction and translation by or on behalf of a person having a right to use a copy of the program is legitimate and compatible with fair practice and must therefore be deemed not to require the authorization of the rightholder;

Whereas an objective of this exception is to make it possible to connect all components of a computer system, including those of different manufacturers, so that they can work together;

Whereas such an exception to the author's exclusive rights may not be used in a way which prejudices the legitimate interests of the rightholder or which conflicts with a normal exploitation of the program;

Whereas, in order to remain in accordance with the provisions of the Berne Convention for the Protection of Literary and Artistic Works, the term of protection should be the life of the author and fifty years from the first of January of the year following the year of his death or, in the case of an anonymous or pseudonymous work, 50 years from the first of January of the year following the year in which the work is first published;

Whereas protection of computer programs under copyright laws should be without prejudice to the application, in appropriate cases, of other forms of protection; whereas, however, any contractual provisions contrary to Article 6 or to the exceptions provided for in Article 5 (2) and (3) should be null and void;

Whereas the provisions of this Directive are without prejudice to the application of the competition rules under Articles 85 and 86 of the Treaty if a dominant supplier refuses to make information available which is necessary for interoperability as defined in this Directive;

Whereas the provisions of this Directive should be without prejudice to specific requirements of Community law already enacted in respect of the publication of interfaces in the telecommunications sector or Council Decisions relating to standardization in the field of information technology and telecommunication;

Whereas this Directive does not affect derogations provided for under national legislation in accordance with the Berne Convention on points not covered by this Directive,

HAS ADOPTED THIS DIRECTIVE:

Article 1. Object of protection

1. In accordance with the provisions of this Directive, Member States shall protect computer programs, by copyright, as literary works within the meaning of the Berne Convention for the Protection of Literary and Artistic Works. For the purposes of this Directive, the term 'computer programs' shall include their preparatory design material.

2. Protection in accordance with this Directive shall apply to the expression in any form of a computer program. Ideas and principles which underlie any element of a computer program, including those which underlie its interfaces, are not protected by copyright under this Directive.

3. A computer program shall be protected if it is original in the sense that it is the author's own intellectual creation. No other criteria shall be applied to determine its eligibility for protection.

Article 2. Authorship of computer programs

1. The author of a computer program shall be the natural person or group of natural persons who has created the program or, where the legislation of the Member State permits, the legal person designated as the rightholder by that legislation. Where collective works are recognized by the legislation of a Member State, the person considered by the legislation of the Member State to have created the work shall be deemed to be its author.

2. In respect of a computer program created by a group of natural persons jointly, the exclusive rights shall be owned jointly.

3. Where a computer program is created by an employee in the execution of his duties or following the instructions given by his employer, the employer exclusively shall be entitled to exercise all economic rights in the program so created, unless otherwise provided by contract.

Article 3. Beneficiaries of protection

Protection shall be granted to all natural or legal persons eligible under national copyright legislation as applied to literary works.

310

Article 4.　Restricted Acts

Subject to the provisions of Articles 5 and 6, the exclusive rights of the rightholder within the meaning of Article 2, shall include the right to do or to authorize:

(a) the permanent or temporary reproduction of a computer program by any means and in any form, in part or in whole. Insofar as loading, displaying, running, transmission or storage of the computer program necessitate such reproduction, such acts shall be subject to authorization by the rightholder;

(b) the translation, adaptation, arrangement and any other alteration of a computer program and the reproduction of the results thereof, without prejudice to the rights of the person who alters the program;

(c) any form of distribution to the public, including the rental, of the original computer program or of copies thereof. The first sale in the Community of a copy of a program by the rightholder or with his consent shall exhaust the distribution right within the Community of that copy, with the exception of the right to control further rental of the program or a copy thereof.

Article 5.　Exceptions to the restricted acts

1.　In the absence of specific contractual provisions, the acts referred to in Article 4(a) and (b) shall not require authorization by the rightholder where they are necessary for the use of the computer program by the lawful acquirer in accordance with its intended purpose, including for error correction.

2.　The making of a back-up copy by a person having a right to use the computer program may not be prevented by contract insofar as it is necessary for that use.

3.　The person having a right to use a copy of a computer program shall be entitled, without the authorization of the rightholder, to observe, study or test the functioning of the program in order to determine the ideas and principles which underlie any element of the program if he does so while performing any of the acts of loading, displaying, running, transmitting or storing the program which he is entitled to do.

Article 6.　Decompilation

1.　The authorization of the rightholder shall not be required where reproduction of the code and translation of its form within the meaning of Article 4 (a) and (b) are indispensable to obtain the information necessary to achieve the interoperability of an independently created computer program with other programs, provided that the following conditions are met:

(a) these acts are performed by the licensee or by another person having a right to use a copy of a program, or on their behalf by a person authorized to [do] so;

(b) the information necessary to achieve interoperability has not previously been readily available to the persons referred to in subparagraph (a); and (c) these acts are confined to the parts of the original program which are necessary to achieve interoperability.

2. The provisions of paragraph 1 shall not permit the information obtained through its application:

(a) to be used for goals other than to achieve the interoperability of the independently created computer program;

(b) to be given to others, except when necessary for the interoperability of the independently created computer program; or

(c) to be used for the development, production or marketing of a computer program substantially similar in its expression, or for any other act which infringes copyright.

3. In accordance with the provisions of the Berne Convention for the protection of Literary and Artistic Works, the provisions of this Article may not be interpreted in such a way as to allow its application to be used in a manner which unreasonably prejudices the right holder's legitimate interests or conflicts with a normal exploitation of the computer program.

Article 7.   Special measures of protection

1. Without prejudice to the provisions of Articles 4, 5 and 6, Member States shall provide, in accordance with their national legislation, appropriate remedies against a person committing any of the acts listed in subparagraphs (a), (b) and (c) below:

(a) any act of putting into circulation a copy of a computer program knowing, or having reason to believe, that it is an infringing copy;

(b) the possession, for commercial purposes, of a copy of a computer program knowing, or having reason to believe, that it is an infringing copy;

(c) any act of putting into circulation, or the possession for commercial purposes of, any means the sole intended purpose of which is to facilitate the unauthorized removal or circumvention of any technical device which may have been applied to protect a computer program.

2. Any infringing copy of a computer program shall be liable to seizure in accordance with the legislation of the Member State concerned.

3. Member States may provide for the seizure of any means referred to in paragraph 1 (c).

Article 8.   Term of protection

1. Protection shall be granted for the life of the author and for fifty years after his death or after the death of the last surviving author; where the computer program is an anonymous or pseudonymous work, or where a legal person is designated as the author by national legislation in accordance with Article 2 (1),

the term of protection shall be fifty years from the time that the computer pro-gram is first lawfully made available to the public. The term of protection shall be deemed to begin on the first of January of the year following the abovementioned events.

2.   Member States which already have a term of protection longer than that provided for in paragraph 1 are allowed to maintain their present term until such time as the term of protection for copyright works is harmonized by Community law in a more general way.

Article 9.   Continued application of other legal provisions

1.   The provisions of this Directive shall be without prejudice to any other legal provisions such as those concerning patent rights, trade-marks, unfair competition, trade secrets, protection of semi-conductor products or the law of contract. Any contractual provisions contrary to Article 6 or to the exceptions provided for in Article 5 (2) and (3) shall be null and void.

2.   The provisions of this Directive shall apply also to programs created before 1 January 1993 without prejudice to any acts concluded and rights acquired before that date.

Article 10.   Final provisions

1.   Member States shall bring into force the laws, regulations and adminis-trative provisions necessary to comply with this Directive before 1 January 1993. When Member States adopt these measures, the latter shall contain a reference to this Directive or shall be accompanied by such reference on the occasion of their official publication. The methods of making such a reference shall be laid down by the Member States.

2.   Member States shall communicate to the Commission the provisions of national law which they adopt in the field governed by this Directive.

Article 11

This Directive is addressed to the Member States.

B. Directive 96/9/EC of the European Parliament and of the Council of 11 March 1996 on the legal protection of databases

THE EUROPEAN PARLIAMENT AND THE COUNCIL OF THE EUROPEAN UNION,

Having regard to the Treaty establishing the European Community, and in particular Article 57 (2), 66 and 100a thereof,

Having regard to the proposal from the Commission,

Having regard to the opinion of the Economic and Social Committee,

Acting in accordance with the procedure laid down in Article 189b of the Treaty,

(1) Whereas databases are at present not sufficiently protected in all Member States by existing legislation; whereas such protection, where it exists, has different attributes;

(2) Whereas such differences in the legal protection of databases offered by the legislation of the Member States have direct negative effects on the functioning of the internal market as regards databases and in particular on the freedom of natural and legal persons to provide on-line database goods and services on the basis of harmonized legal arrangements throughout the Community; whereas such differences could well become more pronounced as Member States introduce new legislation in this field, which is now taking on an increasingly international dimension;

(3) Whereas existing differences distorting the functioning of the internal market need to be removed and new ones prevented from arising, while differences not adversely affecting the functioning of the internal market or the development of an information market within the Community need not be removed or prevented from arising;

(4) Whereas copyright protection for databases exists in varying forms in the Member States according to legislation or case-law, and whereas, if differences in legislation in the scope and conditions of protection remain between the Member States, such unharmonized intellectual property rights can have the effect of preventing the free movement of goods or services within the Community;

(5)   Whereas copyright remains an appropriate form of exclusive right for authors who have created databases;

(6)   Whereas, nevertheless, in the absence of a harmonized system of unfair-competition legislation or of case-law, other measures are required in addition to prevent the unauthorized extraction and/or re-utilization of the contents of a database;

(7)   Whereas the making of databases requires the investment of considerable human, technical and financial resources while such databases can be copied or accessed at a fraction of the cost needed to design them independently;

(8)   Whereas the unauthorized extraction and/or re-utilization of the contents of a database constitute acts which can have serious economic and technical consequences;

(9)   Whereas databases are a vital tool in the development of an information market within the Community; whereas this tool will also be of use in many other fields;

(10)   Whereas the exponential growth, in the Community and worldwide, in the amount of information generated and processed annually in all sectors of commerce and industry calls for investment in all the Member States in advanced information processing systems;

(11)   Whereas there is at present a very great imbalance in the level of investment in the database sector both as between the Member States and between the Community and the world's largest database-producing third countries;

(12)   Whereas such an investment in modern information storage and processing systems will not take place within the Community unless a stable and uniform legal protection regime is introduced for the protection of the rights of makers of databases;

(13)   Whereas this Directive protects collections, sometimes called 'compilations', of works, data or other materials which are arranged, stored and accessed by means which include electronic, electromagnetic or electro-optical processes or analogous processes;

(14)   Whereas protection under this Directive should be extended to cover non-electronic databases;

(15)   Whereas the criteria used to determine whether a database should be protected by copyright should be defined to the fact that the selection or the arrangement of the contents of the database is the author's own intellectual creation; whereas such protection should cover the structure of the database;

(16)   Whereas no criterion other than originality in the sense of the author's intellectual creation should be applied to determine the eligibility of the database for copyright protection, and in particular no aesthetic or qualitative criteria should be applied;

(17)   Whereas the term 'database' should be understood to include literary, artistic, musical or other collections of works or collections of other material such as texts, sound, images, numbers, facts, and data; whereas it should cover collections of independent works, data or other materials which are systematically or methodically arranged and can be individually accessed; whereas this means that a recording or an audiovisual, cinematographic, literary or musical work as such does not fall within the scope of this Directive;

316

(18)   Whereas this Directive is without prejudice to the freedom of authors to decide whether, or in what manner, they will allow their works to be included in a database, in particular whether or not the authorization given is exclusive; whereas the protection of databases by the sui generis right is without prejudice to existing rights over their contents, and whereas in particular where an author or the holder of a related right permits some of his works or subject matter to be included in a database pursuant to a non-exclusive agreement, a third party may make use of those works or subject matter subject to the required consent of the author or of the holder of the related right without the sui generis right of the maker of the database being invoked to prevent him doing so, on condition that those works or subject matter are neither extracted from the database nor re-utilized on the basis thereof;

(19)   Whereas, as a rule, the compilation of several recordings of musical performances on a CD does not come within the scope of this Directive, both because, as a compilation, it does not meet the conditions for copyright protection and be-cause it does not represent a substantial enough investment to be eligible under the sui generis right;

(20)   Whereas protection under this Directive may also apply to the materials necessary for the operation or consultation of certain databases such as thesaurus and indexation systems;

(21)   Whereas the protection provided for in this Directive relates to databases in which works, data or other materials have been arranged systematically or methodically; whereas it is not necessary for those materials to have been physically stored in an organized manner;

(22)   Whereas electronic databases within the meaning of this Directive may also include devices such as CD-ROM and CD-i;

(23)   Whereas the term 'database' should not be taken to extend to computer programs used in the making or operation of a database, which are protected by Council Directive 91/250/EEC of 14 May 1991 on the legal protection of computer programs;

(24)   Whereas the rental and lending of databases in the field of copyright and related rights are governed exclusively by Council Directive 92/100/EEC of 19 November 1992 on rental right and lending right and on certain rights related to copyright in the field of intellectual property;

(25)   Whereas the term of copyright is already governed by Council Directive 93/98/EEC of 29 October 1993 harmonizing the term of protection of copyright and certain related rights;

(26)   Whereas works protected by copyright and subject matter protected by related rights, which are incorporated into a database, remain nevertheless protected by the respective exclusive rights and may not be incorporated into, or extracted from, the database without the permission of the rightholder or his successors in title;

(27)   Whereas copyright in such works and related rights in subject matter thus incorporated into a database are in no way affected by the existence of a separate right in the selection or arrangement of these works and subject matter in a database;

(28)   Whereas the moral rights of the natural person who created the database belong to the author and should be exercised according to the legislation of the Member States and the provisions of the Berne Convention for the Protection of Literary and Artistic Works; whereas such moral rights remain outside the scope of this Directive;

(29)   Whereas the arrangements applicable to databases created by employees are left to the discretion of the Member States; whereas, therefore nothing in this Directive prevents Member States from stipulating in their legislation that where a database is created by an employee in the execution of his duties or following the instructions given by his employer, the employer exclusively shall be entitled to exercise all economic rights in the database so created, unless otherwise provided by contract;

(30)   Whereas the author's exclusive rights should include the right to determine the way in which his work is exploited and by whom, and in particular to control the distribution of his work to unauthorized persons;

(31)   Whereas the copyright protection of databases includes making databases available by means other than the distribution of copies;

(32)   Whereas Member States are required to ensure that their national provisions are at least materially equivalent in the case of such acts subject to restrictions as are provided for by this Directive;

(33)   Whereas the question of exhaustion of the right of distribution does not arise in the case of on-line databases, which come within the field of provision of services; whereas this also applies with regard to a material copy of such a database made by the user of such a service with the consent of the rightholder; whereas, unlike CD-ROM or CD-i, where the intellectual property is incorporated in a material medium, namely an item of goods, every on-line service is in fact an act which will have to be subject to authorization where the copyright so provides;

(34)   Whereas, nevertheless, once the rightholder has chosen to make available a copy of the database to a user, whether by an on-line service or by other means of distribution, that lawful user must be able to access and use the database for the purposes and in the way set out in the agreement with the rightholder, even if such access and use necessitate performance of otherwise restricted acts;

(35)   Whereas a list should be drawn up of exceptions to restricted acts, taking into account the fact that copyright as covered by this Directive applies only to the selection or arrangements of the contents of a database; whereas Member States should be given the option of providing for such exceptions in certain cases; whereas, however, this option should be exercised in accordance with the Berne Convention and to the extent that the exceptions relate to the structure of the database; whereas a distinction should be drawn between exceptions for private use and exceptions for reproduction for private purposes, which concerns provisions under national legislation of some Member States on levies on blank media or recording equipment;

(36)   Whereas the term 'scientific research' within the meaning of this Directive covers both the natural sciences and the human sciences;

(37)   Whereas Article 10 (1) of the Berne Convention is not affected by this Directive;

(38)   Whereas the increasing use of digital recording technology exposes the database maker to the risk that the contents of his database may be copied and rearranged electronically, without his authorization, to produce a database of identical content which, however, does not infringe any copyright in the arrangement of his database;

(39)   Whereas, in addition to aiming to protect the copyright in the original selection or arrangement of the contents of a database, this Directive seeks to safeguard the position of makers of databases against misappropriation of the results of the financial and professional investment made in obtaining and collection the contents by protecting the whole or substantial parts of a database against certain acts by a user or competitor;

(40)   Whereas the object of this sui generis right is to ensure protection of any investment in obtaining, verifying or presenting the contents of a database for the limited duration of the right; whereas such investment may consist in the deployment of financial resources and/or the expending of time, effort and energy;

(41)   Whereas the objective of the sui generis right is to give the maker of a database the option of preventing the unauthorized extraction and/or re-utilization of all or a substantial part of the contents of that database; whereas the maker of a database is the person who takes the initiative and the risk of investing; whereas this excludes subcontractors in particular from the definition of maker;

(42)   Whereas the special right to prevent unauthorized extraction and/or re-utilization relates to acts by the user which go beyond his legitimate rights and thereby harm the investment; whereas the right to prohibit extraction and/or re-utilization of all or a substantial part of the contents relates not only to the manufacture of a parasitical competing product but also to any user who, through his acts, causes significant detriment, evaluated qualitatively or quantitatively, to the investment;

(43)   Whereas, in the case of on-line transmission, the right to prohibit re-utilization is not exhausted either as regards the database or as regards a material copy of the database or of part thereof made by the addressee of the transmission with the consent of the rightholder;

(44)   Whereas, when on-screen display of the contents of a database necessitates the permanent or temporary transfer of all or a substantial part of such contents to another medium, that act should be subject to authorization by the rightholder;

(45)   Whereas the right to prevent unauthorized extraction and/or re-utilization does not in any way constitute an extension of copyright protection to mere facts or data;

(46)   Whereas the existence of a right to prevent the unauthorized extraction and/or re-utilization of the whole or a substantial part of works, data or materials from a database should not give rise to the creation of a new right in the works, data or materials themselves;

(47)   Whereas, in the interests of competition between suppliers of information products and services, protection by the sui generis right must not be afforded in such a way as to facilitate abuses of a dominant position, in particular as regards the creation and distribution of new products and services which have an intellectual, documentary, technical, economic or commercial added value;

whereas, therefore, the provisions of this Directive are without prejudice to the application of Community or national competition rules;

(48) Whereas the objective of this Directive, which is to afford an appropriate and uniform level of protection of databases as a means to secure the remuneration of the maker of the database, is different from the aim of Directive 95/46/ EC of the European Parliament and of the Council of 24 October 1995 on the protection of individuals with regard to the processing of personal data and on the free movement of such data, which is to guarantee free circulation of personal data on the basis of harmonized rules designed to protect fundamental rights, notably the right to privacy which is recognized in Article 8 of the European Convention for the Protection of Human Rights and Fundamental Freedoms; whereas the provisions of this Directive are without prejudice to data protection legislation;

(49) Whereas, notwithstanding the right to prevent extraction and/or re-utilization of all or a substantial part of a database, it should be laid down that the maker of a database or rightholder may not prevent a lawful user of the database from extracting and re-utilizing insubstantial parts; whereas, however, that user may not unreasonably prejudice either the legitimate interests of the holder of the sui generis right or the holder of copyright or a related right in respect of the works or subject matter contained in the database;

(50) Whereas the Member States should be given the option of providing for exceptions to the right to prevent the unauthorized extraction and/or re-utilization of a substantial part of the contents of a database in the case of extraction for private purposes, for the purposes of illustration for teaching or scientific research, or where extraction and/or re-utilization are/is carried out in the interests of public security or for the purposes of an administrative or judicial procedure; whereas such operations must not prejudice the exclusive rights of the maker to exploit the database and their purpose must not be commercial;

(51) Whereas the Member States, where they avail themselves of the option to permit a lawful user of a database to extract a substantial part of the contents for the purposes of illustration for teaching or scientific research, may limit that permission to certain categories of teaching or scientific research institution;

(52) Whereas those Member States which have specific rules providing for a right comparable to the sui generis right provided for in this Directive should be permitted to retain, as far as the new right is concerned, the exceptions traditionally specified by such rules;

(53) Whereas the burden of proof regarding the date of completion of the making of a database lies with the maker of the database;

(54) Whereas the burden of proof that the criteria exist for concluding that a substantial modification of the contents of a database is to be regarded as a substantial new investment lies with the maker of the database resulting from such investment;

(55) Whereas a substantial new investment involving a new term of protection may include a substantial verification of the contents of the database;

(56) Whereas the right to prevent unauthorized extraction and/or re-utilization in respect of a database should apply to databases whose makers are nationals or habitual residents of third countries or to those produced by legal persons not established in a Member State, within the meaning of the Treaty, only

if such third countries offer comparable protection to databases produced by nationals of a Member State or persons who have their habitual residence in the territory of the Community;

(57) Whereas, in addition to remedies provided under the legislation of the Member States for infringements of copyright or other rights, Member States should provide for appropriate remedies against unauthorized extraction and/or re-utilization of the contents of a database;

(58) Whereas, in addition to the protection given under this Directive to the structure of the database by copyright, and to its contents against unauthorized extraction and/or re-utilization under the sui generis right, other legal provisions in the Member States relevant to the supply of database goods and services continue to apply;

(59) Whereas this Directive is without prejudice to the application to databases composed of audiovisual works of any rules recognized by a Member State's legislation concerning the broadcasting of audiovisual programmes;

(60) Whereas some Member States currently protect under copyright arrangements databases which do not meet the criteria for eligibility for copyright protection laid down in this Directive; whereas, even if the databases concerned are eligible for protection under the right laid down in this Directive to prevent unauthorized extraction and/or re-utilization of their contents, the term of protection under that right is considerably shorter than that which they enjoy under the national arrangements currently in force; whereas harmonization of the criteria for determining whether a database is to be protected by copyright may not have the effect of reducing the term of protection currently enjoyed by the rightholders concerned; whereas a derogation should be laid down to that effect; whereas the effects of such derogation must be confined to the territories of the Member States concerned,

HAVE ADOPTED THIS DIRECTIVE:

Chapter I. Scope

Article 1. Scope

1. This Directive concerns the legal protection of databases in any form.

2. For the purposes of this Directive, 'database' shall mean a collection of independent works, data or other materials arranged in a systematic or methodical way and individually accessible by electronic or other means.

3. Protection under this Directive shall not apply to computer programs used in the making or operation of databases accessible by electronic means.

Article 2. Limitations on the scope

This Directive shall apply without prejudice to Community provisions relating to:

(a) the legal protection of computer programs;

(b) rental right, lending right and certain rights related to copyright in the field of intellectual property;

(c) the term of protection of copyright and certain related rights.

Chapter II. Copyright

Article 3. *Object of protection*

1. In accordance with this Directive, databases which, by reason of the selection or arrangement of their contents, constitute the author's own intellectual creation shall be protected as such by copyright. No other criteria shall be applied to determine their eligibility for that protection.

2. The copyright protection of databases provided for by this Directive shall not extend to their contents and shall be without prejudice to any rights subsisting in those contents themselves.

Article 4. *Database authorship*

1. The author of a database shall be the natural person or group of natural persons who created the base or, where the legislation of the Member States so permits, the legal person designated as the rightholder by that legislation.

2. Where collective works are recognized by the legislation of a Member State, the economic rights shall be owned by the person holding the copyright.

3. In respect of a database created by a group of natural persons jointly, the exclusive rights shall be owned jointly.

Article 5. *Restricted acts*

In respect of the expression of the database which is protectable by copyright, the author of a database shall have the exclusive right to carry out or to authorize:

(a) temporary or permanent reproduction by any means and in any form, in whole or in part;

(b) translation, adaptation, arrangement and any other alteration;

(c) any form of distribution to the public of the database or of copies thereof. The first sale in the Community of a copy of the database by the rightholder or with his consent shall exhaust the right to control resale of that copy within the Community;

(d) any communication, display or performance to the public;

(e) any reproduction, distribution, communication, display or performance to the public of the results of the acts referred to in (b).

Article 6. *Exceptions to restricted acts*

1.   The performance by the lawful user of a database or of a copy thereof of any of the acts listed in Article 5 which is necessary for the purposes of access to the contents of the databases and normal use of the contents by the lawful user shall not require the authorization of the author of the database. Where the lawful user is authorized to use only part of the database, this provision shall apply only to that part.

2.   Member States shall have the option of providing for limitations on the rights set out in Article 5 in the following cases:

(a) in the case of reproduction for private purposes of a non-electronic database;

(b) where there is use for the sole purpose of illustration for teaching or scientific research, as long as the source is indicated and to the extent justified by the non-commercial purpose to be achieved;

(c) where there is use for the purposes of public security or for the purposes of an administrative or judicial procedure;

(d) where other exceptions to copyright which are traditionally authorized under national law are involved, without prejudice to points (a), (b) and (c).

3.   In accordance with the Berne Convention for the protection of Literary and Artistic Works, this Article may not be interpreted in such a way as to allow its application to be used in a manner which unreasonably prejudices the right-holder's legitimate interests or conflicts with normal exploitation of the database.

Chapter III. Sui Generis Right

Article 7. *Object of protection*

1.   Member States shall provide for a right for the maker of a database which shows that there has been qualitatively and/or quantitatively a substantial invest-ment in either the obtaining, verification or presentation of the contents to pre-vent extraction and/or re-utilization of the whole or of a substantial part, evaluated qualitatively and/or quantitatively, of the contents of that database.

2.   For the purposes of this Chapter:

(a) 'extraction' shall mean the permanent or temporary transfer of all or a substantial part of the contents of a database to another medium by any means or in any form;

(b) 're-utilization' shall mean any form of making available to the public all or a substantial part of the contents of a database by the distribution of copies, by renting, by on-line or other forms of transmission. The first sale of a copy of a database within the Community by the rightholder or with his consent shall exhaust the right to control resale of that copy within the Community; Public lending is not an act of extraction or re-utilization.

3.   The right referred to in paragraph 1 may be transferred, assigned or granted under contractual licence.

4.   The right provided for in paragraph 1 shall apply irrespective of the eligibility of that database for protection by copyright or by other rights. Moreover, it shall apply irrespective of eligibility of the contents of that database for protection by copyright or by other rights. Protection of databases under the right provided for in paragraph 1 shall be without prejudice to rights existing in respect of their contents.

5.   The repeated and systematic extraction and/or re-utilization of insubstantial parts of the contents of the database implying acts which conflict with a normal exploitation of that database or which unreasonably prejudice the legitimate interests of the maker of the database shall not be permitted.

Article 8.   Rights and obligations of lawful users

1.   The maker of a database which is made available to the public in whatever manner may not prevent a lawful user of the database from extracting and/or re-utilizing insubstantial parts of its contents, evaluated qualitatively and/or quantitatively, for any purposes whatsoever. Where the lawful user is authorized to extract and/or re-utilize only part of the database, this paragraph shall apply only to that part.

2.   A lawful user of a database which is made available to the public in whatever manner may not perform acts which conflict with normal exploitation of the database or unreasonably prejudice the legitimate interests of the maker of the database.

3.   A lawful user of a database which is made available to the public in any manner may not cause prejudice to the holder of a copyright or related right in respect of the works or subject matter contained in the database.

Article 9.   Exceptions to the sui generis right

Member States may stipulate that lawful users of a database which is made available to the public in whatever manner may, without the authorization of its maker, extract or re-utilize a substantial part of its contents:

(a) in the case of extraction for private purposes of the contents of a non-electronic database;

(b) in the case of extraction for the purposes of illustration for teaching or scientific research, as long as the source is indicated and to the extent justified by the non-commercial purpose to be achieved;

(c) in the case of extraction and/or re-utilization for the purposes of public security or an administrative or judicial procedure.

Article 10.   Term of protection

1.   The right provided for in Article 7 shall run from the date of completion of the making of the database. It shall expire fifteen years from the first of January of the year following the date of completion.

2.   In the case of a database which is made available to the public in whatever manner before expiry of the period provided for in paragraph 1, the term of protection by that right shall expire fifteen years from the first of January of the year following the date when the database was first made available to the public.

3.   Any substantial change, evaluated qualitatively or quantitatively, to the contents of a database, including any substantial change resulting from the accumulation of successive additions, deletions or alterations, which would result in the database being considered to be a substantial new investment, evaluated qualitatively or quantitatively, shall qualify the database resulting from that investment for its own term of protection.

Article 11.   Beneficiaries of protection under the sui generis right

1.   The right provided for in Article 7 shall apply to database whose makers or rightholders are nationals of a Member State or who have their habitual residence in the territory of the Community.

2.   Paragraph 1 shall also apply to companies and firms formed in accordance with the law of a Member State and having their registered office, central administration or principal place of business within the Community; however, where such a company or firm has only its registered office in the territory of the Community, its operations must be genuinely linked on an ongoing basis with the economy of a Member State.

3.   Agreements extending the right provided for in Article 7 to databases made in third countries and falling outside the provisions of paragraphs 1 and 2 shall be concluded by the Council acting on a proposal from the Commission. The term of any protection extended to databases by virtue of that procedure shall not exceed that available pursuant to Article 10.

Chapter IV.   Common Provisions

Article 12.   Remedies

Member States shall provide appropriate remedies in respect of infringements of the rights provided for in this Directive.

Article 13.   Continued application of other legal provisions

This Directive shall be without prejudice to provisions concerning in particular copyright, rights related to copyright or any other rights or obligations subsisting in the data, works or other materials incorporated into a database, patent rights, trade marks, design rights, the protection of national treasures, laws on restrictive practices and unfair competition, trade secrets, security, confidentiality, data protection and privacy, access to public documents, and the law of contract.

Article 14. *Application over time*

1.   Protection pursuant to this Directive as regards copyright shall also be available in respect of databases created prior to the date referred to [sic] Article 16 (1) which on that date fulfil the requirements laid down in this Directive as regards copyright protection of databases.

2.   Notwithstanding paragraph 1, where a database protected under copyright arrangements in a Member State on the date of publication of this Directive does not fulfil the eligibility criteria for copyright protection laid down in Article 3 (1), this Directive shall not result in any curtailing in that Member State of the remaining term of protection afforded under those arrangements.

3.   Protection pursuant to the provisions of this Directive as regards the right provided for in Article 7 shall also be available in respect of databases the making of which was completed not more than fifteen years prior to the date referred to in Article 16 (1) and which on that date fulfil the requirements laid down in Article 7.

4.   The protection provided for in paragraphs 1 and 3 shall be without prejudice to any acts concluded and rights acquired before the date referred to in those paragraphs.

5.   In the case of a database the making of which was completed not more than fifteen years prior to the date referred to in Article 16 (1), the term of protection by the right provided for in Article 7 shall expire fifteen years from the first of January following that date.

Article 15. *Binding nature of certain provisions*

Any contractual provision contrary to Articles 6 (1) and 8 shall be null and void.

Article 16. *Final provisions*

1.   Member States shall bring into force the laws, regulations and administrative provisions necessary to comply with this Directive before 1 January 1998.

When Member States adopt these provisions, they shall contain a reference to this Directive or shall be accompanied by such reference on the occasion of their official publication. The methods of making such reference shall be laid down by Member States.

2.   Member States shall communicate to the Commission the text of the provisions of domestic law which they adopt in the field governed by this Directive.

3.   Not later than at the end of the third year after the date referred to in paragraph 1, and every three years thereafter, the Commission shall submit to the European Parliament, the Council and the Economic and Social Committee a report on the application of this Directive, in which, inter alia, on the basis of

specific information supplied by the Member States, it shall examine in particular the application of the sui generis right, including Articles 8 and 9, and shall verify especially whether the application of this right has led to abuse of a dominant position or other interference with free competition which would justify appropriate measures being taken, including the establishment of non-voluntary licensing arrangements. Where necessary, it shall submit proposals for adjustment of this Directive in line with developments in the area of databases.

Article 17.

This Directive is addressed to the Member States.

C. Directive 2001/29/EC of the European Parliament and of the Council of 22 May 2001 on the harmonisation of certain aspects of copyright and related rights in the information society

THE EUROPEAN PARLIAMENT AND THE COUNCIL OF THE EUROPEAN UNION,

Having regard to the Treaty establishing the European Community, and in particular Articles 47(2), 55 and 95 thereof,

Having regard to the proposal from the Commission,

Having regard to the opinion of the Economic and Social Committee,

Acting in accordance with the procedure laid down in Article 251 of the Treaty,

Whereas:

(1) The Treaty provides for the establishment of an internal market and the institution of a system ensuring that competition in the internal market is not distorted. Harmonisation of the laws of the Member States on copyright and related rights contributes to the achievement of these objectives.

(2) The European Council, meeting at Corfu on 24 and 25 June 1994, stressed the need to create a general and flexible legal framework at Community level in order to foster the development of the information society in Europe. This requires, inter alia, the existence of an internal market for new products and services. Important Community legislation to ensure such a regulatory framework is already in place or its adoption is well under way. Copyright and related rights play an important role in this context as they protect and stimulate the development and marketing of new products and services and the creation and exploitation of their creative content.

(3) The proposed harmonisation will help to implement the four freedoms of the internal market and relates to compliance with the fundamental principles of law and especially of property, including intellectual property, and freedom of expression and the public interest.

(4)   A harmonised legal framework on copyright and related rights, through increased legal certainty and while providing for a high level of protection of intellectual property, will foster substantial investment in creativity and innovation, including network infrastructure, and lead in turn to growth and increased competitiveness of European industry, both in the area of content provision and information technology and more generally across a wide range of industrial and cultural sectors. This will safeguard employment and encourage new job creation.

(5)   Technological development has multiplied and diversified the vectors for creation, production and exploitation. While no new concepts for the protection of intellectual property are needed, the current law on copyright and related rights should be adapted and supplemented to respond adequately to economic realities such as new forms of exploitation.

(6)   Without harmonisation at Community level, legislative activities at national level which have already been initiated in a number of Member States in order to respond to the technological challenges might result in significant differences in protection and thereby in restrictions on the free movement of services and products incorporating, or based on, intellectual property, leading to a re-fragmentation of the internal market and legislative inconsistency. The impact of such legislative differences and uncertainties will become more significant with the further development of the information society, which has already greatly increased transborder exploitation of intellectual property. This development will and should further increase. Significant legal differences and uncertainties in protection may hinder economies of scale for new products and services containing copyright and related rights.

(7)   The Community legal framework for the protection of copyright and related rights must, therefore, also be adapted and supplemented as far as is necessary for the smooth functioning of the internal market. To that end, those national provisions on copyright and related rights which vary considerably from one Member State to another or which cause legal uncertainties hindering the smooth functioning of the internal market and the proper development of the information society in Europe should be adjusted, and inconsistent national responses to the technological developments should be avoided, whilst differences not adversely affecting the functioning of the internal market need not be removed or prevented.

(8)   The various social, societal and cultural implications of the information society require that account be taken of the specific features of the content of products and services.

(9)   Any harmonisation of copyright and related rights must take as a basis a high level of protection, since such rights are crucial to intellectual creation. Their protection helps to ensure the maintenance and development of creativity in the interests of authors, performers, producers, consumers, culture, industry and the public at large. Intellectual property has therefore been recognised as an integral part of property.

(10)   If authors or performers are to continue their creative and artistic work, they have to receive an appropriate reward for the use of their work, as must producers in order to be able to finance this work. The investment required to

produce products such as phonograms, films or multimedia products, and services such as "on-demand" services, is considerable. Adequate legal protection of intellectual property rights is necessary in order to guarantee the availability of such a reward and provide the opportunity for satisfactory returns on this investment.

(11)   A rigorous, effective system for the protection of copyright and related rights is one of the main ways of ensuring that European cultural creativity and production receive the necessary resources and of safeguarding the independence and dignity of artistic creators and performers.

(12)   Adequate protection of copyright works and subject-matter of related rights is also of great importance from a cultural standpoint. Article 151 of the Treaty requires the Community to take cultural aspects into account in its action.

(13)   A common search for, and consistent application at European level of, technical measures to protect works and other subject-matter and to provide the necessary information on rights are essential insofar as the ultimate aim of these measures is to give effect to the principles and guarantees laid down in law.

(14)   This Directive should seek to promote learning and culture by protecting works and other subject-matter while permitting exceptions or limitations in the public interest for the purpose of education and teaching.

(15)   The Diplomatic Conference held under the auspices of the World Intellectual Property Organisation (WIPO)   in December 1996 led to the adoption of two new Treaties, the "WIPO Copyright Treaty" and the "WIPO Performances and Phonograms Treaty", dealing respectively with the protection of authors and the protection of performers and phonogram producers. Those Treaties update the international protection for copyright and related rights significantly, not least with regard to the so-called "digital agenda", and improve the means to fight piracy world-wide. The Community and a majority of Member States have already signed the Treaties and the process of making arrangements for the ratification of the Treaties by the Community and the Member States is under way. This Directive also serves to implement a number of the new international obligations.

(16)   Liability for activities in the network environment concerns not only copyright and related rights but also other areas, such as defamation, misleading advertising, or infringement of trademarks, and is addressed horizontally in Directive 2000/31/EC of the European Parliament and of the Council of 8 June 2000 on certain legal aspects of information society services, in particular electronic commerce, in the internal market ('Directive on electronic commerce'), which clarifies and harmonises various legal issues relating to information society services including electronic commerce. This Directive should be implemented within a timescale similar to that for the implementation of the Directive on electronic commerce, since that Directive provides a harmonised framework of principles and provisions relevant inter alia to important parts of this Directive. This Directive is without prejudice to provisions relating to liability in that Directive.

(17)   It is necessary, especially in the light of the requirements arising out of the digital environment, to ensure that collecting societies achieve a higher level of rationalisation and transparency with regard to compliance with competition rules.

(18)   This Directive is without prejudice to the arrangements in the Member States concerning the management of rights such as extended collective licences.

(19)   The moral rights of rightholders should be exercised according to the legislation of the Member States and the provisions of the Berne Convention for the Protection of Literary and Artistic Works, of the WIPO Copyright Treaty and of the WIPO Performances and Phonograms Treaty. Such moral rights remain outside the scope of this Directive.

(20)   This Directive is based on principles and rules already laid down in the Directives currently in force in this area, in particular Directives 91/250/EEC, 92/100/EEC, 93/83/EEC, 93/98/EEC and 96/9/EC, and it develops those principles and rules and places them in the context of the information society. The provisions of this Directive should be without prejudice to the provisions of those Directives, unless otherwise provided in this Directive.

(21)   This Directive should define the scope of the acts covered by the reproduction right with regard to the different beneficiaries. This should be done in conformity with the acquis communautaire. A broad definition of these acts is needed to ensure legal certainty within the internal market.

(22)   The objective of proper support for the dissemination of culture must not be achieved by sacrificing strict protection of rights or by tolerating illegal forms of distribution of counterfeited or pirated works.

(23)   This Directive should harmonise further the author's right of communication to the public. This right should be understood in a broad sense covering all communication to the public not present at the place where the communication originates. This right should cover any such transmission or retransmission of a work to the public by wire or wireless means, including broadcasting. This right should not cover any other acts.

(24)   The right to make available to the public subject-matter referred to in Article 3(2)   should be understood as covering all acts of making available such subject-matter to members of the public not present at the place where the act of making available originates, and as not covering any other acts.

(25)   The legal uncertainty regarding the nature and the level of protection of acts of on-demand transmission of copyright works and subject-matter protected by related rights over networks should be overcome by providing for harmonised protection at Community level. It should be made clear that all rightholders recognised by this Directive should have an exclusive right to make available to the public copyright works or any other subject-matter by way of interactive on-demand transmissions. Such interactive on-demand transmissions are characterised by the fact that members of the public may access them from a place and at a time individually chosen by them.

(26)   With regard to the making available in on-demand services by broadcasters of their radio or television productions incorporating music from commercial phonograms as an integral part thereof, collective licensing arrangements are to be encouraged in order to facilitate the clearance of the rights concerned.

(27)   The mere provision of physical facilities for enabling or making a communication does not in itself amount to communication within the meaning of this Directive.

(28) Copyright protection under this Directive includes the exclusive right to control distribution of the work incorporated in a tangible article. The first sale in the Community of the original of a work or copies thereof by the rightholder or with his consent exhausts the right to control resale of that object in the Community. This right should not be exhausted in respect of the original or of copies thereof sold by the rightholder or with his consent outside the Community. Rental and lending rights for authors have been established in Directive 92/100/EEC. The distribution right provided for in this Directive is without prejudice to the provisions relating to the rental and lending rights contained in Chapter I of that Directive.

(29) The question of exhaustion does not arise in the case of services and on-line services in particular. This also applies with regard to a material copy of a work or other subject-matter made by a user of such a service with the consent of the rightholder. Therefore, the same applies to rental and lending of the original and copies of works or other subject-matter which are services by nature. Unlike CD-ROM or CD-I, where the intellectual property is incorporated in a material medium, namely an item of goods, every on-line service is in fact an act which should be subject to authorisation where the copyright or related right so provides.

(30) The rights referred to in this Directive may be transferred, assigned or subject to the granting of contractual licences, without prejudice to the relevant national legislation on copyright and related rights.

(31) A fair balance of rights and interests between the different categories of rightholders, as well as between the different categories of rightholders and users of protected subject-matter must be safeguarded. The existing exceptions and limitations to the rights as set out by the Member States have to be reassessed in the light of the new electronic environment. Existing differences in the exceptions and limitations to certain restricted acts have direct negative effects on the functioning of the internal market of copyright and related rights. Such differences could well become more pronounced in view of the further development of transborder exploitation of works and cross-border activities. In order to ensure the proper functioning of the internal market, such exceptions and limitations should be defined more harmoniously. The degree of their harmonisation should be based on their impact on the smooth functioning of the internal market.

(32) This Directive provides for an exhaustive enumeration of exceptions and limitations to the reproduction right and the right of communication to the public. Some exceptions or limitations only apply to the reproduction right, where appropriate. This list takes due account of the different legal traditions in Member States, while, at the same time, aiming to ensure a functioning internal market. Member States should arrive at a coherent application of these exceptions and limitations, which will be assessed when reviewing implementing legislation in the future.

(33) The exclusive right of reproduction should be subject to an exception to allow certain acts of temporary reproduction, which are transient or incidental reproductions, forming an integral and essential part of a technological process and carried out for the sole purpose of enabling either efficient transmission in a

network between third parties by an intermediary, or a lawful use of a work or other subject-matter to be made. The acts of reproduction concerned should have no separate economic value on their own. To the extent that they meet these conditions, this exception should include acts which enable browsing as well as acts of caching to take place, including those which enable transmission systems to function efficiently, provided that the intermediary does not modify the information and does not interfere with the lawful use of technology, widely recognised and used by industry, to obtain data on the use of the information. A use should be considered lawful where it is authorised by the rightholder or not restricted by law.

(34)   Member States should be given the option of providing for certain exceptions or limitations for cases such as educational and scientific purposes, for the benefit of public institutions such as libraries and archives, for purposes of news reporting, for quotations, for use by people with disabilities, for public security uses and for uses in administrative and judicial proceedings.

(35)   In certain cases of exceptions or limitations, rightholders should receive fair compensation to compensate them adequately for the use made of their protected works or other subject-matter. When determining the form, detailed arrangements and possible level of such fair compensation, account should be taken of the particular circumstances of each case. When evaluating these circumstances, a valuable criterion would be the possible harm to the rightholders resulting from the act in question. In cases where rightholders have already received payment in some other form, for instance as part of a licence fee, no specific or separate payment may be due. The level of fair compensation should take full account of the degree of use of technological protection measures referred to in this Directive. In certain situations where the prejudice to the rightholder would be minimal, no obligation for payment may arise.

(36)   The Member States may provide for fair compensation for rightholders also when applying the optional provisions on exceptions or limitations which do not require such compensation.

(37)   Existing national schemes on reprography, where they exist, do not create major barriers to the internal market. Member States should be allowed to provide for an exception or limitation in respect of reprography.

(38)   Member States should be allowed to provide for an exception or limitation to the reproduction right for certain types of reproduction of audio, visual and audio-visual material for private use, accompanied by fair compensation. This may include the introduction or continuation of remuneration schemes to compensate for the prejudice to rightholders. Although differences between those remuneration schemes affect the functioning of the internal market, those differences, with respect to analogue private reproduction, should not have a significant impact on the development of the information society. Digital private copying is likely to be more widespread and have a greater economic impact. Due account should therefore be taken of the differences between digital and analogue private copying and a distinction should be made in certain respects between them.

(39)   When applying the exception or limitation on private copying, Member States should take due account of technological and economic developments,

in particular with respect to digital private copying and remuneration schemes, when effective technological protection measures are available. Such exceptions or limitations should not inhibit the use of technological measures or their enforcement against circumvention.

(40) Member States may provide for an exception or limitation for the benefit of certain non-profit making establishments, such as publicly accessible libraries and equivalent institutions, as well as archives. However, this should be limited to certain special cases covered by the reproduction right. Such an exception or limitation should not cover uses made in the context of on-line delivery of protected works or other subject-matter. This Directive should be without prejudice to the Member States' option to derogate from the exclusive public lending right in accordance with Article 5 of Directive 92/100/EEC. Therefore, specific contracts or licences should be promoted which, without creating imbalances, favour such establishments and the disseminative purposes they serve.

(41) When applying the exception or limitation in respect of ephemeral recordings made by broadcasting organisations it is understood that a broadcaster's own facilities include those of a person acting on behalf of and under the responsibility of the broadcasting organisation.

(42) When applying the exception or limitation for non-commercial educational and scientific research purposes, including distance learning, the non-commercial nature of the activity in question should be determined by that activity as such. The organisational structure and the means of funding of the establishment concerned are not the decisive factors in this respect.

(43) It is in any case important for the Member States to adopt all necessary measures to facilitate access to works by persons suffering from a disability which constitutes an obstacle to the use of the works themselves, and to pay particular attention to accessible formats.

(44) When applying the exceptions and limitations provided for in this Directive, they should be exercised in accordance with international obligations. Such exceptions and limitations may not be applied in a way which prejudices the legitimate interests of the rightholder or which conflicts with the normal exploitation of his work or other subject-matter. The provision of such exceptions or limitations by Member States should, in particular, duly reflect the increased economic impact that such exceptions or limitations may have in the context of the new electronic environment. Therefore, the scope of certain exceptions or limitations may have to be even more limited when it comes to certain new uses of copyright works and other subject-matter.

(45) The exceptions and limitations referred to in Article 5(2), (3) and (4) should not, however, prevent the definition of contractual relations designed to ensure fair compensation for the rightholders insofar as permitted by national law.

(46) Recourse to mediation could help users and rightholders to settle disputes. The Commission, in cooperation with the Member States within the Contact Committee, should undertake a study to consider new legal ways of settling disputes concerning copyright and related rights.

(47) Technological development will allow rightholders to make use of technological measures designed to prevent or restrict acts not authorised by the

rightholders of any copyright, rights related to copyright or the sui generis right in databases. The danger, however, exists that illegal activities might be carried out in order to enable or facilitate the circumvention of the technical protection provided by these measures. In order to avoid fragmented legal approaches that could potentially hinder the functioning of the internal market, there is a need to provide for harmonised legal protection against circumvention of effective technological measures and against provision of devices and products or services to this effect.

(48)   Such legal protection should be provided in respect of technological measures that effectively restrict acts not authorised by the rightholders of any copyright, rights related to copyright or the sui generis right in databases without, however, preventing the normal operation of electronic equipment and its technological development. Such legal protection implies no obligation to design devices, products, components or services to correspond to technological measures, so long as such device, product, component or service does not otherwise fall under the prohibition of Article 6. Such legal protection should respect proportionality and should not prohibit those devices or activities which have a commercially significant purpose or use other than to circumvent the technical protection. In particular, this protection should not hinder research into cryptography.

(49)   The legal protection of technological measures is without prejudice to the application of any national provisions which may prohibit the private possession of devices, products or components for the circumvention of technological measures.

(50)   Such a harmonised legal protection does not affect the specific provisions on protection provided for by Directive 91/250/EEC. In particular, it should not apply to the protection of technological measures used in connection with computer programs, which is exclusively addressed in that Directive. It should neither inhibit nor prevent the development or use of any means of circumventing a technological measure that is necessary to enable acts to be undertaken in accordance with the terms of Article 5(3) or Article 6 of Directive 91/250/EEC. Articles 5 and 6 of that Directive exclusively determine exceptions to the exclusive rights applicable to computer programs.

(51)   The legal protection of technological measures applies without prejudice to public policy, as reflected in Article 5, or public security. Member States should promote voluntary measures taken by rightholders, including the conclusion and implementation of agreements between rightholders and other parties concerned, to accommodate achieving the objectives of certain exceptions or limitations provided for in national law in accordance with this Directive. In the absence of such voluntary measures or agreements within a reasonable period of time, Member States should take appropriate measures to ensure that rightholders provide beneficiaries of such exceptions or limitations with appropriate means of benefiting from them, by modifying an implemented technological measure or by other means. However, in order to prevent abuse of such measures taken by rightholders, including within the framework of agreements, or taken by a Member State, any technological measures applied in implementation of such measures should enjoy legal protection.

(52)   When implementing an exception or limitation for private copying in accordance with Article 5(2)(b), Member States should likewise promote the use of voluntary measures to accommodate achieving the objectives of such exception or limitation. If, within a reasonable period of time, no such voluntary measures to make reproduction for private use possible have been taken, Member States may take measures to enable beneficiaries of the exception or limitation concerned to benefit from it. Voluntary measures taken by rightholders, including agreements between rightholders and other parties concerned, as well as measures taken by Member States, do not prevent rightholders from using technological measures which are consistent with the exceptions or limitations on private copying in national law in accordance with Article 5(2)(b), taking account of the condition of fair compensation under that provision and the possible differentiation between various conditions of use in accordance with Article 5(5), such as controlling the number of reproductions. In order to prevent abuse of such measures, any technological measures applied in their implementation should enjoy legal protection.

(53)   The protection of technological measures should ensure a secure environment for the provision of interactive on-demand services, in such a way that members of the public may access works or other subject-matter from a place and at a time individually chosen by them. Where such services are governed by contractual arrangements, the first and second subparagraphs of Article 6(4) should not apply. Non-interactive forms of online use should remain subject to those provisions.

(54)   Important progress has been made in the international standardisation of technical systems of identification of works and protected subject-matter in digital format. In an increasingly networked environment, differences between technological measures could lead to an incompatibility of systems within the Community. Compatibility and interoperability of the different systems should be encouraged. It would be highly desirable to encourage the development of global systems.

(55)   Technological development will facilitate the distribution of works, notably on networks, and this will entail the need for rightholders to identify better the work or other subject-matter, the author or any other rightholder, and to provide information about the terms and conditions of use of the work or other subject-matter in order to render easier the management of rights attached to them. Rightholders should be encouraged to use markings indicating, in addition to the information referred to above, inter alia their authorisation when putting works or other subject-matter on networks.

(56)   There is, however, the danger that illegal activities might be carried out in order to remove or alter the electronic copyright-management information attached to it, or otherwise to distribute, import for distribution, broadcast, communicate to the public or make available to the public works or other protected subject-matter from which such information has been removed without authority. In order to avoid fragmented legal approaches that could potentially hinder the functioning of the internal market, there is a need to provide for harmonised legal protection against any of these activities.

(57)   Any such rights-management information systems referred to above may, depending on their design, at the same time process personal data about the consumption patterns of protected subject-matter by individuals and allow for tracing of on-line behaviour. These technical means, in their technical functions, should incorporate privacy safeguards in accordance with Directive 95/46/EC of the European Parliament and of the Council of 24 October 1995 on the protection of individuals with regard to the processing of personal data and the free movement of such data.

(58)   Member States should provide for effective sanctions and remedies for infringements of rights and obligations as set out in this Directive. They should take all the measures necessary to ensure that those sanctions and remedies are applied. The sanctions thus provided for should be effective, proportionate and dissuasive and should include the possibility of seeking damages and/or injunctive relief and, where appropriate, of applying for seizure of infringing material.

(59)   In the digital environment, in particular, the services of intermediaries may increasingly be used by third parties for infringing activities. In many cases such intermediaries are best placed to bring such infringing activities to an end. Therefore, without prejudice to any other sanctions and remedies available, rightholders should have the possibility of applying for an injunction against an intermediary who carries a third party's infringement of a protected work or other subject-matter in a network. This possibility should be available even where the acts carried out by the intermediary are exempted under Article 5. The conditions and modalities relating to such injunctions should be left to the national law of the Member States.

(60)   The protection provided under this Directive should be without prejudice to national or Community legal provisions in other areas, such as industrial property, data protection, conditional access, access to public documents, and the rule of media exploitation chronology, which may affect the protection of copyright or related rights.

(61)   In order to comply with the WIPO Performances and Phonograms Treaty, Directives 92/100/EEC and 93/98/EEC should be amended,
HAVE ADOPTED THIS DIRECTIVE:

Chapter I.   Objective and Scope

Article 1.   Scope

1.   This Directive concerns the legal protection of copyright and related rights in the framework of the internal market, with particular emphasis on the information society.

2.   Except in the cases referred to in Article 11, this Directive shall leave intact and shall in no way affect existing Community provisions relating to:

(a) the legal protection of computer programs;

(b) rental right, lending right and certain rights related to copyright in the field of intellectual property;

(c) copyright and related rights applicable to broadcasting of programmes by satellite and cable retransmission;

(d) the term of protection of copyright and certain related rights;

(e) the legal protection of databases.

Chapter II. Rights and Exceptions

Article 2. *Reproduction right*

Member States shall provide for the exclusive right to authorise or prohibit direct or indirect, temporary or permanent reproduction by any means and in any form, in whole or in part:

(a) for authors, of their works;

(b) for performers, of fixations of their performances;

(c) for phonogram producers, of their phonograms;

(d) for the producers of the first fixations of films, in respect of the original and copies of their films;

(e) for broadcasting organisations, of fixations of their broadcasts, whether those broadcasts are transmitted by wire or over the air, including by cable or satellite.

Article 3. *Right of communication to the public of works and right of making available to the public other subject-matter*

1.   Member States shall provide authors with the exclusive right to authorise or prohibit any communication to the public of their works, by wire or wireless means, including the making available to the public of their works in such a way that members of the public may access them from a place and at a time individually chosen by them.

2.   Member States shall provide for the exclusive right to authorise or prohibit the making available to the public, by wire or wireless means, in such a way that members of the public may access them from a place and at a time individually chosen by them:

(a) for performers, of fixations of their performances;

(b) for phonogram producers, of their phonograms;

(c) for the producers of the first fixations of films, of the original and copies of their films;

(d) for broadcasting organisations, of fixations of their broadcasts, whether these broadcastsare transmitted by wire or over the air, including by cable or satellite.

3.   The rights referred to in paragraphs 1 and 2 shall not be exhausted by any act of communication to the public or making available to the public as set out in this Article.

Article 4. Distribution right

1.   Member States shall provide for authors, in respect of the original of their works or of copies thereof, the exclusive right to authorise or prohibit any form of distribution to the public by sale or otherwise.

2.   The distribution right shall not be exhausted within the Community in respect of the original or copies of the work, except where the first sale or other transfer of ownership in the Community of that object is made by the rightholder or with his consent.

Article 5. Exceptions and limitations

1.   Temporary acts of reproduction referred to in Article 2, which are transient or incidental [and] an integral and essential part of a technological process and whose sole purpose is to enable:

(a) a transmission in a network between third parties by an intermediary, or

(b) a lawful use of a work or other subject-matter to be made, and which have no independent economic significance, shall be exempted from the reproduction right provided for in Article 2.

2.   Member States may provide for exceptions or limitations to the reproduction right provided for in Article 2 in the following cases:

(a) in respect of reproductions on paper or any similar medium, effected by the use of any kind of photographic technique or by some other process having similar effects, with the exception of sheet music, provided that the rightholders receive fair compensation;

(b) in respect of reproductions on any medium made by a natural person for private use and for ends that are neither directly nor indirectly commercial, on condition that the rightholders receive fair compensation which takes account of the application or non-application of technological measures referred to in Article 6 to the work or subject-matter concerned;

(c) in respect of specific acts of reproduction made by publicly accessible libraries, educational establishments or museums, or by archives, which are not for direct or indirect economic or commercial advantage;

(d) in respect of ephemeral recordings of works made by broadcasting organisations by means of their own facilities and for their own broadcasts; the preservation of these recordings in official archives may, on the grounds of their exceptional documentary character, be permitted;

(e) in respect of reproductions of broadcasts made by social institutions pursuing non-commercial purposes, such as hospitals or prisons, on condition that the rightholders receive fair compensation.

3.   Member States may provide for exceptions or limitations to the rights provided for in Articles 2 and 3 in the following cases:

(a) use for the sole purpose of illustration for teaching or scientific research, as long as the source, including the author's name, is indicated, unless this turns out to be impossible and to the extent justified by the non-commercial purpose to be achieved;

(b) uses, for the benefit of people with a disability, which are directly related to the disability and of a non-commercial nature, to the extent required by the specific disability;

(c) reproduction by the press, communication to the public or making available of published articles on current economic, political or religious topics or of broadcast works or other subject-matter of the same character, in cases where such use is not expressly reserved, and as long as the source, including the author's name, is indicated, or use of works or other subject-matter in connection with the reporting of current events, to the extent justified by the informatory purpose and as long as the source, including the author's name, is indicated, unless this turns out to be impossible;

(d) quotations for purposes such as criticism or review, provided that they relate to a work or other subject-matter which has already been lawfully made available to the public, that, unless this turns out to be impossible, the source, including the author's name, is indicated, and that their use is in accordance with fair practice, and to the extent required by the specific purpose;

(e) use for the purposes of public security or to ensure the proper performance or reporting of administrative, parliamentary or judicial proceedings;

(f) use of political speeches as well as extracts of public lectures or similar works or subject-matter to the extent justified by the informatory purpose and provided that the source, including the author's name, is indicated, except where this turns out to be impossible;

(g) use during religious celebrations or official celebrations organised by a public authority;

(h) use of works, such as works of architecture or sculpture, made to be located permanently in public places;

(i) incidental inclusion of a work or other subject-matter in other material;

(j) use for the purpose of advertising the public exhibition or sale of artistic works, to the extent necessary to promote the event, excluding any other commercial use;

(k) use for the purpose of caricature, parody or pastiche;

(l) use in connection with the demonstration or repair of equipment;

(m) use of an artistic work in the form of a building or a drawing or plan of a building for the purposes of reconstructing the building;

(n) use by communication or making available, for the purpose of research or private study, to individual members of the public by dedicated terminals on the premises of establishments referred to in paragraph 2(c) of works and other subject-matter not subject to purchase or licensing terms which are contained in their collections;

(o) use in certain other cases of minor importance where exceptions or limitations already exist under national law, provided that they only concern analogue uses and do not affect the free circulation of goods and services within the Community, without prejudice to the other exceptions and limitations contained in this Article.

4.   Where the Member States may provide for an exception or limitation to the right of reproduction pursuant to paragraphs 2 and 3, they may provide similarly for an exception or limitation to the right of distribution as referred to in Article 4 to the extent justified by the purpose of the authorised act of reproduction.

5.   The exceptions and limitations provided for in paragraphs 1, 2, 3 and 4 shall only be applied in certain special cases which do not conflict with a normal exploitation of the work or other subject-matter and do not unreasonably prejudice the legitimate interests of the rightholder.

Chapter III.   Protection of Technological Measures and Rights-Management Information

Article 6.   Obligations as to technological measures

1.   Member States shall provide adequate legal protection against the circumvention of any effective technological measures, which the person concerned carries out in the knowledge, or with reasonable grounds to know, that he or she is pursuing that objective.

2.   Member States shall provide adequate legal protection against the manufacture, import, distribution, sale, rental, advertisement for sale or rental, or possession for commercial purposes of devices, products or components or the provision of services which:

(a) are promoted, advertised or marketed for the purpose of circumvention of, or

(b) have only a limited commercially significant purpose or use other than to circumvent, or

(c) are primarily designed, produced, adapted or performed for the purpose of enabling or facilitating the circumvention of, any effective technological measures.

3.   For the purposes of this Directive, the expression "technological measures" means any technology, device or component that, in the normal course of its operation, is designed to prevent or restrict acts, in respect of works or other subject-matter, which are not authorised by the rightholder of any copyright or any right related to copyright as provided for by law or the sui generis right provided for in Chapter III of Directive 96/9/EC. Technological measures shall be deemed "effective" where the use of a protected work or other subject-matter is controlled by the rightholders through application of an access control or protection process, such as encryption, scrambling or other transformation of the work or other subject-matter or a copy control mechanism, which achieves the protection objective.

4.   Notwithstanding the legal protection provided for in paragraph 1, in the absence of voluntary measures taken by rightholders, including agreements between rightholders and other parties concerned, Member States shall take

appropriate measures to ensure that rightholders make available to the beneficiary of an exception or limitation provided for in national law in accordance with Article 5(2)(a), (2)(c), (2)(d), (2)(e), (3)(a), (3)(b) or (3)(e) the means of benefiting from that exception or limitation, to the extent necessary to benefit from that exception or limitation and where that beneficiary has legal access to the protected work or subject-matter concerned.

A Member State may also take such measures in respect of a beneficiary of an exception or limitation provided for in accordance with Article 5(2)(b), unless reproduction for private use has already been made possible by rightholders to the extent necessary to benefit from the exception or limitation concerned and in accordance with the provisions of Article 5(2)(b) and (5) [sic] without preventing rightholders from adopting adequate measures regarding the number of reproductions in accordance with these provisions.

The technological measures applied voluntarily by rightholders, including those applied in implementation of voluntary agreements, and technological measures applied in implementation of the measures taken by Member States, shall enjoy the legal protection provided for in paragraph 1.

The provisions of the first and second subparagraphs shall not apply to works or other subject-matter made available to the public on agreed contractual terms in such a way that members of the public may access them from a place and at a time individually chosen by them.

When this Article is applied in the context of Directives 92/100/EEC and 96/9/EC, this paragraph shall apply mutatis mutandis.

Article 7. Obligations concerning rights-management information

1. Member States shall provide for adequate legal protection against any person knowingly performing without authority any of the following acts:

(a) the removal or alteration of any electronic rights-management information;

(b) the distribution, importation for distribution, broadcasting, communication or making available to the public of works or other subject-matter protected under this Directive or under Chapter III of Directive 96/9/EC from which electronic rights-management information has been removed or altered without authority, if such person knows, or has reasonable grounds to know, that by so doing he is inducing, enabling, facilitating or concealing an infringement of any copyright or any rights related to copyright as provided by law, or of the sui generis right provided for in Chapter III of Directive 96/9/EC.

2. For the purposes of this Directive, the expression "rights-management information" means any information provided by rightholders which identifies the work or other subject-matter referred to in this Directive or covered by the sui generis right provided for in Chapter III of Directive 96/9/EC, the author or any other rightholder, or information about the terms and conditions of use of the work or other subject-matter, and any numbers or codes that represent such information.

The first subparagraph shall apply when any of these items of information is associated with a copy of, or appears in connection with the communication to the public of, a work or other subject matter referred to in this Directive or covered by the sui generis right provided for in Chapter III of Directive 96/9/EC.

Chapter IV.　Common Provisions

Article 8.　Sanctions and remedies

1.　Member States shall provide appropriate sanctions and remedies in respect of infringements of the rights and obligations set out in this Directive and shall take all the measures necessary to ensure that those sanctions and remedies are applied. The sanctions thus provided for shall be effective, proportionate and dissuasive.

2.　Each Member State shall take the measures necessary to ensure that rightholders whose interests are affected by an infringing activity carried out on its territory can bring an action for damages and/or apply for an injunction and, where appropriate, for the seizure of infringing material as well as of devices, products or components referred to in Article 6(2).

3.　Member States shall ensure that rightholders are in a position to apply for an injunction against intermediaries whose services are used by a third party to infringe a copyright or related right.

Article 9.　Continued application of other legal provisions

This Directive shall be without prejudice to provisions concerning in particular patent rights, trade marks, design rights, utility models, topographies of semi-conductor products, type faces, conditional access, access to cable of broadcasting services, protection of national treasures, legal deposit requirements, laws on restrictive practices and unfair competition, trade secrets, security, confidentiality, data protection and privacy, access to public documents, the law of contract.

Article 10.　Application over time

1.　The provisions of this Directive shall apply in respect of all works and other subject-matter referred to in this Directive which are, on 22 December 2002, protected by the Member States' legislation in the field of copyright and related rights, or which meet the criteria for protection under the provisions of this Directive or the provisions referred to in Article 1(2).

2. This Directive shall apply without prejudice to any acts concluded and rights acquired before 22 December 2002.

Article 11.   Technical adaptations

1. Directive 92/100/EEC is hereby amended as follows:
   (a) Article 7 shall be deleted;
   (b) Article 10(3) shall be replaced by the following: "3. The limitations shall only be applied in certain special cases which do not conflict with a normal exploitation of the subject-matter and do not unreasonably prejudice the legitimate interests of the rightholder."

2. Article 3(2) of Directive 93/98/EEC shall be replaced by the following: "2. The rights of producers of phonograms shall expire 50 years after the fixation is made. However, if the phonogram has been lawfully published within this period, the said rights shall expire 50 years from the date of the first lawful publication. If no lawful publication has taken place within the period mentioned in the first sentence, and if the phonogram has been lawfully communicated to the public within this period, the said rights shall expire 50 years from the date of the first lawful communication to the public.

However, where through the expiry of the term of protection granted pursuant to this paragraph in its version before amendment by Directive 2001/29/EC of the European Parliament and of the Council of 22 May 2001 on the harmonisation of certain aspects of copyright and related rights in the information society the rights of producers of phonograms are no longer protected on 22 December 2002, this paragraph shall not have the effect of protecting those rights anew."

Article 12.   Final provisions

1. Not later than 22 December 2004 and every three years thereafter, the Commission shall submit to the European Parliament, the Council and the Economic and Social Committee a report on the application of this Directive, in which, inter alia, on the basis of specific information supplied by the Member States, it shall examine in particular the application of Articles 5, 6 and 8 in the light of the development of the digital market. In the case of Article 6, it shall examine in particularwhether that Article confers a sufficient level of protection and whether acts which are permitted by law are being adversely affected by the use of effective technological measures. Where necessary,in particular to ensure the functioning of the internal market pursuant to Article 14 of the Treaty, it shall submit proposals for amendments to this Directive.

2. Protection of rights related to copyright under this Directive shall leave intact and shall in no way affect the protection of copyright.

3. A contact committee is hereby established. It shall be composed of representatives of the competent authorities of the Member States. It shall be chaired by a representative of the Commission and shall meet either on the initiative of the chairman or at the request of the delegation of a Member State.

4. The tasks of the committee shall be as follows:

(a) to examine the impact of this Directive on the functioning of the internal market, and to highlight any difficulties;

(b) to organise consultations on all questions deriving from the application of this Directive;

(c) to facilitate the exchange of information on relevant developments in legislation and case-law, as well as relevant economic, social, cultural and technological developments;

(d) to act as a forum for the assessment of the digital market in works and other items, including private copying and the use of technological measures.

Article 13. Implementation

1. Member States shall bring into force the laws, regulations and administrative provisions necessary to comply with this Directive before 22 December 2002. They shall forthwith inform the Commission thereof.

When Member States adopt these measures, they shall contain a reference to this Directive or shall be accompanied by such reference on the occasion of their official publication. The methods of making such reference shall be laid down by Member States.

2. Member States shall communicate to the Commission the text of the provisions of domestic law which they adopt in the field governed by this Directive.

Article 14. Entry into force

This Directive shall enter into force on the day of its publication in the Official Journal of the European Communities.

Article 15. Addressees

This Directive is addressed to the Member States.

Part IV
Case and Note Updates

Chapter 1. Copyright in Context

B. The History of U.S. Copyright Law

Page 29. Insert the following at the end of the table:

Year	Amendment
2008	Prioritizing Resources and Organization for Intellectual Property Act (PRO-IP Act). Provided that registration requirements do not apply to criminal infringement actions; specified that exportation of infringing copies is infringing; created the post of Intellectual Property Enforcement Coordinator in the Department of Justice to address counterfeiting and piracy issues; and created the Office of the Intellectual Property Enforcement Representative within the Executive Office of the President. (*See infra* Chapter 6.)
2008	Vessel Hull Design Protection Amendments. Expanded definition of articles entitled to special design protection. (*See* Chapter 4 of the casebook.)

C. The Growing Role of International Treaties and Institutions

Page 40. At the end of the first paragraph, insert the following:

On January 26, 2009, a WTO Panel issued a report on a third copyright-related TRIPS dispute. In *China—Measures Affecting the Protection and Enforcement of Intellectual Property Rights*, WT/DS362/R (Jan. 26, 2009), the U.S. filed a complaint at the WTO against China, alleging a number of ways in which China's laws fall short of the protection and enforcement provisions required by the TRIPS Agreement. Pertinent aspects of this case will be discussed in Chapters 3.A, 6.E, and 10.G *infra* pages 365.66, 516, and 499-500, respectively.

Page 42. In the Notes and Questions, replace Questions 3 and 4 with the following:

3. In 2007, the WIPO General Assembly adopted the "Development Agenda" in response to concerns expressed by developing countries about, among other things, the need for a more balanced approach to WIPO's fundamental mission of promoting the harmonization of international intellectual property rights. It consists of 45 recommendations divided into six clusters, many directed at re-orienting WIPO's operational philosophy and its technical assistance programs. *See* <http://www.wipo.int/ip-development/en/agenda/recommendations.html>.

The Development Agenda is viewed by scholars, commentators, and many international consumer advocacy groups as an important response to long-standing complaints by developing and least-developed countries about WIPO's singular dedication to achieving stronger levels of protection globally without consideration of the public policy objectives that inform the regulation of intel-lectual property rights in most industrially advanced countries. Although the Development Agenda has been widely regarded as a victory for the developing and least-developed countries, it remains unclear how its adoption will transform the substantive obligations of prevailing intellectual property treaties such as the TRIPS Agreement and other, recently concluded, free trade agreements (FTAs) that embody high standards for global intellectual property protection. There are also questions about the extent to which WIPO's core mission to strengthen and promote intellectual property protection can realistically be altered to accom-modate norms that promote access to, and dissemination of, knowledge-based goods.

4. In addition to adopting the WIPO Development Agenda, WIPO member states also established a Committee on Development and Intellectual Property (CDIP). The CDIP is charged with the task of developing a framework for implementation of the recommendations. Do you think developing and least-developed countries will be the sole beneficiaries? For example, under the Cluster B recommendations (dealing with norm-setting, flexibilities, public policy, and the public domain), WIPO is required to "consider the preservation of the public domain . . . and deepen [its] analysis of the implications and benefits of a rich and accessible public domain" in carrying out its norm-setting activities. Is the pres-ervation of a strong public domain an issue of significance solely to developing and least-developed countries?

Chapter 2. Authors, Writings, and Progress

A. The Elements of Copyrightable Subject Matter

Page 54. In the Notes and Questions, insert new Question 6 and renumber Question 6 as Question 7:

6. How would the *MAI* reasoning apply to streamed video content stored in buffer memory in increments of 1.2 seconds, and continually overwritten? Cablevision used such an arrangement to enable a "remote DVR" system. First, Cablevision split its programming data stream into two identical streams. One stream was transmitted to Cablevision's customers, and the other was routed through a buffering device called the Broadband Media Router (in 1.2-second increments) and then through the "primary ingest buffer" in Cablevision's remote DVR data center (in 0.1-second increments). If a customer wished to record a particular program to watch later, a dedicated copy for that customer would be created and stored in server space allocated to that customer. Otherwise, the programming data continued to pass through buffer memory, continually overwritten by new programming data. In *Cartoon Network LP v. CSC Holdings, Inc.*, 536 F.3d 121 (2d Cir. 2008), *petition for cert. filed*, 77 U.S.L.W. 3229 (Oct. 6, 2008), the court held that the programming data stored in Cablevision's buffers were not fixed. The court observed:

> The Act . . . provides that a work is "'fixed' in a tangible medium of expression when its embodiment . . . is sufficiently permanent or stable to permit it to be reproduced . . . *for a period of more than transitory duration.*" . . . We believe that this language plainly imposes two distinct but related requirements: the work must be embodied in a medium (the "embodiment requirement"), and it must remain thus embodied "for a period of more than transitory duration" (the "duration requirement"). . . .
>
> [W]e construe *MAI Systems* and its progeny as holding that loading a program into a computer's RAM *can* result in copying that program. We do not read *MAI Systems* as holding that, as a matter of law, loading a program into a form of RAM

always results in copying. Such a holding would read the "transitory duration" language out of the definition. . . . It appears the parties in *MAI Systems* simply did not dispute that the duration requirement was satisfied; this line of cases simply concludes that when a program is loaded into RAM, the embodiment requirement is satisfied. . . .

Id. at 127-28 (emphasis in original). Do you agree with the court's reading of the statute? Is the court correct in concluding that its interpretation of the statutory definition is consistent with the *MAI* court's interpretation?

Page 56. Replace the paragraph that begins "In 2004, defendants in two separate actions . . ." with the following:

Other cases have addressed the "limited Times" challenge to the anti-bootlegging provisions. In *KISS Catalog v. Passport International Productions*, 405 F. Supp. 2d 1169 (C.D. Cal. 2005), the court concluded that it was "unlikely" that Congress had the power pursuant to the Copyright Clause to adopt §1101(a)(3), the civil prohibition, but nonetheless concluded that the Commerce Clause empowered Congress to adopt that provision. Whether the unlimited duration was fundamentally inconsistent with the Copyright Clause did not need to be addressed, according to the court, so long as there was "an alternative source of constitutional authority." *Id.* at 1175.

In *United States v. Martignon*, 492 F.3d 140 (2d Cir. 2007), the Court acknowledged that the express limitations on congressional power in one clause can, "in limited instances . . . apply externally to another clause." *Id.* at 144. The court reasoned that "Congress exceeds its power under the Commerce Clause by transgressing limitations of the Copyright Clause only when (1) the law it enacts is an exercise of the power granted Congress by the Copyright Clause and (2) the resulting law violates one or more specific limits of the Copyright Clause." *Id.* at 149. To determine when a law should be considered an exercise of Congress' Copyright Clause power, the court focused on the word "secure" contained in that clause and the history and context of the clause. It held that to be an exercise of Copyright Clause authority the law must create, bestow, or allocate property rights in expression. At issue in *Martignon* was the criminal prohibition, §2319A. That law, the Second Circuit concluded, does not create or bestow any rights on an author or a creator of expression, but rather "creates a power in the government to protect the interest of performers from commercial predations." *Id.* at 151. Because the law was not an exercise of authority pursuant to the Copyright Clause, the limitations in that clause did not apply, and the court determined the provision was a lawful exercise of Congress' Commerce Clause authority.

The *Martignon* court specified that it was expressing "no opinion on Section 1101's constitutionality." *Id.* at 152 n.8. Additionally "because no commercial motive is required for a Section 1101 violation" the court specifically limited its holding to Section 2319A. *Id.* Under the Second Circuit's approach, would §1101 be constitutional?

Page 65. *Insert the following after the Notes and Questions:*

Mannion v. Coors Brewing Company
377 F. Supp. 2d 444 (S.D.N.Y. 2006)

KAPLAN, J.: . . .

FACTS

Jonathan Mannion is a freelance photographer who specializes in portraits of celebrity athletes and musicians in the rap and rhythm-and-blues worlds. In 1999 he was hired by SLAM, a basketball magazine, to photograph basketball star Kevin Garnett in connection with an article. . . . The article, entitled "Above the Clouds," appeared as the cover story of the December 1999 issue of the magazine. It was accompanied by a number of Mannion's photographs of Garnett, including the one at issue here (the "Garnett Photograph"), which was printed on a two-page spread introducing the article.

The Garnett Photograph . . . is a three-quarter-length portrait of Garnett against a backdrop of clouds with some blue sky shining through. The view is up and across the right side of Garnett's torso, so that he appears to be towering above earth. He wears a white T-shirt, white athletic pants, a black close-fitting cap, and a large amount of platinum, gold, and diamond jewelry ("bling bling" in the vernacular), including several necklaces, a Rolex watch and bracelet on his left wrist, bracelets on his right wrist, rings on one finger of each hand, and earrings. His head is cocked, his eyes are closed, and his heavily-veined hands, nearly all of which are visible, rest over his lower abdomen, with the thumbs hooked on the waistband of the trousers. The light is from the viewer's left, so that Garnett's right shoulder is the brightest area of the photograph and his hands cast slight shadows on his trousers. As reproduced in the magazine, the photograph cuts off much of Garnett's left arm.

In early 2001, defendant Carol H. Williams Advertising ("CHWA") began developing ideas for outdoor billboards that would advertise Coors Light beer to young black men in urban areas. One of CHWA's "comp boards"—a "comp board" is an image created by an advertising company to convey a proposed design—used a manipulated version of the Garnett Photograph and superimposed on it the words "Iced Out" ("ice" being slang for diamonds) and a picture of a can of Coors Light beer (the "Iced Out Comp Board"). CHWA obtained authorization from Mannion's representative to use the Garnett Photograph for this purpose.

The Iced Out Comp Board . . . used a black-and-white, mirror image of the Garnett Photograph, but with the head cropped out on top and part of the fingers cropped out below. CHWA forwarded its comp boards to, and solicited bids for the photograph for the Coors advertising from, various photographers including Mannion, who submitted a bid but did not receive the assignment.

Coors and CHWA selected for a Coors billboard a photograph (the "Coors Billboard") . . . that resembles the Iced Out Comp Board. The Coors Billboard depicts, in black-and-white, the torso of a muscular black man, albeit a model other than Garnett, shot against a cloudy backdrop. The pose is similar to that in the Garnett Photograph, and the view also is up and across the left side of the torso. The model in the billboard photograph also wears a white T-shirt and white athletic pants. The model's jewelry is prominently depicted; it includes a necklace of platinum or gold and diamonds, a watch and two bracelets on the right wrist, and more bracelets on the left wrist. The light comes from the viewer's right, so that the left shoulder is the brightest part of the photograph, and the right arm and hand cast slight shadows on the trousers. . . .

Mannion subsequently noticed the Coors Billboard at two locations in the Los Angeles area. He . . . brought this action for infringement in February of 2004. The parties each move for summary judgment.

DISCUSSION

DETERMINING THE PROTECTIBLE ELEMENTS OF THE GARNETT PHOTOGRAPH . . .

The first question must be: in what respects is the Garnett Photograph protectible? . . .

1. Protectible Elements of Photographs . . .

It sometimes is said that "copyright in the photograph conveys no rights over the subject matter conveyed in the photograph." But this is not always true. It of course is correct that the photographer of a building or tree or other pre-existing object has no right to prevent others from photographing the same thing. That is because originality depends upon independent creation, and the photographer did not create that object. By contrast, if a photographer arranges or otherwise creates the subject that his camera captures, he may have the right to prevent others from producing works that depict that subject.

Almost any photograph "may claim the necessary originality to support a copyright." Indeed, ever since the Supreme Court considered an 1882 portrait by the celebrity photographer Napoleon Sarony of the 27-year-old Oscar Wilde, courts have articulated lists of potential components of a photograph's originality. These lists, however, are somewhat unsatisfactory.

First, they do not deal with the issue, alluded to above, that the nature and extent of a photograph's protection differs depending on what makes that photograph original.

Second, courts have not always distinguished between decisions that a photographer makes in creating a photograph and the originality of the final product. Several cases, for example, have included in lists of the potential components of photographic originality "selection of film and camera," "lens and filter selection," and "the kind of camera, the kind of film, [and] the kind of lens." Having considered the matter fully, however, I think this is not sufficiently precise. Decisions about film, camera, and lens, for example, often bear on whether an image is original. But the fact that a photographer made such choices does not alone make the image original. "Sweat of the brow" is not the touchstone of copyright. Protection derives from the features of the work itself, not the effort that goes into it. . . .

A photograph may be original in three respects. They are not mutually exclusive.

a. Rendition

First, "there may be originality which does not depend on creation of the scene or object to be photographed . . . and which resides [instead] in such specialties as angle of shot, light and shade, exposure, effects achieved by means of filters, developing techniques etc." I will refer to this type of originality as originality in the rendition because, to the extent a photograph is original in this way, copyright protects not *what* is depicted, but rather *how* it is depicted. . . .

b. Timing

A photograph may be original in a second respect. "[A] person may create a worthwhile photograph by being at the right place at the right time." I will refer to this type of originality as originality in timing.

. . . A modern work strikingly original in timing might be *Catch of the Day*, by noted wildlife photographer Thomas Mangelsen, which depicts a salmon that appears to be jumping into the gaping mouth of a brown bear at Brooks Falls in Katmai National Park, Alaska. An older example is Alfred Eisenstaedt's photograph of a sailor kissing a young woman on VJ Day in Times Square, the memorability of which is attributable in significant part to the timing of its creation.

Copyright based on originality in timing is limited by the principle that copyright in a photograph ordinarily confers no rights over the subject matter. Thus, the copyright in *Catch of the Day* does not protect against subsequent photographs of bears feasting on salmon in the same location. Furthermore, if another photographer were sufficiently skilled and fortunate to capture a salmon at the precise moment that it appeared to enter a hungry bear's mouth — and others have tried, with varying degrees of success — that photographer, even if inspired by Mangelsen, would not necessarily have infringed his work because Mangelsen's copyright does not extend to the natural world he captured.

In practice, originality in timing gives rise to the same type of protection as originality in the rendition. In each case, the image that exhibits the originality, but not the underlying subject, qualifies for copyright protection.

c. Creation of the Subject

The principle that copyright confers no right over the subject matter has an important limitation. A photograph may be original to the extent that the photographer created "the scene or subject to be photographed." This type of originality, which I will refer to as originality in the creation of the subject, played an essential role in *Rogers v. Koons* [960 F.2d 301(2d Cir. 1992)] and *Gross v. Seligman* [212 F. 930 (2d Cir. 1914)].

In *Rogers*, the court held that the copyright in the plaintiff's photograph *Puppies*, which depicted a contrived scene of the photographer's acquaintance, Jim Scanlon, and his wife on a park bench with eight puppies on their laps, protected against the defendants' attempt to replicate precisely, albeit in a three dimensional sculpture, the content of the photograph. Although the Circuit noted that *Puppies* was original because the artist "made creative judgments concerning technical matters with his camera and the use of natural light"—in other words, because it was original in the rendition—its originality in the creation of the subject was more salient. The same is true of the works at issue in *Gross v. Seligman*, in which the Circuit held that the copyright in a photograph named *Grace of Youth* was infringed when the same artist created a photograph named *Cherry Ripe* using "the same model in the identical pose, with the single exception that the young woman now wears a smile and holds a cherry stem between her teeth."

* * * * * *

To conclude, the nature and extent of protection conferred by the copyright in a photograph will vary depending on the nature of its originality. Insofar as a photograph is original in the rendition or timing, copyright protects the image but does not prevent others from photographing the same object or scene. . . .

By contrast, to the extent that a photograph is original in the creation of the subject, copyright extends also to that subject. Thus, an artist who arranges and then photographs a scene often will have the right to prevent others from duplicating that scene in a photograph or other medium.[65]

2. Originality of the Garnett Photograph

There can be no serious dispute that the Garnett Photograph is an original work. The photograph does not result from slavishly copying another work and therefore is original in the rendition. Mannion's relatively unusual angle and distinctive lighting strengthen that aspect of the photograph's originality. His composition—posing man against sky—evidences originality in the creation of the subject. Furthermore, Mannion instructed Garnett to wear simple and plain clothing and as much jewelry as possible, and "to look 'chilled out.'" His orchestration of the scene contributes additional originality in the creation of the subject.

Of course, there are limits to the photograph's originality and therefore to the protection conferred by the copyright in the Garnett Photograph. For example, Kevin Garnett's face, torso, and hands are not original with Mannion, and Mannion therefore may not prevent others from creating photographic portraits

---

65. I recognize that the preceding analysis focuses on a medium—traditional print photography—that is being supplanted in significant degree by digital technology. These advancements may or may not demand a different analytical framework.

of Garnett. Equally obviously, the existence of a cloudy sky is not original, and Mannion therefore may not prevent others from using a cloudy sky as a backdrop.

The defendants, however, take this line of reasoning too far. They argue that it was Garnett, not Mannion, who selected the specific clothing, jewelry, and pose. In consequence, they maintain, the Garnett Photograph is not original to the extent of Garnett's clothing, jewelry, and pose. They appear to be referring to originality in the creation of the subject.

There are two problems with the defendants' argument. The first is that Mannion indisputably orchestrated the scene, even if he did not plan every detail before he met Garnett, and then made the decision to capture it. The second difficulty is that the originality of the photograph extends beyond the individual clothing, jewelry, and pose viewed in isolation. It is the entire image — depicting man, sky, clothing, and jewelry in a particular arrangement — that is at issue here, not its individual components. . . .

NOTES AND QUESTIONS

1. How helpful is the *Mannion* court's taxonomy of originality in photographs? How distinct are the different dimensions of originality described by the court? Was the photograph in *Sarony* original in rendition, original in creation of the subject, or both?

2. Does assessment of originality in "rendition" or "creation of the subject" violate the *Bleistein* non-discrimination principle?

3. Consider whether and to what extent copyright would (or should) protect the following:

    a. a photograph by acclaimed documentary photographer Walker Evans of riders on the New York City subway;

    b. photographs on a restaurant menu depicting dishes available at the restaurant;

    c. the photograph on your driver's license.

4. Should the *Mannion* taxonomy be used for other types of works? Would it have been helpful in evaluating the lithographs in *Bleistein*?

Pages 70-72. Delete **The Bridgeman Art Library v. Corel Corp., Ltd.** *and the Notes and Questions and insert the following:*

Meshwerks, Inc. v. Toyota Motor Sales U.S.A., Inc.
528 F.3d 1258 (10th Cir. 2008)

GORSUCH, J.: . . . [Toyota and its advertising agency, Saatchi & Saatchi, hired Grace & Wild, Inc., to supply digital models of Toyota's vehicles for its model-year 2004 advertising campaign.] . . . G&W subcontracted with Meshwerks to assist with two initial aspects of the project—digitization and modeling. Digitizing involves collecting physical data points from the object to be portrayed. In the case of Toyota's vehicles, Meshwerks took copious measurements of Toyota's vehicles by covering each car, truck, and van with a grid of tape and running an articulated arm tethered to a computer over the vehicle to measure all points of intersection in the grid. Based on these measurements, modeling software then generated a digital image resembling a wire-frame model. . . .

At this point, however, the on-screen image remained far from perfect and manual "modeling" was necessary. Meshwerks personnel fine-tuned or, as the company prefers it, "sculpted," the lines on screen to resemble each vehicle as closely as possible. Approximately 90 percent of the data points contained in each final model, Meshwerks represents, were the result not of the first-step measurement process, but of the skill and effort its digital sculptors manually expended at the second step. For example, some areas of detail, such as wheels, headlights, door handles, and the Toyota emblem, could not be accurately measured using current technology; those features had to be added at the second "sculpting" stage, and Meshwerks had to recreate those features as realistically as possible by hand, based on photographs. Even for areas that were measured, Meshwerks faced the challenge of converting measurements taken of a three-dimensional car into a two-dimensional computer representation; to achieve this, its modelers had to sculpt, or move, data points to achieve a visually convincing result. The purpose and product of these processes, after nearly 80 to 100 hours of effort per vehicle, were two-dimensional wire-frame depictions of Toyota's vehicles that appeared three-dimensional on screen, but were utterly unadorned—lacking color, shading, and other details. Attached to this opinion as Appendix A are sample screenprints of one of Meshwerks' digital wire-frame models.

With Meshwerks' wire-frame products in hand, G&W then manipulated the computerized models by, first, adding detail, the result of which appeared on screen as a "tightening" of the wire frames, as though significantly more wires had been added to the frames, or as though they were made of a finer mesh. Next, G&W digitally applied color, texture, lighting, and animation for use in Toyota's advertisements. An example of G&W's work product is attached as Appendix B to this opinion. . . .

[Meshwerks sued Toyota, Saatchi & Saatchi, and G&W, asserting that it had contracted for only a one-time use of its models and that subsequent, unauthorized uses infringed its copyrights in the models. The district court granted defendants' motion for summary judgment, and Meshwerks appealed.]

II . . .

A . . .

What exactly does it mean for a work to qualify as "original"? In *Feist [Publications, Inc. v. Rural Telephone Service Co.*, 499 U.S. 340 (1991)], the Supreme Court clarified that the work must be "independently created by the author (as opposed to copied from other works)." *Id.* at 345 . . . ; see also *Burrow-Giles Lithographic Co. v. Sarony*, 111 U.S. 53, 58 . . . (1884) (the work for which copyright protection is sought must "owe[ ] its origin" to the putative copyright holder) (internal quotation omitted). In addition, the work must "possess[ ] at least some minimal degree of creativity," *Feist*, 499 U.S. at 345. . . . [5]

The parties focus most of their energy in this case on the question whether Meshwerks' models qualify as independent creations, as opposed to copies of Toyota's handiwork. But what can be said, at least based on received copyright doctrine, to distinguish an independent creation from a copy? And how might that doctrine apply in an age of virtual worlds and digital media that seek to mimic the "real" world, but often do so in ways that undoubtedly qualify as (highly) original? . . .

[P]hotography was initially met by critics with a degree of skepticism: a photograph, some said, "copies everything and explains nothing," and it was debated whether a camera could do anything more than merely record the physical world. . . . [In *Burrow-Giles*], the Court indicated [that] photographs are copyrightable, if only to the extent of their original depiction of the subject. Wilde's image [was] not copyrightable; but to the extent a photograph reflects the photographer's decisions regarding pose, positioning, background, lighting, shading, and the like, those elements can be said to "owe their origins" to the photographer, making the photograph copyrightable, at least to that extent.

As the Court more recently explained in *Feist*, the operative distinction is between, on the one hand, ideas or facts in the world, items that cannot be copyrighted, and a particular expression of that idea or fact, that can be. . . . So, in the case of photographs, for which Meshwerks' digital models were designed to serve as practically advantageous substitutes, authors are entitled to copyright protection only for the "incremental contribution," *SHL Imaging, Inc.* [*v. Artisan House, Inc.*], 117 F. Supp. 2d at 311 [(S.D.N.Y. 2000)] (internal quotation omitted), represented by their interpretation or expression of the objects of their attention.

B

Applying these principles, evolved in the realm of photography, to the new medium that has come to supplement and even in some ways to supplant it, we think Meshwerks' models are not so much independent creations as (very good) copies of Toyota's vehicles. . . .

---

5. The two pertinent concepts—independent creation and minimal creativity—are intertwined and overlap, at least to some degree: After all, if something qualifies as an independent creation (that is, it is more than a copy) won't it also usually betray some minimal degree of creativity? Still, though the independent test imputed by the creativity requirement is low, it does exist. *Feist*, 499 U.S. at 345, 362. . . .

1

Key to our evaluation of this case is the fact that Meshwerks' digital wire-frame computer models depict Toyota's vehicles without any individualizing features: they are untouched by a digital paintbrush; they are not depicted in front of a palm tree, whizzing down the open road, or climbing up a mountainside. Put another way, Meshwerks' models depict nothing more than un-adorned Toyota vehicles—the car as car. See Appendix A.... [I]n short, its models reflect none of the decisions that can make depictions of things or facts in the world, whether Oscar Wilde or a Toyota Camry, new expressions subject to copyright protection.

The primary case on which Meshwerks asks us to rely actually reinforces this conclusion. In *Ets-Hokin v. Skyy Spirits, Inc.*, 225 F.3d 1068 (9th Cir.2000) (*Skyy I*), the Ninth Circuit was faced with a suit brought by a plaintiff photographer who alleged that the defendant had infringed on his commercial photographs of a Skyy-brand vodka bottle. The court held that the vodka bottle, as a "utilitarian object," a fact in the world, was not itself (at least usually) copyrightable. *Id.* at 1080 (citing 17 U.S.C. §101). At the same time, the court recognized that plaintiff's photos reflected decisions regarding "lighting, shading, angle, background, and so forth," *id.* at 1078, and to the extent plaintiff's photographs reflected such original contributions the court held they could be copyrighted. In so holding, the Ninth Circuit reversed a district court's dismissal of the case and remanded the matter for further proceedings, and Meshwerks argues this analysis controls the outcome of its case.

But *Skyy I* tells only half the story. The case soon returned to the court of appeals, and the court held that the defendant's photos, which differed in terms of angle, lighting, shadow, reflection, and background, did not infringe on the plaintiff's copyrights. *Ets-Hokin v. Skyy Spirits, Inc.*, 323 F.3d 763, 765 (9th Cir.2003) (*Skyy II*). Why? The only constant between the plaintiff's photographs and the defendant's photographs was the bottle itself, *id.* at 766, and an accurate portrayal of the unadorned bottle could not be copyrighted. . . .

The teaching of *Skyy I* and *II*, then, is that the vodka bottle, because it did not owe its origins to the photographers, had to be filtered out to determine what copyrightable expression remained. And, by analogy—though not perhaps the one Meshwerks had in mind—we hold that the unadorned images of Toyota's vehicles cannot be copyrighted by Meshwerks and likewise must be filtered out. To the extent that Meshwerks' digital wire-frame models depict only those un-adorned vehicles, having stripped away all lighting, angle, perspective, and "other ingredients" associated with an original expression, we conclude that they have left no copyrightable matter. . . .

Confirming this conclusion as well is the peculiar place where Meshwerks stood in the model-creation pecking order. On the one hand, Meshwerks had nothing to do with designing the appearance of Toyota's vehicles, distinguishing them from any other cars, trucks, or vans in the world. . . . On the other hand, how the models Meshwerks created were to be deployed in advertising—including the backgrounds, lighting, angles, and colors—were all matters left to those (G & W, Saatchi, and 3D Recon) who came after Meshwerks left the scene. . . . [8]

It is certainly true that what Meshwerks accomplished was a peculiar kind of copying. It did not seek to recreate Toyota vehicles outright—steel, rubber, and all; instead, it sought to depict Toyota's three-dimensional physical objects in a two-dimensional digital medium. But we hold, as many before us have already suggested, that, standing alone, "[t]he fact that a work in one medium has been copied from a work in another medium does not render it any the less a 'copy.'" Nimmer on Copyright §8.01[B]. . . . After all, the putative creator who merely shifts the medium in which another's creation is expressed has not necessarily added anything beyond the expression contained in the original. . . .

In reaching this conclusion, we do not for a moment seek to downplay the considerable amount of time, effort, and skill that went into making Meshwerks' digital wire-frame models. But, in assessing the originality of a work for which copyright protection is sought, we look only at the final product, not the process, and the fact that intensive, skillful, and even creative labor is invested in the process of creating a product does not guarantee its copyrightability. *See Feist,* 499 U.S. at 359-60. . . .

2

Meshwerks' intent in making its wire-frame models provides additional support for our conclusion. "In theory, the originality requirement tests the putative author's state of mind: Did he have an earlier work in mind when he created his own?" Paul Goldstein, Goldstein on Copyright §2.2.1.1. If an artist affirmatively sets out to be unoriginal—to make a copy of someone else's creation, rather than to create an original work—it is far more likely that the resultant product will, in fact, be unoriginal. . . . Of course, this is not to say that the accidental or spontaneous artist will be denied copyright protection for not intending to produce art; it is only to say that authorial intent sometimes can shed light on the question of whether a particular work qualifies as an independent creation or only a copy.

In this case, the undisputed evidence before us leaves no question that Meshwerks set out to copy Toyota's vehicles, rather than to create, or even to add, any original expression. The purchase order signed by G & W asked Meshwerks to "digitize and model" Toyota's vehicles, and Meshwerks' invoice submitted to G & W for payment reflects that this is exactly the service Meshwerks performed. Aplt's App. at 113, 115. Meshwerks itself has consistently described digitization and modeling as an attempt accurately to depict real-world, three-dimensional objects as digital images viewable on a computer screen. *See, e.g., id.* at 369 ("the graphic sculptor is not intending to 'redesign' the product, he or she is attempting to depict that object in the most realistic way"). . . .

---

8. We are not called upon to, and do not, express any view on the copyrightability of the work products produced by those who employed and adorned Meshwerks' models.

C

Although we hold that Meshwerks' digital, wire-frame models are insufficiently original to warrant copyright protection, we do not turn a blind eye to the fact that digital imaging is a relatively new and evolving technology and that Congress extended copyright protection to "original works of authorship fixed in any tangible medium of expression, *now known or later developed.*" 17 U.S.C. §102(a) (emphasis added). . . .

Digital modeling can be, surely is being, and no doubt increasingly will be used to create copyrightable expressions. Yet, just as photographs can be, but are not per se, copyrightable, the same holds true for digital models. There's little question that digital models can be devised of Toyota cars with copyrightable features, whether by virtue of unique shading, lighting, angle, background scene, or other choices. The problem for Meshwerks in this particular case is simply that the uncontested facts reveal that it wasn't involved in any such process. . . . For this reason, we do not envision any "chilling effect" on creative expression based on our holding today. . . .

NOTES AND QUESTIONS

1. Can *Alfred Bell* and *Meshwerks* be construed consistently? Should copyright protect the result of "[a] copyist's bad eyesight or defective musculature, or a shock caused by a clap of thunder"? After *Feist* (decided in 1991), does it? Would you argue that, just like a mezzotint, a digital model always contains more than a merely trivial variation of the original?

2. Is it appropriate to consider intent in determining originality? If so, what type of intent counts? If Meshwerks had created its digital models for an art exhibit rather than for an advertising campaign, should the result change? Why, or why not?

3. If "minimal creativity" means something more than "independently created," how much more is required? Consider whether, after *Feist*, copyright would protect the following:

    a. digital photographs of public domain paintings;
    b. digital photographs of public domain sculptures;
    c. an Andy Warhol painting of a Campbell's soup can;
    d. a design for a calendar using particular petroglyph symbols as the middle two zeros in the year "2000";
    e. the images identified by the *Meshwerks* court as G&W's work product.

4. In *Bridgeman Art Library, Ltd. v. Corel Corp.*, 36 F. Supp. 2d 191 (S.D.N.Y. 1999), Bridgeman had been authorized to prepare and sell color reproductions of public domain paintings residing in museum and private collections. Corel allegedly copied Bridgeman's color transparencies to produce its own CD-ROM

product. The court dismissed Bridgeman's copyright infringement claim, ruling that the transparencies did not contain the required "distinguishable variation," but reflected only "slavish copying." Do you agree with the court's conclusion? If so, are the works in hypotheticals b and c, above, distinguishable?

5. Both *Alfred Bell* and *Bridgeman* involved the preparation of "derivative works"—works based on preexisting works. The 1976 Act makes separate provision for the copyrightability of derivative works; the 1909 Act did not use that terminology, but allowed copyright protection for "reproductions of a work of art." As discussed in Section A.4.a in the casebook, there is a debate about whether the threshold originality requirement should be determined differently for such works. For now, note that the *Bridgeman* decision effectively permitted the copying of images of underlying works in the public domain, while the *Alfred Bell* decision had the opposite effect. Which outcome is more likely to promote progress?

6. Many photographs, including a large number in the public domain, are held in private collections and made available to the public only as digital replicas. For example, Corbis, a company founded by Bill Gates, acquired the Bettman Archive's collection of 16.5 million photographs, including 30 years' worth of United Press International photographs. To preserve the originals, Corbis has buried them in an underground, climate-controlled storage facility. Digital reproductions are available via license. Can Corbis copyright the digital images? Would it make any difference to your answer if Corbis digitally watermarks each image? If Corbis cannot copyright the digital images, should it be able to place contractual restrictions on access to and use of them?

B. Who is an Author?

Page 110. In the Notes and Questions, insert a new Question 8 and renumber Question 8 as Question 9:

8. In *Darden v. Peters*, 488 F.3d 277 (4th Cir. 2007), the plaintiff had taken a U.S. Census map, added color and shading to give the map a three-dimensional effect, selected a font for labeling the states and added additional labels as well. The Copyright Office rejected the application for registration and the Fourth Circuit agreed, concluding that: "Additions to the preexisting maps such as color, shading, and labels using standard fonts and shapes fall within the narrow category of works that lack even a minimum level of creativity...." *Id.* at 287. The court noted that the contributions Darden alleged to constitute original authorship elements resembled the examples set forth in regulations issued by the Copyright Office of the types of works that lack a minimum level of creativity: "[w]ords and short phrases such as names, titles, and slogans; familiar symbols or designs; mere variations of typographic ornamentation, lettering or coloring; mere listing of ingredients or contents." 37 C.F.R. §202.1(a); *see supra* page 78 of

the casebook. Why was Darden's map denied protection when Mason's maps were granted protection? In his application for registration Darden described his work as "a derivative work that . . . was based on preexisting 'US Census black and white outline maps.'" Does the difference in treatment lie solely in Darden's designation of his map as a "derivative work" instead of a compilation?

Page 117. In the Notes and Questions, insert new Question 6 and renumber Questions 6-8 as Questions 7-9:

6. Recently the Second Circuit held that a joint owner of a copyright cannot retroactively transfer his ownership interest to a defendant who has been sued by the other joint owner of the copyright. *Davis v. Blige,* 505 F.3d 90 (2d Cir. 2007). The court viewed the retroactive transfer as "an attempt to cut off the accrued rights of the other owner to sue for infringement," *id.* at 97, and concluded that permitting retroactive transfer would "violate basic principles of tort and contract law, and undermine the policies embodied by the Copyright Act." *Id.* at 98. It worried that permitting such retroactive assignments or even licenses would inject uncertainty and unpredictability into determinations of copyright ownership and authorization, creating "substantial mischief." *Id.* at 105. Do you agree? If such mischief resulted from a grant by one co-owner, would it be possible instead to require the authorizing co-owner to account to his other co-owners?

Page 125. In the Notes and Questions, insert new Question 3 and renumber Questions 3-4 as Questions 4-5:

3. In 2005 the American Law Institute adopted The Restatement (Third) of Agency, which is meant to supersede The Restatement (Second) of Agency. The wording of many of the sections has changed significantly and a different numbering scheme has been implemented. Section 7.07 is the parallel to old §220, and it no longer contains the list of factors that the Supreme Court looked to in *Reid.* Should a change in the Restatement affect how courts analyze whether an individual is an employee or an independent contractor for purposes of determining whether a work is a work made for hire?

Chapter 3. Acquiring, Keeping, and Transferring Copyright

A. Formalities

Page 150.   In the Notes and Questions:

a.   Insert new Question 4 and renumber Questions 4-8 as Questions 5-9:

4. Article 4.1 of the Chinese Copyright Law provides that "[w]orks the publication and/or dissemination of which are prohibited by law shall not be protected by this Law." On August 13, 2007, the U.S. initiated a formal complaint at the WTO against China, claiming that Article 4.1 denies copyright protection to certain categories of works, including those that fail to satisfy "content review." *See China — Measures Affecting the Protection and Enforcement of Intellectual Property Rights*, WT/DS362/R ¶7.16 (Jan. 26, 2009). The U.S. also claimed that such content review is, in effect, a "formality" to which copyrighted works in China are subject. *Id.* ¶7.145. In response, China argued that Article 4.1 merely denies "copyright protection" with respect to enforceability of such works, but not "copyright," which vests at the moment of creation. *Id.* ¶¶7.17, 7.21, 7.54. China also argued that Article 4.1 denies protection to, *inter alia*, works whose contents are unconstitutional or immoral. *Id.* ¶¶7.17, 7.53.

The WTO Panel found that China's law was not in compliance with the TRIPS Agreement. It noted examples of prohibited content in authorial works contained in a variety of Chinese Administrative Regulations such as the Regulations on the Administration of Audiovisual Products and the Regulations on the Administration of Publications. In these Regulations, prohibited content includes content that "jeopardize[s] the unification, sovereignty and territorial integrity of the State"; "propagate[s] cults and superstition"; or "jeopardize[s] social ethics or fine national cultural traditions." *Id.* Under the plain language of Article 4.1, authors of works that are prohibited from publication or distribution in China are denied the full panoply of rights required by the Berne Convention and TRIPS Agreement. The

Panel concluded that China's copyright law denies protection to certain classes of works in violation of Article 5(1) of the Berne Convention, as incorporated by Article 9 (1) of the TRIPS Agreement. *Id.* ¶¶7.50, 7. 60. Do you agree?

Having already ruled that Article 4.1 of China's Copyright Law has the effect of denying copyright protection to certain classes of works, the WTO Panel chose to exercise "judicial economy" and did not rule directly on the question whether submission of an authorial work to content review constitutes a formality under the Berne Convention and TRIPS Agreement. *Id.* ¶¶7.191, 7.192. Are content restrictions "formalities" proscribed under Article 5(2) of the Berne Convention? Australia, Canada, and the European Community joined the U.S. to argue that content review is an impermissible formality of China's Copyright Law. *Id.* ¶¶7.149, 7.151, 7.152.

b. At the end of renumbered Question 6, insert the following:

The Fourth Circuit recently held that the applicable standard of review of Copyright Office decisions is the "abuse of discretion" standard followed under the Administrative Procedure Act. *Darden v. Peters*, 488 F.3d 277 (4th Cir. 2007) (rejecting argument that a *de novo* standard should be applied to review of Copyright Office decisions).

c. Replace renumbered Question 9 with the following:

9. Failure to comply with the deposit requirements by submitting a later revised version of the work sought to be registered can result in a lack of copyright protection. *See, e.g,. Geoscan, Inc. v. Geotrace Techs., Inc.*, 226 F.3d 387, 393 (5th Cir. 2000) (dismissing lawsuit for failure to submit deposit copies of the source code of the original program). This deposit requirement can pose practical problems for authors of works that are updated frequently, such as computer programs or websites. Why do you think the court imposed this requirement?

B. Duration

Page 152. At the end of the paragraph preceding the Notes and Questions, insert the following:

; *Van Cleef & Arpels Logistics, S.A. v. Landau Jewelry*, 583 F. Supp. 2d 461, 465 (S.D.N.Y. 2008) (failure to file a notice of intent under the URAA "does not alter the legal inevitability of restoration").

Page 152.   In the Notes and Questions, replace Question 3 with the following:

3. A federal district court in Colorado recently ruled that that the restoration provision is unconstitutional, *Golan v. Holder*, 2009 WL 928327 (D. Colo. Apr. 3, 2009), while the D.C. Circuit has rejected similar arguments of unconstitutionality, *Luck's Music Library, Inc. v. Gonzales*, 407 F.3d 1262 (D.C. Cir. 2005). These challenges are discussed in Question 7 on pages 168-69 of the casebook, as replaced in this supplement below.

Pages 156-58.   In the Notes and Questions, insert new Question 2 and renumber Questions 2-4 as Questions 3-5:

2. For foreign works, the duration rules may sometimes seem more complicated, particularly since important consideration must be given to events that took place outside the U.S. In *Societe Civile Succession v. Renoir*, 549 F.3d 1182 (9th Cir. 2008), the plaintiff, a French trust, sued for copyright infringement of sculptures co-authored by the famous French artist Pierre-Auguste Renoir and one of his assistants, Richard Guino. *Societe Civile Succession* (SCS) obtained the copyrights pursuant to a settlement agreement between Renoir's family and Guino's family. However, Renoir's great-grandson, a defendant in this case, was not part of the settlement agreement.

The sculptures were first published in France no later than 1917 in Renoir's name, but there was no American-style notice affixed to the works. In 1984, SCS obtained U.S. copyright registrations for the sculptures and indicated that they were either first published in England in 1983 or unpublished. The court held that publication without copyright notice in a foreign country does not place a work in the public domain in the U.S. Further, because the sculptures were never published with a copyright notice, they did not fall under the 1909 Act. Consequently, "the sculptures were neither protected by copyright nor injected into the public domain." *Id.* at 1187. Ultimately, the court held that U.S. copyright protection for the sculptures began upon registration in 1984 and therefore was governed by the rules of the 1976 Act. Thus, the sculptures are protected for the life of the last surviving author, Guino, who died in 1973, plus 70 years (i.e., until 2043).

Does this outcome make sense? Is it possible that a work can be "neither fish nor fowl"—i.e., not protected by copyright but not in the public domain? Does the court's reasoning point to a loophole in the duration rules or merely to the excesses of the prior system of formalities?

Page 168.   In the Notes and Questions, replace Question 7 with the following:

7. Two lawsuits filed on behalf of different plaintiffs have raised constitutional challenges to §104A of the Copyright Act, which restores copyright to eligible

foreign works. In the first, *Lucks' Music Library, Inc. v. Gonzales*, 407 F.3d 1262 (D.C. Cir. 2005), the court rejected the plaintiff's constitutional challenges to §104A, relying heavily on the Supreme Court's opinion in *Eldred*. In the second lawsuit, the courts relied on *Eldred* to reach the opposite result.

The lead plaintiff in the second lawsuit, Mr. Lawrence Golan, conducted a small college orchestra that, following enactment of §104A, had to pay royalties to perform restored works by Shostakovich, Prokofiev, and others. The district court initially rejected Golan's constitutional arguments, but the Tenth Circuit reversed the district court's First Amendment holding. The court instructed that a law removing works from the public domain "alters the traditional contours of copyright protection and requires first amendment scrutiny." *Golan v. Gonzales*, 501 F.3d 1179, 1187 (10th Cir. 2007). On remand, the district court concluded that §104A is content-neutral, and therefore subject to only intermediate constitutional scrutiny, but that the restoration rules are "'substantially broader than necessary'" to effectuate the important government goal of achieving compliance with the Berne Convention. *Golan v. Holder*, 2009 WL 928327, at *8-*9 (D. Colo. Apr. 3, 2009) (quoting *Ward v. Rock Against Racism*, 491 U.S. 781, 800 (1989)). According to the court, the Berne Convention imposes no requirement that restored copyrights be given protection perfectly equivalent to that given copyrights still in force; therefore, Congress could have granted much broader protection to reliance parties than §104A provides. *See id*. An appeal of the district court's ruling is expected.

Page 169. *In the Notes and Questions, replace Question 9 with the following:*

9. In January 2005, several members of Congress requested that the Copyright Office undertake a review of potential problems posed by so-called orphan works, i.e., "copyrighted works whose owners are difficult or even impossible to locate." They expressed a concern that public access to such works might be impeded because of the high transaction costs involved in locating the copyright owners and the uncertainty associated with using the works without permission. In January 2006, the Copyright Office submitted a final report to Congress in which it concluded that sufficient ground exists for a "meaningful legislative solution" to address the orphan works problem. Among other things, the Report recommended that Congress amend the Copyright Act to limit the scope of monetary remedies and injunctive relief available for infringement of copyright in an orphan work. *See* Report on Orphan Works, *http://www.copyright.gov/orphan/orphan-report-full.pdf*. Do you think these recommendations effectively address disincentives to use orphan works? If adopted, would they sufficiently ameliorate the concerns associated with long copyright terms? What other recommendations would you suggest?

C. Renewals and Terminations of Transfers

Pages 175-77. In the Notes and Questions, insert new Question 3 and renumber Questions 3-5 as Questions 4-6:

3. As described on pages 154-55 of the casebook, in 1992 Congress passed the Copyright Renewal Act (CRA), which made renewal automatic. Previously, the requirement of filing a renewal certificate meant that many works that no longer had commercial significance lost their copyright protection because the owner did not take the affirmative step required to extend it. After passage of the CRA, no affirmative action was required for copyright protection to extend the full 75 (now 95) years. Works that routinely had passed into the public domain after 28 years now receive protection for 95 years. After the Supreme Court decided *Eldred v. Ashcroft*, pages 159-67 in the casebook, Internet archivists filed a constitutional challenge to the CRA. They asserted that the change from an opt-in system of renewal to one of automatic renewal altered the "traditional contours of copyright protection" and therefore required First Amendment scrutiny. *Kahle v. Gonzales*, 487 F.3d 697 (9th Cir. 2007). Holding that the CRA "placed existing copyrights in parity with those of future works," the Ninth Circuit dismissed the plaintiffs' claims. *Id.* at 700.

Page 182. Delete Question 4 and insert the following:

Note on "Agreements to the Contrary"

Recall that the renewal term provided by the 1909 Act was meant to provide authors with an opportunity to renegotiate assignments made before the full value of a work was known. However, the ability to transfer the contingent interest in the renewal term meant that such transfers became standard in industry contracts and significantly undermined the purpose of the renewal term as a second bite at the apple. With the termination provisions, Congress provided a stronger right for authors and their statutory heirs. Both §203 and §304 provide that "termination of the grant may be effected notwithstanding any agreement to the contrary, including any agreement to make a will or to make any future grant." 17 U.S.C. §§203(a)(5), 304(c)(5), 304(d)(1). The Supreme Court has characterized the termination right as inalienable. *Stewart v. Abend*, 495 U.S. 207, 230 (1990).

Just what constitutes an "agreement to the contrary"? It seems clear that an agreement that the author will not seek to exercise her termination rights would qualify. What if the parties to an oral agreement many years later dispute copyright ownership and, in settling that dispute, agree that the work was created as a "work made for hire"? Recall that works made for hire are not subject to termination rights. Should the settlement agreement characterizing the work as a work made for hire be considered "an agreement to the contrary"? The Second Circuit has concluded that "an agreement made subsequent to a work's creation that declares that it is a work created for hire" is an agreement to the contrary and, therefore, does not bar a subsequent lawsuit seeking to terminate the oral assignment of copyright. *Marvel Characters Inc. v. Simon*, 310 F.3d 280 (2d Cir. 2002). The court determined that:

> Any other construction of §304(c) would thwart the clear legislative purpose and intent of the statute. If an agreement between an author and publisher that a work was created for hire were outside the purview of §304(c)(5), the termination provision would be rendered a nullity; litigation-savvy publishers would be able to utilize their superior bargaining position to compel authors to agree that a work was created for hire in order to get their works published.

Id. at 290-91.

Questions about what constitutes an "agreement to the contrary" also arise when the parties to a transfer of copyright renegotiate their agreement without using the formal statutory process for terminating the initial transfer. If the purpose of the statute is to permit authors and their heirs an opportunity to renegotiate the terms once the full value of the work is known, would it be appropriate to characterize that newly renegotiated agreement as "an agreement to the contrary" because it effectively cuts off the statutory termination right? Should it matter how many years had passed since the time of the first agreement or whether the terms of the new agreement are more favorable to the author?

In *Milne ex rel. Coyne v. Stephen Slesinger, Inc.*, 430 F.3d 1036 (9th Cir. 2005), *cert. denied*, 548 U.S. 904 (2006), the granddaughter and heir to the copyrights of A.A. Milne relating to the character Winnie the Pooh sought to terminate an agreement made by Milne in 1930. In 1983, however, the granddaughter's father (Christopher Robin Milne) had entered into a new agreement with the assignee that expressly acknowledged the potential right to terminate the 1930 agreement and sought to replace that agreement with the new one. The Ninth Circuit held that the 1930 agreement had been contractually terminated by the 1983 agreement. The court rejected the argument that the 1983 agreement was "an agreement to the contrary." Citing the Act's legislative history, it reasoned that Congress "did not intend for the statute to 'prevent the parties to a transfer or license from voluntarily agreeing at any time to terminate an existing grant and negotiating a new one.'" *Id.* at 1045 (quoting H.R. Rep. No. 94-1476, at 127, 1976 U.S.C.C.A.N. at 5743). The court noted that the terms of the 1983 agreement were far more favorable to the heirs and that the granddaughter had benefited from this new agreement.

The Second Circuit reached a similar conclusion in *Penguin Group v. Steinbeck*, 537 F.3d 193 (2d Cir. 2008), concerning a 1994 agreement in which John Steinbeck's third wife and widow terminated a 1938 agreement and re-granted rights to the publisher. In a lawsuit brought by Steinbeck's descendants from a prior marriage seeking to terminate the 1938 agreement and recapture the copyrights, the court determined that the 1994 agreement was not an "agreement to the contrary" but was, instead, a valid contractual termination that ended the 1938 agreement.

The 1994 agreement was not only more favorable to the widow, but it also obligated the publisher to publish some of her writings. As with the 1938 agreement, the 1994 agreement did not provide any royalties to the descendants.

The statute provides that a further grant "of any right covered by a terminated grant is valid only if it is made after the effective date of the termination." 17 U.S.C. §§203(b)(4), 304(c)(6)(D), 304(d)(1). An exception is made for a further grant to the original grantee or the original grantee's successor in interest, so long as such further grant is made "after the notice of termination has been served." *Id.* §§203(b)(4), 304(c)(6)(D), 304(d)(1). Should these statutory provisions affect interpretation of agreements that are voluntarily renegotiated outside the formalities of the termination process? The *Steinbeck* court relied on the fact that the authors' heirs renegotiated the agreements "while wielding the threat of termination," even though the statutory formalities for vesting the termination rights through service of notice were not completed prior to the execution of the renegotiated agreement. *Steinbeck*, 537 F.3d at 202; *see also Milne*, 430 F.3d at 1045 (noting that while Christopher Robin Milne "presumably could have served a termination notice, he elected instead to use his leverage to obtain a better deal").

D. Mechanics of Transfers

Pages 183-88. *Replace Section D.1 with the following:*

1. Express versus Implied Transfers

Section 204 of the Copyright Act prescribes a particular form for the effective transfer of copyright ownership rights. This section states in part:

> §204. Execution of transfers and other documents
> (a) A transfer of copyright ownership, other than by operation of law, is not valid unless an instrument of conveyance, or a note or memorandum of the transfer, is in writing and signed by the owner of the rights conveyed or such owner's duly authorized agent.

17 U.S.C. §204. In essence, §204 is a statute of frauds requirement, providing that any purported transfer of a copyright interest must be stated in writing, signed by the copyright owner.

As you learned in your first-year contracts class, putting agreements in writing is good practice: it requires the parties to articulate and clarify their thinking, minimizes misunderstandings, and emphasizes the seriousness of the promises undertaken. The Ninth Circuit has resisted suggestions that the writing requirement of §204 should bend to arguments about industry custom:

> Section 204's writing requirement is not unduly burdensome; it necessitates neither protracted negotiations nor substantial expense. The rule is really quite simple: If the

copyright holder agrees to transfer ownership to another party, that party must get the copyright holder to sign a piece of paper saying so. It doesn't have to be the Magna Charta; a one-line pro forma statement will do.

Effects Assocs., Inc. v. Cohen, 908 F.2d 555, 557 (9th Cir.1990) (rejecting defendant's "argument that . . . Moviemakers do lunch, not contracts").

What happens if the writing requirement is not satisfied? Section 101 of the Copyright Act defines a "transfer of ownership" as "an assignment, mortgage, exclusive license, or any other conveyance, alienation, or hypothecation of a copyright or of any of the exclusive rights comprised in a copyright, whether or not it is limited in time or place of effect, but not including a nonexclusive license." Thus, a "transfer," which the statute requires be in writing, does not include a nonexclusive license. When should a court imply such a license? Other than being nonexclusive, what should the terms of that license be?

Asset Marketing Systems, Inc. v. Gagnon
542 F.3d 748 (9th Cir. 2008)

SMITH, J.: . . . From May 1999 to September 2003, Gagnon [doing business as "Mister Computer"] was an at-will, independent contractor for [Asset Marketing Systems, Inc. (AMS)], hired to assist with its information technology needs. Subsequently, Gagnon was asked to develop custom software for AMS. AMS was Gagnon's largest client, accounting for 98% of his business. Jay Akerstein, a partner at AMS who later became the Chief Operating Officer, was Gagnon's primary contact. Over the course of their four-year relationship, AMS paid Gagnon over $2 million, $250,000 of which was for custom software development and computer classes. Gagnon developed six computer programs for AMS.

In May 2000, AMS and Gagnon entered a Technical Services Agreement (TSA), which was scheduled to expire on April 30, 2001. The TSA, printed on Mister Computer letterhead, set forth Gagnon's fees and the services to be provided. The services included "Custom Application Programming — Consultant will provide Contractor with specific add-on products to enhance Contractor's current in-house database application," and mentioned nothing about a license. The TSA was not renewed, though the relationship continued.

AMS claims that on June 12, 2002, Gagnon signed a Vendor Nondisclosure Agreement (NDA).[1] The NDA would have given AMS ownership of all intellectual property developed for AMS by Gagnon. Gagnon claims that the document is a forgery and that his signature cannot be authenticated.

In June 2003, Gagnon proposed that AMS execute an Outside Vendor Agreement (OVA). The OVA included a Proprietary Rights clause providing:

> Client agrees that all designs, plans, specifications, drawings, inventions, processes, and other information or items produced by Contractor while performing services under this agreement will be the property of Contractor and will be licensed to Client

---

1. The NDA was located and produced six months into the litigation.

on a non-exclusive basis as will any copyrights, patents, or trademarks obtained by Contractor while performing services under this agreement. On request and at Contractor's expense, Client agrees to help Contractor obtain patents and copyrights for any new developments. This includes providing data, plans, specifications, descriptions, documentation, and other information, as well as assisting Contractor in completing any required application or registration. Any source code or intellectual property will remain the property of Contractor. Trademarks, service marks, or any items identifying said Company shall remain the Company's said property. Contractor will allow Company non exclusive, unlimited licensing of software developed for Company.

Akerstein declined to execute the OVA, but countered with a redlined version of the OVA, which substantially rewrote the Proprietary Rights clause to read:

Contractor agrees that all designs, plans, specifications, drawings, inventions, processes, and other information or items produced by Contractor while performing services under this agreement will be the sole property of Client. Any source code or intellectual property agreed to and documented as Contractor's will remain the property of Contractor.

By the end of June 2003, AMS had decided to terminate Gagnon's services. AMS extended an employment offer to Gagnon, but he declined to accept the offer. AMS and Gagnon then discussed an exit strategy, and by late July, the parties had set a target exit date of September 15, 2003.

In August 2003, Gagnon responded to Akerstein's redlined OVA draft with a letter asserting that his "position has always been that Asset Marketing Systems shall be entitled to unlimited software licensing as long as my company had a business relationship with Asset Marketing Systems." The parties never executed the OVA.

In a letter to AMS dated September 18, 2003, Gagnon demanded $1.75 million for AMS to have the right to continue to use the programs and $2 million for Gagnon's agreement not to sell or disclose the programs to AMS's competitors.

In a letter dated September 23, 2003, AMS terminated its relationship with Gagnon. According to AMS, a consultant identified numerous problems with Gagnon's work. It also stated:

Recently, we had discussed employee and intellectual property issues which have yet to be resolved. Despite the foregoing, I learned that we did not have copies of the source code for the software we developed and that copies of our SalesLogix software and our entire database may be maintained by you and your agents offsite.

The letter then demanded:

In connection with that separation, you must immediately provide any and all copies of the source code for all software developed by and on behalf of Asset Marketing Systems immediately. You are not authorized to utilize that software which we believe is owned and all copyrights belong to Asset Marketing Systems. Furthermore, despite your claimed ownership in that copyright, we believe that Asset Marketing Systems' trade secrets are embedded and utilized throughout that software which would preclude use by you as well.

We also demand that you return to us any copies of the SalesLogix software or Asset Marketing databases, programs or other materials that may have come into your possession during our relationship. . . .

In October 2003, Gagnon sent AMS a cease and desist letter, asserting that the use of the programs was unauthorized. . . . Gagnon demanded that AMS certify that it had undertaken to remove "all original and derivative source code" and all related files for the programs from AMS computers.

AMS responded by asserting that Gagnon could not unilaterally stop AMS from continuing to use and update the programs because it had an irrevocable license to use, copy, and modify the programs based on the course of conduct of the parties over the past two-and-a-half years. . . .

Gagnon alleges that AMS's continued use of the six programs constitutes copyright infringement because the programs were used by AMS without its obtaining a license or Gagnon's permission. AMS asserts three defenses to Gagnon's copyright infringement claim: an implied license, a transfer of copyright ownership via the NDA, and 17 U.S.C. §117. We hold that AMS has an implied unlimited license for the programs, and we do not reach the other defenses asserted by AMS.

Though exclusive licenses must be in writing, 17 U.S.C. §204, grants of nonexclusive licenses need not be in writing, and may be granted orally or by implication. *Foad Consulting Group, Inc. v. Azzalino*, 270 F.3d 821, 825-26 (9th Cir. 2001). We have previously considered the grant of an implied license in the context of movie footage and architectural drawings. *Id.; Effects Assocs., Inc. v. Cohen*, 908 F.2d 555, 558 (9th Cir. 1990).

In *Effects Associates*, a movie producer hired Effects Associates to create certain special effects for a movie. Though the film footage containing the special effects was used without the producer's obtaining a written license from Effects Associates, we found that an implied license had been granted because the footage was created at the producer's request with the intent that it be used in the film with no warning that use of the footage would constitute infringement. We determined that "[t]o hold that Effects did not at the same time convey a license to use the footage . . . would mean that plaintiff's contribution to the film was 'of minimal value,' a conclusion that can't be squared with the fact that Cohen paid Effects almost $56,000 for this footage." *Id.* at 559.

Thus, we have held that an implied license is granted when "(1) a person (the licensee) requests the creation of a work, (2) the creator (the licensor) makes that particular work and delivers it to the licensee who requested it,[4] and (3) the

---

4. Though delivery of a copy of software does not compel the conclusion that Gagnon granted AMS a license, it is a relevant factor that we may consider. *See* 17 U.S.C. §202; *Effects*, 908 F.2d at 558 n. 6 (recognizing that delivery is not dispositive, but "one factor that may be relied upon in determining that an implied license has been granted").

licensor intends that the licensee-requestor copy and distribute his work." *I.A.E., Inc. v. Shaver*, 74 F.3d 768, 776 (7th Cir. 1996) (citing *Effects*, 908 F.2d at 558-59) (footnote added). We apply the same analysis we did in *Effects* to implied licenses for computer programs. The last prong of the *Effects* test, however, is not limited to copying and distribution; instead we look at the protected right at issue — here, whether Gagnon intended that AMS use, retain, and modify the programs.

1. AMS Requested the Creation of the Programs

Gagnon argues that AMS never specifically requested that he create the programs, but "rather relayed its needs to Mr. Gagnon and he satisfied them by providing either computer hardware or computer software at his discretion." We find this interpretation of "request" to be strained. Gagnon did not create the programs on his own initiative and market them to AMS; rather, he created them in response to AMS's requests. Moreover, after prototype software was developed, he made changes to the programs in response to Akerstein and other AMS employees' requests. No genuine issue of material fact remains as to whether AMS requested the programs.

2. Gagnon Created the Software for AMS and Delivered It

Though Gagnon argues that the programs could be converted for use by another company, Gagnon admitted that the programs were created specifically for AMS and that AMS paid for the work related to drafting of the programs as well as some related costs. It is, therefore, undisputed that Gagnon created these programs for AMS.

The remaining question is whether Gagnon delivered the programs to AMS. We agree with the district court that Gagnon delivered them when he installed them onto the AMS computers and stored the source code on-site at AMS. Gagnon argues that even if he had installed the programs onto the AMS computers, he never delivered the source code so that AMS could modify the code. If AMS did not have the right to modify the code, it may have infringed Gagnon's copyright by exceeding the scope of its license. Gagnon primarily points to AMS's inability to locate the code on its own computer systems after his services were terminated to show that AMS did not possess the code. But, as we explain below, Gagnon's conduct manifested an objective intent to give AMS an unlimited license at the time of creation; thus, when he stored the source code at AMS, the code was delivered.

3. Gagnon's Intent as Manifested by His Conduct

Gagnon argues that he never intended that AMS would retain and modify the programs he delivered. Gagnon misunderstands the inquiry into intent, and we conclude that his conduct did manifest an intent to grant a license. The relevant intent is the licensor's objective intent at the time of the creation and delivery of the software as manifested by the parties' conduct. *See Effects*, 908 F.2d at 559 n. 6 (noting that "every objective fact concerning the transaction" supported the finding that an implied license existed). The First and Fourth Circuits consider the following factors to determine such an intent:

> (1) whether the parties were engaged in a short-term discrete transaction as opposed to an ongoing relationship; (2) whether the creator utilized written contracts . . . providing that copyrighted materials could only be used with the creator's future involvement or express permission; and (3) whether the creator's conduct during the creation or delivery of the copyrighted material indicated that use of the material without the creator's involvement or consent was permissible.

[*John G. Danielson, Inc. v. Winchester–Conant Props., Inc.*, 322 F.3d 26, 41 (1st Cir.2003).] We find this approach to be persuasive.

Gagnon and AMS had an ongoing service relationship in which Gagnon provided technical support for all computer-related problems at AMS; he also created certain custom software applications at AMS's request. The relationship of the parties indicates neither an intent to grant nor deny a license without Gagnon's future involvement.

Several documents exist, however, that reflect the parties' objective intent: the TSA, signed by both parties, the OVA submitted by Gagnon, and Gagnon's letter objecting to Akerstein's proposed changes to the OVA.[6] Courts have looked to contracts, even if unexecuted, as evidence of the intent of the party submitting the contract. *See Johnson v. Jones*, 149 F.3d 494, 501 (6th Cir.1998) (finding no license where architect submitted contracts containing express provision that drawings could not be used by others except with agreement and compensation).

The TSA, signed by both parties in 2000 and printed on Mister Computer letterhead, stated only that Gagnon "will provide" AMS "specific add-on products." Nothing in the TSA indicates Gagnon's understanding or intent that continued use of the custom application programming undertaken by Gagnon would be prohibited after the TSA terminated. . . . Like the special effects creators in *Effects Associates*, Gagnon was well paid for his services. Under the circumstances, it defies logic that AMS would have paid Gagnon for his programming services if AMS could not have used the programs without further payment pursuant to a separate licensing arrangement that was never mentioned in the TSA, and never otherwise requested at the time. This is especially so because custom software is far less valuable without the ability to modify it and because the TSA was set to expire in one year; one would expect some indication of the need for future licensing if the custom programs were to become unusable after the TSA expired.

The OVA submitted by Gagnon, but never executed, did not evidence any intent by Gagnon to limit AMS's use of the programs. Gagnon argues that the clause, "Client agrees that [intellectual property] produced by Contractor while performing services under this agreement will be the property of Contractor and

---

6. We do not consider the NDA, allegedly signed by Gagnon, because Gagnon contests its validity and argues that his signature was forged, creating a factual dispute inappropriate for resolution on summary judgment.

will be licensed to Client on a non-exclusive basis as will any copyrights, patents, or trademarks obtained by Contractor while performing services under this agreement . . . ," means that his license was conditioned on a continuing relationship with AMS. We disagree. The clause "while performing services under this agreement" modifies the production of the intellectual property and the obtainment of copyrights. Furthermore, the contract then expressly stated, "Contractor will allow Company non-exclusive, unlimited licensing of software developed for Company," eliminating any ambiguity.

Moreover, Gagnon and AMS did not discuss a licensing agreement until their relationship was ending. Gagnon delivered the software without any caveats or limitations on AMS's use of the programs. Even if Gagnon and his employees maintained the software and had primary control over the code, they programmed on-site at AMS on AMS computers to which key AMS personnel had access — conduct that does not demonstrate an intent to retain sole control. The first time Gagnon expressed a contrary intent was in his letter to Aker[stein] sent after AMS had decided to terminate Gagnon's services. . . .

4. Scope and Irrevocability of Implied License

For the reasons outlined, we hold that Gagnon granted AMS an unlimited, nonexclusive license to retain, use, and modify the software. Furthermore, because AMS paid consideration, this license is irrevocable. *See Lulirama Ltd., Inc. v. Axcess Broad. Servs., Inc.*, 128 F.3d 872, 882 (5th Cir.1997). "[A] nonexclusive license supported by consideration is a contract." *Lulirama*, 128 F.3d at 882; *see also Effects*, 908 F.2d at 559 n. 7 (an implied license is a "creature of law, much like any other implied-in-fact contract"). If an implied license accompanied by consideration were revocable at will, the contract would be illusory.

NOTES AND QUESTIONS

1. As *AMS* shows, parties do not always put their arrangements in writing. Is it good policy for courts to imply a nonexclusive license? Does the *AMS* decision set out appropriate considerations for determining when such a license should be implied?

2. Are there other instances in which courts should imply a license? The application of copyright to the Internet has raised many questions about how to determine the appropriate balance between owners and users of copyrighted works. Recall *MAI Systems Corp. v. Peak Computer, Inc.*, 991 F.2d 511 (9th Cir. 1993), discussed in Chapter 2.A.1.a, pages 51-53 of the casebook, in which the court held that a RAM copy, created by loading software from a hard disk into the CPU of a computer, satisfies the fixation requirement. Based on an extension of the *MAI* reasoning, routine activities such as forwarding e-mail or downloading documents from the web would each involve multiple acts of copyright infringement. Could courts hold that such activities are protected by an implied license?

3. In *AMS*, the delivery of tangible copies embodying the copyrighted work was a factor the court considered in determining whether to imply a license. Does that make sense? Remember that copyright ownership is distinct from ownership of the underlying object in which the copyrightable expression is fixed. *See* 17 U.S.C. §202. For example, ownership of the copyright in a novel or a painting does not entail ownership of a physical copy of the novel or painting. Similarly, ownership of a physical copy of a novel or a painting does not equal, and cannot be taken to imply, ownership of the copyright in that novel or painting. We return to this distinction in Chapter 5 when we examine the first sale doctrine.

4. In addition to §204's provisions governing transfers, a copyright also may be transferred by "operation of law." Section 201(d)(1) recognizes transfers by will (which would satisfy the writing requirement) as well as by intestate succession, which is governed by state law. Note, however, that intestate succession to the copyright is distinct from intestate succession to the termination interest, which is governed by §§203 and 304.

5. Although the statute provides that an exclusive license constitutes a transfer of ownership, at least one court has ruled that an exclusive licensee is not equivalent to a copyright owner. *Gardner v. Nike, Inc.*, 279 F.3d 774 (9th Cir. 2002). In that case the Ninth Circuit held that an exclusive licensee may not transfer the licensed rights without the consent of the original licensor because "§201(d)(2) only conferred the 'protections and remedies' afforded a copyright owner under the 1976 Act, not the rights." *Id.* at 779. A logical implication from *Gardner* is that rights obtained pursuant to any license, including an exclusive license, may not be sublicensed without authorization from the copyright owner. Would that rule be good policy?

6. Section 205 of the Copyright Act provides for recordation of transfers of copyright with the Copyright Office. Prior to U.S. ratification of the Berne Convention, recordation was a pre-suit requirement if the copyright claimant was a transferee of the exclusive rights. The 1988 amendments to the Copyright Act, occasioned by the Berne Convention, dispensed with this prerequisite to filing a copyright action. However, recordation remains useful for a variety of purposes. A recorded copyright document serves the important function of providing constructive notice of the facts stated in the document so long as the document or attached materials identify the work in question and the work has been registered. Recordation is also important for determining a superior claim as between two conflicting copyright transfers.

7. In today's information economy, many companies' major assets are primarily intangible. Yet these firms need to raise money as much as, if not more than, their counterparts with tangible assets. These firms often offer their intangible assets, including their copyrights, as security for a loan. If the firm fails to repay the loan, the secured party can "repossess" the collateral (the property serving as security). Certain issues arise, however, when the collateral consists of copyrights.

State law, specifically Article 9 of the Uniform Commercial Code (UCC), governs the creation and enforcement of many, if not most, security interests. Article 9 typically requires that a notice (called a financing statement) be filed in the appropriate location within the state that Article 9 rules select. This filing "perfects" the security interest and generally safeguards the secured party against conflicting claims to the collateral that may be raised by a later claimant. As state law, Article 9 is subject to preemption by federal law. Authorities generally agree that to perfect a security interest in a copyright, the secured party should file with the Copyright Office. Section 205 of the Copyright Act provides for recordations of transfers, and the definition of "transfer" includes "hypothecation," which in turn encompasses the grant of a security interest.

However, the Copyright Act provides that recording a transfer gives constructive notice only if the copyright has been registered. 17 U.S.C. §205(c)(2). Ideally, then, a lender should always require that a copyright registration be filed before concluding the secured transaction. In some cases this is difficult because the work itself is in flux; for example, software under development changes daily. In those cases, filing under "regular" Article 9 rules may be sufficient, but it is not guaranteed.

Unfortunately, there are other complications. One controversial case held that even when the collateral is not the copyright itself, but rather the royalties generated by the copyright, the filing should still be made with the Copyright Office. *See In re National Peregrine, Inc.*, 116 B.R. 194 (C.D. Cal. 1990). This conflicts with provisions of Article 9 that would label the royalties "accounts" and permit perfection in them to be achieved by a state law filing.

Page 200. In the Notes and Questions, insert new Question 4:

4. The National Institutes of Health (NIH) has adopted a policy requiring that all final manuscripts reporting the results of federally funded research be provided to the NIH in electronic form to be made available to the public "no later than 12 months after the official date of publication." *See* U.S. Dep't of Health & Human Services, National Institutes of Health, Revised Policy on Enhancing Public Access to Archived Publications Resulting from NIH-Funded Research, NOT-OD-08-033. Scientific publishers have opposed that decision, arguing that members of the public may gain access to papers published in their journals from a variety of other sources. They have supported proposed legislation that would forbid federal agencies from imposing any condition requiring "the transfer or license to or for a Federal agency" of rights to make copyrighted works available to the public. Fair Copyright in Research Works Act, H.R. 6845, 110th Cong., 2d Sess. Would you support enactment of such a bill? Why, or why not?

Page 200. Insert the following after the Notes and Questions:

Jacobsen v. Katzer
535 F.3d 1373 (Fed. Cir. 2008)

HOCHBERG, J.: . . .

I.

Jacobsen manages an open source software group called Java Model Railroad Interface ("JMRI"). Through the collective work of many participants, JMRI created a computer programming application called DecoderPro, which allows model railroad enthusiasts to use their computers to program the decoder chips that control model trains. DecoderPro files are available for download and use by the public free of charge from an open source incubator website called Source-Forge;. . . . The downloadable files contain copyright notices and refer the user to a "COPYING" file, which clearly sets forth the terms of the Artistic License.

Katzer/Kamind offers a competing software product, Decoder Commander, which is also used to program decoder chips. During development of Decoder Commander, one of Katzer/Kamind's predecessors or employees is alleged to have downloaded the decoder definition files from DecoderPro and used portions of these files as part of the Decoder Commander software. The Decoder Commander software files that used DecoderPro definition files did not comply with the terms of the Artistic License. Specifically, the Decoder Commander software did not include (1) the authors' names, (2) JMRI copyright notices, (3) references to the COPYING file, (4) an identification of SourceForge or JMRI as the original source of the definition files, and (5) a description of how the files or computer code had been changed from the original source code. The Decoder Commander software also changed various computer file names of DecoderPro files without providing a reference to the original JMRI files or information on where to get the Standard Version.

Jacobsen moved for a preliminary injunction, arguing that the violation of the terms of the Artistic License constituted copyright infringement. . . . The District Court found that Jacobsen had a cause of action only for breach of contract, rather than an action for copyright infringement based on a breach of the conditions of the Artistic License. . . .

II. . . .

A.

. . . Open Source software projects invite computer programmers from around the world to view software code and make changes and improvements to it. Through such collaboration, software programs can often be written and debugged faster and at lower cost than if the copyright holder were required to do all of the work independently. In exchange and in consideration for this collaborative work, the copyright holder permits users to copy, modify and distribute the software code subject to conditions that serve to protect downstream users and to keep the code accessible. By requiring that users copy and restate the license and attribution information, a copyright holder can ensure that recipients of the redistributed computer code know the identity of the owner as well as the scope of the license granted by the original owner. The Artistic License in this case also requires that changes to the computer code be tracked so that downstream users know what part of the computer code is the original code created by the copyright holder and what part has been newly added or altered by another collaborator.

Traditionally, copyright owners sold their copyrighted material in exchange for money. The lack of money changing hands in open source licensing should not be presumed to mean that there is no economic consideration, however. There are substantial benefits, including economic benefits, to the creation and distribution of copyrighted works under public licenses that range far beyond traditional license royalties. For example, program creators may generate market share for their programs by providing certain components free of charge. Similarly, a programmer or company may increase its national or international reputation by incubating open source projects. Improvement to a product can come rapidly and free of charge from an expert not even known to the copyright holder. . . .

B.

The parties do not dispute that Jacobsen is the holder of a copyright for certain materials distributed through his website. Katzer/Kamind also admits that portions of the DecoderPro software were copied, modified, and distributed as part of the Decoder Commander software. Accordingly, Jacobsen has made out a prima facie case of copyright infringement. Katzer/Kamind argues that they cannot be liable for copyright infringement because they had a license to use the material. Thus, the Court must evaluate whether the use by Katzer/Kamind was outside the scope of the license. . . . The copyrighted materials in this case are downloadable by any user and are labeled to include a copyright notification and a COPYING file that includes the text of the Artistic License. The Artistic License grants users the right to copy, modify, and distribute the software:

> provided that [the user] insert a prominent notice in each changed file stating how and when [the user] changed that file, and provided that [the user] do at least ONE of the following:
>
> a) place [the user's] modifications in the Public Domain or otherwise make them Freely Available . . .
> b) use the modified Package only within [the user's] corporation or organization.
> c) rename any non-standard executables so the names do not conflict with the standard executables, which must also be provided, and provide a separate manual page for each nonstandard executable that clearly documents how it differs from the Standard Version, or
> d) make other distribution arrangements with the Copyright Holder.

The heart of the argument on appeal concerns whether the terms of the Artistic License are conditions of, or merely covenants to, the copyright license. Generally, a "copyright owner who grants a nonexclusive license to use his copyrighted material waives his right to sue the licensee for copyright infringement" and can sue only for breach of contract. *Sun Microsystems, Inc., v. Microsoft Corp.*, 188 F.3d 1115, 1121 (9th Cir.1999); . . . . If, however, a license is limited in scope and the licensee acts outside the scope, the licensor can bring an action for copyright infringement . . . .

Thus, if the terms of the Artistic License allegedly violated are both covenants and conditions, they may serve to limit the scope of the license and are governed by copyright law. If they are merely covenants, by contrast, they are governed by contract law. . . .

III.

The Artistic License states on its face that the document creates conditions: "The intent of this document is to state the *conditions* under which a Package may be copied." (Emphasis added.) The Artistic License also uses the traditional language of conditions by noting that the rights to copy, modify, and distribute are granted *"provided that"* the conditions are met. Under California contract law, "provided that" typically denotes a condition . . . .

The District Court interpreted the Artistic License to permit a user to "modify the material in any way" and did not find that any of the "provided that" limitations in the Artistic License served to limit this grant. The District Court's interpretation of the conditions of the Artistic License does not credit the explicit restrictions in the license that govern a downloader's right to modify and distribute the copyrighted work. The copyright holder here expressly stated the terms upon which the right to modify and distribute the material depended and invited direct contact if a downloader wished to negotiate other terms. These restrictions were both clear and necessary to accomplish the objectives of the open source licensing collaboration, including economic benefit. . . .

In this case, a user who downloads the JMRI copyrighted materials is authorized to make modifications and to distribute the materials "provided that" the user follows the restrictive terms of the Artistic License. A copyright holder can grant the right to make certain modifications, yet retain his right to prevent other modifications. Indeed, such a goal is exactly the purpose of adding conditions to a license grant. . . .

It is outside the scope of the Artistic License to modify and distribute the copyrighted materials without copyright notices and a tracking of modifications from the original computer files. If a downloader does not assent to these conditions stated in the COPYING file, he is instructed to "make other arrangements with the Copyright Holder." Katzer/Kamind did not make any such "other arrangements." The clear language of the Artistic License creates conditions to protect the economic rights at issue in the granting of a public license. These conditions govern the rights to modify and distribute the computer programs and files included in the downloadable software package. The attribution and modification transparency requirements directly serve to drive traffic to the open source incubation page and to inform downstream users of the project, which is a significant economic goal of the copyright holder that the law will enforce. Through this controlled spread of information, the copyright holder gains creative collaborators to the open source project; by requiring that changes made by downstream users be visible to the copyright holder and others, the copyright holder learns about the uses for his software and gains others' knowledge that can be used to advance future software releases.

IV.

. . . Having determined that the terms of the Artistic License are enforceable copyright conditions, we remand to enable the District Court to determine whether Jacobsen [is entitled to a preliminary injunction.] . . .

NOTES AND QUESTIONS

1. Note the court's emphasis on modification and distribution of the program in violation of the license terms. It is copyright infringement to modify or distribute the program without statutory authorization or a license to do so. Thus, modification or distribution without complying with the license — i.e., acting outside its scope — is an infringement. This will become clearer to you after you study the §106 rights, including the rights to make derivative works and to distribute copies of a work.

2. The question whether a particular contractual provision is a covenant or condition is a matter of state contract law. Do you recall from your contracts class what the tests are for distinguishing a covenant and a condition and the difficulty in doing so? Does the case provide sufficient guidance?

3. The court seems to categorize cases neatly into two categories — those involving conditions (governed by copyright law) and those involving covenants (governed by contract law). Doesn't the case involve a breach of contract as well as copyright infringement? According to at least two commentators, "[a] breach of a mere covenant entitles the licensor to damages perhaps, but does not support an infringement claim so long as the licensee continues to perform within the license scope. On the other hand, breach of a scope provision entitles the licensor to both a contract remedy and an infringement claim, providing of course that there can be no double recovery." Raymond T. Nimmer & Jeff C. Dodd, Modern Licensing Law 2007 edition, §§11:24-27, 11:54, at 1114-23, 1197-1209 (2006). This suggests that a plaintiff could claim both breach of contract and copyright infringement for violation of a scope provision, as Jacobsen did in this case.

Pages 205-07.   In the Notes and Questions,

a.   At the end of Question 2, insert the following:

Some plaintiffs objected to the settlement in this class action litigation, arguing that the named plaintiffs, who owned registered copyrights, failed adequately to represent the interests of unnamed class members, who owned unregistered copyrights. On appeal, the Second Circuit reversed the district court's approval of the class and of the settlement. The court held that the district court lacked jurisdiction to certify a class consisting of claims arising from the infringement of unregistered copyrights and to approve a settlement with respect to those claims. In re *Literary Works in Electronic Databases Copyright Litigation*, 509 F.3d 116 (2d Cir. 2007). The court vacated the opinion and remanded the case for further proceedings. In March 2009, the Supreme Court granted certiorari to address whether the lack of registration defeats federal subject matter jurisdiction. *Reed Elsevier, Inc. v. Muchnick*, 129 S. Ct. 1523 (2009).

b.   Replace Question 3 with the following:

3. After *Tasini*, what factors should be relevant in determining the scope of the collective work publisher's revision privilege under §201(c)? In *Greenberg v. National Geographic Society*, 533 F.3d 1244 (11th Cir. 2008) (en banc), the court drew two fundamental lessons from *Tasini*: "First, the concept of 'revision' necessarily includes some elements of novelty or 'newness' . . . and second, consideration of the context in which the contributions are presented is critical in determining whether that novelty is sufficient to defeat the publisher's §201(c) privilege." *Id.* at 1251. The product at issue in the case was The Complete National Geographic (CNG), a series of CD-ROMs containing each monthly issue of the magazine as it was originally published from 1888 through 1996. The court rejected the plaintiff's argument that aggregating editions into a larger collective work took the new collective work outside the privilege. The product contained a 25-second introductory montage of individual cover images as a "virtual cover" for the product, allowed readers to flip through the pages of the magazine, to zoom in on a particular page, and to digitally search the magazine articles. The court concluded that these new elements did not take the CNG outside the §201(c) privilege. The individual author contributions were presented as digital replicas of the pages of the magazine, two pages at a time with the fold in the middle and the page numbers in the exact same place as in the print version. The "new elements," the court noted, were a by-product of the digital medium. The court noted that "[a]s technology progresses and different mediums are created through which copyrightable works are introduced to the public, copyright law must remain grounded in the premise that a difference in form is not the same as a difference in substance." *Id.* at 1257. *See also Faulkner v. Nat'l Geographic Soc'y*, 409 F.3d 16 (2d Cir. 2005).

c. Insert new Question 6:

6. Note that to be eligible for the rights granted in §201(c), the works at issue must be classified as collective works. In *Jarvis v. K2, Inc.,* 486 F.3d 526 (9th Cir. 2007), the plaintiff had created several thousand photographic images for use in advertisements for defendant's products. After the relationship soured, the plaintiff sued for copyright infringement. Among the acts of infringement alleged by the plaintiff were the creation of four different collages containing 24 of plaintiff's images along with other images. The district court concluded that the collages did not constitute infringements because of the collective right privilege. On appeal, the Ninth Circuit determined that the collages constituted derivative works rather than collective works and thus were outside the scope of the collective right privilege. *Id.* at 531-32. The court first quoted the statutory definitions and then turned to legislative history indicating that in collective works the separate elements "remain unintegrated and disparate." *Id.* at 531 (quoting H.R. Rep. No. 94-1476, at 122 (1976), *reprinted in* 1976 U.S.C.C.A.N. 5659, 5737). The court noted that the collages did not merely compile the plaintiff's images, but "shrank, expanded, distorted, overlaid and otherwise edited the original images, while also combining them with photos taken by other photographers, additional graphics, the K2 logo and marketing slogans." *Id.*

Chapter 4. Protected Works and Boundary Problems

A. Useful Articles with Pictorial, Graphic, or Sculptural Aspects

Pages 224-26. In the Notes and Questions, insert new Question 6 and renumber Questions 6-8 as Questions 7-9:

6. May one claim copyright in a useful article with pictorial, graphic, or sculptural aspects based on a copyright registration in a two-dimensional drawing? In *Eliya v. Kohl's Dept. Stores*, 2006 WL 2645196 (S.D.N.Y. Sept. 13, 2006), the plaintiff shoe designer and manufacturer alleged that defendant Kohl's had infringed his copyright by making shoes similar to a two-dimensional shoe design registered with the Copyright Office. The court held that Eliya could assert an infringement claim based on the two-dimensional registration, but that the design elements delineated in the drawing—stitching, borders, and sole patterns—were neither physically nor conceptually separable.

Page 232. Delete §1301(b)(2) and insert the following:

(2) A "useful article" is a vessel hull or deck, including a plug or a mold, which in its normal use has an intrinsic utilitarian function that is not merely to portray the appearance of the article or to convey information. An article which normally is part of a useful article shall be deemed to be a useful article. . . .

Page 234. In the Notes and Questions:

a. Delete the last two sentences of Question 2 and insert the following:

Elsewhere, however, the VHDPA states that "[t]he design of a vessel hull, deck, or combination of a hull and deck, including a plug or a mold, is subject to protection under this chapter, notwithstanding section 1302(4)." *Id.* §1301(a)(2). What, then, is the point of §1302(4)?

b. Insert the following at the end of Question 3:

In the 110th session of Congress, bills were introduced that would amend the VHDPA to provide protection for registered fashion designs for a three-year period. H.R. 2033, 110th Cong.' 1st Sess., S. 1957, 110th Cong., 2d Sess. The bills demonstrate how Congress could use the VHDPA as a template for extending protection to other types of design. They would amend §1301 by defining "fashion design" as "the appearance as a whole of an article of apparel, including its ornamentation," and extending the protections in §1301(a) to "fashion design."

Reread Notes 7-8 on page 226 of the casebook. Is VHDPA-type protection for fashion designs desirable as a policy matter? For a recent discussion of that question, see Kal Raustiala & Christopher Sprigman, *The Piracy Paradox: Innovation and Intellectual Property in Fashion Design*, 92 Va. L. Rev. 1687 (2006) (examining why the fashion industry thrives despite the lack of protection and arguing that copying may promote innovation there), and Randal C. Picker, *Of Pirates and Puffy Shirts: A Comment on "The Piracy Paradox: Innovation and Intellectual Property in Fashion Design,"* available at *http://ssrn.com/abstract_id=959727* (2007) (arguing that the situation is more complex than Raustiala & Sprigman suggest and expressing skepticism that copying of fashion design leads to more innovation).

C. Architectural Works

Page 276. Before the Notes and Questions, insert the following:

Intervest Construction, Inc. v. Canterbury Estate Homes, Inc.
554 F.3d 914 (11th Cir. 2008)

BIRCH, J.: . . .

In this copyright infringement action the appellant contends that the district court erred when it examined the two floor-plans at issue . . . emphasizing the differences between the two . . .

I. BACKGROUND

. . . [T]he floor plan for The Westminster was created in 1992 as a work-made-for-hire by Intervest Construction, Inc. ("Intervest"). The putatively infringing floor-plan, The Kensington, was created in 2002 by Canterbury Estate

Homes, Inc. ("Canterbury"). Each floor-plan depicts a four-bedroom house, with one bedroom being denominated as a "master" bedroom or suite. Each floor plan includes a: two-car garage; living room; dining room; "family" room; foyer; "master" bathroom; kitchen; second bathroom; nook; and porch/patio. Each floor-plan also reflects certain "elements" common to most houses: doors; windows; walls; bathroom fixtures (toilet, tub, shower, and sink); kitchen fixtures (sink, counter, refrigerator, stovetop, and pantry/cabinets); utility rooms and fixtures (washer, dryer, and sink); and closets. A cursory examination of the two floor-plans reveals that the square footage of both is approximately the same. Also, as is common to houses, there are placements of entrances, exits, hallways, openings, and utilities (furnace, air conditioner, hot water heater, and telephone hardware).

After identifying all of these unassigned components and elements of the floor-plans, the district court undertook a careful comparative analysis of the selection, coordination, and arrangement of these common components and elements. The district court focused upon the dissimilarities in such coordination and arrangement: [Eds. — The court then proceeded with a lengthy comparison of the floor plans. A few excerpts from that comparison are included below.]

> First, Canterbury represents that the square footage of the rooms in the two designs is different, and visual examination of the floor plans appears to confirm that. . . .
>
> Second, the garage in The Westminster has a front entrance, while The Kensington's has a side entrance. Further, Intervest's design has an attic access from the garage, while Canterbury's version has a "bonus room" above the garage, something The Westminster lacks entirely. Moreover, the inside air conditioning unit and water heater are placed differently in the two floor plans. Additionally, The Kensington has two windows in the garage, while The Westminster has none. In The Westminster, there is a bedroom closet to the left of the utility room, whereas in The Kensington, there is a hallway in that location. . . .
>
> Proceeding to the center portion of the homes, the nooks in the two plans are markedly different. In that regard, [The Westminster's] nook feeds into a ninety degree angle adjacent to the Porch and has windows looking both to the outside and to the Porch. On the other hand, [The Kensington's] design is rounded into the porch and is completely made of glass. There is no window to the outside or into the Covered Patio. Moreover, the entrance from the Nook into the Living Room in [The Westminster's] design has an elongated wall which travels much further into the Living Room than in [The Kensington's] design, and also fails to break inward at a ninety degree angle like in [The Kensington's] design. . . .
>
> The kitchens in the two plans are also substantially different. In that connection, the wall placement in the southeast corner of the kitchens is significantly different. [The Kensington's] design pushes this wall further into the Living Room and pushes the Kitchen Counter much further north than in [The Westminster's] design. This allows [The Kensington's] design to have a much larger Pantry than [The Westminster's] design. . . .
>
> . . . Additionally, in The Kensington's master bath, "the doors to the walk-in closets . . . are solid and open in different directions than those [in the Westminster], which uses a retractable door." . . . Finally, the sinks in the master bath are placed differently in the two designs. In The Kensington, the sinks are centered; in The Westminster, they are not." [Eds. — Internal citations have been omitted.] . . .

II. DISCUSSION

Since we are dealing with a specific type of copyrightable work, here an architectural work, we begin by examining the statutory definition of an "architectural work," to wit: "the design of a building as embodied in any tangible medium of expression, including a building, architectural plans or drawings. The work includes the overall form as well as the arrangement and composition of spaces and elements in the design, but does not include individual standard features." 17 U.S.C. §101 (2008). A review of the legislative history discloses that such "individual standard features" include "common windows, doors, and other staple building components." H.R.Rep. No. 101-735 (1990) *as reprinted in* 1990 U.S.C.C.A.N. 6935, 6949. Including the phrase "the arrangement and composition of spaces and elements in the design" demonstrates Congress' appreciation that "creativity in architecture frequently takes the form of a selection, coordination, or arrangement of unprotectible elements into an original, protectible whole." *Id.* Accordingly, while individual standard features and architectural elements classifiable as ideas or concepts are not themselves copyrightable, an architect's original combination or arrangement of such elements may be. . . . Thus, the definition of an architectural work closely parallels that of a "compilation" under the statute, that is: "[A] work formed by the collection and assembling of preexisting materials or of data that are selected, coordinated, or arranged in such a way that the resulting work as a whole constitutes an original work of authorship." 17 U.S.C. §101. The Supreme Court . . . and our court . . . [have] indicated that the compiler's choices as to selection[,] coordination, or arrangement are the only portions of a compilation, or here, architectural work, that are even entitled to copyright protection. Accordingly, any similarity comparison of the works at issue here must be accomplished at the level of protected expression . . . that is, the *arrangement* and *coordination* of those common elements ("selected" by the market place, i.e., rooms, windows, doors, and "other staple building components"). In undertaking such a comparison it should be recalled that the copyright protection in a compilation is "thin." . . . Moreover, as the Second Circuit has noted, the substantial similarity inquiry is "narrowed" when dealing with a compilation. . . .

. . . Thus, when viewed through the narrow lens of compilation analysis only the original, and thus protected arrangement and coordination of spaces, elements and other staple building components should be compared. . . .

. . . [A]s noted above, while a creative work is entitled to the most protection, a compilation is entitled to the least, narrowest or "thinnest" protection. . . . Accordingly, when courts have examined copyright infringement claims involving compilations the definition of "substantial similarity" has been appropriately modified to accentuate the narrower scope of protection available. . . .

III. CONCLUSION

. . . Given that the plans at issue were protected by compilation copyrights which were "thin," the district court correctly determined that the differences in the protectable expression were so significant that, as a matter of law, no reasonable properly-instructed jury of lay observers could find the works substantially similar. . . .

Page 276.   In the Notes and Questions, insert the following at the end of Question 1:

The Fourth Circuit in *Nelson-Salabes* emphasized the similarities of the architectural design plans at issue, while the Eleventh Circuit in *Intervest* emphasized the dissimilarities of the floor plans at issue. Which approach is more consistent with the language and legislative history of the AWCPA?

E.   Databases

Page 304.   In the Notes and Questions, insert the following at the end of Question 2:

In another case involving the copyrightability of prices, the Second Circuit considered whether commodity futures prices circulated by the commodity exchange at the close of each day's trading were meant to reflect "how the market *should* value . . . or *will* value" the commodity futures as "an empirical reality, an economic fact about the world that [the plaintiff was] seeking to discover," or whether the plaintiff was "creating predictions or estimates." *New York Mercantile Exch., Inc. v. Intercontinental Exch., Inc.*, 497 F.3d 109, 115 (2d Cir. 2007) (emphasis in original). Recognizing that it is often difficult to determine the line between *creation*, which would be copyrightable, and *discovery*, which would not, the court ruled that even if the prices were copyrightable, the merger doctrine barred plaintiff's infringement claim.

Chapter 5. The Statutory Rights of Copyright Owners

B. The Reproduction Right

Page 345.   Insert the following after the Notes and Questions:

Mannion v. Coors Brewing Company
377 F. Supp. 2d 444 (S.D.N.Y. 2006)

[Review the excerpt from the *Mannion* case, pages 353-57 *supra*. Recall that the court identified three different ways originality can be expressed in photographs. In the excerpt below, the court considers the role of the idea/expression dichotomy in assessing the copyrightability of photographs and then considers how to compare photographs to determine if they are substantially similar.]

KAPLAN, J: . . .

THE IDEA/EXPRESSION DIFFICULTY

Notwithstanding the originality of the Garnett Photograph, the defendants argue that the Coors Billboard does not infringe because the two, insofar as they are similar, share only "the generalized idea and concept of a young African American man wearing a white T-shirt and a large amount of jewelry."

It is true that an axiom of copyright law is that copyright does not protect "ideas," only their expression. Furthermore, when "a given idea is inseparably tied to a particular expression" so that "there is a 'merger' of idea and expression," courts may deny protection to the expression in order to avoid conferring a monopoly on the idea to which it inseparably is tied. But the defendants' reliance on these principles is misplaced.

The "idea" (if one wants to call it that) postulated by the defendants does not even come close to accounting for all the similarities between the two works, which extend at least to angle, pose, background, composition, and lighting. It is possible to imagine any number of depictions of a black man wearing a white T-shirt and "bling bling" that look nothing like either of the photographs at issue here.

This alone is sufficient to dispose of the defendants' contention that Mannion's claims must be rejected because he seeks to protect an idea rather than its expression. But the argument reveals an analytical difficulty in the case law about which more ought to be said. One of the main cases upon which the defendants rely is *Kaplan v. Stock Market Photo Agency, Inc.,* [133 F. Supp. 2d 317 (S.D.N.Y. 2001)] in which two remarkably similar photographs of a businessman's shoes and lower legs, taken from the top of a tall building looking down on a street below . . . were held to be not substantially similar as a matter of law because all of the similarities flowed only from an unprotected idea rather than from the expression of that idea.

But what is the "idea" of Kaplan's photograph? Is it (1) a businessman contemplating suicide by jumping from a building, (2) a businessman contemplating suicide by jumping from a building, seen from the vantage point of the businessman, with his shoes set against the street far below, or perhaps something more general, such as (3) a sense of desperation produced by urban professional life?

If the "idea" is (1) or, for that matter, (3), then the similarities between the two photographs flow from something much more than that idea, for it would have been possible to convey (1) (and (3)) in any number of ways that bear no obvious similarities to Kaplan's photograph. (Examples are a businessman atop a building seen from below, or the entire figure of the businessman, rather than just his shoes or pants, seen from above.) If, on the other hand, the "idea" is (2), then the two works could be said to owe much of their similarity to a shared idea. . . .

The idea/expression distinction arose in the context of literary copyright. . . . And it makes sense to speak of the idea conveyed by a literary work and to distinguish it from its expression. To take a clear example, two different authors each can describe, with very different words, the theory of special relativity. The words will be protected as expression. The theory is a set of unprotected ideas. . . .

In the visual arts, the distinction breaks down. For one thing, it is impossible in most cases to speak of the particular "idea" captured, embodied, or conveyed by a work of art because every observer will have a different interpretation.[80] Furthermore, it is not clear that there is any real distinction between the idea in a work of art and its expression. An artist's idea, among other things, is to depict a particular subject in a particular way. As a demonstration, a number of cases from this Circuit have observed that a photographer's "conception" of his subject is copyrightable. By "conception," the courts must mean originality in the rendition, timing, and creation of the subject — for that is what copyright protects in photography. But the word "conception" is a cousin of "concept," and both are

---

80. In cases dealing with toys or products that have both functional and design aspects, courts sometimes use "idea" to refer to a gimmick embodied in the product. . . . This case does not concern any kind of gimmick, and the Court ventures no opinion about the applicability of the idea/expression dichotomy to any product that embodies a gimmick, including toys or other objects that combine function and design.

akin to "idea." In other words, those elements of a photograph, or indeed, any work of visual art protected by copyright, could just as easily be labeled "idea" as "expression." . . .

. . . [A]t what point do the similarities between two photographs become sufficiently general that there will be no infringement even though actual copying has occurred? . . . [T]this question is precisely the same, although phrased in the opposite way, as one that must be addressed in all infringement cases, namely whether two works are substantially similar with respect to their protected elements. It is nonsensical to speak of one photograph being substantially similar to another in the rendition and creation of the subject but somehow not infringing because of a shared idea. Conversely, if the two photographs are not substantially similar in the rendition and creation of the subject, the distinction between idea and expression will be irrelevant because there can be no infringement. The idea/expression distinction in photography, and probably the other visual arts, thus achieves nothing beyond what other, clearer copyright principles already accomplish.

I recognize that those principles sometimes may pose a problem like that Judge Hand identified with distinguishing idea from expression in the literary context. As Judge Hand observed, however, such line-drawing difficulties appear in all areas of the law. The important thing is that the categories at issue be useful and relevant, even if their precise boundaries are sometimes difficult to delineate. In the context of photography, the idea/expression distinction is not useful or relevant.

. . .

COMPARISON OF THE COORS BILLBOARD AND THE GARNETT PHOTOGRAPH

The next step is to determine whether a trier of fact could or must find the Coors Billboard substantially similar to the Garnett Photograph with respect to their protected elements.

Substantial similarity ultimately is a question of fact. "The standard test for substantial similarity between two items is whether an 'ordinary observer, unless he set out to detect the disparities, would be disposed to overlook them, and regard [the] aesthetic appeal as the same.'" . . . The Second Circuit sometimes has applied a "more discerning observer" test when a work contains both protectible and unprotectible elements. The test "requires the court to eliminate the unprotectible elements from its consideration and to ask whether the protectible elements, standing alone, are substantially similar." . . . The Circuit, however, is ambivalent about this test. In several cases dealing with fabric and garment designs, the Circuit has cautioned that:

> "a court is not to dissect the works at issue into separate components and compare only the copyrightable elements. . . . To do so would be to take the "more discerning" test to an extreme, which would result in almost nothing being copyrightable because original works broken down into their composite parts would usually be little more than basic unprotectible elements like letters, colors and symbols." [*Boisson*, 273 F.3d at 272.]

Dissecting the works into separate components and comparing only the copyrightable elements, however, appears to be exactly what the "more discerning observer" test calls for.

The Circuit indirectly spoke to this tension in the recent case of *Tufenkian Import/Export Ventures, Inc. v. Einstein Moomjy, Inc.,* 338 F.3d 127 (2d Cir. 2003). There the trial court purported to use the more discerning observer test but nonetheless compared the "total-concept-and-feel" of carpet designs. . . .

In light of these precedents, the Court concludes that it is immaterial whether the ordinary or more discerning observer test is used here because the inquiries would be identical. The cases agree that the relevant comparison is between the protectible elements in the Garnett Photograph and the Coors Billboard, but that those elements are not to be viewed in isolation.

The Garnett Photograph is protectible to the extent of its originality in the rendition and creation of the subject. Key elements of the Garnett Photograph that are in the public domain—such as Kevin Garnett's likeness—are not replicated in the Coors Billboard. Other elements arguably in the public domain—such as the existence of a cloudy sky, Garnett's pose, his white T-shirt, and his specific jewelry—may not be copyrightable in and of themselves, but their existence and arrangement in this photograph indisputably contribute to its originality. Thus the fact that the Garnett Photograph includes certain elements that would not be copyrightable in isolation does not affect the nature of the comparison. The question is whether the aesthetic appeal of the two images is the same.

The two photographs share a similar composition and angle. The lighting is similar, and both use a cloudy sky as backdrop. The subjects are wearing similar clothing and similar jewelry arranged in a similar way. The defendants, in other words, appear to have recreated much of the subject that Mannion had created and then, through imitation of angle and lighting, rendered it in a similar way. The similarities here thus relate to the Garnett Photograph's originality in the rendition and the creation of the subject and therefore to its protected elements.

There of course are differences between the two works. The similarity analysis may take into account some, but not all, of these. It long has been the law that "no plagiarist can excuse the wrong by showing how much of his work he did not pirate." [*Id.* at 132-33 (quoting *Sheldon v. Metro-Goldwyn Pictures Corp.,* 81 F.2d 49, 56 (2d Cir. 1936)) (internal quotation marks omitted)]. Thus the addition of the words "Iced Out" and a can of Coors Light beer may not enter into the similarity analysis.

Other differences, however, are in the nature of changes rather than additions. One image is black and white and dark, the other is in color and bright. One is the mirror image of the other. One depicts only an unidentified man's torso, the other the top three-fourths of Kevin Garnett's body. The jewelry is not identical. One T-shirt appears to fit more tightly than the other. These changes may enter the analysis because "[i]f the points of dissimilarity not only exceed the points of similarity, but indicate that the remaining points of similarity are, within the context of plaintiff's work, of minimal importance . . . then no infringement results."

The parties have catalogued at length and in depth the similarities and differences between these works. In the last analysis, a reasonable jury could find substantial similarity either present or absent. . . .

396

NOTES AND QUESTIONS

1. Do you agree with the *Mannion* court's conclusion that "other, clearer copyright principles" render the idea/expression distinction superfluous in cases involving visual artworks? How does the court separate protectible and un-protectible elements of the Garnett photograph? How should a jury do this?

Page 349. In the Notes and Questions, insert new Question 5:

5. In *BUC International Corp. v. International Yacht Council Ltd.*, 489 F.3d 1129 (11th Cir. 2007), BUC registered a copyright in a directory of yacht listings designed to facilitate broker access to industry information regarding the sale of used yachts. The International Yacht Council (IYC), a coalition of professional yacht broker associations, created an on-line multiple listing service for yacht listings. Vessel listings were placed on the IYC site by MLS Solutions, which obtained its listings from brokers, most of whom were BUC licensees. These brokers simply copied their BUC listings and sent them to IYC for posting. Ruling on a disputed jury instruction regarding the appropriate standard for infringement of factual compilations, the court stated:

> "The nuances of the 'substantial similarity' test vary, . . . depending on the nature of the copyrighted work at issue. For example, in cases involving a compilation, 'substantial similarity' imparts a narrowed construction. . . . [T]he components of a compilation are generally in the public domain, and a finding of substantial similarity or even absolute identity as to matters in the public domain will not suffice to prove infringement. What must be shown is substantial similarity between those elements, and only those elements, that provide copyrightability to the allegedly infringed compilation. Given the teachings of *Feist*, it is the original selection and arrangement of the collected data that bear legal significance for factual compilations. . . . By comparison, the 'virtual identicality' standard calls for a greater degree of similarity between the copyrighted work and the allegedly infringing work than does 'substantial similarity.' 'Virtual identicality,' as adopted in this circuit, applies to 'claims of compilation copyright infringement of nonliteral elements of a computer program.'" *BUC Int'l Corp.*, 489 F.3d at 1148 (internal citations omitted).

What policy concerns might justify application of different infringement standards to different kinds of compilations? Should the virtual identicality standard be applied to all works with significant amounts of non-copyrightable content?

Page 363. In the Notes and Questions, insert new Question 4 and renumber Question 4 as Question 5:

4. In *Storage Technology Corp. v. Custom Hardware Engineering & Consulting Inc.*, 421 F.3d 1307 (Fed. Cir. 2005), the defendant service company left copies of

plaintiff's code in its customer's RAM for the duration of its maintenance contract. The court held that "maintenance" as used in §117(c) has a "much broader temporal connotation" than "repair" as used in §117(d). According to the court, "maintenance, or servicing, was meant to encompass monitoring systems for problems, not simply fixing a single, isolated malfunction." *Id.* at 1312. Concluding that the protection of §117 ceases only when maintenance ends, the court stated that "[i]t would run counter to [Congress's] objective to construe section 117(c) narrowly to apply only to companies that performed repair in discrete, temporally isolated stages, rather than to construe the statute to apply to repair and maintenance services generally, so long as the companies' only reason for copying the software at issue was to fix and maintain the machines on which the software was running." *Id.* at 1313.

C. The Distribution Right

Page 368. *Before the Notes and Questions, insert the following:*

Capitol Records, Inc. v. Thomas
579 F. Supp. 2d 1210 (D. Minn. 2008)

DAVIS, C.J.:

I. INTRODUCTION

. . . The Court has sua sponte raised the issue of whether it erred in instructing the jury that making sound recordings available for distribution on a peer-to-peer network, regardless of whether actual distribution was shown, qualified as distribution under the Copyright Act.

II. BACKGROUND

Plaintiffs are recording companies that owned or controlled exclusive rights to copyrights in sound recordings, including 24 at issue in this lawsuit. On April 19, 2006, Plaintiffs filed a Complaint against Defendant Jammie Thomas alleging that she infringed Plaintiffs' copyrighted sound recordings pursuant to the Copyright Act, 17 U.S.C. §§101, 106, 501-505, by illegally downloading and distributing the recordings via the online peer-to-peer file sharing application known as Kazaa. Plaintiffs sought injunctive relief, statutory damages, costs, and attorney fees. In Jury Instruction No. 15, the Court instructed: "The act of making copyrighted sound recordings available for electronic distribution on a peer-to-peer network, without license from the copyright owners, violates the copyright owners' exclusive right of distribution, regardless of whether actual distribution has been shown." On October 4, 2007, the jury found that Thomas had willfully infringed on all 24 of Plaintiffs' sound recordings at issue, and awarded Plaintiffs statutory damages in the amount of $9,250 for each willful infringement. On October 5, the Court entered judgment on the jury's verdict. . . .

On May 15, 2008, the Court issued an Order stating that it was contemplating granting a new trial on the grounds that it had committed a manifest error of law in giving Jury Instruction No. 15.

III.   DISCUSSION . . .

C.   STATUTORY FRAMEWORK

The Copyright Act provides that "the owner of copyright under this title has the exclusive rights to do and to authorize any of the following: . . . (3) to distribute copies or phonorecords of the copyrighted work to the public by sale or other transfer of ownership, or by rental, lease, or lending." 17 U.S.C. §106(3). The Act does not define the term "distribute." . . .

D.   PLAIN MEANING OF THE TERM "DISTRIBUTION"

. . . Each party asserts that the Court should adopt the plain meaning of the term "distribution;" however, they disagree on what that plain meaning is. Thomas and her supporters argue that the plain meaning of the statute compels the conclusion that merely making a work available to the public does not constitute a distribution. Instead, a distribution only occurs when a defendant actually transfers to the public the possession or ownership of copies or phonorecords of a work. Plaintiffs and their supporters assert that making a work available for distribution is sufficient.

1.   Statutory Language

Starting with the language in §106(3), the Court notes that Congress explains the manners in which distribution can be effected: sale, transfer of ownership, rental, lease, or lending. The provision does not state that an offer to do any of these acts constitutes distribution. Nor does §106(3) provide that making a work available for any of these activities constitutes distribution. An initial reading of the provision at issue supports Thomas's interpretation.

2.   Secondary Sources

The ordinary dictionary meaning of the word "distribute" necessarily entails a transfer of ownership or possession from one person to another. *See, e.g., Merriam-Webster's Collegiate Dictionary* (10th ed.1999) (defining "distribute" as, among other things, "1: to divide among several or many: APPORTION . . . 2 . . . b: to give out or deliver esp. to members of a group"). Additionally, the leading copyright treatises conclude that making a work available is insufficient to establish distribution. *See, e.g.,* 2-8 *Nimmer on Copyright,* §8.11[A] (2008); 4 *William F. Patry, Patry on Copyright,* §13.11.50 (2008).

3.   *Opinion of the Register of Copyrights*

Register of Copyrights, Marybeth Peters, has opined to Congress that making a copyrighted work available violates the distribution right. . . . However, opinion letters from the Copyright Office to Congress on matters of statutory interpretation are not binding. . . .

4.   *Use of the Term in Other Provisions of the U.S. Code*

As Plaintiffs note, in other provisions of federal copyright law, Congress has explicitly defined "distribute" to include offers to distribute. . . . The differing definitions of "distribute" within copyright law demonstrate that there is not one uniform definition of the term throughout copyright law. . . . However, the Court notes that when Congress intends distribution to encompass making available or offering to transfer, it has demonstrated that it is quite capable of explicitly providing that definition within the statute. In this case, Congress provided the means by which a distribution occurs — "by sale or other transfer of ownership, or by rental, lease, or lending" — without also providing that a distribution occurs by an offer to do one of those actions, as it did in §901(a)(4). While the Copyright Act does not offer a uniform definition of "distribution," the Court concludes that, in light of the examined provisions, Congress's choice to not include offers to do the enumerated acts or the making available of the work indicates its intent that an actual distribution or dissemination is required in §106(3). . . .

The Court's examination of the use of the term "distribution" in other provisions of the Copyright Act, as well as the evolution of liability for offers to sell in the analogous Patent Act, lead to the conclusion that the plain meaning of the term "distribution" does not include[] making available and, instead, requires actual dissemination. . . .

E.   WHETHER "DISTRIBUTION" IS SYNONYMOUS WITH "PUBLICATION"

Plaintiffs advocate that, within the Copyright Act, the term "distribution" is synonymous with the term "publication."

> "Publication" is the distribution of copies or phonorecords of a work to the public by sale or other transfer of ownership, or by rental, lease, or lending. The offering to distribute copies or phonorecords to a group of persons for purposes of further distribution, public performance, or public display, constitutes publication. A public performance or display of a work does not of itself constitute publication. 17 U.S.C.

§101. Under this definition, making sound recordings available on Kazaa could be considered distribution.

The first sentence of the definition of "publication" and §106(3) are substantially identical. However, there is additional language in the definition of "publication." Relying primarily on legislative history, Plaintiffs assert that the sentence defining publication as "[t]he offering to distribute copies or phonorecords to a group of persons for purposes of further distribution, public performance, or public display" should also apply to the definition of distribution. . . .

Plaintiffs note that the text of §106 grants a copyright owner the following five exclusive rights: "(1) to reproduce the copyrighted work . . . (2) to prepare derivative works . . . (3) to distribute copies of the work . . . (4) . . . to perform the copyrighted work publicly; and (5) . . . to display the work publicly." 17 U.S.C. §106. However, the House and Senate Committees evaluating the Copyright Act, described the following five rights: "the exclusive rights of reproduction, adaptation, *publication*, performance, and display." *Elektra Entm't Group, Inc. v. Barker*, 551 F. Supp. 2d 234, 241 (S.D.N.Y.2008) (quoting H.R. Rep. No. 94-1476, at 61 (1976); S. Rep. No. 94-473, at 57 (1976)) (emphasis added in *Barker*). The Committee Reports identified the "Rights of Reproduction, Adaptation, and Publication" as "[t]he first three clauses of section 106." *Id.* (quoting H.R. Rep. at 61; S. Rep. at 57). Also, the House Committee Report stated that §106(3) "'establishes the exclusive right of publication' and governs 'unauthorized public distribution'—using the words 'distribution' and 'publication' interchangeably within a single paragraph." *Id.* (citing H.R. Rep. at 62; S. Rep. at 58).

The Court does not find . . . snippets of legislative history to be dispositive of the definition of distribution. Nowhere in this legislative history does Congress state that distribution should be given the same broad meaning as publication. In any case, even if the legislative history indicated that some members of Congress equated publications with distributions under §106(3), that fact cannot override the plain meaning of the statute. . . .

F. EXISTENCE OF A PROTECTED RIGHT TO AUTHORIZE DISTRIBUTION

Plaintiffs and their supporters also take the position that authorizing distribution is an exclusive right protected by the Copyright Act. They base this argument on the fact that §106 states "the owner of copyright under this title has the exclusive rights **to do** and **to authorize** any of the following . . . (3) to distribute. . . ." (emphasis added). Plaintiffs claim that the statute grants two separate rights—the right to "do" distribution and the right to "authorize" distribution. Therefore, making sound recordings available on Kazaa violates the copyright owner's exclusive right to authorize distribution.

The Court concludes that the authorization clause merely provides a statutory foundation for secondary liability, not a means of expanding the scope of direct infringement liability. . . .

H.   HOTALING V. CHURCH OF JESUS CHRIST OF LATTER-DAY SAINTS

In *Hotaling [v. Church of Jesus Christ of Latter-Day Saints,* 118 F.3d 199 (4th Cir.1997)], the Fourth Circuit held that "a library distributes a published work, within the meaning of the Copyright Act, when it places an unauthorized copy of the work in its collection, includes the copy in its catalog or index system, and makes the copy available to the public." *Id.* at 201. . . . [T]he Fourth Circuit did not analyze any case law to support its conclusion that making the copyrighted materials available for distribution constituted distribution. Nor did it conduct any analysis of §106(3). Instead, the court was guided by equitable concerns. Some courts have applied the principle articulated in *Hotaling,* to conclude that merely making a work available for others to download over a peer-to-peer network may constitute a distribution. . . . *Hotaling* is [not] consistent with the logical statutory interpretation of §106(3), the body of Copyright Act case law, and the legislative history of the Copyright Act. . . .

Finally, while the Court does not adopt the deemed-disseminated theory based on *Hotaling* it notes that ***direct*** proof of actual dissemination is not required by the Copyright Act. Plaintiffs are free to employ circumstantial evidence to attempt to prove actual dissemination. . . .

Pages 368-69.   In the Notes and Questions:

a. Delete Questions 1-2, insert the following, and renumber Questions 3-5 as Questions 4-6:

1. Do you agree with the *Capitol Records* court's interpretation of §106(3)? *Capital Records* reflects the majority position among courts who have addressed the question what constitutes "distribution" in the digital context. Most courts have held that merely making files available for sharing via a peer-to-peer network does not violate the distribution right. *See, e.g., Atlantic v. Howell,* 554 F. Supp. 2d 976 (D. Ariz. 2008); *London Sire-Records Inc, v. Doe 1,* 542 F. Supp. 2d 153 (D. Mass. 2008). Further, several of these courts have explicitly criticized *Hotaling* as inconsistent with the Copyright Act. In *Elektra Entertainment Group Inc. v. Barker,* 551 F. Supp. 2d 234 (S.D.N.Y. 2008), the court noted that *Hotaling* "did not cite any precedent in holding that making copyrighted works available to the public constitutes infringement" and that its interpretation of §106(3) "even if sound public policy, is not grounded in the statute." *Id.* at 243.

2. What does the *Capital Records* court mean when it states that the court in *Hotaling* "was guided by equitable concerns"? Can you distinguish the reasoning in *Hotaling* from these recent decisions interpreting §106(3)? Perhaps a central problem between *Hotaling* and these on-line cases is simply that the role and function of libraries and peer-to-peer networks cannot reasonably be analogized. Should the interpretation of the distribution right vary based on the environment in which an infringing act allegedly has taken place?

3. As a matter of policy, should Congress amend §106(3) to broaden its scope? Why, or why not? How would you draft such an amendment?

b. Delete the last sentence of renumbered Question 4 and insert the following:

Under the *Capitol Records* interpretation of §106(3), is the U.S. in compliance with its obligations under the WCT? *See Arista Records LLC v. Greubel*, 453 F. Supp. 2d 961, 969 n.10 (N.D. Tex. 2006) (acknowledging the treaty compliance question but declining to address it while ruling on a motion to dismiss).

c. In renumbered Question 5, delete the following:

"Given the *Bertelsmann* court's ruling, is it appropriate for the USTR to apply such pressure? Why might it do so?"

Page 374. In the Notes and Questions, insert the following at the end of Question 2:

In *Brilliance Audio, Inc. v. Haights Cross Communications*, 474 F.3d 365 (6th Cir. 2007), the court considered whether the record rental exception to the first sale doctrine applies to all sound recordings or only to sound recordings of musical works. The defendants purchased and repackaged retail editions of plaintiff's audio books and then distributed the works by, among other things, renting them in direct competition with the plaintiff. The court reviewed the legislative history of §109 and determined that Congress intended to address only concerns related to rental of musical recordings. *Id.* at 371-73. It reasoned, further, that an exception to the first sale doctrine "should be construed narrowly because it upsets the traditional bargain between the rights of copyright owners and the personal property rights of an individual who owns a particular copy." *Id.* at 373.

Do you agree that audiobooks are distinguishable enough from sound recordings of musical works to justify excluding them from the ambit of §109(b)(1)(A)? Should Congress expand the scope of this exception?

Page 374. Insert the following after the Notes and Questions:

Vernor v. Autodesk, Inc.
555 F. Supp. 2d 1164 (W.D. Wash. 2008)

JONES, J.: . . . Mr. Vernor makes his living selling goods on eBay, the well-known internet auction site. He has two packages of Autodesk's copyrighted AutoCAD software, and hopes to sell them on eBay. He brought this action for declaratory relief because Autodesk's past actions give him reason to believe that Autodesk will try to stop his sales. [Mr. Vernor previously had sold three packages of AutoCAD software that he had purchased at garage sales and office sales and Autodesk had tried to stop those sales. Autodesk's actions led to Mr. Vernor's suspension from eBay, but he was reinstated after he protested the suspension.]

By tracing the serial numbers on the packages, Autodesk has determined that both were originally transferred from Autodesk to [a Seattle architecture firm, Cardwell/Thomas Associates ("CTA")] in a settlement of an unrelated dispute. According to the Settlement Agreement, CTA paid just over $44,000. Autodesk shipped the packages to CTA; CTA eventually resold some of the packages to Mr. Vernor, including the two AutoCAD packages that Mr. Vernor now possesses.

In the Settlement Agreement, CTA agreed to "adhere to all terms of the [attached] Autodesk Software License Agreement." The License Agreement ("License") is substantially identical to one included inside each AutoCAD package. The License Agreement grants a "nonexclusive, nontransferable license to use the enclosed program . . . according to the terms and conditions herein." The License . . . [regulates the] number of computers on which [a] user can install software, number of users, software copying, and copying of documentation. . . . It also imposes several "Restrictions," including a prohibition on "rent, lease, or transfer [of] all or part of the Software, Documentation, or any rights granted hereunder to any other person without Autodesk's prior written consent." . . . [It] also prohibit[s] use outside of [the] western hemisphere, modification or reverse-engineering of software, and removing labels. . . .

III. ANALYSIS. . . .

B. MR. VERNOR IS ENTITLED TO THE PROTECTION OF THE FIRST SALE DOCTRINE.

1. *If It Applies, the First Sale Doctrine Immunizes Mr. Vernor.*

If there were no License, there is no dispute that Mr. Vernor's resale of the AutoCAD packages would be legal. The first sale doctrine permits a person who owns a lawfully-made copy of a copyrighted work to sell or otherwise dispose of the copy. . . . 17 U.S.C. §109(a). There is no dispute that the copy of Autodesk software contained in each AutoCAD package was lawfully made. If there were no License, there would be no dispute that CTA owned the AutoCAD packages at issue, that Mr. Vernor now owns the packages, and that he can dispose of them as he wishes. . . .

Autodesk's motion [for summary judgment] turns on its assertion that, because of the License, the transfer of AutoCAD packages to CTA was not a sale. Without a sale, there can be no "first sale." Or, phrased in the language of §109(a), without a sale, CTA was not an "owner of a . . . copy" of Autodesk software. If CTA was not an owner within the meaning of the statute, Mr. Vernor is also not an owner within the meaning of §109(a).

Autodesk correctly asserts that mere possession of a copyrighted copy pursuant to a license is not a sale, and thus not a basis to invoke the first sale doctrine. . . . Indeed, the Copyright Act itself declares that the first sale doctrine does not "extend to any person who has acquired possession of the copy or phonorecord from the copyright owner, by rental, lease, loan, or otherwise, without acquiring ownership of it." 17 U.S.C. §109(d).

The critical dispute here, however, is whether Autodesk's transfer of AutoCAD packages to CTA was a sale or a mere transfer of possession pursuant to a license. If the transaction was a sale, then the restrictions of the License give rise, at most, to a breach of contract claim:

> "first sale" buyer's disregard of restriction on resale does not make buyer — or subsequent buyer an infringer; [a] copyright holder's remedy is suit for breach of contract containing the restrictions.

Denbicare U.S.A. Inc. v. Toys 'R' Us, Inc., 84 F.3d 1143, 1152 (9th Cir. 1996). If Autodesk sold the AutoCAD packages, then the License's ban on transferring the software is of no consequence under the Copyright Act. *Id.*

2. *What is a Sale? The Ninth Circuit Answers in* Wise.

No bright-line rule distinguishes mere licenses from sales. Several principles govern. The court must analyze the "arrangement at issue and decide whether it should be considered a first sale." [*United States v.*] *Wise*, 550 F.2d [1180,] 1189 [(9th Cir. 1977)]. The label placed on a transaction is not determinative.

Wise charts a path to distinguishing sales from non-sales in determining if the first sale doctrine applies. The *Wise* court considered numerous transfer contracts between movie studios and recipients of movie prints, and found that almost all of them were licenses, loans, or other non-sale transactions. Many of the contracts "reserved title to the film prints" in the studio, and required that the recipients return the prints following the expiration of a fixed term. *Wise*, 550 F.2d at 1190. Those contracts were labeled "licenses," and all transferred "only limited rights for the exhibition or distribution of the films for a limited purpose and for a limited period of time." In some contracts, the studios did not expressly reserve title to the film print. Nonetheless, the court found that this omission was not determinative because "the general tenor of the entire agreement [was] inconsistent" with a sale. . . .

When the *Wise* court considered three types of contracts that allowed the recipient to keep the film print, however, it found sales. One contract allowed a television network receiving the film prints to retain one print, without restrictions on its resale. Another contract, for the sale of a film print to actress Vanessa Redgrave ("the Redgrave Contract"), required Ms. Redgrave to pay a fee to receive a film print that was subject to draconian transfer restrictions. Ms. Redgrave could use the print only for her "personal use and enjoyment," was required to retain possession of the print "at all times," and could not sell, lease, license, or loan the print to any other person. Despite the absolute bar on transferring the film, the court found that the "transaction strongly resembl[ed] a sale with restrictions on the use of the print." The court held that the defendant could rely on the first sale doctrine with respect to his later sales of the print. Finally, the court found that film prints transferred solely for salvage or destruction were sold.

In comparing the transactions found to be sales in *Wise* with those that were not, the critical factor is whether the transferee kept the copy acquired from the copyright holder. When the film studios required that prints be returned, the court found no sale. When the studios did not require the transferee to return the prints, the court found a sale. Even a complete prohibition on further transfer of the print (as in the Redgrave Contract), or a requirement that the print be salvaged or destroyed, was insufficient to negate a sale where the transferee was not required to return the print.

Taking direction solely from *Wise*, the court concludes that the transfer of AutoCAD packages from Autodesk to CTA was a sale. Like the Redgrave Contract, the Settlement Agreement and License allowed CTA to retain possession of the software copies in exchange for a single up-front payment. Like the Redgrave Contract, the Settlement Agreement and License imposed onerous restrictions on transfer of the AutoCAD copies. Similar to the salvage transactions in *Wise*, the License required CTA to destroy the software in the event that it purchased a software upgrade.[5] Under *Wise*, however, this is a "sale with restrictions on use," and is a sufficient basis to invoke the first sale doctrine.

3. *A Trio of Ninth Circuit Decisions Reaches Results Contrary to* Wise.

As far as the court is aware, *Wise* is the only Ninth Circuit precedent analyzing what constitutes a "sale" for purposes of invoking the first sale doctrine. In the more than 30 years since *Wise*, no Ninth Circuit opinion has questioned it, much less overruled it. It retains vitality in recent Ninth Circuit jurisprudence. Three opinions issued after *Wise*, however, consider the same "sale" question in a different context, and arrive at contrary results. . . .

As with the first sale doctrine, courts have determined that a person becomes an "owner of a copy" of software under §117 only in certain transactions.

In *MAI Sys. Corp. v. Peak Computer, Inc.*, 991 F.2d 511 (9th Cir. 1993), the court considered a software license that controlled the use of the software, and declared that "any possession" of the software "not expressly authorized under this License" is prohibited. The court devoted its attention to whether the use of the software by an unlicensed repair service violated the plaintiff's copyright. In a single footnote, without analysis or explanation, the court declared that "[S]ince

---

5. Autodesk presents evidence that, before CTA sold the AutoCAD packages to Mr. Vernor, it bought upgraded AutoCAD software. Autodesk asserts that the License required CTA to destroy the AutoCAD packages, and barred their resale. This contention is fodder for a breach of contract claim against CTA, but it does not affect Mr. Vernor. . . .

MAI licensed its software, [its] customers do not qualify as 'owners' of the software and are not eligible for protection under §117." *Id.* at 519 n. 5. The court did not cite *Wise*.

In *Triad Sys. Corp. v. Southeastern Express Co.*, 64 F.3d 1330, 1333 (9th Cir. 1995), the court tacitly assumed that licensees could not invoke §117. . . .

Finally, in *Wall Data* [*Inc. v. Los Angeles County Sheriff's Dep't*, 447 F.3d 769, 785 (9th Cir. 2006)], the court briefly analyzed a purported license agreement to determine if it was a sale that would permit the invocation of §117. The license agreement imposed restrictions on copying the software, restrictions on the number of users, and restrictions on transferring the software on computers within the licensed entity. The license imposed no limits on re-sale of the software. *Id.* The court concluded that the restrictions were "sufficient to classify the transaction as a grant of license to Wall Data's software, and not a sale of Wall Data's software." *Id.* at 785 (citing *MAI*). The court reasoned that "such restrictions would not be imposed on a party who owned the software." *Id.* The court did not cite *Wise*.

If the court were to apply this trio of precedent (the "*MAI* trio") to the license before it, it would conclude that Autodesk did not sell AutoCAD copies to CTA. . . .

4.   The Court Must Follow Wise, Not the MAI Trio.

The court holds that it must follow *Wise*, and not the *MAI* trio. Where opinions of three-judge Ninth Circuit panels conflict, the court must rely on the earliest opinion. *United States v. Rodriguez-Lara*, 421 F.3d 932, 943 (9th Cir. 2005). . . .

Because the conflict between *Wise* and the *MAI* trio places the court in the uncomfortable position of choosing which Ninth Circuit precedent to follow, the court has considered possibilities for avoiding the conflict. As the court explains below, it finds the conflict unavoidable. . . .

[T]he court considers, but rejects, the possibility that the analysis of whether a "first sale" has occurred might be different for purposes of §109 (at issue in *Wise*) and §117 (at issue in the *MAI* trio). The court rejects the possibility because both statutes use the same "owner of a . . . copy" language.[8] The court presumes that identical phrases used within the Copyright Act have identical meaning. Nothing before the court overcomes the presumption in this case.

The court also concludes that it cannot distinguish *Wise* because it was a criminal case, and the government carried the burden of proving the absence of a first sale. No Ninth Circuit decision addresses who bears the burden to prove a first sale or the absence thereof in a civil case. . . .

---

8. Section 117(a) uses the phrase "owner of a copy," whereas §109(a) uses the phrase "owner of a particular copy." There is no suggestion that the word "particular" makes a material difference.

Finally, although the court recognizes the tsunami of technological change between the decisions in *Wise* and the *MAI* trio, it finds that the change provides no basis to avoid the conflict between the decisions. . . .

[A]lthough technology has changed, the question at the core of this case is not technological. Mr. Vernor does not seek to take advantage of new technology to ease copying, he seeks to sell a package of physical objects which contain copies of copyrighted material. The essential features of such sales vary little whether selling movie prints via mail (as in *Wise*) or software packages via eBay.

For the reasons stated above, the court follows the *Wise* course and concludes that the transfer of AutoCAD packages from Autodesk to CTA was a sale with contractual restrictions on use and transfer of the software. Mr. Vernor may thus invoke the first sale doctrine, and his resale of the AutoCAD packages is not a copyright violation. . . .

D. AUTODESK HAS NOT ESTABLISHED THAT ITS LICENSE BINDS MR. VERNOR OR HIS CUSTOMERS.

Although Mr. Vernor's resale of AutoCAD packages is not a copyright violation, he is concerned that Autodesk asserts he is contractually bound by the License. In reviewing Autodesk's motion and its reply, the court finds a few suggestions that Autodesk believes that the License binds Mr. Vernor. . . .

Not only has Autodesk failed to surmount the thorny issues of privity and mutual assent inherent in its contention that its License binds Mr. Vernor and his customers, it has ignored the terms of the License itself. The Autodesk License is expressly "nontransferable." Autodesk does not explain how a nontransferable license can bind subsequent transferees. . . .

If Autodesk believes that the License binds Mr. Vernor or his customers, it must file a new motion addressing that argument. . . .

NOTES AND QUESTIONS

1. Do you agree with the court's analysis in *Vernor*? The focus in *United States v. Wise* on the importance of a right to continued possession of the copy has influenced other courts as well. In *UMG Recordings, Inc. v. Augusto*, 558 F. Supp. 2d 1055 (C.D. Cal. 2008), the court looked past the copyright owner's characterization of the transaction as a "license" to the "economic realities of the transaction." The plaintiff had sent promotional CDs to music industry insiders. The CDs contained a label that stated:

This CD is the property of the record company and is licensed to the intended recipient for personal use only. Acceptance of this CD shall constitute an agreement to comply with the terms of the license. Resale or transfer of possession is not allowed and may be punishable under federal and state laws.

The defendant had obtained copies of the CDs and, as in *Vernor*, was selling them on eBay, advertising them as "rare collectibles not available in stores." The court noted that nothing required the recipient to return the promotional CDs to UMG and there were no consequences if the CDs were lost or destroyed. The court noted that the only benefit to the purported "license" was to restrain transfer, a purpose that the Supreme Court had rejected 100 years ago. *Id.* at 1061 (citing *Bobbs-Merrill Co. v. Straus*, 210 U.S. 339 (1908)).

2. Autodesk was attempting to use contracts to restrict resale of copies of its software. Because Mr. Vernor never installed the copies of the software on any computers, he did not encounter the license agreements, ubiquitous with computer software, that require the user to click "I Agree." On the other hand, the company from whom he had purchased the copies, CTA, had entered into a settlement agreement, binding itself to the License Agreement. The court seems to indicate that Autodesk could pursue a claim of breach of contract against CTA. Should Autodesk also be able to claim copyright infringement against CTA? Would it matter how the settlement agreement was worded? Recall *Jacobsen v. Katzer*, 535 F.3d 1373 (Fed. Cir. 2008), *supra* pages 380-83. In that case the Federal Circuit concluded that when a licensee failed to comply with a condition in the agreement, the license no longer protected the licensee from a claim of infringement. Would the *Vernor* court's conclusion that CTA was an "owner" and not a licensee for purposes of §109(a) affect the viability of a copyright infringement claim by Autodesk against CTA?

3. There is a lot at stake in the determination of who constitutes an owner of a copy and who constitutes a mere licensee. Some software products retail for hundreds, if not thousands, of dollars. If copyright owners can control the subsequent transfer of copies of such software, they will not need to compete with "used" copies of their own products. Should copyright owners be protected against such competition? Is there any reason to treat copies of computer software differently than used books?

Pages 376-77.   Insert new Question 6:

6. The Copyright Office recently completed a study of the challenges that digital technologies raise for libraries, and issued a report recommending a series of amendments designed to harmonize §108 with the library community's emerging consensus about "best practices" in the digital age. The Section 108 Study Group Report is available at <http://www.section108.gov/>.

Pages 382-84.   Replace Questions 5-9 with the following:

5. Justice Ginsburg noted in her concurrence in *L'anza* that the Court was not "resolv[ing] cases in which the allegedly infringing imports were manufactured abroad." *Quality King Distribs., Inc. v. L'anza Research Int'l, Inc.*, 523 U.S. 135, 154

(1998). If a copy is lawfully made abroad, is §109(a) a defense to a claim of unlawful importation under §602? According to the Ninth Circuit, the answer is "no". *See Omega S.A. v. Costco Wholesale Corp.*, 541 F.3d 982 (9th Cir. 2008), *petition for cert. filed*, 77 U.S.L.W. 3657 (U.S. May 18, 2009) (No. 08-1423). There, Omega manufactured watches with a copyrighted design engraved on the underside. The manufacture occurred in Switzerland, and Omega sold watches to authorized distributors overseas. "Unidentified third parties eventually purchased the watches and sold them to . . . a New York company, which in turn sold them to Costco. Costco then sold [them] to consumers in California." *Id.* at 984. The court held that " . . . the application of §109(a) to foreign-made copies would impermissibly apply the Copyright Act extraterritorially in a way that the application of the statute after foreign sales does not. . . . To characterize the making of copies overseas as 'lawful[] . . . under [Title 17]' [§109(a)] would be to ascribe legality under the Copyright Act to conduct that occurs entirely outside the United States, notwithstanding the absence of a clear expression of congressional intent in favor of extraterritoriality." *Id.* at 988. Is this decision consistent with *L'anza*? Consistent with the wording of §§109 and 602? Should Omega itself, as the copyright owner and manufacturer of the watches at issue, be able to use copyright law to prevent their resale in the U.S.? To the extent the *Omega* court's decision provides greater protection to foreign-made copies of works protected by U.S. copyrights than to domestic-made copies, is it sensible as a policy matter?

6. Internationally, rules regarding the effect of exhaustion principles on gray market imports vary. (Recall that the TRIPS Agreement does not mandate that countries adopt rules on exhaustion.) In *Silhouette International Schmied GmbH & Co. KG v. Hartlauer Handelsgesellschaft mbH*, 2 C.M.L.R. 953 (1998), a trademark case, the European Court of Justice (ECJ) interpreted the governing law as requiring pure territoriality. The plaintiff, Silhouette, an Austrian company, produces high-end eyeglasses. Silhouette sold a consignment of eyeglass frames in a discontinued style to a Bulgarian company, which agreed that the frames would be sold only in Bulgaria or other former Eastern bloc countries. Instead, the frames were purchased by Hartlauer, a discount retailer operating within Austria. The Austrian courts ruled that under traditional principles of Austrian law, Silhouette's sale of the frames would have exhausted its trademark rights. However, they referred to the ECJ (the high court of the then European Community) the question whether an intervening European trademark directive, now incorporated into Austrian law, had altered the operation of exhaustion principles. The ECJ concluded that under the directive, exhaustion applied only if the goods were sold within the countries of the European Community, but not if they were sold in a country outside the Community.

The language of the more recent EU directive on copyright harmonization suggests that the same principles will apply to exhaustion of rights under copyright law. Directive 2001/29/EC of the European Parliament and of the Council of 22 May 2001 on the harmonisation of certain aspects of copyright and related rights in the information society, 2001 O.J. (L. 167) 10, art. 4(2).

7. Some academics argue that gray markets in copyrighted and/or trademarked goods can be efficient because they promote the acquisition of these

goods by more consumers and at lower prices. *See, e.g.*, Nancy T. Gallini & Aidan Hollis, *A Contractual Approach to the Gray Market*, 19 Int'l Rev. L. & Econ. 1 (1999); Shubha Ghosh, *An Economic Analysis of the Common Control Exception to Gray Market Exclusion*, 15 U. Pa. J. Int'l Bus. L. 373 (1994). Other commentators respond that copyright and trademark protection are territorial by design, and that this is appropriate because the price discrimination that territoriality enables — that is, charging relatively affluent consumers in the U.S. and other industrialized countries more for the same goods — enables producers and distributors to provide consumers in these countries with "extras" such as warranty service, and increases incentives to produce, distribute, and promote products. Copyright owners also argue that gray market goods unfairly constrain their profit margins by forcing them to compete against their own products. *See, e.g.*, Richard S. Higgins & Paul H. Rubin, *Counterfeit Goods*, 29 J.L. & Econ. 211 (1986); William M. Landes & Richard A. Posner, *Trademark Law: An Economic Perspective*, 30 J.L. & Econ. 265 (1987); Elin Dugan, Note, *United States of America, Home of the Cheap and the Gray: A Comparison of Recent Court Decisions Affecting the U.S. and European Gray Markets*, 33 Geo. Wash. Int'l L. Rev. 397, 409-11 (2001) (summarizing manufacturers' arguments). Who has the better argument? If you agree with the gray market critics, are you more persuaded by territoriality concerns or by the price discrimination argument? (If the latter, have you ever shopped at a discount store like Costco, Sam's Club, or the Price Club?)

8. How should copyright law respond to distribution of copies across national borders via the Internet? Digital delivery is increasingly the mechanism of choice for software distribution to individual purchasers and may soon become more widely used for distribution of other kinds of works. Does §602(a) as currently worded allow such distribution by foreign copyright holders? Should it?

9. In 2008, Congress amended §602(a) to specify that unauthorized *exportation* of copies or phonorecords is also an infringement of copyright actionable under §501. Why do you think Congress made this change? Is it good policy?

10. In the digital era, some of the copyright industries have taken matters into their own hands and are selling "region-coded" entertainment goods. The technology for region-coding was developed by the video game industry to combat large-scale counterfeiting that was perceived as particularly acute in Southeast Asia and China. The industry reasoned that if video game cartridges purchased in Asia would not play on video game consoles sold in North America or Europe, counterfeiters would have more difficulty gaining a foothold in the industry's most lucrative markets. More recently, however, a number of the copyright industries have realized that region-coding technologies can also be used to control gray market imports. The movie industry, for example, sells region-coded DVDs under a series of cooperative licensing agreements with manufacturers of home DVD players. Under the new region-coding agreements, regions perceived as harboring counterfeiters are no longer the exclusive targets. DVDs manufactured in Europe will not work on DVD players sold in North America, and vice versa.

What do you think of these arrangements? If copyright law does not prohibit the imports, is it good policy to allow the affected industries to adopt technological protections that have that effect? We return to the interaction between copyright law and technological protection in Chapter 8.

D. The Right to Prepare Derivative Works

Page 400. In the Notes and Questions, insert the following at the end of Question 3(c):

See Clean Flicks of Colo., LLC v. Soderbergh, 433 F. Supp. 2d 1236 (D. Colo. 2006) (holding that edited movies are unauthorized copies but not unauthorized derivative works because the infringing copies were not used in a transformative manner).

E. Moral Rights: The American Version

Page 423. In the Notes and Questions, insert new Question 2 and renumber Questions 2-6 as 3-7:

2. Reread the definition of a "work of visual art" in §101 of the Copyright Act. How much flexibility does this definition provide in determining what constitutes a work of visual art? Is a wildflower garden created by a famous artist and maintained as a public exhibit for over 20 years a work of visual art? Is it a sculpture? Is it a work of applied art? *See Kelley v. Chicago Park Dist.,* No. 04-C-07715 (N.D. Ill. Sept. 14, 2007) (directing the parties to brief whether a display of wildflowers by an artist is a copyrightable sculpture and whether the nature of the display entitles it to protection under VARA). How should courts apply VARA to new art forms?

Page 426. In the Notes and Questions, insert new Question 5:

5. On remand, the district court found Dastar liable for infringement of Doubleday's copyright in the Eisenhower book and the Ninth Circuit affirmed. *See Twentieth Century Fox Film Corp. v. Entertainment Distrib.,* 429 F.3d 869 (9th Cir. 2005), *cert. denied sub nom. Dastar Corp. v. Random House, Inc.,* 126 S. Ct. 2932 (2006).

F.   The Public Performance and Public Display Rights

Pages 431-32.   Delete the Notes and Questions and insert the following:

Cartoon Network LP v. CSC Holdings, Inc.
536 F.3d 121 (2d Cir. 2008), *petition for cert. filed,* **77 U.S.L.W. 3229 (Oct. 6, 2008)**

WALKER, J.: . . . In March 2006, Cablevision, an operator of cable television systems, announced the advent of its new "Remote Storage DVR System." As designed, the RS-DVR allows Cablevision customers who do not have a stand-alone DVR to record cable programming on central hard drives housed and maintained by Cablevision at a "remote" location. RS-DVR customers may then receive playback of those programs through their home television sets, using only a remote control and a standard cable box equipped with the RS-DVR software. Cablevision notified its content providers, including plaintiffs, of its plans to offer RS-DVR, but it did not seek any license from them to operate or sell the RS-DVR.

Plaintiffs, which hold the copyrights to numerous movies and television programs, sued Cablevision for declaratory and injunctive relief. They alleged that Cablevision's proposed operation of the RS-DVR would directly infringe their exclusive rights to both reproduce and publicly perform their copyrighted works. . . .

I.   OPERATION OF THE RS-DVR SYSTEM

Cable companies like Cablevision aggregate television programming from a wide variety of "content providers"—the various broadcast and cable channels that produce or provide individual programs—and transmit those programs into the homes of their subscribers via coaxial cable. At the outset of the transmission process, Cablevision gathers the content of the various television channels into a single stream of data. Generally, this stream is processed and transmitted to Cablevision's customers in real time. Thus, if a Cartoon Network program is scheduled to air Monday night at 8pm, Cartoon Network transmits that program's data to Cablevision and other cable companies nationwide at that time, and the cable companies immediately re-transmit the data to customers who subscribe to that channel.

Under the new RS-DVR, this single stream of data is split into two streams. The first is routed immediately to customers as before. The second stream flows into a device called the Broadband Media Router ("BMR") . . . which buffers the data stream, reformats it, and sends it to the "Arroyo Server," which consists, in relevant part, of two data buffers and a number of high-capacity hard disks. The entire stream of data moves to the first buffer (the "primary ingest buffer"), at which point the server automatically inquires as to whether any customers want to record any of that programming. If a customer has requested a particular program, the data for that program move from the primary buffer into a secondary buffer, and then onto a portion of one of the hard disks allocated to that customer. As new data flow into the primary buffer, they overwrite a corresponding quantity of data already on the buffer. The primary ingest buffer holds no more than 0.1 seconds of each channel's programming at any moment. Thus, every tenth of a second, the data residing on this buffer are automatically erased and replaced. The data buffer in the BMR holds no more than 1.2 seconds of programming at any time. While buffering occurs at other points in the operation of the RS-DVR, only the BMR buffer and the primary ingest buffer are utilized absent any request from an individual subscriber.

As the district court observed, "the RS-DVR is not a single piece of equipment," but rather "a complex system requiring numerous computers, processes, networks of cables, and facilities staffed by personnel twenty-four hours a day and seven days a week." . . . To the customer, however, the processes of recording and playback on the RS-DVR are similar to that of a standard set-top DVR. Using a remote control, the customer can record programming by selecting a program in advance from an on-screen guide, or by pressing the record button while viewing a given program. A customer cannot, however, record the earlier portion of a program once it has begun. To begin playback, the customer selects the show from an on-screen list of previously recorded programs. . . . The principal difference in operation is that, instead of sending signals from the remote to an on-set box, the viewer sends signals from the remote, through the cable, to the Arroyo Server at Cablevision's central facility. . . . In this respect, RS-DVR more closely resembles a VOD [Video on Demand] service, whereby a cable subscriber uses his remote and cable box to request transmission of content, such as a movie, stored on computers at the cable company's facility. . . . But unlike a VOD service, RS-DVR users can only play content that they previously requested to be recorded.

Cablevision has some control over the content available for recording: a customer can only record programs on the channels offered by Cablevision (assuming he subscribes to them). Cablevision can also modify the system to limit the number of channels available and considered doing so during development of the RS-DVR. . . .

II. THE DISTRICT COURT'S DECISION

In the district court, plaintiffs successfully argued that Cablevision's proposed system would directly infringe their copyrights in three ways. First, by briefly storing data in the primary ingest buffer and other data buffers integral to the function of the RS-DVR, Cablevision would make copies of protected works and thereby directly infringe plaintiffs' exclusive right of reproduction under the Copyright Act. Second, by copying programs onto the Arroyo Server hard disks (the "playback copies"), Cablevision would again directly infringe the reproduction right. And third, by transmitting the data from the Arroyo Server hard disks to its RS-DVR customers in response to a "playback" request, Cablevision would directly infringe plaintiffs' exclusive right of public performance. . . . Agreeing with all three arguments, the district court awarded summary declaratory judgment to plaintiffs and enjoined Cablevision from operating the RS-DVR system without obtaining licenses from the plaintiff copyright holders. . . .

DISCUSSION . . .

[The court of appeals held that the data stored in the buffers were not "fixed" because they were not embodied in the storage medium for a period of more than transitory duration. As to the copies stored on the Arroyo Server hard disks, it held that they were "made" by Cablevision's customers, who supplied the volitional conduct that caused them to be created. You will learn about the role of volitional conduct in distinguishing between direct infringers and parties liable, if at all, on a theory of indirect infringement, in Chapter 6 of the casebook. — Eds.]

III.   TRANSMISSION OF RS-DVR PLAYBACK

Plaintiffs' final theory is that Cablevision will violate the Copyright Act by engaging in unauthorized public performances of their works through the playback of the RS-DVR copies. . . . Section 101, the definitional section of the Act, explains that

> [t]o perform or display a work "publicly" means (1) to perform or display it at a place open to the public or at any place where a substantial number of persons outside of a normal circle of a family and its social acquaintances is gathered; or (2) to transmit or otherwise communicate a performance or display of the work to a place specified by clause (1) or to the public, by means of any device or process, whether the members of the public capable of receiving the performance or display receive it in the same place or in separate places and at the same time or at different times.

[17 U.S.C.] §101.

The parties agree that this case does not implicate clause (1). Accordingly, we ask whether these facts satisfy the second, "transmit clause" of the public performance definition: Does Cablevision "transmit . . . a performance . . . of the work . . . to the public"? *Id.* No one disputes that the RS-DVR playback results in the transmission of a performance of a work — the transmission from the Arroyo Server to the customer's television set. Cablevision contends that . . . the transmission is not "to the public" under the transmit clause. . . .

The statute itself does not expressly define the term "performance" or the phrase "to the public." It does explain that a transmission may be "to the public . . . whether the members of the public capable of receiving the performance . . . receive it in the same place or in separate places and at the same time or at different times." *Id.* This plain language instructs us that, in determining whether a transmission is "to the public," it is of no moment that the potential recipients of the transmission are in different places, or that they may receive the transmission at different times. The implication from this same language, however, is that it is relevant, in determining whether a transmission is made to the public, to discern who is "capable of receiving" the performance being transmitted. . . .

The legislative history of the transmit clause supports this interpretation. The House Report on the 1976 Copyright Act states that

> [u]nder the bill, as under the present law, a performance made available *by transmission to the public at large* is "public" even though the recipients are not gathered in a single place, and even if there is no proof that any of the *potential recipients* was operating his receiving apparatus at the time of the transmission. The same principles apply whenever the *potential recipients of the transmission* represent a limited segment of the public, such as the occupants of hotel rooms or the subscribers of a cable television service.

H.R.Rep. No. 94-1476, at 64-65 (1976), *reprinted in* 1976 U.S.C.C.A.N. 5659, 5678 (emphases added). . . .

From the foregoing, it is evident that the transmit clause directs us to examine who precisely is "capable of receiving" a particular transmission of a performance. Cablevision argues that, because each RS-DVR transmission is made using a single unique copy of a work, made by an individual subscriber, one that can be decoded exclusively by that subscriber's cable box, only one subscriber is capable of receiving any given RS-DVR transmission. This argument accords with the language of the transmit clause. . . .

The district court, in deciding whether the RS-DVR playback of a program to a particular customer is "to the public," apparently considered all of Cablevision's customers who subscribe to the channel airing that program and all of Cablevision's RS-DVR subscribers who request a copy of that program. Thus, it concluded that the RS-DVR playbacks constituted public performances because "Cablevision would transmit the *same program* to members of the public, who may receive the performance at different times, depending on whether they view the program in real time or at a later time as an RS-DVR playback." . . . In essence, the district court suggested that, in considering whether a transmission is "to the public," we consider not the potential audience of a particular transmission, but the potential audience of the underlying work (i.e., "the program") whose content is being transmitted.

We cannot reconcile the district court's approach with the language of the transmit clause. That clause speaks of people capable of receiving a particular "transmission" or "performance," and not of the potential audience of a particular "work." Indeed, such an approach would render the "to the public" language surplusage. Doubtless the *potential* audience for every copyrighted audiovisual work is the general public. As a result, any transmission of the content of a copyrighted work would constitute a public performance under the district court's interpretation. But the transmit clause obviously contemplates the existence of non-public transmissions; if it did not, Congress would have stopped drafting that clause after "performance."

On appeal, plaintiffs offer a slight variation of this interpretation. They argue that both in its real-time cablecast and via the RS-DVR playback, Cablevision is in fact transmitting the "same performance" of a given work: the performance of the work that occurs when the programming service supplying Cablevision's content transmits that content to Cablevision and the service's other licensees. . . .

Thus, according to plaintiffs, when Congress says that to perform a work publicly means to transmit . . . a performance . . . to the public, they really meant "transmit . . . the 'original performance' . . . to the public." The implication of this theory is that to determine whether a given transmission of a performance is "to the public," we would consider not only the potential audience of that transmission, but also the potential audience of any transmission of the same underlying "original" performance.

Like the district court's interpretation, this view obviates any possibility of a purely private transmission. Furthermore, it makes Cablevision's liability depend, in part, on the actions of legal strangers. Assume that HBO transmits a copyrighted work to both Cablevision and Comcast. Cablevision merely retransmits the work from one Cablevision facility to another, while Comcast retransmits the program to its subscribers. Under plaintiffs' interpretation, Cablevision would still be transmitting the performance to the public, solely because Comcast has transmitted the same underlying performance to the public. . . .

We do not believe Congress intended such odd results. Although the transmit clause is not a model of clarity, we believe that when Congress speaks of transmitting a performance to the public, it refers to the performance created by the act of transmission. Thus, HBO transmits its own performance of a work when it transmits to Cablevision, and Cablevision transmits its own performance of the same work when it retransmits the feed from HBO. . . .

In sum, none of the arguments advanced by plaintiffs or the district court alters our conclusion that, under the transmit clause, we must examine the potential audience of a given transmission by an alleged infringer to determine whether that transmission is "to the public." And because the RS-DVR system, as designed, only makes transmissions to one subscriber using a copy made by that subscriber, we believe that the universe of people capable of receiving an RS-DVR transmission is the single subscriber whose self-made copy is used to create that transmission.

Plaintiffs contend that it is "wholly irrelevant, in determining the existence of a public performance, whether 'unique' *copies* of the same work are used to make the transmissions." . . . But plaintiffs cite no authority for this contention. And our analysis of the transmit clause suggests that, in general, any factor that limits the *potential* audience of a transmission is relevant. . . .

Indeed, we believe that *Columbia Pictures Industries, Inc. v. Redd Horne, Inc.,* 749 F.2d 154 (3d Cir.1984), relied on by both plaintiffs and the district court, supports our decision to accord significance to the existence and use of distinct copies in our transmit clause analysis. . . .

. . . In concluding that Maxwell's violated the transmit clause, that court explicitly relied on the fact that defendants showed the same copy of a work seriatim to its clientele, and it quoted [the Nimmer] treatise emphasizing the same fact. . . .

Unfortunately, neither the *Redd Horne* court nor Prof. Nimmer explicitly explains *why* the use of a distinct copy affects the transmit clause inquiry. But our independent analysis confirms the soundness of their intuition: the use of a unique copy may limit the potential audience of a transmission and is therefore relevant to whether that transmission is made "to the public." . . .

Given that each RS-DVR transmission is made to a given subscriber using a copy made by that subscriber, we conclude that such a transmission is not "to the public," . . . .

This holding, we must emphasize, does not generally permit content delivery networks to avoid all copyright liability by making copies of each item of content and associating one unique copy with each subscriber to the network, or by giving their subscribers the capacity to make their own individual copies. We do not address whether such a network operator would be able to escape any other form of copyright liability, such as liability for unauthorized reproductions or liability for contributory infringement. . . .

[The court directed that summary judgment be granted in favor of Cablevision.]

NOTES AND QUESTIONS

1. Consider the following hypotheticals. Which clause(s) of the statutory definition of "publicly" does each implicate, and how should each be decided? Do the *Redd Horne* analysis and the *Cartoon Network* analysis appear to dictate different outcomes in any of the hypotheticals?

   a. Rentals from the store desk of videotapes that are then taken by customers to individual viewing booths, placed in separate video players located in each booth, and played under the control of the customers.
   b. Rentals from a hotel desk of DVDs for viewing in the individual hotel rooms, when each room is equipped with a DVD player and the guest controls the playing of the DVD.
   c. Rentals from a hotel desk of DVDs for viewing in the individual hotel rooms, when the DVD player is located at the front desk.
   d. Rentals of DVDs and portable DVD players in airports, when the DVDs are watched in-flight and then returned, along with the players, at travelers' destination airports.

2. In *Cartoon Network*, why shouldn't the characterization of a performance depend on "the potential audience of any transmission of the same underlying 'original' performance"? From the perspective of the content provider, what distinguishes Cablevision's RS-DVR service from a video-on-demand service?

3. In determining whether particular transmissions are public, is it appropriate to consider whether or not unique copies were used? Why, or why not?

Based on the legislative history quoted in the *Redd Horne* opinion, how do you think the 1976 Congress would have answered that question? Should any performance transmitted over a one-to-many infrastructure count as "public"?

4. Why do you think the plaintiffs in *Redd Horne* and *Cartoon Network* objected to the services that the defendants provided? From a practical standpoint, how would each defendant's service affect the market for the copyrighted works?

5. As the *Redd Horne* court observes, the first sale doctrine of §109(a) limits only the copyright owner's right of public distribution, not the right of public performance. Therefore, when someone rents or even purchases a copy of a music CD or a motion picture DVD, lawful possession of that copy does not give him the right to publicly perform the copyrighted work embodied in it. The notion that "It's my copy; I can do with it what I want" is thus not entirely true. There are other limiting doctrines in copyright law that may allow for certain public performances, see pages 436-41 and Chapter 7 in the casebook, but the first sale doctrine will not.

Page 435. Insert the following immediately before the Notes and Questions:

Perfect 10, Inc. v. Amazon.com, Inc.
508 F.3d 1146 (9th Cir. 2007)

Ikuta, J.: . . .

Google operates a search engine, a software program that automatically accesses thousands of websites . . . and indexes them within a database stored on Google's computers. When a Google user accesses the Google website and types in a search query, Google's software searches its database for websites responsive to that search query. Google then sends the relevant information from its index of websites to the user's computer. . . .

The Google search engine that provides responses in the form of images is called "Google Image Search." In response to a search query, Google Image Search identifies text in its database responsive to the query and then communicates to users the images associated with the relevant text. Google's software cannot recognize and index the images themselves. Google Image Search provides search results as a webpage of small images called "thumbnails," which are stored on Google's servers. The thumbnail images are reduced, lower-resolution versions of full-sized images stored on third-party computers.

When a user clicks on a thumbnail image, the user's browser program interprets HTML instructions on Google's webpage. These HTML instructions direct the user's browser to cause a rectangular area (a "window") to appear on the user's computer screen. The window has two separate areas of information. The browser fills the top section of the screen with information from the Google webpage, including the thumbnail image and text. The HTML instructions also give the user's browser the address of the website publisher's computer that stores the full-size version of the thumbnail. By following the HTML instructions to access the third-party webpage, the user's browser connects to the website publisher's computer, downloads the full-size image, and makes the image appear at the bottom of the window on the user's screen. Google does not store the images that fill this lower part of the window and does not communicate the images to the user; Google simply provides HTML instructions directing a user's browser to access a third-party website. However, the top part of the window (containing the information from the Google webpage) appears to frame and comment on the bottom part of the window. Thus, the user's window appears to be filled with a single integrated presentation of the full-size image. . . . The processes by which the webpage directs a user's browser to incorporate content from different computers into a single window is referred to as "in-line linking." . . .

Google also stores webpage content in its cache. For each cached webpage, Google's cache contains the text of the webpage as it appeared at the time Google indexed the page, but does not store images from the webpage. . . . Google may provide a link to a cached webpage in response to a user's search query. However, Google's cache version of the webpage is not automatically updated when the webpage is revised by its owner. So if the webpage owner updates its webpage to remove the HTML instructions for finding an infringing image, a browser communicating directly with the webpage would not be able to access that image. However, Google's cache copy of the webpage would still have the old HTML instructions for the infringing image. Unless the owner of the computer changed the HTML address of the infringing image, or otherwise rendered the image unavailable, a browser accessing Google's cache copy of the website could still access the image where it is stored on the website publisher's computer. In other words, Google's cache copy could provide a user's browser with valid directions to an infringing image even though the updated webpage no longer includes that infringing image.

In addition to its search engine operations, Google generates revenue through a business program called "AdSense." Under this program, the owner of a website can register with Google to become an AdSense "partner." The website owner then places HTML instructions on its webpages that signal Google's server to place advertising on the webpages that is relevant to the webpages' content. Google's computer program selects the advertising automatically by means of an algorithm. AdSense participants agree to share the revenues that flow from such advertising with Google. . . .

Google also generated revenues through an agreement with Amazon.com that allowed Amazon.com to in-line link to Google's search results. Amazon.com gave its users the impression that Amazon.com was providing search results, but Google communicated the search results directly to Amazon.com's users. Amazon.com routed users' search queries to Google and automatically transmitted Google's responses (i.e., HTML instructions for linking to Google's search results) back to its users.

Perfect 10 markets and sells copyrighted images of nude models. Among other enterprises, it operates a subscription website on the Internet. Subscribers pay a monthly fee to view Perfect 10 images in a "members' area" of the site. Subscribers must use a password to log into the members' area. Google does not include these password-protected images from the members' area in Google's index or database. Perfect 10 has also licensed Fonestarz Media Limited to sell and distribute Perfect 10's reduced-size copyrighted images for download and use on cell phones.

Some website publishers republish Perfect 10's images on the Internet without authorization. Once this occurs, Google's search engine may automatically index the webpages containing these images. . . .

DIRECT INFRINGEMENT

• • •

The district court held that Perfect 10 was likely to prevail in its claim that Google violated Perfect 10's display right with respect to the infringing thumbnails. . . . However, the district court concluded that Perfect 10 was not likely to prevail on its claim that Google violated . . . [Perfect 10's display right] with respect to its full-size infringing images. . . .

A. DISPLAY RIGHT

• • •

We have not previously addressed the question when a computer displays a copyrighted work for purposes of section 106(5). Section 106(5) states that a copyright owner has the exclusive right "to display the copyrighted work publicly." The Copyright Act explains that "display" means "to show a copy of it, either directly or by means of a film, slide, television image, or any other device or process. . . ." 17 U.S.C. §101. Section 101 defines "copies" as "materials objects, other than phonorecords, in which a work is fixed by any method now known or later developed, and from which the work can be perceived, reproduced, or otherwise communicated, either directly or with the aid of a machine or device." *Id.* Finally, the Copyright Act provides that "[a] work is 'fixed' in a tangible medium of expression when its embodiment in a copy or phonorecord, by or under the authority of the author, is sufficiently permanent or stable to permit it to be perceived, reproduced, or otherwise communicated for a period of more than transitory duration." *Id.*

We must now apply these definitions to the facts of this case. A photographic image is a work that is "'fixed' in a tangible medium of expression," for purposes of the Copyright Act, when embodied (i.e., stored) in a computer's server (or hard disk, or other storage device). . . . The computer owner shows a copy "by means of a . . . device or process" when the owner uses the computer to fill the computer screen with the photographic image stored on that computer, or by communicating [sic] the stored image electronically to another person's computer. . . . In sum, based on the plain language of the statute, a person displays a photographic image by using a computer to fill a computer screen with a copy of the photographic image fixed in the computer's memory. There is no dispute that Google's computers store thumbnail versions of Perfect 10's copyrighted images and communicate copies of those thumbnails to Google's users. Therefore, Perfect 10 has made a prima facie case that Google's communication of its stored thumbnail images directly infringes Perfect 10's display right.

Google does not, however, display a copy of full-size infringing photographic images for purposes of the Copyright Act when Google frames in-line linked images that appear on a user's computer screen. Because Google's computers do not store the photographic images, Google does not have a copy of the images for purposes of the Copyright Act. In other words, Google does not have any "material objects . . . in which a work is fixed . . . and from which the work can be perceived, reproduced, or otherwise communicated" and thus cannot communicate a copy. 17 U.S.C. §101.

. . . Providing the[] HTML instructions is not equivalent to showing a copy. First, the HTML instructions are lines of text, not a photographic image. Second, HTML instructions do not themselves cause infringing images to appear on the user's computer screen. The HTML merely gives the address of the image to the user's browser. The browser then interacts with the computer that stores the infringing image. It is this interaction that causes an infringing image to appear on the user's computer screen. . . .

Perfect 10 argues that Google displays a copy of the full-size images by framing the full-size images, which gives the impression that Google is showing the image within a single Google webpage. While in-line linking and framing may cause some computer users to believe they are viewing a single Google webpage, the Copyright Act, unlike the Trademark Act, does not protect a copyright holder against acts that cause consumer confusion. . . .[7]

Nor does our ruling that a computer owner does not display a copy of an image when it communicates only the HTML address of the copy erroneously collapse the display right in section 106(5) into the reproduction right set forth in section 106(1). Nothing in the Copyright Act prevents the various rights protected in section 106 from overlapping. . . .

Because Google's cache merely stores the text of webpages, our analysis of whether Google's search engine program potentially infringes Perfect 10's display and distribution rights is equally applicable to Google's cache. Perfect 10 is not likely to succeed in showing that a cached webpage that in-line links to full-size infringing images violates such rights. For purposes of this analysis, it is irrelevant whether cache copies direct a user's browser to third-party images that are no longer available

---

7. Perfect 10 also argues that Google violates Perfect 10's right to display full-size images because Google's in-line linking meets the Copyright Act's definition of "to perform or display a work 'publicly.'" 17 U.S.C. §101. This phrase means "to transmit or otherwise communicate a performance or display of the work to . . . the public, by means of any device or process, whether the members of the public capable of receiving the performance or display receive it in the same place or in separate places and at the same time or at different times." *Id*. Perfect 10 is mistaken. Google's activities do not meet this definition because Google transmits or communicates only an address which directs a user's browser to the location where a copy of the full-size image is displayed. Google does not communicate a display of the work itself.

on the third party's website, because it is the website publisher's computer, rather than Google's computer, that stores and displays the infringing image. . . .

[The court also concluded that Google's display of thumbnail images was fair use. For that portion of the opinion, see pages 450–53, *infra*.]

AMAZON.COM

. . . The district court concluded that Perfect 10 was unlikely to succeed in proving that Amazon.com was a direct infringer, because it merely in-line linked to the thumbnails on Google's servers and to the full-size images on third-party websites. . . .

We agree that Perfect 10 has not shown a likelihood that it would prevail on the merits of its claim that Amazon.com directly infringed its images. Amazon.com communicates to its users only the HTML instructions that direct users' browsers to Google's computers (for thumbnail images) or to a third party's computer (for full-size infringing images). Therefore, Amazon.com does not display . . . a copy of the thumbnails or full-size images to its users. . . .

Page 435. In the Notes and Questions:

a. Delete Question 2.

b. Insert new Questions 1-2, and renumber Questions 1 and 3 as Questions 3-4:

1. Do you agree that the plain language of the Act mandates rejection of Perfect 10's claims for direct infringement with respect to the full-size images? The district court reached the same conclusion, but used a different approach. The court considered two possible tests for what constitutes a display. The "server" test defines "'display' as the act of *serving* content over the web" — i.e., physically sending ones and zeroes over the internet to the user's browser. *Perfect 10 v. Google, Inc.,* 416 F. Supp. 2d 828, 839 (C.D. Cal. 2006) (emphasis in original). The "incorporation" test defines "'display' as the mere act of incorporating content into a webpage that is then pulled up by the browser." *Id.* The court found the server test preferable because it "is based on what happens at the technological-level[;] . . . neither invites copyright infringing activity by a search engine . . . nor flatly precludes liability for such activity[;] . . . website operators can readily understand the server test and courts can apply it relatively easily[; and it] . . . maintains, however uneasily, the delicate balance for which copyright law strives — i.e., between encouraging the creation of creative works and encouraging the dissemination of information." *Id.* at 843-44. Which approach do you prefer, the district court's or the Ninth Circuit's? Do you agree with the district court that a server test is preferable as a matter of policy?

2. Review Question 1, page 402 *supra*. Perfect 10 also asserted a claim against Google for direct infringement of its distribution right. It argued that, like users of peer-to-peer file-sharing services and like the library in *Hotaling v. Church of Jesus Christ of Latter Day Saints,* pages 365-67 in the casebook, Google made the infringing full-size images "available" to its users. The court rejected that argument, reasoning that "Google does not own a collection of Perfect 10's full-size images and does not communicate these images to the computers of people using Google's search engine." It concluded that therefore "the 'deemed distribution' rule does not apply to Google." *Perfect 10, Inc. v. Amazon.com, Inc.,* 508 F.3d at 1162. Do you agree with this reasoning? If copyright law is to adopt a "deemed distribution" rule, how broadly should that rule extend?

G. Copyright and the Music Industry

Pages 448-49. In the Notes and Questions:

a. Insert new Question 2 and renumber Questions 2-3 as Questions 3-4:

2. The Copyright Office has ruled that cellular phone ringtones that are excerpts of preexisting sound recordings "fall squarely within the scope of the statutory license" under §115 and constitute DPDs. *In the Matter of Mechanical & Digital Phonorecord Delivery Rate Adjustment Proceeding,* U.S. Copyright Office, No. RF 2006-1 (Oct. 16, 2006). If additional material is added, the ringtone may be a derivative work and thus ineligible for the §115 mechanical license. *Id.* Songwriters, represented by the National Music Publishers Association, the Songwriters Guild of America, and the Nashville Songwriters Association International, had argued that all ringtones are derivative works. Why do you think the Copyright Office ruled as it did? Do you think the ruling is a sound one?

b. Insert new Question 5:

5. What activities are covered by a mechanical license under §115? Imagine that you are a manufacturer of a karaoke device, which you hope to sell to restaurants and bars around the world. What kinds of licenses do you need? Does it make a difference whether you put the recordings on cassettes or compact discs or embed them in a microchip, which, when plugged into a television, displays the lyrics of the song on the television screen in real time? Does a mechanical license entitle you to print or display the song lyrics in real time? If not, what other kind of license do you need and why? *See Leadsinger Inc. v. BMG Music Publishing,* 512 F.3d 522 (9th Cir. 2008) (holding that a karaoke device that displays lyrics is not a

phonorecord but an audiovisual work excluded from §115's compulsory licensing scheme.)

Page 463.   In the Notes and Questions, insert new Question 5:

5. XM, a licensed satellite radio broadcaster, offered a new service to its subscribers called "XM+MP3." The service was facilitated by special devices that made it possible for subscribers to receive XM radio broadcasts, make digital downloads for private personal use, store MP3 files the subscribers may already own or acquire from a third party, and store up to 50 hours of broadcast music (about 1,000 songs) for unlimited replay so long as the users maintained a subscription with XM. Users of the service could also transfer music files from their personal computer onto the XM+MP3 player to create indexed personal libraries of sound recordings and personalized playlists. In a lawsuit filed against XM by major record labels, XM asserted that it was statutorily immune from suit for copyright infringement based on the AHRA. The parties disputed whether the XM+MP3 players are "digital audio recording devices" (DARDs) under the AHRA. According to the court, however, even if the devices qualified as DARDs, the AHRA only offers immunity for actions based on the distribution of such devices and not "absolute immunity" from copyright litigation. A license to broadcast music is not "a . . . wholesale, blanket protection for any and all conduct." The court noted that the allegations by the Plaintiffs were not based on the XM+MP3 players, but on the fact that XM was acting as an unauthorized content deliverer to those devices. *See Atlantic Recording Corp. v. XM Satellite Radio,* No. 06-Civ.-3733 (S. D.N.Y. Jan. 19, 2007) (memorandum and order) at 15, 20. Do you agree with the court's interpretation of the AHRA? Is there any way XM can offer these services without violating the Copyright Act? What other defenses might you raise on behalf of XM?

Page 468.   Insert the following at the end of the Note on the Small Webcaster Settlement Act of 2002:

In March 2007, a panel of Copyright Royalty Judges issued a determination concerning the royalty rate to be paid to sound recording copyright owners for webcasting. The panel abandoned the percentage-of-revenue scheme in favor of a per-performance, per-listener escalating royalty rate for all stations that exceed a monthly aggregate-tuning-hours threshold. Additionally, it imposed a $500-per-channel fee on all commercial webcasters. Webcasters derided the panel's royalty rate determination, asserting that the rates favored the music industry and would drive them out of business. Congress intervened again, adopting the Webcaster Settlement Act, which authorized SoundExchange to negotiate alternative rates and terms with the webcasters.

In March 2009, the Copyright Office announced that SoundExchange had reached agreements with the Corporation for Public Broadcasting (CPB), the

National Association of Broadcasters (NAB), and several small webcasters, including Attention Span Radio, Blogmusik, Born Again Radio, Music Justice, My Jazz Network, and Voice of Country. U.S. Copyright Office, *Notification of Agreements Under the Webcaster Settlement Act of 2008*, 74 Fed. Reg. 9293 (Mar. 3, 2009). The Copyright Office published the different agreements as appendices to the official notice appearing in the Federal Register and indicated that the rates and terms in the agreements are "available to any webcasters meeting the respective eligibility conditions of the agreements as an alternative to the rates and terms of any determination by the Copyright Royalty Judges." *Id.* at 9293. Thus, entities engaged in webcasting that require a license from the sound recording copyright owner can look to these agreements and, if they meet the qualifications, can elect to pay either the royalties set by the March 2007 Copyright Royalty Judges or those established under the negotiated agreements.

Under the CPB agreement, the total license fee for the January 1, 2005, through December 31, 2010, term of the agreement was set at $1.85 million. The NAB license is applicable to businesses engaged in webcasting that own and operate one or more FCC-licensed terrestrial AM or FM radio stations. The NAB license covers the period from January 1, 2006, through December 31, 2015, and requires each broadcaster to pay an annual nonrefundable fee of $500 for each of its channels, with a maximum fee of $50,000 (for 100 or more channels or stations) and an escalating, per-performance royalty rate set beginning at $0.0008 in 2006 and ending at $0.0025 in 2015.

The final agreement negotiated by SoundExchange covers "Eligible Small Webcasters," defined as webcasters that have annual gross revenues of not more than $1.25 million. In addition to an annual fee ranging from $500 to $2,000, webcasters pay a royalty rate based on a percentage of revenue. For small webcasters that do not exceed 5 million aggregate tuning hours per month, the royalty rate for the period from January 1, 2006, through December 31, 2015, is the greater of either (1) 10% of the webcaster's first gross revenue in excess of $250,000 and 12% of any annual gross revenue exceeding $250,000, or (2) 7% of the webcaster's annual expenses. For transmissions exceeding five million aggregate tuning hours per month, small webcasters will need to pay either the rates that were set by the March 2007 panel determination, or "the then-applicable commercial webcasting rates under Sections 112(e) and 114." *Id.* at 9303.

In an effort to have sufficient data to determine the payment of royalties collected to sound recording copyright owners, each of the agreements requires the reporting of significant data to SoundExchange, with an exception limited to "Microcasters," who pay a $100 annual "proxy fee" and then do not report details relating to what sound recordings they webcasted. Among other requirements, to qualify as a Microcaster an entity must have gross revenues that do not exceed $5,000 and gross expenses that do not exceed $10,000, and during the applicable year the entity must not expect to make eligible nonsubscription transmissions exceeding 18,067 aggregate tuning hours.

Page 469. In the Notes and Questions, insert new Question 3 and renumber Questions 3-6 as 4-7:

3. On December 18, 2007, senior members of the Senate and House Judiciary Committees introduced bipartisan legislation to provide owners of sound recording copyrights with full performance rights covering the use of their sound recordings by over-the-air broadcasters. If enacted, the proposed Performance Rights Act would remove a longstanding limitation that benefits conventional radio stations. The proposed bill, which has enjoyed broad support, including from quarters traditionally resistant to the expansion of copyright rights, would amend §106(6) of the Copyright Act to read as follows: "in the case of sound recordings, to perform the copyrighted work publicly by means of an audio transmission." As drafted, the bill provides relief for noncommercial radio stations, including public, educational and religious stations, by giving those stations the option of a nominal, annual flat fee. It provides similar relief for commercial stations whose annual revenue is under $1.25 million, which currently comprise approximately three-fourths of all music radio stations. Finally, the proposed legislation seeks to amend the §114 statutory license for digital public performances to ensure the preservation of royalties payable to songwriters or copyright owners of underlying musical works. Most other industrialized countries already provide similar protection for performance rights for sound recordings.

Chapter 6. The Different Faces of Infringement

A. Direct Infringement

Page 477. In the Notes and Questions, insert the following at the end of Question 4:

In declining to find Cablevision liable for direct infringement of the reproduction right based on copies of programming stored at the request of customers of its remote DVR service (*see* page 413 *supra*), the Second Circuit offered a slightly different analysis of the direct liability problem presented by networked digital services:

> There are only two instances of volitional conduct in this case: Cablevision's conduct in designing, housing, and maintaining a system that exists only to produce a copy, and a customer's conduct in ordering that system to produce a copy of a specific program. In the case of a VCR, it seems clear — and we know of no case holding otherwise — that the operator of the VCR, the person who actually presses the button to make the recording, supplies the necessary element of volition, not the person who manufactures, maintains, or, if distinct from the operator, owns the machine. We do not believe that an RS-DVR customer is sufficiently distinguishable from a VCR user to impose liability as a direct infringer on a different party for copies that are made automatically upon that customer's command.
>
> . . . In determining who actually "makes" a copy, a significant difference exists between making a request to a human employee, who then volitionally operates the copying system to make the copy, and issuing a command directly to a system, which automatically obeys commands and engages in no volitional conduct. . . . Here, by selling access to a system that automatically produces copies on command, Cablevision more closely resembles a store proprietor who charges customers to use a photocopier on his premises, and it seems incorrect to say, without more, that such a proprietor "makes" any copies when his machines are actually operated by his customers. . . .
>
> Our refusal to find Cablevision directly liable on these facts is buttressed by the existence and contours of the Supreme Court's doctrine of contributory liability in

the copyright context. After all, the purpose of any causation-based liability doctrine is to identify the actor (or actors) whose "conduct has been so significant and important a cause that [he or she] should be legally responsible." W. Page Keeton et al., *Prosser and Keeton on Torts* §42, at 273 (5th ed.1984). But here, to the extent that we may construe the boundaries of direct liability more narrowly, the doctrine of contributory liability stands ready to provide adequate protection to copyrighted works.

Cartoon Network LP v. CSC Holdings, Inc., 536 F.3d 121, 131-32 (2d Cir. 2008), *petition for cert. filed*, 77 U.S.L.W. 3229 (Oct. 6, 2008). Is the Second Circuit's analysis more persuasive than the Fourth Circuit's? Do you agree that the nature of Cablevision's involvement in the recording of copies makes an indirect liability inquiry more appropriate? Revisit this question after you read the next two sections of this chapter in the casebook.

B. Vicarious Liability and Contributory Infringement

Page 487. In the Notes and Questions, insert new Questions 6 and 7 and renumber Question 6 as Question 8:

6. What level of control is necessary to satisfy the requirements for vicarious liability? In *Perfect 10, Inc. v. Amazon.com*, 508 F.3d 1146 (9th Cir. 2007), pages 419-23 *supra*, the Ninth Circuit specified that there must be "both a legal right to stop or limit the directly infringing conduct, as well as the practical ability to do so." In that case, Google had contracts with some of the alleged third party infringers through its AdSense partnership program. The contracts specified that Google could terminate the contracts if the partners "violate others' copyright[s]." *Id.* at 1173. The court concluded that these contracts did not give Google the right to stop the third parties' direct infringement, but rather gave Google only the right to terminate the relationship. In light of this ruling, what types of contractual clauses might satisfy the Ninth Circuit? Will an arms-length contractual relationship ever create a sufficient legal right to control the infringing activity of another?

Concerning the practical ability to control the infringing activity of another, Perfect 10 argued that Google could have managed its operations to avoid including infringing websites in its search results. The court rejected this argument as an attempt to blur the distinction between vicarious liability and contributory liability. It noted that "contributory liability is based on the defendant's failure to stop its own actions which facilitate third-party infringement, while vicarious liability is based on the defendant's failure to cause a third party to stop its directly infringing activities." Google's failure to change its operations was relevant to the claim of contributory infringement only. Is this an appropriate way to analyze allegations of a defendant's failure to act?

The *Perfect 10* court did not address the second element required for vicarious liability: direct financial benefit. If the potential for vicarious liability can be eliminated through an arm's-length contractual relationship with the only consequence for infringing activity being termination of the contract, does it matter how much of a "draw" the infringing material creates? Is this consistent with *Fonovisa*? Should there be an inverse relationship between the two elements necessary for vicarious liability, so that when there is significant evidence of direct financial benefit the level of control need not be as high? Would that blur the line between vicarious liability and contributory liability?

7. Around the same time that it sued Google and Amazon.com, Perfect 10 filed a separate lawsuit against Visa and other credit card processing entities, asserting that the credit card entities were indirectly liable for copyright infringement by third-party websites for whom they processed payments. Perfect 10 alleged that it had repeatedly notified the credit card entities of the infringement and that their own rules required them to terminate payment services for businesses that conducted illegal activity. In *Perfect 10, Inc. v. Visa International Service Ass'n*, 494 F.3d 788 (9th Cir. 2007), a divided Ninth Circuit panel upheld dismissal of Perfect 10's contributory infringement and vicarious liability claims.

The majority opinion began by observing that "[w]e evaluate Perfect 10's claims with an awareness that credit cards serve as the primary engine of electronic commerce and that Congress has determined it to be the "policy of the United States — (1) to promote the continued development of the Internet . . . and (2) to preserve the vibrant and competitive free market that presently exists [for online services].'" *Id.* at 794 (quoting 47 U.S.C. §§230(b)(1), (2)). The majority reasoned that the credit card entities' payment processing services did not materially contribute to the alleged infringement because they lacked a "direct connection" to the infringing conduct. *Id.* at 797. It distinguished the services provided by Google, Amazon.com, and Napster on the ground that they "allowed users to locate and obtain infringing material," *id.* at 796. The majority further observed that although credit card payment systems "make it easier for such an infringement to be profitable, and . . . therefore have the effect of increasing such infringement" the infringement could still occur without use of the payment systems. *Id.* at 798. As to vicarious liability, the majority concluded that, just as Google's right to terminate an AdSense contract did not give it the right and ability to control infringement by third-party websites (see Question 6, *supra*), the credit card entities were not in a position to control the infringing conduct simply because they could have stopped processing the payments. *Id.* at 803-04.

In a lengthy dissent, Judge Kozinski argued that these conclusions were flatly inconsistent with the rules developed in the circuit's previous indirect liability cases. On the test for material contribution, he observed:

My colleagues recognize, as they must, that helping consumers locate infringing content can constitute contributory infringement, but they consign the means of payment to secondary status. . . . But why is *locating* infringing images more central to infringement than *paying* for them? If infringing images can't be found, there can be no infringement; but if infringing images can't be paid for, there can be no infringement either. Location services and payment services are equally central to infringement. . . .

. . . As the majority admits, if Google were unwilling or unable to serve up infringing images, consumers could use Yahoo!, Ask.com, Microsoft Live Search, A9.com, or AltaVista instead. . . . Even if none of these were available, consumers could still locate websites with infringing images through e-mails from friends, messages on discussion forums, . . . peer-to-peer networking using BitTorrent or eDonkey, offline and online advertisements . . . , disreputable search engines hosted on servers in far-off jurisdictions or even old-fashioned word of mouth. . . .

The majority's attempt to distinguish location services from payment services by trying to show that there are viable alternatives for the latter but not the former cuts entirely against them. As plaintiff alleges, and as experience tells us, there are numerous ways of locating infringing images on the Internet, but there are no adequate substitutes for credit cards when it comes to paying for them. . . . If it mattered whether search engines or credit cards are more important to peddling infringing content on the Internet, credit cards would win hands down.

But it doesn't matter. Material assistance turns on whether the activity in question "substantially assists" infringement. *Amazon*, 487 F.3d at 729. It makes no difference whether the primary infringers might do without it by finding a workaround. . . .

Id. at 812-14.

As to vicarious liability, Judge Kozinski began by observing that the credit card entities' fee structures ensured that "they take a cut of virtually every sale of pirated material." *Id.* at 816. He further observed that, unlike Google's AdSense contracts, the credit card entities' own regulations require investigation of claims of illegal conduct by participating merchants and "strictly prohibit members from servicing illegal businesses." *Id.* at 817.

Do you agree with the majority, or with Judge Kozinski? Did the court apply more lenient standards to the credit card entities than it did to the on-line search companies? From a policy standpoint, would extending indirect liability to entities that provide financial services to alleged infringers be a good idea? Why, or why not?

C. Liability of Device Manufacturers

Page 501. In the Notes and Questions, insert new Question 10:

10. On remand in *Grokster*, the district court granted the copyright owners' motion for summary judgment against defendant StreamCast Networks on the question of liability, relying on the inducement theory outlined by the Supreme Court. (In a 2005 settlement, defendant Grokster agreed to cease distributing its client application and to stop supporting its existing network.) Plaintiffs then requested that the court permanently enjoin StreamCast from operating its Morpheus network or any similar network "until there is a 'robust and secure means exhaustively to' stop infringement," and require StreamCast to "'use all

technologically feasible means to prevent or inhibit' infringement" by users of existing versions of the Morpheus software. *Metro-Goldwyn-Mayer Studios, Inc. v. Grokster, Ltd.,* 518 F. Supp. 1197 (C.D. Cal. 2007). In response, StreamCast asserted that plaintiffs' proposal effectively would require enjoining it from continued distribution of its software. It argued, further, that requiring filtering would be inconsistent with a line of patent cases in which, although defendants had been found liable for inducing infringement, courts refused to *enjoin* the sale of products that were staple articles of commerce suitable for substantial noninfringing use. *Id.* at 1231-32.

Observing that "[t]here is a distinction between forbidding distribution of a technology capable of substantial noninfringing uses and simply requiring sufficient efforts to minimize the prospective infringement that would otherwise be induced," the court rejected StreamCast's argument against a court-imposed filtering requirement. It reasoned that StreamCast's own actions had so closely associated the Morpheus software with copyright infringement that "continued distribution of Morpheus alone [, without filtering,] constitutes infringement." *Id.* at 1235. The court also noted that the Ninth Circuit had affirmed a district court order requiring Napster to implement acoustical fingerprinting and filtering technologies. The court ruled, however, that since perfect filtering was not technically possible, plaintiffs' proposed wording set the bar too high. It ordered "StreamCast to reduce Morpheus' infringing capabilities, while preserving its core noninfringing functionality, as effectively as possible." *Id.* at 1236. It also ruled that StreamCast had no duty to filter out particular works until it had been given sufficient notice of those works' presence on its network. The court reserved authority to alter the injunction's terms in response to future events, and indicated that it would appoint a special master to oversee implementation. What do you think of the court's solution?

D. On-line Service Provider Liability

Page 504.   In the Notes and Questions:

a. Insert the following at the end of Question 2:

See also Field v. Google, Inc., 412 F. Supp. 2d 1106, 1124 (D. Nev. 2006) (Google's retention in cache of indexed pages for periods ranging from 14 to 20 days was "transient").

b. Insert the following at the end of Question 4:

In 2008, Congress passed the Higher Education Opportunity Act, Pub. L. No. 110-315, which is directed at lowering tuition costs and streamlining the financial aid process. Buried in this lengthy piece of legislation is a provision requiring colleges to develop a plan to block peer-to-peer file-sharing and to offer students an alternative to illegal downloading as a condition of being able to get federal financial aid for students. *See* 20 U.S.C. §1094(a)(29). Is this a wise use of educational institutions' limited resources?

Pages 505-08.   Replace Questions 1-5 with the following:

1. Section 512 does not shelter an OSP that fails to adopt and reasonably implement a policy for terminating repeat infringers. Read 17 U.S.C. §512(i) and identify its requirements. Are the OSPs in the following hypotheticals eligible to invoke §512's safe harbors?

   a. The OSP establishes a copyright policy but does not communicate the policy to its users until after it is sued for copyright infringement, and it terminates repeat infringers by blocking their passwords but not their IP addresses. *See A&M Records, Inc. v. Napster, Inc.*, 2000 WL 573136 (N.D. Cal. May 12, 2000) (holding grant of summary judgment on the applicability of §512 inappropriate because genuine issues of material fact existed regarding the defendant's compliance with §512(i)).

   b. The OSP adopts a policy that does not use the term "repeat infringer" or otherwise track the statutory language but that prohibits violations of copyright law and provides for penalties ranging from removal of individual items to termination of service. Pursuant to the policy, the OSP has canceled "millions of listings," issued warnings of possible termination, and terminated some users. However, it has not "conduct[ed] active investigation of possible infringement or ma[de] a decision regarding difficult infringement issues." *See Corbis Corp. v. Amazon.com, Inc.*, 351 F. Supp. 2d 1090, 1101-04 (W.D. Wash. 2004) (OSP eligible to invoke §512).

   c. The OSP changes the e-mail address designated for receipt of notifications of claimed infringement but does not immediately inform the Copyright Office of the change. *See Ellison v. Robertson*, 357 F.3d 1072, 1080 (9th Cir. 2004) (delay of approximately six months raised a triable issue of material fact regarding the OSP's eligibility for a safe harbor, and also regarding whether the OSP should have known of the infringing activity).

   d. The OSP does not respond to the plaintiff's takedown notices because they lack the required statement under penalty of perjury, but the OSP has received notices about the same allegedly infringing websites from other copyright holders. *See Perfect 10, Inc. v. CCBill LLC*, 488 F.3d 1102 (9th Cir.) (lack of response to defective notices does not raise genuine issue of material fact concerning "reasonably implementing a repeat infringer policy," but court must consider how OSP responded to notices from other copyright owners), *cert. denied*, 128 S. Ct.709 (2007).

2. Obviously, whether an OSP has reasonably implemented a policy to terminate repeat infringers hinges in part on what the OSP knows about the activities

of its subscribers. Section 512(c) defines three situations in which an OSP is charged with knowledge. Two of these situations—actual knowledge and receipt of a compliant takedown notice—are easily understood. The third situation, "awareness of facts or circumstances from which infringing activity is apparent," §512(c)(1)(A)(ii), is more difficult. Are there situations or "red flags" that should create a presumption of knowledge? In *Perfect 10, Inc. v. CCBill LLC*, 488 F.3d 1102 (9th Cir.), *cert. denied*, 128 S. Ct. 709 (2007), the plaintiff argued that any of the following three conditions should be *per se* red flags: (1) defective takedown notices; (2) suspicious names of subscribers' websites (such as "illegal.net" and "stolencelebritypics.com"); and (3) the presence of password-hacking information on subscribers' websites. The court rejected all three of these arguments. It held that defective notices cannot be deemed to impart the required awareness. *Id.* at 1114. Noting that sites that traffic in titillating pictures may attempt to increase their salacious appeal with words like "illegal" or "stolen," it refused to "place the burden of determining whether photographs are actually illegal on a service provider." *Id.* Finally, it noted that one could not know whether a site offering password-hacking information enabled infringement without verifying that the passwords worked. The court was unwilling to place such a burden on service providers. What do you think of the court's conclusions? Are there other situations that should create red flags?

The *CCBill* litigation involved a claim of §512 safe harbor immunity. Without the protection of the safe harbor, a court would analyze liability under contributory infringement doctrine, which requires a showing of knowledge of the infringing activity. Should the standard for what constitutes knowledge under contributory infringement doctrine be different from the standard for what constitutes knowledge under the statutory safe harbor? In *Perfect 10, Inc. v. Amazon.com* 508 F.3d 1146 (9th Cir. 2007), the Ninth Circuit held that in light of the Supreme Court's opinion in *Grokster*, contributory infringement liability is for those who are actively encouraging infringement and that "a computer system operator can be held contributorily liable if it 'has *actual* knowledge that *specific* infringing material is available using its system.'" *Id.* at 1172 (quoting *A&M Records, Inc. v. Napster*, 239 F.3d 1004, 1022 (9th Cir. 2001)). Does the standard in §512(c)(1)(A)(ii) mean that a defendant could lose the safe harbor protection but then, nonetheless, avoid liability for contributory infringement because the requisite level of knowledge is not present? Does that result make sense? Why, or why not?

3. Does an OSP's implementation of a copyright compliance policy under §512 make its conduct "volitional" and therefore subject to a claim of direct infringement under *Netcom*'s reasoning? In *CoStar Group, Inc. v. LoopNet, Inc.*, 373 F.3d 544 (4th Cir. 2004), which involved allegedly infringing copies of photographs of commercial real estate listings, the court concluded that it does not:

> . . . After expressly warranting that he has "all necessary rights and authorizations from the . . . copyright owner of the photographs," the subscriber uploads the photograph into a folder in LoopNet's system. The photograph is then transferred to the RAM of one of LoopNet's computers for review. A LoopNet employee reviews the photo for two purposes: (1) to block photographs that do not depict commercial real

estate, and (2) to block photographs with obvious signs that they are copyrighted by a third party. If the photograph carries a copyright notice or represents subject matter other than commercial real estate, the employee deletes the photograph; otherwise, she clicks a button marked "accept," and LoopNet's system automatically associates the photograph with the subscriber's web page for the property listing, making it available for use. Unless a question arises, this entire process takes "a few seconds."

Although LoopNet engages in volitional conduct to block photographs measured by two grossly defined criteria, this conduct, which takes only seconds, does not amount to "copying," nor does it add volition to LoopNet's involvement in storing the copy. The employee's look is so cursory as to be insignificant, and . . . tends only to lessen the possibility that LoopNet's automatic electronic responses will inadvertently enable others to trespass on a copyright owner's rights. . . . LoopNet can be compared to an owner of a copy machine who has stationed a guard by the door to turn away customers who are attempting to duplicate clearly copyrighted works. LoopNet has not by this screening process become engaged as a "copier" of copyrighted works. . . .

To the extent that LoopNet's intervention in screening photographs goes further than the simple gatekeeping function described above, it is because of CoStar's complaints about copyright violations. Whenever CoStar has complained to LoopNet about a particular photograph, LoopNet has removed the photograph, and the property listing with which the photograph was associated has been marked. The next time the user tries to post a photograph to accompany that listing, LoopNet conducts a manual side-by-side review to make sure that the user is not reposting the infringing photograph. CoStar and other copyright holders benefit significantly from this type of response. If they find such conduct by an ISP too active, they can avoid it by adding a copyright notice to their photographs, which CoStar does not do. . . .

Id. at 556. What do you think of this reasoning?

4. Google uses automated tools called "bots" to index websites. Google's bots copy pages and store them for up to 20 days in temporary storage called cache. When a user enters a query into Google for which an indexed page is relevant, the Google search engine will return both a link to the version of the page in the Google cache as well as a link to the actual page. A site owner can use certain codes to indicate to a bot that it does not wish the page to be indexed or does not wish the indexing site, i.e., Google, to use a cached link.

Does Google infringe websites' copyrights when it copies pages into its cache or when it serves a user a copy of a cached page? In *Field v. Google, Inc.*, 412 F. Supp. 2d 1106 (D. Nev. 2006), the plaintiff challenged the latter practice, though not the initial copying. (Why not?) Citing *LoopNet*, the court reasoned: "[W]hen a user requests a Web page contained in the Google cache by clicking on a 'Cached' link, it is the user, not Google, who creates and downloads a copy of the cached Web page. Google is passive in this process. . . . The automated, non-volitional conduct by Google in response to a user's request does not constitute direct infringement under the Copyright Act." *Id.* at 1115. What do you think of this reasoning?

The court also held that even if Google had engaged in direct infringement, it could assert the defense of implied license. Plaintiff's failure to follow the in-dustry standard (of which it was aware) of including certain code to indicate an unwillingness to have its web pages available from cache could be "reasonably interpreted as the grant of a license to Google for that use." *Id.* at 1116. Do you agree?

5. What does "storage at the direction of the user of material" mean in §512(c) (1)? For example, can an OSP take advantage of §512(c)(1) if it converts files uploaded by users to another format? In *Io Group, Inc. v. Veoh Networks, Inc.*, 586 F. Supp. 2d 1132 (N.D. Cal. 2008), the court held that Veoh was not precluded from using §512(c) simply because its software automatically converted user-submitted content into Flash format. The court relied on §512's language, noting that while §512(k)(1)(A) defines "service provider" narrowly to preclude modification to the content of material the OSP receives, that definition does not apply to §512(c): Rather, the broader definition of §512(k)(1)(B), which lacks such a limitation, applies. The court also stated: " . . . Veoh does not itself actively participate or supervise the uploading of files. Nor does it preview or select the files before the upload is completed. Instead, video files are uploaded through an automated process which is initiated entirely at the volition of Veoh's users." *Id.* at 1148. Would the court have held differently if the conversion to Flash format had not been automatic? Would §512(c) be available to Veoh if its software created still-image files from users' content to use as icons for search results? (Yes. *Id.* at 1146-48). What if Veoh's software: (i) automatically created copies of small parts of the original file; (ii) allowed users to access uploaded files by streaming; and (iii) allowed users to download entire video files? *See UMG Recordings, Inc. v. Veoh Networks, Inc.*, 2008 WL 5423841, at *7-*9 (C.D. Cal. 2008) (" . . . §512(c) does not require that the infringing conduct constitute storage in its own right. Rather the infringing conduct must occur *as a result of the storage*. . . . [T]he language in the remainder of §512(c) *"presupposes* that the service provider will be providing access to the user's material.") (emphasis in original).

6. From the perspective of an Internet user, what do you make of the notification, counternotification, and subpoena procedures established by §512? Do they reflect an appropriate balancing of the various interests affected? If not, what changes would you recommend?

7. Now assess the notification requirements from the OSP's perspective. Consider first the requirement that the notification identify the allegedly infringing material and provide "information reasonably sufficient to permit the service provider to locate the material." 17 U.S.C. §512(c)(3)(A)(iii). What does this mean in practice? If you were in-house counsel to the OSP in each of the following hypotheticals, how would you respond?

   a. A letter sent to eBay.com states that counterfeit copies of a work are being traded on eBay, but does not provide the relevant eBay item numbers. *See Hendrickson v. eBay, Inc.*, 165 F. Supp. 2d 1082, 1090 (C.D. Cal. 2001) (notification insufficient).

   b. A letter sent to Amazon.com identifies "all *Manson* DVDs" as infringing. *See Hendrickson v. Amazon.com, Inc.*, 298 F. Supp. 2d 914, 916 (C.D. Cal. 2003) (notification sufficient).

   c. A letter sent to an on-line payment service that processes subscriptions to client sites offering pornographic content asserts that the client sites contain infringing images, but does not identify the precise sites or the precise images. *See Perfect 10, Inc. v. CCBill, LLC*, 340 F. Supp. 2d 1077 (C.D. Cal. 2004) (notification insufficient).

d. A letter sent to a provider of Internet hosting services identifies two hosted sites that it asserts were created for the sole purpose of displaying the copyrighted works, and states that essentially all of the images at those sites are infringing. *See ALS Scan, Inc. v. RemarQ Communities, Inc.*, 239 F.3d 619, 625 (4th Cir. 2001) (notification sufficient).

Are all of these decisions consistent with each other?

When an OSP receives a notice that substantially complies with the statutory requirements, for how long must it monitor its system for the infringing material identified therein? *See Hendrickson*, 298 F. Supp. 2d at 917 (no obligation to detect items posted nine months after the date of the notice). The House Report accompanying §512 stated that the "legislation is not intended to discourage the service provider from monitoring its service for infringing material." H.R. Rep. No. 105-796, *reprinted in* 1998 U.S.C.C.A.N. 645, 649. Do you think OSPs will, in fact, monitor their services? Read §512(m) before you answer.

8. Finally, consider the notification requirements from the perspective of a copyright holder. First, what constitutes a "good faith belief" under §512(c)(3)(A)(v)? If a website contains statements like "'Join to download full length movies online now!'" followed by graphics depicting the copyright owner's films, must the copyright owner verify that, in fact, its material can be downloaded? *See Rossi v. Motion Picture Ass'n of Am.*, 391 F.3d 1000, 1002-06 (9th Cir. 2004) (good faith requirement is subjective, and copyright owner need not investigate whether its copyrighted movies were actually available for download before sending notification to the OSP).

Second, what would constitute a "knowing[] material[] misrepresent[ation]" under §512(f)? How would you apply this standard in a case in which the copyright owner sends a notice knowing that parts of the material identified are not copyrighted, and that any infringement likely would be excused under the fair use doctrine? In *Online Policy Group v. Diebold, Inc.*, 337 F. Supp. 2d 1195 (N.D. Cal. 2004), the court assessed a notification sent by Diebold, a manufacturer of electronic voting machines, demanding the removal from the Internet of copied portions of an archive of e-mail exchanged among Diebold employees that revealed serious technical problems with Diebold's machines. The court concluded that Diebold had violated the statute:

> "Knowingly" means that a party actually knew, should have known if it acted with reasonable care or diligence, or would have had no substantial doubt had it been acting in good faith, that it was making misrepresentations. . . . "Material" means that the misrepresentation affected the ISP's response to a DMCA letter. . . .
> . . . No reasonable copyright holder could have believed that [the material] was protected by copyright, and there is no genuine issue of fact that Diebold knew—and indeed that it specifically intended . . . that its [notices] would result in prevention of publication of that content. The representations were material in that they resulted in

removal of the content from websites. . . . The fact that Diebold never actually brought suit against any alleged infringer suggests strongly that Diebold sought to use [§512] . . . as a sword to suppress publication of embarrassing content rather than as a shield to protect its intellectual property.

Id. at 1204.

Are *Rossi* and *Online Policy Group* consistent with one another? Do the different standards they articulate for "good faith belief" and "knowing material misrepresentation," respectively, comport with the policy considerations animating §512?

9. Can failure to consider the applicability of fair use constitute a basis for a claim of knowing material misrepresentation under §512(f)? At least one court has answered "yes," making clear that there are constraints on a copyright owner's use of takedown notices. In *Lenz v. Universal Music Corp.*, 572 F. Supp. 2d 1150 (N.D. Cal. 2008), the court held that "to proceed under the DMCA with 'a good faith belief that use of the material in the manner complained of is not authorized by the copyright owner, its agent, or the law,' the owner *must* evaluate whether the material makes fair use of the copyright." *Id.* at 1154 (emphasis added).

10. At least two major Internet access providers appear to have deployed "deep packet inspection" technologies to analyze, and sometimes block, traffic passing through their networks. Deep packet inspection examines bits of digital information to determine which application generated the information, and can also be used to identify digital watermarks. After subscribers of the cable and Internet provider Comcast discovered a network utility that hampered use of the popular BitTorrent P2P file-sharing protocol, Comcast admitted that it had deliberately interfered with subscribers' BitTorrent downloads. According to Comcast, this helped it to manage competing demands for bandwidth. In March 2008, following an investigation by the Federal Communications Commission, Comcast announced that it would no longer engage in the challenged practice, and pledged to come up with other traffic management solutions, although it did not indicate what those solutions might be.

Is deep packet inspection by Internet access providers a good solution to the problem of on-line copyright infringement? Why, or why not? Review §512(a), the statutory safe harbor for transitory digital network communications. If an OSP engages in deep packet inspection, will it lose eligibility to claim the safe harbor? If so, is that result appropriate?

Page 508. Insert the following before the Note on Identifying the Direct Infringer:

NOTE ON OSPs AND USER-GENERATED CONTENT

Many Internet users rely on the Internet to distribute content that they have created. Web platforms like YouTube and Flickr, which did not exist when Congress enacted §512, were designed specifically as venues for such user-generated content. Today, those sites and many others like them receive millions of visitors daily. Those visits translate into substantial advertising revenue for the OSPs that operate the sites.

Often, user-generated content includes material drawn from preexisting copyrighted works. The uses of preexisting materials are so diverse as to defy description. Sometimes, the user-generated work is a mashup — a work that combines two preexisting works to create something that blends the two. Sometimes, users edit excerpts from single works, adding, deleting or substituting elements. Many users create works of "fan fiction," inserting new characters and storylines into the fictional universes of popular movies, television shows, and books. Others remix sounds and images from a variety of sources. In some user-generated works, copyrighted musical recordings provide soundtracks for video of users dancing, singing, or simply going about their daily activities. Sometimes, too, users simply repost snippets of copyrighted movies and television broadcasts that they find particularly interesting (or particularly annoying).

Web platforms for user-generated content have drawn considerable attention from the major copyright industries. Representatives of these industries argue that such sites function principally to enable uncontrolled distribution of infringing copies of their works, and that many of the user-generated works described above also infringe their copyrights.

In February 2007, Viacom served YouTube with 100,000 §512 takedown notices for allegedly infringing content uploaded by users. Some industry observers think Viacom expected the sheer number of notices to bring YouTube to the bargaining table, and hoped that YouTube would agree to use content filtering tools approved by Viacom. Instead, YouTube simply processed the notices and, where indicated, took down the infringing materials. Viacom then sued YouTube, asserting that YouTube should be held liable for repeated acts of copyright infringement committed by its users. Shortly after the lawsuit was filed, Google acquired YouTube, so the lawsuit now pits Viacom's resources against Google's. Discovery is underway, with no sign of an imminent settlement.

In addition, the major copyright industries have sought to engage the OSP industry in negotiations that would yield privately-agreed methods of policing for copyright infringement. In 2007, a group of major copyright owners including Disney, Fox, Microsoft, NBC Universal, and Viacom released a document titled "Copyright Principles for UGC Services," <http://www.ugcprinciples.com/>. According to the proposed principles, Web platforms for user-generated content should implement "effective content identification technology . . . with the goal of eliminating from their services all infringing user-uploaded audio and video content for which Copyright Owners have provided Reference Material." *Id.*, ¶3. The proposed principles define "effective content identification technology" as any technology that is both "commercially reasonable" and "highly effective, in relation to other technologies commercially available at the time of implementation." *Id.* The technology should automatically block user uploads for which a copyright owner has provided "reference data for content required to establish a match with user-uploaded content" unless the copyright owner has instructed that matches should be handled in some other way. *Id.* ¶3(a)-(c).

Pursuant to the proposed principles, a UGC service may undertake "manual (human) review of all user-uploaded audio and video content in lieu of, or in addition to, use of Identification Technology, if feasible and if such review is as effective as Identification Technology in achieving the goal of eliminating infringing content." *Id.* ¶3(f). UGC services also must give copyright owners that register with them access to "commercially reasonable enhanced searching and identification means" to search for infringing content themselves. *Id.* ¶5. The proposed principles state that "Copyright Owners and UGC services should cooperate to ensure that the Identification Technology is implemented in a manner that effectively balances legitimate interests in (1) blocking infringing user-uploaded content, (2) allowing wholly original and authorized uploads, and (3) accommodating fair use." *Id.* ¶3(d).

As of this writing, only a handful of OSPs have endorsed the proposed principles. Web platforms like YouTube argue that the provisions of §512 provide sufficient protection for copyright owner interests, and that they respond promptly to copyright owners' takedown notices.

NOTES AND QUESTIONS

1. Assume that discovery shows that YouTube has always acted promptly to process §512 takedown notices and remove infringing materials. How would you rule on Viacom's indirect copyright infringement claims against Google/YouTube, and why?

2. If you represented Google/YouTube in the Viacom lawsuit, what terms would you want included in any settlement? What terms would you want if you represented Viacom?

3. What do you think of the "Copyright Principles for UGC Services"? If you represented a Web platform for user-generated content, would you favor adoption? If UGC platforms all decided to adopt the copyright industries' filtering proposal, would that be an efficient solution to the problem of online copyright infringement? Would such a solution be fair to users? In response to the Principles, a group of nonprofit organizations offered a competing proposal, titled "Fair Use Principles for User Generated Video Content." We will consider that proposal in Chapter 7, *infra*, after you have learned about fair use.

Pages 510-11: In the Notes and Questions, insert new Question 6:

6. Recently, the RIAA announced that it was suspending its strategy of suing individuals suspected of exchanging infringing files via peer-to-peer networks. *See Music Industry to Drop Mass Suits*, Wall St. J., Dec. 27, 2008, *available at* 2008 WLNR 24774194 (stating that the recording industry had filed suit against "about 35,000 people since 2003"). Album sales, however, continued to decline, and suits against individuals generally did not result in good publicity for the RIAA. The RIAA recently changed tactics by entering into agreements with OSPs. The RIAA will

notify an OSP when it suspects the OSP's customer is infringing. The OSP in turn will inform its customer of the RIAA's notice and request that the customer cease its infringement. Failure to do so may result in slower service or a cessation of service altogether. *See generally id.* What are the pros and cons of this approach from the RIAA's perspective? From the OSP's perspective? What incentive would an OSP have to enter into such an agreement?

E. Criminal Infringement

Page 516.   In the Notes and Questions, insert new Question 3:

3. Recall from pages 512-13 of the casebook that criminal copyright infringement is also now a prominent feature of international copyright law, a development that can be attributed largely to U.S. efforts during the Uruguay Round negotiations. Under the TRIPS Agreement, all WTO members must provide criminal procedures and penalties for "wilful . . . copyright piracy on a commercial scale." *See* TRIPS Agreement art. 61. However, the Agreement does not define what constitutes "commercial scale" or how to determine when a Member's national law violates this provision. In *China—Measures Affecting the Protection and Enforcement of Intellectual Property Rights,* WT/DS362/R (Jan. 26, 2009), the U.S. claimed that China's domestic legislation was inconsistent with TRIPS Article 61, because its criminal procedures and penalties do not apply unless certain thresholds are met. For example, the Chinese criminal law applies criminal penalties for acts of copyright infringement "if the amount of illegal gains is relatively large, or if there are other serious circumstances. . . ." *Id.* ¶7.408 (quoting Section 217 of China's Criminal Law). Pursuant to related legislation, serious circumstances are deemed to exist when the number of illegally reproduced or distributed copyrighted works exceeds 500 copies. *Id. See also* ¶7.409. Applying normal rules of treaty interpretation, the Panel concluded that Article 61 embodies a "relative standard" and that the TRIPS Agreement "does not mandate specific forms of legislation." The Panel

> may not simply assume that a Member must give its authorities wide discretion to determine what is on a commercial scale in any given case, and may not simply assume that thresholds, including numerical tests, are inconsistent with the relative benchmark in the first sentence of Article 61 of the TRIPS Agreement. As long as a Member in fact provides for criminal procedures and penalties to be applied in cases of wilful . . . copyright piracy on a commercial scale, it will comply with this obligation. If it is alleged that a Member's method of implementation does not so provide in such cases, that allegation must be proven with evidence.

Id. ¶7.602. The Panel concluded that the U.S. had failed to establish the claimed violation of the TRIPS Agreement. *Id.* ¶7.669. Should criminal thresholds be deemed *per se* violations of the TRIPS Agreement?

Pages 520-21: In the Note on Internet-Era Amendments to the Copyright Felony Provisions, insert the following before the last paragraph:

The push to strengthen criminal copyright enforcement next produced the Prioritizing Resources and Organization for Intellectual Property ("PRO-IP") Act of 2008, which reorganized the Department of Justice to create the Intellectual Property Enforcement Division, headed by an enforcement officer reporting directly to the Deputy Attorney General; authorized the appointment of "intellectual property attachés" to be posted to U.S. embassies abroad; established the Office of the Intellectual Property Enforcement Representative within the Executive Office of the President; and gave the head of that office comprehensive advisory authority over domestic and international enforcement policy. In addition, the PRO-IP Act amended §411 to specify that registration of copyright is a prerequisite for filing a civil infringement lawsuit. Therefore, registration is not a prerequisite for commencing a criminal prosecution.

Page 522. In the Notes and Questions, insert the following at the end of Question 3:

Determining the "retail value" of a work is relevant for meeting the threshold requirement for certain types of criminal infringement, as well as for establishing whether the offense is a felony or a misdemeanor. The Fourth Circuit has determined that "retail value" refers to the greater of (1) the "prices assigned to commodities and goods for sale at the retail level at the time of sales at issue," or (2) "prices of commodities and goods determined by actual transactions between willing buyers and willing sellers at the retail level." *United States v. Armstead*, 524 F.3d 442, 446 (4th Cir. 2008). The court rejected the defendant's argument that because the defendant had sold bootleg copies of DVDs to undercover agents for $5 each, that was the "going rate" between willing buyers and willing sellers. The government had introduced evidence showing $19 as the minimum retail price for the DVDs at issue.

Whether bootleg sales have a one-for-one correspondence to lost retail sales for the copyright owner is a hotly debated issue. While the courts calculate the "retail value" for purposes of criminal liability based on the price of legitimate copies, they sometimes use different valuations in other contexts. For example, the Federal Mandatory Victims Restitution Act requires proof of the actual loss suffered. One court reasoned:

> It is a basic principle of economics that as price increases, demand decreases. Customers who download music and movies for free would not necessarily spend money to acquire the same product. . . . I am skeptical that customers would pay $7.22 or $19 for something they got for free. Certainly 100% of the illegal downloads . . . did not result in the loss of a sale. . . .

United States v. Dove, 585 F. Supp. 2d 865, 870 (W.D. Va. 2008).

Chapter 7. Another Limitation on Copyright: Fair Use

B. The Different Faces of Fair Use

Page 556. Insert the following immediately before the Notes and Questions:

Bill Graham Archives v. Dorling Kindersley Limited
448 F.3d 605 (2d Cir. 2006)

RESTANI, J.: . . .

BACKGROUND

In October of 2003, [Dorling Kindersley ("DK")] published *Grateful Dead: The Illustrated Trip* ("Illustrated Trip"), in collaboration with Grateful Dead Productions, intended as a cultural history of the Grateful Dead. The resulting 480-page coffee table book tells the story of the Grateful Dead along a timeline running continuously through the book, chronologically combining over 2000 images representing dates in the Grateful Dead's history with explanatory text. A typical page of the book features a collage of images, text, and graphic art designed to simultaneously capture the eye and inform the reader. Plaintiff [Bill Graham Archives ("BGA" or "Appellant")] claims to own the copyright to seven images displayed in *Illustrated Trip*, which DK reproduced without BGA's permission.

Initially, DK sought permission from BGA to reproduce the images. In May of 2003, the CEO of Grateful Dead Productions sent a letter to BGA seeking permission. . . . BGA responded by offering permission in exchange for Grateful Dead Productions' grant of permission to BGA to make CDs and DVDs out of concert footage in BGA's archives. Next, DK directly contacted BGA seeking to negotiate a license agreement, but the parties disagreed as to an appropriate license fee. Nevertheless, DK proceeded with publication of *Illustrated Trip* without entering a license fee agreement with BGA. Specifically, DK reproduced seven artistic images originally depicted on Grateful Dead event posters and tickets. BGA's seven images are displayed in significantly reduced form and are accompanied by captions describing the concerts they represent.

When DK refused to meet BGA's post-publication license fee demands, BGA filed suit for copyright infringement. . . . [T]he district court determined that DK's reproduction of the images was fair use and granted DK's motion for summary judgment.

DISCUSSION

I. PURPOSE AND CHARACTER OF USE

. . .

[W]e agree with the district court that DK's actual use of each image is transformatively different from the original expressive purpose. Preliminarily, we recognize, as the district court did, that *Illustrated Trip* is a biographical work documenting the 30-year history of the Grateful Dead. While there are no categories of presumptively fair use, *see Campbell v. Acuff-Rose Music, Inc.*, 510 U.S. at 584 . . . courts have frequently afforded fair use protection to the use of copyrighted material in biographies, recognizing such works as forms of historic scholarship, criticism, and comment that require incorporation of original source material for optimum treatment of their subjects. . . . No less a recognition of biographical value is warranted in this case simply because the subject made a mark in pop culture rather than some other area of human endeavor. . . .

In the instant case, DK's purpose in using the copyrighted images at issue in its biography of the Grateful Dead is plainly different from the original purpose for which they were created. Originally, each of BGA's images fulfilled the dual purposes of artistic expression and promotion. The posters were apparently widely distributed to generate public interest in the Grateful Dead and to convey information to a large number [of] people about the band's forthcoming concerts. In contrast, DK used each of BGA's images as historical artifacts to document and represent the actual occurrence of Grateful Dead concert events featured on *Illustrated Trip*'s timeline.

In some instances, it is readily apparent that DK's image display enhances the reader's understanding of the biographical text. In other instances, the link between image and text is less obvious; nevertheless, the images still serve as historical artifacts graphically representing the fact of significant Grateful Dead concert events selected by the *Illustrated Trip*'s author for inclusion in the book's timeline. We conclude that both types of uses fulfill DK's transformative purpose of enhancing the biographical information in *Illustrated Trip*, a purpose separate and distinct from the original artistic and promotional purpose for which the images were created. . . . [B]ecause DK's use of the disputed images is transformative both

446

when accompanied by referencing commentary and when standing alone, we agree with the district court that DK was not required to discuss the artistic merits of the images to satisfy this first factor of fair use analysis.

This conclusion is strengthened by the manner in which DK displayed the images. First, DK significantly reduced the size of the reproductions. . . . While the small size is sufficient to permit readers to recognize the historical significance of the posters, it is inadequate to offer more than a glimpse of their expressive value. In short, DK used the minimal image size necessary to accomplish its transformative purpose.

Second, DK minimized the expressive value of the reproduced images by combining them with a prominent timeline, textual material, and original graphical artwork, to create a collage of text and images on each page of the book. To further this collage effect, the images are displayed at angles and the original graphical artwork is designed to blend with the images and text. Overall, DK's layout ensures that the images at issue are employed only to enrich the presentation of the cultural history of the Grateful Dead, not to exploit copyrighted artwork for commercial gain. . . .

Third, BGA's images constitute an inconsequential portion of *Illustrated Trip*. The extent to which unlicensed material is used in the challenged work can be a factor in determining whether a biographer's use of original materials has been sufficiently transformative to constitute fair use. . . . Although our circuit has counseled against considering the percentage the allegedly infringing work comprises of the copyrighted work in conducting *third-factor* fair use analysis, . . . several courts have done so, *see, e.g., Harper*, 471 U.S. at 565-66 . . . (finding the fact that quotes from President Ford's unpublished memoirs played a central role in the allegedly infringing magazine article, constituting 13% of that article, weighed against a finding of fair use). . . . We find this inquiry more relevant in the context of *first-factor* fair use analysis.

In the instant case, the book is 480 pages long, while the BGA images appear on only seven pages. Although the original posters range in size from 13" × 19" to more than 19" × 27", the largest reproduction of a BGA image in *Illustrated Trip* is less than 3" × 4½", less than $\frac{1}{20}$ the size of the original. And no BGA image takes up more than one-eighth of a page in a book or is given more prominence than any other image on the page. In total, the images account for less than one-fifth of one percent of the book. . . . [W]e are aware of no case where such an insignificant taking was found to be an unfair use of original materials.

Finally, as to this first factor, we briefly address the commercial nature of *Illustrated Trip*. . . . Even though *Illustrated Trip* is a commercial venture, we recognize that "nearly all of the illustrative uses listed in the preamble paragraph of §107 . . . are generally conducted for profit. . . ." *Campbell*, 510 U.S. at 584. . . . Moreover, "[t]he crux of the profit/nonprofit distinction is not whether the sole motive of the use is monetary gain but whether the user stands to profit from exploitation of the copyrighted material without paying the customary price." *Harper*, 471 U.S. at 562. . . . Here, *Illustrated Trip* does not exploit the use of BGA's images as such for commercial gain. Significantly, DK has not used any of BGA's images in its commercial advertising or in any other way to promote the sale of the book. *Illustrated Trip* merely uses pictures and text to describe the life of the Grateful Dead. By design, the use of BGA's images is incidental to the commercial biographical value of the book. . . .

II. NATURE OF THE COPYRIGHTED WORK

. . .

We agree with the district court that the creative nature of artistic images typically weighs in favor of the copyright holder. We recognize, however, that the second factor may be of limited usefulness where the creative work of art is being used for a transformative purpose. . . . Here, we conclude that DK is using BGA's images for the transformative purpose of enhancing the biographical information provided in *Illustrated Trip*. Accordingly, we hold that even though BGA's images are creative works, which are a core concern of copyright protection, the second factor has limited weight in our analysis because the purpose of DK's use was to emphasize the images' historical rather than creative value.

III. AMOUNT AND SUBSTANTIALITY OF THE PORTION USED

. . .

The district court determined that even though the images are reproduced in their entirety, the third fair use factor weighs in favor of DK because the images are displayed in reduced size and scattered among many other images and texts. In faulting this conclusion, Appellant contends that the amount used is substantial because the images are copied in their entirety. Neither our court nor any of our sister circuits has ever ruled that the copying of an entire work *favors* fair use. At the same time, however, courts have concluded that such copying does not necessarily weigh against fair use because copying the entirety of a work is sometimes necessary to make a fair use of the image. *See . . . Nunez v. Caribbean Int'l News Corp.*, 235 F.3d 18, 24 (1st Cir. 2000). . . .

Here, DK used BGA's images because the posters and tickets were historical artifacts that could document Grateful Dead concert events and provide a visual context for the accompanying text. To accomplish this use, DK displayed reduced versions of the original images and intermingled these visuals with text and original graphic art. As a consequence, even though the copyrighted images are copied in their entirety, the visual impact of their artistic expression is significantly limited because of their reduced size. . . .

IV. EFFECT OF THE USE UPON THE MARKET FOR OR VALUE OF
THE ORIGINAL

. . .

In the instant case, the parties agree that DK's use of the images did not impact BGA's primary market for the sale of the poster images. Instead, we look to whether DK's unauthorized use usurps BGA's potential to develop a derivative market. Appellant argues that DK interfered with the market for licensing its images for use in books. Appellant contends that there is an established market for licensing its images and it suffered both the loss of royalty revenue directly from DK and the opportunity to obtain royalties from others. . . .

[W]e look at the impact on potential licensing revenues for "traditional, reasonable, or likely to be developed markets." [*American Geophysical Union v.*] *Texaco,* [*Inc.*] 60 F.3d [913,] at 930 [(2d Cir. 1995)]. In order to establish a traditional license market, Appellant points to the fees paid to other copyright owners for the reproduction of their images in *Illustrated Trip.* Moreover, Appellant asserts that it established a market for licensing its images, and in this case expressed a willingness to license images to DK. Neither of these arguments shows impairment to a traditional, as opposed to a transformative market. . . .

Here . . . we hold that DK's use of BGA's images is transformatively different from their original expressive purpose. In a case such as this, a copyright holder cannot prevent others from entering fair use markets merely "by developing or licensing a market for parody, news reporting, educational or other transformative uses of its own creative work." *Castle Rock,* 150 F.3d at 146 n. 11. "[C]opyright owners may not preempt exploitation of transformative markets. . . ." *Id.* Moreover, a publisher's willingness to pay license fees for reproduction of images does not establish that the publisher may not, in the alternative, make fair use of those images. *Campbell,* 510 U.S. at 585 n. 18 . . . (stating that "being denied permission to use [or pay license fees for] a work does not weigh against a finding of fair use"). Since DK's use of BGA's images falls within a transformative market, BGA does not suffer market harm due to the loss of license fees. . . .

Pages 556-59. In the Notes and Questions:

a. Insert new Question 5 and renumber Questions 5-7 as Questions 6-8:

5. Do you agree that DK's use of BGA's images was transformative? Should courts treat the inclusion of images in a biographical account differently from the inclusion of text (*see New Era*)? Note the *BGA* court's conclusion that DK minimized its use of the expressive aspect of the images by reducing their size. Should this matter? If DK had reproduced full-page versions of the images, should the fair use analysis change?

Should the scope of fair use be the same for a biography of a pop culture movement (*BGA*) as for the biography of a religious (*New Era*) or political (*Harper & Row*) leader? Is *BGA* consistent with those cases and with the treatment of popular culture in *Castle Rock*?

b. Insert the following at the end of Question 6 (now Question 7):

g. Jeff Koons is a visual artist who incorporates images from popular media and commercial advertising into his art. His painting "Niagara" depicts four pairs of women's lower legs and feet hovering over images of various confectionary treats like a brownie sundae. He adapted a photograph from a fashion magazine for one of the pairs of legs. According to Koons, the work is intended as a commentary on how popular images mediate basic needs. *See Blanch v. Koons,* 467 F.3d 244 (2d Cir. 2006) (fair use).

Pages 573-75.   Replace the Note on Internet Search Engines and the Notes and Questions with the following:

Perfect 10, Inc. v. Amazon, Inc.
508 F.3d 1146 (9th Cir. 2007)

[Review pages 419-23 *supra* for the facts of this case. The district court held that Google's display of thumbnail versions of infringing copies of Perfect 10's images most likely was not fair use. *Perfect 10 v. Google, Inc.,* 416 F. Supp. 2d 828 (C.D. Cal. 2006). The court concluded that "[t]he first, second, and fourth fair use factors weigh slightly in favor of P10. The third weighs in neither party's favor." *Id.* at 851. What follows is the Ninth Circuit's holding on the fair use issue.]

IKUTA, J.: . . .

FAIR USE DEFENSE

. . . Google contends that its use of thumbnails is a fair use of the images and therefore does not constitute an infringement of Perfect 10's copyright. . . .

In applying the fair use analysis in this case, we are guided by *Kelly v. Arriba Soft Corp.,* which considered substantially the same use of copyrighted photographic images as is at issue here. *See* 336 F.3d 811 [(9th Cir. 2003)]. In *Kelly,* a photographer brought a direct infringement claim against Arriba, the operator of an Internet search engine. The search engine provided thumbnail versions of the photographer's images in response to search queries. *Id.* at 815-16. We held that Arriba's use of thumbnail images was a fair use primarily based on the transformative nature of a search engine and its benefit to the public. *Id.* at 818-22. We also concluded that Arriba's use of the thumbnail images did not harm the photographer's market for his image. *Id.* at 821-22.

In this case, the district court determined that Google's use of thumbnails was not a fair use and distinguished *Kelly. Perfect 10,* 416 F. Supp. 2d [828, 845-51 (C.D. Cal. 2006)]. We consider these distinctions in the context of the four-factor fair use analysis.

Purpose and character of the use. . . . As noted in *Campbell,* a "transformative work" is one that alters the original work "with new expression, meaning, or message." *Campbell* [v. *Acuff-Rose Music, Inc.*], 510 U.S. [569, 579 (1994)]. . . .

Google's use of thumbnails is highly transformative. In *Kelly,* we concluded that Arriba's use of thumbnails was transformative because "Arriba's use of the images serve[d] a different function than Kelly's use — improving access to information on the [I]nternet versus artistic expression." *Kelly,* 336 F.3d at 819. Although an image may have been created originally to serve an entertainment, aesthetic, or informative function, a search engine transforms the image into a pointer directing a user to a source of information. Just as a "parody has an obvious claim to transformative value" because "it can provide social benefit, by shedding light on an earlier work, and, in the process, creating a new one," *Campbell,* 510 U.S. at 579, a search engine provides social benefit by incorporating an original work into a new work, namely, an electronic reference tool. Indeed, a search engine may be more transformative than a parody because a search engine provides an entirely new use for the original work, while a parody typically has the same entertainment purpose as the original work. . . . In other words, a search engine puts images "in a different context" so that they are "transformed into a new creation." [citation omitted].

The fact that Google incorporates the entire Perfect 10 image into the search engine results does not diminish the transformative nature of Google's use. As the district court correctly noted, *Perfect 10,* 416 F. Supp. 2d at 848-49, we determined in *Kelly* that even making an exact copy of a work may be transformative so long as the copy serves a different function than the original work, *Kelly,* 336 F.3d at 818-19. For example, the First Circuit has held that the republication of photos taken for a modeling portfolio in a newspaper was transformative because the photos served to inform, as well as entertain. *See [Nun]ez v. Caribbean Int'l News Corp.,* 235 F.3d 18, 22-23 (1st Cir. 2000). . . . Here, Google uses Perfect 10's images in a new context to serve a different purpose.

The district court nevertheless determined that Google's use of thumbnail images was less transformative than Arriba's use of thumbnails in *Kelly* because Google's use of thumbnails superseded Perfect 10's right to sell its reduced-size images for use on cell phones. *See Perfect 10,* 416 F. Supp. 2d at 849. The district court stated that "mobile users can download and save the thumbnails displayed by Google Image Search onto their phones," and concluded "to the extent that users may choose to download free images to their phone rather than purchase [Perfect 10's] reduced-size images, Google's use supersedes [Perfect 10's]." *Id.*

Additionally, the district court determined that the commercial nature of Google's use weighed against its transformative nature. *Id.* Although *Kelly* held that the commercial use of the photographer's images by Arriba's search engine was less exploitative than typical commercial use, and thus weighed only slightly against a finding of fair use, *Kelly,* 336 F.3d at 818-20, the district court here distinguished *Kelly* on the ground that some website owners in the AdSense program had infringing Perfect 10 images on their websites, *Perfect 10,* 416 F. Supp. 2d at 846-47. The district court held that because Google's thumbnails "lead users to sites that directly benefit Google's bottom line," the AdSense program increased the commercial nature of Google's use of Perfect 10's images. *Id.* at 847. . . .

We note that the superseding use in this case is not significant at present: the district court did not find that any downloads for mobile phone use had taken place. *See Perfect 10,* 416 F. Supp. 2d at 849. Moreover, while Google's use of thumbnails to direct users to AdSense partners containing infringing content adds a commercial dimension that did not exist in *Kelly,* the district court did not determine that this commercial element was significant. *See id.* at 848-49. The district court stated that Google's AdSense programs as a whole contributed "$630 million, or 46% of total revenues" to Google's bottom line, but noted that this figure did not "break down the much smaller amount attributable to websites that contain infringing content." *Id.* at 847 & n. 12 (internal quotation omitted).

We conclude that the significantly transformative nature of Google's search engine, particularly in light of its public benefit, outweighs Google's superseding and commercial uses of the thumbnails in this case. . . .

Therefore, this factor weighs heavily in favor of Google.

The nature of the copyrighted work. With respect to the second factor, "the nature of the copyrighted work," . . . our decision in *Kelly* is directly on point. There we held that the photographer's images were "creative in nature" and thus "closer to the core of intended copyright protection than are more fact-based works." *Kelly,* 336 F.3d at 820 (internal quotation omitted). However, because the photos appeared on the Internet before Arriba used thumbnail versions in its search engine results, this factor weighed only slightly in favor of the photographer. *Id.*

Here, the district court found that Perfect 10's images were creative but also previously published. *Perfect 10,* 416 F. Supp. 2d at 850. The right of first publication is "the author's right to control the first public appearance of his expression." *Harpers & Row* [*Publishers v. Nation Enters.*] 471 U.S. [539, 564 (1985)]. Because this right encompasses "the choices of when, where, and in what form first to publish a work," *id.,* an author exercises and exhausts this one-time right by publishing the work in any medium. . . . Once Perfect 10 has exploited this commercially valuable right of first publication by putting its images on the Internet for paid subscribers, Perfect 10 is no longer entitled to the enhanced protection available for an unpublished work. Accordingly the district court did not err in holding that this factor weighed only slightly in favor of Perfect 10. *See Perfect 10,* 416 F. Supp. 2d at 849-50.

The amount and substantiality of the portion used. . . . In *Kelly,* we held Arriba's use of the entire photographic image was reasonable in light of the purpose of a search engine. *Kelly,* 336 F.3d at 821. Specifically, we noted, "[i]t was necessary for Arriba to copy the entire image to allow users to recognize the image and decide whether to pursue more information about the image or the originating [website]. If Arriba only copied part of the image, it would be more difficult to identify it, thereby reducing the usefulness of the visual search engine." *Id.* Accordingly, we concluded that this factor did not weigh in favor of either party. *Id.* Because the same analysis applies to Google's use of Perfect 10's image, the district court did not err in finding that this factor favored neither party.

Effect of use on the market. . . . In *Kelly,* we concluded that Arriba's use of the thumbnail images did not harm the market for the photographer's full-size images. *See Kelly,* 336 F.3d at 821-22. We reasoned that because thumbnails were not a substitute for the full-sized images, they did not harm the photographer's ability to sell or license his full-sized images. *Id.* The district court here followed *Kelly*'s reasoning, holding that Google's use of thumbnails did not hurt Perfect 10's market for full-size images. *See Perfect 10,* 416 F. Supp. 2d at 850-51. We agree.

Perfect 10 argues that the district court erred because the likelihood of market harm may be presumed if the intended use of an image is for commercial gain. However, this presumption does not arise when a work is transformative because "market substitution is at least less certain, and market harm may not be so readily inferred." *Campbell,* 510 U.S. at 591. As previously discussed, Google's use of thumbnails for search engine purposes is highly transformative, and so market harm cannot be presumed.

Perfect 10 also has a market for reduced-size images, an issue not considered in *Kelly.* The district court held that "Google's use of thumbnails likely does harm the potential market for the downloading of [Perfect 10's] reduced-size images onto cell phones." *Perfect 10,* 416 F. Supp. 2d at 851 (emphasis omitted). The district court reasoned that persons who can obtain Perfect 10 images free of charge from Google are less likely to pay for a download, and the availability of Google's thumbnail images would harm Perfect 10's market for cell phone downloads. *Id.* As we discussed above, the district court did not make a finding that Google users have downloaded thumbnail images for cell phone use. This potential harm to Perfect 10's market remains hypothetical. We conclude that this factor favors neither party.

Having undertaken a case-specific analysis of all four factors, we now weigh these factors together "in light of the purposes of copyright." *Campbell,* 510 U.S. at 578; *see also Kelly,* 336 F.3d at 818. . . . In this case, Google has put Perfect 10's thumbnail images (along with millions of other thumbnail images) to a use fundamentally different than the use intended by Perfect 10. In doing so, Google has provided a significant benefit to the public. Weighing this significant transformative use against the unproven use of Google's thumbnails for cell phone downloads, and considering the other fair use factors, all in light of the purpose of copyright, we conclude that Google's use of Perfect 10's thumbnails is a fair use. . . . [W]e vacate the preliminary injunction regarding Google's use of thumbnail images.

NOTES AND QUESTIONS

1. Did Arriba or Google transform the plaintiffs' works or simply their context? Should your answer to this question affect the fair use analysis?

2. Do *Arriba* and *Perfect 10* mean that search engines should never worry about copyright infringement claims? After *Perfect 10,* what arguments can a copyright owner make about a visual search engine's effects on the potential market for or value of its works? What evidence might demonstrate such effects? Should such evidence change the result of the fair use analysis?

What if the search engine is also a comparison shopping service—i.e., the search engine makes copies of web pages and extracts product and pricing information? When a user enters the name of a product, the engine returns a list of what sites are offering it for sale and at what price. *See Ticketmaster Corp. v. Tickets. com, Inc.,* 2000 WL 1887522, at *3 (C.D. Cal. 2000) (stating that it would likely excuse the copying of web pages as a step in creating the database containing uncopyrighted product and pricing information as fair, citing *Sony v. Connectix* and "certain prior cases" as authority for its view).

3. Is the *Perfect 10* court's analysis of the four factors consistent with the analysis of courts in the other cases you have read?

Pages 596-97. In the Notes and Questions, insert new Question 4 and renumber Questions 5-6 as Questions 6-7:

4. Is the *Bill Graham Archives* case, pages 445–49, *supra*, consistent with *Texaco*? The *BGA* court stated, "Here, unlike in *Texaco*, we hold that DK's use of BGA's images is transformatively different from their original expressive purpose." *Bill Graham Archives v. Dorling Kindersley Ltd.*, 448 F.3d 605, 614 (2d Cir. 2006). The *BGA* court also distinguished *Texaco* because that case "involved direct evidence that the allegedly infringing use [, copying by researchers,] would cause the owner [, the scientific journals,] to lose license revenues derived from a substantially similar use." *Id.* at n.6. Do you find these distinctions persuasive? In particular, does the concept of "transformative markets" assist in determining what market harm is relevant under the fourth factor?

Page 599-600. In the Notes and Questions:

a. At the end of Question 1, insert the following:

c. A video editing company edits feature films to remove profanity, nudity and other content deemed inappropriate for a family audience. All copies of the films edited are obtained from customers or authorized retailers. The company sells or rents the edited films via its website or through retailers. Purchasers must buy one copy of the original unedited film for every edited version bought; the company purchases an authorized copy of the film for every edited version it rents. *See Clean Flicks of Colorado, LLC v. Soderbergh*, 433 F. Supp. 2d 1236 (D. Colo. 2006) (no fair use).

b. Insert new Question 5:

5. In an attempt to quantify the "fair use economy," the Computer & Communications Industry Association commissioned an economic study of the benefits that flow from fair use. The study, released in September 2007, uses the same methodology recommended by WIPO in its guidelines on measuring the economic contribution of the copyright industries. It concludes that in 2006 the "fair use industries"—a diverse group including computer and peripheral equipment manufacturers, audio and video equipment manufacturers, Internet publishers, Internet service providers, Web search companies, and electronic shopping companies—generated revenues of $4.5 trillion, value added of $2.2 trillion, a payroll of $1.2 trillion, and exports of $194 billion. The fair use industries

accounted for 16.6% of the U.S. current dollar GDP and 18.3% of U.S. economic growth. *Fair Use in the U.S. Economy: Economic Contribution of Industries Relying on Fair Use* (2007), <http://www.ccianet.org/artmanager/uploads/1/FairUseStudy-Sep12.pdf>. Do these figures alter any of your answers to Questions 1-4?

Page 602.   Insert the following new Notes and Questions:

4. Review the *Note on OSPs and User-Generated Content*, pages 439-41 *supra*. Consider the following examples of user-generated content, all available on YouTube as of this writing. If the creators of these video clips were sued for copyright infringement, could they successfully invoke the fair use doctrine? How would you analyze each example?

   a.   A short video of a toddler dancing to the song "Let's Go Crazy," by Prince;
   b.   A music video of Michael Jackson's "Thriller" performed by prison inmates in the Philippines;
   c.   A video of two students in a dorm room somewhere in China lip-synching to the song "That Way," by the Backstreet Boys;
   d.   A mashup juxtaposing the soundtrack from *Brokeback Mountain* with clips from the *Back to the Future* movies in a way that suggests forbidden love between Marty McFly and Doc Brown;
   e.   A video titled "Chad Vader, Day Shift Manager," that shows *Star Wars'* evil Lord Vader managing a supermarket;
   f.   A mashup combining Apple Computer's famous "1984" Superbowl ad, which included Orwellian scenes of factory workers watching a video presentation by a demagogic leader, with footage of 2008 Democratic presidential candidate Hillary Clinton.

5. If YouTube were to adopt the filtering protocols recommended in the copyright industries' "Copyright Principles for UGC Services," how would each of the videos in Question 4 be treated? Do the proposed principles appear to give a UGC service the flexibility to manually review videos automatically selected for blocking and elect not to block certain of those videos? If you worked as in-house counsel for a UGC service that had adopted the proposed principles, would you recommend that approach? Why, or why not?

6. In response to the copyright industries' proposal, a group of nonprofit organizations issued a counterproposal titled "Fair Use Principles for User Generated Video Content," <http://www.eff.org/files/UGC_Fair_Use_Best_Practices_0.pdf>. According to this proposal, automated content filters should be designed to incorporate protections for fair use. The proposal suggests a "three strikes" design for filtering technologies, so that user generated video content would be removed only if:

   (1)   the video track matches the video track of a copyrighted work submitted by a content owner;

(2) the audio track matches the audio track of that *same* copyrighted work; and

(3) nearly the entirely (e.g., 90% or more) of the challenged content is comprised of a single copyrighted work (i.e., a "ratio test").

> If filtering technologies are not reliably able to establish these "three strikes," further human review by the content owner should be required before content is taken down or blocked.

Fair Use Principles, *supra*, ¶2(a). What do you think of this proposal? If YouTube adopted the nonprofit organizations' proposed fair use principles, how would each of the videos in Question 4 be treated?

7. Under either proposal, manual review of the videos by the Web platform's legal staff might occur. (Do you see when and how this might happen under each proposal?) If you were responsible for manually reviewing and evaluating §512 takedown notices received by YouTube, how would you evaluate each of the videos in Question 4?

Page 602.   After the Notes and Questions, insert the following:

Note on the Google Library Project Settlement

In 2004, Google announced a project to create a searchable database containing every book that it could find. Users would be able to search the database for specific books or for books about topics of interest to them. Unlike a digital catalog, which relies on titles and keywords, the database would allow searches on the full text of included works, and would have the capability to return full-text search results. Several leading university libraries, including those at Harvard and the University of Michigan, granted Google access to scan their collections. Google stated that it would accommodate copyright interests by designing its system to return full-text search results only for public domain works. For books still under copyright, searches would return only small excerpts. After several publishers complained to Google, Google offered any copyright owner that objected to the inclusion of its works the opportunity to opt out.

The Author's Guild and several of its individual members filed a class action lawsuit against Google, arguing that the preparation of digitally scanned copies infringed their members' copyrights. Google's answer asserted a variety of defenses, including fair use. Subsequently, five member companies of the Association of American Publishers filed a separate lawsuit against Google. Before the disputes could be litigated, however, the parties agreed on a settlement, which as of this writing is awaiting the court's approval.

The settlement agreement requires Google to make cash payments to all class members whose books have been scanned, and to establish a series of payment-based models for access to the book search service by institutional users and members of the public. Google may offer some free public access via university and public libraries but may provide no more than one terminal per public library building or per 10,000 students, and it must charge users a per-page fee to print search results. The agreement creates a registry to locate copyright holders and disburse payments. At any time within the first 27 months after court approval and notice to class members, a copyright holder may request removal of particular books. Alternatively, at any time the copyright holder may change a book's status from "display" to "non-display," which means that a search result can display only standard bibliographic information for that book. However, any book that is commercially available as of the date of court approval must be classified initially as a non-display book. The book may be given "display" status only if the copyright owner requests it, or if Google can make a subsequent showing that the book is no longer commercially available. The agreement imposes on Google a duty to maintain technical security of its database according to standards to be developed by Google and host institutions and approved by the registry. Finally, the agreement allows Google to benefit from most future legislative changes to the Copyright Act but specifically excludes future changes to the fair use doctrine.

NOTES AND QUESTIONS

1. If the Google dispute had been litigated to a judgment, how do you think the court would have ruled on the fair use question? Is Google's use of the books "transformative"? In what way? How would Google's planned database have affected the actual or potential market for the books included in it?

2. Focus now on the "opt-out" system that Google devised. Should such a system weigh in favor of holding Google's copying to be fair use? Why, or why not? Should the Copyright Act be amended to allow some types of copying subject to an opt-out rule? For discussion of this question, see Oren Bracha, *Standing Copyright Law on Its Head? The Googlization of Everything and the Many Faces of Property*, 85 Tex. L. Rev. 1799 (2007).

3. What do you think of the terms of the settlement agreement between Google and the author and publisher plaintiffs? If you were the judge charged with reviewing the agreement, are there any terms that would give you pause?

4. Why do you think the settlement agreement restricts Google's ability to take advantage of future changes to the fair use doctrine? How might the agreement affect Google's participation in future copyright litigation over the meaning of fair use? How might it affect Google's lobbying behavior?

Chapter 8. Technological Protections

B. The Digital Millennium Copyright Act

Page 617. In the Notes and Questions, insert the following at the end of Question 1:

Disabling the region coding would enable users to play DVDs lawfully purchased in other countries. Would this violate §1201? See Sony Computer Entm't Am., Inc. v. Divineo Inc., 81 U.S.P.Q.2d 1045 (N.D. Cal. 2006) (holding that even though "mod chips" for video game consoles enabled some lawful uses, they had the "primary purpose" of circumventing Sony's authentication system).

Page 623. Delete the last sentence of Question 8, and replace it with the following:

For a list of DMCA-related disputes and warnings, visit the Electronic Frontier Foundation's web site at *http://www.eff.org* and search on "DMCA consequences."

Pages 623-24. Insert the following at the end of the Note on Library of Congress Rulemakings Under §1201:

The third rulemaking, completed in 2006, continued the pattern of narrowly-defined exemptions established by the first two rulemakings. The Copyright Office reiterated the requirement that proponents of exemptions prove by a preponderance of the evidence a "substantial adverse effect" on noninfringing uses. U.S. Copyright Office, Exemption to Prohibition on Circumvention of Copyright Protection Systems for Access Control Technologies: Final Rule, 71 Fed. Reg. 68,472, 68,473 (Nov. 27, 2006), codified at 37 C.F.R. §201.40. Rather than focusing solely on effects on particular works, however, the Copyright Office concluded that in some circumstances "a particular class of copyrighted works" may be defined "by reference to the type of user who may take advantage of the exemption or by reference to the type of use of the work that may be made pursuant to the exemption." Id.

Based on these criteria, the Copyright Office renewed, and in one case narrowed, three of the four previously existing exemptions. It concluded that only libraries and archives would be affected by lack of access to computer programs and video games in obsolete formats, and so narrowed the existing exemption for those works to cover only circumvention for purposes of preservation or archival reproduction. It declined to renew the exemption for lists of filtering criteria, on the ground that proponents of the exemption had relied solely on the record from the previous rulemaking and had adduced no evidence of current need. It also approved three new exemptions: one for audiovisual works included in libraries of college or university film/media studies departments, "when circumvention is accomplished for the purpose of making compilations of portions of those works for educational use in the classroom by media studies or film professors," id. at 68,474; one for computer programs that enable mobile phones to connect to wireless telephone networks, "when circumvention is accomplished for the sole purpose of lawfully connecting" to a network other than the one for which the phone was originally programmed, id. at 68,476; and one for audio and audio-visual works distributed in CD format and protected by technological measures that "create or exploit security flaws or vulnerabilities . . . when circumvention is accomplished solely for the good faith testing, investigating, or correcting such security flaws or vulnerabilities," id. at 68,477.

Pages 626-27. In the Notes and Questions:

a. Insert the following at the end of Question 1:

What do you think of the Copyright Office's conclusion that exemptions may be defined in part by classes of users? Is that approach supported by the statutory language? How does it affect the scope of approved exemptions?

b. Insert new Question 4 and renumber Questions 4-8 as Questions 5-9:

4. Legislation introduced in the 109th Congress proposed amending §1201 to allow both circumvention of technological measures and manufacture and distribution of circumvention tools where such actions are "necessary to make a noninfringing use" of a protected work and where "the copyright owner fails to make available the necessary means to make such noninfringing use without additional cost or burden" to the user. H.R. 4536, 109th Cong., 1st Sess., §5. Legislation introduced in the 110th Congress, titled the FAIR USE Act, proposes amending §1201 to add a list of specific exemptions to the circumvention ban and

the device bans. The list includes, inter alia, gaining access to a public domain work, gaining access to "a work of substantial public interest solely for purposes of criticism, comment, news reporting, scholarship, or research," and enabling transmittal of a work within a "home or personal network." H.R. 1201, 110th Cong., 1st Sess., §3(b). Would you support either of these proposals?

Page 639. In the Notes and Questions, in Question 6:

Change the citation to read Davidson & Assoc., Inc. v. Jung, 422 F.3d 630 (8th Cir. 2005).

D. Protection for Copyright Management Information

Page 643. Insert the following after Kelly v. Arriba Soft Corp.:

IQ Group, Ltd. v. Wiesner Publishing, LLC
409 F. Supp. 2d 587 (D.N.J. 2006)

[IQ, an online advertising firm, distributed ads for two insurance companies, National Senior Associate Company ("NSAC") and Capital Care, Inc. IQ included its own logo and a hyperlink to copyright information on its own web site in the ads. Both NSAC and Capital Care subsequently hired Wiesner to distribute ads for them. Wiesner distributed the same ads that IQ had formerly distributed, but it removed the IQ logo and the hyperlink to IQ's web site. IQ registered copyright in the ads and then sued Wiesner, NSAC, and Capital Care, alleging copyright infringement and violation of §1202. Wiesner moved for summary judgment on IQ's §1202 claim.]

GREENAWAY, J.: . . .
Wiesner argues that the logo and hyperlink cannot fall within the scope of the statute, as set out in 17 U.S.C. §1202(c), and asks the Court to rule on this as a matter of law.

The DMCA provision at issue, 17 U.S.C. §1202(c), defines "copyright management information" in eight categories. IQ contends that the logo falls within category 2 ("[t]he name of, and other identifying information about, the author of a work"), category 3 ("[t]he name of, and other identifying information about, the copyright owner of the work"), and category 7 ("[i]dentifying numbers or symbols referring to such information or links to such information"). IQ contends as well that the hyperlink falls within categories 3 and 7, and that the hyperlink points to a website containing information falling within category 6 ("[t]erms and conditions for use of the work"). . . .

1. THE DMCA IN THE FRAMEWORK OF TRADEMARK AND COPYRIGHT LAW

In effect, IQ asks this Court to construe the DMCA so as to allow a logo, functioning as a service mark, to come within the definition of copyright management information which, by operation of the DMCA, would act to protect the copyright of its owner. . . .

Looking only at the literal language of the statute, IQ's construction is not implausible: a logo in an email, to the extent that it operates as a trademark or service mark, could communicate information that indicates the source of the email. It is a symbol that refers to identifying information, so a very broad interpretation of §1202(c) might conceivably include a logo. The problem is that this construction allows a trademark to invoke DMCA protection of copyrights. . . .

The Supreme Court cautioned against blurring the boundaries between trademark law and copyright law in Dastar Corp. v. Twentieth Century Fox Film Corp., 539 U.S. 23 . . . (2003). . . . The Court warned that disregarding the trademark/copyright law distinction "would create a species of mutant copyright law." Id. at 34. . . .

. . . [R]ather than an interpretation of the Lanham Act, as in Dastar, IQ here seeks an interpretation of the DMCA that would blur the boundaries between copyright and trademark. Following Dastar, this Court rejects this argument. . . .

2. THE DMCA: STATUTORY INTERPRETATION OF §1202

. . .

The text of §1202 appears to define "copyright management information" quite broadly, to the point that the section, read literally, applies wherever any author has affixed anything that might refer to his or her name. Examination of the legislative history, as well as extrinsic sources, however, shows that the statute should be subject to a narrowing interpretation.

Law professor Julie E. Cohen has written widely on the DMCA and on copyright management information. See generally Julie E. Cohen, Copyright and The Jurisprudence of Self-Help, 13 Berkeley Tech. L.J. 1089 (1998). Cohen explains that, traditionally, authors have relied on copyright law to define and protect their legal rights. Now, however, new technologies can control access to works, such that technology attached to the work itself defines and protects the legal rights of the copyright owner. The DMCA directly protects not the copyrights, but the technological measures that protect the copyrights. In Cohen's view, copyright management information ("CMI") is limited to components of such technological measures.[1] This central insight is confirmed by examination of the history of §1202.

---

1. See also Julie E. Cohen, *A Right to Read Anonymously: A Closer Look at Copyright Management in Cyberspace*, 28 Conn. L. Rev. 981, 984 (1996) ("new digital monitoring and metering technologies define the burgeoning field of 'copyright management'").

It is frequently stated that Congress enacted the DMCA in order to implement the World Intellectual Property Organization ("WIPO") Copyright Treaty and the WIPO Performances and Phonograms Treaty. H.R. Rep. No. 105-551 (1998). It is true that enactment of the DMCA brought United States copyright law into compliance with these treaties. Id. Thus, the WIPO treaties are useful in understanding §1202.

The WIPO treaties mandated protection of copyright management information. According to Severine Dusollier, WIPO protected CMI as part of "a double protection for technical measures." S. Dusollier, Some Reflections on Copyright Management Information and Moral Rights, 25 Colum. J.L. & Arts 377, 382 (2003). In the framework of the WIPO treaties, technical measures such as CMI are components of automated copyright protection systems: "As digital identification systems and other technologies that enable the marking and protection of works have started to develop, rightholders have feared that these technological tools might themselves be cracked by other technologies or machines, or that they might be easily modified or removed." Id. The WIPO treaties, and hence the DMCA, protect CMI so as to protect the technological measures of copyright protection themselves. This echoes the understanding of the DMCA expressed by Cohen, supra.

Although many view the DMCA as implementing the WIPO treaties, in fact, §§1201 and 1202 were drafted prior to the treaties. President Clinton established the Information Infrastructure Task Force ["IITF"] in 1993 with the mandate to develop comprehensive information technology policies and programs that would promote the development of the national information infrastructure ("NII"). . . .

Released in September, 1995, and known as the "White Paper," the Report [of the IITF's Working Group on Intellectual Property Rights] presented a draft of §§1201and 1202, and discussed the rationale for these sections:

> Systems for managing rights in works are being contemplated in the development of the NII. These systems will serve the functions of tracking and monitoring uses of copyrighted works as well as licensing of rights and indicating attribution, creation and ownership interests. A combination of file- and system-based access controls using encryption technologies, digital signatures and steganography[2] are, and will continue to be, employed by owners of works to address copyright management concerns. . . .
>
> To implement these rights management functions, information will likely be included in digital versions of a work (i.e., copyright management information) to inform the user about the authorship and ownership of a work (e.g., attribution information) as well as to indicate authorized uses of the work (e.g., permitted use information). For instance, information may be included in an "electronic envelope" containing a work that provides information regarding authorship, copyright ownership, date of creation or last modification, and terms and conditions of authorized uses. As measures for this purpose become incorporated at lower levels (e.g., at the operating system level), such information may become a fundamental component of a file or information object.

---

2. As explained in the Report, steganography is digital watermarking. (*Id.* 188.)

Once information such as this is affiliated with a particular information object (e.g., data constituting the work) and readily accessible, users will be able to easily address questions over licensing and use of the work. For example, systems for electronic licensing may be developed based on the attribution or permitted use information associated with an information object.

(Id. 191-192.)

The White Paper understood "copyright management information" to be information about authorship, ownership, and permitted uses of a work that is included in digital versions of the work so as to implement "rights management functions" of "rights management systems." Such systems are conceived of as electronic and automated within the environment of a computer network. . . .

The White Paper demonstrates that the Working Group on Intellectual Property Rights, in drafting §1202, understood this section to protect the integrity of automated copyright management systems functioning within a computer network environment. . . .

The draft legislation presented in the White Paper was introduced in both houses of Congress immediately upon its release as the "The National Information Infrastructure Copyright Protection Act" ("NIICPA"). . . . As Congress developed the DMCA, the NIICPA was incorporated into it. Section[] . . . 1202 underwent no significant revision between drafting in 1995 and enactment in 1998 under section 103 of the DMCA, Public Law 105-304.

The Congressional committees which considered the DMCA published a number of reports on the Act relevant to §§1201 and 1202. There is little discussion, however, of §1202. The Senate Committee Report provides this commentary:

> Rights management information is "information which identifies the work, the author of the work, the owner of any right in the work, or information about the terms and conditions of use of the work . . . which is attached to a copy of a work or appears in connection with communication of the work to the public." Art. 12. Rights management information is more commonly referred to in the U.S. as copyright management information (CMI). The purpose of CMI is to facilitate licensing of copyright for use on the Internet and to discourage piracy.
>
> [CMI] is an important element in establishing an efficient Internet marketplace in copyrighted works free from governmental regulation. Such information will assist in tracking and monitoring uses of copyrighted works, as well as licensing of rights and indicating attribution, creation and ownership.
>
> Under the bill, CMI includes such items as the title of the work, the author, the copyright owner, and in some instances, the writer, performer, and director. CMI need not be in digital form, but CMI in digital form is expressly included.

S. Rep. No. 105-190 (1998). Viewed alone, this gives only a vague idea as to what copyright management information is and how it functions. It is, however, consistent with the understanding established supra, as it emphasizes the role of such information in facilitating licensing on the Internet, discouraging piracy, and establishing an efficient Internet marketplace. There is nothing to suggest that the

Senate Committee understood §1202 differently from the Working Group, as protecting the integrity of automated copyright management systems functioning within a computer network environment.

Similarly, the House Committee stated: "A new 'Section 1202' to the Copyright Act is required by both WIPO Treaties to ensure the integrity of the electronic marketplace by preventing fraud and misinformation." H.R. Rep. No. 105-551 (1998). This committee report, in addressing a different DMCA section, states: "It may, in appropriate circumstances include the absence of customary indicia of ownership or authorization, such as a standard and accepted digital watermark or other copyright management information." Id. This shows that Congress viewed a digital watermark as an example of copyright management information. . . .

This interpretation of §1202 makes sense additionally because it fits §1201 with §1202, and with chapter 12 as a whole. . . .

. . . [T]raditionally, the rights of authors have been managed by people, who have controlled access and reproduction. Through scientific advances, we now have technological measures that can control access and reproduction of works, and thereby manage the rights of copyright owners and users. Section 1202 operates to protect copyright by protecting a key component of some of these technological measures. It should not be construed to cover copyright management performed by people, which is covered by the Copyright Act, as it preceded the DMCA; it should be construed to protect copyright management performed by the technological measures of automated systems.

Under this interpretation of §1202, this Court must determine whether the information removed by Wiesner from the NSAC and Capital Care ads functioned as a component of an automated copyright protection or management system. IQ has presented no evidence on this matter that creates a genuine issue as to a material fact for trial. This Court finds no genuine issue as to a material fact and therefore Wiesner is entitled to judgment as a matter of law. . . .

[The court also denied IQ's motion for summary judgment on its copyright infringement claim against Wiesner because copyright ownership of the ads was disputed.]

Pages 643-44. In the Notes and Questions, renumber Question 3 as Question 4 and insert the following as Question 3:

3. In *McClatchey v. Associated Press*, 82 U.S.P.Q.2d 790 (W.D. Pa. 2007), the court held that as a matter of statutory construction, §1202 must protect non-digital information: ". . . Section 1202(c) defines the term [copyright management information] broadly to include 'any' of the information set forth in the eight categories, 'including in digital form.' To avoid rendering those terms superfluous, the statute must also protect non-digital information." Id. at 1195. In *McClatchey*, the plaintiff had used a computer program to place a title and copyright notice on a photograph she had taken. The defendant allegedly took a photo of plaintiff's photograph and cropped it to remove the title and copyright notice. The court refused to grant summary judgment to the defendant. Would

the IQ Group court agree with this holding? Which court's interpretation of §1202 is more convincing? How would you apply each to the following hypotheticals:

    a. IQ placed copyright notices on the ads themselves and Wiesner removed the information.

    b. Textile Co. placed a copyright notice on its fabric's selvage (the border of the fabric that is cut off and discarded) and when it sold the fabric, also attached a tag stating that the design was a copyrighted work of Textile Co. Ya-Ya Brand Inc. purchased the fabric, removed the selvage and the tag, and resold the fabric. See Textile Secrets Int'l, Inc. v. Ya-Ya Brand Inc., 524 F. Supp. 2d 1184 (C.D. Cal. 2007) (notice and tag not covered by §1202).

    c. Review the Note on Open Source Software and Creative Commons, pages 198-200 of the casebook. When selecting a particular Creative Commons license, the author may "attach" the license to the work by embedding code that will generate the license symbol, a short description of the license, and a hyperlink to the full description of the license on the Creative Commons website. Joe downloads a work made available under a Creative Commons license and removes the information.

E.   Converging Technologies: Digital Television and the Broadcast Flag

Page 646.   In the Notes and Questions, insert new Question 5:

5. Some music industry interests have proposed that Congress mandate the creation of an "audio broadcast flag" for digital radio transmissions. Like the video broadcast flag proposal, this one failed to make significant headway prior to the 2006 congressional elections. Would you support an "audio broadcast flag" requirement? Are the policy considerations identical?"

Chapter 9. State Law Theories of Protection, and Their Limits

C. The Right of Publicity

Pages 683-84. In the Notes and Questions, insert new Question 5:

5. In *Facenda v. N.F.L. Films, Inc.*, 542 F.3d 1007 (3d Cir. 2008) the estate of John Facenda sued NFL Films for violation of Pennsylvania's statutory right of publicity for its use of Facenda's voice in a program about the making of the video game Madden NFL '06. Facenda had signed a release granting NFL Films "the unequivocal rights to use the audio and visual film sequences" he had recorded "or any part of them . . . in perpetuity and by whatever media or manner NFL Films . . . sees fit, provided, however, such use does not constitute an endorsement of any product or service." *Id.* at 1012. The court held that §301 did not preempt the right of publicity claim because the Pennsylvania statute required an extra element—a showing of commercial value. Additionally, the court looked to *Midler* for support in holding that Facenda's voice was not within the subject matter of copyright.

In finding no implied preemption, the court adopted a test suggested by the Nimmer copyright treatise. The first prong of the test considers whether the copyrighted work was used for "purposes of trade'" or in an expressive work: Nimmer argues that courts generally have held the right of publicity claim not preempted in the former case and preempted in the latter. 1 Nimmer on Copyright §1.01[B][3][b][iv][I], at 1-88.2(9) to (11). The court found NFL Films' use of the sequences in a "22-minute promotional piece akin to advertising [did] not count as an expressive work . . . suggest[ing] that conflict preemption [would be] inappropriate. . . . " *Facenda*, 542 F.3d at 1030.

Under the second prong of the test, courts are to consider the effect of a contract, and particularly

the purposes of the use to which the plaintiff initially consented when signing over the copyright in a contract. . . . [T]he proper question in cases involving advertising and a contract . . . is whether the plaintiff "collaborated in the creation of a copyrighted advertising product." 1 Nimmer on Copyright §1.01[B][3][b][iv][II], at 1-88.2(20). If the plaintiff did [so] collaborate . . . then the party holding the copyright is in a very strong position to contend that allowing the plaintiff to assert a right of publicity against use of its likeness in advertising would interfere with the rights it acquired.

Id. at 1030. The court found that Facenda had not consented to use of the sequences in advertisements for football video games and that the release "did not implicitly waive his right to publicity, the core of which is the right not to have one's identity used in advertisements." *Id.* at 1031.

The *Facenda* court considered its holding consistent with *Laws*. Do you agree? What do you think of Nimmer's test? How should NFL Films revise its release form to avoid this problem in the future?

E. Contract

Pages 699-718. Replace Section E with the following:

Contracts involving copyrighted material are ubiquitous. Indeed, all of the copyright industries described in Chapter 1 of the casebook rely on the existence and enforcement of more or less intricate contractual arrangements to order their affairs. The legislative history of §301 indicates that at least some members of Congress did not intend the 1976 Act to preempt claims for breach of contract. However, because one can infer little from that history, questions of preemption of contractual terms continue to arise.

In cases involving claims of breach of contract and defenses of copyright preemption, it is important to keep separate arguments about the existence of the contract itself. As you learned in your first-year contracts class, if there is no enforceable contract, there can be no breach. Furthermore, even if the contract is enforceable generally, a court may refuse to enforce particular terms under contract law doctrines such as unconscionability. Preemption of the breach of contract claim is a different kind of defense. A defense based on preemption argues that even if there is an otherwise enforceable contract, a court may not entertain the state law claim of breach of contract because it is preempted by the Copyright Act.

When applying an extra-element style of preemption analysis under §301, some courts analyze the act that allegedly constitutes the breach: If that act violates one of the exclusive rights under §106 (such as copying), a court may hold the breach of contract claim preempted. In contrast, where the allegedly breaching act does not also infringe a §106 right, the court may hold the breach of contract claim not preempted. For example, in *National Car Rental System Inc. v. Computer Associates International, Inc.*, 991 F.2d 426 (8th Cir.), *cert. denied*, 510 U.S. 861 (1993), the court held that a claim alleging that the defendant breached a software license agreement by using the program to process data for third parties was not preempted:

> CA [i.e., Computer Associates,] does not claim that National is doing something that the copyright laws reserve exclusively to the copyright holder, or that the use restriction is breached "by the mere act of reproduction, performance, distribution or display." Instead . . . CA must be read to claim that National's or EDS's processing of data for third parties is the . . . act [prohibited under their contract]. None of the exclusive copyright rights grant CA that right of their own force. Absent the parties' agreement, this restriction would not exist. Thus, CA is alleging that the contract creates a right not existing under the copyright law, a right based upon National's promise, and that it is suing to protect that contractual right.

Id. at 433. To similar effect is *Kabehie v. Zoland*, 102 Cal. App. 4th, 513 (2002). There, the court explained:

> . . . A right that is qualitatively different from copyright includes a right to payment, a right to royalties, or any other independent covenant. . . . If, however, the promise is equivalent to copyright, the breach of the promise is not the extra element making the action qualitatively different from copyright. In such a case, there is simply no consideration for the promise. The promisor has merely agreed to do that which the promisor is already obligated to do under federal copyright law.

Id. at 528.

Other courts take a different approach, focusing not on the act that constitutes the breach but rather on the existence of the contract itself. These courts hold that the distinguishing characteristics of a contract — i.e., existence of a promise, mutual assent, and consideration — render a cause of action for breach of contract qualitatively different from one for copyright infringement. *See, e.g., Taquino v. Teledyne Monarch Rubber*, 893 F.2d 1488, 1501 (5th Cir. 1990) ("contract promise" renders breach of contract action qualitatively different from copyright infringement claim); *Architectronics, Inc. v. Control Sys., Inc.*, 935 F. Supp. 425, 438-39 (S.D.N.Y. 1996) (same). Using this type of analysis, the contract claim would rarely be preempted.

Note on Contract Formation Issues and Preemption Analysis

The most difficult preemption questions involving contracts have arisen as a result of contracting practices rarely used before enactment of the 1976 Act. As you learned in Chapter 4 of the casebook, software is easily copied and software providers were uncertain whether they could successfully claim intellectual property protection for the information embodied in mass-marketed software products. They began to distribute their software with "end user license agreements" (EULAs) that prohibited end users from engaging in a variety of practices, some of which would be permissible under the Copyright Act. More recently, other providers of digital content also have begun to adopt the practice of using

EULAs. These take a variety of forms, including agreements printed on the package itself (shrinkwraps), electronic agreements allegedly accepted by the user's clicking "I agree" (clickwraps), and electronic agreements allegedly accepted by some act like downloading (browsewraps).

Are any of these "agreements" enforceable under contract law? Some early cases labeled shrinkwraps contracts of adhesion unenforceable in the absence of a state statute. In recent years, however, courts have become increasingly willing to hold, in particular, shrinkwrap and clickwrap agreements to be enforceable contracts under the common law of contract or the Uniform Commercial Code (UCC).

In *ProCD, Inc. v. Zeidenberg*, 86 F.3d 1447 (7th Cir. 1996), the court addressed a preemption challenge to a contract action based on a shrinkwrap EULA. *ProCD* marketed a database on CD-ROM that contained a white-pages directory that the court assumed was not copyrightable. ProCD charged one price to commercial users and a lower one to consumers. Those who purchased the consumer package were prohibited from engaging in commercial use of the database under the terms of a license "encoded on [] CD-ROM disks as well as printed in the manual, and which appear[ed] on a user's screen every time the software [ran]." *Id.* at 1450. Zeidenberg purchased the consumer version and used it commercially by marketing the database on the Internet for a lower price than ProCD charged for its commercial version. The court held the license an enforceable contract and the breach of contract action not preempted. Although the *ProCD* court rested its holding on §301 of the Copyright Act and cited both *National Car Rental* and *Taquino* favorably, it did not emphasize either the nature of the act breaching the agreement or the existence of a promise, mutual assent, or consideration. The court stated:

> Rights "equivalent to any of the exclusive rights within the general scope of copyright" are rights established *by law* — rights that restrict the options of persons who are strangers to the author. Copyright law forbids duplication, public performance, and so on, unless the person wishing to copy or perform the work gets permission; silence means a ban on copying. A copyright is a right against the world. Contracts, by contrast, generally affect only their parties; strangers may do as they please, so contracts do not create "exclusive rights."

Id. at 1454 (emphasis in original).

This approach is reminiscent of the cases under the Supremacy Clause that you read in Section 9.A of the casebook. One theme that runs through those cases is that a state may not constitutionally employ a scheme of protection that essentially competes with a federal system of protection. Because contracts only affect the parties to them, state enforcement of them should not implicate such concerns. The *ProCD* ruling extends this traditional view to shrinkwrap contracts. At the same time, the *ProCD* court "refrain[ed] from adopting a rule that anything with the label 'contract' is necessarily outside the preemption clause: the variations and possibilities are too numerous to foresee. . . . [S]ome applications of the law of contract could interfere with the attainment of national objectives and therefore come within the domain of §301(a). But general enforcement of shrinkwrap licenses . . . does not create such interference." *Id.* at 1455.

NOTES AND QUESTIONS

1. Are the *National Car Rental* and *ProCD* approaches consistent? If not, which do you find more persuasive? Is it possible to reconcile them? Note that *National Car Rental* involved a copyrighted program and *ProCD* an uncopyrighted database. One might frame *National Car Rental* as raising the question whether one can enter into restrictive contracts that provide more protection to copyrighted material than copyright law would. *ProCD* raises the question whether parties can create private copyright-like rights in data that the public federal law has deemed unworthy of protection. Should both situations be assessed in the same way for preemption purposes?

2. What pro-competitive function did the contract in *ProCD* serve? Did the contract in *National Car Rental* also serve a pro-competitive function?

3. In *ProCD*, the court envisions copyright and contract as co-existing in part because contracts bind only the parties to them and thus do not create rights against the world in the same way that copyright law does. Is that the case even in *ProCD*? When the contract is encoded on a CD-ROM, even the person who picks the CD up on the street will have to accept the terms of the license before using the software. Should this matter to the preemption analysis? Should negotiated agreements be assessed differently from standard-form agreements in a preemption analysis? If either the rightful possessor or the person who finds the CD on the street employs techniques to circumvent the license and obtain access to the software without agreeing to the terms, is the DMCA violated?

4. The majority of commentators disagreed vehemently with both *ProCD*'s contract and copyright law holdings. Consider the following, written by Professor Niva Elkin-Koren:

> . . . [R]estrictions imposed by copyright law are limited and reflect the balance between the need to induce creation and the need to guarantee public access to information. If copyright owners are free to use contractual agreements to restrict use, and are then able to use copyright to prevent any use that is not subject to these restrictions, owners are gaining absolute monopoly over their works.
>
> When owners exercise absolute monopoly, users' choices become very limited. . . . [V]aluable uses . . . may not occur under a contractual regime. . . .
>
> [T]he low standard of assent that *ProCD* . . . held to be sufficient for contract formation does not promote competition over the terms.

Niva Elkin-Koren, *Copyright Policy and the Limits of Freedom of Contract*, 12 Berkeley Tech. L.J. 93, 109-10 (1997).

Professor Elkin-Koren stresses that markets for information are different from markets for other products. "[O]nce information is produced, it is socially optimal to maximize its use by the public. To the extent that on-line dissemination replaces current distribution channels . . . this information could become subject to license restrictions. In the absence of alternatives . . . our current capacity to access information at low cost will be restricted." *Id.* at 111. She argues that contractual restrictions coupled with on-line distribution featuring fees for every use will hamper creativity and cause information deprivation and inequality. *Id.* at 112. Do you agree? If so, what should copyright law or any other law do about it? More specifically, how should these concerns affect the preemption analysis?

5. Another way to understand the preemption issue in the contractual context is as a conflict between two schools of thought. Professor O'Rourke describes them as follows:

> One view . . . contends that copyright merely provides a bundle of rights to copyright owners to help them avoid the transaction costs of contracting with each purchaser of the copyrighted material. In this model, copyright functions much like . . . a boilerplate contract to govern the parties' relationship in the absence of a contrary agreement. Nothing prevents the parties from . . . creating their own property rights through private contract. . . .
>
> Another view . . . argues that copyright represents a legislative scheme carefully balanced to advance the public interest by providing an incentive to authors to create while safeguarding the free flow of the information on which such creativity is based. In this model, there are immutable rules around which the parties cannot contract because the public interest cannot be sacrificed on the altar of two-party agreements. The problem is in defining exactly which provisions of the copyright law are immutable and which are not, in a manner more definitive than simply stating, "We know immutable rules when we see them." . . .

Maureen A. O'Rourke, *Copyright Preemption After the* ProCD *Case: A Market-Based Approach*, 12 Berkeley Tech. L.J. 53, 77-79 (1997).

Is there a happy medium between the two extremes? Professor O'Rourke argues that there is. Instead of a blanket rule for or against preemption, she suggests that courts should integrate market considerations into the preemption inquiry to determine whether the particular term is reasonable within the particular market and what impact it has on the incentives of others to create similar works. *See id.* at 88-89 (styling this a "reverse" fair use inquiry). Would a market-based preemption test make sense as a policy matter? Is there any authority for such an approach in the statute or the Supremacy Clause?

6. Review the Note on Open Source Software and Creative Commons, Chapter 3.D, pages 198-200 of the casebook. The open source and creative commons movements rely on a combination of copyright law and contract to enforce norms of openness. Are "copyleft" licenses, which require licensees to distribute their derivative works under the same copyleft terms, enforceable? Don't they restrict the licensee's freedom to exercise its own copyright rights and user privileges? Under the GNU General Public License (GPL) offered by the Free Software Foundation, identifiable sections of the new work that are not derived from copyleft protected programs need not be distributed under the GNU GPL if those identifiable sections are distributed as separate works. <http://www.fsf.org/licensing/licenses/gpl.txt>. Does this clause fully address concerns you might have about the enforceability of such a copyleft license?

7. The National Conference of Commissioners on Uniform State Laws (NCCUSL) worked for a number of years on a uniform law to govern transactions in software and computer information products, many (if not most) of which are copyrighted. The eventual result of NCCUSL's efforts was the Uniform Computer Information Transactions Act (UCITA), which was adopted in only two states and is now widely regarded as unsuccessful. The American Law Institute (ALI) has since undertaken a Principles project in the area of software contracting. Like UCITA, the Principles would permit contract formation as in the *ProCD* case. Principles of the Law of Software Contracts §§2.01-2.02 (Proposed Final Draft 2009). Although the Principles do not direct a court to hold any particular provisions of negotiated or standard-form contracts preempted, they note: "[P]reemption issues are heightened when software is distributed under take-it-or-leave-it standard-form agreements that, by virtue of state enforcement, more closely resemble state legislation competing with the federal scheme than a bargain between two parties." *Id.* §1.09 cmt. a. They also attempt to provide extensive commentary and illustrations to help a court analyze preemption questions. *Id.* §1.09.

8. Keep in mind that if the copyrighted work is sold rather than licensed (see the discussion of the first sale doctrine, *supra* pages 403-08), the issue whether copyright law preempts a breach of contract action simply does not arise.

Remember also that it is critical to consider how the particular court analyzes the question of the appropriate cause of action. Recall the *Jacobsen* case excerpted *supra* pages 380-83. If a claim is based on a covenant, then breach of contract is the appropriate action. If it is based on a condition, then some courts would say that the appropriate cause of action is in copyright infringement. Others would permit both the contract and copyright causes of action to proceed so long as the recovery is not duplicative and the breach of contract action not preempted.

Note on Contractual Provisions Against Reverse Engineering

The *Kewanee Oil* case that you read on pages 657-60 of the casebook held that patent law does not preempt enforcement of an appropriate state trade secret law. There, the Court emphasized that there is little risk of inventors' choosing state trade secret law over the federal patent law in part because trade secret law does not preclude discovery of the secret by independent means or by reverse engineering.

As you know, software providers often rely on trade secret protection. Many also distribute only the object code version of programs. A programmer can reverse engineer object code to discover information about how the program works.

Providers thus often include provisions against reverse engineering in both EU-LAs and negotiated agreements.

In *Vault Corp. v. Quaid Software Ltd.*, 847 F.2d 255 (5th Cir. 1988), the court addressed copyright preemption challenges to Louisiana's Software License Enforcement Act, which allowed software providers to enforce certain terms so long as they were contained in a license that accompanied the software. At issue specifically was whether Vault could enforce a shrinkwrap license's prohibition, authorized by the statute, against decompilation and disassembly (both types of reverse engineering) that the statute authorized. The Fifth Circuit stated:

> In *Sears, Roebuck & Co. v. Stiffel Co.*, 376 U.S. 225 . . . (1964), the Supreme Court held that "[w]hen state law touches upon the area of [patent or copyright statutes], it is 'familiar doctrine' that the federal policy 'may not be set at naught, or its benefits denied' by the state law." . . . Section 117 of the Copyright Act permits an owner of a computer program to make an adaptation of that program [under certain circumstances.] The provision in Louisiana's License Act, which permits a software producer to prohibit the adaptation of its licensed computer program by decompilation or disassembly, conflicts with the rights of computer program owners under §117 and clearly "touches upon an area" of federal copyright law. For this reason . . . we hold that at least this provision of Louisiana's License Act is preempted by federal law, and thus that the restriction in Vault's license agreement against decompilation or disassembly is unenforceable.

Id. at 269-70.

As you read in Chapter 7 of the casebook, pages 562-70, over time courts began to consider reverse engineering a fair use under certain circumstances. Also over time, the Federal Circuit clarified that it considers software patentable subject matter. *See In re Bilski*, 545 F.3d 943 (Fed. Cir. 2008) (en banc) (clarifying the proper test to apply to determine patent eligibility in the software context); *Eolas Techs., Inc. v. Microsoft Corp.*, 399 F.3d 1325, 1339 (Fed. Cir. 2005); *AT&T v. Excel Commc'ns*, 172 F.3d 1352 (Fed. Cir. 1999); *State St. Bank & Trust v. Signature Fin. Servs.*, 149 F.3d 1368 (Fed. Cir. 1998). Given *Vault* and these other trends, many thought a copyright preemption challenge to a breach of contract claim based on a EULA provision banning reverse engineering would likely succeed. Consider the following case.

Bowers v. Baystate Technologies, Inc.
320 F.3d 1317 (Fed. Cir.), *cert. denied*, 539 U.S. 928 (2003)

[Bowers marketed patented software under a license that prohibited reverse engineering. Baystate marketed competing patented software and sued Bowers for a declaratory judgment of non-infringement, invalidity, or unenforceability of the Bowers patent. Bowers counterclaimed for, *inter alia*, copyright infringement and breach of contract, alleging that Baystate had reverse engineered Bowers' software in violation of the agreement. The jury found Baystate had infringed Bowers' copyright and breached the contract. Baystate appealed.]

RADER, J. . . . Baystate contends that the Copyright Act preempts the prohibition of reverse engineering embodied in Mr. Bowers' shrink-wrap license agreements. . . . This court holds that, under First Circuit law,* the Copyright Act does not preempt or narrow the scope of Mr. Bowers' contract claim.

Courts respect freedom of contract and do not lightly set aside freely-entered agreements. . . . The First Circuit does not interpret [§301] to require preemption as long as "a state cause of action requires an extra element, beyond mere copying, preparation of derivative works, performance, distribution or display." *Data Gen. Corp. v. Grumman Sys. Support Corp.*, 36 F.3d 1147, 1164, 32 USPQ2d 1385, 1397 (1st Cir.1994) . . .

The First Circuit has not addressed expressly whether the Copyright Act preempts a state law contract claim that restrains copying. . . . [M]ost courts to examine this issue have found that the Copyright Act does not preempt contractual constraints on copyrighted articles. *See, e.g., ProCD, Inc. v. Zeidenberg*, 86 F.3d 1447 . . . (7th Cir.1996).

. . . This court believes that the First Circuit would follow the reasoning of *ProCD* and the majority of other courts to consider this issue. This court, therefore, holds that the Copyright Act does not preempt Mr. Bowers' contract claims.

In making this determination, this court has left untouched the conclusions reached in *Atari Games v. Nintendo* regarding reverse engineering as a statutory fair use exception to copyright infringement. *Atari Games Corp. v. Nintendo of America, Inc.*, 975 F.2d 832 . . . (Fed.Cir.1992). In *Atari*, this court stated that . . . "[t]he legislative history of section 107 suggests that courts should adapt the fair use exception to accommodate new technological innovations." *Atari*, 975 F.2d at 843. This court noted "[a] prohibition on all copying whatsoever would stifle the free flow of ideas without serving any legitimate interest of the copyright holder." *Id.* Therefore, this court held "reverse engineering object code to discern the unprotectable ideas in a computer program is a fair use." *Id.* Application of the First Circuit's view distinguishing a state law contract claim having additional elements of proof from a copyright claim does not alter the findings of *Atari*. Likewise, this claim distinction does not conflict with the expressly defined circumstances in which reverse engineering is not copyright infringement under 17 U.S.C. §1201(f) (section of the Digital Millennium Copyright Act) and 17 U.S.C. §906 (section directed to mask works).

Moreover, while the Fifth Circuit has held a state law prohibiting all copying of a computer program is preempted by the federal Copyright Act, *Vault Corp. v. Quaid Software, Ltd.*, 847 F.2d 255 (5th Cir.1988), no evidence suggests the First Circuit would extend this concept to include private contractual agreements supported by mutual assent and consideration. The First Circuit recognizes contractual waiver of affirmative defenses and statutory rights. . . . Thus, case law indicates the First Circuit would find that private parties are free to contractually forego the limited ability to reverse engineer a software product under the ex-

---

* [When dealing with issues that are outside the exclusive jurisdiction of the Federal Circuit, the court applies the law of the circuit from which the appeal is taken, here, the First Circuit. — Eds.]

emptions of the Copyright Act. Of course, a party bound by such a contract may elect to efficiently breach the agreement in order to ascertain ideas in a computer program unprotected by copyright law. Under such circumstances, the breaching party must weigh the benefits of breach against the arguably de minimus [*sic*] damages arising from merely discerning non-protected code. . . .

In this case, the contract unambiguously prohibits "reverse engineering." . . .

The record amply supports the jury's finding of a breach of that agreement. . . .

DYK, Circuit Judge, concurring in part and dissenting in part.

I join the majority opinion except insofar as it holds that the contract claim is not preempted by federal law. . . . The majority's approach permits state law to eviscerate an important federal copyright policy reflected in the fair use defense, and the majority's logic threatens other federal copyright policies as well. I respectfully dissent.

I . . .

The test for preemption by copyright law, like the test for patent law preemption, should be whether the state law "substantially impedes the public use of the otherwise unprotected" material. *Bonito Boats, Inc. v. Thunder Craft Boats, Inc.*, 489 U.S. 141, 157, 167 . . . (1989) (state law at issue was preempted because it "substantially restrict[ed] the public's ability to exploit ideas that the patent system mandates shall be free for all to use."); *Sears, Roebuck & Co. v. Stiffel Co.*, 376 U.S. 225, 231-32 . . . (1964). *See also Eldred v. Ashcroft*, 537 U.S. 186 . . . (2003) (applying patent precedent in copyright case). In the copyright area, the First Circuit has adopted an "equivalent in substance" test to determine whether a state law is preempted by the Copyright Act. *Data Gen. Corp. v. Grumman Sys. Support Corp.* 36 F.3d 1147, 1164-65 (1st Cir.1994). . . . "[A]n action is equivalent in substance to a copyright infringement claim [and thus preempted by the Copyright Act] where the additional element merely concerns *the extent to which* authors and their licensees can prohibit unauthorized copying by third parties." *Id.* at 1165 (emphasis in original).

II . . .

We correctly held in *Atari Games Corp. v. Nintendo of America, Inc.*, 975 F.2d 832, 843 (Fed.Cir.1992), that reverse engineering constitutes a fair use under the Copyright Act. The Ninth and Eleventh Circuits have also ruled that reverse engineering constitutes fair use. *Bateman v. Mnemonics, Inc.*, 79 F.3d 1532, 1539 n. 18 (11th Cir.1996); *Sega Enters. Ltd. v. Accolade, Inc.*, 977 F.2d 1510, 1527-28 (9th Cir.1992). No other federal court of appeals has disagreed.

We emphasized in *Atari* that an author cannot achieve protection for an idea simply by embodying it in a computer program. . . . [T]he fair use defense for reverse engineering is necessary so that copyright protection does not "extend to any idea, procedure, process, system, method of operation, concept, principle, or discovery, regardless of the form in which it is described, explained, illustrated, or embodied in such work," as proscribed by the Copyright Act. 17 U.S.C. §102(b) (2000).

III

A state is not free to eliminate the fair use defense. Enforcement of a total ban on reverse engineering would conflict with the Copyright Act itself by protecting otherwise unprotectable material. If state law provided that a copyright holder could bar fair use of the copyrighted material by placing a black dot on each copy of the work offered for sale, there would be no question but that the state law would be preempted. A state law that allowed a copyright holder to simply label its products so as to eliminate a fair use defense would "substantially impede" the public's right to fair use and allow the copyright holder, through state law, to protect material that the Congress has determined must be free to all under the Copyright Act. *See Bonito Boats*, 489 U.S. at 157....

I nonetheless agree with the majority opinion that a state can permit parties to contract away a fair use defense or to agree not to engage in uses of copyrighted material that are permitted by the copyright law, if the contract is freely negotiated.... A freely negotiated agreement represents the "extra element" that prevents preemption of a state law claim that would otherwise be identical to the infringement claim barred by the fair use defense of reverse engineering. *See Data Gen.*, 36 F.3d at 1164-65.

However, state law giving effect to shrinkwrap licenses is no different in substance from a hypothetical black dot law. Like any other contract of adhesion, the only choice offered to the purchaser is to avoid making the purchase in the first place.... State law thus gives the copyright holder the ability to eliminate the fair use defense in each and every instance at its option. In doing so, as the majority concedes, it authorizes "shrinkwrap agreements . . . [that] are far broader than the protection afforded by copyright law."...

IV

There is, moreover, no logical stopping point to the majority's reasoning.... If by printing a few words on the outside of its product a party can eliminate the fair use defense, then it can also, by the same means, restrict a purchaser from asserting the "first sale" defense, embodied in 17 U.S.C. §109(a), or any other of the protections Congress has afforded the public in the Copyright Act. That means that, under the majority's reasoning, state law could extensively undermine the protections of the Copyright Act.

V

The Fifth Circuit's decision in *Vault* directly supports preemption of the shrinkwrap limitation. The majority [misreads *Vault*. There,] the Fifth Circuit held that the specific provision of state law that authorized contracts prohibiting reverse engineering, decompilation, or disassembly of computer programs was preempted by federal law because it conflicted with a portion of the Copyright Act and because it "'touche[d] upon an area' of federal copyright law." 847 F.2d at 269-70 (quoting *Sears, Roebuck*, 376 U.S. at 229, 84 S.Ct. 784). From a preemption standpoint, there is no distinction between a state law that explicitly validates a contract that restricts reverse engineering (*Vault*) and general common law that permits such a restriction (as here). On the contrary, the preemption clause of the Copyright Act makes clear that it covers "any such right or equivalent right in any such work *under the common law or statutes of any State*." 17 U.S.C. §301(a) (2000) (emphasis added).

I do not read *ProCD, Inc. v. Zeidenberg*, 86 F.3d 1447 (7th Cir.1996), the only other court of appeals shrinkwrap case, as being to the contrary . . . The court saw the licensor as legitimately seeking to distinguish between personal and commercial use. . . . The court also emphasized that the license "would not withdraw any information from the public domain" because all of the information on the CD-ROM was publicly available. *Id.* at 1455.

The case before us is different from *ProCD*. The Copyright Act does not confer a right to pay the same amount for commercial and personal use. It does, however, confer a right to fair use, 17 U.S.C. §107, which we have held encompasses reverse engineering.

ProCD and the other contract cases are also careful not to create a blanket rule that all contracts will escape preemption. The court in that case emphasized that "we think it prudent to refrain from adopting a rule that anything with the label 'contract' is necessarily outside the preemption clause." . . .

I conclude that *Vault* states the correct rule; that state law authorizing shrinkwrap licenses that prohibit reverse engineering is preempted; and that the First Circuit would so hold because the extra element here "merely concerns *the extent to which* authors and their licensees can prohibit unauthorized copying by third parties." *Data Gen.*, 36 F.3d at 1165 (emphasis in original). I respectfully dissent.

NOTES AND QUESTIONS

1. Do you find the majority or the dissent in *Bowers* more convincing? Why? Do they arrive at different results because the majority focuses on §301 and the dissent on constitutional principles? Are you persuaded by the dissenter's contention that his argument is consistent with *ProCD*?

2. Would the *Vault* court have agreed with the Seventh Circuit if it had been presented with the facts of *ProCD*? *Vault* involved a preemption challenge to a state statute, while *ProCD* involved a preemption challenge to a private contract. Should this make a difference to the preemption analysis?

3. The dissent in *Bowers* would make a distinction between standard-form and negotiated agreements. Indeed, an argument that such a distinction matters has been implicit in much of this section. Should the distinction matter? One could argue that standard-form contracts permit mass-markets to form and that licensees should be deemed to have consented to terms unless the terms are unenforceable under general contract law. Thus, mass-market contracts should not

be treated differently in a preemption analysis than negotiated contracts. Do you agree? If not, articulate the reasons why you disagree.

4. Reread Note 6, Chapter 4.B, page 268 of the casebook. There we excerpted part of an article by Professor Samuelson et al., arguing that the law should protect some amount of lead time for developers to permit them to recoup their investments. In *Vault*, Vault had developed a program to prevent unauthorized copying of computer programs—customers (software vendors) would place programs on diskettes loaded with Vault's program and purchasers would need that version of the diskette to be in the drive for the vendor's program to run. Quaid developed a product that defeated Vault's protection mechanism and allowed the production of functional copies. Should Vault have been allowed to use contract law to give it sufficient protection to innovate in the first place?

How about ProCD? Zeidenberg marketed the database in direct competition with ProCD and at a lower price because Zeidenberg did not incur the costs of gathering the data. Should ProCD be able to define its own protection by contract or should it have to rely on any protection misappropriation law might give it?

5. By now, you have read *Sega Enterprises Ltd. v. Accolade, Inc.*, 977 F.2d 1510 (9th Cir. 1992), Chapter 7, pages 562-66 of the casebook. In *Sega*, the court held that §117 did not authorize disassembly of object code because such a use goes "far beyond that contemplated by CONTU and authorized by section 117." *Id.* at 1520. Is this holding consistent with *Vault*? Which court do you think is correct? In *Sega*, the court did, however, determine that in certain circumstances fair use permits the reproduction of computer software that occurs in the course of disassembly. Should it make a difference in determining preemption if the contractual clause at issue negates an express provision of the copyright statute, such as §117, or a judicial application of the fair use doctrine?

6. Fair use, of course, encompasses many acts in addition to reverse engineering under certain circumstances. In practice, very few contracts literally prohibit fair use, perhaps because fair use is so hard to define in advance of litigation. Instead, firms often try to enter into negotiated or standard-form contracts that spell out permitted and prohibited uses in detail. Some of the prohibited uses might be fair under certain circumstances. What should a court do with a preemption challenge to a breach of contract claim based on an act that copyright law would consider fair? Should courts find that the Copyright Act preempts claims of contract breach concerning clauses that purport to prohibit some types of fair use (e.g., restrictions that purport to prevent a purchaser from criticizing the copyrighted work) but not others? Does it matter for purposes of preemption that the jury had concluded that Baystate's product, allegedly created after disassembling Bowers's copyrighted software, infringed the plaintiff's copyrights? Should the merits of the infringement case affect the analysis of the preemption question?

7. Amazon recently introduced the latest version of the Kindle, its e-book reader. The Kindle now has a read-aloud feature—i.e., the Kindle itself will read

a book aloud. The Authors Guild objected to this feature, concerned that it would undercut the market for audiobooks. The Guild advised its members to negotiate contracts that would prohibit Amazon from allowing the Kindle to read their books aloud. If Amazon were to breach such a provision, how would you analyze the argument that the author's breach of contract claim is preempted by copyright law?

Chapter 10. The Copyright Infringement Lawsuit

A. Proper Court

Page 741. In the Notes and Questions, insert new Question 6:

6. Although some plaintiffs prefer to sue for breach of contract, many prefer to sue for copyright infringement when a defendant exceeds the scope of a license. A copyright infringement claim provides, *inter alia,* access to the federal courts and an array of remedies that a state breach of contract action does not. A copyright plaintiff may also assert a separate claim for breach of contract, although it may not recover twice for the same injury.

How does one know if a particular breach of a license agreement gives rise to an action for breach of contract or copyright infringement, or both? In *Sun Microsystems, Inc. v. Microsoft Corp.,* 188 F.3d 1115 (9th Cir. 1999), Sun sued Microsoft for copyright infringement based on Microsoft's failure to comply with a license provision requiring Microsoft's products to be compatible with certain Sun specifications. The Ninth Circuit stated: "Whether this is a copyright or contract case turns on whether the compatibility provisions help define the scope of the license." *Id.* at 1121. The question whether a provision is a license restriction (or condition) or a separate covenant is governed by state law. *Id.* at 1122. On remand, the district court held that under California law, the compatibility provisions were contractual covenants rather than license restrictions, relying on the language and structure of the agreement: the license was not conditional on compliance with the compatibility requirements, and the agreement's remedial scheme that provided for notice and a right to cure in the event of breach would be frustrated if Sun could sue immediately for copyright infringement. *Sun Microsystems, Inc. v. Microsoft Corp.,* 81 F. Supp. 2d 1026, 1032-33 (N.D. Cal. 2000). The appropriate cause of action was thus in breach of contract rather than copyright infringement.

Consider the following hypothetical: Ticketmaster's web site provides that its use is governed by terms available on the site and that continuing past the home page constitutes assent to those terms. The terms of use include limitations on the number of visits a user may make, a prohibition on commercial use, and prohibitions covering the use of automated devices to access the site, the use of any devices that interfere with the proper working of the site, and any other action that imposes an unreasonable burden on Ticketmaster's servers. The agreement further states "You do not have permission to access this Site in any way that violates these terms of use." RMG uses spiders to access Ticketmaster's web site, visits the site more than the terms of use permit, and causes Ticketmaster's servers to crash. Ticketmaster's in-house counsel asks you whether it should sue RMG for breach of contract, copyright infringement, or both. How would you analyze this question? Is there a contract? If so, what does it say? Since accessing a web site necessarily involves copying it, do all terms of use effectively limit the scope of a visitor's license, making any violation of those terms an act of copyright infringement? *See generally Ticketmaster L.L.C. v. RMG Techs., Inc.,* 507 F. Supp. 2d 1096 (C.D. Cal. 2007) (holding that the terms of use created a non-exclusive license and use of the web site in excess of the authorization granted therein is infringement). Do you agree?

What if the terms of use forbade circumvention of certain technological controls that Ticketmaster uses to limit access? Would violation of those terms give Ticketmaster a cause of action under the DMCA? For breach of contract? Both? *See id.* (holding that conduct violated the DMCA and not addressing viability of breach of contract action).

Page 743. In the Notes and Questions, insert the following at the end of Question 1:

As noted in Chapter 3, *supra* Supplement page 384, the Supreme Court recently granted certiorari in *In re Literary Works in Electronic Databases Copyright Litigation*, 509 F.3d 116 (2d Cir. 2007). The case involves a class action settlement relating to both registered and unregistered copyrights. In reversing the district court's approval of the class and of the settlement, the Second Circuit held that the court lacked jurisdiction to certify a class consisting of claims arising from the infringement of unregistered copyrights or to approve a settlement with respect to those claims. The Supreme Court's review is "limited to the following question: Does 17 U.S.C. §411(a) restrict the subject matter jurisdiction of the federal courts over copyright infringement actions?" *Reed Elsevier, Inc. v. Muchnick*, 129 S. Ct. 1523 (2009).

B. Proper Timing

Page 743. In the Notes and Questions, replace Question 1 with the following:

1. The question of what constitutes registration pursuant to §411 continues to divide the courts. In a lengthy opinion in *La Resolana Architects, PA v. Clay Realtors Angel Fire*, 416 F.3d 1195 (10th Cir. 2005), the Tenth Circuit adopted the so-called

"registration approach." Yet in *Prunté v. Universal Music Group*, 484 F. Supp. 2d 32 (D.D.C. 2007), the plaintiff offered as proof of ownership of a valid copyright a copy of a copyright preregistration form and an e-mail response from the Copyright Office indicating receipt of the plaintiff's application and fees. Noting that "[t]here is a split of authority among courts as to whether such evidence is sufficient to allow one to bring suit for copyright infringement," the district court disagreed with the Tenth Circuit and held that the application approach "is the correct [approach] and is in harmony with the language of the Copyright Act." *Id.* at 40. Which approach do you think is more faithful to the language of §411?

D. Proper Defendants

Page 758. Insert the following at the end of the Notes and Questions:

Note on the Sovereign Immunity of the United States

Chavez and the *Florida Prepaid* cases address state sovereign immunity. What about cases against the U.S.? May the U.S. assert a defense of sovereign immunity? Court decisions have established that the U.S. is not subject to suit by state governments or individuals in the absence of its consent. Congress, however, may choose to waive the sovereign immunity of the U.S. and has generally done so in copyright infringement cases:

> [W]henever the copyright in any work protected under the copyright laws of the United States shall be infringed by the United States, by a corporation owned or controlled by the United States, or by a contractor, subcontractor, or any person, firm, or corporation acting for the Government and with the authorization or consent of the Government, the exclusive action which may be brought for such infringement shall be an action by the copyright owner against the United States in the Court of Federal Claims for the recovery of his reasonable and entire compensation as damages for such infringement, including the minimum statutory damages as set forth in section 504(c) of title 17, United States Code.

28 U.S.C. §1498(b). This section generally limits recovery to infringements committed not more than three years before the filing of an infringement complaint or counterclaim for infringement.

Congress's waiver of the U.S.'s sovereign immunity is subject to important limitations where the copyright owner is (or was) a government employee: "[A] government employee shall have a right of action against the Government . . . except where he was in a position to order, influence, or induce use of the copyrighted work by the Government." *Id.* Also, a copyright owner has no cause of action against the government when the copyrighted work was "prepared as part of the official functions of the employee, or in the preparation of which Government time, material, or facilities were used:" *Id*. In *Blueport Co. v. United States*, 533 F.3d 1374, 1380-81 (Fed. Cir. 2008), *cert. denied*, ___ U.S. ___, 2009 WL 160640, the court held that these limitations are jurisdictional in nature — i.e., if a claim falls outside the scope of the statute's limited waiver of sovereign immunity, the court has no jurisdiction to hear the case. Thus, the federal government does not have to raise sovereign immunity as an affirmative defense and the party alleging infringement has the burden of showing that its claim is not jurisdictionally barred.

The *Blueport* case involved Air Force Sergeant Mark Davenport, who taught himself computer programming skills sufficient to enable him to write a database system in off-hours and with his own resources. He shared the program with his colleagues, posted it on an Air Force web page, and gave presentations to Air Force officers to convince them to adopt it. The Air Force became concerned about its dependence on a program, access to which was controlled by a single person. Davenport refused to give the Air Force the source code and instead assigned his rights to Blueport. Blueport sued the Air Force for copyright infringement after the Air Force hired a contractor to revise the object code. The Federal Circuit held that the Court of Federal Claims lacked jurisdiction over the case because Davenport was in a position to "order, influence, or induce" the Air Force's use of the program. *Id*. at 1382.

NOTES AND QUESTIONS

1. Why do you think the U.S. has waived sovereign immunity in copyright cases when the states have not generally done so?

2. How would you analyze the question whether the U.S. has waived sovereign immunity under the DMCA? In *Blueport*, Davenport had written an automatic expiration date into each version of the program. The Air Force extended the date by modifying the object code, so Blueport also brought a DMCA claim. The court held that the U.S. had not waived sovereign immunity for DMCA claims. The DMCA contains no such waiver, and "a claim for violation of the DMCA is not . . . a subset of claims for copyright infringement" and thus is not covered by the waiver in 28 U.S.C. §1498(b). 533 F.3d 1374, 1383-84 (Fed. Cir. 2008), *cert. denied*, ___ U.S. ___, 2009 WL 160640.

Page 758. In the Notes and Questions, insert new Question 7:

7. The United States government also enjoys the protection of sovereign immunity but has expressly consented to suit in the Court of Federal Claims for alleged infringements of copyrights. 28 U.S.C. §1498(b). That express statutory waiver of sovereign immunity does not, however, apply to claims for monetary relief brought pursuant to the DMCA. *See Blueport Co. v. United States*, 71 Fed. Cl. 768 (2006).

F.   International Issues

Page 768.   In the Notes and Questions:

a.   At the end of Question 5, insert the following:

After a rehearing en banc, the Ninth Circuit reversed the district court decision, but the judges disagreed on the reason for reversal. *Yahoo! Inc. v. La Ligue Contre le Racisme et l'anti-sémitisme*, 433 F.3d 1199 (9th Cir. 2006). Some thought the case was not ripe for adjudication, while others would have dismissed for lack of personal jurisdiction over the French organization.

b.   Replace Questions 6-7 with the following and renumber Question 7 as Question 8:

6. Questions about the standard for enforcement of foreign judgments are likely to continue to arise in U.S. courts. In *Sarl Louis Feraud International v. Viewfinder, Inc.*, 489 F.3d 474 (2d Cir. 2007), the court addressed the question whether a French judgment against a web site operator should be enforced under New York's Uniform Foreign Money Judgment Recognition Act. Several design houses had filed suit against Viewfinder in Paris for posting photographs of fashion shows at which the designers' fashions were exhibited. *Id.* at 476-77. The French court issued a default judgment against Viewfinder, finding that the photos had been posted without authorization and that Viewfinder had "committed 'parasitism' under French law because it had 'take[n] advantage of plaintiff's reputation and commercial efforts creating confusion. . . .'" *Id.* at 477.

The district court held the French judgment unenforceable as repugnant to New York's public policy because it violated Viewfinder's First Amendment rights. *Id.* at 477-78. The Second Circuit vacated the judgment and set forth the mode of analysis the district court is to use on remand:

> In deciding whether the French Judgments are repugnant to the public policy of New York, the district court should first determine the level of First Amendment protection required by New York public policy when a news entity engages in the unauthorized use of intellectual property [like that] at issue here. Then, it should determine whether the French intellectual property regime provides comparable protections.

Id. at 481-82.

Is this a helpful analysis? Should the district court enforce the judgment if it finds that the use would be fair under U.S. law? What if the use would not be fair? Review note 3 on page 767 of the casebook. What if the designs at issue would not be copyrightable under U.S. law? Should a court apply the same principles to choice of law issues as to the issue of enforcement of a foreign judgment?

7. Even beyond the on-line environment, the question of jurisdiction is important in an era in which many transactions cross national borders. To reduce legal uncertainty, parties to such transactions often include jurisdictional provisions in their contracts, and similar provisions may appear in end user shrinkwrap and clickwrap licenses. The Hague Conference on Private International Law's Draft Convention on Jurisdiction and Foreign Judgments in Civil and Commercial Matters, finalized in 2005, attempted to promulgate uniform rules for interpreting choice of forum clauses and recognizing and enforcing foreign judgments. In general, it required that choice of forum clauses be enforced and foreign judgments honored, but it excluded from its ambit choice of forum clauses in consumer contracts involving natural persons. The Draft Convention did not attract much support. The Conference then drafted a Convention on Choice of Court Agreements limited to business to business contracts and excluding disputes regarding the validity of registered intellectual property rights. To date, only Mexico has adopted this Convention.

The American Law Institute (ALI) recently gave final approval to a work entitled "Intellectual Property: Principles Governing Jurisdiction, Choice of Law, and Judgments in Transnational Disputes." The Principles generally require the enforcement of choice of forum and choice of law agreements with special safeguards in the case of mass-market agreements. In such agreements, the clause at issue must be "reasonable and readily accessible to the nondrafting party at the time the agreement was concluded. . . ." Principles §§202, 302. The Principles provide a list of factors for a court to consider in determining reasonableness. *See id.* The Principles also do not permit application of "particular rules of foreign law . . . if such application leads to a result in the forum State that is repugnant to the public policy in that State." *Id.* §322. With respect to enforcement of judgments, the Principles provide that a court should enforce a judgment rendered by a foreign court if the foreign court applied the Principles to the case. *Id.* §401(1)(a). Otherwise, the court should determine enforceability based on its ordinary rules regarding enforcement of foreign judgments. *Id.* §401(1)(b). The Principles do not become law unless and until a court adopts them. Should courts do so?

G. Civil Remedies

Pages 769-76. Replace Section G.1 with the following:

1. Injunctions

Read §502, which authorizes injunctions in copyright cases. In the U.S., injunctive relief is rooted in well-established principles of equity. This remedy can be traced back to the British Courts of Equity, where injunctions were readily granted in copyright cases.

In the U.S., in non-copyright cases, courts balance four factors in determining whether to grant an injunction. Although the precise formulation of these factors varies, a plaintiff generally must show: "(1) that it has suffered an irreparable injury; (2) that remedies available at law, such as monetary damages, are inadequate to compensate for that injury; (3) that, considering the balance of hardships between the plaintiff and defendant, a remedy in equity is warranted; and (4) that the public interest would not be disserved by a permanent injunction." *eBay Inc. v. MercExchange, L.L.C.,* 547 U.S. 388, 391 (2006).

Historically, courts were willing to grant preliminary injunctions in copyright cases without engaging in a detailed analysis of each of the traditional four factors. The Second Circuit's view in the following quote exemplifies this approach:

> [A] preliminary injunction can be granted if [the] plaintiff shows irreparable injury, combined with either a probability of success on the merits, or a fair ground for litigation and a balance of the hardships in his favor. In copyright cases, however, if probable success — a prima facie case of copyright infringement — can be shown, the allegations of irreparable injury need not be very detailed, because such injury can normally be presumed when a copyright is infringed.

Wainwright Sec., Inc. v. Wall St. Transcript Corp., 558 F.2d 91, 94 (2d Cir. 1977), *cert. denied,* 434 U.S. 1014 (1978).

Permanent injunctions were likewise common, as were judicial statements like, "When a copyright plaintiff has established a threat of continuing infringement, he is *entitled* to an injunction." *Walt Disney Co. v. Powell,* 897 F.2d 565, 567 (D.C. Cir. 1990) (emphasis in original). Indeed, a court's authority to grant a permanent injunction historically has been very broad, extending to unregistered works and, in appropriate cases, to future works and works not in suit. *See Olan Mills, Inc. v. Linn Photo Co.,* 23 F.3d 1345 (8th Cir. 1994).

In *eBay Inc. v. MercExchange, L.L.C.,* 547 U.S. 388 (2006), the Supreme Court ruled that courts must evaluate the traditional four factors before granting an injunction in a patent infringement case. The Patent Act provides that courts may "grant injunctions in accordance with the principles of equity to prevent the violation of any right secured by patent, on such terms as the court deems reasonable." 35 U.S.C. §283. The Court rejected both the asserted "'general rule,' unique to patent disputes, 'that a permanent injunction will issue once infringement and validity have been adjudged,'" and statements indicating that denials of injunctions should be rare. *eBay,* 547 U.S. at 393-94. It held that an injunction should be granted only after weighing the four factors, and also noted that the "decision to grant or deny permanent injunctive relief is an act of equitable discretion by the . . . court." *Id.* at 391.

The Court observed that the rule it announced for patent cases was:

> consistent with our treatment of injunctions under the Copyright Act. Like a patent owner, a copyright holder possesses "the right to exclude others from using his property." . . . Like the Patent Act, the Copyright Act provides that courts 'may' grant injunctive relief "on such terms as it may deem reasonable to prevent or restrain

infringement of a copyright." 17 U.S.C. §502(a). . . . And as in our decision today, this Court has consistently rejected invitations to replace traditional equitable considerations with a rule that an injunction automatically follows a determination that a copyright has been infringed. *See, e.g., New York Times Co. v. Tasini,* 533 U.S. 483, 505 . . . (2001) (citing *Campbell v. Acuff-Rose Music, Inc.,* 510 U.S. 569, 578 n. 10 . . . (1994)). . . .

Id. at 392.

What are the implications of *eBay* for copyright litigants? Consider the following three opinions, one pre-*eBay* and two applying the *eBay* approach.

Abend v. MCA, Inc.
863 F.2d 1465 (9th Cir. 1988)

[Review the facts of *Stewart v. Abend* on page 170 of the casebook. Recall that the Supreme Court held that the work was infringing, but did not disturb the Ninth Circuit's opinion about appropriate remedies. Here is that portion of the Ninth Circuit's opinion.]

PREGERSON, J.: . . . We are mindful that this case presents compelling equitable considerations which should be taken into account by the district court in fashioning an appropriate remedy in the event defendants fail to establish any equitable defenses. Defendants invested substantial money, effort, and talent in creating the "Rear Window" film. Clearly the tremendous success of that venture initially and upon re-release is attributable in significant measure to, inter alia, the outstanding performances of its stars — Grace Kelly and James Stewart — and the brilliant directing of Alfred Hitchcock. The district court must recognize this contribution in determining Abend's remedy.

The district court may choose from several available remedies for the infringement. Abend seeks first an injunction against the continued exploitation of the "Rear Window" film. 17 U.S.C. §502(a) provides that the court "*may . . .* grant temporary and final injunctions on such terms as it may deem reasonable to prevent or restrain infringement of a copyright." Defendants argue . . . that a finding of infringement presumptively entitles the plaintiff to an injunction, citing Professor Nimmer. *See* 3 M. Nimmer, Nimmer on Copyright §14.06[B] at 14-55 to 14-56.2 (1988). However, Professor Nimmer also states that "where great public injury would be worked by an injunction, the courts might . . . award damages or a continuing royalty instead of an injunction in such special circumstances." *Id.* at 14-56.2.

We believe such special circumstances exist here. The "Rear Window" film resulted from the collaborative efforts of many talented individuals other than Cornell Woolrich, the author of the underlying story. The success of the movie resulted in large part from factors completely unrelated to the underlying story, "It Had To Be Murder." It would cause a great injustice for the owners of the film if the court enjoined them from further exhibition of the movie. An injunction would also effectively foreclose defendants from enjoying legitimate profits derived from exploitation of the "new matter" comprising the derivative work, which is given express copyright protection by section 7 of the 1909 Act. Since defendants could not possibly separate out the "new matter" from the underlying work, their right to enjoy the renewal copyright *in the derivative work* would be rendered meaningless by the grant of an injunction. We also note that an injunction could cause public injury by denying the public the opportunity to view a classic film for many years to come.

This is not the first time we have recognized that an injunction may be an inappropriate remedy for copyright infringement. In *Universal City Studios v. Sony Corp. of America,* 659 F.2d 963, 976 (9th Cir. 1981), *rev'd on other grounds,* 464 U.S. 417 ... we stated that Professor Nimmer's suggestion of damages or a continuing royalty would constitute an acceptable resolution for infringement caused by in-home taping of television programs by VCR — "time-shifting." *See also Sony Corp. v. Universal City Studios,* 464 U.S. 417, 499-500 (1984) (Blackmun, J., dissenting).

As the district court pointed out in the *Sony* case, an injunction is a "harsh and drastic" discretionary remedy, never an absolute right. . . . Abend argues nonetheless that defendants' attempts to interfere with his production of new derivative works can only be remedied by an injunction. We disagree. Abend has not shown irreparable injury which would justify imposing the severe remedy of an injunction on defendants. Abend can be compensated adequately for the infringement by monetary compensation. 17 U.S.C. §504(b) provides that the copyright owner can recover actual damages and "any profits of the infringement that are *attributable to the infringement* and are not taken into account in computing the actual damages." (Emphasis added.) The district court is capable of calculating damages caused to the fair market value of plaintiff's story by the re-release of the film. Any impairment of Abend's ability to produce new derivative works based on the story would be reflected in the calculation of the damage to the fair market value of the story. . . .

Phelps & Associates v. Galloway
492 F.3d 532 (4th Cir. 2007)

NIEMEYER, J.:

After R. Wayne Galloway began construction of his retirement home on Lake Wylie, near Charlotte, North Carolina, using architectural plans designed and copyrighted by Christopher Phelps & Associates, LLC ("Phelps & Associates"), without permission, Phelps & Associates commenced this action against Galloway for copyright infringement. Phelps & Associates sought damages . . . and injunctive relief. A jury found that Galloway infringed Phelps & Associates' copyright and awarded it $20,000 in damages. . . . The district court thereafter declined to enter an injunction, finding that the jury verdict had made Phelps & Associates "whole". . . . Phelps & Associates appeals, requesting a new trial on damages and the entry of an injunction prohibiting the future lease or sale of the infringing house and mandating the destruction or return of the infringing plans. . . .

Insofar as Phelps & Associates suggests that it is *entitled* to injunctive relief, we reject the argument. *See eBay Inc. v. MercExchange, L.L.C.,* — U.S. —, 126 S.Ct.

1837, 1839 . . . (2006). . . . [The Court there said, "] A plaintiff must demonstrate: (1) that it has suffered an irreparable injury; (2) that remedies available at law, such as monetary damages, are inadequate to compensate for that injury; (3) that, considering the balance of hardships between the plaintiff and defendant, a remedy in equity is warranted; and (4) that the public interest would not be disserved by a permanent injunction.["] *Id.* at 1839. Moreover, the Court reiterated that even upon this showing, whether to grant the injunction still remains in the "equitable discretion" of the court. . . .

Phelps & Associates' . . . request for equitable relief, that Galloway be permanently enjoined from leasing or selling the completed house, is argued with the following syllogism: First, the completed house is an infringing copy of Phelps & Associates' copyrighted work. *See* 17 U.S.C. §101. *Second,* as the copyright holder, Phelps & Associates has the exclusive right to "distribute" its copyrighted work "by sale or other transfer of ownership." *See id.* §106(3). *Therefore,* Galloway may never lease or sell the house without infringing Phelps & Associates' copyright. *See id.* §501(a). Because it is likely that Galloway will lease or sell the house, Phelps & Associates believes this lease or sale should be foreclosed by a permanent injunction.

We agree with Phelps & Associates that Galloway will inevitably sell or transfer his house within the period during which Phelps & Associates still holds the copyright—i.e. 95 years, *see* 17 U.S.C. §302(c)—and that such a sale could, absent this action, expose Galloway to further relief, *see id.* §106(3); *id.* §501(a); *cf. id.* §109(a) (permitting resale of "lawfully made" copies) . . . But Phelps & Associates has requested relief for that inevitable transaction now *in this action,* as part of the panoply of remedies available under the Copyright Act, and therefore entitlement to that relief can be and is resolved in this action under the principles of *eBay,* 126 S.Ct. at 1839.

The first two *eBay* criteria for injunctive relief—irreparable injury and the inadequacy of monetary damages—have most likely been demonstrated. Irreparable injury often derives from the nature of copyright violations, which deprive the copyright holder of intangible exclusive rights. Damages at law will not remedy the continuing existence of Phelps & Associates' design in the Galloway house. Moreover, while the calculation of future damages and profits for each future sale might be possible, any such effort would entail a substantial amount of speculation and guesswork that renders the effort difficult or impossible in this case. Accordingly, we conclude that Phelps & Associates most likely has satisfied the first two *eBay* factors.

When considering the third and fourth factors, however—the balance of hardships and the public interest—Phelps & Associates' showing has fallen short.

First, Phelps & Associates has been fully and adequately compensated for the copying and use of its design as manifested in the single Galloway house. . . . A sale of the house would not be a second copy or manifestation of the design, but merely a transfer of the structure in which the design was first copied. An injunction against sale would but slightly benefit Phelps & Associates' legitimate entitlements because the infringing house would retain the same form and location, remaining a permanent nuisance to the copyright regardless of whether there is an injunction. An injunction against sale would neither undo the prior

490

infringement, nor diminish the chances of future copying. At the same time, a permanent injunction would impose a draconian burden on Galloway, effectively creating a *lis pendens* on the house and subjecting him to contempt proceedings simply for selling his own property.

Second, a house or building, as an expression of the architect's copyrighted plans, usually has a predominantly functional character. . . . This is the same reason that Congress manifested an expectation that injunctions will not be routinely issued against substantially completed houses whose designs violated architectural copyrights. H.R.Rep. No. 101-735, at 13-14 (1990), *reprinted in* 1990 U.S.C.C.A.N. 6935, 6944 (explaining that buildings "are the only form of copyrightable subject matter that is habitable"). Those considerations are at their strongest when the architectural structure is completed and inhabited by the infringer, as here. While Galloway infringed the copyright, he now is living in a "copy" of the architectural work. His interest in remaining there, with the same rights as other homeowners to alienate his property, is substantial and, in this case, trumps Phelps & Associates' interests in any injunction prohibiting a lease or sale of the house.

Third, an injunction against sale of the house would be overbroad, as it would encumber a great deal of property unrelated to the infringement. The materials and labor that went into the Galloway house, in addition to the swimming pool, the fence, and other non-infringing features, as well as the land underneath the house, would be restrained by the requested injunction. As such, the injunction would take on a fundamentally punitive character, which has not been countenanced in the Copyright Act's remedies. . . . In a similar vein, the requested injunction would undermine an ancient reluctance by the courts to restrain the alienability of real property. . . . For these reasons, the public interest would be disserved by the entry of an injunction.

Finally, ultimate discretion to grant any such injunctive relief rests with the district court, and for the reasons enumerated, we conclude that deference to the district court's refusal is appropriate in the absence of any showing that such refusal was otherwise an abuse of discretion. *See eBay,* 126 S.Ct. at 1839. . . .

Phelps & Associates relies upon *Sony Corporation of America v. Universal City Studios, Inc.,* 464 U.S. 417, 446 n. 28 . . . (1984), to argue that the refusal to issue an injunction against future leases and sales of the Galloway house amounts to a judicially-created compulsory license, which is disfavored. The reliance on *Sony,* however, is misplaced. The remedies under the Copyright Act do not resemble a license because the Copyright Act remedies are far broader than simply requiring a defendant to make license payments. Under the Copyright Act, a copyright holder is entitled to both actual damages — the market price of the license — *and* disgorgement of the infringer's profits, which might be immensely greater than the price of a license. *See* 17 U.S.C. §504. Moreover, the infringer takes the risk that the district court will order, in its discretion, the destruction or other disposition of the infringing article. *See id.* §503(b). In the garden-variety piracy case, such orders are routinely issued. . . . Given the risks attendant to infringement, denying an injunction is not equivalent to a compulsory license. *See Walker v. Forbes, Inc.,* 28 F.3d 409, 412 (4th Cir.1994) ("By stripping the infringer not only of the licensing fee but also of the profit generated as a result of the use of the infringed item, the law makes clear that there is no gain to be made from taking someone else's intellectual property without their consent"). While granting an injunction to destroy an infringing article might be usual with respect to personal property, especially in the garden-variety music or movie piracy case, refusing to order destruction or the inalienability of property is also consistent with the Copyright Act's remedial scheme and does not amount to a compelled license.

For all of these reasons, we affirm the district court's order denying an injunction against the future lease or sale of Galloway's house. . . .

[The court remanded to the district court to consider whether, in light of the *eBay* factors, it should grant an injunction ordering the destruction of copies of the plans.] . . .

Metro-Goldwyn-Mayer Studios v. Grokster
518 F. Supp. 2d 1197 (N.D. Cal. 2007)

[Review the facts of this case at pages 490-99 of the casebook. After articulating a theory of liability for inducement of infringement, the Supreme Court remanded the case to the district court, which found defendants liable on that theory. In this opinion, the district court addresses whether the plaintiffs are entitled to injunctive relief.]

WILSON, J.: . . . Under 17 U.S.C. §502(a), this Court is empowered to grant a permanent injunction "as it may deem reasonable to prevent or restrain infringement of a copyright." . . .

Before applying *eBay*, it must be noted that Plaintiffs also ask this Court first to apply an arguably different (and perhaps more permissive) permanent injunction test. Prior to *eBay*, in *MAI Sys. Corp. v. Peak Computer, Inc.*, 991 F.2d 511, 520 (9th Cir.1993), the Ninth Circuit stated that "[a]s a general rule, a permanent injunction will be granted when liability has been established and there is a threat of continuing violations." Consistent with the Ninth Circuit, Nimmer writes, "[i]t is uncontroversial that a 'showing of past infringement and a substantial likelihood of future infringement' justifies issuance of a permanent injunction." 4 Melville B. Nimmer & David Nimmer, *Nimmer on Copyright*, §14.06[B] & n. 76.1 . . . ; *see also id.* §14.06[B] ("Because a permanent injunction is issued only after liability is established, its issuance probably does not require a showing of irreparable injury.").

In light of this two-part rule (past infringement + likelihood of future infringements), Plaintiffs have asked for a permanent injunction. However, this Court has doubts that *MAI's* "general rule" regarding permanent injunctions survives *eBay*. In *eBay*, the Supreme Court rejected the Federal Circuit's "general rule" in patent cases that "courts will issue permanent injunctions against patent infringement absent exceptional circumstances." 126 S. Ct. at 1839-40. . . . This Court can identify no place for a separate and distinct two-part *MAI* test or "general rule" that could circumvent *eBay*. . . .

The first question to address is whether Plaintiffs "ha[ve] suffered an irreparable injury." *eBay*, 126 S.Ct. at 1839. . . . [T]he Tenth Circuit has observed that "irreparable harm is often suffered when the injury can[not] be adequately atoned for in money, or when the district court cannot remedy [the injury] following a final determination on the merits." *Prairie Band [of Potawatomi Indians v. Pierce]*, 253 F.3d [1234,] at 1250 [(10th Cir. 2001)]. . . .

The parties dispute whether, in light of *eBay*, irreparable harm can be presumed. . . . Other courts have in the past presumed the existence of irreparable injury upon the establishment of liability in copyright cases. . . .

Yet, these cases were all decided prior to the Supreme Court's decision in *eBay*. The *eBay* Court held that it is Plaintiffs who "must demonstrate" (meaning, have the burden of proof) that the traditional factors favor a permanent injunction. 126 S. Ct. at 1839. The Supreme Court also highlighted that it has "consistently rejected" the rule that "an injunction automatically follows" an infringement holding. *Id.* at 1840. Given Plaintiffs' burden of proof and the inability of a district court to "automatically" issue injunctions, it is perhaps unclear in *eBay's* wake whether a permanent injunction can be granted based on a rebuttable presumption of irreparable harm. . . .

. . . [T]he *eBay* district court has subsequently decided that there can be no presumption of irreparable harm in the permanent injunction context. *See Merc-Exchange, L.L.C. v. eBay, Inc.*, 500 F. Supp. 2d 556, 568 (E.D. Va. 2007) ("[A] review of relevant caselaw, as well as the language of the Supreme Court's decision, supports defendants' position that such presumption no longer exists."). This view appears to have been followed by perhaps every court expressly considering *eBay*. . . .

This Court agrees with StreamCast, and these district courts, that the presumption of irreparable harm no longer inures to the benefit of Plaintiffs. The *eBay* Court plainly stated that Plaintiffs "must demonstrate" the presence of the traditional factors, and therefore have the burden of proof with regard to irreparable harm. . . .

Irreparable harm cannot be established solely on the fact of past infringement. Additionally, it must also be true that the mere likelihood of future infringement by a defendant does not by itself allow for an inference of irreparable harm. As to the latter, future copyright infringement can always be redressed via damages, whether actual or statutory. *See* 17 U.S.C. §504. . . .

"[I]rreparable harm may not be presumed[, but] [i]n run-of-the-mill copyright litigation, such proof should not be difficult to establish. . . ." 6 [William F.] Patry, [*Patry on Copyrights,*] . . . §22:74. Thus, Plaintiffs may establish an irreparable harm stemming from the infringement (e.g., loss of market share, reputational harm). It is also possible that some qualitative feature about the infringement itself, such as its peculiar nature, could elevate its status into the realm of "irreparable harm."

StreamCast accepts that certain harms caused by infringement, such as loss of brand recognition and market share, can amount to irreparable harm. . . . However, StreamCast rejects the argument that copyright infringement can itself ever represent irreparable harm. StreamCast asserts that "[i]f damages can be calculated, the injury is not irreparable . . . — the Copyright Act specifically provides for statutory damages, which are calculable assuming Plaintiffs can prove direct infringement of their works, and a basis for the range requested." . . . This Court has doubts regarding StreamCast's position. In *eBay*, Chief Justice Roberts indicated that irreparable harm can result from the infringement itself, depending upon the circumstances of the case:

> From at least the early 19th century, courts have granted injunctive relief upon a finding of infringement in the vast majority of patent cases. This "long tradition of equity practice" is not surprising, given the difficulty of protecting a right to exclude through monetary remedies that allow an infringer to use an invention against the patentee's wishes — a difficulty that often implicates the first two factors of the traditional four-factor test.

126 S.Ct. at 1841 (Roberts, C.J., concurring); . . . And "[l]ike a patent owner, a copyright holder possesses 'the right to exclude others from using his property.'" [*Id.*] at 1840. . . .

This Court also recognizes that a competing *eBay* concurrence took issue with Chief Justice Roberts's "right to exclude" language. Justice Kennedy explained his view that "the existence of a right to exclude does not dictate the remedy for a violation of that right." *eBay*, 126 S.Ct. at 1842 (Kennedy, J., concurring). This Court agrees, since a contrary conclusion would come close to permitting a presumption of irreparable harm. This Court also observes that Justice Kennedy's statement was made primarily in the context of certain recent developments in the patent field that are wholly inapplicable to this lawsuit. For example, this is simply not a case in which the copyright infringement represents "but a small component of the product the companies seek to produce," such that "legal damages may well be sufficient to compensate for the infringement." *Id.* As this Court previously held, StreamCast's entire business was built around the fundamental premise that Morpheus would be utilized to infringe copyrights, including those owned by Plaintiffs. Furthermore, Justice Kennedy emphasized that "[t]he equitable discretion over injunctions . . . is well suited to allow courts to adapt to the rapid technological and legal developments. . . ." *Id.* Given the technological aspects of the infringement induced by StreamCast, and the flexibility conferred by the Copyright Act, this Court is persuaded that its bases for finding irreparable harm, *infra*, are supported by both Chief Justice Roberts's and Justice Kennedy's concurrences.

In light of this authority, the Court concludes that certain qualities pertaining to the nature of StreamCast's inducement of infringement are relevant to a finding of irreparable harm. . . .

The irreparable harm analysis centers on two basic themes: (1) StreamCast has and will continue to induce far more infringement than it could ever possibly redress with damages; and (2) Plaintiffs' copyrights (especially those of popular works) have and will be rendered particularly vulnerable to continuing infringement on an enormous scale due to StreamCast's inducement. The Court agrees with both arguments, and each is independently sufficient to support [a] finding of irreparable harm in this case.

First, the Court must ask whether a particular defendant's probable inability to pay damage constitutes irreparable harm. In the ordinary case, "merely

494

alleging an opponent's inability to pay damages does not constitute irreparable harm." *Rosewood Apartments Corp. v. Perpignano*, 200 F. Supp. 2d 269, 278 (S.D.N.Y. 2002). But "[i]n some limited circumstances, parties have demonstrated such a strong likelihood that their opponent will be unable to pay that courts have awarded them equitable relief." *Id.* . . . The rationale in such cases must be that an award of monetary damages will be meaningless, and the plaintiff will have no substantive relief, where it will be impossible to collect an award for past and/or future infringements perpetrated by a defendant.

Plaintiffs have not yet sought an award of statutory damages. Additionally, Plaintiffs have not provided this Court with specific evidence as part of this motion demonstrating that StreamCast would be unable to pay damages for the infringements it has induced in the past, and could continue to induce in the future. But such evidence is not necessary here. Based on the undisputed evidence at summary judgment of massive end-user infringement, it is highly likely that the award of statutory damages that ultimately befalls StreamCast in this case will be enormous (especially considering the potential relationship between inducement and a finding of willfulness), and would far outstrip the amount of revenue the company has garnered in recent years. . . . This Court's conclusion would also be the same even if Plaintiffs chose to forgo a damages award as part of this lawsuit. This is because the amount of infringement that StreamCast could induce in the future is so staggering that the recoverable statutory damages would very probably be well beyond StreamCast's anticipated resources. Because it is extremely unlikely that StreamCast will be able to compensate Plaintiffs monetarily for the infringements it has induced in the past, or the infringements it could induce in the future through Morpheus, Plaintiffs have and will continue to suffer irreparable harm.

Second, the Court agrees with Plaintiffs' claim that a substantial number of their copyrighted works have and would continue to become irreparably exposed to infringement on a tremendous scale due to StreamCast's inducement. This inducement greatly erodes Plaintiffs' ability to enforce their exclusive rights. *See A & M Records, Inc. v. Napster, Inc.*, 239 F.3d 1004, 1029 (9th Cir.2001) (rejecting Napster's request for compulsory royalties as opposed to injunctive relief because "Plaintiffs would lose the power to control their intellectual property"). It also promises no realistic mechanism through which statutory damages can be collected for all of the inevitable subsequent infringements occurring outside of the Morpheus System and Software. . . .

The Court is aware that Plaintiffs can seek an award of statutory damages from StreamCast for infringements occurring through the Morpheus System and Software (ignoring for now the likely reality regarding StreamCast's ability to pay). However, Plaintiffs cannot recover damages from StreamCast for the inevitable derivative infringements that will occur outside of Morpheus, with copyrighted content originally acquired within it, as a consequence [of] StreamCast's inducement. Even numerous lawsuits against direct infringers will necessarily prove to be insufficient under these conditions. *Cf. Grokster*, 545 U.S. at 929-30, 125 S.Ct. 2764 ("When a widely shared service or product is used to commit infringement, it may be impossible to enforce rights in the protected work effectively against all direct infringers. . . ."). Indeed, the very need to file multiple lawsuits as a consequence of StreamCast's inducement is itself supportive of an irreparable harm finding.

In sum, Plaintiffs have offered two independently sufficient grounds for a finding of irreparable harm. . . .

[The court found the other three eBay factors also favored the plaintiffs, and concluded that a permanent injunction should issue.]

NOTES AND QUESTIONS

1. Do you prefer the four-factor test, a presumption in favor of injunctive relief in cases of infringement or some other rule? Do you think injunctions will be more difficult to obtain in copyright cases after *eBay*? Is that result appropriate? Note that the TRIPS Agreement only requires that injunctive relief be available, not that courts must award such relief. Do you think that either *Phelps* or *Grokster* would have been decided differently pre-*eBay*? Why, or why not?

2. Are you persuaded by the *Grokster* court's analysis of the irreparable harm factor? Are there circumstances in which probable inability to pay damages would not (or should not) constitute irreparable harm? What other circumstances might demonstrate irreparable harm to a copyright owner? What kinds of infringing activity can't be remedied by an award of monetary damages?

If a court finds that the four-factor test is satisfied, how broadly should its remedial powers extend? Are there circumstances under which it would be appropriate for courts to grant injunctions covering unregistered copyrights, or copyrights not before the court?

3. Would it ever be appropriate (and permitted under *eBay*) for courts to presume irreparable harm in the preliminary injunction context once the plaintiff has shown likely success on the merits? Of what value is a preliminary injunction to a copyright plaintiff?

4. Before the *eBay* case, some scholars had argued that preliminary injunctions could violate the First Amendment:

> . . . [W]hen a court concludes that the defendant's expression is probably not substantially similar to the plaintiff's expression, or is probably a fair use, the court should never issue a preliminary injunction, even if the balance of hardships tilts in the plaintiff's favor. Likewise when the court concludes that the case is genuinely close: erroneously failing to enjoin speech is better than erroneously enjoining speech, especially when erroneous failure to enjoin speech is remediable by a damages award. . . .
>
> . . . Thus, a court should not enter a preliminary injunction unless it is clearly convinced that the speech falls within the copyright exception (*i.e.*, that it's substantially similar to the plaintiff's expression and is not a fair use). . . .

Mark A. Lemley & Eugene Volokh, *Freedom of Speech and Injunctions in Intellectual Property Cases*, 48 Duke L.J. 147, 215-16 (1998).

Does *eBay* resolve this objection?

5. To avoid tension with First Amendment principles, why not refuse preliminary injunctions as a matter of course and simply order monetary compensation? In *Suntrust Bank v. Houghton Mifflin Co.*, 252 F.3d 1165 (11th Cir. 2001), discussed in the Note on Fair Use and the First Amendment, page 560 of the casebook, the court vacated a preliminary injunction on First Amendment grounds, stating that the injunction was an unconstitutional prior restraint. In a subsequent opinion clarifying that First Amendment protections for the defendant's parody were preserved via the fair use doctrine, the court ruled that any injury resulting from the alleged infringement could be adequately remedied by money damages. *Suntrust Bank v. Houghton Mifflin Co.*, 268 F.3d 1257, 1263 (11th Cir. 2001). Should courts do this more often in fair use cases? In other infringement cases?

6. Did the courts' decisions in *Abend* and *Phelps* effectively create compulsory licenses? Do you find the *Phelps* court's rejection of the "compulsory license" characterization convincing? Why, or why not? Since Congress has instituted compulsory licenses elsewhere in the Copyright Act, would it be appropriate for a court to impose such a license without prior congressional authorization?

7. In economic terms, a compulsory license scheme is described as a liability regime. Liability rules allow use by third parties but require compensation for such use. In contrast, property rules allow the property owner to preclude unauthorized uses by third parties, and to receive both injunctive and monetary relief. Recall the goals of copyright, which you studied in Chapter 1. Which model—a property regime or a liability regime—is more consistent with copyright objectives? Would you argue, along with Chief Justice Roberts, that the nature of the right protected by a patent or copyright regime is the right to exclude, or are you persuaded by Justice Kennedy's distinction between rights and remedies? Is either model mandated by the language of the Intellectual Property Clause?

Universal City Studios, Inc. v. Reimerdes
111 F. Supp. 2d 294 (S.D.N.Y. 2000), aff'd sub nom.
Universal City Studios, Inc. v. Corley, 273 F.3d 429
(2d Cir. 2001)

[Review the facts of this case beginning on page 609 of the casebook.]

KAPLAN, J.: . . .

B. Permanent Injunction and Declaratory Relief

Plaintiffs seek a permanent injunction barring defendants from posting DeCSS on their web site and from linking their site to others that make DeCSS available.

The starting point, as always, is the statute. The DMCA provides in relevant part that the court in an action brought pursuant to its terms "may grant temporary and permanent injunctions on such terms as it deems reasonable to prevent or restrain a violation. . . ." [*See* 17 U.S.C. §1203(b)(1). — Eds.] Where statutes in substance so provide, injunctive relief is appropriate if there is a reasonable likelihood of future violations absent such relief and, in cases brought by private plaintiffs, if the plaintiff lacks an adequate remedy at law.

In this case, it is quite likely that defendants, unless enjoined, will continue to violate the Act. Defendants are in the business of disseminating information to assist hackers in "cracking" various types of technological security systems. And while defendants argue that they promptly stopped posting DeCSS when enjoined preliminarily from doing so, thus allegedly demonstrating their willingness to comply with the law, their reaction to the preliminary injunction in fact cuts the other way. Upon being enjoined from posting DeCSS themselves, defendants encouraged others to "mirror" the information — that is, to post DeCSS — and linked their own web site to mirror sites in order to assist users of defendants' web site in obtaining DeCSS despite the injunction barring defendants from providing it directly. While there is no claim that this activity violated the letter of the preliminary injunction, and it therefore presumably was not contumacious, and while its status under the DMCA was somewhat uncertain, it was a studied effort to defeat the purpose of the preliminary injunction. In consequence, the Court finds that there is a substantial likelihood of future violations absent injunctive relief.

There also is little doubt that plaintiffs have no adequate remedy at law. The only potential legal remedy would be an action for damages under Section 1203(c), which provides for recovery of actual damages or, upon the election of the plaintiff, statutory damages of up to $2,500 per offer of DeCSS. Proof of actual damages in a case of this nature would be difficult if not virtually impossible, as it would involve proof of the extent to which motion picture attendance, sales of broadcast and other motion picture rights, and sales and rentals of DVDs and video tapes of movies were and will be impacted by the availability of DVD decryption technology. Difficulties in determining what constitutes an "offer" of DeCSS in a world in which the code is available to much of the world via Internet postings, among other problems, render statutory damages an inadequate means of redressing plaintiffs' claimed injuries. Indeed, difficulties such as this have led to the presumption that copyright and trademark infringement cause irreparable injury, i.e., injury for which damages are not an adequate remedy. The Court therefore holds that the traditional requirements for issuance of a permanent injunction have been satisfied. Yet there remains another point for consideration.

Defendants argue that an injunction in this case would be futile because DeCSS already is all over the Internet. They say an injunction would be comparable to locking the barn door after the horse is gone. And the Court has been troubled by that possibility. But the countervailing arguments overcome that concern.

To begin with, any such conclusion effectively would create all the wrong incentives by allowing defendants to continue violating the DMCA simply because others, many doubtless at defendants' urging, are doing so as well. Were that the law, defendants confronted with the possibility of injunctive relief would be well advised to ensure that others engage in the same unlawful conduct in order to set up the argument that an injunction against the defendants would be futile because everyone else is doing the same thing.

Second, and closely related, is the fact that this Court is sorely "troubled by the notion that any Internet user . . . can destroy valuable intellectual property rights by posting them over the Internet." While equity surely should not act where the controversy has become moot, it ought to look very skeptically at claims that the defendant or others already have done all the harm that might be done before the injunction issues.

The key to reconciling these views is that the focus of injunctive relief is on the defendants before the Court. If a plaintiff seeks to enjoin a defendant from burning a pasture, it is no answer that there is a wild fire burning in its direction. If the defendant itself threatens the plaintiff with irreparable harm, then equity will enjoin the defendant from carrying out the threat even if other threats abound and even if part of the pasture already is burned.

These defendants would harm plaintiffs every day on which they post DeCSS on their heavily trafficked web site and link to other sites that post it because someone who does not have DeCSS thereby might obtain it. They thus threaten plaintiffs with immediate and irreparable injury. They will not be allowed to continue to do so simply because others may do so as well. In short, this Court, like others tha[t] have faced the issue[], is "not persuaded that modern technology has withered the strong right arm of equity." Indeed, the likelihood is that this decision will serve notice on others that "the strong right arm of equity" may be brought to bear against them absent a change in their conduct and thus contribute to a climate of appropriate respect for intellectual property rights in an age in which the excitement of ready access to untold quantities of information has blurred in some minds the fact that taking what is not yours and not freely offered to you is stealing. Appropriate injunctive and declaratory relief will issue simultaneously with this opinion. . . .

NOTES AND QUESTIONS

1. Would *Reimerdes* be decided the same way after *eBay*? Should *eBay*'s analysis apply to injunctions under the DMCA?

2. What are the policy implications of injunctive relief under §1201 when the technologically-protected material may not be copyrightable subject matter? The *Reimerdes* court justifies its award of permanent injunctive relief in large part based on the defendants' encouragement of others to set up mirror sites for DeCSS after the preliminary injunction issued. Is this justification for the permanent injunction consistent with First Amendment principles?

Page 777. In the Notes and Questions, insert new Question 2:

2. In *China—Measures Affecting the Protection and Enforcement of Intellectual Property Rights*, WT/DS362/R (Jan. 26, 2009), the U.S. argued that China's customs measures dealing with the destruction or disposal of infringing goods were inconsistent with Article 59 of the TRIPS Agreement, which provides, in part, that "competent authorities shall have the authority to order the destruction or disposal

of infringing goods in accordance with the principles set out in Article 46." Under the Chinese Customs Intellectual Property Rights Regulations and Implementing Measures, infringing goods seized by customs authorities may be: (1) donated to social welfare bodies for use in social public welfare undertakings; (2) sold to the rightholder; or (3) if neither of these two options is available, auctioned. All infringing features of the goods must be eradicated before an auction. *Id.* ¶7.194.

The U.S. argued that this disposal scheme impermissibly constrains the authority of Chinese authorities to destroy infringing goods and that the priority accorded the three disposal options allows such goods to enter channels of commerce. The WTO Panel rejected the argument, observing that "the obligation that competent authorities 'shall have the authority' to make certain orders is not an obligation that competent authorities shall exercise that authority in a particular way, unless otherwise specified." *Id.* ¶7.238.

Read Articles 46 and 59 of the TRIPS Agreement. In your view, does the Chinese disposal scheme violate the letter or spirit of these provisions? Why should seizure and impoundment of infringing goods be required in all WTO member countries, especially if the goods can be used for public benefit? Such goods could be donated to rural schools, orphanages, or public libraries. What effect, if any, would such redemptive uses have on authorial incentives?

Page 784. In the Notes and Questions:

a. Insert the following at the end of Question 3:

Consider the following hypothetical: Defendant Bad Boy Entertainment (BBE) produces a rap album called "Ready to Die" containing 17 tracks. The title track infringes Bridgeport Music, Inc.'s copyright in "Singing in the Morning" by sampling that song. Bridgeport is able to prove BBE's profits from the album. How would you apportion those profits to the infringement? *See Bridgeport Music, Inc. v. Justin Combs Publ'g*, 507 F.3d 470, 483-84 (6th Cir. 2007) (upholding jury's adoption of the plaintiffs' methodology which divided the album's profits by its number of tracks). The court observed, "[t]he jury acted within its province when it rejected defendants' argument[s] that plaintiffs' allocation included profits attributable to non-infringing elements of the song 'Ready to Die' . . . [and] that the song was memorable (and successful) because of certain [other] lyrics." *Id.* Do you agree? Should a court instead require a plaintiff further to apportion profits based on the fraction of the entire song that the infringing sample represents?

b. Insert the following at the end of Question 4:

In *Bridgeport Music, Inc. v. Justin Combs Publishing*, 507 F.3d 470, 486-88 (6th Cir. 2007), the jury awarded $366,939 in compensatory damages and $3.5 million in punitive damages. The court reviewed the punitive damages award de novo and held that it violated the due process clause under Supreme Court precedent. *Id.* at

486 (citing *State Farm Mut. Auto Ins. Co. v. Campbell*, 538 U.S. 408 (2003), and *BMW v. Gore*, 517 U.S. 559 (1996)). According to those cases, the constitutionality of punitive damages awards is to be assessed by considering "the reprehensibility of defendants' conduct, the disparity between plaintiffs' harm and the award, and a comparison of the award and civil penalties in comparable cases." *Id.* at 486. The court found that intentional malice or deceit was not enough to make the defendants' conduct "reprehensible" and that the 9.5:1 ratio of punitive damages to compensatory damages was excessive. *Id.* at 486-90.

Page 794.   In the Notes and Questions:

a.   Insert the following at the end of Question 4:

In *WB Music v. RTV Communications Group*, 445 F.3d 538 (2d Cir. 2006), the defendant had created seven different compilation CDs that contained a total of 13 different copyrighted musical works owned by the plaintiffs. The final sentence of §504(c)(1) provides that "[f]or the purposes of this subsection, all the parts of a compilation or derivative work constitute one work." Acknowledging that the statute was ambiguous as to whether that sentence refers to the infringed work or to the allegedly infringing work, the court determined that it defined what constituted "one work" belonging to the plaintiff. Therefore, the proper award in the case was 13 times the statutory amount, not seven times the statutory amount.

b.   Insert new Question 5 and renumber Question 5 as Question 6:

5. The DMCA provides for statutory damages "as the court considers just" "for each violation of section 1201 in the sum of not less than $200 or more than $2,500 per act of circumvention [and] for each violation of section 1202 in the sum of not less than $2,500 or more than $25,000." 17 U.S.C. §1203(c)(3). What does "violation" mean? In *McClatchey v. Associated Press*, 83 U.S.P.Q.2d 1095 (W.D. Pa. 2007) (*see supra* page 465 for the facts), the defendant removed the plaintiff's copyright management information and distributed its photograph to 1,147 subscribers. Removal of the information constituted one violation. Addressing AP's distribution of the photo to subscribers, the court stated: "In essence the term 'each violation' is best understood to mean 'each violative act performed by Defendant.' . . . [T]he Court concludes that AP committed only one alleged violative act by distributing the . . . photograph to its . . . subscribers, even though there were 1,147 recipients." *Id.* at 1101. In arriving at this result, the court refused to incorporate the limitations of §504(c) into §1203(c)(3) because its language differs from that of §504. *Id.* Instead, the court looked to cases interpreting 47 U.S.C. §605, which prohibits intercepting certain communications, and elaborating the role of statutory damages under that statute: "Presumably, plaintiffs will elect statutory damages only when that calculation exceeds their actual damages. . . . Congress would not have intended to make the statutory damages windfall totally

independent of the defendant's conduct. Where one act by Defendant results in mass infringement, it is more likely that actual damages will yield the more favorable recovery." *Id*. Do you agree with the court's approach?

c. Insert the following paragraph at the end of newly renumbered Question 6:

Would you change your answer in the context of liability for file-sharing? As we discuss in the casebook on pages 508-10 and in Question 4 on page 510, the Recording Industry Association of America has sued thousands of individuals for sharing music over peer-to-peer networks. In late 2007, a jury found an individual file-sharer liable for 24 instances of willful infringement. *Capitol Records Inc. v. Thomas*, 2007 WL 2826645 (D. Minn. Oct. 1, 2007) (Special Verdict Form). The jury awarded a total of $222,000 in statutory damages to the plaintiffs, setting the amount of damages for each infringement at $9,250. *Id*. The plaintiffs did not request a particular amount, and the jury did not explain how it arrived at the $9,250 per song figure, although one of the plaintiffs' attorneys believes the amount reflects a compromise, and that some jurors would have been willing to award the $150,000 maximum. *Industry's Lead Counsel in Music-Sharing Suits Discusses Procedural Aspects of Campaign*, 23 No. 9 Ent. L. & Fin. 1 (2007). Had those jurors prevailed, the amount of damages would have been $3,600,000.

The defendant has requested a new trial on damages to determine actual damages and whether the damages awarded by the jury violated the Due Process Clause. Alternatively, the defendant has requested the court to order remittitur, reducing the damages to reflect the limitations of *State Farm* and *Gore* (*see* page 501 *supra*). *Capitol Records, Inc.*, 2007 WL 4586690 (D. Minn. Oct. 15, 2007) (Defendant's Motion for New Trial, Or In the Alternative, for Remittitur). What do you think the appropriate figure is for statutory damages per song in cases of music file-sharing? Is it relevant that one can generally purchase songs on the Internet for about $1.00, and that the record labels receive about 70 cents per song? *See id*.

d. Insert new Question 7:

7. It is important to remember that for copyright owners, eligibility to recover attorneys' fees is dependent on timely registration. Specifically, §412 provides that:

> no award of statutory damages or of attorney's fees . . . shall be made for — (1) any infringement of copyright in an unpublished work commenced before the effective date of its registration; or (2) any infringement of copyright commenced after first publication of the work and before the effective date of its registration, unless such registration is made within three months after the first publication of the work.

17 U.S.C. §412. In a case that does not involve the three-month publication grace period, what happens when infringement begins, then registration occurs, and subsequent to the registration the infringement continues? Can a successful plaintiff in a lawsuit seeking recovery for post-registration infringements avoid the bar against statutory damages and attorneys' fees? Generally, the first act of infringement in a series of ongoing infringements of the same kind marks the commencement of one continuing infringement under §412. *See Derek Andrew, Inc. v. Poof Apparel Corp.*, 528 F.3d 696, 700-01 (9th Cir. 2008) (collecting cases). In *Derek Andrew*, the Ninth Circuit held that the mere fact that copies of the infringing garment tag were "attached to new garments made and distributed after the date of registration did not transform those distributions into separate and distinct infringements." *Id.* at 701. The court reversed the district court's award of statutory damages and attorneys' fees under the Copyright Act.